Teaching Social Competence

A Practical Approach for Improving Social Skills in Students At-Risk

Teaching Social Competence

A Practical Approach for Improving Social Skills in Students At-Risk

Dennis R. Knapczyk
Indiana University

Paul Rodes
Indiana University

Brooks/Cole Publishing Company
I(T)P™ An International Thomson Publishing Company

Pacific Grove • Albany • Bonn • Boston • Cincinnati • Detroit • London • Madrid • Melbourne
Mexico City • New York • Paris • San Francisco • Singapore • Tokyo • Toronto • Washington

Sponsoring Editor: *Vicki Knight*
Editorial Associate: *Lauri Ataide*
Marketing Team: *Carolyn Crockett* and *Margaret Parks*
Production Editor: *Penelope Sky*
Production Assistant: *Tessa McGlasson*
Manuscript Editor: *Patterson Lamb*
Permissions Editor: *May Clark*
Interior Design: *Detta Penna* and *Jamie Sue Brooks*
Cover Design: *Detta Penna*
Cover Photo: *Mary Kate Denny/PhotoEdit*
Photo Editor: *Kathleen Olson*
Typesetting: *ColorType, Inc.*
Printing and Binding: *Malloy Lithographing, Inc.*

For more information, contact:

BROOKS/COLE PUBLISHING COMPANY
511 Forest Lodge Road
Pacific Grove, CA 93950
USA

International Thomson Publishing Europe
Berkshire House 168-173
High Holborn
London WC1V 7AA
England

Thomas Nelson Australia
102 Dodds Street
South Melbourne, 3205
Victoria, Australia

Nelson Canada
1120 Birchmount Road
Scarborough, Ontario
Canada M1K 5G4

International Thomson Editores
Campos Eliseos 385, Piso 7
Col. Polanco
11560 México D. F. México

International Thomson Publishing GmbH
Königswinterer Strasse 418
53227 Bonn
Germany

International Thomson Publishing Asia
221 Henderson Road
#05-10 Henderson Building
Singapore 0315

International Thomson Publishing Japan
Hirakawacho Kyowa Building, 3F
2-2-1 Hirakawacho
Chiyoda-ku, Tokyo 102
Japan

Printed in the United States of America

10 9 8 7 6 5 4 3 2 1

Library of Congress Cataloging-in-Publication Data

Knapczyk, Dennis R.,
Teaching social competence: a practical approach for improving social skills in students at risk/
Dennis R. Knapczyk, Paul Rodes.
p. cm.
Includes bibliographical references and index.
ISBN 0-534-33894-1
1. Social skills—Study and teaching—United States. 2. Special education—United States.
I. Rodes, Paul. II Title.
HM299.K53 1996 95–32751
371.9-dc20 CIP

THIS BOOK IS PRINTED ON ACID-FREE RECYCLED PAPER

This book is dedicated to my parents,
who always wanted a writer in the family;
and, of course, to Susan and the kids.

D.R.K.

To my parents and to Shari;
and to Barbara Was, John Horan, Jane Syburg, Tom Gerencher,
and all the memorable teachers who
first shaped my understanding of education.

P.G.R.

Brief Contents

PART ONE Social Competence and the Social Skills Curriculum 1

1 Social Competence and Social Expectations 3
2 Describing Expectations for Social Behavior 27
3 Describing Standards for Meeting Expectations 57

PART TWO Assessing Social Skills 79

4 Planning a Survey Level Assessment 81
5 Summarizing Survey Level Assessment Results and Selecting Target Skills for Interventions 115
6 Conducting a Specific Level Assessment *Part I: Assessing Basic Abilities* 143
7 Conducting a Specific Level Assessment *Part II: Assessing Component Steps* 173
8 Conducting a Specific Level Assessment *Part III: Assessing Performance Conditions* 195

PART THREE Planning and Implementing Interventions for Teaching Social Competence 225

9 Setting Instructional Goals and Brainstorming Procedures 227
10 Developing and Refining Intervention Plans 259
11 Monitoring the Intervention 295
12 Analyzing Intervention Results and Determining Next Steps 327

PART FOUR Broader Applications in the Teaching of Social Competence 365

13 Streamlining the Process of Social Competence 367
14 Teaching Social Competence to Groups of Students 405
15 Teaching Social Competence within and across Grade Levels 432

APPENDIX A Expectations for Social Behavior 453
APPENDIX B Resources and Teaching Materials for Social Skills Instruction 479
REFERENCES 481
INDEX 487

Contents

PART ONE Social Competence and the Social Skills Curriculum 1

CHAPTER 1 *Social Competence and Social Expectations 3*

Looking at Social Competence 3

Social Competence and Social Incompetence 5

Case Study: Three Students in Mrs. Armstrong's Class 6

Focusing on Competence 7

The Complexity of Social Demands 8

Social Demands and Situations 9

Social Demands and People 10

Explicit and Implicit Demands 13

A Short Activity 14

Need for a Systematic Approach 14

Expectations for Social Behavior 17

Advantages of Looking at Expectations 18

Summary 22

CHAPTER 2 *Describing Expectations for Social Behavior 27*

Social Competence and the Social Skills Curriculum 27

Functions of a Social Skills Curriculum 28

Defining a Social Skills Curriculum 30

Step 1: Listing Settings and Situations 30

Step 2: Taking Notes on Social Demands 37

Step 3: Listing Expectations for Each Situation 43

Benefits and Uses of the Social Skills Curriculum 49

Assessing Problems in Social Behavior 49

Clarifying the Goals of Interventions 49

Expanding the Scope of an Instructional Program 50

Summary 51

CHAPTER 3 *Describing Standards for Meeting Expectations 57*

Social Competence and Standards 57

Advantages of Identifying Standards 58
To Make the Curriculum Operational 58
To Aid in Assessing Behavior 58
To Clarify Instructional Goals 60
Elements That Make Up Standards for Social Expectations 62
Units of Measure 62
Criterion Levels 66
Identifying and Describing Standards for Expectations 67
Identifying Units of Measure 68
Identifying Criterion Levels 71
Identifying Standards in Different Situations 71
Using Standards to Evaluate Social Behavior 73
Standards As Source of Student Difficulty 73
Standards Applied Collectively 73
Summary 74

PART TWO Assessing Social Skills 79

CHAPTER 4 *Planning a Survey Level Assessment 81*
Overview of Survey Level Assessment 82
Principles of a Survey Level Assessment 83
Need for Personalized Assessment 84
Need to Assess under Natural Conditions 84
Need for Teacher-Developed Assessment 85
Advantages of Assessing with the Social Skills Curriculum 85
Planning a Survey Level Assessment 86
Steps in Planning the Assessment 86
Step 1: Choose a Student to Assess 87
Step 2: Choose Situations in Which to Assess 88
Step 3: Choose Expectations to Assess 91
Step 4: Describe the Standards for Measuring Performance 95
Step 5: Choose Assessment Procedures 97
Step 6: Prepare to Record Assessment Results 102
Step 7: Schedule the Assessment 103
Conducting a Survey Level Assessment 107
Stay Focused 107
Remain within Your Limits 107
Keep Outside Observers Unobtrusive 108
Summary 109

CHAPTER 5 *Summarizing Survey Level Assessment Results and Selecting Target Skills for Interventions 115*
Tallying the Results of a Survey Level Assessment 115
Record Results Using Prescribed Units of Measure 115
Keep a Daily Record of Results 116
Record Additional Information That May Affect the Students' Behavior 119

Compiling a List of Expectations Not Met 120
Setting Priorities Among Expectations Not Met 120
An Approach for Setting Priorities 120
Considerations in Setting Priorities 121
Using the Guidelines 128
Defining Target Skills for Interventions 129
The Need for Further Assessment 132
The Need for Further Investigation of Target Skills 136
Summary 137

CHAPTER 6 ***Conducting a Specific Level Assessment Part I: Assessing Basic Abilities 143***
Overview of Basic Abilities Assessment 144
Basic Abilities and Planning Interventions 144
Basic Abilities and Problems in Social Behavior 146
Preparing a Basic Abilities Assessment 148
Step 1: Listing Information about the Student and the Target Skill 149
Step 2: Listing the Basic Abilities to Be Assessed 149
Step 3: Formulating Questions about Basic Abilities 158
Step 4: Planning and Scheduling Assessment Procedures 160
Conducting a Basic Abilities Assessment 163
Summarizing the Results of a Basic Abilities Assessment 164
Entering Assessment Results on the Worksheet 165
Recording Comments and Conclusions 165
Setting the Directions for Interventions 166
Summary 167

CHAPTER 7 ***Conducting a Specific Level Assessment Part II: Assessing Component Steps 173***
Overview of a Component Steps Assessment 173
Importance of Behavioral Patterns and Component Steps in Achieving Social Competence 175
Building More Complex Social Skills 175
Combining Steps to Form Behavioral Patterns 176
Broadening the Scope of Social Interactions 176
Component Steps and Problems in Social Behavior 177
Failure to Perform Essential Steps 177
Failure to Combine Steps into Behavioral Patterns 178
Preparing a Component Steps Assessment 178
Step 1: Listing Information about the Student and the Target Skill 179
Step 2: Listing the Component Steps for the Target Skill 179
Step 3: Planning and Scheduling the Assessment Procedures 184
Conducting a Component Steps Assessment 185
Assessing All the Component Steps 186
Summarizing the Results of an Assessment 187
Tallying Results 187

Commenting on Performance 188
Listing the Findings from the Assessment 188
Summary 189

CHAPTER 8 *Specific Level Assessment Part III: Assessing Performance Conditions 195*
Overview of a Performance Conditions Assessment 195
Performance Conditions and Social Behavior 196
Importance of Assessing Performance Conditions 196
The Focus of Performance Conditions Assessment 198
Types of Guidelines Set by Performance Conditions 198
Time: When Should Performance Occur? 198
Location: Where Should Performance Take Place? 199
People: With Whom Should Performance Take Place? 199
Amount: How Much Performance Is Necessary? 199
Materials: What Resources Should Be Used for Performance? 200
Performance Conditions and Problems in Social Behavior 200
Problems with Placement and Reaction 200
Examples of Problems with Placement and Reaction 201
Performance Conditions and Inconsistent Behavior 202
Preparing a Performance Conditions Assessment 203
Step 1: Listing Information about the Student and the Target Skill 203
Step 2: Checking Off General Performance Issues to Investigate 209
Step 3: Describing Specific Questions to Assess 212
Step 4: Planning and Scheduling Assessment Procedures 213
Conducting a Performance Conditions Assessment 215
Watching for Environmental Factors That Affect Performance 215
Thinking Ahead to Intervention Procedures 216
Summarizing the Results of an Assessment 217
Recording Results and Comments on the Worksheet 217
Listing the Findings from the Assessment 218
Summary 219

PART THREE Planning and Implementing Interventions for Teaching Social Competence 225

CHAPTER 9 *Setting Instructional Goals and Brainstorming Procedures 227*
Consolidating Instructional Goals from a Specific Level Assessment 227
Reviewing the Findings 227
Consolidating and Selecting Instructional Goals 230
Finalizing Instructional Goals 232
Procedures for Teaching Social Skills 234
Directions 236
Rehearsal 237

Modeling 240
Prompting 244
Brainstorming Intervention Procedures 247
Step 1: Listing Basic Information and Instructional Goals 252
Step 2: Making a Separate Page for Each Goal 252
Step 3: Checking Off Instructional Approaches to Consider 252
Step 4: Brainstorming Intervention Ideas for Each Goal 253
Summary 253

CHAPTER 10 ***Developing and Refining Intervention Plans 259***
Organizing Intervention Plans 259
Sequencing Instructional Goals 260
Identifying Promising Intervention Procedures 261
Ten Ways to Develop Intervention Procedures 262
Elaborate and Expand on Key Ideas 262
Combine and Coordinate Individual Procedures 263
Involve Colleagues in Planning 263
Match Intervention Plans to Assessment Results 265
Build on Students' Strengths 265
Promote Student Involvement and Independence 266
Integrate Procedures Into the Regular Routine 267
Make Procedures Flexible 267
Consult Published Resources for Additional Ideas 267
Keep Procedures Simple 268
Address Complex Goals 269
Chaining 269
Shaping 271
Increasing Student Incentive 272
Incentive Derives from Students' Understanding of Outcomes 273
Highlight Natural Outcomes 274
Add Rewards for Performance 277
Coordinating and Scheduling Intervention Procedures 280
Integrating Intervention Procedures 280
Scheduling the Intervention 285
Summary 268

CHAPTER 11 ***Monitoring the Intervention 295***
Benefits of Monitoring Interventions 295
Preparing to Monitor Interventions 297
Step 1: Listing Basic Information about the Monitoring Activities 297
Step 2: Entering the Target Skill 300
Step 3: Entering the Standard for the Original Priority Expectation 300
Step 4: Specifying a Level of Confidence for Monitoring the Standards 303
Step 5: Choosing Other Issues for Monitoring 306
Step 6: Listing Procedures for Monitoring 313
Step 7: Providing Spaces for Recording Results 315

Summary 322

CHAPTER 12 *Analyzing Intervention Results and Determining Next Steps* 327
When Interventions Are Working As Planned 328
Sandy's Intervention: A Progress Report 328
Deciding What to Do Next 330
When Interventions Are Not Working As Planned 338
Alfred's Intervention: A Progress Report 339
Deciding What to Do Next 341
Making a Checklist of Scenarios and Options 352
Granville's Intervention: A Progress Report 356
Deciding What to Do Next 357
Summary 358

PART FOUR **Broader Applications in Teaching Social Competence** 365

CHAPTER 13 *Streamlining the Teaching of Social Competence* 367
When to Use a Systematic Approach 367
Addressing the Most Difficult and Long-Standing Behavior Problems 368
Working on New Problems 368
Working with Students Having Severe Learning and Behavior Problems 369
Streamlining the Assessment and Intervention Process 370
Mrs. Armstrong's New Interventions 371
Reviewing the Steps in the Intervention Planning Process 371
Part I: The Social Skills Curriculum and the Survey Level Assessment 372
Part II: Specific Level Assessment 378
Part III: Developing and Conducting Interventions 384
Using a Worksheet to Guide Streamlining 392
Description of Student Behavior and Circumstances 398
Outline of Steps in the Assessment and Intervention Process 398
Notes on How to Complete Each Step 398
Summary 399

CHAPTER 14 *Teaching Social Competence to Groups of Students* 405
Adapting the Intervention Approach to Groups of Students 405
Step 1: Choosing the Settings, Situations, and Groups You Will Address 406
Step 2: Identifying Expectations to Consider Addressing 407
Step 3: Assigning Priorities and Choosing Target Skill(s) 414
Step 4: Listing Key Abilities, Steps, and Conditions for Target Skills 415
Step 5: Conducting Informal Assessment and Listing Instructional Goals for Lessons 416
Step 6: Brainstorming Procedures for Addressing Instructional Goals 417
Step 7: Developing and Improving Lesson Plans 417
Step 8: Coordinating and Scheduling Lesson Plans 423
Step 9: Preparing Monitoring Procedures 424
Summary 425

CHAPTER 15 *Collaboration in Teaching Social Competence 431*
Coordinating Social Skills Instruction with Other Settings 431
Working with Personnel within the Same Grade Level 432
Working with Personnel across Grade Levels and Schools 434
Deciding What to Accomplish by Coordinating Social Skills Instruction 436
Collaborating with Personnel within a Single Grade Level 436
Collaborating with Personnel across Grade Levels or Schools 438
Using a Worksheet to List Objectives 440
Suggestions for Approaching Other Personnel 442
Using the Direct Approach 442
Using the Indirect Approach 442
Coordinating Social Expectations among Settings 444
Working from the Similarities in Social Expectations 445
Working from the Differences in Social Expectations 445
Coordinating Instructional Activities among Settings 447
Summary 448

APPENDIX A **Expectations for Social Behavior 453**

APPENDIX B **Resources and Teaching Materials for Social Skills Instruction 479**

REFERENCES 481

INDEX 487

WORKSHEETS 499

Preface

The procedures outlined in *Teaching Social Competence* have been field-tested and fine-tuned by nearly 600 teachers and other education professionals. The primary audience for the course has been general and special education teachers, but it has also included principals, guidance counselors, teaching assistants, school board members, and parents. Our techniques have been adapted and applied in classes from preschool through high school, in settings as varied as math class and playground, in public, parochial, and special education facilities. Our procedures can be used to set instructional goals and develop interventions for almost any student who has difficulty with social interactions—from the general education student whose behavior is a little too aggressive, awkward, or shy to the student whose social problems are compounded by physical, mental, or emotional disabilities.

Improving the behavior of students who are not socially competent is vital to educational programming. Although we usually recognize that social development is a normal part of the learning and maturation process, we often underestimate just how much it affects students' overall success in school. Problems in social behavior result in poor interactions with classmates and teachers; affect students' motivation, self-esteem, and self-image; diminish academic achievement; and lead to students missing many positive educational and social experiences.

Despite their importance, social skills are rarely taught systematically. Most students acquire them incidentally, by watching and imitating others, learning from trial and error, and interpreting environmental cues that indicate what behaviors are acceptable. Some students, however, though capable of achieving social competence, find it difficult to learn indirectly. Our formal approach will be particularly helpful to such children. A student who has learning or cognitive disabilities, a diminished self-concept, an attention deficit, or other problems will benefit from learning deliberate, rehearsed strategies for social interactions. These strategies help children develop a uniform pattern of behavior that is appropriate in a wide variety of social situations.

A formal approach to teaching social skills is also helpful in addressing chronic social problems. Students with poor social skills may become defiant and quarrelsome, behaving in ways that further impede their social progress. For example, a strongly aggressive student who is rejected by peers may be provoked to even more extreme behavior and as a consequence may be segregated, losing the influence of favorable role models. When students' social skill deficits are long-standing and severe, a step-by-step approach that includes behavior management can help them overcome the motivational problems that often result from a history of enduring others' negative reactions.

We do not offer a universal panacea for troubled students—or, for that matter, for frustrated teachers. It is difficult to predict whether specific students with problems in social behavior will ever be truly successful in their interactions. Teachers are naturally limited in how much they can modify their classroom routines to accommodate students who have major skill deficits. But it is important to recognize that even in severe cases most students can improve their social performance if we can find an effective way of teaching them. This may involve systematic coordinated efforts by school personnel, who must bear in mind the students' potential regardless of their current school placements and academic and personal histories.

A Practical Approach

In *Teaching Social Competence* we explain how you can help students improve their interactions with teachers and classmates. Instead of focusing on students' problems, we stress the importance of understanding how social skills work in particular school settings. When you can identify the key social skills most students use every day, you can target specific areas where a less skilled student needs help. Our techniques can be integrated into the ongoing activities of normal school settings, thus addressing students' problems in the context in which they occur.

Although many of the concepts we present may seem complex, the basic premise behind them is quite simple: the most important thing you can do for students who have problems in social interaction is to look closely and analytically at their behavior and understand the source of their difficulties. The best way to understand the problems most students face is first to identify the skills used by more successful students and then to assess whether specific children are able to act in the same ways. You gain a clear idea of the needs of at-risk or mildly disabled students when you compare their behavior with that of more competent students, and you can then devise precise and effective interventions that will help them improve their social behavior.

Organization

In each chapter, we provide detailed instructions and guidelines for carrying out each stage or task in the assessment and intervention process.

In Part I we discuss competent social behavior and the importance of proficient social skills in school settings. We introduce the idea that social demands form a broad-based social skills curriculum and explain how you can identify the social demands that make up this curriculum in your own setting.

In Part II we explain how to assess a student who has trouble achieving social competence and to define a single clear goal that will give focus to intervention planning. We also consider why a student may not meet a particular social demand, using a three-part process that allows you to examine (a) the student's proficiency in the basic abilities that relate to the demand; (b) how the student performs in trying to meet the demand, and (c) the student's attention to the environmental conditions of the demand.

In Part III we discuss how to develop and implement different types of interventions and how to monitor their results. We also consider options for continuing, fading, and modifying the procedures, depending on the student's progress.

In Part IV we look at some of the ways you can modify or extend the process of assessment and intervention and at how you can adapt the ideas in the text to your actual practice. Finally, we suggest opportunities for using our concepts and techniques in collaborative efforts between teachers in different classrooms and even across grade levels and schools.

Activities and Worksheets

We have supplied a variety of forms that follow a systematic sequence from one chapter to the next in a step-by-step process for analyzing social skills in your students, assessing individual needs, and developing concrete interventions. Although the activities and worksheets have been developed for a college-level preservice teacher course, they are also intended for teachers in the field, and so we have included deliberately extensive details. Our intention was not to burden teachers with extra work but to emphasize each key element in the planning process by linking it to a realistic teaching activity.

Case Study and Examples

Throughout the book, a fifth-grade case study that reflects the experiences of actual teachers shows how our concepts can be applied to real-life school situations. Of course, our methods can be adapted to a wide variety of levels and circumstances; at the end of every chapter, two examples illustrate other settings.

We hope you will easily use the guidelines, worksheets, activities, and examples as the basis of effective strategies for helping your students improve their social competence.

Acknowledgments

We would like to acknowledge the teachers and other school personnel who participated in the courses for which we developed this text. We drew many of our best examples from their worksheets.

We also thank the associate instructors who helped plan course activities and who made valuable suggestions for revising the text: Thomas Brush, Terri Marché, Carrie Chapman, Mary Lou Morton, Laura Versaci, Jeannie Glendenning, Jeannie Brush, Mary Ann Champion, Lori Hubbard, and James Orr. Special thanks go to Mary Lou Morton for helping compile the appendix and to Frances and Emily Knapczyk for their work on the index.

Finally, we appreciate the thoughtful responses of the following reviewers: Janis Chadsey-Rusch, University of Illinois; Christine Cheney, University of Nevada; Tim Lewis, University of Oregon; Keith Storey, San Francisco State University; and George Sugai, University of Oregon.

Dennis R. Knapczyk
Paul Rodes

Teaching Social Competence

A Practical Approach for Improving Social Skills in Students At-Risk

PART ONE

Social Competence and the Social Skills Curriculum

In Part I we introduce the concept of social competence and consider the types of demands students must meet to be proficient in their social interactions. One way to describe the demands for being socially competent is as kind of a "social skills curriculum," similar to the academic curriculum you use in subject matter areas like reading or math. In the subsequent chapters, we draw many parallels between the explicit and well-documented academic curricula you are already using in your teaching and the implicit and "hidden" social skills curriculum that is also important to your students' success in school. An important first step in teaching social competence will be to identify and list this curriculum, because—like any other curriculum—it can serve as a framework for determining whether students have the skills they need at a particular age or grade level, and for deciding where to focus instruction.

In Chapter One we discuss social competence and social skills, and show that these concepts can be defined in terms of the demands for social behavior that typical students encounter in their everyday interactions at school. We explain how social demands are set in school and emphasize the value of closely observing and considering the complex network of demands that students in your own school settings negotiate daily.

In Chapter Two we explore the idea of a social skills curriculum and discuss how it pertains to students' achieving social competence. We show how you can describe or list the social skills curriculum for your particular classroom or school setting, and how you can use it in planning instruction and developing interventions for improving students' social behavior.

Chapter Three explains how to identify the standards for the individual demands in a social skills curriculum. These standards indicate the level of social behavior students display in their interactions. Whereas a social skills curriculum describes *what* students must do in their social interactions, standards signify *how much* the students must actually do these things to achieve social competence.

As a unit, the chapters in Part I are designed to give you a clearer and more detailed understanding of the network of social demands that typical students meet every day. This should lay the groundwork for your identifying the types of problems individual students may have in their interactions, and for planning procedures to improve their behavior.

CHAPTER 1

Social Competence and Social Expectations

"Granville is too aggressive." "Sandy is too shy and withdrawn to talk with her classmates." "Alfred means well, but he plays the clown all the time. He probably does not get enough attention at home." When teachers think of social skills, they usually think in terms of problems like these. Almost any teacher can name a half dozen students who have difficulty participating in social interactions with peers or adults. It is less often, however, that we consider the nature and complexity of skilled, competent social behavior. What are social skills? How are they judged? Who sets social demands, and how do students recognize and react to them? To understand the way social behavior is constructed and patterned in school settings, we must think beyond our problem students and their unskilled performance, and look at the ways average students show competence in their everyday social interactions. In this chapter, we look closely at what social skills are and consider the complex demands students must meet to achieve social competence.

Looking at Social Competence

Students must display an enormous range of behavior to reach even an average level of social competence. Social competence encompasses the broad array of perceptions, judgments, and behaviors that enable students to be successful in their social interactions (Campbell & Siperstein, 1994). Students demonstrate social competence by such actions as the following:

- Exchanging greetings with adults
- Conversing with classmates
- Recognizing positive and negative reactions to behavior
- Accepting criticism or praise from teachers

- Responding to teasing or derogatory comments
- Dealing with the aggressive acts of schoolmates

Social competence includes both verbal and nonverbal behavior—from participating in class discussions and conversing on current topics and trends to interpreting body language and using facial expressions and gestures.

The ability to use these skills correctly determines students' social competence. *Social competence* is thus a broader and more inclusive term than *social skills* because it refers not simply to discrete actions and abilities, but to the overall quality and adequacy of the behavior students display in their interactions. Social competence is actually an evaluative term that reflects the judgments people make about behavior: students show they are socially competent by acting in ways compatible with and acceptable to those around them. To achieve social competence, then, students must have the skills to meet the demands of the people with whom they interact on a day-to-day basis (McFall, 1982). Obviously, average students' social behavior need not be exceptional, but it must at least be adequate for the circumstances they are in for other people to view them as competent.

The individual skills and actions students must master to show social competence are those that allow them to initiate, sustain, adapt, alter, and discontinue interactions as conditions dictate. These skills allow students to engage in inter-

Social skills are crucial to successful school performance.

actions that are socially acceptable and personally satisfying. Students who have a good repertoire of social skills are able to attain outcomes that are mutually beneficial to participants in an interaction and to achieve goals that are challenging and gratifying (Combs & Slaby, 1977; Dowrick, 1986; Merrell, 1994).

Social Competence and Social Incompetence

Although learning competent social behavior is one of the most important achievements students attain in school, it rarely receives the attention we give to incompetent behavior (Howell, Fox, & Morehead, 1993; Nichols, 1992). As teachers, we usually take socially competent behavior for granted because it fits in well with the circumstances students are in and conforms to our expectations. We may be aware that particular students are socially accepted and reasonably well liked by peers and adults, but we rarely consider the range of skills and abilities they regularly employ to achieve this status. On the other hand, our attention is easily drawn to students' unskilled behavior because these actions do not correspond to what we usually expect. Learning and behavior problems are more noticeable than skilled performance because they disrupt the natural flow of classroom activities and school routines. Consequently, both we and our students usually know which children are not competent in their interactions because their behavior differs from that of the peer group in some significant way.

Furthermore, we often characterize or label the transgressing students' behavior according to the problems in their interactions. For example, we may describe student behavior as "immature," "disruptive," "inattentive," "aggressive," or "withdrawn." We can usually support our use of these labels by citing examples of the students' classroom and school behavior; by describing their past exploits; or by referring to their school records, test scores, and reports (Campbell & Claus, 1982). In addition, we often attribute the difficulties students have in their social interactions to some type of disability or to factors such as immaturity, cultural diversity, or home environment (Dowrick, 1986). By doing so, we try to "explain away" the problems by labeling them, as if the explanation itself provides an adequate solution to the difficulties the students are experiencing.

In short, our natural inclination is often to attribute to students the characteristics of their behavior, and to view the problem behavior as "the problem student." Unfortunately, this response can impede our efforts to help students overcome their difficulties in social interactions, as we tend to react to the students' unacceptable behavior rather than to identify the social skills we need to teach them so they can behave more appropriately. To increase students' social competence, we must do more than document their problems or guess at the causes of their failures; we must focus on the skills they need to learn to be successful in their interactions (Scales, 1990).

To illustrate this approach to improving social competence, the following section presents a case study of a teacher who is considering the social problems of three students in her class. We show how she can best help these three by gaining a better understanding of the social skills used by the more competent students in her class. We refer to this case study and these three students throughout the text to give concrete examples of the concepts and procedures involved in teaching social competence.

Case Study: Three Students in Mrs. Armstrong's Class

Mrs. Armstrong is a fifth-grade homeroom, social studies, and language arts teacher at Madison Elementary School. She is in the teacher's lounge talking with Mr. Wagner, the fifth-grade math and science teacher, and Ms. Hernandez, one of the school's special education teachers. They are comparing notes on this year's students, and Mrs. Armstrong is explaining that she is worried about the progress of several students in her class.

Most of Mrs. Armstrong's class is performing pretty much as she would expect, but she is perplexed by a few students who have displayed a range of social problems over the past quarter. She is describing some of these problems to Mr. Wagner, who teaches many of the same students in his classes, and to Ms. Hernandez, who provides special education services to one of them. She explains that these are not the only students who need extra help in her class, but the approaches that are successful with the other students do not seem to work for these few. She is particularly concerned about three students.

One of them, **Granville,** has been in special education for the past few years because of his behavioral problems. This year he has been mainstreamed in Mrs. Armstrong's and Mr. Wagner's classes, but he still receives some individualized help from Ms. Hernandez. Granville gets D's and F's in most of his schoolwork, even though his achievement test scores show that he should be doing much better. Mrs. Armstrong and some of the other teachers describe him as aggressive, quick-tempered, and a bully. He calls classmates names, makes obscene and threatening gestures, and hits and pushes other students. Few of Granville's classmates choose to interact with him, but some will tease him and provoke his outbursts.

Mrs. Armstrong has noticed that Granville shows respect for her, follows her directions, and participates adequately in most classroom activities; but she usually has to separate him from the other students during small group lessons because he does not interact well with classmates on cooperative tasks. During class breaks, recess times, and art and gym periods, Granville actively seeks out other students, but his interactions often end in verbal and physical confrontations.

Mrs. Armstrong senses that Granville would very much like to get along with his classmates, but he goes about it the wrong way. She has repeatedly reprimanded him and used "time out" and other disciplinary techniques to try to reach him, but his behavior has not changed appreciably over the school year. It is clear that Granville's problems in interacting with classmates are adversely affecting his school work.

Sandy is usually well behaved and never displays the kind of aggressive behavior that Granville shows. However, Mrs. Armstrong is worried that Sandy is overly quiet and unsociable in school. She seems to need constant reassurance that she is doing her work correctly, even though she rarely asks questions when she actually does need help. Although Sandy can read fairly well and has the potential to work at grade level, she earns D's in most of her academic subjects.

Mrs. Armstrong feels that Sandy's difficulties with her schoolwork are related more to her lack of self-esteem, poor motivation, and social immaturity than to limitations in her academic ability. Sandy does not like to participate in class discussions or group activities and seems generally uninterested in instructional lessons. Mrs. Armstrong suspects that Sandy receives little support at home, and, as a result, she is far too dependent on her teachers for approval even though she is as reluctant to initiate interactions with them as with her classmates.

Alfred interacts well with Mrs. Armstrong, but he acts silly when he is around his classmates. He is clearly attempting to gain peer approval by his clowning, but his classmates are more likely to reject him as "too weird." When Alfred talks with classmates, he tends to interrupt, repeat himself frequently, and speak too loudly and insistently. Furthermore, he chooses topics of conversation that are either too immature or too esoteric for his peers. Alfred does not seem to play organized games very well, so during recess classmates rarely ask him to participate in their activities. As a result of these problems, Alfred has few friends, and other students tend to shun him or tease him for not fitting in. Alfred's social problems have also begun to affect his schoolwork, as he does not take much interest in classroom activities and bothers his neighbors rather than paying attention or doing his assignments.

Mrs. Armstrong tells Mr. Wagner and Ms. Hernandez that she has tried to spend extra time with Granville, Sandy, and Alfred by working with them individually. She keeps a close watch on how they are doing on assignments, and she encourages them to interact more positively with schoolmates in classroom and recess activities. However, Mrs. Armstrong senses that the additional time and attention she gives these students is having little positive impact on their behavior because she is failing to get at the real sources of their problems. Mrs. Armstrong is afraid that if she cannot find a new approach for helping these three students, they will not be able to meet the demands of the sixth grade when they move on to Jefferson Middle School next year.

Focusing on Competence

As Mrs. Armstrong has discovered, addressing complex or challenging problems in social behavior can be difficult, using the kind of informal or haphazard approach she has tried so far with Granville, Sandy, and Alfred. Moreover, if she tries further to classify and label the source of the students' difficulties, she is likely to be no closer to helping them. To address the problems of students like Granville, Sandy, and Alfred, we need a complete shift in focus. Rather than cataloging and analyzing the problems they display, we must identify the specific social skills they need to learn.

This shift brings our approach to social problems into line with the way we usually address difficulties in the academic areas, such as in English or math. For example, when Mrs. Armstrong works with students who have problems in reading or social studies, she does not spend time labeling their mistakes, or searching for causes. Instead, she determines which parts of the subject area pose particular difficulties for the students, and which major facts or skills they need to learn. In the same way, then, when she focuses on the social problems of her students, she does not need to label Granville's aggressive personality so much as to decide on better alternatives to teach him; nor will speculations on the effects of Sandy's home life prove as helpful to her instruction as a clear analysis of the class participation and conversational skills Sandy needs to learn.

Therefore, the best way to address problems in social competence is to focus on *competent,* rather than incompetent, behavior. When students show significant problems in their social behavior—problems that seem resistant to ordinary remedial methods—the best approach is to identify *what students must do* to match their behavior to the demands of school settings (Wasik, 1990). Instead of asking "What's wrong with these students?" we need to ask "What must these students learn to improve their behavior?" The first question will lead us down blind alleys and waste our efforts on obscure problems. The second question will help us set goals for interventions that focus on substituting skilled behavior for unskilled behavior.

The effectiveness of social skills instruction, just as that of academic instruction, depends far more on a thorough understanding of the subject or skill area itself than on a listing of the students' problems (Scales, 1990). By identifying the skills average students use to meet the social demands of their teachers and classmates, we can determine what we should teach the students who need to improve their social competence. Our approach in this text, therefore, begins by looking not at the problem behaviors of high-risk students like Sandy, Alfred, and Granville, but rather at the socially competent behavior of typical students. In describing the everyday social interactions of average, competent students, we can lay the foundation for setting goals and finding solutions for students who have not effectively learned these vital social skills.

The Complexity of Social Demands

Although "the everyday social behavior of average students" may sound like a simple subject, social behavior can be an enormously complicated area to understand and describe. One of the most important things to recognize about social skills is that they represent extremely complex performance. Every day, ordinary students respond to an intricate network of social demands, skillfully using prescribed patterns to negotiate a maze of changing situations and settings (Kasen, Johnson, & Cohen, 1990). Because most students learn social behavior incidentally in the course of their growth and schooling, this process can look deceptively natural and straightforward. Consequently, we often overlook the complicated perceptions, judgments, and skills that are required to interact at even a minimum level of competence.

For example, on the school playground during a typical recess period, students in Mrs. Armstrong's fifth-grade class talk with one another on many different topics, using a variety of language patterns. They may speak differently with friends than with other classmates, with boys than with girls, and with peers than with adults. At the same time, the students have to show proficiency in certain games, demonstrate familiarity with current fads and trends, and negotiate conflicts without getting into fights. Failure to meet any one of these demands can result in loss of status, rejection by peers, punishment by adults, or even physical violence.

To perform competently in circumstances like these, students must be able to tailor their interactions to the various standards for acceptable behavior. They must pay close attention to the constantly changing conditions that indicate which interactions to engage in and what form the interactions should take (Kronick, 1981; Salvia & Hughes, 1990). For instance, the content and tone of the fifth graders' conversations can change markedly as the participants, topics, or locations of the conversations shift. Similarly, while playing games on the playground, the students may need to draw on significantly different types of skills as the size and composition of the play groups change during the recess period, or as the game progresses toward a conclusion. They must recognize these changes and adapt their behavior to ensure that their interactions continue to be effective.

Students must also be able to predict the outcomes of their actions, assess their effectiveness, and modify their behavior as circumstances in the environment dictate (Fagan, Long, & Stevens, 1975; Renshaw & Asher, 1982). During conversations or games, for example, students must anticipate the reactions their comments or actions will elicit, must judge from actual reactions whether their performance is appropriate, and must continue the activity or modify their behavior as the situation may warrant. Failure to recognize the way one's behavior is perceived can accentuate unskilled performance and turn minor mistakes into major blunders and awkward behavior patterns. In short, ordinary social competence is made up of a significant array of skills, which must be constantly adapted to many changing factors. In the next sections, we discuss in more detail some of the elements that contribute to the complexity of social demands.

Social Demands and Situations

The activities in which students take part during the school day create different demands on their social behavior (Campbell & Siperstein, 1994). In general, these school situations fall into two categories. In *structured situations*—those that involve close supervision or specific directions from adults—social behavior is typically defined by the nature of the activity, and the opportunities students have to interact are somewhat restricted. For example, during Mrs. Armstrong's presentation of an instructional lesson, her students' interactions are mostly limited to asking questions and volunteering answers. The content of the interactions is generally restricted to the topic of the lesson, and the students' choice of what to say and do is considerably reduced by her direction.

On the other hand, in *unstructured situations*—those that involve less strict supervision or an absence of formal tasks and activities—student interactions can take a broader variety of forms. Unstructured situations can include transition times between classroom activities, passing time in the school hallways, lunchtime in the cafeteria, recess, and any other nondirected or noninstructional times. In these situations, students typically have many more opportunities to interact, and many choices of how to behave. During class breaks, Mrs. Armstrong's students might or might not seek out classmates for conversation. They can select whom to approach or avoid, decide on the content of their interactions, and choose the form the interaction takes.

Thus, the demands for interacting appropriately in structured and in unstructured situations are usually very different. Students must be able to distinguish clearly between these demands and adapt their behavior to respond to them. Mrs. Armstrong's students typically change their behavior significantly as they move from one situation to another. They become much quieter and stop clowning as they move from the playground area or school hallway into Mrs. Armstrong's classroom. At the same time, most of them are able to recognize certain social demands that carry over to both structured and unstructured settings, such as responding politely to adults, or avoiding physical conflicts. Students who have trouble recognizing and responding to these variations in social demands as they move between structured and unstructured situations can exhibit inappropriate and inconsistent behavior and can stand out noticeably from their more competent peers.

Social Demands and People

Social demands are further complicated by the different people who affect the shape that interactions take. In most school settings, social demands are set or influenced by teachers and administrators, by classmates, and by the values and perceptions of the individual students themselves. In this section, we look at some of the complexities these different people can add to the demands for social behavior.

Demands Established by School Personnel

Many of the social demands in school are initiated or shaped by the teachers and other personnel who oversee student behavior. Most of the behavior of Mrs. Armstrong's students conforms to the rules and guidelines she sets for her class. Their behavior is further affected by such factors as the teaching approaches she uses, the activities she schedules, and the grouping arrangements she sets up (Campbell & Siperstein, 1994).

Other school personnel who also establish demands for Mrs. Armstrong's students may include the following:

- Other teachers who work with her students
- Staff who supervise students' passing time in the hallways
- Administrative personnel who set guidelines for behavior throughout the school building and grounds
- Playground supervisors who oversee recess times
- Cafeteria workers who monitor lunchtime activities
- Maintenance workers who set standards for cleanliness of the school building

To achieve social competence, Mrs. Armstrong's students must become skilled at internalizing and responding to the demands of their teachers. As the students move from one setting or circumstance to another, they must understand and adapt to the array of demands that other school personnel place on their behavior as well.

When Mrs. Armstrong and Mr. Wagner compared notes on their students' behavior in their classrooms, they discovered that they have some different demands for social performance. For instance, Mrs. Armstrong feels that clowning around disrupts the flow of her teaching lessons, and she does not tolerate any outlandish comments or sarcastic remarks. On the other hand, Mr. Wagner uses a more relaxed teaching format, and he permits his students to joke with him and tease one another during some of the class activities. When they consider the differences in their demands, the teachers are surprised at how skillfully and naturally most of the students in the class modify their behavior as they move from one class to the other. But they also realize that these differences may be a significant source of difficulty for less aware or less skilled students.

Demands Established by Classmates

School personnel are not the only source of social demands in school. Classmates and peers set requirements for social behavior that can be as crucial to students' overall success as those set by their teachers. Furthermore, these peer-set demands are often far more inflexible and exacting than those of adults (Brendtro, Brokenleg, & Van Brockern, 1990; Downs & Rose, 1991). While such requirements are usually unstated, they are nonetheless clearly prescribed—and often set in stone—by prevailing practices.

The demands of classmates and peers are most apparent in unstructured situations—during activities like playing games, holding conversations, working together on class assignments, and engaging in other informal social interactions. In these situations peers set standards for the number of interactions in which students engage, their content and form, and their location and context. For example, during recess periods, fifth graders in Mrs. Armstrong's class expect classmates to talk on particular topics, play certain games proficiently, and use specific language patterns. Students who do not perform to the demands of the group may be ignored, teased, shunned, and excluded from activities and interactions. Even though Mrs. Armstrong feels that some of these demands are not really appropriate and would like students to show more tolerance and sensitivity toward one another, she realizes that the students must meet these requirements, at least to a minimal level, to make friends and to be accepted by their peer groups. Furthermore, Mrs. Armstrong must be able to identify these peer-set demands so she can help students like Granville, Sandy, and Alfred improve their behavior when they interact with classmates.

Demands Self-Established by Students

To further complicate this picture, individual students also set demands for their own behavior (Bauer & Sapona, 1991). They usually encounter very few problems in their performance when these demands correspond to those of their teachers

Social demands are set by many people in school settings.

and classmates, and when they have the skills to meet them. But sometimes the requirements students have for their own social behavior are unrealistic, impracticable, or not commensurate with their ability. Problems in social behavior will often occur when students require behavior of themselves that does not match what is expected by their teachers and classmates or that is not in keeping with their capabilities.

Sandy may have very high aspirations for her classroom participation but may not have the conversational skills or the experiential background to meet these demands. As a consequence, she may feel that she is a failure if she is not a central contributor in group activities, and may give up trying to do well at all. Similarly, Alfred may envision himself as class leader, but he may not have the leadership skills that classmates expect of someone who takes this role. Thus, some of his inept interactions with classmates may result from his awkward attempts at exercising leadership. In cases such as Sandy's and Alfred's, the mismatch between the demands students establish for themselves and their ability to meet these demands may be a far greater source of frustration and embarrassment than any of the requirements set by their teachers and classmates.

Although self-determined demands are among the most important factors affecting social behavior, they are often the most difficult to identify. Interviewing students or closely observing how they react to their own performance can sometimes uncover discrepancies between the demands they place on their behavior and their actual ability level. But sometimes this information is almost impossible to obtain. Nevertheless, when you weigh the complexity of the social behavior students must demonstrate, it is always important to consider the impact of their own demands on their behavior. Students whose responses indicate discouragement or low self-esteem often are asking more of themselves than they can achieve. Therefore, helping students set and meet realistic demands for their behavior is often a very important aspect of improving their social competence.

Explicit and Implicit Demands

Another factor adding to the complexity of social demands is the manner in which these demands are communicated to students. Many social rules are stated or written explicitly. For example, in Mrs. Armstrong's fifth-grade classroom, students are expected to obey the rules she sets out for the class, to avoid arguments during small group work, and to contribute their ideas to class discussions. These demands are explicit because Mrs. Armstrong communicates them to her students and posts them on the bulletin board.

But many other demands for social behavior are implicit, subjective in nature, and established more by conventional practices than by stated rules (Campbell & Siperstein, 1994). Mrs. Armstrong's setting includes many demands that are unstated or understood for the class, and how well students meet these demands affects how successful they are in her classroom. Implicit demands regulate the way students

- greet her when they enter the classroom
- seek out help in doing their work
- ask for and share school supplies
- cooperate with one another when working on assigned tasks
- talk with one another before and after class begins

Peer-set demands in particular are likely to be implicit, involving areas such as the topics students choose for conversation during free time; the local conventions and adaptations they use in games and sports; and the current mannerisms, gestures, and language patterns they employ in speech. Although these requirements are never written or expressed in any formal manner, success in making friends and achieving status in peer groups depends on students' ability to recognize and to meet demands like these.

Therefore, to meet *all* the social demands for Mrs. Armstrong's class, students must not only follow posted rules and comply with her verbal instructions, but they must also extend greetings, share supplies, cooperate on assignments, converse with classmates, and meet many other demands that are never explicitly stated. Many social behavior problems may be attributed to students' failure to recognize and meet many of these "understood" demands. Therefore, when you consider the social demands of your settings, you should look carefully for the basic skills students must have to meet these unstated but nonetheless crucial demands.

A Short Activity

You can gain a sense of how complicated social behavior is by looking at what students do in everyday school situations. Spend five or ten minutes watching the typical interactions of students and listing about ten distinct social behaviors or actions you see. Look at both a structured and an unstructured situation to get a sense of the different social demands for each.

Mrs. Armstrong decided to observe the behavior of her fifth-grade students during a social studies activity in her classroom and in the hallway during a break between class periods. In each situation, she observed for a few minutes, then listed on a worksheet ten things she had seen the students do. Figure 1.1 shows the worksheet Mrs. Armstrong filled out.

During the map coloring activity, Mrs. Armstrong was surprised to note how much quiet interaction—much of it nonverbal—went on between herself and the students through eye contact and facial expressions. In the hallway, conversely, she noted that the interactions tended to be broader and more verbal, and often involved physical contact.

Notice that Mrs. Armstrong concentrated on social behaviors that seemed typical or average in these situations. At the same time, of course, she would also have seen a lot of problem behavior—students talking too loudly, pushing or fighting, sitting alone rather than with a group, and so on. But her principle focus was *competent* performance, to gain an understanding of what is involved in displaying typical social behavior. In the same way, it is a good idea for you to focus on examples of average, competent social behavior to get a better sense of the hundreds of little things that ordinary students do every day to form friendships, to avoid conflicts, to communicate with teachers, and in short, to promote and maintain a comfortable, productive social environment in which to interact and learn.

Need for a Systematic Approach

Once we begin to examine the intricate network of skills and actions that make up social competence, we see that this is not an area we can approach haphazardly. Social demands are complex, and we need to address problems in social behavior carefully and systematically, as a quick or impulsive approach may miss the source of the students' problems. If Mrs. Armstrong wants to design an intervention to help Alfred replace his clownish behavior with more mature responses, she may be overwhelmed by the wide-ranging social skills issues that Alfred's behavior

Figure 1.1 Mrs. Armstrong's list of social behavior

Worksheet 1.1: Observing Social Behavior	Page 1 of 2
Name: *Mrs. Armstrong*	Date: *Sept. 2*

Structured situation: *5th-grade social studies—map coloring activity—small groups*

Behaviors observed:

1. *Students are whispering to their neighbors.*
2. *A few students borrow crayons or markers from others.*
3. *Students often ask their neighbors why they are using a certain color.*
4. *Many students ask the teacher questions and show the teacher their maps.*
5. *Students raise eyebrows, smile, and so on, at teacher's response.*
6. *Some light verbal teasing goes on among students and among teacher and students.*
7. *Some students visit with friends on their way to the wastebasket or pencil sharpener.*
8. *Most raise their hands to signal the teacher when they have finished the task.*
9. *Students who have finished converse quietly; most make plans for lunch and recess, or discuss the assignment they just did.*
10. *Two friends make funny faces at each other from across the room and mouth words silently.*

Figure 1.1 *(continued)*

Worksheet 1.1: Observing Social Behavior	Page 2 of 2
Name: *Mrs. Armstrong*	Date: *Sept. 2*

Unstructured situation: *Hallway (early morning)—5th-grade students*

Behaviors observed:

1. *Students gossip and talk about previous evening's events, TV shows, etc.*
2. *Several students greet the principal as they come into the building. "Good Morning, Ms. Guindling."*
3. *Several boys are talking in a group while two boys are jamming on "air" guitars.*
4. *Teasing—one girl is gently pulling on the hair of the girl in front of her.*
5. *Most students are talking very loudly—not paying much attention to teachers.*
6. *Students line up to use the drinking fountain; there is some playful pushing, but most just talk to the others in line.*
7. *Two boys were taking turns trying to pick each other up.*
8. *Students pass notes—usually if from a boy to a girl or girl to a boy, they are given to a third person who passes it on. Also girls write notes to other girls.*
9. *A student closes his friend's locker before the friend has finished using it, so he'll have to open it again. (This seems to be the "in" thing right now.)*
10. *Students go into classroom in groups (boys with boys, girls with girls).*

represents. How extensive is his problem behavior? Are there some social areas where his performance is already average or competent? Is he better at meeting peer-set demands than at meeting his teachers' demands? Are Alfred's problems motivational, or does he simply lack the skills to improve? Which of his problem areas should she address first: Conversations? Game-playing? Classroom behavior? In which locations should she direct her attention: The playground? The classroom? The cafeteria? And during what times: During class work? Independent time? Recess? Even after she has answered these questions, how can she be sure she has considered the full range of Alfred's social behavior and not overlooked something central?

While she is thinking about how, when, and where to help Alfred change his behavior, what about Granville and Sandy? Will she need to start all over with them? All these questions point to the need for a deliberate, well-planned approach to addressing problems in social behavior. You cannot begin to answer these types of questions for your own circumstances without a broad-based, systematic consideration of all the issues pertaining to the difficulties students face. We have found that you cannot make a detailed examination of these considerations without first gaining a complete understanding of what social competence entails in your particular circumstances. Thus the first step in identifying problems in social behavior is to look closely at the expectations for social behavior in your school and to understand what students must do to meet them. We explain what social expectations are in the next section.

Expectations for Social Behavior

To define the requirements for social competence in useful, concrete language, we speak of the demands placed on students' behavior in terms of *expectations*. Expectations are reflected in the behaviors students display in competent interactions. By this term we do not mean to express the hopes or attitudes we have for student performance (as in "high expectations"), but rather to indicate the demands or requirements for minimally competent behavior that students are expected to meet. Note that expectations apply to all facets of school performance, not just social skills (Brophy & Good, 1986; Good & Weinstein, 1986). When Mrs. Armstrong's students complete a homework assignment, read a passage in their textbook, or pass a test or quiz, they are meeting particular expectations for academic competence in her class. Table 1.1 shows examples of expectations in some academic areas.

The idea of expectations goes beyond the rules and regulations that we ask students to follow, however, and is broader than the skills that enable them to master subject matter content. In this text, of course, our focus is the expectations for social behavior. These may include such diverse areas as playing games, conversing with classmates, showing respect for teachers, and setting personal goals and knowing how to attain them. Some expectations may involve the use of fairly basic skills, such as greeting a teacher at the start of a class period or asking a simple question about an assignment. Others may require much more sophisticated skills, like giving a class presentation on a science project, leading a small group discussion, or building lasting friendships with schoolmates. Table 1.2 gives examples of social expectations for different school settings. Notice that these descriptions are quite similar to the academic expectations described in Table 1.1.

The distinction characterizing these items as expectations is that *students must actually demonstrate these behaviors to show competence in their social interactions.* Expectations represent the skills and actions that advance students' social maturity and academic achievement, promote their friendships with classmates, enhance their overall independence, and relate to the other indicators of school success. As the list in Table 1.2 implies, being successful in school depends on much more than gaining knowledge in academic subject matter; having a good repertoire of social skills is just as likely to contribute to students' success as is having good academic skills.

Advantages of Looking at Expectations

A comparison of Tables 1.1 and 1.2 suggests that expectations can help us understand and quantify social requirements in much the same way that we normally understand and quantify academic requirements. By using them, we can develop a consistent and objective measure for judging students' social competence and for identifying skill deficits and instructional goals for students who display problem behavior. In the following section we explain what expectations are and discuss the reasons for and advantages of studying them.

Expectations Are Realistic

The first important point about expectations is that they are *minimum* requirements for being competent in school. We tend to think of expectations as what we ask our students to do. In reality, however, students who succeed at an average level may be doing considerably less than we think. For example, Mrs. Armstrong

TABLE 1.1 Examples of academic expectations for school settings

Setting: Social Studies Class	*Setting: Math Class*
Passes test on Bill of Rights	Brings completed homework to class
Recites names and capitals of states	Answers questions correctly during drill
Completes two-page report on state of choice	Passes quiz on base numbers
Answers questions on text during class	Multiplies single-digit fractions
Completes and turns in homework assignment	Shows all work on homework problems

TABLE 1.2 Examples of social expectations for school settings

Setting: Social Studies Class	*Setting: School Playground*	*Setting: All School Settings*
Works with partner on homework assignment	Asks peers to play games or share in recess activities	Establishes friendships with peers
Works cooperatively with peers	Follows local rules when playing games	Cooperates with instructional personnel
Asks for help when having difficulty with an assignment	Plays with peers without fighting	Ignores peer verbal/physical aggression
Answers questions when called on	Participates in peer play groups	Shares peer interaction problems with teacher
Participates in class discussion	Enters conversations without interrupting	Accepts constructive criticism given by peers or teachers
Remains quiet during a class activity	Encourages teammates during games	
Shares materials and supplies with peers	Converses on age-appropriate topics	
Interacts with peers other than close friends		

would like her students to play games together and avoid conflicts every day during the recess period. But in reality, her average fifth graders may join in cooperative activities only about 50% of the time and may avoid conflicts only about three days out of five to maintain their friendships and further their social development. If an average student can achieve a minimum level of competence under these conditions, then behaving correctly every day is not really an expectation of the setting, despite Mrs. Armstrong's wishes.

Looking at the minimum demands for behavior in this way can help you rethink the social requirements of your class and clarify your understanding of what students actually need to do to be socially competent. In other words, expectations define the realistic, minimum demands for passing a class or making a few friends rather than describing the theoretical or ideal requirements for earning an A+ or being the most popular student in school. In practical terms, this view of expectations will help you set goals that bring your students up to a competent level of social interaction based on well-defined criteria for achieving success in the setting. Furthermore, it avoids the danger of creating a wider gap between your students' current performance level and the ideal social performance that is too often perceived by both students and teachers as unattainable. Thus, rather than trying to make Alfred the most popular fifth grader, Mrs. Armstrong should focus instead on helping him hold up his end of a conversation so he can make one or two friends or at least be accepted by his peer groups.

Expectations describe observable social behavior.

Expectations Are Objective

Another important point about expectations is that we can describe them in terms of observable behavior rather than vague or arbitrary qualities. Too often, we tend to think of social performance in subjective and unmeasurable terms such as "having a positive attitude" or "being interested in group activities." When we make such judgments, however, we cannot see our students' attitudes or measure their interest; what we are really considering are the specific actions that demonstrate these qualities. We judge behavior like this by such factors as whether students watch what is going on, offer encouragement to peers, add pertinent comments to discussions, and work in cooperation with their group. Thus, we really evaluate whether students *act* interested, not whether they *are* interested.

In Tables 1.1 and 1.2, expectations are described in terms of the external signs that demonstrate that students meet the requirements of a situation, not as inner states of mind (Kruger, 1990). Thus, we can judge student behavior in quantifiable and objective terms, based on actual observation. This description also has important implications for helping students improve their social skills. It would be a daunting task, after all, for Mrs. Armstrong to teach Sandy "not to be withdrawn" or "to have a better self-image." If instead she focuses on more objective, observable goals, such as "starts conversations with peers" or "smiles and comments when teacher talks to her," she can direct Sandy's instruction toward skills that offer genuine, definable progress—giving her a far bigger boost than a more general approach to her problems could ever achieve.

Expectations Are Impersonal

Another notable feature of expectations is that they represent the demands that *all* students in a setting have to meet and not simply the demands for particular students who are having problems in social interactions. This point is important because we usually think of expectations as varying according to the abilities of each student. Remember, however, we are no longer using the term *expectation* to mean what is predicted or hoped for, but rather to indicate the minimal, average requirements for competence. Although we may be able to guess which students will exceed or fall short of this level, the basic level that defines competence remains the same for all the students.

In some cases, you may need to set intermediate steps or objectives for students who are far from meeting some particular expectations. But even here you are not changing the expectation for those students; you are just indicating the intermediate steps or subskills they must learn before reaching a fully competent level. And by setting your sights on the level of skilled behavior that is typical of students in the setting, you are assured of setting functional and realistic goals for the students who have not yet achieved this level. Your judgments about their potential will be accurate and impartial, and you will avoid demanding too much—or too little—of them.

Expectations Are Localized

As we mentioned above, social demands are set by specific situations and people in the school environment. Because expectations are based on the behavior of actual students, they are tailored to the specific demands of each setting in which they are described. Describing expectations thus has advantages over using standardized catalogs or social skills inventories, which too often overlook regional, cultural, and economic factors important in defining social norms.

In many respects Mrs. Armstrong's students act like other fifth-grade children across the country. But important elements of their behavior might be affected by the school's location, the students' cultural background, and local economic and social conditions. A deliberate effort by Mrs. Armstrong to account for such factors when using standardized materials could easily ensnare her in a morass of assumptions and prejudices. But because expectations are based on the observable behavior of children in the setting, they can account for local conditions naturally and automatically without relying on Mrs. Armstrong's personal judgments and biases.

Expectations Are Positive

The greatest advantage in looking at expectations brings our discussion of social skills full circle. Earlier in this chapter, we discussed the importance of focusing on competent rather than incompetent behavior. Instead of asking "What's wrong with this student?" we pointed to the need to ask "What must this student learn to improve his or her behavior?" Expectations allow us to answer that question by redefining student problems in terms of the competent behavior the student needs to learn, focusing on positive attainable skills rather than on failures (Campbell & Siperstein, 1994).

If Mrs. Armstrong looks only at Alfred's problem behavior, she might focus on items like these:

- Goes out of turn during playground games
- Talks too loudly in the cafeteria
- Talks on immature subjects
- Does not sit still during teaching lessons
- Acts silly and immature around peers
- Clowns around and bothers neighbors during class

To redefine these problem areas, Mrs. Armstrong could look at the way most of Alfred's classmates behave in each of these same circumstances. She might come up with the following list of expectations that apply to the problems Alfred shows in his behavior:

- Takes turns in playground games
- Keeps voice below overall noise level of cafeteria
- Talks on age-appropriate subjects
- Stays in seat during teaching lessons
- Uses age-appropriate body language and gestures in peer group
- Whispers quietly to neighbor during class

This approach may seem like little more than a semantic shift, but it is nonetheless important. Now, instead of reciting a laundry list of complaints about Alfred, Mrs. Armstrong can begin to concentrate her efforts on the particular skills he needs to learn—skills that his competent peers have already mastered in their day-to-day interactions, and skills that will improve his behavior. Thus, rather than analyzing vague or uncontrollable factors such as self-esteem, emotional disturbance, or lack of support at home, expectations can clarify the areas of behavior you are trying to improve so you can use these areas as the goals for the interventions (Cohen & Fish, 1993). Expectations are the observable, positive behaviors that average, typical students use to participate in interactions with adults and schoolmates. In the next chapter, we show you how you can identify and list these expectations for your own settings.

❍ Summary

Looking at Social Competence

1. Social competence encompasses a broad range of perceptions, judgments, and behaviors.
2. To improve social competence, we must focus on the skills students need to learn to be successful in their interactions.

3. Social skills instruction depends on a clear and thorough understanding of the way typical students show social competence.

The Complexity of Social Demands

1. In order to perform competently, students must be able to
   a. attend to environmental conditions
   b. have and use required skills
   c. adapt behavior to changing circumstances
   d. predict the outcomes of their actions
   e. evaluate the effectiveness of their behavior
2. The demands for interacting in structured situations—those supervised by adults—and in unstructured situations are usually very different.
3. Social demands are set by teachers and other school personnel, by classmates and peers, and by individual students themselves.
4. Social demands can be explicit—clearly communicated to students—or they can be implicit—suggested by the circumstances in which students interact.
5. A systematic approach to social skills instruction can help to focus interventions on the skills students need to learn to improve their competence.

Expectations for Social Behavior

1. Expectations are reflected in the behaviors students display to show competence in their interactions.
2. Expectations for achieving social competence and for achieving academic competence are comparable in that they both require observable behaviors.
3. Expectations provide a tool for obtaining clear measures of social behavior and for setting goals for students who have yet not achieved social competence.
4. Expectations pertain to the minimum requirements for competence.
5. Expectations are observable and measurable.
6. Expectations apply to everyone in the setting, not just to students who show problems in their behavior.
7. Expectations help to turn problem behavior into instructional goals.

Examples for Chapter One

In the text we use the fictional case study of Mrs. Armstrong to illustrate key concepts and techniques. In reality the procedures we describe have been tested and used by teachers and other personnel in a wide variety of school settings. Here and at the end of each chapter we present actual examples of their work, to show how the approaches we outline have been applied in different settings. We have changed the names on the worksheets and added commentary in the margins, but otherwise these examples are drawn directly from real-life cases.

Example 1a

This worksheet from a first-grade teacher shows how Mrs. Armstrong's technique can be applied in a lower-elementary setting.

Worksheet 1.1: Observing Social Behavior — Page 1 of 2

Name: *Mrs. Torrez* Date: *Sept. 2*

Structured situation: *1st-grade classroom—spelling activity*

Behaviors observed:

1. *Children fidget, pick at shoelaces & Velcro fasteners while listening to directions.*

It is often helpful to look for body language to see how students interact during structured activities. →

2. *Several students move closer to favorite classmates when teacher chooses partners.*
3. *Students answer the teacher's questions in chorus.*
4. *Students talk quietly with their partners during the game.*
5. *Groups get louder when the teacher is attending to another student.*

Citing specific quotes or actions can add helpful detail to your lists. →

6. *Students act the words out—each group plans how they will do it. ("Okay, I'll pretend to drive the car, and you sit in the back seat." "No, I want to drive too . . . .")*
7. *Students react strongly to teacher attention—smile, tell her their plans, etc.*
8. *Students raise hands and talk out when they think they know the word being acted out. ("Oh! I know!")*
9. *Class claps for each group when the act is completed.*

Student–teacher bonds play a particularly important role in the social behavior of younger children. Make sure you note the ways students interact with adults in the situation. →

10. *Most students reaffirm their performance with the teacher after the activity is done. ("How did we do?" "How did we do?" etc.)*

Example 1b

This ninth-grade teacher's worksheet shows Mrs. Armstrong's technique applied in a high school setting.

Gender plays a significant—and evolving—role in the social patterns set by students. This is usually an important factor to note when describing social behavior.

With older students you can often gain valuable knowledge about social roles and behavior by simply asking them questions. Frequently you will find that students are quite insightful and eager to talk about their social expectations.

Notice that typical social activity may often involve behavior of which teachers and other adults would disapprove.

Just as in the elementary setting, physical interaction and body language are important components of social behavior at the high school level.

Worksheet 1.1: Observing Social Behavior — Page 2 of 2

Name: *Ms. Burnham* Date: *Sept. 2*

Unstructured situation: *Cafeteria—9th-grade lunch*

Behaviors observed:

1. *Students wave and greet one another as they enter the cafeteria.*
2. *Students sit with their friends at tables—mostly groups of girls and groups of boys, but some are mixed.*
3. *Certain groups go to certain areas in the cafeteria. (I had some students explain the groups. They include "preps," "snobs," "wavers," "skaters," "druggers," and "hoods.")*
4. *Students talk about what they are doing after school, other people, etc.*
5. *A lot of nasty talk—things they would get into trouble for saying in class.*
6. *Students share food and drinks with friends.*
7. *Three girls are laughing as they tease a friend about a crush she has on a boy.*
8. *A group of girls is laughing and looking admiringly at a boy who is talking and entertaining them.*
9. *Among the boys, a lot of body contact when talking to friends (hitting on the arm, etc.).*
10. *A boy and girl are holding hands—he is walking her to her next class.*

Mr. Wagner's Case Study

Mrs. Armstrong's worksheets and the examples at the end of the chapter provide models for the procedures we describe. But we would also like to illustrate pitfalls and mistakes that can diminish the effectiveness of these techniques. Accordingly, at the end of each chapter we present a negative example from Mr. Wagner's work, showing typical problems in the application of the procedures in the text.

Mr. Wagner's Behavior List

Mr. Wagner's worksheet shows some of the pitfalls to avoid when looking at student behavior. His list is strongly focused on the rules and procedures he has established for class start-up and does not really address the students' social interactions in this situation. Note also that his list is geared more toward what Mr. Wagner *wants* the students to do than toward what he actually sees them doing.

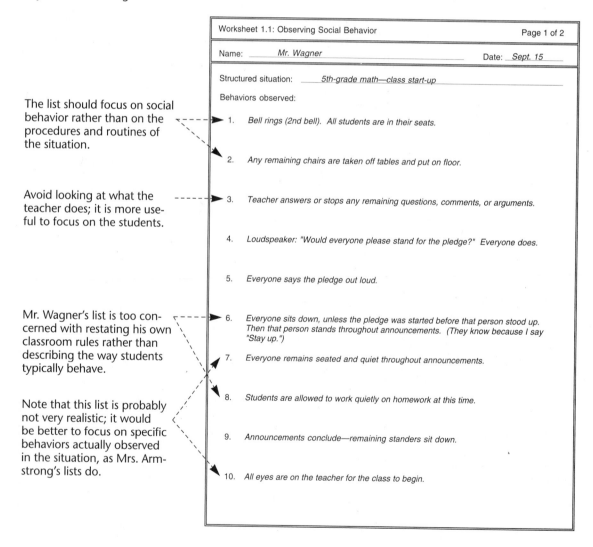

Worksheet 1.1: Observing Social Behavior — Page 1 of 2

Name: *Mr. Wagner* Date: *Sept. 15*

Structured situation: *5th-grade math—class start-up*

Behaviors observed:

The list should focus on social behavior rather than on the procedures and routines of the situation. (→ 1, 2)

1. *Bell rings (2nd bell). All students are in their seats.*
2. *Any remaining chairs are taken off tables and put on floor.*

Avoid looking at what the teacher does; it is more useful to focus on the students. (→ 3)

3. *Teacher answers or stops any remaining questions, comments, or arguments.*
4. *Loudspeaker: "Would everyone please stand for the pledge?" Everyone does.*
5. *Everyone says the pledge out loud.*

Mr. Wagner's list is too concerned with restating his own classroom rules rather than describing the way students typically behave. (→ 6, 8)

6. *Everyone sits down, unless the pledge was started before that person stood up. Then that person stands throughout announcements. (They know because I say "Stay up.")*
7. *Everyone remains seated and quiet throughout announcements.*
8. *Students are allowed to work quietly on homework at this time.*

Note that this list is probably not very realistic; it would be better to focus on specific behaviors actually observed in the situation, as Mrs. Armstrong's lists do. (→ 7, 10)

9. *Announcements conclude—remaining standers sit down.*
10. *All eyes are on the teacher for the class to begin.*

CHAPTER 2

Describing Expectations for Social Behavior

The demands for competent social behavior are as central to success in school as any of the subject matter demands teachers set for academic achievement. In fact, the array of expectations governing social behavior can be described as a broad, unwritten curriculum—one that is every bit as rigid and as important to students' success in school as the written curricula in reading, writing, and mathematics (Brophy & Good, 1986; Good & Weinstein, 1986). Like the academic curricula, the social skills curriculum is already firmly in place when students enter their age or grade-level placement (Hamilton, 1983).

In this chapter, we explain many of the features and uses of a social skills curriculum. We also show how you can identify and catalog the expectations that make up the social skills curriculum in your school settings.

Social Competence and the Social Skills Curriculum

Describing social competence as a curriculum represents an important shift in thinking about planning social skills instruction. Traditionally, we think of social competence as a vague set of interlocking attitudes and interaction patterns rather than as a clearly defined set of skills with a well-defined instructional sequence. By describing social competence as a curriculum of key skills, we can undertake the teaching of social skills with the same kind of deliberate approach we use for academic instruction (Cartledge & Milburn, 1986). When teaching mathematics, we look to the mathematics curriculum to tell us what the students should have learned already and what they need to work on next. In developing social competence, we can look to the social skills curriculum to tell us what skills students should be able to use and what skills they still need to learn.

There is, of course, a catch. In the academic curriculum, the skills students need are already outlined by a commercially designed, lab-tested, school board–approved series of textbooks, manuals, and instructional aids. By comparison, our inventory for the social skills curriculum is usually rather sketchy and poorly articulated, consisting perhaps of a short list of classroom rules and a general sense of what it means to behave "like fifth- (or first-, or ninth-) grade students." If the social skills curriculum is to be an explicit, well-organized, and useful guide to instruction, we must first fully and clearly describe the specific skills for being socially competent. This chapter shows you how.

Functions of a Social Skills Curriculum

Because we use curricula in schools every day, it is easy to think of them simply as instructional guides. But curricula have several key functions that we seldom consider, even if we understand them intuitively. Therefore, before we present a method for identifying and listing the social skills in a curriculum, in the following sections we explain the functions that a social skills curriculum might have in a school program. It will be important for you to keep these functions in mind when you begin to describe the social skills curriculum that applies to your own setting.

Defining Content of Instruction

The most obvious use of a curriculum is to define what we teach our students. A mathematics curriculum, for example, outlines a series of topics, skills, and lessons that students should learn over the course of the year, and the elements it contains directly determine what our students do in math class during the school day. A social skills curriculum serves the same function. We already know that social skills instruction makes up a large part of our teaching. Every time we encourage a child to share, offer advice to an awkward teen, prompt a quiet student to speak up in class discussion, or try to tame the unruly behavior of the class clown, we are teaching social skills. But just what are we teaching? Unlike mathematics, there is no guidebook in this area to tell us what page we are on. This is why we must use actual, typical student behavior as the basis for describing a curriculum for social skills. By looking carefully at what the average students are learning, we can get a more solid view of what we are teaching and become more aware of the content of social skills instruction in our settings.

Describing Age-Appropriate Behavior

Another function of a curriculum is to describe the performance requirements for a particular age or grade level. When we say that students have achieved "a tenth-grade reading level" or "a third-grade math level," we are referring to specific skills defined by the reading and mathematics curricula as appropriate for those ages. In the same way, students must become skilled at participating in the interactions and performing the social behaviors that are typical of their age group if they are to be judged socially competent by their teachers and peers.

The unwritten social skills curriculum that specifies this age-appropriate behavior can be surprisingly rigid. Ten-year-old children, for example, must usually select games, activities, and conversational topics that are very different from those that seven-year-old children or thirteen-year-old adolescents choose.

Mrs. Armstrong has noticed that her fifth-grade students use the playground equipment differently from the way the third graders do. Although most of them still like the swings, they consider the teeter-totter "babyish," and they use the monkey bars and slide mostly to try daring or difficult tricks. Students who fail to recognize these distinctions and who fail to meet the expectations for "acting their age" risk being shunned by classmates, excluded from peer interactions, or perceived as either immature or pretentious. A well-documented curriculum of social skills clarifies the requirements for acting one's age by defining the behavior that is appropriate for students of a particular age or grade level.

Defining Minimum Levels of Behavior

We emphasized in Chapter One that expectations indicate the *minimum* requirements for social performance—the behavior that is considered "acceptable" or average by people in the school environment (McFall, 1982). This indication is also a normal function of academic curricula, which set clear minimum requirements for passing each subject. To earn a passing grade in Mrs. Armstrong's social studies class, her students must obtain an average score of 70% correct on homework, quizzes, and tests, and complete a group project and an oral report. In the same way, the social skills curriculum indicates the minimum performance necessary for showing competence. As with academic curricula, behavior that does not meet the expectations of the social skills curriculum can lead a student to "fail" by having too many confrontations with classmates and teachers, not having any friends, being referred to school special services, or losing interest in school and eventually dropping out (Cohen & Fish, 1993; Howell, Fox, & Morehead, 1993; Walker, Colvin, & Ramsey, 1995).

Such results are cumulative; social competence, like academic competence, is not determined by meeting any single expectation but by overall performance across a wide range of social demands and conditions. Students who show problems in their behavior will often behave as acceptably and appropriately as the other students in the setting. However, the number of times they exhibit this behavior will usually fall well below the level their teachers and schoolmates consider the absolute minimum for being socially competent. Because it offers a broad-based foundation for judging this overall performance, the social skills curriculum can provide a valuable yardstick for identifying the problems individual students may have in their interactions, both in the types and the amounts of behavior they display.

Specifying Conditions for Using Skills

Most curricula also indicate the conditions in which students are to use their skills, stating *what* students are to do and *when* they are to do it. To meet the requirements for mathematics, for example, students must know not only how to perform specific operations but also how to perform them properly under different circumstances such as in different types of problems, instructional formats, or assigned activities. In the same way, the social skills curriculum defines the kinds and amounts of behavior that are adequate and appropriate for each of the various situations students encounter in their day-to-day routines and interactions.

Students must use their conversational skills in very different ways depending on whether they are participating in a class discussion, a lunchtime conversation, or a game on the playground. These performance conditions indicate to students when they should add comments to a conversation or how many comments they should make to hold up their end of the discussion. Thus, students must not only have a sufficient repertoire of conversational skills but must also be able to use them under the right conditions and match them effectively to the demands of the situation. The social skills curriculum is a valuable tool for keeping track of these shifting requirements as students move from situation to situation.

To use a social skills curriculum as you use academic curricula, you must first describe the social skills and behaviors that make up the curriculum. In the next section, we explain how to identify the social skills curriculum that is in place in your own school settings.

Defining a Social Skills Curriculum

Defining a social skills curriculum is not so much a decision-making process as it is a fact-finding mission. For this reason, it is useful to structure the task with a worksheet, one that is flexible enough to include the variety of skills and behaviors that social competence involves, but rigid enough to give your work structure and organization. In this section, we show how to complete such a worksheet and use as an example the one Mrs. Armstrong prepared for her fifth-grade class. The steps in the process are listed in Table 2.1.

Step 1: Listing Settings and Situations

To identify the expectations that make up the social skills curriculum, we must begin by developing a manageable system to categorize the dozens of demands expected of students. The academic curricula accomplish this kind of organization by dividing expectations into broad subject areas (English, math, chemistry) and individual topics (parts of speech, long division, the periodic table). This approach is sometimes applied to social skills as well, breaking instruction into such areas as problem solving, interpersonal skills, situational perception, and anger control (Goldstein, 1988).

TABLE 2.1 Steps in defining a social skills curriculum

Step 1:	List situations
Step 2:	Observe and take notes on social demands
Step 3:	Define expectations for each situation

Although dividing social skills into topics in this way might aid in organizing instruction, it does not help to fulfill many of the other functions of a curriculum. Unlike long division or the periodic table, which students use at a specific time of day and at a specific point in the semester, social expectations such as asking for assistance, talking with classmates, or sharing materials and ideas take place in many different settings and contexts throughout the school day (Good & Weinstein, 1986; Greenwood & Carta, 1987; Knoff, 1990). A topic-by-topic approach may be helpful for planning classroom lessons on social skills, but it will be of little use for tracking how well students apply their social skills under varying conditions, or for determining the areas in which their social behavior may not be meeting minimum requirements for competence.

For these reasons, we have found that the best way to organize and categorize social expectations is by the *situations* or the activities that make up the regular routine of each school *setting*. To clarify these terms, think of settings as the basic locations and time periods that make up the school environment, such as Mrs. Armstrong's fifth-grade social studies class, Mr. Wagner's fifth-grade math class, lunchtime in the cafeteria, or recess on the playground. Each of these settings can be further divided into specific situations characterizing the activities that usually take place, such as small group work, independent study, conversation at cafeteria tables, and organized games (Bauer & Sapona, 1991; Cairns, 1986).

Important Features of Settings and Situations

Following are several important features of settings and situations that can affect social behavior.

Settings and situations create opportunities for social interactions. Settings and situations are the environmental conditions that give students opportunities to engage in social interactions (Campbell & Siperstein, 1994). Most student behavior reflects specific opportunities to interact with other people, such as in a classroom when the teacher calls on them or during a recess game when friends are close by. Within school settings, these situations set the tone and define the content of student interactions.

For example, students in Mrs. Armstrong's classroom act much more aggressively and boisterously on the playground during game situations than they do in the classroom. Playground situations naturally create many opportunities for students to form groups of different sizes and types, to disagree about rules, and to discuss a more varied set of topics, because the activities during recess are far less structured and the performance demands are more implicit. In contrast, behavior is much more subdued in the classroom during instructional lessons because students do not have the same types of opportunities to engage in such free-ranging behavior. The structured nature of the classroom in terms of lessons, instructional formats, seating arrangements, and management style does not give students the same opportunities for performance.

Settings and situations define the expectations for social behavior. Different settings and situations also affect the level and type of behavior that people judge as

Social expectations vary from one situation to another.

competent or not competent (Asher, Oden, & Gottman, 1977). As a result, the expectations for social behavior, and the social skills curriculum, will vary from setting to setting and from situation to situation. In Mrs. Armstrong's social studies class, for example, the students interact quite differently depending on the activities that are taking place. They display one type of behavior when they first enter the room during class start-up time, and others during announcements, group work, or homework review. Similarly, when they play football or basketball on the playground, their actions are different from the ones they display when they walk around the playground in conversational groups or when they wait in line to come into the building. In short, social behavior is closely linked to—and is often defined by—the situations in which the social interactions take place (Asher, Oden, & Gottman, 1977; Howell, Fox, & Morehead, 1993).

In summary, the settings and situations that make up students' normal routine make an ideal structuring device for a curriculum of social expectations. They give you a context for describing expectations and for categorizing them by the circumstances to which they apply.

Describing Settings and Situations

Describing settings is a very straightforward process; you simply indicate the locations for which you would like to specify a social skills curriculum. For example, Mrs. Armstrong has decided to describe the social skills curriculum for her fifth-grade social studies class and for the playground area where the fifth graders have recess.

Describing situations is usually a more complicated task, because the conditions for social behavior can be quite varied and flexible. Most situations can be characterized by the activity that is taking place, such as working on an assignment, passing from one classroom to another, or playing an organized game in gym. These activities can usually be further described and clarified by one or more of the following dimensions:

Group size, such as large group, small group, or individual

Format of the activities, such as lecture, class discussion, lining up in the hallway, or sitting at cafeteria tables

Tasks or pastimes in which students engage, such as taking a test, reading silently, working on a project, eating lunch, or playing an organized game

The best approach for describing the situations in most settings is to list the activities that make up the usual routine of the setting (Greenwood & Carta, 1987; Kounin, 1983). Mrs. Armstrong can list the situations for her social studies class like this:

Class start-up time and announcements

Homework grading and review

Teacher presentation and instruction

Large group discussion

Small group discussion/activity (groups of 5 to 7 students; at tables in back of room)

Independent work time (students work alone or in pairs)

Class dismissal

As this outline shows, a chronological list of the normal activities in the setting effectively organizes the different situations in which the students' interactions take place. Note that in creating her list, Mrs. Armstrong's aim was not so much to describe every activity that happens in her class as to break the class period down into a few broad categories in which the social interactions are fairly distinctive. Likewise, there is no need to be absolutely strict in describing a chronological routine. Mrs. Armstrong may rarely have a large group discussion, a small group activity, and independent work time all on the same day. However, she included them all on her list because they represent three main categories of activities that occur in her classroom regularly.

As you list situations, it is also important to identify the true beginning and ending points in the routine, or the transitions that lead into and out of the setting. Mrs. Armstrong has listed "class start-up" and "class dismissal" as the beginning and ending activities for her social studies class period, as the interactions taking place during these times often set the tone for the entire class period. You should include situations like these in your list, because a significant amount of social interaction can occur during these normal transition times.

This kind of clearly structured routine can often be used to describe fairly informal settings as well, as long as the types of interactions that take place conform to a specific sequence of activities. Mrs. Armstrong might describe the situations for lunchtime in the cafeteria like this:

Entering cafeteria

In the food line (takes about 5 minutes)

At tables: eating time (about 10 minutes; in groups of 4–10 students)

At tables: having conversations and socializing after finishing lunch

Leaving cafeteria

Her list outlines the sequence of activities that typify the cafeteria setting during the students' lunch period.

Sometimes you may need a different approach to describe unstructured settings because the activities may not follow a prescribed chronology or routine. Mrs. Armstrong has noticed that during recess her students do not conduct activities in any particular sequence, but go from one type of social situation to another quite freely. On some days, the entire class might play a single organized game for the entire recess, whereas on other days, they might interact in smaller groups and participate in a number of activities at once. In a setting like this, rather than describing situations in terms of a regular schedule, you can list them by the types of activities taking place (conversational groups, team sports or games, informal play), the size of the group (pairs, small group, large group), or the specific areas in the setting where the interactions occur (playground equipment area, ball field, line-up area). Mrs. Armstrong might list the recess situations as follows:

Lining up to go outside

Playing organized games (large group or entire class plays; rules are specific)

Playing catch and other less organized games (usually in groups of 2–4)

Playing on playground equipment

Conversing informally with peers (usually in groups of 2–3)

Lining up to go inside

By listing situations according to activity, group size, or location, Mrs. Armstrong can organize and clarify the demands even for settings that do not fall into a prescribed and well-organized routine.

Worksheets for Settings and Situations

After considering the different settings, situations, and activities in which student interactions take place, you can start filling out a worksheet for the social skills curriculum. The first task is to list the situations for each setting you wish to investigate. Limit your scope at first, since identifying the social expectations in each situation is a fairly time-consuming process. You might start with a single setting—your homeroom classroom or one of your subject matter time periods, for example—and describe that one group of situations before you try other settings you are less familiar with.

On the other hand, you might also want to list the situations for a nonacademic setting your students are in, such as the cafeteria or the playground. By observing student behavior during these times, you can broaden the scope of the curriculum by clarifying the ways students choose activities, pick friends to interact with, converse with teachers and classmates about nonschool topics, handle disagreements, or seek out or avoid attention for certain actions. Identifying expectations like these in unstructured settings will allow you to include skills that enhance students' status in their peer groups, aid them in pursuing their personal interests and goals, and meet other peer-set or self-set expectations. Figure 2.1 shows the first page of Mrs. Armstrong's worksheet, with situations listed for her fifth-grade social studies class and for fifth-grade recess on the playground.

We should interject a note at this point for special education teachers and personnel. If you teach in a self-contained classroom or otherwise separate location, it is important to identify situations that typify *mainstream* settings for students in the same age groups you are working with rather than situations that characterize your own special education setting. The social skills curriculum you develop must be based on the social interactions and expectations of average students in a typical school environment if it is to serve as a referent for minimum, age-appropriate social behavior. This principle parallels the way in which special educators are

Figure 2.1 Mrs. Armstrong's list of situations.

Worksheet 2.1, Part 1: The Social Skills Curriculum—SITUATIONS

Name: *Mrs. Armstrong* Date: *Sept. 9*

Setting #1 (structured): *5th-grade social studies class*

Situations/Activities:

Class start-up time and announcements

Homework grading and review

Teacher presentation and instruction

Large group discussion

Small group discussion /activity (groups of 5 to 7 students; at tables in back of room)

Independent work time (students work alone or in pairs)

Class dismissal

Setting #2 (unstructured): *5th-grade recess*

Situations/Activities:

Lining up to go outside

Playing organized games (large group or entire class plays)

Playing tag and other nonorganized games (usually in groups of 3–6)

Playing on playground equipment

Conversing informally with peers (usually in groups of 2–5)

Lining up to go inside

encouraged to use academic curricula as well (Howell, Fox, & Morehead, 1993; Kameenui & Simmons, 1990).

Ms. Hernandez teaches a mathematics group in her special education resource room at Madison Elementary, and Granville is one of the students in the group. When Ms. Hernandez measures the performance of these students and sets goals for their instruction, she relies on the fifth-grade mathematics curriculum that Mr. Wagner uses in his classroom as a referent for deciding what skills and concepts to assess and teach. Even if the instructional objectives she sets for her students are lower than those listed in the mainstream curriculum, they nonetheless reflect the directions and goals established in the mainstream curriculum.

In the same way, if Ms. Hernandez wishes to prepare a social skills curriculum to assess and to plan instruction for the students in her class, she would look to the mainstream social skills curriculum to obtain a clear referent. She may, for instance, choose to work with Mr. Wagner and identify the social curriculum for his fifth-grade math class. She may also look at the expectations that Mrs. Armstrong's students meet in the cafeteria, to broaden her focus. Even if the behavior of the students in special education is well below the average level of the other students, the curriculum from these mainstream settings will provide a valuable yardstick for assessing her students' skills and for setting incremental objectives for their progress.

In summary, describing situations for each setting you are concerned with is an effective way to organize the various expectations that apply to your students. After you have listed the situations on your social skills curriculum worksheet, you are ready to begin the primary task: describing the skills and actions that define the social expectations for each situation.

Step 2: Taking Notes on Social Demands

Identifying the expectations for social behavior for the various situations you have listed can be quite daunting if you do not approach it systematically. Although some of the expectations that apply to students' social behavior will be immediately apparent and easy to describe, many others will not. One reason for this is that we often become so fixed in our teaching routines and so focused on our day-to-day responsibilities that we do not take the time to clarify many of the expectations students must meet (Lehr & Harris, 1988). In some instances, we just assume that students know what the expectations are, and we disregard the complexities involved in students' understanding them or in acquiring the skills to meet them. Furthermore, as mentioned in Chapter One, we often do not consider the full array of peer-defined expectations that can be every bit as demanding as our own requirements of students.

Conducting Direct Observations

For these reasons, it is a good idea before listing expectations to take a closer look at the situations you are concerned with, to get a complete and realistic picture of what the students are doing. Conducting direct observations is a very useful way of preparing to list expectations for a situation, because your notes can add both precision and breadth to the social skills curriculum. In addition to helping you verify the demands you are already aware of, these observations will also give you valuable new insights into the behavior of your students. Mrs. Armstrong already has a good idea of what her students do in her social studies class and on the playground. But when she conducts closer observations, she is likely to find that some of her assumptions about the students' behavior are not entirely accurate, or that the rules and demands they actually respond to are rather different from the ones she would have listed for them. When she looks more closely at the students' social interactions, she is likely to be surprised at the range and complexity of their behavior and to notice many expectations she had not considered before. This is why conducting observations is so crucial to obtaining a full and accurate listing of the social skills curriculum.

When you conduct observations in the settings, you should make a separate page of notes for each of the situations you have listed in step one above. In this way, you will be ready to describe and classify the expectations you see according to the situations to which they apply. Figure 2.2 shows two of the pages of notes Mrs. Armstrong added to her social skills curriculum worksheet. Note that these two pages cover only two of the situations she has listed; her complete worksheet would include similar pages for all of the situations she listed in step one.

When you conduct these observations, your primary focus should be on the average behavior of the students and the types of skills they use to meet the expectations of the setting, rather than on behavior that is unusual, distracting, or exemplary. Your goal is to capture the range of normal, competent behavior that you see displayed. The following sections offer a guide for what to look for as you conduct your observations and add your notes to the social skills curriculum worksheet.

Look for the basic activity sequence or rules that students follow in the situation. Perhaps the most obvious features you will observe are the basic activity sequence and the rules students follow as they progress through the situation. These demands are usually the easiest to describe, as they are often set by teacher instructions and tend to follow the natural flow of the activity. Pay particular attention to elements of the situation that involve social interaction, as when students share comments after a formal teacher presentation. The following questions are important guides when you watch for the rules and activity sequence that students follow in the situation:

- What is the basic routine of the activity? What kinds of interaction does the activity involve?
- Who leads the activity? How are decisions made on what will be done?
- What types of cooperation does the activity require?
- What basic rules govern the students' social behavior? Are these rules explicit or implicit? Do most students follow the rules?
- Do students seem to set their own rules in the situation?

Figure 2.2 A portion of Mrs. Armstrong's notes for her situations.

Worksheet 2.1, Part 2: The Social Skills Curriculum—NOTES Page *3* of *13*

Name: *Mrs. Armstrong* Date: *Sept. 11*

Setting: *5th-grade social studies*

Situation: *Teacher presentation and instruction*

Notes on social requirements:

- *Students quiet down when they see me hold up worksheets. Several ask if they can help hand them out.*

- *Most students are very curious about the worksheets ("what are those?"). They pay attention when I introduce the activity.*

- *When I ask questions, most raise their hand, wave it eagerly (even if they haven't thought of the answer yet!—mostly an "ooh, choose me!" attitude).*

- *As I go through the questions on the worksheet, most students take notes.*

- *Many look to neighbor's sheet to check their progress.*

- *Several students exchange glances and looks with neighbor after we go over each item, plus occasional whispers ("what did you put down?" "I knew that one").*

- *A lot of physical behavior when they're reading the worksheets and listening—curling feet under desks, playing with hair, tapping pencils.*

- *One girl doesn't appear to be listening, so I call on her for a question. She jumps, then starts to answer the previous question on the page before she realizes which one we are on. She then listens and volunteers attentively for the rest of the class.*

- *When one student is called on for an answer, the others usually give whispers or glances of encouragement. Sometimes they try to whisper the answer, but I correct them.*

- *Once in a while someone asks for clarification, typically raising a hand first. I usually try to respond with praise ("good question").*

- *I end by instructing class to finish the worksheet on their own. Students compare notes, make comments to each other as they make transition to independent work time (many of the comments are about nonacademic subjects—who they want to sit with at lunch, etc.).*

Figure 2.2 *(continued)*

Worksheet 2.1, Part 2: The Social Skills Curriculum—NOTES Page *9* of *13*

Name: *Mrs. Armstrong* Date: *Sept. 14*

Setting: *5th-grade recess*

Situation: *Playing tag and other nonorganized games*

Notes on social requirements:

- *Jump rope—student who brings out the rope picks other students to turn the rope. They are the first to jump.*
- *Students (all girls) stand in line to jump rope. While in line, they talk about their clothes, their hair, who their friends are, who they like, etc.*
- *Students take turns jumping.*
- *Students encourage one another's jumping—they clap when someone does well.*
- *When conflict arises, usually the leader of the group settles the argument. Sometimes the student who loses the argument will quit, but usually she will just wait her turn.*
- *Most students move quickly and easily from one activity or game to another.*
- *Tag—usually the rules are decided and bases are set before the game begins. Usually they say things like "you boys chase us girls" or "the building is base."*
- *During the game, participants continue to make new rules ("Once you've been tagged, you go to jail").*
- *Rules are usually decided by "leaders" (most popular students), but are proposed by anybody.*
- *When a fight starts to break out at one point, the "leader" and other students break it up themselves—they don't refer it to the teacher.*
- *Once in a while the students go to teacher if they can't resolve an argument. (But they'll only go to their own teacher—going to the playground supervisor isn't "cool.")*
- *When teacher blows whistle to get a student's attention, the student usually stops.*
- *Students discuss action of the game at end of period as they line up.*

Look for the ways students interact with adults in the situation. An important aspect of any school situation is how students interact with teachers and other adults who are present. Although we are usually aware of these interactions, we seldom consider them from the students' point of view, especially when we are actively involved in the interactions ourselves. When you observe in a situation, keep in mind the following questions:

- In what ways do students interact with adults?
- How do students respond to adult greetings or interactions?
- How do students ask questions or initiate interactions?
- What are typical topics for student-adult interactions?
- What cues do students respond to when interacting with adults, such as when the adults are preoccupied with other students or activities? Are the cues given verbally? Visually?

Look for the ways students interact with one another. You should also pay attention to student-student interactions in the situation. This observation can require some fairly subtle techniques, as you may need to look for such details as the way students converse quietly or communicate nonverbally, the unwritten social

In what ways do students typically interact in each school situation?

rules they set for themselves, and the little details of their behavior that help them fit in with their peer group. Issues you should consider include these:

- What kinds of interactions do students engage in?
- How do students initiate interactions? How do they join interactions that are already in progress?
- What are typical topics for student-student interactions?
- When do the interactions take place?
- How do students indicate interest or lack of interest during interactions?
- What kinds of body language or nonverbal communication do students employ?
- How do students show friendship in the situation? How do they build friendships?

As you look over the notes Mrs. Armstrong took in Figure 2.2, notice that many of the issues and questions listed above are reflected in her observations. Of course, she would not be able to account for every one of these issues in her notes. But by using these general questions as a guide, she can be sure that she is obtaining a detailed and broadly representative set of notes on her students' social behavior.

Guidelines for Conducting Observations

When you observe, you must be able to pay careful attention to what the students are doing. Often, accomplishing this aim during the normal routines of your setting is difficult, as you may be too burdened with teaching and supervising to devote much time to observation. One way to alleviate this problem is to conduct your observation for very short periods over the space of several days, and to use your notes to summarize what you see. Another approach is to schedule activities that require relatively little supervision or direction from you, leaving you freer to observe the students. You must be sure when you do this, however, that you choose activities that are still fairly typical of the situation so that the students' interactions will follow their normal patterns.

Another solution is to have somebody else conduct the observations for you. Mrs. Armstrong could ask Ms. Hernandez to stop by her social studies class one day to help her observe the students. She would have to inform Ms. Hernandez of precisely what she is looking for in each situation—perhaps by giving her a list of issues or questions like the ones presented above—so that Ms. Hernandez could record useful and complete information when she observes the class. Because Ms. Hernandez already visits the classroom periodically to make observations, her presence would not substantially affect the students' behavior.

In nonclassroom settings, such as the hallways or the cafeteria, you should observe the interactions yourself, if possible. You may also find it helpful to talk with other school personnel who supervise these settings or to ask the students themselves about their behavior, such as what games they usually play during recess or what they like to talk about during lunchtime (Cartwright & Cartwright, 1984).

Remember to remain as unobtrusive as possible during your observations so that students will be encouraged to behave naturally. It is best to act as if you are not paying particular attention to the behavior you are observing. One way to do this is to appear to be busy at some other task such as reading a handout, filling out a form, or grading student papers. The students are likely to pay less attention to you, and you can begin to watch what they do without drawing much notice.

Using Video for Observations

Videotaping is a very effective substitute for direct observation when making the observations yourself is not practical or feasible. This technique is especially useful when you conduct a detailed analysis of your own classroom, as it allows you to fulfill your normal role and responsibilities during class time, and then later look more closely at how the students interact with you and with one another. You will find that videotaping is actually superior to direct observation when you are looking at a large number of different behaviors in the same setting or during the same time span.

When you use video, it is helpful to set up the camera two or three days ahead of time so the students can get used to having the camera in the room. Video is also helpful for observing your students in other settings, especially when you cannot schedule time to observe there yourself. For example, Mrs. Armstrong and Mr. Wagner would like to observe in each other's classroom, but they feel this would be distracting to the students and it would be very difficult to schedule. Instead, they plan to videotape several of their small group activities and view the tapes together. They believe the videotaped samples will give them additional insight into the more implicit expectations that govern these activities.

In summary, conducting careful, complete observations will help you to compile a broad and accurate picture of the skills students use to interact in their daily situations. By adding your notes to your social skills curriculum worksheet, you will be able to begin defining and listing the specific expectations that students meet in each of these situations. Next, we discuss how to describe these expectations.

Step 3: Listing Expectations for Each Situation

The central part of developing the social skills curriculum is describing the actual expectations that students meet to show social competence in each situation. This activity follows very naturally from the previous one; once you have compiled notes on the social behavior of students, you can state the expectations that this behavior represents by listing the specific skills or actions that students use to complete tasks or participate in interactions. This list should be based on your knowledge of the students' behavior and on the observations and notes you have already taken on the social requirements of the situation. For example, in the social studies classroom during teacher presentation, Mrs. Armstrong can define the expectations in terms of what typical students do during this time period: they listen to the teacher's explanation, answer questions when called on, speak loud enough so other students can hear their answer, and so on. For organized games during recess, Mrs. Armstrong can state the expectations in terms of the skills students use or the rules they usually follow: they take turns, handle disagreements by making compromises, yell encouragement to one another, and so on.

Figure 2.3 presents two pages from Mrs. Armstrong's worksheet listing the expectations she defined for these situations. As before, this figure shows only a part of Mrs. Armstrong's worksheet; the complete set would include pages for all the situations she listed in step one. Notice that Mrs. Armstrong has left blank a portion of the worksheet, labeled "standards." We will explain how to fill out this section in Chapter Three. The expectations Mrs. Armstrong has listed are drawn fairly directly from the notes she took earlier (shown in Figure 2.2). In this way, she can ensure that the expectations she lists accurately reflect the behavior that is actually taking place rather than what she would like to take place.

Guidelines for Listing Expectations

Although listing expectations sounds like a simple task, it can be trickier than simply writing out the things students should do. The following suggestions will help you prepare a precise and useful list of expectations for your situations. You may also refer to Appendix A for examples of expectations lists for a variety of situations at different ages and grade levels. These examples can serve as models for the lists you prepare for your own settings.

Describe expectations in positive terms. When you list expectations, use positive rather than negative phrasing. Depicting expectations in this way will focus your attention on what students *do,* not on what they should not do. If you use positive wording, such as "initiates interactions with peers" or "takes turn during game," rather than negative terms such as "doesn't interrupt" or "doesn't play out of turn," you can define the skills that students must have to show competence instead of the misbehavior that creates problems for them. When you follow this guideline, your assessments of student behavior and your plans for interventions and instructional lessons will be consistent with the social skills curriculum.

Describe expectations in terms of observable behavior. You should describe expectations so as to depict clearly what students do in the setting, and to allow you and others to observe and measure their behavior reliably (Good & Weinstein, 1986; Solity & Bull, 1987). This kind of observable, behavioral description is an important advantage of looking at expectations for social behavior rather than at attitudes or other unobservable, poorly defined constructs. Expectations such as "raises hand to ask questions," "ignores peer comments," or "talks quietly with neighbors" are described in terms of behavior that you can actually see and record. The first column in Table 2.2 presents several examples from Mrs. Armstrong's social skills curriculum that are defined behaviorally. The second column contains similar items that are described in vague, nonbehavioral terms. Mrs. Armstrong would find it difficult to judge whether students are actually doing the things described in the second column.

As Table 2.2 demonstrates, describing expectations for social interactions in behavioral or observable terms will allow you to make valid and objective judgments about your students' performance (McFall, 1982). Furthermore, these

Figure 2.3 A portion of Mrs. Armstrong's social skills curriculum.

Worksheet 2.1, Part 3: The Social Skills Curriculum—EXPECTATIONS Page *3* of *13*

Name: *Mrs. Armstrong* Date: *Sept. 18*

Setting: *5th-grade social studies*

SITUATION: *Teacher presentation and instruction*

EXPECTATIONS	STANDARDS (Covered in Chapter Three)	
	Units of Measure	Criterion Level
Pays attention to teacher (eye contact)		
Responds to correction by paying better attention		
Volunteers answers to teacher questions		
Takes notes on teacher presentation		
Checks progress against neighbor's notes		
Communicates with neighbor (on topic) by glances and occasional whispers		
Encourages others (quietly) who are called on		
Asks questions when help is needed		
Raises hand before speaking		
Interacts quietly with neighbors before beginning independent work		

Figure 2.3 *(continued)*

Worksheet 2.1, Part 3: The Social Skills Curriculum—EXPECTATIONS Page *9* of *13*

Name: *Mrs. Armstrong* Date: *Sept. 21*

Setting: *5th-grade recess*

SITUATION: *Playing tag and other nonorganized games*

EXPECTATIONS	STANDARDS (Covered in Chapter Three)	
	Units of Measure	Criterion Level
Jump Rope:		
Stands in line to wait turn to jump		
Interacts with others while waiting in line		
Talks on "cool" subjects (clothes, hair, etc.)		
Takes turn jumping		
Negotiates conflicts with leader		
Accepts judgment of group/leader		
Encourages others who are jumping		
Moves freely between activities or games		
Tag:		
Helps set rules before game begins		
Offers new rules during game		
Helps resolve conflicts within group		
Asks teacher, not aide, to settle arguments		
Avoids fighting		
Stops and pays attention when teacher blows whistle		
Discusses action of game with others as period ends		

TABLE 2.2 **Examples of Mrs. Armstrong's expectations defined behaviorally and nonbehaviorally**

Behavioral Terms	*Nonbehavioral Terms*
Initiates a conversation about school events	Gets along with classmates
Contributes at least 1 example to the group's project	Participates in small group activities
Follows rules for recess games	Acts appropriately during recess
Shares materials for social studies projects	Works well with other students

descriptions will help you to focus interventions on the specific skills students need to learn, and to evaluate clearly whether students are successful in acquiring them (Sugai & Tindal, 1993).

When possible, list expectations in chronological order. It is usually helpful to organize the expectations for a situation according to the general sequence of the activity. You should first identify the starting and ending expectations for the situation. Starting points are usually defined by such demands as "enters classroom quietly," "initiates greeting with peer or group," or "lines up to choose teams." Ending points include such demands as "returns quickly to desk," "finishes conversation with a friendly salutation," or "lines up to return to class." Once you have described the expectations for the beginning and ending points of the activity, you should be able to fill in the rest of the expectations fairly easily by following the outline of the activity from beginning to end.

Of course, certain expectations may apply throughout a situation, and some situations may be less chronologically rigid than others; in such cases, you can list the expectations in any order that is easy to follow without worrying about placing them in a specific sequence. The main objective is to get the expectations listed on the page; making the list chronological is a good way to organize your thoughts, but it is not essential to this task. As Figure 2.3 shows, Mrs. Armstrong has listed the expectations in roughly chronological order, but many of the items do not fall into any prescribed sequence.

Delete items that are not true expectations. By the time you get this far, you should have a fairly extensive list of the various expectations that define social competence in each setting and situation you are concerned with. As you review your list of expectations one last time, make sure that each item in the curriculum is truly a requirement for showing competence, not merely incidental behavior. Even in a tightly defined social situation, the average student has a certain amount of leeway in deciding what to do, so you may see things that are not true expectations. If you come across social behaviors that are optional rather than required, you should delete them from the curriculum. For example, some students may say "Thank you" after they are handed instructional materials, and although it is nice that they say this, it may not really be a requirement for social competence in the situation. Therefore, the key question for each expectation you list is whether it truly is needed for students to display social competence.

Be sure the list reflects the full array of expectations for the situation. Finally, take an objective look at each situation to make sure you have gained a complete picture of what it takes for students to be socially competent there. We stressed focusing on the way students actually behave rather than on how you want them to behave. As teachers, we are strongly inclined to view social expectations as the collection of rules we have for our class: remain quiet, stay in seat, keep hands and feet to self, and so on. Such rules may indeed be part of the social expectations in a setting, but they are usually limited in scope, describing only a part of what students need to do to be socially competent.

To check the breadth and completeness of your lists of expectations, we propose you consider two theoretical tests. The first is "the Sandy test." Sandy seldom breaks Mrs. Armstrong's classroom rules, and yet, as we read in Chapter One, her social performance is clearly substandard in the class. Therefore, when Mrs. Armstrong looks over her social skills curriculum, she must be sure that she has included not just the rules and requirements for keeping out of trouble, but also the expectations for typical, active participation in each setting. You can use this "Sandy test" to review your own curriculum by asking yourself, "If Sandy were in my class, would she meet all these expectations?" If the answer is yes, you need to consider other demands for social behavior that require students to take initiative in the activities and to play an active role in the situation.

The second test we propose is "the alien test." It goes like this: suppose a space alien showed up in Mrs. Armstrong's class, disguised as a human fifth grader. The alien's academic skills are fine, but he has no knowledge of fifth-grade social requirements. If he used Mrs. Armstrong's social skills curriculum as a guide for how to behave in the setting, would her lists of expectations give him a fairly good idea of how to act, or would there be significant gaps? Although this scenario is a little silly, it can be effective in helping you review your curriculum list from the perspective of a complete outsider. By asking yourself the question, "If I were a space alien, would this list of expectations give me enough information to interact competently?" you can spot gaps or omissions you might otherwise overlook.

After using these guidelines and suggestions to review your lists of expectations, you will have completed the steps for developing the social skills curriculum for your settings. This curriculum will give you a functional, accurate accounting of the skills your students demonstrate and the actions they perform in school situations to show social competence. Now, rather than having a vague or general notion of what students must do, you have a well-documented catalog of social skills. The following section discusses some of the uses you may find for this curriculum once you have completed it.

Benefits and Uses of the Social Skills Curriculum

The expectations for social behavior in your settings will give you a new understanding of both the problems your instruction must address and the goals the instruction should have. In this section we discuss several ways you can use the social skills curriculum to design instructional plans and interventions for improving your students' social behavior.

Assessing Problems in Social Behavior

An important use of the social skills curriculum is to measure how well individual students meet the expectations for social behavior. Your knowledge of the curriculum will allow you to compare a student's actual behavior to the expectations for a setting, and thus to identify and handle problems with precision and accuracy. You will understand better the skill deficits that contribute to students' not meeting expectations, and be able to generate effective solutions for overcoming these deficits. A specific benefit is that you will be able to pinpoint the behavior a student should use to substitute for a problem behavior, and to recognize the skills a student must acquire to meet expectations successfully. When Mrs. Armstrong looks closely at the aggressive behavior Granville shows when he has disagreements with his classmates, she can compare her observations to the information she has listed in the curriculum for how the other students negotiate their disagreements without being aggressive. This information will help her decide what specific skills Granville needs to learn in order to replace his aggressive behavior with more effective negotiating skills.

The information from the social skills curriculum will also allow you to capitalize on the students' strengths and areas of competence when you plan instruction. When Mrs. Armstrong considers the expectations for her classroom and the school playground, she may discover that Granville, Sandy, and Alfred are already proficient in many skills that she can use as the foundation for her interventions. Granville, for example, may have some very good leadership and athletic skills; Sandy may have a knack for helping other students with their schoolwork; and Alfred may have a well-developed sense of humor. Mrs. Armstrong may be able to use these positive skills to design interventions that are tailored to the individual needs and abilities of the students and to take advantage of the many valuable skills they have already acquired. Part II in the text explains the process of conducting an assessment using the social skills curriculum.

Clarifying the Goals of Interventions

The individual expectations that make up the social skills curriculum can function as the goals of interventions for students who do not meet them, because they highlight the disparity between competent behavior and the students' actual behavior. Thus the skills that enable students to overcome this disparity would become the primary focus of an intervention. As an example, Mrs. Armstrong has identified expectations for students talking during recess activities about topics that are interesting and pertinent to them, such as the gossip about the latest rock group or their favorite movies. She may find that Alfred usually selects topics that are not age appropriate for fifth graders, such as the cartoons he watches after school, and that his classmates consider these subjects too babyish or uninteresting for them. The gap between Alfred's actual behavior and the demands of the social skills curriculum acts as a barrier between him and his classmates, impeding their social interactions. Removing this barrier can be a goal of Mrs. Armstrong's intervention for Alfred.

Clarifying the goals of interventions in terms of the social skills curriculum can also help you concentrate on developing larger patterns of behavior rather than on addressing individual rule violations and misbehaviors. For example, with Sandy, Mrs. Armstrong can direct her attention to addressing the skill deficits that are at the source of the problems instead of centering on the attributes of her problems, such as poor self-esteem or shyness. Mrs. Armstrong could work with Sandy on such areas as improving her ability to greet teachers on entering the classroom, to establish eye contact with them when they speak to her, or to smile when they praise her work. These types of skills, drawn from the social skills curriculum, can provide the framework for a positive, far-reaching intervention for Sandy. We discuss the use of the social skills curriculum to plan interventions for individual students in Parts III and IV of the text.

Expanding the Scope of an Instructional Program

The social skills curriculum you define for your classroom or grade level can also broaden your overall teaching curriculum, as you can use it to set goals and objectives for your class instruction in much the same way you use the academic curriculum to set goals and objectives in the subject matter areas (Howell & Morehead, 1987; Salvia & Hughes, 1990; Tanner & Tanner, 1990). The social skills curriculum can provide a framework or a resource for planning instructional lessons and learning exercises for all your students. The expectations for social behavior can then become an integral part of your classroom and grade-level instructional program, and you can direct your teaching lessons toward helping all the students improve their social interactions, not just those with the most noticeable behavior problems. By following this curriculum, you and other personnel in your school can promote a school environment in which all students learn to act responsibly and with greater independence and self-assurance. Mrs. Armstrong and Mr. Wagner, in their long-range plans for the school year, intend to use their social skills curriculum to plan and coordinate teaching activities for all their students, not just Granville, Sandy, and Alfred. They hope that doing so can help to improve student behavior even before problems in their interactions arise. In Part IV we explore several different approaches for using the social skills curriculum to expand and coordinate instructional programs beyond a single classroom or school setting.

❍ Summary

Social Competence and the Social Skills Curriculum

1. The expectations that govern social behavior can be viewed as a broad, unwritten curriculum.
2. Social skills instruction can be approached in the same way as academic instruction.
3. Like any curriculum, the social skills curriculum can serve the following functions:
   a. define the content of instruction
   b. describe age-appropriate behavior
   c. define minimum levels of behavior
   d. define the conditions for using skills

The Social Skills Curriculum Worksheet

1. The first step in developing a social skills curriculum is to break down each setting into the specific situations or activities in which the students interact.
2. Settings and situations create opportunities for social interactions and define social expectations.
3. When listing situations, the following principles apply:
   a. Most situations can be described in terms of the basic routine of the setting.
   b. Situations are best described in terms of tasks and activities, group sizes, or locations.
   c. Special education teachers should list the situations for mainstream school settings rather than their own settings.
4. The second step in developing a social skills curriculum is to take notes on the social requirements for each situation.
5. Direct observation can be used to obtain information about
   a. the basic activity sequence or rules that students follow
   b. the ways students interact with adults
   c. the ways students interact with one another
6. The following guidelines apply to conducting observations:
   a. devote full attention to the students' behavior
   b. consider having somebody else conduct the observation
   c. remain as unobtrusive as possible
   d. use videotape for observations when possible
7. The third step in preparing a curriculum is to list expectations for each situation.

8. The following guidelines apply in this step:
   a. describe expectations in positive terms
   b. describe expectations in terms of observable behavior
   c. list expectations in chronological order
   d. delete items that are not true expectations
   e. include the full array of demands for the setting

Benefits and Uses of the Social Skills Curriculum

1. The social skills curriculum can be used to assess problems in social behavior.
2. The social skills curriculum can clarify the goals of interventions.
3. The social skills curriculum can expand the scope of an instructional program.

Examples for Chapter Two

Example 2a

This worksheet of a preschool teacher shows some of the social expectations typical of young children in a playground situation.

Worksheet 2.1, Part 3: The Social Skills Curriculum—EXPECTATIONS Page *8* of *9*

Name: *Mr. Jordan* Date: *Sept. 19*

Setting: *Preschool recess*

SITUATION: *Playing in small groups*

EXPECTATIONS	STANDARDS (*Covered in Chapter Three*)	
	Units of Measure	Criterion Level
1. Chats and laughs with peers		
2. Participates in tag or running games ("I'll catch you!" "I'm faster than you!")		
3. Maneuvers without hurting others		
4. Plays creatively with peers		
5. Expresses self dramatically (pretending to be animals, etc.)		
6. Offers suggestions or instructions for play to others ("Crawl like this.")		
7. Discusses plans for activity with others (who takes what role)		
8. Copies actions of peers		
9. Calls for teacher attention ("Watch me!" "He caught me!")		
10. Teases opposite sex (boys chase girls)		
11. Squeals, laughs, and runs randomly		
12. Mixes and mingles with several other children		
13. Tells others about what he or she is doing		

Including examples with expectations can help to clarify the behavior indicated. (→ items 2 and 5)

Your lists should note the kinds of interactions students use to accomplish tasks or complete activities. (→ items 6 and 7)

Include expectations that indicate the moods or attitudes students typically display in the situation. (→ item 11)

Example 2b

This high school teacher's worksheet shows social expectations typical of the students in this academic situation.

Older students often employ quiet or subtle interactions to help accomplish academic tasks.

Clarify expectations by noting the behavioral signs that define them.

Include the student-set expectations that are typical in the situation, not just the teacher-set demands.

Worksheet 2.1, Part 3: The Social Skills Curriculum—EXPECTATIONS Page 2 of 12

Name: *Mrs. Pajakowski* Date: *Sept. 20*

Setting: *9th-grade careers class*

SITUATION: *Independent work on board assignment*

EXPECTATIONS	STANDARDS (Covered in Chapter Three)	
	Units of Measure	Criterion Level
1. Begins work without prompting		
2. Asks questions about activity		
3. Raises hand before asking question		
4. Checks work quietly with neighbors		
5. Shares supplies with classmates		
6. Pays attention when teacher speaks (eye contact)		
7. Laughs at appropriate times (with teacher and classmates)		
8. Negotiates for more time to finish work		
9. Talks quietly with neighbors		
10. Talks on age-appropriate, current topics		
11. Listens to what other students say		
12. Checks appearance		
13. Talks about activity ("did you finish?")		

Mr. Wagner's Case Study

Mr. Wagner's List of Expectations

Mr. Wagner decided to follow Mrs. Armstrong's lead and make a list of the expectations for social behavior in his math class and in the cafeteria. As before, however, his worksheets have some deficiencies.

This page from his cafeteria list shows that Mr. Wagner is still too strongly focused on the rules and procedures in the situation, and that these expectations describe the demands for student interaction in a vague and fairly superficial manner.

Worksheet 2.1, Part 3: The Social Skills Curriculum—EXPECTATIONS Page *6* of *9*

Name: *Mr. Wagner* Date: *Sept. 26*

Setting: *5th-grade cafeteria*

SITUATION: *Going through food line*

EXPECTATIONS	STANDARDS (Covered in Chapter Three)	
	Units of Measure	Criterion Level
1. Enters cafeteria quietly		
2. No pushing in line		
3. Don't hold up line		
4. Interacts with peers		
5. Respects others		
6. Selects food		
7. Pays cashier		
8. Looks for a place to sit, goes to a table, and sits down with friends		

Items like this often are not realistic—most students probably talk with, laugh with, and tease one another as they enter the cafeteria. (→ 1)

The negative phrasing in these items contributes to the list's emphasis on rules. It is better to use positively phrased examples of what typical students *do*. (→ 2, 3)

Avoid broad or vague phrasing, and express the expectations in observable, behavioral terms. (→ 4, 5)

Mr. Wagner's list focuses too much on the procedures or mechanics of the situation and not enough on student interactions. (→ 6, 7)

Avoid combining several actions in a single expectation. (→ 8)

CHAPTER 3

Describing Standards for Meeting Expectations

Defining the social skills curriculum for school settings gives us a powerful tool for understanding and judging social competence. But one important element is still missing. The expectations we have listed for each situation describe *what* students must do, but they do not define *how much* they must do or *how well* they must do it to show social competence. As Chapter One pointed out, the *amount* or *level* of behavior students should use in their interactions is often as important as the actual actions the behavior involves. In this chapter, we address how much or how well students should behave by discussing standards. We explain how standards relate to social competence, and show how you can identify standards for the expectations in your social skills curriculum.

Social Competence and Standards

Standards are important in defining social competence because they indicate the minimum level of performance that meets expectations (Burden & Byrd, 1994). Behavior that equals or exceeds the standards meets the demands of the situation; behavior that is below the standards does not. Thus, standards represent the dividing line between behavior that is average, proficient, or satisfactory, and behavior that is below average, not proficient, or unsatisfactory (Howell & Morehead, 1987; McFall, 1982). They provide the essential basis for judging what level of behavior is competent.

Without clearly defined standards, it would be very difficult to assess and teach the behavior described in the social skills curriculum in an unbiased and systematic manner. You already use standards to evaluate academic skills in your everyday teaching (Howell, Fox, & Morehead, 1993). If, for example, you say that students must earn at least 65% on a test in order to pass it, the standard for meeting the expectation "answers test questions" is "answers 65% of the questions correctly." Test scores that are at or above this level are "passing," or meet the expectation; scores that are below 65% are "failing," or do not meet the expectation.

Whereas standards for academic skills are usually stated very clearly and explicitly, those for social behavior are usually less obvious to students and teachers alike, and thus are much more difficult to identify and describe. This does not mean, however, that no standards are in effect. On the contrary, standards apply to each skill in the entire spectrum of behavior included in the social skills curriculum. You and your students probably make unconscious judgments about the appropriateness and adequacy of social behavior every day based on these unstated standards. For example, how do you know which students have a problem with talking too loud or with not paying attention? After all, most students raise their voices or become inattentive once in a while. Yet most teachers have a good sense of which students have a particular problem in these areas. There must, therefore, be a fairly clear dividing line between normal "once in a while" misbehavior and behavior that indicates a real problem. That dividing line is the standard, and we show in this chapter how to identify it clearly for all the expectations in the social skills curriculum so you can make reliable and unbiased judgments about student behavior.

❍ Advantages of Identifying Standards

In the following section we discuss the reasons it is important to identify the standards for the expectations in the social skills curriculum.

To Make the Curriculum Operational

Clearly defined standards make the social skills curriculum functional and pragmatic because they indicate the real level of behavior students must attain to meet expectations. When Mrs. Armstrong describes an expectation, such as "converses on age-appropriate subjects" or "cooperates on group work," she is merely expressing ideas or loose descriptions of general student behavior. But these descriptions do not help her apply the expectations to individual, realistic cases of student behavior under a particular set of circumstances. How much cooperation is needed? How much age-appropriate conversation is required? Granville, Sandy, and Alfred converse appropriately sometimes, and they cooperate under certain conditions: Is that what these expectations demand, or must the students do more? Obviously, Mrs. Armstrong cannot really use these expectations as a description of typical or average student behavior until she defines an average or minimal *level* for them, making them both functional and realistic. Standards serve this purpose.

To Aid in Assessing Behavior

Standards enable you to use the expectations in the social skills curriculum to assess student behavior and to decide whether you need to plan interventions. With standards, you can evaluate precisely whether students have acquired and are able to use their social skills to a competent level (Howell, Fox, & Morehead, 1993). Table 3.1 illustrates the need for standards by presenting several observations Mrs. Armstrong has made of her students and some questions she has about their performance. These questions cannot be answered without a well-defined standard that indicates just how much student behavior is required in each circumstance.

Table 3.2 lists the standards that apply to the examples presented in Table 3.1. You can see that stating the standards for each circumstance now allows a precise evaluation of the students' behavior, answering the questions posed in the previous table.

The standard for Mrs. Armstrong's class indicates that Alfred's behavior (four questions per day) does meet the demands for asking questions in this situation. In contrast, the standard for playing cooperatively on the playground indicates that Alfred's performance (30% of the recess period) does not meet the demands of this setting. By clearly defining standards, you can make useful judgments from observations that would otherwise be meaningless.

Standards help to evaluate whether a student's behavior is adequate or competent.

TABLE 3.1 Questions showing the need to specify standards

Expectation	*Performance Observed*
Setting: Mrs. Armstrong's 5th-Grade Social Studies Class	
Asks questions related to class work	Alfred asks about 4 questions each day.
Question: Would Alfred's performance meet the expectation for Mrs. Armstrong's class?	
Setting: Mrs. Armstrong's 5th-Grade Social Studies Class	
Works with classmates on assignments	Sandy stays on task for 85% of most activities and completes about 50% of the assigned work. Her average for correct work is 60%.
Question: Would Sandy's performance meet the expectation for Mrs. Armstrong's class?	
Setting: Cafeteria Area: 5th Graders	
Returns greetings of teachers and classmates	Granville returns about 60% of the greetings.
Question: Would Granville's performance meet the expectation for the cafeteria?	
Setting: Playground Area: 5th Graders	
Plays cooperatively with peers	Alfred plays cooperatively an average of 30% of the recess periods.
Question: Would Alfred's performance meet the expectation for the playground area?	

To Clarify Instructional Goals

Standards provide an unbiased referent not only for assessing student behavior but also for designing and evaluating instructional procedures (Burden & Byrd, 1994). You can use the standards for social expectations to clarify and operationalize the goals of instruction in much the same way you use the standards for academic expectations. If a student is consistently not working up to the academic standard for learning a list of spelling words or for performing a mathematics operation, you would design activities or exercises to help the student reach at least the minimum level specified in your spelling or math curriculum. In the same way, Mrs. Armstrong can use the standards described in Table 3.2 not only to evaluate each student's behavior but also to set and clarify the goals for interventions where they are needed. If Mrs. Armstrong decides to plan an intervention to address Alfred's problem in playing cooperatively on the playground, she can use the 50% standard to pinpoint the level of cooperative play that Alfred must attain to

TABLE 3.2 Examples of standards that clarify whether students meet expectations

Setting: Mrs. Armstrong's 5th-Grade Social Studies Class

Expectation	*Standard*
Asks questions related to class work	Asks an average of 1–2 questions each day.

Evaluation: Alfred's asking 4 questions a day meets the expectation for Mrs. Armstrong's class.

Setting: Mrs. Armstrong's 5th-Grade Social Studies Class

Expectation	*Standard*
Works with classmates on assignments	Stays on task for 75% of activity. Completes 50% of assigned work with 65% accuracy.

Evaluation: Sandy's on-task level of 85% and work completion of 50% meet the expectation for Mrs. Armstrong's class. Sandy's average accuracy of 60% correct does not meet the expectation.

Setting: Cafeteria Area: 5th Graders

Expectation	*Standard*
Returns greetings of teachers and classmates	Returns greetings about 90% of the time.

Evaluation: Granville's average of 60% does not meet the expectation for the cafeteria.

Setting: Playground Area: 5th Graders

Expectation	*Standard*
Plays cooperatively with peers	Plays cooperatively an average of 50% of the recess period.

Evaluation: Alfred's average of 30% does not meet the expectation for the playground.

meet the demands of the setting and design her intervention to achieve that level of performance. Furthermore, she can judge the effectiveness of this intervention by whether it helps Alfred reach the 50% level.

In summary, it is important to identify the standards for social behavior because they are a natural feature of the expectations for social competence. As Chapter One indicated, one characteristic of expectations is that they describe average or minimal competence rather than ideals or exemplary behavior. To use them in a realistic manner, you need to add to your description of each expectation an accurate estimate of the level of behavior that is average or minimally competent. In other words, the main difference between Tables 3.1 and 3.2 is that the second table, with its precise specification of standards, gives a much better picture of the expectations for average competence than the simple expectations in Table 3.1. Unless you similarly define the standards that apply to the expectations for your own settings, you will be left with an incomplete understanding of your social skills curriculum.

Elements That Make Up Standards for Social Expectations

We have focused so far on how standards relate to meeting expectations for social behavior; here we explain the elements that go into defining them. You can state standards for social behavior in terms of two elements:

- *units of measure* that indicate how behavior is quantified
- a *criterion level* that specifies a number or amount of the measurement unit that separates meeting the expectation from not meeting it

Table 3.3 shows standards separated into units of measure and criterion levels. Note in the examples that the measurement units indicate *how you would quantify or count the behavior,* and the criteria define *what levels the behavior must reach* for it to meet the expectation. Each of these components is explained in the next sections.

Units of Measure

Units of measure refer to the scale or the type of numbers you would use to keep track of students' behavior when judging whether their performance is competent or minimally average (Zirpoli & Melloy, 1993). Units of measure answer the question "what do you *count* or look for when you evaluate student behavior?" For academic expectations, units of measure are usually well defined. For exam-

TABLE 3.3 Examples of standards separating units of measure and criteria

	Standards	
Expectation	*Units of Measure*	*Criteria*
Answers questions about topic of day's class	Number of correct answers	At least 1 per class
Uses class time to work with other students on assignments	Amount of time on task	At least 20 minutes per class
Chooses age-appropriate activities	Number of inappropriate activities chosen	No more than 3 per week
Initiates conversations with peers	Number of initiations	At least 2 per each class break
Shares instructional supplies with classmates	Percentage of times sharing supplies when asked	At least 90% of times requested

ple, you probably keep an accurate count of the number of times students hand in their homework, the number of correct answers they give on assignments and tests, and the number of steps they complete on projects. These counting procedures indicate the types of measurement units you use to determine whether students are meeting the demands for their academic work.

In the area of social skills, however, student behavior is usually measured very informally, and you will need to look more closely to see how performance is actually quantified. Remember that with every expectation for social behavior, there is some means by which people in the setting quantify the behavior, even if it is very informal. You generally know, for example, which students do and do not meet social expectations based on how much or how little they perform a particular behavior: how loudly they talk, how often they converse with peers, how many fights they get in, and so on. Although you may not make an actual tally of these numbers, you nonetheless keep track of them in the back of your mind. Classmates also judge the adequacy and effectiveness of other students' behavior based on the same types of informal measures. The informal numbers you and others use to evaluate the behavior are the units of measure.

In Mrs. Armstrong's social studies class, students are expected to ask questions when they need help, to contribute to small group discussions, and to assist one another with assignments during independent work time. Mrs. Armstrong keeps an informal mental count of this behavior, as she generally knows which students meet the demands. She also knows that other students keep track of these behaviors, because they complain to her if Granville does not contribute enough to the small group tasks, or if Alfred acts silly too often when they ask for his help.

Types of Units of Measure

Most units of measure for evaluating the competence of social behavior can be categorized according to four types of expectations or demands: expectations of frequency, of duration, of rate, and of occurrence (Cartwright & Cartwright, 1984; Kerr & Nelson, 1989). Examples of these categories are given in Table 3.4.

Expectations of frequency. Expectations of frequency place demands on *how much* or *how many* of a particular behavior meet the social expectation (Foster, Bell-Dolan, & Burge, 1988). Keeping track of behavior for frequency expectations typically involves recording the number of times students complete a specified set of actions (Kruger, 1990). In classroom settings, for example, measurement units for frequency could include the number of questions students ask or answer, the number of times they greet their teachers, and the number of conversations they initiate with their classmates.

Expectations of duration. Expectations of duration are judged by *how long* performance must last in order to meet the demands of a situation. Duration expectations specify the amount of time students take to perform a behavior or task, and they are measured by comparing the time at which the behavior begins (or is expected to begin) to the time at which behavior ends (or is expected to end) (Kazdin, 1989; Kerr & Nelson, 1989). Some examples of duration measures are

TABLE 3.4 Examples of different types of measurement units that apply to expectations

Expectation	Units of Measure
Frequency Expectations:	
Asks questions related to class work	Number of questions asked
Participates in class discussions	Number of comments or contributions
Initiates interactions with peers	Number of interactions initiated
Duration Expectations:	
Plays cooperatively during recess	Number of minutes spent playing
Stays on task during independent work time	Number of minutes on task
Works with classmates on small group projects	Number of minutes spent working
Rate Expectations:	
Initiates conversations with peers during lunchtime	Number of times initiating conversations during a 20-minute lunch period
Contributes to small group brainstorming activity	Number of ideas contributed during 10-minute activity
Completes running drill in gym class	Number of laps completed in 2 minutes
Occurrence Expectations:	
Gives assistance to classmates when asked	Ratio of times giving assistance (responses) to times assistance is requested (opportunities)
Ignores peer physical/verbal aggression	Ratio of times ignoring aggression (responses) to times aggression is shown toward student (opportunities)
Follows teacher's written and verbal directions	Ratio of number of compliances (responses) to number of directions given (occurrences)

the amount of time students work together to come up with a topic for a project, the number of minutes they play together during recess, and the amount of time they talk on a particular conversational topic.

Expectations of rate. Rate expectations specify *how quickly* or *how regularly* performance should take place. You normally use measures of rate when the expectation involves questions of speed, and the units of measure typically count the number of times students perform a behavior or task within a specified time period (Cartwright & Cartwright, 1984; Zirpoli & Melloy, 1993). In measuring rate, you note both the number of behaviors or tasks students complete *and* the time interval in which this occurs. Examples of units of measure for rate are the number of times students share materials or offer assistance to one another in ten minutes, the number of gym drills they take part in during a forty-minute class, and the number of greetings they give during a five-minute transitional period.

Expectations of occurrence. Occurrence expectations involve the most complex type of measurement units because they are judged by *whether* performance actually occurs *when it is needed.* Expectations of occurrence place demands on how students react to specific opportunities for performance, such as whether they respond calmly when peers tease them or whether they ask for help when they need it. Thus, people measure occurrence when they *compare* the number of times a student performs a particular behavior competently to the number of specific opportunities he or she has to perform it (Cartwright & Cartwright, 1984). If the student acts correctly when presented with an opportunity, you would note an occurrence; if the student does not, you would note a nonoccurrence. The results are then expressed as a ratio or a percentage. For example, you could summarize a student's behavior in terms of responding correctly to teasing eight out of ten times or 80% of the times teased.

You probably use measurement units for occurrence in your subject matter areas when you evaluate test papers and worksheet assignments. You may express test results as the ratio of correct answers given to problems assigned—for example, 15 out of 20; or as a percentage, 75%. These units of measure compare student performance (correct answers) to opportunities for performance (questions assigned).

Occurrence measures can apply to many types of social expectations as well. For example, when students are asked a question, when they are greeted by a classmate, or when they are confronted by an aggressive peer (opportunities to perform), they are usually expected to answer the question, acknowledge the greeting, or adequately handle the confrontation (behavior performed). You would typically measure these expectations with ratios or percentages, such as the percentage of questions answered, percentage of greetings acknowledged, and percentage of confrontations handled peacefully.

Selecting a Measurement System

When you decide on the units of measure to specify for an expectation, you should follow the natural way the behavior is evaluated or counted in the situation. The units of measure you specify for each expectation should correspond to the manner in which teachers or classmates evaluate the behavior under normal performance conditions. If people (you, classmates, other teachers, supervisors) usually keep track of the number of times students perform a set of actions, such as the number of assignments they complete or the number of ideas they contribute to group discussions (frequency expectations), then you should describe the standards using units that measure the number of times, the number of responses, or the number of completions. Thus for the expectation "pays attention to teacher," Mrs. Armstrong should use the "number of times not paying attention" as the units of measure because this is the way she usually determines whether students have problems in paying attention during her presentations.

Similarly, if people naturally keep track of the amount of time students spend completing activities, such as the time they take to go to a learning center after an activity is assigned or the time they spend playing games during recess (duration expectations), you should describe the standards with measurement units such as the amount of time taken or the amount of time spent in an activity. Thus for the playground expectation "moves freely between activities or games," Mrs. Armstrong plans to count the "number of minutes remaining alone" because this is usually what she notices when students have difficulty moving between or joining recess activities. Expectations that are usually judged by how often behavior occurs within a specified time period, such as the number of off-task distractions within a 20-minute activity (rate expectations), should be described with such units as number of times per minute or per hour. Finally, for expectations that are evaluated in terms of whether students perform when given an opportunity, such as how often they respond when questioned in a discussion or whether they react nonaggressively to teasing (occurrence expectations), you should describe the standards using measurement units such as ratio of questions answered to questions asked or percentage of teasing reacted to properly.

For some expectations there may be two or more types of measurement units that apply at the same time, because the behaviors that denote competence are closely related, or because the expectation involves more than one type of demand. For example, when Mrs. Armstrong's students work on a group assignment in class, they are supposed to stay on task for a specific amount of time within their group and at the same time reach a specific level of accuracy in their work to obtain a passing grade. When evaluating an expectation like this, Mrs. Armstrong would usually use units of measure both for how long the students work on the assignment (duration) *and* for how well they perform it (frequency, occurrence, or rate). Therefore, you will need to look closely at the way expectations are normally evaluated in each situation so you can choose the most accurate units of measure to define their standards.

Criterion Levels

The second component of a standard is the criterion level. Criterion levels denote the dividing line in the units of measure that differentiates between meeting and not meeting the demands of the setting (Wolery, Bailey, & Sugai, 1988). With academic skills, this point is usually easy to see. For example, to earn a passing grade in her social studies class, Mrs. Armstrong's students are expected to attain an average percentage score of 70% on weekly quizzes, homework assignments, and the midterm project. Scores averaging 70% or higher meet the demands and are judged competent (or in this case, "passing"), whereas scores of less than 70% do not meet the demands and are considered incompetent (or "failing"). Therefore, Mrs. Armstrong's criterion level for earning a passing grade on quizzes and

Criterion levels indicate the amount of social behavior that is average or typical.

assignments is 70% because it indicates the point at which students meet the expectation for these activities.

With social behavior, it is sometimes more difficult to designate a specific level of behavior that meets an expectation because of the informal way social demands are measured and evaluated. Remember that the criterion level should correspond to the *minimal average level of performance actually displayed by your students* under a particular set of circumstances. Often our inclination is to define standards in terms of what we teachers find acceptable or unacceptable in the setting, or in terms of our own standards for student behavior, when the standards are actually set by classmates or other people. Resisting this impulse is important as it tends to move the social skills curriculum from the realm of the actual to the realm of the ideal, thereby making the curriculum less useful for assessing behavior and planning interventions. For this reason, you should do your best to match criterion levels to the level of performance among the average or typical students. In the next section we discuss how you can achieve this.

Identifying and Describing Standards for Expectations

Identifying standards can be one of the most difficult aspects of describing social behavior because they attempt to quantify an area of performance that we usually consider only in vague terms. In this section, we explain some of the finer points of identifying standards and give a few tips for describing them in a clear and natural manner.

To make the social skills curriculum as functional and useful as possible, you should list standards for all the expectations you have identified. After completing the process presented in Chapter Two for identifying and listing expectations, you can enter the units of measure and criterion levels next to each of the expectations on the worksheet. Figure 3.1 shows two pages of the worksheet that Mrs. Armstrong completed, with standards recorded next to the expectations she listed before. Note that this is simply a more complete version of the worksheet presented in Figure 2.1.

Identifying Units of Measure

When you identify the units of measure for each expectation, your object is to stay as close as possible to the way the behavior is normally judged in the setting. Remember that units of measure answer the question "*what do I count?*" If the expectation is "converses with peers," you need to ask yourself, "what do I (or my students) naturally count, or keep track of, to tell how much a student converses?" The units in this case are likely to be "minutes spent conversing" or "number of conversations." As this example illustrates, one way to ascertain the measurement units people use to evaluate behavior is by closely observing the activities and interactions, and by thinking about how people keep track of the students' behavior—whether they watch for the number of questions asked, the number of comments contributed, or the amount of time spent working cooperatively. To discover how social behavior is measured outside your classroom or in settings less familiar to you, such as on the playground or in the cafeteria, you could confer with the adults or students in these settings or closely observe the activities and interactions taking place to see how people make judgments about the competence of the behavior.

One point you should observe when describing units of measure for standards is that many social behaviors are easier to measure in negative rather than positive terms. Even though the expectations themselves should be described in positive terms, it is often more natural to count exceptions or violations than incidents of compliance. If Mrs. Armstrong is trying to define units of measure for expectations such as "handles disagreements diplomatically" and "returns greetings to teachers and classmates," she would find it difficult to measure the positive behavior, because it would require keeping track of every potential disagreement the students resolve or every time they respond to a greeting. It will be much easier for Mrs. Armstrong to describe measurement units in terms of the "number of unresolved or boisterous disagreements" or "number of times not returning a greeting." These units of measure have the added advantage of being much closer to the natural way people usually judge social behavior; as we pointed out in Chapter One, incompetent behavior is much more quickly recognized than competent behavior.

Note, however, that these negative measures still apply to expectations for competent behavior. When Mrs. Armstrong defines a standard for the expectation

Figure 3.1 Mrs. Armstrong's social skills curriculum showing standards added.

Worksheet 2.1, Part 3: The Social Skills Curriculum—EXPECTATIONS Page *3* of *13*

Name: *Mrs. Armstrong* Date: *Sept. 18*

Setting: *5th-grade social studies*

SITUATION: *Teacher presentation and instruction*

EXPECTATIONS	STANDARDS	
	Units of Measure	Criterion Level
Pays attention to teacher (eye contact)	*# of times not paying attention*	*No more than 2 per class*
Responds to correction by paying better attention	*# of times not paying attention after correction*	*No more than 1 per week*
Volunteers answers to teacher questions	*% of time volunteering for teacher's questions*	*At least 85%*
Takes notes on teacher presentation	*# of notes on page*	*At least 1/3 page*
Checks progress against neighbor's notes	*# of times glancing at neighbor's notes*	*At least 2 per class*
Communicates with neighbor (on topic) by glances and occasional whispers	*# of glances, whispers, nonverbal signs*	*At least 4 per class*
Encourages others (quietly) who are called on	*# of times encouraging others*	*At least 3 per class*
Asks questions when help is needed	*# of time asking questions when help needed (i.e., work incomplete or incorrect)*	*At least 75%*
Raises hand before speaking	*# of times speaking out without raising hand*	*No more than 2 per class*
Interacts quietly with neighbors before beginning independent work	*# of times interacting before beginning work*	*At least 3 days per week*

Figure 3.1 *(continued)*

Worksheet 2.1, Part 3: The Social Skills Curriculum—EXPECTATIONS Page *9* of *13*

Name: *Mrs. Armstrong* Date: *Sept. 21*

Setting: *5th-grade recess*

SITUATION: *Playing tag and other nonorganized games*

EXPECTATIONS	STANDARDS (Covered in Chapter Three)	
	Units of Measure	Criterion Level
Jump Rope:		
Stands in line to wait turn to jump	*# of times out of line*	*No more than 2 per week*
Interacts with others while waiting in line	*% of time interacting*	*At least 50%*
Talks on "cool" subjects (clothes, hair, etc.)	*# of times talking on "uncool" subjects* *# of comments on "cool" subjects*	*No more than 1 per week/* *At least 1 per day*
Takes turn jumping	*# of times going out of turn*	*No more than 2 per week*
Negotiates conflicts with leader	*# of times arguing with leader*	*No more than 1 per day*
Accepts judgment of group/leader	*# of times leaving in anger*	*No more than 1 per week*
Encourages others who are jumping	*# of encouragements given*	*At least 3 per day*
Moves freely between activities or games	*# of minutes remaining alone before joining another activity*	*No more than 3 minutes*
Tag:		
Helps set rules before game begins	*# of times joining in "rules" conversation*	*At least 3 times per week*
Offers new rules during game	*# of new rules offered*	*At least 1 per day*
Helps resolve conflicts within group	*# of conflicts left unresolved*	*No more than 2 per week*
Asks teacher, not aide, to settle arguments	*# of times referring to aide*	*No more than 1 per week*
Avoids fighting	*# of times fighting*	*No more than 1 per 2 weeks*
Stops and pays attention when teacher blows whistle	*# of times ignoring whistle*	*No more than 2 per week*
Discusses action of game with others as period ends	*# of days conversing with others at end of period*	*At least 3 per week*

"raises hand before speaking" in class discussions, she would probably find it more accurate to use "less than three talk-outs per class" than "complies 85% of the time." Even so, Mrs. Armstrong is essentially defining the same standard for the expectation; the difference is that the first one is a more natural way to measure the performance. In either case, the basic expectation remains the positive "raises hand before speaking."

Identifying Criterion Levels

Once you have determined the units of measure for an expectation, you are ready to identify the criterion level that denotes the line between meeting and not meeting the demand. As we noted above, this criterion level should represent the *minimum* performance that could be considered average or competent for this expectation. To help you determine what this level is, you can refer to the notes you took when observing student behavior to define the social skills curriculum (Chapter Two). The direct observations, videotapes, conferences, and other procedures you used to identify expectations have probably already supplied you with information about the standards for many expectations. However, you should plan follow-up observations, conferences, and other activities to determine or verify the standards in areas where your knowledge or understanding is unclear or imprecise. Again, your goal is to develop a complete and accurate picture of the average level of behavior that meets each of the expectations.

Although the process of defining criterion levels can seem quite tricky at first, it becomes easier with experience. Usually, your own prior knowledge of the activities and demands in the setting can give you a fairly clear idea of what the levels are, especially for expectations you set yourself. In particularly difficult cases, you should make at least a rough estimate of the criterion level, or express it as a range. Mrs. Armstrong found after viewing her videotapes that students contribute comments to class discussions roughly five to eight times per week, depending on the topic of the lesson. Note that Mrs. Armstrong identified this criterion by estimating how many times the average or C-level students perform this behavior, *not* by considering her own wishes or judgments. It is crucial to avoid using standards to restate our own classroom rules and regulations instead of describing what typical students do.

Identifying Standards in Different Situations

Like expectations for social behavior, standards are usually set by the people who oversee activities in a setting or by those who participate in the interactions. Thus, standards can change considerably, depending on the circumstances under which students interact. When you examine the expectations for your circumstances, you may find that the standards for some expectations will vary from setting to setting and from situation to situation. Mrs. Armstrong has discovered that she and other teachers in her school often use different units of measure and criterion levels for the same behavior. For instance, the standard for remaining quiet during class is very different in her social studies class, in Mr. Wagner's science class, and in Mrs. Kellerman's art class, even though all three teachers identify remaining quiet as a requirement in their classes. The standard in Mrs. Armstrong's class is higher than in Mr. Wagner's but lower than in Mrs. Kellerman's. Mrs. Armstrong has also noticed differences in standards within her own classroom as the students move between situations. For example, they are expected to raise their hands and wait to be called on before asking questions or making comments in class. During her presentations of the day's lesson, the standard for this expectation is fairly strict, with average students raising their hand about 85% of the time before speaking. During class discussions, however, they are much more apt to speak out spontaneously, and the standard is about 50%. You will often find variations such as these from grade level to grade level, from one subject matter area to another, and from situation to situation; some of these differences can be very significant.

Therefore, when the same expectation for social behavior applies to several situations, check for differences in the standards across these circumstances. Recognizing these differences can aid both in understanding the problems students may have and in deciding on the circumstances in which to carry out interventions. Table 3.5 shows some of the differences in standards Mrs. Armstrong found between her social studies class and Mr. Wagner's science class.

In summary, listing standards is a fairly straightforward process once the expectations are described and organized by settings and situations. Take care in specifying the standards to give the best estimate of what average or minimally competent students do to meet the expectations.

TABLE 3.5 Examples of how standards can vary in different settings and situations

Expectation	*Setting/Situation*	*Standard*
Answers questions about day's topics	Social studies—teacher presentation	Answers 1–2 questions per class—50% correct
	Social studies—independent work time	Answers 2–3 questions per class—75% correct
	Science—group discussion of class projects	Answers 4–5 questions per class—90% correct
Completes homework assignments	Social studies	Turns in 90% of assignments with 70% accuracy
	Science	Turns in 75% of assignments with 60% accuracy
Greets teacher when entering classroom	Social studies	Once each day
	Science	None: Not an expectation

❍ Using Standards to Evaluate Social Behavior

The social skills curriculum you develop by describing expectations and standards for school settings will give you precise information about the skills and levels of behavior that students must display to achieve social competence. You can now use this information to judge the effectiveness and adequacy of your students' behavior and to establish goals for their interventions. Mrs. Armstrong can use the list of expectations and standards she identified for her social studies class to evaluate Granville's, Sandy's, and Alfred's behavior. She can determine whether Sandy contributes enough to class discussions, whether Granville argues too much in small groups, or whether Alfred makes too many sarcastic comments by observing their performance and comparing the results to the standards for those expectations. If Mrs. Armstrong finds a large gap between the students' behavior and the criteria for average, competent performance, she can use this standard as a guide to decide how many times Sandy should be contributing to class discussions, for instance, and then set this standard as a goal for her intervention. Thus, standards let you make objective and reliable comparisons between the level of the students' behavior and the individual expectations in the social skills curriculum. In Part II of the text we discuss in detail how you can use the curriculum to assess the social behavior of individual students and to set priorities for interventions. Before we move on to assessment, however, let us clarify how standards can affect social behavior and how you can use them to make broader judgments of social competence.

Standards As Source of Student Difficulty

Just as students may show difficulties in responding and adapting to changing expectations as they move from situation to situation, they may also have problems adjusting to differences in the standards, even though they may have the skills they need to meet them (Knoff, 1990; Rose, 1972). Students are often unable to recognize and adjust to the different standards they encounter in moving from one setting, teacher, peer group, or grade level to another. Mrs. Armstrong found this with Alfred's clowning when she holds class discussions, because the standards for this behavior in her classroom are very different from those in Mr. Wagner's. She also suspects that Sandy may have difficulties talking with classmates because of the different standards peer groups set for holding conversations. Therefore, when you identify standards for expectations, you should also consider the degree of difficulty students may be having in understanding and adapting to them. You may be able to easily alleviate some problems in social behavior by clarifying and highlighting the changes in standards that may occur across settings and situations.

Standards Applied Collectively

Although we generally speak of each one as marking the line between average and below-average performance, standards make up a collective measurement system. Usually, we make judgments of social competence on a whole array of behaviors simultaneously. When we say Granville is not meeting the expectations for Mrs. Armstrong's class, we are really speaking of the expectations as an overall group. If he were below the standard on only one or two specific expectations, such as cooperating with peers during group work or responding to teasing from classmates, Mrs. Armstrong would probably think of Granville as a competent student. After all, most students have one or two areas of social behavior that fall just below the dividing line for meeting the expectations. Granville's performance, however, is below the standard for competence for a number of social expectations, and it is the collective nature of this problem behavior that leads people to characterize him as an incompetent or high-risk student. Therefore, when you specify standards for the expectations in your settings, your main goal should be to describe a fairly specific average level of performance for the expectations. While you should strive for accuracy, you should not worry too much about applying the standards to students who show minor variations or discrepancies in their behavior, since these relatively few, barely below-average areas will tend to even out over the full array of expectations for the settings.

Summary

Social Competence and Standards

1. Standards indicate the minimum level of student performance that meets an expectation.
2. Standards provide a basis for judging whether the level of a student's behavior is competent.
3. Standards apply to the entire list of skills included in a social skills curriculum.

Advantages of Identifying Standards

1. Standards specify the actual level of behavior students must attain to meet expectations.
2. Standards provide a way to use expectations to assess student behavior and to decide whether there is a need to plan interventions.
3. Standards clarify instructional goals and give an unbiased referent for judging the effectiveness of instructional activities and interventions.

Elements of Standards

1. Standards can be stated in terms of units of measure and criterion levels.
2. Units of measure indicate the type of numbers people normally use to keep track of student behavior.
3. Units of measure most frequently used to evaluate social behavior are frequency, duration, rate, and occurrence.

4. Criterion levels indicate the amount of behavior that meets the demands of a setting.
5. Criterion levels state the minimum or average level of performance actually displayed by typical students.

Identifying and Describing Standards

1. Standards should be specified for each expectation in the social skills curriculum and should be listed on a worksheet alongside each expectation.
2. Closely observing activities and interactions in a setting will give you a clear indication of the units of measure and criterion levels for expectations.
3. Describing units of measure in negative terms is often helpful because people normally keep track of student behavior in this way.
4. Standards can change from setting to setting and from situation to situation depending on how people in the setting judge the competence of student behavior.

Using Standards to Evaluate Behavior

1. Standards are used to evaluate the effectiveness and adequacy of student behavior.
2. Changes in standards across settings and across situations may cause problems for students in adjusting their behavior.
3. Standards are used collectively rather than individually in judging the social competence of students.

Examples for Chapter Three

Example 3a

This table shows the standards for the preschool example presented in the previous chapter, with some of the measurement units and criterion levels that apply to the social expectations for young children.

Duration measures (such as amount of time talking) can be helpful for counting expectations for conversing and interacting.

The most common measure you are likely to need will be frequency—the # of times performing an action.

Units of measure can help to further clarify an expectation, since they point out more precisely what is being counted.

Worksheet 2.1, Part 3: The Social Skills Curriculum—EXPECTATIONS Page _8_ of _9_

Name: _Mr. Jordan_ Date: _Sept. 19_

Setting: _Preschool recess_

SITUATION: _Playing in small groups_

EXPECTATIONS	STANDARDS (Covered in Chapter Three)	
	Units of Measure	Criterion Level
1. Chats and laughs with peers	*Amount of time in animated conversation*	*At least 3 minutes per recess (avg.)*
2. Participates in tag or running games ("I'll catch you!" "I'm faster than you!")	*Amount of time spent in running activities*	*At least 5 minutes per recess (avg.)*
3. Maneuvers without hurting others	*# of times hurting others*	*No more than 3 per week*
4. Plays creatively with peers	*Amount of time spent in creative play*	*At least 5 minutes per recess (avg.)*
5. Expresses self dramatically (pretending to be animals, etc.)	*# of times acting out dramatic roles*	*At least 4 per week*
6. Offers suggestions or instructions for play to others ("Crawl like this.")	*# of suggestions or instructions offered*	*At least 2 per recess*
7. Discusses plans for activity with others (who takes what role)	*# of times participating in planning roles*	*At least 3 per week*
8. Copies actions of peers	*# of times copying peer actions*	*At least 3 per recess*
9. Calls for teacher attention ("Watch me!" "He caught me!")	*# of times calling for teacher attention*	*At least 3 per week*
10. Teases opposite sex (boys chase girls)	*# of times chasing/running*	*At least 4 per week*
11. Squeals, laughs, and runs randomly	*# of times showing excitement*	*At least 2 per recess*
12. Mixes and mingles with several other children	*# of different children interacted with*	*At least 5 per recess*
13. Tells others about what he or she is doing	*# of verbal statements about activities*	*At least 4 per recess*

Example 3b

This table shows the standards for the high school example presented in the previous chapter with units of measure and criterion levels that are appropriate for a high school setting.

It is usually a good idea to include both positive and negative measures; in this way you are likely to record a broader variety of behavior.

The conditional phrasing here implies a ratio; the criterion level is therefore described accordingly.

Often even a complicated expectation can be counted with a fairly simple unit of measure.

Worksheet 2.1, Part 3: The Social Skills Curriculum—EXPECTATIONS Page 2 of 12

Name: *Mrs. Pajakowski* Date: *Sept 20*

Setting: *9th-grade careers class*

SITUATION: *Independent work on board assignment*

EXPECTATIONS	STANDARDS (Covered in Chapter Three)	
	Units of Measure	Criterion Level
1. Begins work without prompting	*Amount of time taken to begin*	*No more than 2 minutes per activity*
2. Asks questions about activity	*# of questions asked*	*At least 2 per activity*
3. Raises hand before asking question	*# of times not raising hand*	*No more than 1 per activity*
4. Checks work quietly with neighbors	*# of times checking with neighbor*	*At least 2 per activity*
5. Shares supplies with classmates	*Ratio of times sharing to times asked*	*At least 80%*
6. Pays attention when teacher speaks (eye contact)	*# of times not paying attention*	*No more than 1 per activity*
7. Laughs at appropriate times (with teacher and classmates)	*# of times laughing with others*	*At least 2 per activity*
8. Negotiates for more time to finish work	*# of times negotiating for more time (when not finished)*	*At least 3 out of 5 times not finished*
9. Talks quietly with neighbors	*Amount of time talking with neighbors*	*Between 3 and 5 minutes per activity*
10. Talks on age-appropriate, current topics	*# of comments on current subjects*	*At least 2 per activity*
11. Listens to what other students say	*# of times not listening to friends*	*No more than 1 per activity*
12. Checks appearance	*# of times checking appearance*	*At least 4 days per week*
13. Talks about activity ("did you finish?")	*# of comments on activity*	*At least 2 per activity*

Mr. Wagner's Case Study

Mr. Wagner's Standards

With some help from Mrs. Armstrong and Ms. Hernandez, Mr. Wagner has improved his lists of expectations, but he is finding it difficult to define standards for the items he has listed. The page of Mr. Wagner's worksheet presented here includes many of the most common difficulties and errors that arise when listing units of measure and criterion levels.

Standards need to count the behavior of individual students, not the class as a whole.

Make sure you use behavioral terms—you can't count a student's knowledge or attitudes.

Make sure the criterion level is consistent with the units of measure.

These standards contradict the original expectation. These should be "*At least . . .*," not "no more than."

These items can be counted more accurately with positive measures (such as "# of questions asked"), since they both involve specific, observable actions that the students perform.

Use ratios or percentages sparingly as they can be tricky to count. (These two items are easier to count as "# of times not following" and "# of times using age-inappropriate language."

Avoid measures that count what the teacher notices or does rather than what the student does.

Criterion levels of zero, or 100%, are usually unrealistic. Remember that this should be an estimate of typical behavior, not a restatement of school rules.

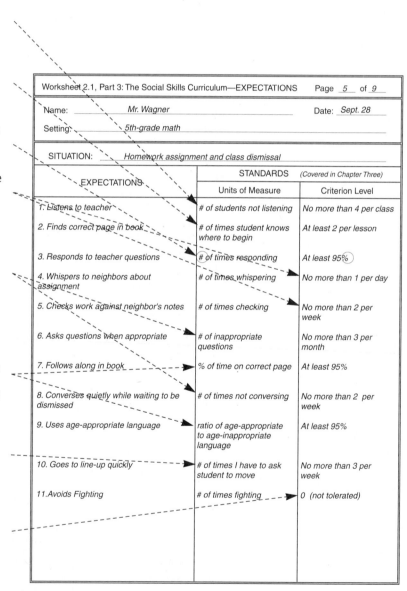

Worksheet 2.1, Part 3: The Social Skills Curriculum—EXPECTATIONS Page 5 of 9

Name: *Mr. Wagner* Date: *Sept. 28*

Setting: *5th-grade math*

SITUATION: *Homework assignment and class dismissal*

EXPECTATIONS	STANDARDS (Covered in Chapter Three)	
	Units of Measure	Criterion Level
1. Listens to teacher	*# of students not listening*	*No more than 4 per class*
2. Finds correct page in book	*# of times student knows where to begin*	*At least 2 per lesson*
3. Responds to teacher questions	*# of times responding*	*At least 95%*
4. Whispers to neighbors about assignment	*# of times whispering*	*No more than 1 per day*
5. Checks work against neighbor's notes	*# of times checking*	*No more than 2 per week*
6. Asks questions when appropriate	*# of inappropriate questions*	*No more than 3 per month*
7. Follows along in book	*% of time on correct page*	*At least 95%*
8. Converses quietly while waiting to be dismissed	*# of times not conversing*	*No more than 2 per week*
9. Uses age-appropriate language	*ratio of age-appropriate to age-inappropriate language*	*At least 95%*
10. Goes to line-up quickly	*# of times I have to ask student to move*	*No more than 3 per week*
11.Avoids Fighting	*# of times fighting*	*0 (not tolerated)*

PART TWO
Assessing Social Skills

In the previous chapters we introduced the concepts of expectations and the social skills curriculum as a way of understanding and documenting the wide array of social behavior students must demonstrate to show competence in their interactions with teachers and classmates. In Part II we explain how these ideas can form the basis for assessing social skills and examining specific problems students may have in their social behavior. *Assessment* is the process of discovering whether students have requisite skills and abilities for meeting expectations, and if they do, whether they use these skills under normal performance conditions (Cone & Hawkins, 1977; Gresham & Elliot, 1984). The results of an assessment can give a precise direction to intervention plans.

In this part of the text, we present a two-phase approach to assessment based on the work of such authors as Choate, Enright, Miller, Poteet, and Rakes (1995), and Howell and Morehead (1987). The first phase is called *survey level assessment,* and the second phase is called *specific level assessment.* This two-level approach can help you assess social behavior efficiently because it allows you to be as general or as specific as you need to be to establish a firm base for planning interventions.

Chapters Four and Five discuss *survey level assessment,* a process that determines which expectations from a social skills curriculum a student does and does not meet. Survey level assessments are broad based, examining a wide variety of performance areas. The results from this process will help you target specific social skills to teach students that will enable them to overcome their most pressing problems. Chapter Four describes the aim of a survey level assessment and outlines a seven-step planning process for conducting such an assessment in your own settings. Chapter Five explains how to summarize and interpret survey level assessment results, and how to use the results to set priorities for further work with the students.

In Chapters Six through Eight, we present *specific level assessment,* which you conduct after identifying the particular social skills that will serve as the target for an intervention. A specific level assessment gives you a detailed look at exactly where and why students are having problems with particular social skills so you can decide what aspects of their performance need to be developed in an intervention. This assessment is more precisely focused than the survey level assessment as it breaks a target behavior or skill into three tightly defined areas of performance: basic abilities, component steps, and performance conditions. Chapters Six through Eight discuss each of these aspects of the specific level assessment.

CHAPTER 4

Planning a Survey Level Assessment

Assessment is a fundamental step in understanding and addressing students' problems in achieving social competence. Careful assessment makes the difference between effective, well-targeted interventions that help students learn the skills they need to develop, and ineffective or misdirected interventions that lead to greater frustration or a renewed sense of failure. When you conduct an assessment of social skills, the results should help you answer your questions about improving the students' behavior so you can begin planning productive, applicable interventions.

Typically, you will find that assessments are used to learn whether something is "wrong" with a student, and to classify problem areas. In far too many cases, school personnel conduct assessments that concentrate on categorizing students according to disability areas or on establishing clinical diagnoses (Hoy & Gregg, 1994; Salvia & Hughes, 1990). But such an approach usually does not help to identify the source of the students' problems or to set goals for their interventions, because most of these assessments fail to point out the specific skills students need to learn to improve their behavior. Furthermore, assessments are often poorly matched to the real issues that need to be investigated, yielding little new information about the students' social behavior. The results only verify what people already know: the students are having difficulties with social interactions. On the other hand, an assessment can be so exhaustive and yield so much information that it is difficult to decide which results are most important or useful in planning further work with the students.

When they are designed carefully, however, assessments can yield valuable information. In this and the following chapters, we describe an approach to assessment that is practical and directly applicable to your students' needs. This approach draws on the social skills curriculum that you have already developed. An assessment based on the information you have gathered about the expectations for social behavior will yield results that show which demands students can and cannot meet and indicate which areas for instruction will have the greatest impact on improving their social competence. Rather than producing a set of numbers that signify whether students are disabled, immature, or maladjusted, an assessment based on the social skills curriculum will (a) reveal the expectations that represent particular problems for students, (b) highlight the specific skills that will improve their behavior, and (c) suggest ways of helping them acquire these skills (Bellack, 1979).

Overview of Survey Level Assessment

The first stage of this assessment is called a *survey level assessment.* Its purpose is to identify the expectations in the social skills curriculum that students do and do not meet. This assessment is especially useful when students have many behavior problems because the results will give you an objective accounting of their skill

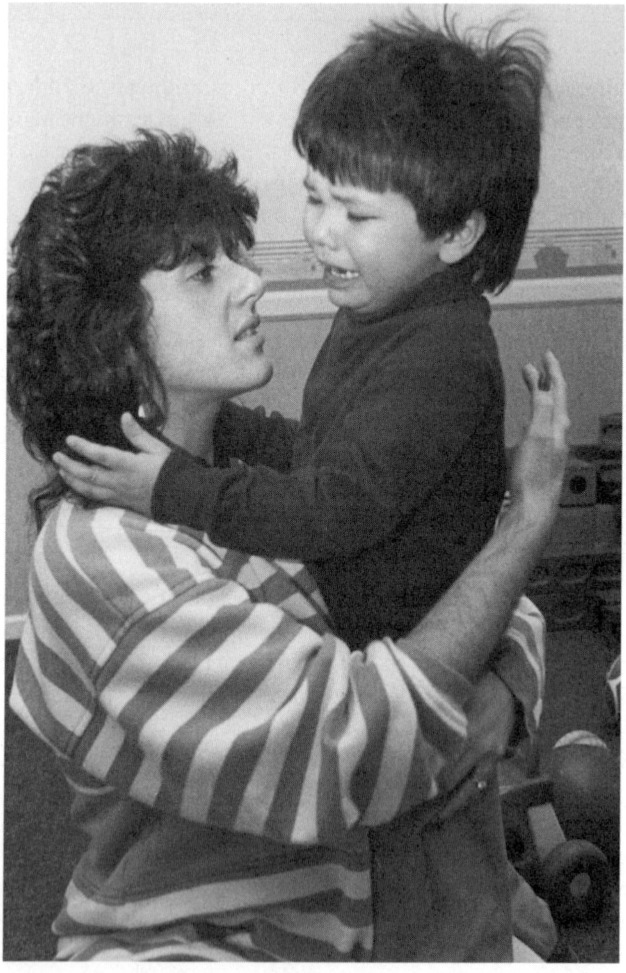

A survey level assessment gives a broad overview of a student's social behavior.

deficits, enabling you to set priorities for their instruction (Howell, Fox, & Morehead, 1993). This is because the assessment is based on a broad understanding of social competence rather than a mere listing of problems.

It will be crucial for Mrs. Armstrong to conduct a survey level assessment of Granville, Sandy, and Alfred before she attempts any extensive interventions with them, because of the many problems they have in their social interactions. With Granville, for instance, her assessment will provide a more specific accounting of his social performance for expectations both in instructional situations, such as asking questions and participating in small group discussions, and in noninstructional situations, such as handling teasing and disagreements on the playground and building more positive relationships with classmates. She wants results that will help her identify the areas of behavior that are the greatest obstacles for Granville, and help her choose the ones she should address first when planning instruction or interventions. Without first assessing Granville's behavior, any effort Mrs. Armstrong makes at setting goals or developing interventions is in danger of being misdirected or wasted entirely.

In this chapter, we explain how to develop a survey level assessment based on the social skills curriculum you identified in Chapters Two and Three, and show how to tailor this assessment to your own needs and circumstances. With the procedures outlined here, you will be able to prepare an assessment to identify and list the expectations an individual student does and does not meet, and to identify the key skills to focus on in developing interventions.

❍ Principles of a Survey Level Assessment

The procedures we outline are fairly extensive and detailed, because a well-designed assessment is the foundation for developing solid interventions. When they are based on reliable assessment results, interventions are much more likely to be dynamic and effective; if they are based on slipshod or cursory assessments, interventions will generally be misdirected and ineffectual. For this reason, we advocate an approach to assessment that is very deliberate and well planned. In the sections that follow, we discuss the principles that underlie this approach and are crucial for ensuring effective, well-directed assessments. Table 4.1 provides an outline of these principles.

TABLE 4.1 Principles for a survey level assessment

A survey level assessment should be:
Personalized
Conducted under natural conditions
Teacher developed

Need for Personalized Assessment

An assessment approach must be flexible so it can be tailored to individual students thus providing an accurate and complete accounting of each student's skill level (Cullen & Pratt, 1992, Zirpoli & Melloy, 1993). The process discussed in this chapter employs the social skills curriculum to produce a personal approach in three ways: (a) you assess only the areas of the curriculum that represent problems or issues for a particular student; (b) you conduct the assessment in the actual situations in which the student's problems occur; and (c) you use procedures that are specifically appropriate for the student and the skills you are assessing (Choate, Enright, Miller, Poteet, & Rakes, 1995). By personalizing the assessment in these ways, you can use the results to design instructional lessons or interventions that are well suited to the characteristics of the individual student.

Mrs. Armstrong will use different areas of her social skills curriculum in assessing Sandy's behavior and Granville's behavior. Sandy displays types of problems quite different from those that cause difficulty for Granville. Mrs. Armstrong will personalize Sandy's assessment by concentrating on skills for conversing with adults and classmates, and by limiting the observations to structured and unstructured classroom settings. With Granville, she may not even look at expectations for interacting with adults because he seems to have very few problems in this area. Instead, she will assess Granville in skills for playing and interacting informally with classmates, and will examine his behavior in both classroom and nonclassroom settings. By tailoring the assessment to each individual student in this way, you will be able to focus much more effectively on the specific skills students need to learn.

Need to Assess under Natural Conditions

An assessment must be conducted under the actual circumstances in which the students' performance typically occurs so you can make an accurate and reliable judgment of whether the students display the expected behavior when it is required (Fish & Massey, 1991; Salvia & Ysseldyke, 1995). The most reliable setting for measuring social behavior will always be the typical or natural performance conditions for the expectations you are concerned with (Cartledge & Cartledge, 1986; Zirpoli & Melloy, 1993). Thus, a fundamental principle in planning an assessment is to conduct the activities as much as possible in the location where the behavior occurs, and to observe the interactions directly as they normally take place.

If Mrs. Armstrong wants to assess Granville's play interactions during recess, she will need to observe his behavior under the normal conditions of the playground setting to get an accurate accounting of his behavior. These conditions will show the skills Granville already uses to interact with playmates as well as the skills he needs to acquire to interact more successfully. This assessment will also indicate the exact circumstances in which he meets and does not meet the social expectations in this setting. If Mrs. Armstrong were to conduct a simulated assessment of

Granville under artificial conditions, the information she would record about his social abilities and behavior would likely be incomplete or even inaccurate because she could not fully re-create the natural conditions for his performance. Under artificial conditions, Granville would probably not act as he usually does, possibly leading Mrs. Armstrong to make incorrect judgments about his skill level.

An assessment is much more accurate, complete, and dependable when it is conducted in the actual circumstances where students interact. Such an assessment lets you examine student performance of the expectations that apply to their behavior, and to determine which skills students must learn to improve their behavior.

Need for Teacher-Developed Assessment

In order to tailor assessment procedures to specific students and situations, you should develop your own assessment procedures rather than relying on commercial materials such as standardized tests, surveys, and inventories. Many of the expectations you will need to examine in your social skills curriculum cannot be easily assessed with commercial materials. Although standardized instruments can be valuable in making clinical diagnoses or obtaining generalized information about behavior, they lack the specificity for assessing many key skill areas. As Cartwright and Cartwright (1984), Howell, Fox, and Morehead (1993), Hoy and Gregg (1994), McFall (1982), Salvia and Hughes (1990), and many others have noted, most expectations for social behavior are established by teachers or classmates, or by students themselves; therefore, they are usually unique to the school settings and situations to which they apply. Commercial materials are unable to describe these demands accurately or completely, because they are developed for a broad audience. They often yield imprecise or incomplete information about the students' skill levels and lead to faulty interventions. Furthermore, commercial materials usually include many items that you may not want to assess at all. It is important, then, to be selective in the commercial materials you use, and to be ready to develop your own procedures to fit the circumstances under which students' interactions take place.

Advantages of Assessing with the Social Skills Curriculum

In addition to satisfying the principles discussed above, assessment using the social skills curriculum offers other advantages. First, the social skills curriculum provides an objective yardstick for measuring student behavior, as it is based on typical or average social performance. Rather than evaluating student behavior in vague or judgmental terms, your assessment can be fairly objective. You will identify and quantify the important features of students' performance, just as when you evaluate performance on a math exercise, a reading assignment, or a social studies report (Choate, Enright, Miller, Poteet, & Rakes, 1995).

A second advantage of using the social skills curriculum is that it allows you to consider a wide array of social expectations when conducting assessments. Because a curriculum documents the full range of social demands that students must meet in school settings, rather than just teacher-set demands and rules, it provides you with a broad-based resource for identifying skill deficits across a full range of situations and demands. Finally, the social skills curriculum provides your assessment with a specific basis for targeting interventions because it consists of actual expectations that typical students must respond to in the settings. In this way, the results of the assessment can be translated quite directly into real-world skills students need to be taught, skills that can serve as concrete and useful goals for interventions.

Thus, the approach we describe for the survey level assessment offers distinct benefits by drawing directly from the social skills curriculum you have already developed for your settings. The following sections discuss the planning process for preparing this type of assessment.

Planning a Survey Level Assessment

Deciding how and where to conduct a survey level assessment can be baffling because of the many questions you may wish to answer and the numerous options available for answering them (Wolery, Bailey, & Sugai, 1988). You can obtain information about the students' skill level through questionnaires, tests, simulated tasks, interviews, and direct observations of behavior. Furthermore, these tools can be used in many different settings and circumstances. In the following sections, we describe a flexible, dynamic framework that addresses all these considerations. As you plan your approach, remember the basic purpose of this assessment: to find out how well the students' performance meets the specific demands of the social skills curriculum.

Steps in Planning the Assessment

Planning a survey level assessment involves a series of fairly complex decisions and determinations; you can simplify the task by breaking it down into several steps, which are listed in Table 4.2.

TABLE 4.2 Steps in planning a survey level assessment

Step 1:	Choose a student to assess
Step 2:	Choose situations in which to assess
Step 3:	Choose expectations to assess
Step 4:	Describe the standards for measuring performance
Step 5:	Choose assessment procedures
Step 6:	Prepare to record assessment results
Step 7:	Schedule the assessment

This step-by-step process will help you build your plan gradually and completely. You will be able to check your work at each stage to ensure that the plans are consistent, and that they correspond with the information you have already obtained in developing a social skills curriculum.

The project can become a bit overwhelming if you do not keep careful track of each step. A useful organizing device is a worksheet that you can use at each stage of the assessment preparation. The worksheet will display in a structured format all the information you will need to conduct the assessment. This level of organization will make the assessment procedure easier to carry out and will also increase the precision of the results you obtain. Most important, the worksheet will help you organize your thinking as you select students to assess; decide on the expectations you will examine; and develop, organize, and schedule the assessment activities.

The worksheet will continue to be a valuable tool after your preparations are complete and the assessment has begun, helping you stay organized as you conduct the assessment and, keeping the activities efficient, well planned, and focused on the expectations you wish to investigate (Cartwright & Cartwright, 1984; Hoy & Gregg, 1994). It will also help you focus on the exact behavior you are looking for, the circumstances in which that behavior is likely to occur, and the way you will record your observations of it. Remember that activities and social interactions often take place so quickly that if you depend on your memory to recall the expectations you are trying to assess or the measurement procedures you are supposed to use, you will be distracted from making an accurate assessment of the students' behavior. The worksheet can help you focus and direct the actual assessment procedures so as to avoid distractions. In the sections that follow, we explain each of the steps in Table 4.2 and show the worksheet Mrs. Armstrong used to complete this process for Granville.

Step 1: Choose a Student to Assess

The first step in conducting a survey level assessment is to select a student to assess. By selecting the student at the beginning of the planning process, you will be able to develop the assessment plan with that particular student in mind. This focus ensures that the procedures you plan will give you detailed and pertinent information about the student, rather than pulling the assessment off into inappropriate, tangential areas. The following guidelines will help with this important first step.

Choose a Student Whose Difficulties Need Particular Attention

Be sure the student you choose for the assessment is an appropriate choice. The survey level assessment process described in this chapter is deliberately detailed and systematic. It is designed to be used with students who exhibit a broad range of problems, or whose problems have resisted simpler, less structured approaches—students such as Granville, Sandy, and Alfred, who have difficult and complicated problems in their social interactions. If you select students whose difficulties are more clear-cut, you will find this kind of assessment to be an exercise in overkill, providing much more detail than you need to develop effective interventions for them. With these students, doing a more specific assessment, which we discuss in Chapters Six, Seven, and Eight, or devising a quick intervention without such extensive preparation, would be more productive. A survey level assessment should be used with students whose performance leaves you with many difficult questions to answer.

Create a Page of the Assessment Worksheet for Entering Information about the Student

Once you have selected the student, you can begin an assessment worksheet by creating a space for key information, such as the student's name and grade. You may wish to add other pertinent information, such as the dates of the assessment, the classes or school settings in which the assessment will take place, and the person or persons conducting the assessment. This step is important because it ensures against the assessor's fading memory that can quickly make a document meaningless if it is not well labeled. Including this background information will allow you to refer to the worksheet weeks or months later and accurately recall specific details about the conditions of the assessment and the student's behavior.

You should also provide a brief description—perhaps a half page—of the students' social behavior, followed by a listing of the major issues or concerns you wish to investigate during the assessment. This information will help you clarify your questions and goals before you begin planning the assessment. Figure 4.1 shows the format Mrs. Armstrong used to enter background information for Granville on the first page of the assessment worksheet. She also added a description of his overall behavior and the concerns she hopes to investigate. This information will allow her to clarify the focus and goals of her assessment as she plans the next steps. Furthermore, this information will help her remember many important details about the assessment activities if she refers to the worksheet in the future.

Step 2: Choose Situations in Which to Assess

Once you have chosen the student to assess, you should identify the situations in which the assessment will take place. A survey level assessment can be intimidating if you set out to collect and list information on a student's social behavior without a clear context for gathering the data. By selecting specific situations in which to assess, you can limit your activities to a few well-chosen areas that will provide a structure for your assessment plans. When completing this task, you should follow the considerations discussed next.

Choose Situations from the Social Skills Curriculum

It is important to ensure that the circumstances of the assessment are as close as possible to the natural conditions in which students interact. For this reason, it is best to select situations for assessment from those you have already defined in the social skills curriculum as natural features of the settings. For example,

Figure 4.1 Mrs. Armstrong's description of Granville's behavior.

Worksheet 4.1, Part 1: Description of Student Behavior

Name: *Mrs. Armstrong* Date: *Sept. 23*

Student to be assessed: *Granville* Grade: *5*

Assessment setting(s): *Social studies class, playground*

Description of student behavior (focus on social skills):

Granville has been described as aggressive, quick tempered, and a bully. He calls classmates names, makes obscene and threatening gestures, and hits and pushes other students. Granville has few real friends among his classmates. Some are afraid of him, but others deliberately tease him and provoke his outbursts.

Granville shows respect for me and his other teachers, and mostly follows directions and participates adequately in classroom activities. But I often have to separate him during small group lessons because he does not interact well with classmates on cooperative tasks. I have repeatedly reprimanded him and used "time out" and other techniques to try to reach him, but his behavior has not changed appreciably over the school year. It is clear that Granville's problems interacting with classmates are adversely affecting his school work.

During class breaks, recess times, and art and gym periods, Granville actively seeks out other students, but his interactions often end in verbal and physical disagreements. He is good at sports, and would probably be fairly popular if he were less aggressive. In addition, he seems to make bad choices in picking playmates. For example, he tries to play with Billy, another 5th grader, but the two of them end up arguing and fighting. I sense that Granville would very much like to get along with his classmates, but he goes about it the wrong way.

Areas or concerns to investigate:

Interacting and cooperating during small group activities

Interactions with neighbors, etc., during classroom activities

Playground interactions

Granville's way of talking to his classmates—his use of greetings, tone, etc.

Mrs. Armstrong had identified the following classroom situations in her social skills curriculum (Chapter Two):

Class start-up time and announcements

Homework grading and review

Teacher presentation and instruction

Large group discussion

Small group discussion/activity

Independent work time

Class dismissal

In preparing an assessment worksheet for her students, Mrs. Armstrong can pick the situations in which to assess their behavior from this list.

Not only will this step ensure that she is basing her assessment plans on the natural conditions of the setting, but it will also allow her to focus only on the situations that interest her for a particular student. Mrs. Armstrong might decide to conduct Granville's assessment only during some of the less structured situations in her classroom, such as class start-up time, small group activity, and class dismissal, because these are the times when he has particular problems. She would not need to include other situations that do not represent a problem for Granville.

Consider All Situations as Possibilities

Although you can choose to assess in some situations and not in others, you should make this decision very carefully; a great deal of significant social behavior takes place in situations you might at first be inclined to overlook. You should consider every setting and situation possible before making your selections. The following are some advantages to assessing in both structured and unstructured situations.

Assessing during classroom lessons and activities. Many of the situations that make up the structured classroom routine can offer opportunities for assessing social interactions (Salvia & Hughes, 1990). Examples include board work activities, class discussions, project presentations, test and quiz study times, and small group work times for assignments. Because these activities usually concentrate on subject matter content, we may overlook the important social expectations that they include, such as asking questions, contributing responses to discussions, complying with directions, sharing supplies and materials, responding to praise or criticism, and offering assistance to classmates (Eisler & Fredericksen, 1980; Greenwood & Carta, 1987).

Such social demands can have a definite impact on a student's school performance, so you should consider these situations carefully when deciding where to focus your assessment. Mrs. Armstrong would probably want to assess Sandy's behavior in many activities like these, as they provide an ideal context for observing Sandy's interactions with adults. She may also include some of these activities in her assessment plans for Granville and Alfred, because they will give her opportunities to observe the boys' interactions with classmates.

Assessing during unstructured or informal activities. Consider less structured or formal situations in your assessment plans because they provide excellent opportunities to observe a wide range of student behavior (Zirpoli & Melloy, 1993). Examples of informal or unstructured activities you could use for assessment are the transition times between instructional lessons, passing times between class periods, and many recess and cafeteria activities. These types of situations allow you to assess the interactions the students themselves select, and to observe the impromptu interactions they have with classmates and teachers. Situations where these activities occur offer many of the best occasions to observe performance in such areas as initiating and sustaining conversations, selecting free-time activities, playing games, cooperating with classmates on assigned tasks, and handling disagreements with schoolmates.

In her plans to assess Granville's and Alfred's behavior, Mrs. Armstrong would most likely include playground situations and other activities where the boys themselves select interactions rather than activities in which the interactions are limited or defined by teachers and supervisors. These activities would provide many of the best opportunities to observe the students' typical interaction patterns with playmates.

Make a Separate Page of the Worksheet for Each Situation

Once you have chosen the situations for the assessment, you should prepare a separate page of the assessment worksheet for each one. This step will make conducting the assessment much easier because it will allow you to organize your procedures according to the students' normal routine and the scheduled activities. This organizational format will also bring your worksheet in line with the social skills curriculum you have already prepared, with each page of the worksheet corresponding to a page of the curriculum.

Figure 4.2 shows two pages of the assessment worksheet Mrs. Armstrong completed for Granville. She entered the situations for each page in the Assessment Situation space. Her complete worksheet would include similar pages for all the situations in which she will access. Note that these pages also provide spaces for completing successive steps in the assessment process.

Step 3: Choose Expectations to Assess

After you have selected the situations, your next step is to choose the specific expectations you plan to assess. For each situation you have chosen, look over the list of expectations on the corresponding page of the social skills curriculum from Chapter Two. As you go through the lists, mark the expectations you have some questions about for the particular student, items for which you want to look at the student's performance more closely. These expectations will be the focus of the survey level assessment. When you pick out the expectations to examine, consider the following recommendations.

Figure 4.2 A portion of Mrs. Armstrong's assessment worksheet for Granville.

Worksheet 4.1, Part 2: Assessment Worksheet

Name: *Mrs. Armstrong* Student : *Granville*

Assessment Situation: *Teacher Presentation* Page *3* of *13*

Expectation	**Units of Measure**	**Criterion Level**	**Procedure**	**Assessment Results** Observations 1st	2nd	3rd	4th	5th	Total
Responds to correction by paying better attention	*# of times not paying attention after correction*	*No more than 1 per week*	*observation/log*						
Volunteers answers for teacher questions	*% of time volunteering for teacher's questions*	*At least 85%*	*video*						
Takes notes on teacher presentation	*# of notes on page*	*At least 1/3 page*	*check notebook*						
Checks progress against neighbor's notes	*# of times glancing at neighbor's notes*	*At least 2 per class*	*video*						
Communicates with neighbor (on topic) by glances and occasional whispers	*# of glances, whispers, nonverbal signs*	*At least 4 per class*	*video*						
Encourages others (quietly) who are called on	*# of times encouraging others*	*At least 3 per class*	*video*						
Asks questions when help is needed	*# of times asking questions when help needed (i.e., work incomplete or incorrect)*	*At least 75%*	*check work; log/ observation*						
Interacts quietly with neighbors before beginning independent work	*# of times interacting before beginning work*	*At least 3 days per week*	*video/observation*						
*Accepts feedback from classmates*** *(** = added for Granville's assessment)*	*# of times arguing about responses*	*No more than 1 per class*	*observation*						

Comments/Notes:

Figure 4.2 *(continued)*

Worksheet 4.1, Part 2: Assessment Worksheet

Name: *Mrs. Armstrong* Student : *Granville*

Assessment Situation: *Playing tag and other nonorganized games* Page *9* of *13*

Expectation	**Units of Measure**	**Criterion Level**	**Procedure**	**Assessment Results** Observations 1st	2nd	3rd	4th	5th	Total
Negotiates conflicts with leader	*# of times arguing with leader*	*No more than 1 per day*	*observation*						
Accepts judgment of group/leader	*# of times leaving in anger*	*No more than 1 per week*	*observation*						
Talks on "cool" subjects (sports, hot TV shows, etc.)	*# of times talking on "uncool" subjects/* *# of comments on "cool" subjects*	*No more than 1 per week* *At least 1 per day*	*observation/ interviews*						
Moves freely between activities or games	*# of minutes remaining alone before joining another activity*	*No more than 3 minutes*	*observation*						
Helps set rules before game begins	*# of times joining in "rules" conversation*	*At least 3 times per week*	*observation/ interviews*						
Offers new rules during game	*# of new rules offered*	*At least 1 per day*	*observation/ interviews*						
Helps resolve conflicts within group	*# of conflicts not resolved within group*	*No more than 2 per week*	*behavior log*						
Avoids fighting	*# of times fighting*	*No more than 1 per week*	*behavior log*						
Discusses action of game with others as period ends	*# of days conversing with others at end of period*	*At least 3 per week*	*observation*						
*Returns greetings in friendly voice (without sarcasm)***	*Ratio of friendly responses to greetings given*	*At least 75%*	*observation/ interviews*						
*Chooses compatible friends to play with***	*# of times playing with incompatible person or group*	*No more than 2 per week*	*observation*						
*(** = added for Granville's assessment)*									

Comments/Notes:

Tailor the Assessment to the Issues You Are Concerned About

Your purpose in completing this step is to select curriculum items that will give you insight into the less obvious areas of a student's performance, or that will allow you to look more closely at the interactions that present particular problems. Thus, you would select expectations that you believe pose the most problems for a student, or that you want to examine in greater detail. It would be pointless to assess the things a student does well. If you know that a student meets an expectation—for example, that he or she asks for help when it is needed—then you have no need to assess that skill. This way of personalizing the assessment will allow you to concentrate on the areas of behavior you are most concerned with.

When assessing Sandy in classroom situations, Mrs. Armstrong may want to look at all the curriculum items that relate to conversing with adults and classmates because she is unsure whether Sandy can meet these expectations. She would also include expectations she knows Sandy has trouble with, such as participating in class discussions or asking for help when needed, because she wants to find out how much difficulty Sandy has in these areas. On the other hand, she would not pick the expectations that she knows Sandy meets, such as following directions or ignoring peer distractions, or expectations that are not particularly significant for Sandy, such as handling peer teasing or sharing materials.

Similarly, when looking at playground activities, Mrs. Armstrong may structure Alfred's assessment to examine both his game-playing skills and his conversational skills with playmates and adults. In contrast, she may decide not to choose many of these expectations with Granville, because she already knows that he can interact very well with adults and that his game-playing skills are excellent. Instead, she may focus specifically on his ability to interact with classmates. Thus, in her plans for assessment Mrs. Armstrong will probably choose to assess very different expectations for Granville, Alfred, and Sandy.

List Expectations on the Assessment Worksheet under the Situations in Which They Apply

Once you have chosen the expectations from the social skills curriculum, you can enter them on the assessment worksheet you are preparing. Figure 4.2 gives an example of this step by showing some of the expectations Mrs. Armstrong entered on her assessment worksheet for Granville. These are items she wants to investigate with him, either because she knows they represent problems for him or because she is not sure whether he meets the demands. Note that Mrs. Armstrong picked out most of these items directly from her social skills curriculum (see Figures 2.3 and 3.1), transferring them to the assessment worksheet.

You may wonder what to do about expectations that apply to more than one situation. It is usually best to assess them in each of the situations so you can compare the students' behavior across the various circumstances in which the expectations apply. This comparison will show whether students can adapt or carry over their skills to a different set of circumstances. For example, in Mrs. Armstrong's classroom, students are expected to volunteer answers during homework review activities, during small group discussions, and during large group presentations. When Mrs. Armstrong plans Sandy's assessment, she should assess her performance under all these conditions, especially since she already knows (or suspects) that Sandy is having problems in these situations. Doing so will help her determine the extent of Sandy's difficulties.

Add Extra Expectations to Personalize the Assessment Further

After you have entered all the pertinent expectations from your social skills curriculum, you should add to each situation any other expectations you may want to look at for the student in question. This step is important because in the original list of expectations you made for the social skills curriculum, you could not possibly list *all* the expectations that apply to each situation. The idea was to obtain an overview of the basic demands that apply to students. Now that you have a particular student in mind, you are likely to think of other expectations for each situation that could yield additional information. These may include items you recognize as significant problems for the student, or simply items you did not think of before but would now like to include on your assessment list.

Add these to the assessment worksheet along with the expectations from the curriculum, but be sure you follow the original guidelines for defining expectations and standards that we discussed in Chapter Two: they must be behaviorally defined, apply to everyone in the setting, represent average levels of performance, and so on. Figure 4.2 includes examples of expectations that were not originally on the social skills curriculum, which Mrs. Armstrong added to Granville's assessment worksheet. For purposes of clarity, these items have been marked with asterisks. Note that although Mrs. Armstrong added these expectations because of questions she had about Granville's performance in particular, she has nevertheless defined them in terms that reflect the average behavior of typical students in the setting. After you have included these items, you will have created a list of expectations for assessment that will be very precisely geared to the performance and problems of the selected student.

Step 4: Describe the Standards for Measuring Performance

The next step in planning the survey level assessment is to identify for each expectation the standard you will use to measure and evaluate the behavior you observe. In Chapter Three, we described the standards for expectations in terms of measurement units and criterion levels. As we explained, units of measure represent the normal way we record, count, or otherwise keep track of a particular behavior; criterion levels provide benchmarks or dividing lines for deciding whether the student's behavior does or does not meet the standards for competent performance. Identifying these elements and listing them on the assessment worksheet will give you ready access to this information so you can determine what to keep track of during the assessment; you can then compare your results to the criterion levels to determine whether the students meet the expectations (Borich, 1988; Kerr & Nelson, 1989). Because it builds on the work you have already done on the social skills curriculum, the task of identifying standards is less daunting than it might appear. When you add standards to your worksheet, you should observe the following guidelines.

Follow the Units of Measure and Criterion Levels Set Out in the Social Skills Curriculum

For the most part, you can identify the units of measure and criterion levels for expectations to be assessed by simply transferring these items to the assessment worksheet directly from the social skills curriculum worksheet. For example, on her social skills curriculum, Mrs. Armstrong described the standards for answering questions during class discussions in terms of a frequency measure—number of times students answer questions. Therefore, in assessing Granville's behavior during discussions, her unit of measure will be the number of times he answers questions. If, instead, the measurement unit had been described in terms of duration—how long the students are to discuss a particular topic—on her assessment worksheet she would describe the units of measure as the number of minutes Granville engages in the discussions.

Similarly, Mrs. Armstrong's curriculum identified the criterion level for answering questions during discussion as at least three times per week. This would be the criterion level for Granville's assessment, and she would include "at least three times per week" in the appropriate column on the assessment worksheet. The second and third columns on Figure 4.2 show examples of units of measure and criterion levels as Mrs. Armstrong entered them on her assessment worksheet.

Make Sure the Standards Are Accurate for Each Separate Situation

As you make these entries, you should attend closely to the settings and situations that apply to each expectation, because for the same expectation you may need to use different measurement procedures to quantify student behavior. For example, when Mrs. Armstrong assesses the expectation "participates in conversations" during small group activities, she might count how many comments students make to the group, as this measure represents the most natural way to judge their participation and can be observed while she supervises the group work. On the other hand, during recess she might measure this expectation by the number of minutes students spend conversing, because the variety of choices students have in their activities and the difficulty of eavesdropping on conversations would make it harder to count the number of comments each student makes. These distinctions would already be apparent in her original social skills curriculum list; she now needs to be careful to note the variations.

Also during this step you should check the numbers you have identified as criterion levels to be sure they supply realistic approximations of the dividing line for competence. You should pay particular attention to expectations that appear in more than one situation; as we noted in Chapter Three, these items may have significantly different criterion levels under changing circumstances. Again, these distinctions should be clear on the original social skills curriculum worksheet, but this step offers you an opportunity to double-check and verify the accuracy of your earlier estimates.

Identify Units of Measure and Criterion Levels for Any New Expectations on the List

A more difficult challenge is to define the standards for the extra expectations you may have added in the previous step, expectations you had not listed earlier in the social skills curriculum. You will now need to add to your worksheet units of measure and criterion levels for these expectations. To complete this task, you may wish to refer to the guidelines for defining measurement units and criterion levels presented in Chapter Three. Remember that even though you thought of these expectations for a particular target student, they nonetheless should represent demands that typical students meet. Therefore, the units of measure should be defined according to the most natural way to measure or count the skill or action, and the criterion levels should reflect minimum competence for the typical or average student rather than what you wish the particular student would do.

Once you have completed this step, you will have finished describing the elements you will be looking for in the assessment. All that remains is to decide how you will look for them.

Step 5: Choose Assessment Procedures

After you have chosen the expectations you will assess with a particular student and have described how they will be measured and judged, you should identify the procedures you will use to conduct the assessment. These procedures can include conducting direct observations, videotaping, examining work samples, and holding interviews with students. Planning these procedures carefully in advance will help prepare you to measure the students' behavior effectively and to record the assessment results accurately.

There are two basic considerations in choosing the procedures for a survey level assessment. The procedures should

1. Allow the students to demonstrate clearly whether they have the skills to meet the expectations you are assessing
2. Permit you to measure the students' behavior easily and accurately, using the units of measure you have defined for each expectation (Hoy & Gregg, 1994)

You should consider the following points when you choose assessment procedures to ensure that they produce a reliable estimate of the students' social skills.

Use Unobtrusive Procedures

The procedures for assessing behavior should be unobtrusive, with little or no interaction between you (and assessment procedures you use) and the students' behavior (Bellack, 1979; Cartwright & Cartwright, 1984). This approach is to ensure the most natural conditions possible. If the students know they are being assessed, or if the assessment procedures affect the way they normally act, the results are likely to be biased and inaccurate. By using assessment procedures that are unobtrusive, such as those that are already a normal part of your teaching or supervisory behavior, the results will more likely show what students actually do under typical performance conditions (Salvia & Hughes, 1990).

In practice, being unobtrusive means using techniques the students will not notice or that will not disrupt or interfere with their actions. For example, Mrs. Armstrong would like to assess Granville's and Alfred's interactions during playground activities and during passing time between classes. If at all possible, she should observe and record their behavior without the students even realizing they are being assessed. To do this, she may have to act preoccupied with some other task, such as grading papers, or look as if she is watching someone else, even though she is being very attentive to Granville's and Alfred's interactions. Her unobtrusive actions will increase the likelihood that the students will act naturally during her observations, even to the point of engaging in misbehavior they would avoid if they realized Mrs. Armstrong was watching them.

Use Other Observers When Necessary

Direct observation of the students' behavior is often the best procedure to use for assessment, but on some occasions you may find that your teaching and supervisory responsibilities take precedence over conducting the assessments and you cannot devote your full attention to the activities. In these instances, it may be helpful to have other school personnel assess the items for you, especially when they will be in the best position to observe the interactions (Hoy & Gregg, 1994).

Other teachers, playground supervisors, instructional assistants, volunteers, and other personnel can help you conduct assessments of your students, but they must be adequately prepared to ensure that the information they collect is accurate and reliable (Nelson, 1977). You must clearly explain the purpose of the assessment and the procedures they are to use so they will (a) recognize the behavior they are to observe, (b) distinguish between appropriate and inappropriate performance of the skills, and (c) understand how they are to record their observations. Before the assessment, observers must become familiar with the setting if it is one they have not been in before, and they must be able to locate and identify the specific students they are observing. It is usually best to have the observers practice the procedures with you so you can compare their observations to those you would make. These practice sessions will give you a chance to fine-tune the assessment procedures and check the reliability of the helpers' observations (Wolery, Bailey, & Sugai, 1988).

Mrs. Armstrong plans to have Mr. Wagner observe some of Alfred's interactions between class periods so she can get a different perspective on his "clowning around" behavior. She will need to indicate clearly what expectations she would like Mr. Wagner to assess, so he can look for specific types of behavior (rather than just generally noting Alfred's clowning). Before conducting the assessment, she will also make one or two preliminary observations with Mr. Wagner to ensure that they have a similar understanding of the expectations they are looking at, and that Mr. Wagner understands how he is to conduct the assessment.

As an aid to outside observers, you should also prepare a separate observation form for them that gives a detailed explanation of the observation procedures. It is especially important that your colleagues clearly understand the types of responses they will be observing and the recording procedures they will use (Hoy & Gregg, 1994). If Mrs. Armstrong has Mr. Wagner record the ratio of times Alfred responds appropriately to peer greetings, Mr. Wagner must understand what constitutes a proper response to the interaction. He must also realize that he is to tally both the opportunities Alfred has to perform the behavior and

Alfred's responses to these opportunities. You can clarify these kinds of details for conducting an assessment by preparing an observation form for the observers.

When you prepare an observation form, you should include the following information:

1. Name of the student being assessed
2. Name of the person doing the observation
3. Days and times during which the assessment will take place
4. Description of the assessment situation
5. Instructions to the observer
6. Description of expectations to be assessed
7. Explanation of the measurement procedures
8. Space to record observations and tally results

Figure 4.3 illustrates the recording form Mrs. Armstrong devised for Mr. Wagner to use when he observes Alfred between class periods. She will review the form with Mr. Wagner before the assessment to clarify each of the items.

Videotape When Possible

Video can provide a valuable tool for assessing the full range of students' social behavior (Dowrick, 1986; Knapczyk, 1989; 1992). Videotaping is useful when direct observation is not feasible, as it alleviates scheduling conflicts and overcomes the need to recruit other observers. It is particularly helpful for observing your own situations when your normal duties make it difficult to pay close attention to students during a class period or a lesson. Mrs. Armstrong may wish to observe Granville and Alfred during small group instructional lessons to assess their social interactions with classmates. Because she would be overseeing the behavior of the entire class, however, it would be difficult for her to obtain an accurate record of some of the expectations she would like to assess. She would find it particularly difficult to keep track of such measures as when the two students' attention fades from activities, how often they converse with classmates, or how many questions they ask and answer. If she videotapes the activities, she could easily and precisely measure these and other skills at a later time.

Videotaping is more than a substitute for observation; adding it to your assessment procedures offers many advantages over direct observation alone. You will often find it much easier to measure students' behavior by reviewing videotaped segments than by conducting on-site direct observations, and the results you obtain are likely to be more precise and reliable. Furthermore, videotaping can yield information that would otherwise be overlooked or difficult to collect. It allows for a complete and detailed observation because the tape can be reviewed as often as necessary (Eby & Kujawa, 1994). It also eliminates the need for the observer to hover over the students and closely supervise the activities in which they engage.

Figure 4.3 Mrs. Armstrong's observation checklist for Mr. Wagner.

Worksheet 4.1 supplement: OBSERVATION FORM

Observer: *Mr. Wagner* Date: *Oct. 3-7*

Student: *Alfred Newman* Grade: *5*

Assessment Situation: *Playing organized games*

Instructions to observer:

This assessment for Alfred is directed primarily at his performance of social skills during game-playing time. Please record his performance of the expectations listed below.

Expectations	Method of Measurement	Results: Observations 1st	2nd	3rd	4th	5th	Total
Initiates interactions with classmates	*Tally number of times Alfred starts an interaction*						
Responds positively to peer greetings (e.g., returns or complies with greetings)	*Tally number of greetings and number of responses*						
Participates actively in play activities (e.g., plays along with classmates and cooperates in activities)	*Record number of minutes Alfred engages in play*						
Follows rules of games being played	*Tally number of times Alfred fails to follow rules*						
Follows directions of group leader	*Tally number of times Alfred fails to follow leader's directions*						
Yells comments, encouragement, instructions during action of game ("Come on! Yeah!" etc.)	*Tally number of on-subject comments Alfred yells*						

Comments/ Observations:

Adding video to your assessment procedures offers significant advantages over direct observation alone.

Videotapes are particularly useful when two or more persons, such as you and another teacher or the student's parents, have questions about a student's skill level and would like to see the behavior together. You could both watch the videotape segment, independently assess the social interactions, compare the assessment results, and discuss plans for possible intervention strategies (Eby & Kujawa, 1994; Knapczyk, 1989).

Although videotaping can initially have reactive effects on student behavior, these effects quickly dissipate as students become accustomed to the videotape equipment. For this reason, it is helpful to set up the camera in advance of the targeted activity and let it run a couple of days before you actually begin collecting the assessment results. By the time the assessment activity begins, the students will be used to being videotaped and will act quite naturally.

Tailor the Procedures to Students' Learning and Performance Characteristics

You should consider the characteristics of the students you are assessing when you devise assessment procedures. Procedures that yield accurate, detailed results with one student can be distracting or misplaced with another. Although Mrs. Armstrong plans to look at several of the same expectations during recess for both Alfred and Granville, she realizes that she may need to use different approaches to assess each student. For Alfred, she may directly observe his behavior on the playground and talk with him about his interactions, because he is usually open and straightforward with her. But Granville is more self-conscious and defensive about his behavior, and he will likely alter his behavior significantly if he knows she is watching him, or he may not give an accurate or reliable verbal account of his interactions. Mrs. Armstrong may need a more indirect approach to assess Granville's behavior, such as watching from a location overlooking the playground area or speaking with the playground supervisors and his teammates about his behavior. In the same way, you should consider the individual characteristics of the students you are assessing as an important factor in deciding what procedures will work best.

Add Assessment Procedures to the Worksheet

After you have decided what procedures you will use in the assessment, you should enter a brief notation of each procedure on the assessment worksheet next to the expectations it will be used to assess. When Mrs. Armstrong videotapes Granville's interactions in the small group, the notations about videotaping that she adds next to each expectation on the worksheet will help her remember when to turn on the camera. They will also remind her to order and set up the equipment ahead of time so it is available when she needs it, and to allow enough time for Granville to become acclimated to being videotaped before she actually conducts the assessment.

The fourth column in Figure 4.2 shows the descriptions of assessment procedures Mrs. Armstrong added to her assessment worksheet. The entries here are written out rather fully for the sake of clarity; on your own worksheet you will probably shorten the descriptions by using codes and abbreviations for the entries.

Match the Procedure to the Expectations Being Assessed

Entering procedures separately for each expectation on the worksheet helps you ensure that your methods are well matched to the issues you wish to examine. Remember that the procedures you choose for each expectation must be appropriate for the measurement units you are counting. If Mrs. Armstrong is counting the number of inappropriate reactions Granville makes to teasing, she must be sure that her observation procedure allows her to keep track of this number. Similarly, if she is planning to count the ratio of answers Sandy gives to questions asked, she must choose a procedure that allows her time to count these items. The procedures she chooses will usually be used for more than one expectation: when she lists "observation" for several expectations during teacher presentation, for instance, that one observation will be directed at all the expectations together. But by entering a description of the procedures separately for each of the expectations on the list, she can ensure for each individual expectation that the approach she has chosen will be sufficient to provide the information she is seeking.

Step 6: Prepare to Record Assessment Results

The last step in devising an assessment worksheet is to provide spaces for recording the results. By adding a space for summarizing the students' behavioral measures, you can tabulate on the worksheet all the information for the entire array of expectations you plan to assess. You can use the spaces on the worksheet for:

- tallying observations
- transcribing test and worksheet scores
- computing daily percentages and totals of observations
- adding comments about other students' behavior
- noting ideas for interventions (Cartwright & Cartwright, 1984)

With this approach, you can enter scores and summaries of work samples, quizzes, and projects on the worksheet and keep the original materials in a separate folder for later review.

Mrs. Armstrong is planning to prepare a note card for Mr. Wagner and herself to record Granville's behavior during recess times. Each day, she will summarize the notations on the card and add the summaries to her worksheet. She plans to keep the note cards in a separate file for later reference. She also wants to have space on the worksheet to list the skills that other students use to meet expectations that are difficult for Granville, and to outline some ideas for intervention techniques. Figure 4.2 shows Mrs. Armstrong's worksheet with a *Results* column and a *Comments* section added to each sheet for entering assessment results and making comments.

Step 7: Schedule the Assessment

Once you have identified the focus of assessment, selected the procedures you will use, and prepared to record the assessment results, all that remains is to decide when the assessment will be carried out. This is not a complicated task, but it does require some planning. To make the best use of your time and to keep the assessment focused and on track, schedule ahead of the time the days for the assessment and the situations and procedures on which you will concentrate. This scheduling step will also help you coordinate any materials or equipment, special activities, or outside observers that will be involved (Howell, Fox, & Morehead, 1993; Merrell, 1994).

When you schedule assessment activities, keep the following considerations in mind.

Provide Multiple Opportunities for Performance

The most important principle in planning an assessment is to allow sufficient opportunities for students to demonstrate whether they meet the expectations and for you to judge the adequacy of their behavior. The more opportunities the students have, the more confidence you will have in the information you obtain (Borich, 1988; Salvia & Ysseldyke, 1995). Howell and Morehead (1987) suggest that to gain an adequate sample of performance, you should give students at least five to ten opportunities to demonstrate whether they have the skills to meet each of the expectations you are concerned with. It is usually best to distribute these opportunities across several days to allow for normal variations in the performance conditions and in the students' behavior (Sugai & Tindal, 1993).

This principle is absolutely crucial for ensuring valid assessment results, for without a broad sample of behavior, the results can be dramatically skewed. For example, Alfred's game-playing behavior is likely to change from day to day. If Mrs. Armstrong were to assess his behavior on only one day, her results might be biased, depending on whether she saw him on a particularly good day or bad day; these results could lead her to make erroneous conclusions about his skill level. Mrs. Armstrong can be sure she gets an accurate picture of Alfred's normal performance by assessing his game-playing skills across several days. Because the procedures she will use are based on the naturally occurring expectations of her social skills curriculum, she can easily conduct this week-long series of observations without disrupting the normal activities on the playground.

When you assess across several days, you can also learn how students respond to a wide array of circumstances. Mrs. Armstrong realizes that recess activities and play groups also will change from day to day and that she will need to schedule her assessment of Alfred across enough days to observe all the activities or play situations she wishes to examine. If she wants to see how Alfred interacts while playing large group games like football, she has a better chance to see one or two football games if she observes the playground setting for an entire week or longer. Similarly, if she wants to observe how Granville responds to peer teasing during the unstructured times before class, she must be sure her assessment takes place over enough days that he encounters this type of interaction several times.

As a general rule, you should replicate assessment activities for any particular expectation over at least three to five occasions. This guideline is only a base number, however; you may have to schedule more repetitions if the initial results are inconclusive. Remember, the primary goal of assessment is to determine accurately whether students meet the expectations you are concerned with. You should base your judgment of how long or how often to make observations on whether you are giving students a full opportunity to show their abilities and whether you can gain a reliable estimate of their performance.

Schedule Assessments for Several Short Periods Rather Than One or Two Long Ones

In addition to providing greater reliability, scheduling several assessments allows you to observe for a number of shorter periods rather than for a few long ones. You can then be more attentive to the students' behavior and to any factors that contribute to their difficulties. With shorter observations, you can avoid the mental fatigue and the distractions that you might experience with an extended assessment, and you can watch more closely for events that may provoke problem behaviors in the students you are observing. In addition, activities planned for shorter time intervals will be easier to incorporate in your own or another teacher's schedule (Salvia & Ysseldyke, 1995).

When Mrs. Armstrong assesses Sandy's participation in classroom activities, it would be difficult for her—or even for an outside observer—to be thoroughly attentive to Sandy's behavior for an entire class period. By limiting each day's observations to ten minutes or so over an entire week, Mrs. Armstrong can pay much closer attention to Sandy's behavior, and note many subtle elements of her performance that she might overlook if she were to attempt a longer but less focused observation.

Develop a Separate Page for Your Assessment Schedule

In addition to the pages you have prepared for each situation, it is helpful to include in the worksheet an overall assessment schedule, so you know ahead of time which situations you will be observing on a particular day, who will be making the observations, when to collect work samples and products, and other considerations that will help the assessment go smoothly and efficiently. An assessment schedule gives you an advanced organizer for your preparations and ensures that the time available for assessment is used effectively, especially when there are many expectations to assess and several different situations in which to conduct observations.

Preparing a schedule need not be a particularly lengthy or involved process. Remember that the assessment worksheet already indicates the situations in which you will carry out the assessment, the expectations you will focus on, and the procedures you will use. All that remains is scheduling the days and times you will assess in each of the situations, and coordinating the procedures and personnel you will use. Mrs. Armstrong plans to prepare an assessment schedule for Granville because she needs to look at several areas of his behavior in both her social studies classroom and on the playground. The assessment worksheet that she prepared for Granville (see Figure 4.2) already provides a clear listing of the expectations she will assess and the procedures she will use during class start-up time, teacher presentation, homework review, and other situations. Now Mrs. Armstrong will schedule and coordinate the assessment activities so she can plan in advance to reserve the video equipment, check Granville's daily assignment record, prepare Mr. Wagner for his observations, and complete the other preparations. The schedule she developed is presented in Figure 4.4.

As Mrs. Armstrong's schedule shows, you should usually include the following information:

1. Name of the student you are assessing
2. Days and times during which the assessment will take place
3. Situations or activities to be assessed during these times
4. Procedures to be conducted within the situations
5. Personnel and supplies needed to conduct the assessment

Note that you can take items 3 and 4 directly from the assessment worksheet.

The schedule indicates that Mrs. Armstrong will spread the assessment over a two-week period to allow for several repetitions of the activities and to pace her observations in order to guard against fatigue and other adverse factors. Her general plan is to focus the first week's activities on the social studies classroom setting and the second week's activities on the playground setting. She may, however, need to continue the assessment into a third week if some of the results in either setting are inconclusive.

Figure 4.4 Mrs. Armstrong's assessment schedule for Granville.

Worksheet 4.1, Part 3: Assessment Schedule Name: *Mrs. Armstrong*

Student: *Granville* Grade: *5* Date: *Sept. 26*

Days/Times	Situations/Procedures	Personnel/Materials
Wk. 1, MTWTF	*Class start-up—direct observation*	*Ms. Hernandez*
Wk. 1, MTWTF	*Homework review, teacher presentation, large group discussion—videotape class and observe; log G.'s behavior, check G.'s notebook*	*Video equipment*
Wk. 1, MWF, and Wk. 2, MW	*Small group discussion/activity—videotape G.'s group, observe, interview. Collect samples of G.'s work.*	*Video equipment Ms. Hernandez*
Wk. 1, MTWTF	*Independent work—direct observation*	
Wk. 1, MTWTF	*Class dismissal—direct observation*	*Ms. Hernandez*
Wk. 2, MTWTF	*Lining up to go outside—direct observation*	
Wk. 2, MTWTF	*Playing organized games, playing nonorganized games—direct observation, behavior log*	*Mr. Wagner*
Wk. 2, MTWTF	*Conversing informally with peers—direct observation, interviews*	*Mr. Wagner*
Wk. 2, MTWTF	*Lining up to go inside—direct observation*	*Mr. Wagner*

Notes:

❍ Conducting a Survey Level Assessment

Once you have completed your preparations, conducting the assessment is fairly straightforward. Your assessment schedule will already tell you which activities to undertake on which days, and the assessment worksheet will guide your procedures and measures in each situation you assess. At this point, the only information we need to add is these final tips for conducting the assessment in an effective manner.

Stay Focused

It is important while conducting an assessment to remain focused on the particular expectations you are examining. This guideline may seem self-evident, but we state it here to stress how easy it will be for you to become distracted from the assessment activities, especially when you are observing many different behaviors or when you are involved in other teaching or supervisory duties. You should periodically review the information on the assessment worksheet to help focus your attention on the items selected for observation. You may also have to adjust your schedule or alter activities so you can give your full attention to making the observations.

When Mrs. Armstrong observes Sandy's interactions during small group times, she must watch for Sandy's contributions to the group, her initiation of peer interactions, her willingness to assume a leadership role, her response to praise or criticism, and any other expectations on the assessment worksheet for that situation. Mrs. Armstrong can avoid being distracted by extraneous factors or by expectations that she is less concerned about by periodically referring to the assessment worksheet and following her plans carefully. This approach will enable her to concentrate on gathering the needed information for the assessment.

Remain within Your Limits

Often you may find you are trying to assess a complex spectrum of expectations that is particularly difficult to observe all at once. You may discover you need to pay attention to several expectations or performance factors during the same activity in order to obtain a complete and accurate measure of the student's abilities and deficits. Mrs. Armstrong, for example, plans to look at Alfred's interactions in game-playing situations on the playground. She wants to obtain information about how he enters a game, how he follows the rules for the games, how he converses with playmates during games, how he responds to criticism, and how he reacts to bystanders. But with the number of skills she is assessing, the time limitations for the activity, and other factors, she sees that it will be impossible for her to make all these observations simultaneously without completely compromising the original intent of the assessment.

Like Mrs. Armstrong, you may find yourself trying to assess too many skills at one time, and realize that you will be unable to conduct an adequate assessment of any of them if you continue as you have planned. In such instances, you can ensure a successful assessment by carefully restructuring the procedures in one of two ways:

1. *Divide your attention.* One approach is to divide your attention among the expectations you wish to assess, looking closely at a few specific expectations during one set of observations and looking at other expectations during another set of observations. By varying the focus of the observations over a few repetitions, you could conduct a complete assessment in all pertinent areas. During some observations, Mrs. Armstrong could look exclusively for how Alfred enters a game situation and how he follows the rules for the games. On other occasions, she could focus primarily on how he converses with playmates, how he handles criticism and disagreements, and how he responds to bystanders. In this way, she will be able to devote her full attention to each of the areas of behavior she wants to assess.

2. *Use other observers.* A second approach is to recruit other observers and plan a division of labor among them. During a single activity, one person could observe how the student performs one set of expectations while another looks at a different set. For example, Mrs. Armstrong could have Mr. Wagner help her observe on the playground. He could watch how Alfred enters games and how he follows the rules for games while she observes his conversational skills, his ability to handle criticism and disagreements, and his response to bystanders. They could then put their findings together to gain a complete picture of Alfred's performance while playing games.

It is important, then, to consider your limitations—and those of other people—in carrying out the assessment procedures so you can plan the procedures to compensate for them.

Keep Outside Observers Unobtrusive

We discussed earlier the importance of conducting assessments in an unobtrusive manner to ensure that the target students do not alter their natural behavior. This issue is particularly important when the assessment involves observers who are not normally present in the setting. You will need to take special precautions when observing in settings that you normally do not frequent, such as another teacher's classroom, the gym, or the school cafeteria. You will also need to make provisions for observers who come into your classroom, and give them directions on how they should act so their presence does not change student behavior from the norm. Outside observers can lessen the effects they may have on student behavior by following these safeguards:

1. *Arrive on site before the activities start* to minimize the attention visitors usually attract when they enter a setting after activities have begun.
2. *Sit or stand in the back of the room* or away from the area where student interactions or activities are taking place.

3. *Remain out of the line of vision* of those being observed and avoid establishing direct eye contact with the students or teachers.

4. *Stay out of the traffic flow* of the activities.

5. *Avoid talking, gesturing, or making sudden movements* that distract the students or instructors, or call attention to the observer.

6. *Allow those in the setting to become acclimated* to the observer before beginning to assess behavior.

7. *Try to look busy* to lessen the students' attention to the observer and to reduce their speculation concerning why they are being watched. Many observers find it helpful to bring outside work or reading to do while they are in the setting because students quickly stop paying attention to visitors who appear preoccupied. After a first few minutes of looking busy, the observer can make the necessary recordings without attracting attention.

Mrs. Armstrong will have Ms. Hernandez help with Granville's assessment during some of her social studies lessons. She will ask Ms. Hernandez to sit at a table area in a back corner of her classroom while she is conducting observations. Ms. Hernandez will plan to arrive a few minutes before the class period begins and will try to look busy so she can avoid interacting with the students. Mrs. Armstrong hopes these preparations will encourage Granville and the other students to act as they normally do during the class, so she and Ms. Hernandez can gain a realistic assessment of Granville's typical performance pattern.

It is important, then, to maintain a focus on the expectations you wish to investigate, to stay within the limits of your ability to make observations, and to apprise outside observers of their roles and responsibilities. In following these guidelines, you will ensure that the assessment provides a valid and reliable survey of the student's behavior. In the next chapter, we explain how to record and summarize assessment results, and how to set priorities for intervention plans.

○ Summary

Overview of Survey Level Assessment

1. The purpose of a survey level assessment is to identify the social expectations students do and do not meet.

2. A survey level assessment is most useful when students have many problems in their social interactions.

Principles of a Survey Level Assessment

1. The assessment approach should be personalized and tailored to individual students.

2. The assessment should be conducted under natural performance conditions to give an accurate and reliable estimate of the students' abilities.

3. A survey level assessment usually includes many teacher-developed procedures.
4. A social skills curriculum can be an important resource for planning a survey level assessment.

Planning a Survey Level Assessment

1. Planning a survey level assessment involves the following steps:
   a. choosing a student
   b. choosing the situations for assessment
   c. choosing the expectations to assess
   d. describing the standards for performance
   e. choosing the procedures for assessment
   f. preparing to record assessment results
   g. scheduling the assessment
2. An assessment worksheet will aid in planning a thorough and reliable assessment, and provide a tool for keeping track of activities and the student's performance.
3. Choose students for assessment whose difficulties need particular attention.
4. A description of the student's behavior and overall performance characteristics should be included on the assessment worksheet.
5. Assessment situations should be chosen directly from the social skills curriculum and can include teaching lessons, classroom activities, and unstructured or informal activities.
6. Expectations should be chosen for assessment because they represent areas of behavior in which more information is needed about the student.
7. Expectations should be entered on the worksheet according to the situations to which they apply.
8. Additional expectations should be added to the worksheet if assessing them can provide valuable information about the student.
9. Standards should follow the units of measure and criterion levels set out in the social skills curriculum.
10. Standards should be described according to the situations to which the expectations apply.
11. The procedures used for assessment should
    a. allow the student to demonstrate clearly whether he or she has the skills to meet expectations
    b. allow the observer to measure the student's behavior easily and accurately
12. Assessment procedures should be unobtrusive; they should not substantially affect the student's natural pattern of behavior.

13. Other observers can assist in helping with the assessment if they are properly prepared for the activities.
14. Videotaping can be used for assessment and can provide information that otherwise could not be obtained.
15. Assessment procedures should be described on the worksheet in a way that matches the expectations being assessed.
16. The assessment worksheet should include spaces for recording and commenting on the student's behavior and summarizing the assessment results.
17. An assessment schedule will help keep the assessment plan well organized.
18. The schedule of activities should provide multiple opportunities for students to demonstrate their skills.
19. Scheduling assessments for short time periods will help to maintain a focus on the expectations that are assessed.
20. An assessment schedule will aid in coordinating activities with other people's schedules.

Conducting a Survey Level Assessment

1. An assessment should stay focused on the particular expectations that are of major concern.
2. It is important to stay within the limits of one's ability to conduct an assessment either by
   a. dividing attention across expectations or
   b. using other observers
3. Other observers assisting with the assessment should follow safeguards to ensure that they do not significantly affect the student's behavior.

Examples for Chapter Four

Example 4a

Ms. Lake is a special education teacher of kindergarten and primary students. Warren spends most of his school day in the general education program. Ms. Lake decided to focus on his behavior during free play time, center time, and other activities in which he interacts with other children. She used this worksheet to describe Warren's social behavior.

For students like Warren, assessment may focus on very basic social expectations. Ms. Lake selected simple items such as "greets classmates by name" and "acknowledges classmates who are nearby." A list of the expectations Warren had difficulty meeting appears at the end of the next chapter.

Learning and behavior problems resulting from disabilities should be described behaviorally.

Descriptions of problems should indicate how they affect or limit students' social interactions.

It is helpful to indicate areas in which students are making progress in their behavior.

The description of student behavior, areas of concern, and expectations to assess (on subsequent worksheet pages) should all be closely linked.

Worksheet 4.1, Part 1: Description of Student Behavior

Name: *Ms. Lake* Date: *Sept. 24*

Student to be assessed: *Warren* Grade: *Kindergarten*

Assessment setting(s): *Playground, free time in classroom*

Description of student behavior *(focus on social skills)*:

Warren is a 5 1/2 year-old developmentally delayed boy who has experienced seizures throughout much of his life. In school he listens and responds to adults, but has few interactions with his peers. He rarely talks with other children or pays attention to what they are doing, even though they may be playing nearby. His language skills are below the level of other 5-year-olds, but are sufficient to communicate with teachers and peers. Because he has problems with balance and coordination, he sometimes bumps or trips over other children, but he doesn't apologize for his actions nor does he accept their help.

Warren is cooperative with his teachers, but ignores directions or suggestions when he doesn't want to follow them. He resists moving from one activity to another, especially if the activity involves playing or working with other children. Sometimes he walks away from an activity rather than join the group. When other children approach him during play time, he usually ignores them but sometimes gets upset and screams or yells. Although his language and social behavior have improved since school began, he lags behind most of his peers.

Areas or concerns to investigate:

Verbal interactions with peers

Playground skills, especially games and activities 5-year-olds typically play

Cooperative play and sharing toys with peers

Following directions of adults

Example 4b

Ms. Santamaria is an eleventh-grade science teacher. For her assessment she selected Alicia, a student who performs well academically but who needs to improve in social behavior. This page shows Ms. Santamaria's description of Alicia's behavior.

Ms. Santamaria focused her assessment on expectations like "stays on topic of discussion," "waits turn to speak," and "acknowledges ideas and suggestions of classmates." A list of the expectations Alicia failed to meet can be found at the end of Chapter Five.

Indicating the context or circumstances in which problems occur can be useful when scheduling assessment activities.

Descriptions of students should also indicate strengths and positive characteristics.

Specific examples often clarify problem behavior.

It is helpful to indicate others' reactions to the students' behavior.

Worksheet 4.1, Part 1: Description of Student Behavior

Name: *Ms. Santamaria* Date: *Sept. 22*

Student to be assessed: *Alicia* Grade: *11*

Assessment setting(s): *Science class/lab*

Description of student behavior *(focus on social skills)*:

Alicia is a high school junior who likes to show off and boss other students. During labs I have many class discussions and Alicia's behavior can be very disruptive. She talks out of turn, makes sarcastic remarks, and acts as if her opinion is the only one that is right. She even criticizes my comments and the examples in the text if she doesn't agree with them. Sometimes her arguments have a lot of merit, so students usually listen closely to what she says.

I also have students do their lab work in pairs and small groups. Alicia does very well in her assignments. She prefers to work alone and is always the first one finished, but then she wanders around the room to see how other students are doing on their activities. Although she tries to be helpful, she comes across as being overly critical and demanding. Once in a while to tease students, she gives them wrong directions, and walks away with a smile. Students constantly complain that she is bothering them, or that they got something wrong because "Alicia said it was okay." She doesn't seem to have any close friends, but she usually gets along with everyone.

Areas or concerns to investigate:

Participating in class discussions—acknowledging others' opinions

Working with partners on labs and projects

Being diplomatic in giving criticism and feedback

Appropriate teasing

Mr. Wagner's Case Study

Mr. Wagner's Description of Granville

Mr. Wagner decided to work with Granville so he could coordinate his efforts with Mrs. Armstrong's. This page, where he describes Granville's behavior, shows some typical problems.

Another step that Mr. Wagner might find difficult is selecting the expectations to assess. A common mistake is failing to focus the assessment on specific areas of concern. For instance, Mr. Wagner might draw his expectations for Granville's assessment directly from the worksheets for his earlier social skills curriculum, and neglect to add any item specifically relevant to Granville. The worksheets for the survey level assessment should reflect the major issues outlined in the description of student behavior.

When describing behavior, avoid vague evaluative terms like "poor attitude" or "unsportsmanlike."

Assessments should be objective. Describing what students actually do (or do not do) is better than speculating on why they do it.

Commenting on a student's family background or other attributes beyond the teachers' control is usually not helpful in planning assessments.

Avoid considering possible intervention procedures before assessments are carried out.

Focus on areas for which it will be helpful to obtain additional information about the student's behavior. It is too soon to set goals for interventions.

Worksheet 4.1, Part 1: Description of student behavior

Name: *Mr. Wagner* Date: *Sept. 30*

Student to be assessed: *Granville* Grade: *5*

Assessment setting(s): *Science class, playground*

Description of student behavior *(focus on social skills)*:

Granville is a physically mature, well-coordinated fifth-grade boy. He is aggressive and uncooperative with his peers both in class and in unstructured settings. He usually has a poor attitude about schoolwork and his behavior during playground games is unsportsmanlike.

Granville's problems are probably related to low self-esteem. He tries to impress other people mostly by imposing his will on them—making himself the center of attention by being bossy, threatening, and intimidating. His brother Orville acted the same way when I had him in fifth grade three years ago, so I think Granville's home life has a lot to do with the way he behaves.

I can usually keep Granville in line when I have him work by himself, but he causes trouble when I have him in a group activity or when he has time to move around the classroom. Mrs. Armstrong reported the same kind of problems in her classroom. Maybe I can try a point reward system with him to get him to follow directions and to work better with other students.

Areas or concerns to investigate:

Stop arguing with the other students

Complete small group activities

Follow teacher directions

CHAPTER 5

Summarizing Survey Level Assessment Results and Selecting Target Skills for Interventions

After you finish the plans for a survey level assessment, carrying out the assessment procedures should be a relatively straightforward process. Your main concern at this point will be keeping track of the results and obtaining the most accurate accounting possible of the students' behavior. After you have completed the assessment, you will be able to summarize and interpret the results in terms of your major concerns about the students.

In this chapter, we explain how to tally and record the assessment results, and how to interpret them according to the standards specified in a social skills curriculum. We also discuss using the results to set priorities among the expectations students do not meet, and defining the target skills for interventions.

Tallying the Results of a Survey Level Assessment

As you make your final preparations for assessment, you should think about how you will record the performance you observe. A precise, reliable system of tallying will make the difference between clear findings and ambiguous ones. In this section, we present some guidelines for tallying and organizing the assessment results. These guidelines will help you to compare the performance you observe to the standards for the expectations and to tell at a glance which expectations the students do not meet.

Record Results Using Prescribed Units of Measure

The units of measure you specified on the assessment worksheet will indicate how you should keep track of the students' performance on each expectation you assess. Thus, entries in the Units of Measure column of the worksheet give you a convenient guide for deciding what to tally as you carry out the assessment activities, and you can record these counts in the Assessment Results column.

Typically, measures of the students' behavior are written on the worksheet as tally marks, averages, grade scores, totals, or other entries that coincide with the units of measure for the expectations. Thus, you should express the results of each day's assessment activities as number counts (had 3 verbal disagreements, raised hand 2 out of 6 times), rates (contributed to discussions 4 times in 30 minutes, played cooperatively 10 out of 25 minutes), or percentages (remained on task 55% of independent work time, returned 10% of greetings). By making sure your recordings correspond to the measurement units, you simplify the process of comparing the assessment results to the standards you described earlier.

Figure 5.1 presents some of the assessment results that Mrs. Armstrong obtained for Granville during teacher presentation and nonorganized games. The figure also illustrates how she matched her recording procedures to the units of measure for the expectations she assessed. For example, with "checks progress against neighbor's notes" (item 4—teacher presentation), the units of measure Mrs. Armstrong stated on her assessment worksheet were "number of times glancing at neighbor's notes." On each day she checked the videotape of Granville, she made a tally mark in the Results column every time he glanced over at his neighbor's work. Likewise, with "moves freely between activities or games" (item 4—nonorganized games), the units of measure specified were "number of minutes remaining alone before joining another activity." During assessment, Mrs. Armstrong tallied the average number of minutes she observed Granville alone between activities each day.

When units of measure are expressed as a ratio or percentage, remember to tally both the opportunities and the occurrences of the expected behavior. For the expectation "returns greetings in a friendly voice (without sarcasm)" (item 10—nonorganized games), Mrs. Armstrong has entered the units of measure "ratio of friendly responses to greetings given." When assessing Granville's performance, she counted both the number of greetings he received and the number of friendly responses he gave, and summarized her tallies as a percentage.

Keep a Daily Record of Results

You should enter separate tallies of the students' behavior on the worksheet each day, even for behaviors you are tracking over an entire week. Keeping daily records in this manner will give you an accurate inventory of each day's entries and allow you to notice any interesting trends in the students' assessment results. For example, if Granville gets into four fights during a week of assessment, it would be important for Mrs. Armstrong to note whether all four took place on the same day or whether they were spread throughout the week. When she interprets the results, she will be able to take a particularly good or bad day into account when she looks at Granville's performance trends over the entire assessment period.

In your daily entries, you should also make notations of variations from natural conditions. For example, you may wish to circle entries for the days on which the student has a cold, a substitute teacher oversees recess activities, a fire drill interrupts a lesson, a new student arrives in the class, or any other extraordinary

Figure 5.1 A portion from Granville's worksheet showing assessment results.

Worksheet 4.1, Part 2: Assessment Worksheet

Name: *Mrs. Armstrong* Student : *Granville*

Assessment Situation: *Teacher Presentation* Page *3* of *13*

Expectation	Units of Measure	Criterion Level	Procedure		Observations 1st	2nd	3rd	4th	5th	Total
Responds to correction by paying better attention	*# of times not paying attention after correction*	*No more than 1 per week*	*observation/log*					/		*1/wk*
Volunteers answers for teacher questions	*% of time volunteering for teacher's questions*	*At least 85%*	*video*	*Q:* *V:*	10 4	15 (14)	7 4	11 7	12 7	*60%****
Takes notes on teacher presentation	*# of notes on page*	*At least 1/3 page*	*check notebook*		1/4	n/a	1/2	1/2	1/4	*avg. 3/8*
Checks progress against neighbor's notes	*# of times glancing at neighbor's notes*	*At least 2 per class*	*video*		/	n/a	/	//		*avg 1****
Communicates with neighbor (on topic) by glances and occasional whispers	*# of glances, whispers, nonverbal signs*	*At least 4 per class*	*video*		///	(~~////~~)	/	//	//	*avg 2****
Encourages others (quietly) who are called on	*# of times encouraging others*	*At least 3 per class*	*video*		~~////~~	n/a	////	/	~~////~~	*avg 4*
Asks questions when help is needed	*# of questions per time help needed (i.e., work incomplete or incorrect)*	*At least 2*	*check work; log/ observation*		/	n/a		/		*avg 1/2****
Interacts quietly with neighbors before beginning independent work	*# of times interacting before beginning work*	*At least 3 days per week*	*video/observation*		/	/	/		/	*4 days*
	# of times arguing about responses	*No more than 1 per class*	*observation*		//		//	///	/	*avg 2****
*(** = added for Granville's assessment)*										*(*** = expectation not met)*

Comments/Notes: *Day 2 a police officer gave a presentation in class. Granville seemed to like having visitors. Granville reacts fine to the teacher during class, but doesn't draw on other students to help him along, and he doesn't like to ask for help; so if he gets lost or behind, he never really catches up .*

Figure 5.1 *(continued)*

Worksheet 4.1, Part 2: Assessment Worksheet	Name: *Mrs. Armstrong*	Student: *Granville*
	Assessment Situation: *Playing tag and other nonorganized games*	Page *9* of *13*

Expectation	Units of Measure	Criterion Level	Procedure	Assessment Results: Observations 1st	2nd	3rd	4th	5th	Total
Negotiates conflicts with leader	*# of times arguing with leader*	*No more than 1 per day*	*observation*	////	/	/	~~////~~		*avg 2 1/2****
Accepts judgment of group/leader	*# of times leaving in anger*	*No more than 1 per week*	*observation*						*none*
Talks on "cool" subjects (sports, hot TV shows, etc.)	*# of times talking on "uncool" subjects/ # of comments on "cool" subjects*	*No more than 1 per week/at least 1 per day*	*observation/ interviews*		/			//	*none/ avg <1****
Moves freely between activities or games	*# of minutes remaining alone before joining another activity*	*No more than 3 minutes*	*observation*	*avg 1 min*	*avg 1.5 min*	*avg 30 min*	*avg 2 min*	*avg 40 sec*	*avg 1.13 min.*
Helps set rules before game begins	*# of times joining in "rules" conversation*	*At least 3 times per week*	*observation/ interviews*	/	/	/	/	/	*5 days*
Offers new rules during game	*# of new rules offered*	*At least 1 per day*	*observation/ interviews*	//	///	/	////		*avg 2*
Helps resolve conflicts within group	*# of conflicts not resolved within group*	*No more than 2 per week*	*behavior log*		/		/		*2/wk*
Avoids fighting	*# of times fighting*	*No more than 1 per week*	*behavior log*		/		//		*3/wk****
Discusses action of game with others as period ends	*# of days conversing with others at end of period*	*At least 3 per week*	*observation*	/	/	/		/	*4/wk*
*Returns greetings in friendly voice (without sarcasm)***	*Ratio of friendly responses to greetings given*	*At least 75%*	*observation/ interviews* G: R:	G: //// R: ///	G: ~~////~~// R: ///	G: ///	G: ///	G: //// R: //	*48%****
*Chooses compatible friends to play with***	*# of times playing with incompatible person or group*	*No more than 2 per week*	*observation*	/	/	/	/		*4/wk****
*(** = added for Granville's assessment)*									*(*** = expectation not met)*

Comments/Notes: *Thursday was a particularly bad day for Granville—he seemed grouchy and got in a big fight with Billy. They carried their argument over to the rest of the day as well, and had to be separated during classroom activities.*

event occurs that can affect a student's behavior. As a general rule, you should not use atypical or exceptional measures from such days in your overall summary of assessment results because they can skew the average score.

For example, during Day 2 of Granville's assessment, Mrs. Armstrong had a police officer visit her class and lead a short class discussion on the effects of drug and alcohol abuse. This was an unusual activity for her class and the students, including Granville, were much more attentive and lively than usual in their discussion. Figure 5.1 shows that on this day, Granville volunteered answers 14 times and communicated with neighbors 6 times during the discussion. Mrs. Armstrong circled these results on her worksheet, because she felt that they did not represent his typical level of class participation. Note that she did not include this day's tally of these items in her computation of the week's average to avoid skewing his average score.

Record Additional Information That May Affect the Students' Behavior

When you conduct an observation, you should watch for particular conditions in the setting that may influence the students' performance. Often, assessment activities can give you new insights about the students' behavior, the source of their problems, and even abilities or skills you had not realized they possessed. You may discover events, such as another student's teasing remarks or unwillingness to share, that seem to provoke or encourage certain problem behaviors. Or you may notice that the students particularly like or dislike certain tasks, activities, or teaching formats.

While Mrs. Armstrong was observing Granville's game playing, she noticed that certain play conditions and actions of classmates seem to affect his behavior. She saw that Granville becomes particularly critical or combative when he starts losing a game or when opponents tease him about the score. But she saw that if he is winning, he is generally supportive of his playmates' mistakes, rarely criticizes their actions, and handles teasing in a playful and good-natured way. These observations are extremely valuable in interpreting the assessment results and in designing further assessments and intervention plans for students. They can give insight into the source of problem behavior and suggest possible solutions for overcoming the problem. Make note of important findings like these by recording your observations and insights in the Comments section of the assessment worksheet.

Figure 5.1 shows some of the comments about Granville's performance that Mrs. Armstrong made on her worksheet. She noted that he seemed to enjoy having a visitor in class, and wrote about his reluctance to seek help on his work. She also recorded an incident in which he and Billy carried over a dispute from the playground to the social studies class, trying to continue the argument all class period.

In summary, you should tally your results from a survey level assessment on a daily basis, and do so in a way that is consistent with the units of measure for the expectations. You should also comment on any important factors or variables that seem to affect the students' performance or that suggest possible intervention strategies.

Compiling a List of Expectations Not Met

After you have completed the assessment and summarized the results, you can determine whether the students meet any single expectation by comparing the results you obtained to the criterion level described on the worksheet. In this section we explain how to make these comparisons so you can compile a complete inventory of the expectations the students do not meet.

When assessment results are tallied to match the units of measure for an expectation, they will be directly comparable to the numbers listed in the Criterion Level column of the worksheet. Now, by comparing the two numbers you can determine whether the performance you assessed meets each expectation. A result that equals or exceeds the criterion level meets the expectation; one that falls below the criterion level does not. For example, during teacher presentation, Granville checked his progress against his neighbor's notes an average of one time per class period. The criterion level on Mrs. Armstrong's worksheet indicates that students should check their neighbor's notes at least two times per period. Based on this comparison, Granville clearly does not meet the expectation. As this illustrates, determining whether students meet an expectation is a simple and straightforward process.

As you go over the assessment results and compare the students' performance to the criterion levels, you should highlight all the expectations the students do not meet, perhaps by placing stars by those items in the Results column. By doing this you will create from your assessment worksheet a detailed, complete, and accurate list of expectations that the students do not meet. This list will help ensure a well-defined focus for further assessment and intervention.

Figure 5.1 shows that Mrs. Armstrong starred the expectations that Granville did not meet. The worksheet indicates that Granville meets the criterion for taking notes and encouraging others but that he does not meet the criterion for volunteering answers, asking questions, and accepting feedback from classmates. After completing her comparisons, Mrs. Armstrong will be able to use the expectations Granville does not meet as a starting point for selecting the social skills to be the focus of her further work with him.

Setting Priorities among Expectations Not Met

A more complicated task than deciding which expectations students do not meet is choosing which problem areas to concentrate on first with interventions. To make this choice, you must set careful priorities among the expectations not met before settling on the focus or target of an intervention (Zirpoli & Melloy, 1993). In this section we explain how to set these priorities.

An Approach for Setting Priorities

As you examine the assessment results and review the expectations the students do not meet, you may feel overwhelmed by the number of problems you need to address. You should realize, however, that working on too many areas simultaneously would be counterproductive. You would be unable to implement, monitor, and evaluate all the interventions you design, and you would end up accomplishing very little in improving the students' social skills—leaving you frustrated and discouraged.

A more practical approach is to establish priorities among problem areas and select specific target skills to work on. You may find it helpful to assign a priority level to each expectation not met:

> *Priority 1 items* are the small group of expectations (no more than two or three) that are most important for improving the students' overall behavior. You will address these areas right away with further assessment and intervention.
>
> *Priority 2 items* are expectations you will address after the students make progress on the priority 1 items and if there is sufficient time in the current school year.
>
> *Priority 3 items* are expectations you will probably not address during this year. If they continue to be problem areas for the students, you can suggest them to the students' future teachers as areas to work on for the next year.

Figure 5.2 shows a partial list of expectations Granville did not meet indicating Mrs. Armstrong's designation for each item on the list as priority 1, 2, or 3.

Considerations in Setting Priorities

When you set priorities, your initial inclination will probably be to designate as priority 1 the most obvious or irritating problems. Mrs. Armstrong may think of Granville's aggressive behavior or Alfred's tendency to talk during class as priority 1 items because these behaviors are most noticeable to her or most disruptive to her teaching. But it is important to resist this impulse, as it can lead to choices that fail to address the students' real or most important needs. Your first concern should instead be placed on the particular expectations that can produce the most profound and broadest improvement in the students' overall social competence.

As you go over the list of expectations the students did not meet, try to anticipate the effect that addressing each problem will have on a variety of performance areas. In going through the list for Granville, Mrs. Armstrong may decide that enhancing his ability to work with classmates on group projects will likely increase the number of assignments he completes and raise his grades on the projects. Additionally, she may think that his having this skill will produce improvements in several other areas of behavior, such as his work habits on other types of classroom assignments, his ability to respond to disagreements and criticism, or even his interactions with teammates in sports games during recess. If so, Mrs. Armstrong's priority would be to teach Granville to work with his classmates rather than to reduce his aggressive behavior, as learning cooperation might have a much greater impact on his overall performance. Similarly, if she thinks that increasing Sandy's question-asking behavior could also improve her attention to instructional activities, her

Figure 5.2 Part of Mrs. Armstrong's prioritized list of expectations Granville does not meet.

Worksheet 5.1: Setting Priorities from Assessment Results

Name: *Mrs. Armstrong* Date: *Oct. 10*

Student: *Granville* Grade: *5*

Expectations not met	Priority level
Works with peers on small group activities	*1*
Ignores teasing and confrontations with classmates	*1*
Initiates and returns greetings of classmates	*2*
Enters conversations without interrupting the flow of conversation	*2*
Asks for help when needed	*2*
Uses age-appropriate strategies for handling rejections and disappointments	*2*
Talks quietly with classmates before class begins	*2*
Talks with peers about "cool" topics	*2*
Ignores distractions by classmates when working on assignments	*2*
Defers to the directions and commands of group leader	*3*
Communicates with neighbor during class	*3*
Remains in assigned area until dismissal	*3*
Accepts criticism from classmates	*3*
Alters performance to correspond to the feelings and wishes of others	*3*
Shares materials and supplies with classmates	

ability to complete assignments, her relationships with teachers, and other key areas, Mrs. Armstrong would give this behavior precedence over others that might not have such significant or generalized effects.

In this section we present some important guidelines for determining which expectations should stand as priorities for further work. Note that these guidelines are *not* listed in order of importance; for any student or problem area, some may assume greater importance than others. When you weigh these guidelines, take into account such variables as the students' age, grade level, interests, abilities, and talents; the characteristics of the students' classmates or peer groups; and the various attributes of the classroom setting and school environment that can influence the students' behavior. You should also consider the "social validity" of the behavioral areas you select—in other words, the potential significance of the skills in improving students' acceptance by adults, peers, and others in the setting (Cartledge & Milburn, 1986; Gresham & Elliott, 1984; Wolf, 1978). Table 5.1 lists the guidelines discussed below.

Expectations that are more functional or frequently used by students should take priority over those that are less functional or less frequently used. Social skills can vary widely in how often students actually need to use them, and how important they are to students' success in a setting (Solity & Bull, 1987; Stainback, Stainback, & Moravec, 1992; Wasik, 1990; Wolery, Bailey, & Sugai, 1988). In instructional situations, expectations such as cooperating with peers, asking for help, and following directions are important because they are central to many aspects of school performance. These skills should generally be ranked before those that may have less impact on students' academic achievement or their participation in instructional lessons. For example, Granville's assessment results indicated that he has problems both in working with other students on assignments and in accepting criticism from peers. As shown in Figure 5.2, Mrs. Armstrong has given precedence to improving his ability to work with other students because she believes this skill is more broadly useful in instructional situations. By comparison,

TABLE 5.1 List of guidelines for setting priorities

Priority should be given to expectations that meet the following guidelines:

Expectations that are functional and frequently used by students

Expectations that are likely to carry over to other settings and situations

Expectations that improve status and relationships with adults and peers

Expectations that have a high value to the students and that may improve their self-esteem

Expectations that are valued by the other people in the setting

Expectations that are prerequisite to or lead up to more advanced skills

she thinks that responding to peer criticism is a less functional skill in her classroom, as she tries to hold such criticism to a minimum.

Similarly, Mrs. Armstrong may discover that on the playground, Alfred has difficulty both with entering conversations without interrupting and with apologizing when he bumps into classmates. She would very likely give priority to improving his conversational skills because he would use these skills much more frequently during playground activities.

Expectations that are more likely to carry over to other settings and situations should take priority over those less likely to transfer. If you address problems that occur in several settings before handling those that happen in only one, you can take advantage of the carryover effects that often result from an intervention (Kerr & Nelson, 1989; Wolery, Bailey, & Sugai, 1988). In this way, you may be able to produce wide-ranging and generalized improvements in the students'

Setting priorities among expectations not met will establish clear directions for further work with students.

behavior. Another advantage is that these expectations are often easier for students to learn because opportunities to work on them occur more often, especially when the conditions of performance are fairly consistent. These opportunities enable students to practice and quickly refine their new skills, and to experience immediate success in their social interactions across a number of school situations.

Mrs. Armstrong has found that Granville has difficulty both in discussing assignments with classmates and remaining in an assigned part of the classroom. Of these two expectations, she has given a higher priority to improving the way he interacts with other students, because she notices that fifth graders use fairly consistent language patterns in talking about assignments, and that Granville could use this skill in a wide variety of school situations. She does not believe that getting Granville to stay in an assigned area would have such broad effects.

With Sandy, Mrs. Armstrong believes that learning to talk about school activities with adults should be given a priority 1 ranking, higher than learning to give a class presentation on current events. She feels that Sandy could easily transfer adult interaction skills to several school settings, because students usually talk the same way to all their teachers and cover the same types of topics with them. Mrs. Armstrong thinks this skill may quickly become a part of Sandy's overall performance pattern and produce notable improvements in her social behavior in several settings.

Expectations that improve status and relationships with adults and peers should be given priority over those that do not produce such improvement. Skills that help students gain self-confidence and experience success in their interactions with peers and adults are more likely to produce generalized improvements in behavior than skills used primarily in independent situations (Cooper, Heron, & Heward, 1987; Renshaw & Asher, 1982). These skills for gaining status in a group and for developing and strengthening relationships often enable students to learn and practice more mature patterns of behavior. Expectations such as sharing materials, cooperating on assigned tasks, and collaborating on projects are especially important because they help students feel they are a part of a group, and because they encourage them to learn from one another's behavior (Johnson & Johnson, 1990; Slavin, 1990; Solomon, Watson, Schaps, Battistich, & Solomon, 1990).

We already mentioned that Mrs. Armstrong is giving priority to improving Granville's work with classmates on assignments because it is a skill he will use very often. She also feels that this skill will improve his status in peer groups, because it will give him a direct and positive means of interacting with his classmates. Similarly, Mrs. Armstrong would give a higher rank to improving Sandy's conversational skills than to improving her independent class work because the conversational expectation would probably have a more positive effect on Sandy's status with teachers and classmates. Although Sandy does need to improve her independent work, it is more critical that she develop stronger relationships with other people in school settings.

Expectations that have a high value to students and that will likely improve their self-esteem and self-image should be given priority over those that do not have as high a value. Skills that help students pursue their own interests and achieve their personal goals should usually be listed before those that pertain to goals selected by others. Students will be more interested in learning these skills, and will use them more often and in a wider array of circumstances (Miller & Harrington, 1990; Peterson & Miller, 1990; Wolery, Bailey, & Sugai, 1988). Especially in cases where students have low self-images, such skills can foster greater self-confidence and independence. They can be used to help students establish better rapport with the adults in the setting, and they encourage a camaraderie and trust between students who wish to learn valued skills and adults who can help them acquire and master these abilities (Lehr & Harris, 1988).

One reason Mrs. Armstrong might give precedence to improving Alfred's game-playing and conversational skills is that these areas are very important to him. She suspects that he will be much more inclined to participate in interventions in these areas than in learning to line up on time after recess and follow the other playground rules imposed by adults. Furthermore, she thinks that if she designs these interventions correctly, she may be able to take advantage of Alfred's interest in learning new play skills to encourage him to follow recess rules and cooperate more with the playground supervisors.

Similarly, Mrs. Armstrong might give priority to improving Sandy's question-asking skills because her inability to obtain help on her schoolwork when she needs it seems to be a source of frustration for her. Improvement here may also give Sandy greater self-esteem by helping her earn better grades. By comparison, Mrs. Armstrong may give a lower ranking to helping Sandy learn to volunteer answers in a large group discussion, another problem area for her. Mrs. Armstrong sees that this latter skill is not as important to Sandy. She also suspects that Sandy may develop it on her own when her self-confidence improves as she asks more questions and gets better grades.

Expectations that are valued and judged especially important by the people in a setting should be given priority over those viewed as less important. When establishing priorities, you must also consider the relative importance of expectations to the other people in the setting (Cooper, Heron, & Heward, 1987; Gresham, 1986). On the playground, classmates may give more value to fitting into social groups than to playing the activities proficiently. Similarly, during class breaks, students in the upper grades may place greater value on using conventional mannerisms and language patterns in their interactions than on the actual topics of the interactions. In the same way, instructional personnel may particularly want their students to participate actively in class discussions or to comply with certain rules or directions. On the other hand, they may place less importance on skills like taking turns to answer questions or on giving formal presentations. It is helpful to know which expectations are viewed in a setting as especially important, as learning these skills can help students fit in better.

With Granville, Mrs. Armstrong has given higher priority to his working on small group activities than to his sharing personal school supplies. One reason is Mrs. Armstrong's strong belief that fifth graders should learn to help one another actively and to combine their talents in completing difficult tasks and projects. On the other hand, she ranked sharing as a lower priority because she feels that fifth graders should have some latitude in deciding whether or not to share things.

Similarly, Mrs. Armstrong may decide to give special consideration to teaching Sandy to greet her teachers and classmates. She knows that the teachers, administrators, and staff at Madison Elementary place particular emphasis on following basic social amenities like greeting other people because they hope to maintain a friendly and personalized school environment. Conversely, she may give a lower priority to helping Sandy participate in large group games on the playground because this skill does not seem to be especially important to Sandy's playmates.

Expectations that lead up to or are prerequisite to more advanced skills should be given priority over those that are not prerequisites. When selecting from among the expectations that students do not meet, you should also consider the more advanced skills students will need to progress satisfactorily in their schooling. Some expectations, such as playing age-appropriate games or being able to change the topic of a conversation, are important because they prepare students for more advanced tasks, like playing cooperatively and conversing comfortably with classmates. Other basic skills, such as complying with the directions of teachers and making personal choices, are important because they help students make successful transitions to future placements, such as to junior and senior high school or to community work settings. Consider giving precedence to these types of skills as you select priority areas for interventions.

With Granville Mrs. Armstrong has given greater priority to more basic skills, like giving greetings and talking on age-appropriate topics, than to the more advanced skill of altering his performance to correspond to the feelings of others. She realizes that Granville must first learn the more elementary conversational skills before he can adapt them to the various circumstances in which he must consider other people's feelings. These basic skills can also serve as the foundation for many other types of social interactions. Similarly, if Mrs. Armstrong sees that Alfred does not understand the fundamental rules for playing recess games like football, she would give this area priority, because knowing how to follow rules provides a foundation for playing many kinds of games and sports. Thus, she might rank following the rules for games higher than showing good sportsmanship, because it is a prerequisite to the more advanced skill and can lead to learning many valuable play skills.

Using the Guidelines

The guidelines presented above are not listed in any particular order, as they are not intended to represent a specific ranking system so much as a series of considerations for you to weigh. As you look over the list of unmet expectations for the students you assessed, you should review these guidelines frequently to help you decide on a priority level for each expectation. Obviously, as you balance these varying considerations, you will need to reflect on the particular characteristics of the students and the setting to decide which guidelines should take precedence

(Cartledge & Milburn, 1986). Mrs. Armstrong found that the first two guidelines were particularly important considerations for Granville. She wants to focus on expectations that have far-ranging effects on his performance, as much of his problem behavior is frequent and widespread. The third and fourth guidelines are particularly important for Sandy, because Mrs. Armstrong would like to work on expectations that improve Sandy's self-esteem and her confidence in peer group interactions. For Alfred, Mrs. Armstrong may give particular attention to the last two guidelines; she wants to choose expectations that will be building blocks as Alfred learns more mature behavior and develops more age-appropriate interactions.

In setting priorities, look closely at expectations for which there are major discrepancies between the standards and the students' observed performance. Mrs. Armstrong feels that Granville's failure to meet the expectation for volunteering answers for teacher questions does fit some of the guidelines she is following (applies across situations, is valued by people in the setting, etc.). But she also notes that while his assessment result (volunteered 60% of the time) fails to meet the criterion (at least 85%), this is not as large a gap as Granville shows for many other expectations. Therefore, she has decided to focus her attention on other expectations that not only fit the guidelines but for which the assessment results suggest a more serious deficit.

Setting priorities will allow you to direct your full attention to a few specific areas of behavior and avoid feeling overwhelmed by the many skills the students need to learn. The guidelines can help as you analyze the expectations the students do not meet, but they should be used in conjunction with, rather than as a replacement for, your knowledge of the students' performance and learning characteristics, and the circumstances of their social interactions.

❍ Defining Target Skills for Interventions

In designating expectations as priority 1 items, you are deciding on the one or two key areas of behavior that will have the greatest impact on improving the students' overall social competence. From now on, we call these areas of behavior *target skills* to indicate the specific skills on which you will focus most of your efforts in working further with the students. They will get first attention in the students' intervention plans and will be the focus of additional assessments to gather more information about the students' abilities and performance characteristics (Howell, Fox, & Morehead, 1993).

A target skill should be defined in terms of one of the expectations you have designated as a priority 1 area so you can keep your tight focus for working with the students. But you may need to redefine the original priority expectation to make it more suitable for working with the student. There are two ways that you should consider revising the target skill: (a) broadening the skill to include related expectations or skill areas, and (b) specifying a single situation or activity in which the skill is used. These approaches are discussed next.

Broadening Target Skills

Because expectations identify discrete social behaviors, you might find the priority 1 item you have selected is fairly limited. You can broaden the scope of the target skill by linking it to areas of behavior that are closely related to the original expectation. Often, when you rank the expectations students do not meet, you will find that the areas you designate as priority 1 are closely tied to some of those ranked priority 2 and priority 3. You can usually rephrase the original expectation to include elements of these closely related expectations, and with your follow-up work in this area, you can increase the potential impact of your intervention without substantially fragmenting your attention to the most important areas of concern.

With Alfred, Mrs. Armstrong may list the following expectation as a priority 1 area for the playground setting:

Follows the rules for playground games

As lower priorities, she may have listed these skills:

Follows the action of games

Cheers and encourages the performance of teammates

Plays the entire game

Stays in game-playing area

Mrs. Armstrong could include elements of these areas of behavior by broadening the original priority 1 expectation to this:

Plays organized games with peers

By expanding the scope of the target skill in this way, she can concentrate on her primary area of concern, helping Alfred learn about game rules, but expand her work to include other closely related skills as well.

For another example of how to define a target skill, look at Mrs. Armstrong's prioritized list of expectations for Granville in Figure 5.2. She has designated the following as one of her priority 1 expectations:

Works with peers on small group activities

In choosing this area, Mrs. Armstrong's goal is to improve Granville's interactions with classmates during small group activities so he completes his assignments on time and works with classmates without becoming domineering, defensive, or combative. Also on Mrs. Armstrong's list are some priority 2 and 3 expectations that are closely related to the goal she has for Granville and that could probably be addressed at the same time without compromising her primary aim. These expectations are listed below:

Enters conversations without interrupting them

Talks with peers about age-appropriate topics

Defers to the directions of a group leader

Accepts criticism from classmates

Target skills are chosen for their potential to improve the students' social competence.

These areas are interrelated, often affecting his interactions with classmates during small group activities, so Mrs. Armstrong could address them all by expanding the original expectation into a single, more inclusive target skill, such as the following:

Cooperates with other students in completing small group activities

This broader skill will enable her to continue her primary focus for Granville and, at the same time, address other important areas of behavior.

Specifying Situations for Target Skills

In cases where a target skill applies to several different settings or situations, you should usually designate one or two of these as the primary context for further work with the students. Limiting the circumstances to a specific activity or interaction will give a clearer direction to any further assessments you do with the students and will make your intervention planning more precise, systematic, and manageable.

With Sandy, Mrs. Armstrong may designate "participates in conversations with teachers and peers" as the priority 1 area for her intervention, but it would be impractical to concentrate on all the different types of conversations that Sandy could have with teachers and peers, and on all the circumstances in which these conversations could take place. Mrs. Armstrong would need to consider the different greetings Sandy would have to use, the different topics she would have to talk about, the different cues she would have to watch for before making comments, and many other factors that can change quickly depending on the conversational conditions. Although Sandy's conversation problems may extend to all these different elements and circumstances, Mrs. Armstrong has neither the time nor the resources to address all of them. Even if she did, Sandy would be overwhelmed by all the new things she would have to learn right away.

A more practical approach is for Mrs. Armstrong to limit the scope of her further work with Sandy to one primary situation, and expand these activities to other areas later on, after Sandy has learned to use her skills under a prescribed set of circumstances. Initially, Mrs. Armstrong might narrow the scope of the target skill to the following:

Participates in conversations with peers during class breaks

This more limited skill would allow Mrs. Armstrong to be much more focused and systematic in her follow-up work with Sandy, avoiding the risk of diffusing her efforts by trying to address too many different variables and circumstances simultaneously.

Similarly with Granville, Mrs. Armstrong will initially limit work on his social interactions to participation in small group projects in her social studies classroom. Later, she will extend her plans for improving Granville's skills to recess activities or to other teachers' classrooms.

Thus, in defining a target skill, you can broaden the original priority expectation to include related performance areas while still giving a tight and concerted aim to your intervention plans. You should also limit the target skill to a single prescribed situation, in order to make your activities more focused and manageable.

The Need for Further Assessment

After you have defined the target skills for your interventions, you will need to look at the students' performance again, more closely, and ask why the students are not meeting these particular social expectations. This further investigation is needed because a survey level assessment, being broad-based in scope, does not allow you to make an in-depth study of the source of students' difficulties in any particular area.

Furthermore, the performance demands for meeting social expectations can be very complicated. Often the sheer number and scope of these behavioral requirements can be significant stumbling blocks for students, affecting their ability to understand and meet the demands for performance (Edwards & O'Toole, 1985). The complexity of social skills required to meet expectations can thus lead to an equally complex range of student problems. It is important to identify the sources of these problems before planning interventions, because these root causes can point to the need for a very systematic approach for improving social skills or for the use of very specific intervention techniques (Cohen & Fish, 1993). If we yield to our first inclination—to attack a problem in its most visible or annoying manifestation—we may never focus on teaching the particular skills that will actually improve the students' behavior.

In the next section, we illustrate the importance of investigating the students' behavior further by discussing the more common problems students may have in meeting social expectations and achieving social competence. Table 5.2 gives an outline of these problems, showing that the main focus of our discussion is on issues and problems related to having—and using—the social skills to meet expectations, and on considerations that will lead to instruction-based interventions. Note that we are not addressing the many other factors that can contribute to poor social behavior in school, such as poverty, medication side effects, inadequate health care, child abuse, and poor parenting practices, as these most often cannot be greatly influenced by school personnel.

Students may not have the requisite skills to interact or to do so successfully. This is a major source of student problems in meeting expectations. Lacking essential skills, students cannot participate effectively in interactions during activities assigned by their teachers or those they select themselves (Asher, Oden, & Gottman, 1977; Cartwright & Cartwright, 1984). This inability is particularly problematic when the students are highly motivated to engage in the activities but become frustrated at their lack of success.

Granville, for example, enjoys associating with classmates and would very much like to talk and play with them. However, he is not skilled in working on classroom projects with them, in conversing on topics they are interested in, or in responding to their teasing and pranks. So, instead of displaying competent social behavior, he hits, pushes, and yells at classmates; acts boastful and shows off; or sulks in another area of the classroom. If we observe these interactions closely, we might discover that Granville wants to have positive interactions, but does not know how to bring them about effectively. Consequently, he behaves in unskilled ways that generate negative reactions from others; these negative reactions make his behavior even worse, reducing other people's perceptions of his social competence even more.

When students show deficits in social skills by displaying inappropriate or disruptive actions, we can usually redefine the problem as a need to learn particular, acceptable behavior that can substitute for their current unacceptable behavior (Knoff, 1990). Redefining a problem in terms of the specific skills and responses

TABLE 5.2 An outline of major problems students may have in meeting social expectations

Students may not meet expectations because they:

- Do not have the required skills to socially interact
- Are unable to match their behavior with the demands of the situation
- Misinterpret or fail to understand the effects their behavior has on others
- Do not value conventional outcomes for their behavior
- Lack interest in the activities in which their social interactions take place

students must learn is one of the most important steps in improving their social competence. We begin by analyzing the types of responses that other, more successful students use in the same situations, and by making the acceptable responses the goals for our interventions (Howell & Morehead, 1987; Knapczyk, 1989; 1992).

Students may not be able to match their behavior to the ongoing demands of the situation. Some students can start an interaction skillfully, but are unable to bring it to a successful conclusion, because they cannot align their behavior with the activities that carry on the interaction, or modify their actions as the conditions in the situation change (Kronick, 1981). The first time Alfred interjects an outlandish comment into a conversation or laughs at another student's serious remarks, the others may think he simply misunderstands what they were saying. But if his behavior continues to be misaligned with the interaction, the other students will likely begin to ignore his comments and stop including him in the conversation altogether, because his behavior breaks the natural flow of the interaction. Thus, even though the interaction may have started out well, Alfred's behavior may become so out of step with the ongoing conditions that it attracts attention for its ineptness. As a result, the other students will look for ways to break off contact with him or they will make him the butt of their jokes.

The problem of misalignment often occurs because students do not recognize their behavior as inappropriate for the circumstances. They fail to pick up subtle cues indicating that they should use a specific type of behavioral pattern or change to a totally new one. Alfred, for example, sometimes adds comments that are not about the current topic of discussion because he does not recognize when students have lost interest in one topic of conversation and have moved on to another. At other times, he may not sense that the mood of the group has shifted and now calls for more serious or conventional behavior. As a result, he does not change his behavior to fit the new demands.

This example illustrates that students may have the individual skills for being successful in interactions but lack the more advanced ability of knowing how or when to use these skills when conditions call for them. Timing or matching one's actions to ongoing circumstances involves attending very closely to the conditions that govern the interactions, especially when they change during the course of the interactions. If students lack this skill, we may need to teach them to attend closely both to their own behavior *and* to the behavior of those around them so their actions stay properly aligned with the situations they are in.

Students may misinterpret or not understand the effects their behavior has on other people (Renshaw & Asher, 1982). They may fail to understand the relationship between their actions and the results of these actions, or think the effects are positive when they are negative. For example, when Alfred makes other students laugh by acting silly, immature, and obnoxious, he may not realize that classmates are laughing at him rather than with him. He may not see that they think he is "weird" and often exclude him from their social groups because of his behavior.

In such cases, students may not need to learn individual behavioral skills, but they do need to acquire the broader skill of recognizing the effects their behavior has on others. When we define a problem in terms of not understanding the consequences of one's actions, we can address a broad range of behavioral problems with a single central focus. Mrs. Armstrong's goal for Alfred could be to make him more aware of how others perceive his behavior and to help him choose more appropriate responses.

Students may be unable or unwilling to give value to conventional outcomes. Many social responses are governed by the impressions students would like to give other people; students usually say or do things to enhance their reputations or to gain recognition for their accomplishments. Trying to impress others serves a very important function in regulating behavior, because interpreting the reactions of others to their behavior gives students a basis for deciding whether to continue, discontinue, or modify their actions (Fagan, Long, & Stevens, 1975). When students see that their actions draw negative attention, they usually stop acting that way and search their behavioral repertoires for alternative responses. In contrast, when students' responses bring about positive attention, they tend to repeat those responses under similar circumstances.

Some students, however, act without regard to the effect their actions have on others (Renshaw & Asher, 1982). For example, Sandy tends to misinterpret and ignore Mrs. Armstrong's feedback about her work, because in the past the individualized attention she received from her teachers brought her embarrassment, criticism, and other negative results. Now she avoids interacting with Mrs. Armstrong and her other teachers altogether, because she places little value on their attention and prefers not to be singled out for routine classroom activities. She may not realize that she is missing the many positive benefits that can come from interacting with her teachers, such as getting a cheery greeting at the start of the school day or obtaining extra help or encouragement with her schoolwork. She may also not see that teachers interpret her actions incorrectly. Her apparent lack of motivation and unusually quiet demeanor may lead them to believe that she has less ability to take part in classroom activities than she actually does; consequently, they may not offer her opportunities to participate in more stimulating and challenging tasks.

Sandy's problem, like Alfred's, is related to her perceptions of the outcomes of her behavior. In this case, her difficulties illustrate that students need both to see and to *value* the results of positive social interactions. As teachers, we often fail to view problems in motivation as possible skill deficits, and we tend to blame students for their lack of interest. It is crucial to understand that students *learn* (or fail to learn) what to desire or value just as they learn any other skill. We may have to teach students like Sandy how to enjoy and take pride in their social interactions and to recognize and celebrate their own accomplishments. In this way, they learn to realize the benefits of being successful and begin to value the attention, recognition, and other positive outcomes of their interactions with adults and classmates.

Students may lack interest in the activities or circumstances in which social interactions take place. A wide variety of activities or tasks provides the context for social interactions, and these events can affect the quality and level of the students' behavior. Students are more likely to engage in positive social interactions when they find the activities and tasks interesting, challenging, or exciting (Asher, Oden & Gottman, 1977; Burden & Byrd, 1994; Harris & Schutz, 1986).

Conversely, the quality of their social interactions usually deteriorates when the activities and tasks become repetitious and boring, or become extremely difficult. In such cases, the most obvious solution is to change the activity to make it more enticing or manageable for students, but sometimes it is more advantageous for students to learn to respond more skillfully to the demands of the activity.

Mrs. Armstrong sometimes gives small groups an extra ten minutes at the end of class to study for quizzes. She has noticed that Granville tends to get into arguments and disagreements during this time and accomplishes very little actual studying. Before addressing his off-task behavior directly, Mrs. Armstrong should consider some other important factors: Does he see any value in studying for tests? Does he have the study skills to use this time effectively? Is he able to work together with his classmates in this type of activity? To make substantial improvements in Granville's social interactions, Mrs. Armstrong may have to teach him both cooperative learning skills and more effective study habits. As he develops an effective strategy for studying and applies these skills with those for working with classmates, Granville's social interactions may improve significantly, and he may use the study time more productively.

Students may be reluctant to interact because they fear or expect negative outcomes. Successful behavior is more likely to be repeated than unsuccessful behavior. But students must also learn to take risks by trying out new behaviors and seeing how well they work so they can continue to develop and refine their social skills. They can gain much valuable experience by trying to interact in new ways, in new situations, and with new people.

Sometimes, however, students are unwilling to enter social interactions that are risky—possibly because they cannot predict whether their responses will be successful or because they have difficulty learning from their mistakes. Not knowing how to take risks can lead to problems in students' social interactions (Raffini, 1993). For example, during class breaks, Sandy would like to talk with some of the other girls and tell them jokes or share in the latest gossip, but she usually remains apart from her classmates because students at her previous school teased and made fun of her. Now, at Madison Elementary School, she is still very hesitant about participating in the give-and-take among classmates because she is unsure how they will respond to her—even though she would probably do just fine if she tried.

In cases like Sandy's, the skill students must develop is to have greater confidence in their abilities. You may have to help students broaden the range of their experiences, or allow them to practice specific behaviors until these are precise and fluent enough to become an integral part of their social interactions. You may also have to give students extra encouragement to try out new interaction patterns, or create opportunities for them to use their skills under supportive and nonthreatening conditions (Eby & Kujawa, 1994).

The Need for Further Investigation of Target Skills

The examples above should suggest the need to address problems in social behavior very carefully and systematically, since a quick or haphazard approach may miss the real source of students' problems. Keep an open mind about the source of students' difficulties in meeting expectations until you have considered all the possibilities. For example, Mrs. Armstrong might try to use a point system with Granville or offer him special privileges to try to help him stay on task and work with classmates on small group activities. But Granville's problem may in fact be more a skill deficit than a motivational issue: perhaps he is unaware of the difficulties his behavior causes, or maybe he has no clear idea of how to improve it. Maybe he needs more background in the assigned material before working in a group situation. Or maybe he must learn to take the suggestions and feedback from his classmates in a less personal and nonjudgmental way. Thus, a motivational approach would not effectively address Granville's problem, whereas an instructional approach focusing on improving his cooperative or negotiating skills probably would.

It is thus important to look for the reason students do not perform a target skill before taking steps to develop an intervention. These follow-up activities will give you a better understanding of the sources of the students' difficulties and help to indicate what your interventions must accomplish (Zirpoli & Melloy, 1993). In the next three chapters, we discuss several different approaches for this type of in-depth investigation.

Summary

Tallying the Results of a Survey Level Assessment

1. Assessment results are described in terms of the units of measures prescribed by the expectations.
2. Keeping daily records of the assessment results will help to maintain an accurate and reliable accounting of the students' behavior.
3. Additional information about variables that affect the students' behavior can clarify results and suggest ideas for interventions.

Compiling a List of Expectations Not Met

1. Expectations not met are determined by comparing the students' assessment results to the standards for the expectations.
2. Expectations not met are those for which the students' behavior falls below criterion levels.
3. Expectations not met can be marked on the assessment worksheet or compiled in a list.

Setting Priorities among Expectations Not Met

1. Assigning priority levels to each expectation not met will give a clear focus to further work with the students.

2. Priority levels should be assigned to expectations based on the following considerations:
   a. expectations that are functional or frequently used
   b. expectations that will carry over to other settings and situations
   c. expectations that improve status and relationships with others
   d. expectations that have high value to students
   e. expectations that are valued by other people
   f. expectations that lead to more advanced skills

3. These guidelines will assist you in choosing the most important areas of behavior for improving students' social competence.

Choosing Target Skills for Interventions

1. Target skills are the specific areas of behavior to be addressed in the students' interventions.

2. Target skills are defined in terms of priority 1 expectations.

3. Target skills can be broadened by adding areas of behavior that are closely related to priority 1 expectations.

4. Target skills should specify performance in a particular setting, situation, or activity.

The Need for Further Assessment

1. It is important to investigate further why students are not meeting social expectations.

2. Students may not meet expectations because they
   a. do not have the requisite skills
   b. cannot match their behavior with the demands of the situation
   c. misinterpret or do not understand the effects of their behavior
   d. are unable or unwilling to give value to outcomes
   e. lack interest in the activities in which social interactions take place
   f. expect or fear negative outcomes

3. Further investigation of why students do not meet expectations will give a clear, direct focus to interventions.

Examples for Chapter Five

Example 5a

This is the prioritized list of expectations not met in the assessment of Warren, whose behavior is described in example 4a. Ms. Lake has given particular priority to skills that will help Warren establish positive interactions with playmates. When setting a target skill for further work with Warren, Ms. Lake broadened her top priority expectation somewhat to "Acknowledges classmates and greets them by name," a fundamental skill that is suited to Warren's needs.

Priority 1 expectations should be among the most frequently used skills in a situation. → Greets classmates by name

The skills used first in an interaction can often be the first areas on which to focus an intervention. → Chooses play area or activity

More complicated or challenging expectations should usually be delayed if the student has difficulty with more basic items. → Talks with playmates about play activity

Lower priority should usually be given to items that simply restate or reinforce classroom rules, as these areas are already addressed in the normal routine of the setting. → Uses toys and equipment for their intended purpose

Worksheet 5.1: Setting Priorities from Assessment Results

Name: *Ms. Lake* Date: *Oct. 5*

Student: *Warren* Grade: *K*

Expectations not met	Priority level
Greets classmates by name	*1*
Chooses play area or activity	*1*
Waits turn to use toys or play equipment	*2*
Verbalizes feelings (rather than reacting physically)	*2*
Shares toys with playmates	*2*
Talks with playmates about play activity	*2*
Moves around area without hurting others	*2*
Laughs/shows humor or excitement	*2*
Stays in supervised play area	*3*
Seeks attention from teacher	*3*
Returns greetings from peers and adults	*3*
Uses toys and equipment for their intended purpose	*3*
Follows adult directions	

Example 5b

Alicia's assessment showed she failed to meet several of Ms. Santamaria's expectations in science class. (Alicia's behavior is described in Example 4b.) Listing her top priorities,Ms. Santamaria defined the target skill for Alicia as "Plans tasks and works cooperatively with partner or group."

Priority 1 expectations should help students fit in with the group.

Discrete behaviors that can quickly improve the student's social performance make good priority 1 expectations.

The most disruptive or annoying problems areas may not always be priority 1 items.

Expectations involving the mechanics or routines of the activity should usually be given a low priority.

Worksheet 5.1: Setting Priorities from Assessment Results

Name: *Ms. Santamaria* Date: *Oct. 9*

Student: *Alicia* Grade: *11*

Expectations not met	Priority level
Divides tasks with partner or group	*1*
Listens to others' comments and opinions	*1*
Reviews assignment with partner or group before beginning work	*2*
Stays on topic of discussion	*2*
Offers suggestions in a diplomatic manner	*2*
Offers positive feedback and praise to classmates	*2*
Follows teacher directions for activities	*2*
Waits turn to speak in discussion	*2*
Acknowledges ideas and suggestions of classmates	*2*
Shows sensitivity to classmates' feelings and moods	*3*
Hands in work and tells teacher when work is completed	*3*
Returns supplies and equipment to storage area	*3*
Stays in assigned area of lab	*3*

Mr. Wagner's Case Study

Mr. Wagner's List of Priorities

After he finished his assessment, Mr. Wagner set priorities for the expectations Granville failed to meet. His list is presented here.

For further work, Mr. Wagner decided to concentrate on Granville's behavior during science class, and set the target skill, "Works on projects with classmates." This is similar to the target skill Mrs. Armstrong set, but you may notice that his phrasing is less focused on the social aspects of group work.

Priorities should be set according to the student's needs, not the teacher's. Look for items that will help the student's social behavior become more successful and fulfilling.

Priority 1 expectations should focus on the social skills that lead to improved academic performance rather than on the academic performance itself. This will give a clearer focus to interventions.

Limit priority 1 expectations to one or two items. Having more than this will make an intervention unfocused and unmanageable.

Many of the expectations Mr. Wagner has assessed are not well targeted to Granville's needs. Determining whether Granville pushes his chair in is not a very effective use of Mr. Wagner's time.

Worksheet 5.1: Setting priorities from assessment results.

Name: *Mr. Wagner* Date: *Oct. 15*

Student: *Granville* Grade: *5*

Expectations not met	Priority level
Completes assignments on time	1
Follows directions for group activity	1
Works on tasks agreed upon by group	1
Avoids fighting or arguing with group members	1
Stays with the group	1
Gets along with group	2
Shares materials with group members	2
Cleans up work area	2
Turns in work when completed	2
Pushes in chair when leaving the work area	3
Brings materials needed for the activity	3
Asks for assistance when needed	3
Moves on to next activity when directed	3

CHAPTER 6

Conducting a Specific Level Assessment

Part I: Assessing Basic Abilities

In the next three chapters, we explain how to conduct a *specific level assessment* of social behavior. This is more precise and individualized than a survey level assessment as it pinpoints *why* students are having difficulty meeting social expectations. In contrast to the survey level, a specific level assessment looks closely and systematically at the students' performance of the target skills you have chosen for attention. The results give structure and purpose to the intervention procedures by showing what must be accomplished to help the students develop the target skills, thereby increasing the efficiency and effectiveness of the intervention plan.

Deciding on a target skill for students gives us only one part of the information we need to design effective interventions, as there may be many different reasons the students fail to perform the skill. In the case study, for example, Mrs. Armstrong has decided that a good target skill for Granville is to improve his level of cooperation with classmates on small group projects. There could be many reasons for his difficulty, however, including one or more of the following problems:

- He may not understand the content of the lesson.
- He may not be able to follow the directions for doing the assignment.
- He may not know how to organize his work to complete the assignment on time.
- He may not be proficient at sharing tasks and making compromises in small group situations.
- He may not coordinate his actions with the actions of the group.
- He may have difficulty deferring to the instructions and judgment of the group leader.
- He may not get along with the particular classmates in his work group.

- He may have difficulty staying on task for the required time to complete his share of the work.
- He may get more enjoyment from arguing and criticizing the other students' work than from doing his own work.

Because of this wide range of possible causes for Granville's problems, Mrs. Armstrong does not know which way to direct her intervention plans. Should she develop a new way to deliver the content or to explain the directions so Granville understands the assignment better? Should she teach him better ways to organize his work time? Should she concentrate on improving his time on task? Should she focus on teaching Granville interpersonal "getting along" skills and plan a series of lessons on sharing and making compromises?

In the next three chapters, we discuss a three-part process of specific level assessment that will help answer questions like these. The three parallel approaches we describe allow you to look at the students' performance from very different perspectives so you can see exactly where students are having problems in their social interactions. In this chapter we explain how to assess the *basic abilities* that students must have in order to be able to perform a target skill. Chapter Seven describes how to assess *component steps,* the sequence of actions students must link together to form the behavioral pattern required by the target skill. Finally, Chapter Eight shows how to assess *performance conditions,* the cues or characteristics of a situation that enable students to align their behavior properly with ongoing activities and interactions. The findings of these three stages of specific level assessment can be coordinated to set instructional goals for a single coherent intervention. The flow chart in Figure 6.1 shows how each stage contributes to a unified set of intervention goals.

Overview of Basic Abilities Assessment

The first approach we present for investigating why students do not meet expectations is to check whether they have the basic abilities they need to acquire and use a specific target skill. *Basic abilities* include the background knowledge and the fundamental behaviors that form the foundation for a more advanced skill. Basic abilities are often described as the pre-skills or prerequisite skills that students must have before they can master an advanced skill (e.g., Borich, 1988; Campbell & Siperstein, 1994; Howell & Morehead, 1987). In this chapter, we describe how to plan, conduct, and summarize an assessment of these basic abilities. We start by explaining what basic abilities are and how they relate to meeting expectations for social behavior.

Basic Abilities and Planning Interventions

Conducting an assessment of basic abilities is an important step in the intervention planning process because it helps to clarify the scope of the intervention. A basic abilities assessment will allow you to determine whether you should direct the

Figure 6.1 Flowchart showing parallel stages of specific level assessment.

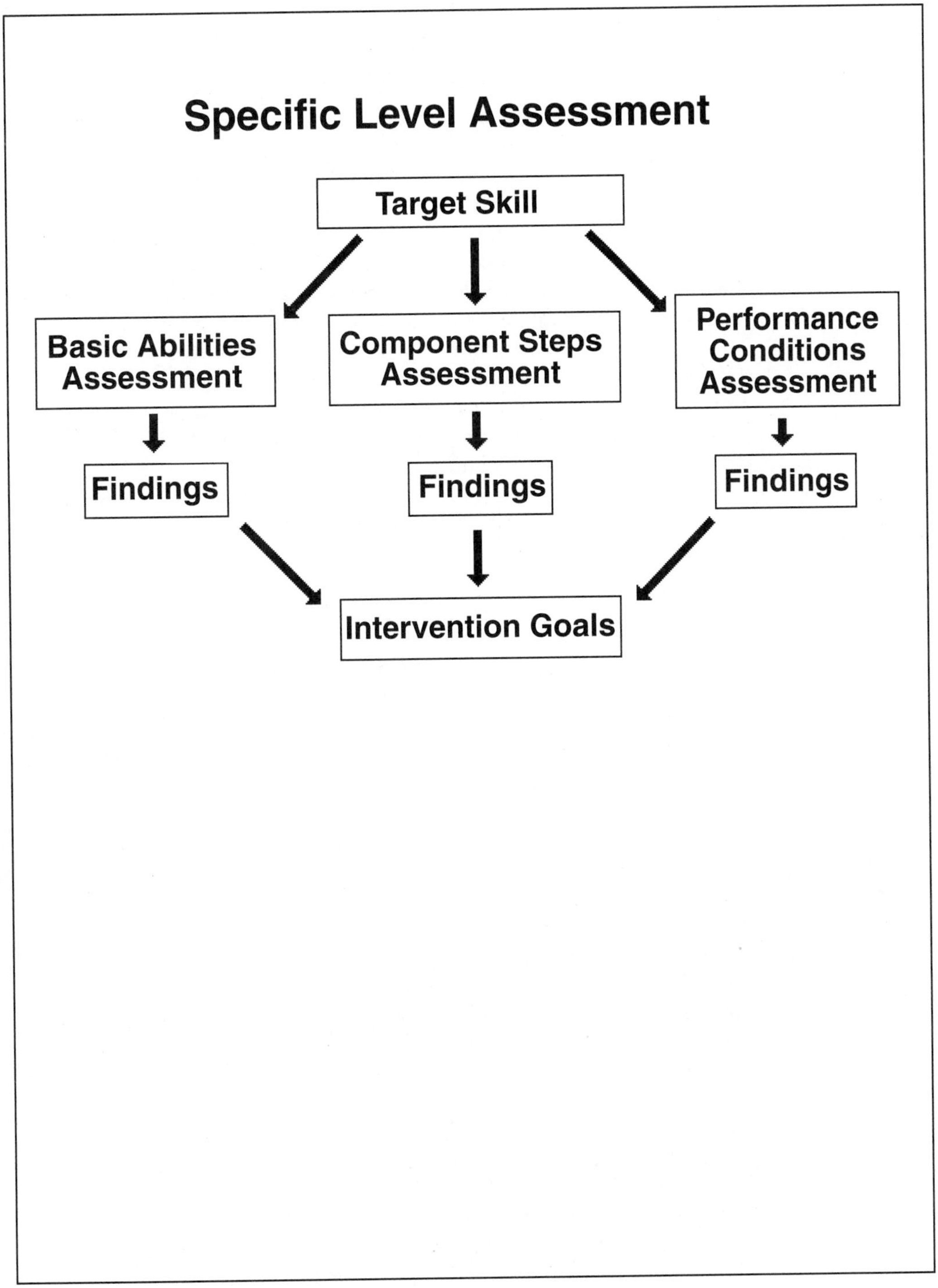

focus of the intervention more broadly toward teaching students the overall target skill, or whether you should first work toward increasing their basic abilities and needs—and work on the target skill later (Hoy & Gregg, 1994). When you see that students lack important basic abilities, you will usually want to focus on these in the students' intervention plan before concentrating more fully on the target skills. In other words, when you look at basic abilities, you are shifting temporarily from a focus on the overall behavior for meeting expectations to a focus on more fundamental skills that will serve as raw materials for learning the larger skill.

In the example we presented above for Granville, we noted that Mrs. Armstrong still had many questions about why he does not work well with classmates on small group activities. Among her concerns were whether she needed to teach Granville how to follow directions, how to break down the tasks into subtasks, and how to understand the material involved in the project. All these questions relate to whether Granville has the *basic abilities* he needs to participate effectively in small group classroom activities. To answer these questions, Mrs. Armstrong needs to conduct a new kind of assessment, one that gives her more information about what Granville is *able or unable* to do in this type of situation, rather than simply looking at what he *does or does not* do (Howell, Fox, & Morehead, 1993). The more clearly she determines the nature and details of Granville's actual abilities, the easier it will be for her to design an intervention that accurately addresses Granville's real needs.

Basic Abilities and Problems in Social Behavior

An assessment of basic abilities will help you to identify and concentrate on the most fundamental problems students may have achieving proficiency in a particular skill. In general, these problems in basic abilities are of two types: (a) students may lack essential background knowledge for using the target skill, or (b) they may lack some fundamental enabling skills that allow them to perform the skill effectively. We discuss these problems next.

Students may lack background knowledge. Students must have certain comprehensive knowledge to use their social skills effectively; problems in social behavior usually arise when students lack this important information (Campbell & Siperstein, 1994; Hoy & Gregg, 1994). As an example, students must know how to read numbers and perform simple mathematics operations before they can participate in activities and exercises that require these skills. They must be able to perform fundamental movement patterns, like running , throwing, and catching, before they can play baseball or football. They must know some key things about a topic before they can discuss it in conversation. These are basic abilities students must have to perform the more advanced skill, and students who lack essential information in these areas will have difficulty with the social behavior based on this background knowledge (Cartledge & Milburn, 1986).

Therefore, one aim of assessing basic abilities is to determine whether students have the requisite background knowledge to perform a target skill. If they lack it, you will know to focus the intervention directly on helping students acquire this knowledge. Based on the results of her survey level assessment, Mrs. Armstrong

A basic abilities assessment examines whether students have the background knowledge and enabling skills needed to use target skills.

may have defined the target skill for Sandy as "converses with peers during play times and classroom transition times." But before she can design an overall intervention to help Sandy talk with her peers, she first needs to consider whether Sandy has the essential background knowledge for holding conversations. In investigating this issue more closely, Mrs. Armstrong will assess whether Sandy has a sufficient understanding of the topics fifth graders talk about so she can add pertinent comments to the conversations. Perhaps Sandy does not talk with other students because she does not have anything relevant to say to them. If Mrs. Armstrong finds that Sandy lacks this basic ability, she will concentrate her intervention on helping Sandy broaden her background and understanding of age-appropriate topics. Furthermore, Mrs. Armstrong will probably need to work on this ability before she tries to increase the frequency or length of Sandy's conversations with classmates, because any effort to address the more advanced skill will not succeed until Sandy has sufficient background knowledge of age-appropriate topics.

Similarly, after analyzing and reviewing the survey level assessment results for Alfred, Mrs. Armstrong may have defined for him the target skill "plays organized games with peers." Now she may question whether he knows how to play some of the games that the other students play. She realizes that knowing and following the rules for sports activities is a prerequisite for playing on teams with other children. If she sees that Alfred is not proficient in playing games, she will want to teach this ability before trying to increase his level of involvement in team play, because it provides the foundation for the more advanced skill.

Students may lack key enabling skills that could help them to meet social expectations more easily. These more generalized basic skills are often used in conjunction with the skills for meeting expectations (Hoy & Gregg, 1994). They are not strictly prerequisites, but students who lack them often have problems using other social skills. For example, if students cannot accept constructive feedback and criticism, they will usually have a difficult time working on small group class projects. If they are unable to extend greetings, they will usually have a hard time starting conversations. Neither accepting constructive feedback nor extending greetings are prerequisites to these other skills; students can work in groups and hold conversations without them. However, lacking these enabling skills can interfere with the students' ability to interact competently in these types of situations. Therefore, you need to determine whether students have these skills; if they are lacking, you may want to develop them before working more broadly on the target skill.

For example, in addition to learning whether Alfred knows the structure and rules of specific sports activities, Mrs. Armstrong may wish to determine whether he has the ability to take turns, pay attention to the action of a game, and work together with teammates on common goals. These last items are not literally necessary before Alfred can begin playing the game, but they are basic abilities that can make his game playing much more effective. And if Mrs. Armstrong sees that he lacks any of these key enabling skills, she will want to help him develop them because they will improve his ability to handle game-playing activities. With Sandy, Mrs. Armstrong may wish to see if she can maintain eye contact with classmates and show appropriate facial expressions while speaking and listening to them. These skills are not essential, but if Sandy develops them, she will have more effective conversations.

Assessing basic abilities, then, will help you pinpoint problems both in fundamental background knowledge and in key enabling skills, problems that may be causing or at least strongly contributing to students' failure to use a target skill. In the remaining sections of the chapter, we explain the steps for carrying out an assessment of basic abilities.

Preparing a Basic Abilities Assessment

As with any other assessment, you should begin an assessment of basic abilities by first preparing detailed plans for your investigation to make sure that your activities are focused and productive. We recommend that you structure your planning by developing a worksheet to help you determine the focus of your investigation and to keep track of important information about the activities. The worksheet will aid you in planning the procedures and in maintaining an accurate record of the results. In the sections that follow, we explain the steps for preparing and filling out a worksheet for basic abilities assessment and show how you can plan your activities to explore the central concerns you have for your own students. Table 6.1 lists the various steps involved in this planning process.

Step 1: Listing Information about the Student and the Target Skill

As preparation for a basic abilities assessment, include information at the top of the worksheet about the students you are planning to assess, such as their names, ages, or grade levels. You should also indicate the target skills you are examining and the person conducting the assessment, if someone other than you. All this information will help you recall important details about the assessment at a later time. Figure 6.2 shows the worksheet Mrs. Armstrong used for assessing Granville's basic abilities.

Step 2: Listing the Basic Abilities to Be Assessed

One of the most challenging tasks in preparing an assessment of basic abilities is to define the specific background knowledge and enabling skills you will investigate. The key to this step is to individualize the list of items, gearing it to the students and circumstances you have in mind (Hoy & Gregg, 1994). Even when you are assessing more than one student on the same target skill, you should develop separate lists of basic abilities, considering the particular questions you have about each student's behavior. The following points will help you keep the list of basic abilities consistent with your questions.

Basic abilities should match the students' overall characteristics. Each target skill has an infinite number of basic abilities you could look at, so the amount of detail you could use to express them can vary greatly. Basic abilities themselves have basic abilities, and these, in turn, have other basic abilities. You can define basic abilities at almost any level of behavior and stage of development you wish to examine, even to the level of very simple body movements.

It is important to select abilities at the right level and in the proper behavioral areas so the assessment is consistent with the learning and performance characteristics of the students you are assessing (Hoy & Gregg, 1994; McLoughlin & Lewis, 1990). Normally, you will assess more fundamental basic abilities with students who are younger, who have more noticeable learning and behavior problems, or who are inexperienced in the target skill area. On the other hand, you will probably not need to be concerned with many of the most basic abilities when you are

TABLE 6.1 Steps in planning a basic abilities assessment

Step 1:	List information about the student and the target skill
Step 2:	List the basic abilities to be assessed
Step 3:	Formulate questions about basic abilities and add them to the worksheet
Step 4:	Plan procedures for assessing basic abilities

Figure 6.2 Mrs. Armstrong's basic abilities worksheet for Granville.

Worksheet 6.1: Basic Abilities Assessment — Page *1* of *6*

Name: *Mrs. Armstrong* Date: *Oct. 14*

Student: *Granville* Grade: *5*

Target skill: *Cooperates with other students in completing small group activities*

Basic abilities to assess:

1) *Is able to understand the content of the activities*
2) *Is able to understand and follow the directions for activities*
3) *Is able to divide activities into subtasks*
4) *Is able to share or assign different subtasks to other group members*
5) ______

Figure 6.2 *(continued)*

Worksheet 6.1 (continued)	Name: *Mrs. Armstrong*	Page *2* of *6*

Basic ability: *(1) Is able to understand content of activity*

Questions to answer about basic ability:

Can Granville understand the basic background of the material? Can he identify the point or purpose of the activity? Can he remember the information he learns? Is he able to apply his knowledge in different ways?

Procedures for answering questions:

- *Give Granville a written test on the background for his social studies activities—include items about that day's lesson.*
- *Discuss recent class content with Granville. Focus on the subjects of activities.*

Personnel/equipment needed:

Make written test

Day	Results:
1	*Granville scored 14/20 on the written test—satisfactory.*
2	*Discussed content with Granville. With prompting, he was able to recognize or identify about 90% of the subjects or events I questioned him about. He seemed frustrated at any gaps, though, and when we talked more he admitted that he didn't like it when other group members acted "like they think they're smarter than me."*
3	
4	
5	

Conclusions/comments:

Granville's background understanding of the material is sufficient for him to take a productive part in the group activities, but it seems to fall short of his own personal goals. G. wants to be the smartest person in the group, and he shows his frustration by criticizing other group members.

Figure 6.2 *(continued)*

Worksheet 6.1 (continued)	Name: *Mrs. Armstrong* Page *3* of *6*

Basic ability: *(2) Is able to understand and follow directions for assignment*

Questions to answer about basic ability:

Can Granville understand and repeat the directions for an activity? Can he follow directions for other types of activities? Can he follow written/oral directions? Can he follow directions for nonacademic tasks?

Procedures for answering questions:

- *Ask Granville questions about directions for a group activity.*
- *Give Granville oral directions for academic and nonacademic tasks, then give him written directions for similar tasks.*

Personnel/equipment needed:

Written directions for tasks.

Day	Results:
1	*Group activity today. I asked Granville about the directions I had given, and he was very sketchy.*
2	
3	*Gave the class oral directions for a solo assignment in the morning. Granville had trouble staying on-task—needed lots of reminding. Gave oral directions for a solo game this afternoon. Granville got started well, but forgot what to do and started wandering and bothering his neighbors.*
4	*Similar activities today, but with written directions. Granville got started well, but then lost track. When prompted to check back to his written directions, he got back on track.*
5	

Conclusions/comments:

Granville has trouble remembering directions. He could do better if he had written directions (or if he wrote them down when he heard them), but only if he learns to check back with the instructions when he gets stuck.

Figure 6.2 *(continued)*

Worksheet 6.1 (continued)	Name: *Mrs. Armstrong*	Page *4* of *6*

Basic ability: *(3) Is able to divide activities into subtasks*

Questions to answer about basic ability:

Can Granville divide a task into substeps? Can he set a strategy for completing different types of tasks? Can he integrate a single subtask into an overall task?

Procedures for answering questions:

- *Discuss different types of tasks with Granville. Ask how he would complete them.*
- *Give the class one academic and one nonacademic task that require substeps.*
- *Check Granville's performance, and ask him about his strategy.*
- *Give him a specific task to do during group activity, and see how he integrates it.*

Personnel/equipment needed:

Plan for activities.

Day	Results:
1	*Granville worked on one subtask (cutting out figures) during the activity. He stayed pretty well on task, but didn't really share his work with others or ask for approval.*
2	*Discussion with Granville. We talked about household tasks like washing the car, and academic tasks like book reports. He could identify different things that needed to be included, but had trouble articulating a coherent sequence.*
3	
4	
5	*Had the class do a three-step social studies activity, and also do a five-step Halloween activity. In each case, Granville seemed to get preoccupied with one or another subtask, and eventually either got frustrated or wandered off task. He couldn't really explain a particular strategy he used.*

Conclusions/comments:

Granville has trouble sequencing a series of subtasks. He can do a single subtask for its own sake, but doesn't have an overall sense of how the parts fit together into an overall set of directions.

Figure 6.2 *(continued)*

Worksheet 6.1 (continued)	Name: *Mrs. Armstrong* Page *5* of *6*

Basic ability: *(4) Is able to share or assign subtasks*

Questions to answer about basic ability:

Can Granville separate a task into jobs for different people? Can he coordinate his own subtasks with those of others? Can he work with adults, if not with peers?

Procedures for answering questions:

- *Coordinate with procedures for basic ability #3.*
- *Discuss how Granville would plan to do tasks if he had others to help him.*
- *Make sure when giving activities for #3, that one involves coordinating some steps with peers, and one with the teacher.*
- *Check how Granville coordinates task with peers in small group.*

Personnel/equipment needed:

Same as #3, above.

Day	Results:
1	*See comments above for #3. Granville didn't really coordinate his task with his peers.*
2	*In our talk, Granville had an easier time planning how to coordinate the household tasks with others, but his plans didn't really use effective cooperation in either type.*
3	
4	
5	*The academic task required me to help and check at one point, while the other required some sharing with peers. With prompting, Granville completed the step with me, but then went back to refining the previous step rather than going on. In the Halloween activity, he never got far enough to work with the others.*

Conclusions/comments:

Granville isn't particularly interested in working with his peers, but he didn't seem to hate the idea either. He will get better at this step if he can learn to follow directions and sequence his tasks more effectively.

Figure 6.2 *(continued)*

Worksheet 6.1 (continued)	Name: *Mrs. Armstrong*	Page *6* of *6*

Findings—instructional goals for intervention:

Learn more effective techniques for following directions.

Learn how to break down tasks and carry out subtasks.

Learn to coordinate and share tasks with others.

assessing students who are older, higher functioning, or more experienced in the performance area.

When Mrs. Armstrong defines basic abilities for assessing Alfred's game-playing skills in a sports activity like football, she must be careful to limit her focus to the areas that are most likely to be problems for a fifth-grade student like Alfred. If she is too zealous in identifying or breaking out the basic abilities, she could end up with items such as these:

- Is able to kick a football
- Is able to run to the goal line
- Is able to identify what team he is on
- Is able to count four downs

These items are indeed basic abilities for playing football, and if Alfred were a kindergarten or first-grade student, or if he had a severe learning disability or motor impairment, some of them might be worth assessing. But because he is a typical fifth grader in most ways, Mrs. Armstrong probably does not have any questions about Alfred's actual *ability* to run to a goal line, to count to four, or to perform the other most basic behaviors—even if he sometimes fails to meet these simple demands when playing. It is important to remember that with basic abilities, you are concerned with questions of what students *are able* to do, not what they actually *do*. Therefore, you should define basic abilities at a level that matches the students' overall cognitive and physical characteristics. In this case, Mrs. Armstrong would pick items that she is more interested in assessing with Alfred such as the following:

- Is able to follow the sequence of rules for playing football
- Is able to follow the offensive play and defensive play of football games
- Is able to coordinate actions with those of teammates
- Is able to make appropriate comments on game action

Similarly, when defining basic abilities for Sandy's assessment, Mrs. Armstrong will probably not be concerned with such basic conversational skills as these:

- Is able to speak English
- Is able to understand spoken words
- Is able to recognize other people
- Is able to respond to questions

These basic abilities for holding conversations could be appropriate for assessment with Sandy if she were a non-English-speaking student, or if Mrs. Armstrong believed she might be language impaired. But as a fairly typical fifth grader, Sandy would already have these skills, and they are thus far too fundamental for her assessment. More appropriate basic abilities to investigate with Sandy might be these:

- Is able to identify the best times to start a conversation
- Is able to select age-appropriate topics

- Is able to respond to verbal and facial cues
- Is able to use animated language and facial expressions

Basic abilities should be limited to those for which you have major concerns. Note in each of the examples given above that there are only a few items Mrs. Armstrong would actually select for each student. For a useful assessment of basic abilities, it is best to limit the list to three to five basic abilities. You may, however, need to expand the list if you have not had many opportunities to work directly with the students and are unsure of their developmental levels. Remember that for this assessment, you are looking only at the students' raw abilities, rather than at problems that may be due to inclination, motivation, timing, or other factors. For example, you would not add any basic abilities that you know the students could use if they really wanted to. Thus, the value of conducting a basic abilities assessment lies in looking carefully at a few key issues about which you have real questions. By overloading the list at the beginning, you risk diluting the effectiveness and depth of your assessment. On the other hand, if you have numerous concerns about the students' basic abilities to perform a target skill you should consider another area to work on, one that is not quite so advanced.

The basic abilities you plan to assess should be added to the assessment worksheet. Figure 6.2 shows the list of basic abilities that Mrs. Armstrong prepared for Granville. For the target skill, "cooperates with other students in completing small group activities," she plans to assess the following:

- Is able to understand the content of the activities
- Is able to understand and follow the directions for the activities
- Is able to divide activities into subtasks
- Is able to share or assign different subtasks to other group members

She feels that this list both reflects what she already knows about Granville's learning and performance characteristics and addresses her major concerns about his ability level.

Figure 6.2 shows a separate page for each of the basic abilities in Granville's assessment. Each of these pages includes spaces for the following:

- Listing questions to investigate for each basic ability
- Describing the procedures for answering these questions
- Scheduling personnel, ordering equipment, developing materials, or making other preparations
- Recording daily results of the assessment
- Summarizing comments on the student's performance of the specific basic ability

Like Mrs. Armstrong, you should prepare a separate worksheet page for each basic ability. This page will be your guide for every step in the assessment of that ability. Keeping each one separate will help you clarify, differentiate, and expand the lines of investigation for each item. We will explain how to complete these activities in the sections that follow.

Step 3: Formulating Questions about Basic Abilities

To establish a clear focus on the issues you want to investigate, it is helpful to prepare a list of *questions* directed toward discovering the students' true abilities—a set of questions for each basic ability you have identified.

Defining questions and adding them to the worksheet will help you tailor the assessment more closely to the particular concerns you may have about the students you are assessing, and will help you to expand or broaden the scope of your probe into the students' raw abilities. The following guidelines and examples will assist you in developing helpful, detailed questions about each of the basic abilities you have designated for assessment.

Ask questions that give a focus and structure to the assessment. The questions you formulate should further define each basic ability area and pinpoint the concerns you want to address. In preparing Sandy's assessment, Mrs. Armstrong will pose questions that guide the focus of her observations in each area of Sandy's behavior. For instance, under the item "Is able to respond to verbal and facial cues," Mrs. Armstrong may enter the following:

- Is Sandy able to recognize pauses in a conversation?
- Can she judge whether a person is pleased or displeased with someone's comment?
- Can she recognize verbal and facial cues when she is in a conversation?
- Can she recognize these cues if she is *not* in the conversation?

These samples show that formulating questions to ask about basic abilities is essentially a brainstorming activity. This is a good place to make guesses, to try out theories, and to think about various possibilities that will help you determine whether students have a particular basic ability. The questions Mrs. Armstrong lists will help her look at each ability area from different angles and get a detailed view in each case of Sandy's proficiencies and limitations.

Some of Mrs. Armstrong's questions for Alfred provide another example of behavioral areas she might want to look at. For the item "Is able to follow the offensive play and defensive play of football games," she may list the following:

- Is Alfred able to explain the rules for particular plays during a game?
- Can he describe and comment on the progress of a football game he is playing?
- Can he describe and comment on a game if he is *not* playing?
- Can he follow the action of other kinds of games (e.g., baseball, basketball)?

Questions like these will give both a focus and a structure to Mrs. Armstrong's assessment and allow her to investigate very specific areas of behavior.

Ask questions that expand the scope of the assessment. Your questions should be exploratory in nature, extending beyond simply finding out whether students are able to perform a distinct skill. Mrs. Armstrong's questions for Sandy and Alfred not only define each basic ability further, but they also broaden the scope of the assessment somewhat by looking at whether the students' abilities are hampered or affected by the circumstances and the people around them. Rather than limiting her investigation to Alfred's ability to follow a football game on the playground, Mrs. Armstrong is interested in discovering whether he can explain the rules for other types of games, like baseball or basketball, or if he is able to follow a game's action under various circumstances, such as when he is a participant, a spectator, or a game official. Your questions can lead you to consider how the students might perform in new, atypical, or idealized situations, helping you learn what they are really capable of doing. Because you are asking questions about what students are *able* to do, rather than what they actually *do*, you need not limit your investigation to behavior displayed under typical or natural conditions.

In fact, probing the range of students' abilities under a variety of circumstances can often be the most important facet of an assessment of basic abilities. Students' full abilities are often masked by the typical context for social interactions—the participants involved, the physical surroundings, and the incentives and disincentives for using skills. If she looks at Alfred's behavior in a variety of sports activities, Mrs. Armstrong may find that he is able to follow the plays in baseball and basketball games because he is especially interested in these sports at the professional level. She may conclude that he has these basic abilities but that he does not apply them to the football games that classmates play during recess. Based on these findings, Mrs. Armstrong could develop an intervention that teaches Alfred to generalize his skills to other games in playground situations or to choose playmates who have the same interests as his.

Similarly, Mrs. Armstrong may expand the scope of Sandy's assessment to see whether she is able to follow conversational cues under a variety of conditions. Mrs. Armstrong may find that Sandy can recognize pauses and breaks in conversations in which she is not involved, but that she cannot identify them when she is engaged directly in the conversations. As a consequence, she may get flustered and act shy because she does not know when to speak. In this case, Mrs. Armstrong would conclude that Sandy does have the ability to recognize the cues, and she would plan her intervention accordingly.

Add questions to the worksheet. Figure 6.2 shows the questions Mrs. Armstrong prepared for Granville's worksheet. Note that she listed questions on a separate page for each of the four basic abilities she is assessing. For example, for the ability "Is able to understand the content of the activities," Mrs. Armstrong listed the following questions:

- Is Granville able to understand the background of the assigned material?
- Can he identify the point or purpose of the activity?
- Can he remember the information he learns?
- Is he able to apply his knowledge in different ways?

You can see from these questions that Mrs. Armstrong has major concerns about Granville's background knowledge in some important areas, such as how well he understands the assigned material, and how much he knows about the particular outcomes she sets for the activities. She also wants to look at some key enabling skills, such as whether he is able to apply his knowledge to different types of activities or different instructional formats. Notice that in this last area, Mrs. Armstrong plans to expand the scope of Granville's assessment to look at how well he uses his knowledge in activities other than small group lessons, such as on workbook assignments or in one-on-one situations with a teacher or another student. On subsequent pages of the worksheet, Mrs. Armstrong entered the other basic abilities she is assessing and listed questions reflecting her major concerns in these areas. The issues she is addressing on these worksheets will give her some very specific areas of investigation.

In summary, defining specific questions to explore about the students' basic abilities will help to give your assessment a clear focus and can expand the scope of investigation to probe more deeply into what each student is able to do. In the next section, we discuss how to identify assessment procedures that will help you to examine these questions in detail.

Step 4: Planning and Scheduling Assessment Procedures

The task in assessing basic abilities is to learn what students are really capable of doing, even if you have to alter the natural performance conditions to get them to show their true abilities. It follows, then, that the procedures you use to assess each basic ability can differ significantly from the procedures in a survey level assessment. With an assessment of basic abilities, you will likely use more individually planned activities, such as having students

- respond to videotaped examples of interactions
- perform specifically designed tasks
- display their behavior under one-on-one, contrived conditions
- engage in role playing and simulation

You could even let the students help you conduct the assessment by holding interviews or discussions with them, or asking them to plan special, high-interest activities.

There are several reasons for using such direct and sometimes obtrusive procedures for this assessment. One is that the procedures you use will be directed specifically at the questions you list for each ability area, so they will usually need to be very precise and tightly focused. At the same time, you need not be too concerned with how consistent the procedures are with the natural performance conditions for the target skill, because you are exploring different possibilities and performance options rather than looking at typical or natural performance. For the same reason, you need not worry about the effects your actions have on the students' behavior, as long as the students show their actual abilities. In fact, there may be times during the assessment when you deliberately use obtrusive, or even intrusive, procedures as a way of motivating students to try their best. You can sometimes tell a great deal about the students' basic abilities and talents by being actively involved in or exerting control over a task or social interaction.

Your intent in making these types of changes from the natural performance circumstances will be (a) to single out the basic abilities from the other behavioral requirements for meeting the expectations and (b) to give students alternative ways to show their abilities. We discuss these goals for assessment procedures in the next sections.

Single out basic abilities from other aspects of performance. This is a major function of the assessment and explains why an assessment of basic abilities is the one time that natural conditions are not a necessary element of the examination procedures. In fact, when you are assessing basic abilities, it is usually *helpful* to vary the circumstances of assessment, changing conditions to factor out other circumstances and areas of behavior in order to get a better view of the students' raw abilities (Howell, Fox, & Morehead, 1993). Students' basic abilities are sometimes masked by their response to what is going on around them. By changing the context of their interactions, you are better able to determine whether their problems are rooted in basic skill deficits or related to other factors, such as to the conditions of the setting or to motivational factors. This out-of-context look at an ability area can be used to heighten the students' attention to one particular aspect of performance, or to make it easier for them to show what they are truly capable of doing. As a result, you obtain a view of their full potential because they can show you what they are capable of doing under the ideal conditions.

Conducting assessment under a variety of conditions will probe the extent of the students' abilities.

To learn whether Sandy is able to recognize cues in conversations, Mrs. Armstrong could videotape a typical conversation between fifth-grade students, show the tape to Sandy, and ask her to identify pauses, prompts, and visual cues. This procedure is precisely geared to answer a specific question about Sandy's abilities and is both more detailed and more focused than any procedures Mrs. Armstrong used earlier in her survey level assessment. More important, this procedure departs significantly from looking at Sandy's behavior under the natural circumstances of the setting, focusing instead on a single aspect of Sandy's raw ability—in this case, the ability to recognize cues. Having Sandy watch a videotape enables Mrs. Armstrong to isolate the important cues for holding conversations and to separate this part of an interaction from the other situational variables that may adversely affect Sandy's behavior. This approach makes it easier for Sandy to display her abilities because she does not have to respond to the many aspects of performance that characterize the natural circumstance. From such an activity, Mrs. Armstrong might discover that Sandy actually does understand conversational cues, but that she normally does not pay close attention to them in actual conversations because she is overly concerned about her personal appearance or language usage. In this way, you can often learn important information about students' abilities by altering performance conditions to isolate particular basic abilities from the distractions and pressures of the natural setting.

Give students alternative ways to show basic abilities. When you plan an assessment, providing alternative ways for students to display their abilities can help you obtain clear and precise answers to the questions you are asking. The example of showing Sandy a videotape of two people having a conversation is one approach Mrs. Armstrong can use to assess Sandy's knowledge of conversational cues. This procedure gives Sandy an opportunity to demonstrate her knowledge and abilities without having to deal with the normal concerns and stresses of typical social interactions. But Mrs. Armstrong should add other procedures as well, to give Sandy the broadest circumstances possible for displaying her entire range of abilities in this area. She could also ask Sandy to watch some of the conversations fifth graders have during transition between lessons and explain what she knows about cues. Mrs. Armstrong could mimic or act out some of the cues herself and ask Sandy to identify the ones she sees. Procedures like these would give Sandy several ways to demonstrate her ability to read cues and thus would help Mrs. Armstrong ensure that she is fully probing the extent of Sandy's capabilities.

Similarly, when assessing Alfred's ability to follow the action of games, Mrs. Armstrong will use a variety of formats. She may, for example, do one or more of the following:

- Pull Alfred out a game he is playing and ask him specific questions about what is going on, or why players did certain things
- Have him look on from the sidelines and comment on a game that is going on
- Have him watch a video of a professional game and explain the action on the screen

- Have him demonstrate particular plays and rules on a board game or on the blackboard

By giving Alfred various ways to show his understanding of game rules, Mrs. Armstrong may discover that he knows much more about game playing than his behavior otherwise indicates. Note that these procedures roughly follow the list of questions Mrs. Armstrong outlined for this basic ability for Alfred. A distinct advantage of having listed a broad range of questions is that they can help you develop a solid variety of procedures for probing the full extent of student capabilities.

Sometimes you may find it useful to give students extra incentives to use their skills to see what role motivation plays in their behavior. Mrs. Armstrong could offer Granville extra privileges or rewards to increase his interest in working with classmates or his motivation to complete the small group projects. With this increased incentive, Granville may give his full attention to demonstrating whether he has the skills needed to earn the reward rather than acting disruptive and combative. Note that none of these procedures will give an accurate picture of the students' normal or typical behavior pattern, but they will yield valuable information about what the students are able to do under ideal conditions. This is the real value of a basic abilities assessment.

Figure 6.2 shows the procedures Mrs. Armstrong has planned for assessing Granville's basic abilities. She will start assessing his understanding of the content of social studies lessons by giving him a written test, and will follow the test with a brief one-on-one discussion of the items to probe his knowledge even further. On the second day, she plans to give him an oral quiz. With these procedures, she hopes to learn whether he is able to demonstrate sufficient knowledge of social studies concepts to complete the small group projects she assigns, and whether he is able to apply this knowledge in the context of different instructional activities. To assess his understanding of directions, she plans to use both oral and written formats and to compare his performance across various types of academic and nonacademic tasks. She would like to see whether Granville responds better to one mode of presentation or type of direction than another, and whether his motivation in completing assignments (high-interest tasks versus low-interest tasks) is a major factor in whether he follows directions. These procedures will allow Mrs. Armstrong to single out each of the basic abilities from the other performance requirements and to give Granville alternative ways to display his abilities. Once you have planned procedures, you will be ready to begin the basic abilities assessment. In the next sections, we discuss guidelines for conducting the assessment activities and for summarizing and interpreting results.

❍ Conducting a Basic Abilities Assessment

When you conduct an assessment of basic abilities, you do not have to be overly concerned with following the strict guidelines described in Chapter Four, because this activity is quite different from a survey level assessment. In many ways, you can be more exploratory and flexible with the procedures you use because the assessment does not have to be tied closely to the natural performance conditions.

Also, you do not have to worry about being unobtrusive or consistent. The accuracy of the results will not be adversely affected if you introduce new ideas or procedures while conducting the assessment, or if you make changes in the activities as you go along.

When Mrs. Armstrong conducts her basic abilities assessment of Sandy, she can use several approaches to determine whether Sandy is able to select age-appropriate topics for conversations, respond to facial expressions, and use the other fundamental skills being measured. Mrs. Armstrong's original plan is to show Sandy a videotape of conversations and have her comment on particular aspects of the presentations. But afterward, if Mrs. Armstrong is still unsure about Sandy's full abilities because Sandy is uncomfortable working in a one-on-one situation like this, she could follow this procedure by having a couple of students, including Sandy, watch the videotape and hold a small group discussion. Mrs. Armstrong could even show the tape to the entire class and give a paper-and-pencil quiz on various aspects of having conversations, or she could structure a role-playing activity. With all these procedures, Mrs. Armstrong's intention would be essentially the same: to learn what Sandy's true abilities are in the areas under study. Similarly with Granville, if Mrs. Armstrong finds that a written quiz or follow-up discussion does not give her a good indication of his ability, she could try other possibilities. For instance, she could assess his knowledge by having a highly respected student give Granville the quiz orally, or she could ask the questions in a game show format that takes advantage of his interest in participating in competitive activities.

As the above examples show, conducting an assessment of basic abilities is likely to be far more exploratory and unstructured than activities you have done before, because the object is to probe the students' proficiency in selected areas rather than to measure their behavior under natural conditions. Therefore, you should feel free to adapt procedures to supplement your information as much as possible so you can discover what the students can do if given the opportunity. But, as with any assessment, you should come away from the activities with concrete and complete information about the students' abilities. Remember that the changes you make in schedules, activities, grouping arrangements, or other aspects of the setting should be done with the purpose of determining whether there is a difference between what students are capable of doing and what they actually do under typical performance conditions. This new information about the students' ability level, contrasted with what you already know about their usual performance pattern, provides the basis for planning an intervention.

After conducting an assessment of basic abilities, you should summarize the results in a way that establishes a focused aim for an intervention. We discuss how to record and interpret results from this assessment in the next section.

Summarizing the Results of a Basic Abilities Assessment

Just as the procedures themselves are more flexible in an assessment of basic abilities, so is the way you record results. It is less crucial to collect numbers or tallies than to arrive at conclusions about how well the students are able to perform the basic skills, because you are looking at abilities rather than measuring performance levels. When Mrs. Armstrong assesses Sandy's ability to judge a person's reaction to a comment she is less concerned with obtaining an accurate count of Sandy's normal behavior than with probing Sandy's ability to make the judgment under some circumstance. Of course, to make this determination, Mrs. Armstrong may decide to count the number of accurate judgments Sandy makes while watching the videotape samples, or to keep a tally of things Sandy fails to see. But she could summarize her findings in other ways as well, such as by entering notes on a log sheet. Regardless of the type of recordings she makes, Mrs. Armstrong needs to determine whether Sandy can judge a person's response to a comment.

Entering Assessment Results on the Worksheet

For the reasons given above, you can use a fairly flexible format for entering the assessment results on the worksheet. As Figure 6.2 shows, the page for each basic ability includes a Results section that is divided into separate days so you can record your observations for each day. For example, one basic ability Mrs. Armstrong assessed with Granville was, "Is able to understand the content of the activities." To check his background knowledge, she gave him a written quiz one day and asked him some questions orally the next. Thus for Day 1, she entered the score for Granville's written test, and for Day 2, she entered comments about his oral interview. Her results in assessing his understanding of directions describe the various problems Granville had both in understanding the directions and remembering them later.

Your recording format, then, should be flexible and versatile enough to accommodate any type of results you are likely to obtain. This type of format allows you to note *any* kind of results, not just the ones you had planned for. Such flexibility is particularly helpful when assessing basic abilities: because of the variety of procedures you can use and the probing nature of the inquiry, basic abilities assessments are likely to spot unexpected problems, talents, and characteristics in students. During her assessment, Mrs. Armstrong may find that Sandy can very accurately interpret the conversational patterns other students use, but cannot replicate these patterns in her own speaking. Or she may discover that Granville has a particular fear of being wrong in front of his peers. Or that Alfred acts immature in playground groups primarily when a particular girl he likes is present. These kinds of observations may not be planned, but by following a fairly loose recording format, Mrs. Armstrong can enter them along with the results of the tests or interviews she conducts each day.

Recording Comments and Conclusions

When you finish assessing each basic ability, you should summarize the observations and conclusions you draw for each one. This procedure allows you to interpret any numbers or other measures you have obtained as well as to clarify and review what you have learned about the students' overall ability in each specific area. In summarizing her assessment of Granville's ability to understand the content of small group projects, Mrs. Armstrong described in the Conclusions/ comments space on the worksheet her judgments and observations about this item. She stated that while his test and oral quiz scores show that Granville knows enough to take an active part in the activities, his level of understanding is not broad enough to meet his own personal goal of being the smartest person in his group. As a result, he shows his frustration at feeling ignorant in front of his classmates by acting overly critical of their work. This valuable information is drawn not so much from the numbers Mrs. Armstrong collected as from her asking Granville about his reluctance to share in the activity with his group.

Discovering new or unexpected knowledge about students' behavior is a fairly typical outcome of a basic abilities assessment. You often uncover information that may be unrelated to the abilities you are looking at but that is nonetheless crucial for understanding why students do not meet expectations and for planning interventions. For example, by having Sandy watch videotaped conversations and discuss them in a small group activity, Mrs. Armstrong may discover that Sandy can, in fact, spot verbal and physical cues. But she may also find that Sandy is very sensitive to criticism and has to be very confident in the accuracy of what she says before she expresses her ideas in a group situation. Mrs. Armstrong should include this information in the Conclusions/comments section, as it gives her helpful directions for planning an intervention.

Setting the Directions for Interventions

When you have finished conducting the assessment and have recorded the results for each basic ability, summarize your overall findings on a separate page of the worksheet. To make the findings as practical and useful as possible, you should express them in terms of specific instructional goals you could plan to focus on with an intervention. In reviewing her assessment results and comments for Alfred, Mrs. Armstrong may have identified three areas to work on with an intervention:

- Learn the fundamental rules for playing games on the playground
- Learn to coordinate his behavior with the actions of his teammates
- Learn to interact with girls he has a crush on

The last page of Figure 6.2 shows the findings Mrs. Armstrong recorded for Granville's assessment. She listed the following instructional goals as a tentative focus for his intervention:

- *Learn more effective skills for following directions.* Mrs. Armstrong noted that Granville has difficulty remembering directions with multiple steps. She thinks he may need to write down directions as teachers give them so he can refer to his notes later as he completes the work.
- *Learn how to break down tasks and carry out subtasks.* Mrs. Armstrong concluded that in writing down directions, Granville must learn to identify the individual steps or subtasks for completing assignments.

- *Learn to coordinate and share tasks with others.* Mrs. Armstrong felt that this skill may possibly improve as Granville learns items 1 and 2. If not, the group leaders could be instructed to be more explicit about the responsibilities they delegate to the other group members. Perhaps, if Granville assumes the role of group leader, he may see the importance of this skill.

Later, Mrs. Armstrong will be able to refer to this list of instructional goals when she develops a comprehensive intervention plan. In Chapter Nine, we explain how she can refine and consolidate these preliminary goals to form the basis for an effective and tightly targeted intervention. But before we arrive at that point, we first discuss two other parallel stages of specific level assessment: assessing component steps and assessing performance conditions.

Summary

The Need for Specific Level Assessment

1. Specific level assessment pinpoints the reasons students are having difficulty performing a target skill.
2. Without a specific level assessment, it is difficult for a teacher to determine what potential sources or causes for problems should be addressed in an intervention.

An Overview of a Basic Abilities Assessment

1. Basic abilities are the background knowledge and fundamental behaviors for performing more advanced skills.
2. An assessment of basic abilities shows whether an intervention should be directed toward a target skill or toward basic abilities for the target skill.
3. An assessment of basic abilities will help to identify two types of problems:
   a. whether students have sufficient background knowledge for the target skill
   b. whether they have the enabling skills for performing the target skills
4. Background knowledge is the essential information that is needed to perform a target skill.
5. Enabling skills allow students to use their skills effectively to meet social expectations.

Preparing an Assessment of Basic Abilities

1. To help you plan and organize the assessment activities and keep track of the assessment results, it is helpful to prepare an assessment worksheet.

2. Planning an assessment of basic abilities involves the following steps:
   a. listing information about the student and target skill
   b. listing the basic abilities to be assessed
   c. formulating questions to assess for each basic ability
   d. planning procedures for assessing the questions
3. When defining and listing basic abilities to assess, you should follow these guidelines:
   a. The list of basic abilities should be individualized, and should be geared to the students' overall learning and performance characteristics.
   b. Basic abilities should be limited to those for which there are major concerns or questions.
4. The following guidelines apply to formulating questions about basic abilities:
   a. The assessment questions should define each basic ability and pinpoint areas of concern to assess.
   b. The questions should give a focus and structure to the assessment activities.
   c. The questions should expand the scope of assessment to inquire broadly into students' capabilities.
5. The procedures for assessing basic abilities should follow these guidelines:
   a. The procedures should involve altering natural performance conditions in order to learn what students are capable of doing.
   b. Procedures should single out or isolate basic abilities from other behavioral requirements.
   c. Procedures should give students alternative ways to demonstrate their abilities.

Conducting an Assessment of Basic Abilities

1. An assessment of basic abilities can vary from the guidelines for a survey level assessment.
2. Procedures can change during the course of the assessment to investigate different issues and hypotheses about the students' performance.

Summarizing the Results of an Assessment

1. Recording formats can be flexible but should be geared to the assessment procedures.
2. Results for each basic ability should be summarized in terms of comments and conclusions about the students' ability in the specific area.
3. Overall findings should be summarized in terms of specific directions or instructional goals for the students' intervention.

Examples for Chapter Six

Example 6a

Mrs. Garrison is a physical education teacher at the elementary level. Her third-grade student is very competitive and aggressive when playing ball during recess, and the target skill she has set for him is "shares play with teammates."

For this skill she identified the following basic abilities:

Is able to follow the actions of teammates.
Is able to accept suggestions and feedback from teammates.
Is able to control level of physical behavior.
Is able to formulate positive comments and praise.

This page from the basic abilities assessment shows that Butch has difficulty recognizing and controlling the force of his physical play. One of the findings Mrs. Garrison derived from this assessment was "Learn to recognize and control physical play."

Basic abilities can involve physical or motor skills.

Procedures should explore different ways in which students can show their abilities.

Results should indicate the circumstances under which students perform more and less effectively.

Students may be unwilling to take part in some assessment activities; this is one reason it is important to give them a variety of opportunities to show their abilities.

Worksheet 6.1 (continued) — Name: *Mrs. Garrison* — Page *4* of *7*

Basic ability: *(3) Is able to to control his level of physical behavior*

Questions to answer about basic ability:

Is Butch able to limit his physical activity? Can he recognize when his play is becoming too rough or aggressive? Can he recognize rough play in other students? Can he stop his physical contact in play situations?

Procedures for answering questions:

• Videotape Butch during team play. Ask him to comment on his own physical behavior and that of others. • Role-play a situation involving physical play. Have Butch and others demonstrate too much contact, just enough, and none at all. • Work one-on-one with Butch to check how well he can execute specific moves and plays. • Have older students work with Butch to see if he can play more appropriately with bigger kids.

Personnel/equipment needed:

Video, activity plan, older students

Day	Results:
1	*Worked alone with Butch, then with small group of boys. He had trouble making subtle moves (running in slow motion, taking baby jumps) but did fine at learning set plays in basketball. He executed the plays well in a practice situation, but went back to hogging the ball and playing roughly in an actual game.*
2	
3	*Showed Butch a video of his play group. He could recognize when other students were pushing or hitting, but got defensive when I showed him examples of his own rough play. He made excuses ("Griffen pushed me first") or said his play was acceptable ("that's how they play in the NBA").*
4	*Did a role play in gym class about playing with good sportsmanship. Butch and others were to demonstrate different levels of physical play, with Butch showing "just right." Butch was reluctant to take part in the role play, and made funny faces to classmates when it was his turn. He told me later he thought it was "dumb."*
5	*Butch and some of his group played with older students today. Butch was much less aggressive with the big kids, but he enjoyed the game a lot. One of the students coached Butch a lot, and he seemed to enjoy the attention. His movements were still fairly rough, but he didn't push as much and shared the ball more.*

Conclusions/comments:

Butch has trouble recognizing the level of his physical play, but he can perform reasonably well under controlled conditions (running practice plays, playing with bigger students). In a regular play situation with children his own age, he has difficulty noticing and controlling his behavior, and is resistant to efforts to teach him to moderate his level of play.

Example 6b

Mr. Eckstein is a high school guidance counselor. He has been working with Miranda, a ninth grader who monopolizes conversations, talking at length on subjects that other students are not interested in. The target skill Mr. Eckstein has chosen is "shares in conversations equally with peers."

Mr. Eckstein's assessment investigated the following basic abilities:

Is able to follow the flow of conversations.
Is able to judge and moderate her tone of voice.
Is able to match conversation topics to different groups.

In this page of his worksheet, Mr. Eckstein focuses on Miranda's ability to follow the flow of a conversation. The results showed that she does have this ability, but does not apply it in actual conversations. Therefore, Mr. Eckstein added the following item to his findings: "Learn to pay attention to the reactions of other group members."

Basic abilities can involve cognitive skills.

Assessment procedures should isolate the specific ability being assessed from other performance requirements.

Improvisation is possible in a basic abilities assessment. Mr. Eckstein added this procedure on Day 4 because he felt it would give him some further insights into Miranda's ability.

Basic abilities assessments often show that students have fairly extensive abilities, but have difficulty drawing on them in typical social situations.

Worksheet 6.1 (continued) Name: *Mr. Eckstein* Page *2* of *6*

Basic ability: *(1) Is able to follow the flow of a conversation*

Questions to answer about basic ability:

Can Miranda indicate the point at which a topic changes in a conversation? Can she specify the topics that were discussed? Can she describe the topic that might be discussed next? Can she recognize reactions and nonverbal cues from others in the conversations?

Procedures for answering questions:

- *After Miranda finishes a conversation, ask her to review the topics that were discussed, and to describe the reactions of the group. Try this with different group sizes and compositions.*
- *Show Miranda a videotaped conversation. Ask her to indicate when the topic changes, and to guess what the next topic discussed might be. Also ask her to interpret the nonverbal reactions of participants.*

Personnel/equipment needed:

Video, conversation groups

Day	Results:
1	*Talked to Miranda after lunch. She was able to name some of the general topics discussed, but had a harder time saying what the different group members had to say about the topics, and could not recall how the conversation had moved from one topic to the next.*
2	
3	*Showed Miranda a videotaped conversation. She could follow the conversation, and was pretty good at predicting where the conversation would go next. She was less skillful at picking out the attitudes of the various participants, but when we went back and reviewed the tape she could interpret the facial expressions fairly well.*
4	*I asked Miranda to sit in a conversation group without talking, and report on her observations. She seemed to enjoy the challenge, and gave a good accounting of the topic and the attitudes of the different students in the group. She was able to describe both verbal and nonverbal responses that she saw.*
5	

Conclusions/comments:

Miranda is able to follow a conversation quite well if she is able to turn her attention to the other group members. Once she is not trying to talk herself, she is able to come up with some solid insights into the attitudes and ideas of her classmates.

Mr. Wagner's Case Study

Mr. Wagner's Basic Abilities Assessment

Mr. Wagner came up with the following basic abilities to investigate for Granville:

Brings proper materials to group.
Reads the assignments.
Understands that his behavior makes classmates angry.
Realizes that he should ask for help when he needs it.

Note that Mr. Wagner focused on Granville's habitual behavior and his level of self-awareness, rather than on his abilities. The list should have been expressed in terms of what Granville is able to do.

A page from Mr. Wagner's assessment is presented below. From the results on this page he drew this finding: "Learn that he should behave toward others as he wants them to behave toward him." Although this goal is admirable, it will be hard to address with a specific instructional intervention, as it is described in terms of broad values rather than precise behavioral objectives.

Avoid focusing the assessment on students' attitudes or values. Concentrate on their actual abilities.

These questions tend more toward preaching at Granville than toward investigating his behavior.

Assessing students under natural circumstances usually adds little new information about their abilities. It is important to vary assessment conditions as much as possible.

Talking with students can sometimes be helpful, but they may often be unable to understand or explain their own behavior and abilities.

This entry indicates the procedure, but fails to include the results.

Mr. Wagner's conclusions are premature, as he has not really explored the limits of Granville's ability. His comments also include statements that are not relevant to this particular ability.

Worksheet 6.1 (continued) | Name: *Mr. Wagner* | Page *4* of *6*

Basic ability: *(3) Understands that his behavior makes classmates angry*

Questions to answer about basic ability:

Can Granville explain why he does the things he does? Can he understand how other people feel about his behavior? Can he recognize other alternatives? Does he think before he acts?

Procedures for answering questions:

- *Watch Granville's behavior during group work. Note any arguments and disagreements, and see how Granville handles them.*
- *Afterward, talk to Granville about the group and ask him how he thinks the other students are reacting. Ask him whether he could think of other ways to handle the situation.*

Personnel/equipment needed:

Day	Results:
1	*Granville got in a dispute with the other group members during a science experiment. I asked him later how he thinks the students felt about that. He got defensive and couldn't really say.*
2	*Granville was a bit better today during group work. I asked him how he felt about getting along with the group, and he said he liked it.*
3	*Talked with Granville about alternatives to arguing in settling disagreements. He said that only "sissies" ask teachers for help. I asked him why he got in so many arguments, but his only answer was "I dunno."*
4	
5	*Had a discussion with Granville after class about "thinking before acting." Asked Granville if he thought about what might happen to him when he starts fighting with classmates on the playground, and told him some better ways he could resolve his disputes.*

Conclusions/comments:

Granville does not seem to have this ability because he cannot understand that his own behavior is what makes the other children avoid him or tease him. A lot of his arguments in class take place because he isn't paying attention and doesn't know what the assignment is. He tries to lok at other students' work or copy their answers, and they get angry with him.

CHAPTER 7

Conducting a Specific Level Assessment
Part II: Assessing Component Steps

In Chapter Six we explained that you can gain important information about why students do not meet expectations by assessing their basic abilities. But lacking basic abilities is only one of the reasons students may have problems in their social behavior. In order to meet expectations, students must also *use* their skills properly by forming behavioral patterns that match the demands of social interactions. In this chapter we present a second, parallel approach to a specific level assessment; it involves looking at the way students link skills together into behavioral patterns. We explain how to analyze the component steps that make up behavioral patterns, and show how to conduct an assessment of these steps and interpret the results.

Overview of a Component Steps Assessment

The target skills you select as priorities for an intervention are actually composed of many skills and actions. Students link these various skills together to form more complicated behavioral patterns (Campbell & Siperstein, 1994; Cartledge & Milburn, 1986). Thus, social skills such as holding a conversation, playing a sports activity, giving a class recitation, and participating in a small group discussion involve a variety of other more fundamental skills that students combine into the behavioral patterns that characterize their interactions. We use the term *behavioral pattern* to refer to the integrated series of actions that students use to meet the requirements of an expectation, and the term *component steps* to refer to the individual actions that make up a behavioral pattern. Component steps are the specific actions, subtasks, or behaviors that students link together to form a more complicated social skill (Howell & Morehead, 1987; Kerr & Nelson, 1989).

You will find that students who have difficulty with a target skill may have problems performing some of the component steps properly even though they have all the basic abilities needed to meet the expectation. In some cases, they may

A component steps assessment examines how well students combine steps into behavioral patterns.

have difficulty with one or more component steps; in other cases, they may know all the component steps but be unable to combine them in a way that meets the requirements of the interaction. In a specific level assessment of component steps, you analyze the sequence of steps involved in using a target skill. Then you use the analysis to determine (a) whether students perform each individual component step, and (b) whether they link all the steps together into the required behavioral pattern. You can use the results of the assessment to design an intervention that will teach students to perform specific component steps and to join them together with the other steps they already know.

Although our discussion of component steps at times seems to parallel the discussion of basic abilities, there are significant differences between the two concepts in assessment. We explained in Chapter Six that an assessment of basic abilities focuses on what students *are able to do;* you examine each ability area to learn whether the students can show proficiency in performing the required fundamental skill. Now we are shifting our focus to address questions of what the students actually *do.* In an assessment of component steps, you look at the students' actual performance of the behavioral patterns they use to meet expectations.

Mrs. Armstrong may find in her basic abilities assessment that Sandy does have sufficient knowledge of age-appropriate topics, but these results would not necessarily mean that Sandy uses this ability when she needs to. She may choose more immature or mundane subjects to talk about when she is in actual conversations with her peers, even though she has the basic ability to speak on age-appropriate subjects. Thus, Sandy may have problems in her conversations because she does not use her skill of selecting topics. Similarly, Mrs. Armstrong may find that Alfred knows the rules for playing games during recess. However, he may still have difficulty meeting the expectation because he does not apply his knowledge of rules in game-playing situations. In cases like these where students have the ability to meet expectations but still have problems with their behavior, you should shift your attention to determining whether they *use* their skills properly by forming behavioral patterns that meet the expectations.

❍ Importance of Behavioral Patterns and Component Steps in Achieving Social Competence

All social skills are made up of component steps and behavioral patterns, even though we do not usually think of them in this way. The dynamics of behavioral patterns, and the steps that form these patterns, can be quite complicated, especially in the area of social behavior. This idea has a parallel in academic areas: we often think of academic skills in terms of their component steps, and we often use instructional materials and teaching methods that highlight the major steps for mastering these skills. For example, we may use worksheets or prepare outlines that show the component steps for skills like computing long division problems, doing a science experiment, or completing a book report. On the other hand, we rarely consider social skills in terms of the individual steps students must go through to show competent social behavior. Therefore, before we explain how to design and conduct an assessment of component steps, we describe in detail what component steps are and discuss several ways they relate to achieving social competence.

Building More Complex Social Skills

In the previous chapter, we described basic abilities as the "raw materials" for meeting an expectation. In a similar way, component steps can be described as the "building blocks" for the complex behavioral patterns students use in their social interactions. Component steps function like the individual bricks in a masonry wall or the sections of fabric in a quilt—and just as with masonry walls and quilts, the behavioral patterns these steps form are often much more complex than they seem at first. The component parts (social skills, bricks, or pieces of fabric) join with one another to make a highly complicated and intricate structure that has many uses and functions beyond those of the individual elements. We can put the component parts together in many different ways or combine them with other parts to form a wide variety of highly distinctive patterns, depending on the demands of the situation or on our preferences. Often we do not realize how complex and elaborate many social skills are until we look closely at the behavioral patterns students use.

Consider the component steps involved when a student talks with a friend during lunchtime. At first glance, this social exchange may seem fairly simple and straightforward—just two friends talking together while eating their lunch. But if you look more closely, you can see how complicated the skill is and how many component steps are required for a successful interaction. At the start of the conversation, the students choose just the right greeting to fit the occasion. Then one student decides on a topic for the conversation, anticipating what the other student's knowledge and interest in the topic will be. The second student joins the conversation, possibly feigning interest in the topic until they can move to another. As the interaction continues, the students direct the conversation to the areas that particularly interest them, each sensing when the other person is losing interest in one area so they can shift to another. They share each other's excitement and enthusiasm with smiles, gestures, and facial expressions, and they handle disagreements and sensitive areas with diplomacy, always keeping within the boundaries of the friendship. Throughout the conversation, they use speech and language patterns that are age appropriate, nonoffensive, and suitable for the situation. Finally, they end the conversation with a salutation that further solidifies their friendship. Thus, even fundamental social skills, like having a casual conversation with a friend, can involve many individual component steps.

Combining Steps to Form Behavioral Patterns

As this example shows, students typically combine individual components into smooth and well-integrated behavioral patterns that make the composite behavior look simple and natural (Cartledge & Milburn, 1986). The entire process usually takes a very short time and requires little effort. The students probably do not even think about the types of skills and actions they are displaying, but their performance requires a very skillful coordination of several factors. Each of the individual elements is well timed and sequenced so that one behavior flows smoothly into the next, and each behavior is aligned with the various phases of the overall interaction. The two students talking together move quickly and easily from greeting one another to selecting a mutually interesting conversational topic, and they make smooth transitions from one topic to another, with each anticipating the other's interests. Furthermore, if they meet another friend as they leave the cafeteria, the students may go through all these steps again, quickly changing their behavior and forming a completely different conversational pattern. Thus, socially competent students are able to link together individual behaviors and actions into increasingly complex and integrated behavioral patterns that fit the demands of an interaction.

Broadening the Scope of Social Interactions

Having a broad repertoire of social skills enables students to participate in many social interactions if they know how and when to use these skills. By combining and re-combining social skills to form behavioral patterns, students gain the abilities to engage in new, more diverse, and more sophisticated interactions; to sustain their interactions for increasingly longer periods of time; and to adapt and modify their behavior to an ever-widening range of performance conditions. The ability to combine component steps into behavioral patterns enables students to align their actions with tne ongoing activities of a social interaction and to pace and adjust their behavior as conditions in the situation dictate. They can use some elements during certain parts of an interaction, others during other parts of the interaction, and hold still others in reserve to be used only under certain special circumstances. For example, a very important aspect of having a conversation with friends is knowing how to handle disagreements and deal with sensitive issues, even though students may use this skill only on certain occasions (such as with only one or two of their more touchy friends). Similarly, during sports activities, knowing how to be a good loser or gracious winner and how to deal with cheating or rule violations are usually important skills to have in reserve. In short, students can achieve tremendous versatility and spontaneity in their interactions by having an array of social skills to draw on, and knowing how and when to use them in a behavioral pattern.

❍ Component Steps and Problems in Social Behavior

Being competent in school requires the ability to combine component steps into behavioral patterns. Invariably, some steps in a pattern are more difficult than others for students to use or link together. An assessment of component steps will help you check how well students use and combine individual social skills. The results you obtain from this type of assessment will help you identify two types of problems: (a) students' failure to perform some essential component step(s), or (b) their failure to integrate or combine the steps to fit the demands of the setting. We discuss each of these problems in the next sections.

Failure to Perform Essential Steps

Often, students who have difficulty with a target skill may be proficient at performing some of the component steps but not others (Cartledge & Milburn, 1986). This could be a problem for Alfred, who has difficulty playing games during recess, and for Granville, who has trouble working cooperatively with classmates. In both instances, the boys may begin the interactions in an acceptable manner but have difficulty bringing them to a successful conclusion. Alfred, for instance, may perform most of the component steps for playing recess games, such as joining the play group, cooperating with the group leader, and reacting appropriately to successes or disappointments. However, he may fail to perform other key steps, such as waiting his turn and paying attention to the action of the game. His lack of proficiency at these specific component steps can be the source of broader problems in his social interactions on the playground. Note that Alfred may very well have the *ability* to perform these steps. His basic abilities assessment may have indicated that he is able to follow the action of the game when he tries, and that he knows how to follow the rules. But he may not actually perform the steps when he should. By conducting an assessment of component steps, Mrs. Armstrong will be able to obtain a more accurate and detailed picture of such lapses in performance.

Similarly, Granville may have difficulty working with classmates because he does not respond well to peer comments and suggestions. Even though he may do well at some steps—finding his work group, following directions, planning and discussing the activity—he will not be successful in the overall activity unless he learns to react appropriately to feedback from his classmates. Students thus will not be competent in their social interactions unless they have learned how and when to use the component steps for meeting expectations. If they have difficulty with some of the important steps, they will not be successful in their interactions regardless of the other skills they exhibit.

Failure to Combine Steps into Behavioral Patterns

Mastering every component step for an interaction does not ensure competent performance. Students must also time and sequence the individual steps and link them all together into a well-organized behavioral pattern so their actions match the demands of the situation. Alfred may use the proper game skills, but he might try to act them out at the wrong times, such as when others are taking their turn, or when play has stopped. His ill-timed behavior may interrupt the natural flow of the games and cause students to avoid playing with him or to make fun of him. Similarly, Granville may do poorly on small group projects not because he lacks the individual skills for doing the work, but because he is unable to time or coordinate his actions with ongoing group activities. Perhaps his behavior does not follow the group's plans or does not correspond with what the group is doing at a particular time. In these examples, Alfred's and Granville's problems occur because they are unable to combine the component steps into an integrated behavioral pattern that fits the demands of the situation.

Thus, even if students perform the individual steps properly, they can experience problems when they fail to integrate component steps effectively into a smooth and coherent pattern of behavior. An assessment of component steps will allow you to examine how well students perform the individual elements involved in meeting a target skill, and also how well they combine these elements into a unified behavioral pattern. In the rest of the chapter, we discuss how to plan, conduct, and summarize such an assessment.

❍ Preparing a Component Steps Assessment

You should start an assessment of component steps by developing a worksheet to ensure that the activities are well planned and to help you keep an accurate record of your results. Table 7.1 illustrates the different steps for preparing an assessment worksheet. We will explain these steps in the sections that follow.

TABLE 7.1 Steps in planning a component steps assessment

Step 1:	List information about the student and the target skill
Step 2:	List the component steps for the target skill
Step 3:	Plan and schedule assessment procedures

Step 1: Listing Information about the Student and the Target Skill

To begin the assessment worksheet, enter the name and grade level of the student you plan to assess, the target skill being investigated, the setting or situation in which the assessment will take place, and any other important information that will help you recall the details of the assessment at some later date. Figure 7.1 shows the worksheet Mrs. Armstrong prepared for Granville. She entered essential information about the assessment at the top of the worksheet.

Step 2: Listing the Component Steps for the Target Skill

Next, you should write in the component steps for the target skill you plan to assess. The list of component steps should correspond to the sequence of actions or subtasks that students usually perform in meeting the social expectations. To make this list, you analyze or break down the target skill according to this sequence of actions; you can then assess the students on their performance of each individual step as well as on whether they link the steps properly. From this analysis and assessment, you can gain a clearer understanding of where in the sequence students have problems in their social behavior (Salvia & Hughes, 1990).

In preparing to assess Alfred's performance of component steps, Mrs. Armstrong developed the following list of steps that a student typically follows when playing organized games during recess:

- Shares in planning game before going outside
- Joins group with appropriate greeting
- Cooperates in choosing teams and deciding on game rules
- Follows directions of group leaders
- Pays attention to game
- Plays proper role in game (waits for turn, stays in position, etc.)
- Takes turn promptly and with proper actions
- Handles success/failure gracefully
- Stops playing when game is over
- Shares in group talk about game after recess

This sequence of steps that the fifth graders go through when they play organized games forms a list of the component actions or subtasks they need to perform the target skill. Although some of the steps listed above would not necessarily be classified as social skills, students still have to perform them properly, in the correct sequence, to be successful in playing organized games during recess.

This kind of analysis will allow you to focus the assessment on any number of problems students may have with the target skill. For example, Alfred may act awkward or clown around during organized games even though he has most of the basic abilities and skills he needs to play proficiently. Mrs. Armstrong could use the list of component steps to assess Alfred's behavior and learn more about

Figure 7.1 Mrs. Armstrong's component steps assessment worksheet for Granville.

Worksheet 7.1: Component Steps Assessment — Page 1 of 2

Name: *Mrs. Armstrong* Date: *Oct. 23*

Student: *Granville* Grade: *5*

Target skill: *Cooperates with other students in completing small group activities*

Procedures for assessing component steps:

Observe and videotape Granville's group during social studies activity, paying attention to Granville's work and level of cooperation. Discuss incidents afterward with Granville in as neutral terms as possible to determine his responses.

Component Steps:

Assessment Results: (enter "+" for successful performance, "o" for unsuccessful performance)

Component Steps	1st	2nd	3rd	4th	5th
1. Listens to or reads description of assignment	o	+	o	+	o
2. Assembles materials for project	+	o	+	+	+
3. Goes to the group assigned	+	o	+	+	+
4. Exchanges greetings with group members	+	o	o	+	o
5. Listens to and follows direction of group leader	o	o	o	+	o
6. Negotiates with group in delegating subtasks	o	o	o	o	o
7. Works on assigned subtasks	o	+	o	o	+
8. Seeks help from group members in completing subtasks	o	o	o	o	o
9. Assists other group members with their subtasks	o	o	o	+	+
10. Handles disagreements and feedback diplomatically	o	+	o	o	o
11. Participates in putting together final project	o	o	o	+	+
12. Returns to seat when activity ends	o	+	+	+	+

Figure 7.1 *(continued)*

Worksheet 7.1 (continued)	Name: *Mrs. Armstrong*	Page 2 of 2

Comments:

- *Granville was in a really bad mood on Day 3—he didn't cooperate with anyone all day.*
- *Granville's behavior really gets off track when it comes time to work and negotiate with group leaders and other group members.*
- *Granville tries to do his work before anyone has discussed it, and he ends up having to redo things or gets in arguments because he's not doing the right task.*

Findings—instructional goals for intervention:

Learn to work with group in planning

Learn to seek help from group members

Learn to coordinate actions with ongoing group activity

Learn to negotiate disagreements

why he acts this way. She will be able to see whether his ungainly or self-conscious behavior is related to a failure in any of the following:

- Cooperating in planning the game
- Listening and following the directions of the team leader
- Paying attention to the game activities
- Taking his turn or playing his proper role in the game
- Performing any other step or combination of steps for meeting the expectation

The worksheet in Figure 7.1 has spaces on the left side for entering the component steps, and shows the list Mrs. Armstrong made for Granville's target skill of cooperating with peers on small group projects. Notice that she sequenced her list in the order in which her students normally perform the skill. The following guidelines will help you analyze component steps.

Specify an activity in which the target skill is used. You should have a specific activity or type of interaction in mind when you analyze the component steps, so your list gives a clear description of the behavioral pattern students use. The activity or interaction you choose should be one that is typical for the students and the setting. If you try instead to develop a single generalized list for several types of activities, your list will not have a clear structure because it will have to account for variations in the steps students go through and in the ways they perform the steps. Such lists are very difficult to use to assess student behavior.

Mrs. Armstrong decided to use football games to provide the framework for listing component steps for playing organized games during recess. Football is a sports activity often played by fifth graders, and Alfred frequently participates in the games. She chose small group activities in which she has students produce a written report or project to give a framework for her analysis of cooperating with students in small groups. Mrs. Armstrong realized that developing a generalized list of component steps for recess games or for small group activities was impractical because she would have to account for too many variations in student behavior.

Identify the starting and ending points of the target skill. Knowing the boundaries of a social interaction is essential when you analyze a target skill, because you will need a complete list of steps to determine where problems in behavior occur. When Mrs. Armstrong first considers the component steps for Sandy's target skill of "converses with peers in informal groups," she may think in only general terms of the topics students talk about. She may at first regard this as a simple skill for fifth graders and assume that Sandy's problem is one of motivation: she simply chooses not to talk very much with classmates. But if she looks more systematically at the beginning and end of this behavioral pattern and considers the skill from the perspective of students, she will discover that holding a conversation includes many preliminary and finishing steps that she had not considered before. In holding an ordinary conversation, a student typically does the following:

- Chooses a person to talk with
- Selects a topic of mutual interest

- Initiates the conversation or joins an ongoing conversation
- Decides on language patterns and gestures to use
- Adds comments about the topic
- Converses on the topic at some length
- Changes the topic when interest or knowledge of the topic ends
- Finishes the conversation when interest in conversing ends or when it is time for another activity
- Ends the conversation with a salutation or appropriate gesture

Thus, in terms of what fifth-grade students actually must do, conversing with peers can be a complicated expectation to meet. Mrs. Armstrong can see from this more complete analysis the importance of finding the beginning and ending points of the interaction, because there are many areas before and after the main interaction takes place where a student like Sandy can get off track.

Note that the individual component steps need not take place at one time, nor be performed in the same location. When Mrs. Armstrong lists the component steps for Alfred's target skill, playing in organized sports, she realizes that the steps actually begin in the classroom while the students are lining up to go outside; during this time, they discuss game rules and begin to choose sides. Furthermore, the sequence ends back in the classroom when students file into the room, put the equipment away, and finish talking about the activities before the start of the next class period. Considering the start and finish of the behavioral pattern will help you spot variations in time and location like these that may be crucial to meeting social expectations.

List the steps in a roughly chronological order. Following the elements of the activity from start to finish is the most effective way to describe a series of component steps. But notice also in the largely chronological examples above, some items may not fit into a rigid order. Often you may find steps that students need to repeat during the interaction, steps that vary in their position in the sequence, or steps that must be performed and sustained throughout most of the interaction.

For instance, Sandy may have to give salutations at several points during the interaction if the group she is interacting with is large and transitory, and she may need to repeat the steps for selecting a language pattern, adding comments, and conversing on the topic every time the topic changes. Similarly, on Alfred's list, steps like paying attention to the game, playing the proper role, and taking turns promptly are not discrete actions that take place once during the activity, but rather they are ongoing behaviors that he must integrate into his performance throughout the game. Thus, while the component steps list should follow a reasonably chronological sequence, there will typically be elements in the list that are not strictly sequential. The rule of thumb in such cases is to stick as closely as possible to the general pattern students follow, but to include all the pertinent component steps even if some do not fit into a tidy progression.

Make sure your analysis of component steps is comprehensive. When you define component steps for assessment, realize that the steps themselves have substeps, and you may need to identify these as well. The amount of detail you use in your analysis should reflect the learning and performance characteristics of the students you are planning to assess. As with a basic abilities assessment, you should avoid breaking a target skill into too many simple steps, as this could make the assessment cumbersome and time-consuming. Rather, the analysis should reflect the areas of behavior that may be problems for the students you are concerned with, so that the results of the assessment are useful in planning interventions.

In listing steps for conversing with peers for Sandy's assessment, Mrs. Armstrong should consider that each of the component steps can be divided into parts. If she thinks Sandy may have difficulty performing a particular step in the interaction, such as "joins an ongoing conversation," she may want to break it down further into such subcomponents as these:

- Identifies the topic of conversation
- Selects a pertinent comment to add
- Decides what language pattern to use for making the comment
- Recognizes and waits for a pause in the conversation
- Interjects the comment into the conversation

Mrs. Armstrong can add these items to her list and use the new list of steps and substeps to conduct a comprehensive assessment of Sandy, identify the skills Sandy has for holding a conversation, and determine exactly where in the sequence Sandy experiences problems in her behavior.

To sum up, breaking down the target skill will help you identify the specific component steps you need to assess so you can find where problems in behavior occur. You analyze the component steps for target skills by listing the various actions students go through to complete an activity, task, or interaction. Be careful to note the beginning and ending points of the activity and follow the general chronological progression of the interaction so the analysis is complete and well organized. Finally, be sure your list includes the issues you wish to investigate for the particular student you will assess. After you have listed the component steps, you should enter the items on an assessment worksheet as shown in Figure 7.1. The next step is to choose procedures that will allow you to observe closely the students' performance of the steps you have listed.

Step 3: Planning and Scheduling the Assessment Procedures

The procedures you use for an assessment of component steps should allow you to accurately measure and judge the students' performance of each component of the target skill. Unlike an assessment of basic abilities, in which you examine what students *are able* to do under ideal conditions, a component skills assessment should let you record as accurately as possible the students' *usual* or *typical* performance. You should already know what the students *can* do; now you are investigating what they actually *do*.

Because of this focus on typical behavior, in this assessment you should stay as close as possible to the natural conditions of performance, for the reasons stated for the survey level assessment in Chapter Four. You conduct an assessment of component steps under the same conditions in which you originally assessed the expectations from the social skills curriculum, but now you will be looking more closely and systematically at the individual actions or steps students use to perform a specific target skill. You will need to observe whether the students are proficient in each of the actions, and whether they sequence and integrate their actions into a behavioral pattern that meets the requirements of the situation. To accomplish this, you can use any of the procedures you used for the survey level assessment in Chapter Four, including direct observation, videotaping, and outside observers as well as interviews, work samples, logs or journals, and other techniques for investigating and recording the students' typical behavior.

All the guidelines presented in Chapter Four for assessing the expectations in the social skills curriculum also apply to an assessment of component steps. As indicated in that chapter, you should conduct an assessment of component steps in as unobtrusive a manner as possible. Videotaping and using other observers are good alternate techniques when you are unable to give your complete and full attention to observing the students' behavior. The worksheet in Figure 7.1 shows a space for recording information about the assessment setting and procedures. The space does not have to be large; you would not write out your entire plan here—just a brief note on the various aspects of the activities. As shown in Figure 7.1, Mrs. Armstrong plans to conduct her assessment in the social studies classroom, and she will use videotapes, direct observations, and interviews as her assessment procedures. Once you have planned your procedures, you will be ready to begin the assessment. In the next section, we discuss issues and guidelines for conducting an effective and accurate assessment.

Conducting a Component Steps Assessment

An assessment of component steps needs to occur in the natural conditions of the activity. With this assessment, however, you will probably find it more challenging to be unobtrusive than during a survey level assessment because of the detail of observation that is needed for each of the component steps. Mrs. Armstrong may find that if she stands close enough to observe each step of Sandy's conversational patterns, the entire group will respond unnaturally to her presence. Similarly, if she tries to get a video camera close enough to record the conversations, the students may act intimidated or awkward. In such cases, you may have to compromise by structuring activities that are as natural as possible while also allowing you to make valid observations. Mrs. Armstrong could start having informal conversations with student groups during which she sits in with Sandy and her friends. After several days, as the students become accustomed to her presence, her observation of Sandy will be less disruptive. This solution may not be ideal, but it will allow Mrs. Armstrong to gain more information about Sandy's behavior than would otherwise be possible.

Assessing All the Component Steps

It is crucial to obtain an adequate assessment of *all* the steps of an activity or interaction. Sometimes, assessing certain component steps is difficult because students have problems in the earlier steps in the sequence that prevent them from completing the remaining steps on their own. But if they do not at least try to perform all the steps, you will not obtain a complete assessment of their behavior. In these cases, you may have to make special provisions.

For example, when Mrs. Armstrong begins her observations of Sandy's conversations with classmates, she may see that Sandy does not initiate conversations successfully. Maybe she uses the wrong greetings and students walk away from her, or perhaps she does not speak up and they ignore her. At this point, Mrs. Armstrong cannot assess the complete sequence of component steps because Sandy does not have an opportunity to go through them. But it is still important for Mrs. Armstrong to learn whether Sandy has difficulty with other steps in the interaction; otherwise her assessment will be incomplete and she will not know whether to include these later steps in Sandy's intervention plan. The only way she can obtain this information is to structure the activity so Sandy can complete the interaction.

Under these circumstances, you should note on the assessment worksheet that the students were unable to complete the step, and then help the students continue

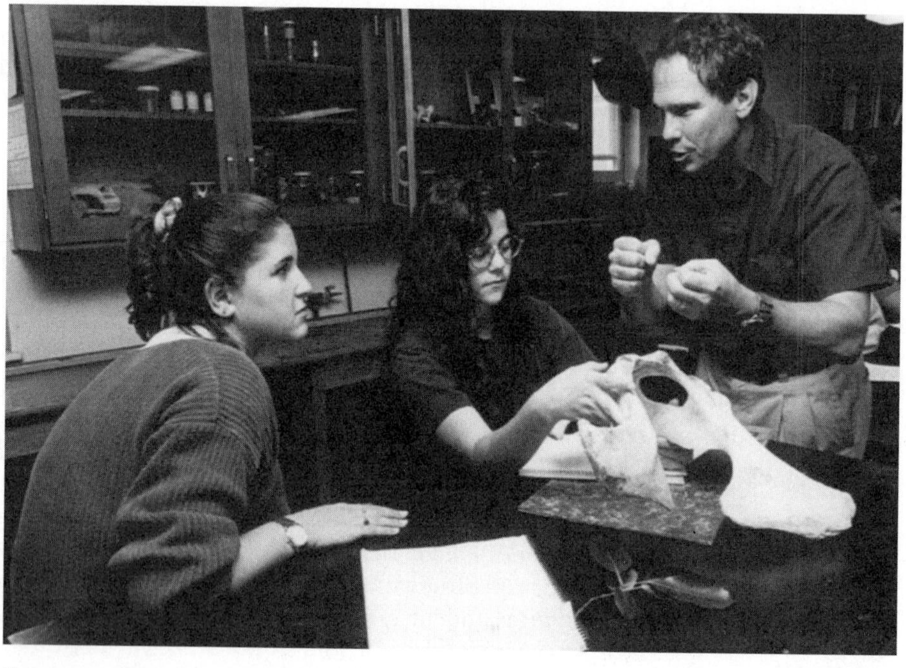

You may need to intervene during an assessment if students get stuck on a particular component step.

with the activity so it can proceed to its natural conclusion. Even though you intervene to give the students assistance through some parts of the interaction, you can still conduct a complete assessment of their behavior. For example, when Mrs. Armstrong sees that Sandy is not successful at initiating a conversation, she may at this point show her the correct skills to use. Then, when Sandy displays the correct behavior, Mrs. Armstrong can back away from the interaction and let it continue. She would intercede again only if Sandy has difficulty with another step. Perhaps Sandy does not respond when the students she is talking with give her cues to comment on a particular topic. Mrs. Armstrong would note this problem on the worksheet and then help Sandy through this step, possibly by asking her a direct question, or by leading the group to another topic about which Sandy is more knowledgeable. Mrs. Armstrong would then pull back and allow the interaction to continue as before. This approach allows you to conduct a thorough assessment of component skills even when the students are unable to perform some of the steps on their own.

With this approach, you will not be totally unobtrusive because your behavior will influence the social interaction. You can nonetheless minimize your effect on the interaction by separating yourself from the activities as much as possible and by interrupting the interaction no more than is absolutely necessary. Furthermore, you should withhold assistance until you are sure the students cannot perform a step. Sometimes students will look to you for guidance on what to do next in the interaction even when they have a pretty good idea. Avoid giving these cues unless the students actually need them. Remember that your overall objective is to preserve the natural flow of the interaction so the students show their typical behavior.

○ Summarizing the Results of an Assessment

The final task in a component steps assessment is to tally the results, record general comments about the students' behavior, and list the findings that can serve as the goals of the intervention.

Tallying Results

You should tally the assessment results as soon after the assessment as possible so the entries are accurate and reliable. As Figure 7.1 illustrates, the list of component steps can be used as a simple checklist for recording results. During Granville's assessment, Mrs. Armstrong entered a "+" (indicating successful performance) or a "o" (indicating an error) for each component step. Her worksheet shows results over five different observations, illustrating the importance of giving the student several performance opportunities to ensure results that reflect typical or average behavior.

As the students progress each day through the steps of the activity, you should mark whether they complete each individual step successfully. Note as errors any instances when (a) the students are unable to perform a step on their own, (b) their attempts to complete a step are incorrect, or (c) you have to give them assistance to complete a step. Mrs. Armstrong's tallies in Figure 7.1 show that Granville had particular difficulties with listening to and following directions of group leaders, negotiating with the group in delegating subtasks, seeking help from group members in completing subtasks, and handling disagreements and feedback in a diplomatic manner.

Commenting on Performance

The worksheet in Figure 7.1 has space for listing overall comments about the assessment results. This space is useful for summarizing major features of the results and for highlighting key steps that present difficulties for the students. In this space you can also describe such factors as (a) the variables that affect the students' behavior, (b) elements of the component steps they do not seem to understand, (c) steps they perform out of sequence, or (d) new insights or conclusions you have made about their performance.

You should also address in the comments how well the students sequence and combine their actions during the assessment. Record whether they use the proper sequence of steps for the interaction, and whether they integrate their behavior into a behavioral pattern that fits the demands of the situation. In her comments about Granville (Figure 7.1), Mrs. Armstrong recorded some of the trends she saw in his behavior. She has also noted, as her tallies indicate, that he had particular difficulty on Day 3 of the assessment, producing results uncharacteristic of his behavior on the other days.

Listing the Findings from the Assessment

After you have recorded your comments for the assessment, you should summarize your overall findings in terms of instructional goals that you might address in the intervention, just as you did for the assessment of basic abilities. When listing specific skills the students need to be taught, consider individual steps in the activity or interaction that they consistently fail to perform on their own. For example, as the Findings section of Figure 7.1 shows, Mrs. Armstrong designated two goals based on specific steps that represent significant difficulties for Granville:

- Learn to seek help from group members
- Learn to negotiate disagreements

She also combined two closely related component steps into a third goal:

- Learn to work with the leader and the group when planning subtasks

You should also designate as instructional goals any aspects of the students' behavior that are poorly timed or out of sequence. Mrs. Armstrong noticed that Granville begins working on subtasks right away, before the group has divided the tasks or discussed how they will be delegated. As a result, he gets into arguments with group members because his work does not fit with the group's plans. Therefore, one of Mrs. Armstrong's findings for Granville is this:

- Learn to sequence work according to the group plan

Finally, consider as goals in the Findings section any problems the students may have aligning their behavioral pattern with the requirements of the situation. This focus of intervention is especially important when the assessment results show that the students can perform many or all of the component steps, but that they are unable to combine the steps into an effective or appropriate pattern. In such cases, indicate that the intervention should teach the students to improve the accuracy and fluency of their behavior. With Granville's extensive problems in performing component steps and in sequencing his actions, Mrs. Armstrong is unlikely to focus on these broader questions of fluency when she sets the immediate goals for his intervention; she would include this area later if it is needed. On the other hand, with Sandy's assessment, she may find that Sandy does complete many of the necessary steps for holding conversations but still appears hesitant and uncertain when she is in a conversational group. One finding from Sandy's assessment could center on helping her learn to organize her thoughts and comments effectively so she can approach conversations in a more self-assured and confident manner.

In summary, keeping a daily tally of the results of the component steps assessment will help you identify specific steps that pose difficulties for students. As you complete the assessment, you should also record comments about these problem areas, noting how well the students sequence and time their performance of the steps as well as any special circumstances or new insights that will help you when you design an intervention. Finally, you should prepare a list of findings that indicates tentative instructional goals for an intervention. Include individual steps the students need to be taught as well as any elements of sequencing or fluency in performance that involve combining actions into behavioral patterns that fit the demands of the situation.

❍ Summary

Overview of an Assessment of Component Steps

1. Target skills are composed of many individual skills and actions.
2. Behavioral patterns are the integrated series of skills and actions for meeting social expectations.
3. Component steps are the skills and actions that make up a behavioral pattern.
4. Students can have difficulty meeting social expectations because they are unable to perform individual component steps and/or are unable to combine the steps into behavioral patterns.

5. Assessments of component steps and basic abilities differ in that the former focus on how students actually behave in their interactions under normal performance conditions.

Importance of Behavioral Patterns and Component Steps in Achieving Social Competence

1. Component steps can help students build more complicated social skills.
2. Component steps can be combined to form different types of behavioral patterns.
3. Component steps and behavioral patterns broaden the scope and the complexity of students' social interactions.

Component Steps and Problems in Social Behavior

1. An assessment of component steps will help to identify two types of problems:
   a. Students may fail to perform component steps
   b. Students may fail to combine and integrate component steps into behavioral patterns.

Preparing a Component Steps Assessment

1. Preparing an assessment of component steps involves the following:
   a. describing pertinent information about the student and the circumstances of the assessment
   b. listing the component steps for the target skill
   c. planning the assessment procedures and schedule
2. An analysis of component steps involves breaking target skills into the sequence of actions or subtasks that students perform in meeting social expectations.
3. An analysis of component skills should indicate the logical starting and ending points of an interaction.
4. An analysis of component steps should take into account the time frame and the location in which the individual steps occur.
5. An analysis of component steps should be comprehensive and complete in helping to identify student problems.
6. An assessment of component skills should be conducted under natural performance conditions to ensure valid and reliable results.

Conducting a Component Steps Assessment

1. Obtaining a complete accounting of all the steps is crucial, even if the students need assistance through some steps.

Summarizing Assessment Results

1. A checklist format is helpful for recording whether students perform each component step correctly.
2. Other information about the students' performance should be noted to help in interpreting the assessment results.
3. The summary of findings from the assessment should give a clear focus to intervention plans.

Examples for Chapter Seven

Example 7a

Mr. Williams is a preschool teacher who is concerned about Wilson, a very shy child who avoids contact with other students during play activities. Mr. Williams would like to teach Wilson to open up a bit to playmates, especially as his verbal skills have not progressed since the beginning of the year. He has set the target skill "Talks and plays with classmates during free play."

This page shows the steps Mr. Williams identified for the skill and the results he recorded for Wilson. On the basis of his observations, Mr. Williams identified the following findings for the assessment:

Learn to select playmates.
Learn to verbalize ideas and feelings about play.
Learn to invite others to play.

Procedures for assessing component steps can usually be simple and direct.

The starting point for many play skills is when a student selects the activity or chooses a playmate.

Note that Wilson had difficulty getting started in the activity, but once Mr. Williams helped him get past the first steps he did well with the rest of the skill. This result is common in component skills assessments.

Use a notation to indicate when students did not have an opportunity to perform a step.

Worksheet 7.1: Component Steps Assessment — Page 1 of 2

Name: *Mr. Williams* Date: *Oct. 25*
Student: *Wilson* Grade: *Preschool*
Target skill: *Talks and plays with classmates during free play*

Procedures for assessing component steps:

Videotape children playing with toys in the play area

Assessment Results: (enter "+" for successful performance, "o" for unsuccessful performance)

Component Steps:	1st	2nd	3rd	4th	5th
1. Chooses playmate(s)	o	o	o	+	o
2. Greets playmate(s)	o	o	o	o	o
3. Talks about what to play	o	o	o	o	o
4. Begins playing at play station	+	+	o	+	o
5. Makes eye contact with others nearby	+	o	+	+	o
6. Invites others to join in	o	o	o	o	o
7. Works together on play project	+	+	+	N	+
8. Shares toys without arguing	+	+	o	+	+
9. Verbalizes thoughts, ideas	o	+	o	o	+
10. Seeks acknowledgment from teacher	o	+	o	+	N
11. Uses positive, friendly language	o	+	o	+	o
12. Uses friendly body language	+	+	+	+	o
13. Listens to playmates/accepts peers' ideas	o	+	+	+	N
14. Helps put toys away when directed by teacher	+	N	+	+	+
15. Goes to assigned area for next activity	+	+	+	+	+

"N" = no opportunity

Example 7b

Mrs. Nemeth is an eleventh-grade history teacher. For John's assessment she has selected the target skill "Participates in large group discussions," because she feels his failure to participate actively in class contributes to his earning poor grades on tests and assignments. The first page of her assessment is presented here.

Based on the steps John had trouble performing, Mrs. Nemeth recorded the following findings on the second page of her worksheet:

Learn to identify opportunities to speak.
Learn to ask questions about topic.
Learn to share opinions and relate topic to personal experiences.

Talking to students after an activity can clarify their performance on key steps.

The assessment results often show clearly where a student's performance breaks down during an activity.

A student may need to perform a step more than once during the activity.

Some steps may not follow a strictly chronological sequence.

Worksheet 7.1: Component Steps Assessment — Page 1 of 2

Name: *Mrs. Nemeth* Date: *Oct. 21*
Student: *John* Grade: *11*
Target skill: *Participates in large group discussions*

Procedures for assessing component steps:

Observe and videotape John during our class discussion of the day's assigned reading. Talk to him afterward to determine his responses and whether he followed the discussion.

Component Steps: / **Assessment Results:** (enter "+" for successful performance, "o" for unsuccessful performance)

Component Steps	1st	2nd	3rd	4th	5th
1. Listens to directions/opening comments	o	+	o	+	+
2. Exchanges glances and facial expressions with peers	+	+	+	+	+
3. Follows sequence of the discussion	o	o	o	+	o
4. Identifies proper time to speak	o	o	o	o	+
5. Gives answers related to topic	o	o	o	+	o
6. Asks relevant questions	o	o	o	o	o
7. Shares opinions	o	o	o	o	o
8. Relates topic to personal experiences	o	o	o	o	o
9. Uses animated language	+	o	+	o	+
10. Changes body position frequently	+	+	+	+	+
11. Responds to verbal and facial cues	+	+	+	+	+
12. Responds positively to classmates' comments	+	o	o	+	o
13. Laughs and smiles at appropriate times	+	+	+	+	+
14. Listens to teacher summary	o	+	o	o	+
15. Proceeds to next activity when directed	+	+	+	+	+

Mr. Wagner's Case Study

Mr. Wagner's Component Steps Assessment

For his component steps assessment, Mr. Wagner listed the steps for working on group projects. Note that his list should include several more items, particularly covering the social dimensions of the activity. Mr. Wagner assessed Granville over the course of a week. On Friday he had the class watch a video, so he didn't have time to do a full group activity. He drew the following findings from his assessment:

> Learn to read the assignment.
> Learn to do own work.
> Learn to stay on task longer.

These findings were not drawn directly from the assessment results, but reflected his impressions as he observed Granville's behavior.

Worksheet 7.1: Component Steps Assessment — Page 1 of 2

Name: *Mr. Wagner* Date: *Oct. 25*
Student: *Granville* Grade: *5*
Target skill: *Works on projects with classmates*

Procedures for assessing component steps:

Observe Granville working with classmates on group projects

Component Steps:	**Assessment Results:** (enter "+" for successful performance, "o" for unsuccessful performance) 1st	2nd	3rd	4th	5th
1. Discusses directions with group members	+	+	o	+	N
2. Chooses subtasks to work on	+	+	+	+	N
3. Works on own subtasks	o	o	o	+	N
4. Seeks help on subtasks	N	N	o	N	N
5. Gives help to members of the group	+	+	+	o	N
6. Completes project on time	o	o	o	+	N
7. Turns in project to teacher	o	+	o	+	o
8. Returns to assigned seat	+	+	+	o	+

"N" = no opportunity

There is no clear starting point for the skill, such as listening to directions or assembling with group members.

Mr. Wagner should have given Granville at least a few opportunities to perform this step.

This list does not provide a full, detailed description of the social aspects of working in a group.

The activity Mr. Wagner had for Day 5 was not helpful for assessing Granville's behavior. Mr. Wagner should have planned another activity or conducted the assessment on another day.

CHAPTER 8

Specific Level Assessment

Part III: Assessing Performance Conditions

With the first two stages of the specific level assessment, we have shown that you can discover a wealth of useful information about students' problems in meeting social expectations by assessing basic abilities and component steps. To this point, however, the techniques we have presented have examined social skills in relative isolation. We have focused primarily on the students and their behavior without taking into account the conditions and circumstances under which their performance takes place. To fully understand the problems students have in their interactions, we must also look at the context in which these interactions occur. In this chapter, we present a third, broader stage of specific level assessment, one that examines the conditions of performance for social behavior. We explain the nature of performance conditions, consider the problems students may have responding to them, and show how to plan and conduct an assessment of them.

Overview of a Performance Conditions Assessment

Students do not behave in a vacuum; their actions are affected by a complex, often bewildering array of environmental variables that surrounds them in their daily school routines and interactions. In the classroom, the hallways, the cafeteria, the playground, and all other settings, students must respond properly to a constantly changing set of circumstances in order to achieve social competence (Cairns, 1986). We call these environmental factors *performance conditions.*

The conditions of performance include the circumstances in which students engage in social behavior, such as the activities that are taking place or the interactions that are already in progress (Cartwright & Cartwright, 1984; Wahler & Fox, 1981). We first introduced the underlying concept of performance conditions in Chapter Two, when we discussed the importance of settings and situations in defining expectations in the social skills curriculum. As we indicated in that chapter, settings and situations set the occasion for student behavior, and create opportunities for students to engage in social interactions (Campbell & Siperstein, 1994; Howell, Fox, & Morehead, 1993). But performance conditions can go beyond a simple consideration of settings and situations. They include not only the broad activities and locations in which the students interact but also such variables as the people nearby, the timing of ongoing events, the layout of the setting, and the overall level of group interaction.

These varying conditions throughout the school environment often shape or even define social expectations, determining where, when, how much, and with whom students should interact to meet the demands of the setting. At the same time, these circumstances influence and help form the expectations students set for themselves and affect the various options they have for meeting these expectations. In sum, the conditions in school settings and situations determine what students must do to meet other people's expectations, and what they can do to pursue their own interests and desires (Zirpoli & Melloy, 1993).

Performance Conditions and Social Behavior

Because they provide the context for social interactions, performance conditions play an important role in prompting and regulating students' social behavior. The physical and behavioral characteristics of a situation help students determine how and when to use a specific social skill, and to anticipate whether using that skill will have the desired effect. These environmental factors establish guidelines for behavior such as when to initiate a particular interaction, what form the interaction should take, how long it should continue, and what outcomes are likely to result when the interaction is completed (Asher, Oden, & Gottman, 1977; Hoy & Gregg, 1994).

For example, fifth graders in Mrs. Armstrong's class participate in both large and small group discussions, and the nature of their participation in these activities depends on factors that are mainly set by the environment. During small group discussions, students can speak to one another more frequently, and their comments can range over more areas than is possible in a larger group. They tend to talk more freely and informally, choose a wider array of topics to discuss, and express more of their personal views and concerns. By comparison, large group discussions are quite limited in scope because they center mostly on the questions Mrs. Armstrong asks about textbook-related topics in history or geography. When students respond to peer comments in the large group, they usually direct their statements to Mrs. Armstrong, and speak more tactfully and cautiously in giving feedback to classmates and in adding comments to the discussion. In this way, performance conditions shift and change throughout the school day; the conditions for taking tests, for completing independent work, and for participating in the other classroom activities each set different guidelines for social behavior.

Importance of Assessing Performance Conditions

Recognizing these shifting performance conditions and reacting properly to them are crucial elements of competent social performance. To participate effectively in school activities, students must respond at the right times, pay attention to the

A performance conditions assessment examines how well students coordinate their behavior with the activities around them.

right things, direct their behavior to the proper places and people, avoid speaking too often or too seldom, and not make comments that are too curt or too long-winded. Furthermore, their behavior must be properly aligned with the actions and interactions of everyone else participating in the activities. When students fail to tailor their performance to the demands of the situation, their behavior can interrupt the natural flow of the activities and attract negative attention. Behavior that disrupts interactions often indicates that students have difficulty recognizing and responding to the performance conditions. A performance conditions assessment can help identify problems students may have adapting or integrating their behavior with ongoing circumstances.

Some of the problems Granville, Alfred, and Sandy have performing their target skills may arise from difficulties in responding correctly to the conditions of performance. Granville may speak too forcefully or critically to the peers in his group, or he may make too many argumentative and belligerent comments. Alfred may disrupt the play activity by leaving the play area too often to talk to other students, or he may interrupt the game with too many silly and immature comments. Sandy may have particular difficulty conversing with popular classmates, or she may not respond quickly enough to the group's cues for input. Each of these problems arises not necessarily because the students' behavior is incorrect but because it does not fit the circumstances they are in at that time. By conducting a performance conditions assessment with Granville, for example, Mrs. Armstrong can gain useful information about why he is not responding properly to the environmental variables that indicate what he should or should not do during small group discussions. She may discover that the problems occur because he acts without considering or recognizing the performance conditions that pertain to small group activities, or because he does not know how to adapt or apply his skills properly to these conditions.

The Focus of Performance Conditions Assessment

In a performance conditions assessment, you investigate how well students coordinate their actions with the flow of ongoing activities and the circumstances around them. The conditions of performance provide important guidelines for achieving social competence, as they establish the boundaries and the form for acceptable student behavior. Therefore, when you assess performance conditions you concentrate less on the conditions themselves than on how well students recognize and react to them.

The most helpful way to think about and describe performance conditions is by the parameters or dimensions they set for student behavior. The assessment is based not on what the conditions *are*, but on how they shape or define the expectations that are in effect when social interactions take place. Thus, rather than cataloging or enumerating the various conditions that exist when the target skill is being used, we prepare for a performance conditions assessment by looking at the ways these conditions set requirements or guidelines for how the target skill should be used. In the next section, we discuss several types of parameters that performance conditions set for students' social behavior.

Types of Guidelines Set by Performance Conditions

The performance conditions of a setting set guidelines for student behavior in roughly five areas: time, location, people, amount, and materials. The conditions in effect at any given moment help students negotiate the following issues relating to their expected performance.

Time: When Should Performance Occur?

The performance conditions in a situation indicate how students should time their behavior to bring it in line with the events and interactions that are taking place in the setting (Zirpoli & Melloy, 1993). For instance, should they act before, during, or after someone else acts? How should prior actions affect what they do next? How should they get ready for the next set of activities? Students need to time the start of their behavior and coordinate their actions to align with ongoing activities and interactions. During class discussions, Mrs. Armstrong's students must wait for an appropriate opening to make a comment, such as after Mrs. Armstrong asks a question or after another student finishes a statement. If a student wants to talk more informally with a friend, he or she must wait for a transition time or a break rather than speaking out during the discussion. On the other hand, students can usually communicate briefly with their neighbors using glances and whispers as long as they time their behavior carefully to coincide with distractions or transitions between speakers. Thus, when students engage in an interaction, they must watch conditions closely to ensure that their behavior is timed correctly and coordinated properly with other people's actions.

Location: Where Should Performance Take Place?

Performance conditions also indicate the location or the relative position in which students should place or direct their actions. Students must select the appropriate location for their actions, matching their behavior to the physical surroundings as well as to the position of others in the situation. When Mrs. Armstrong asks the students to line up for recess, they must go to the area of the classroom where the line is usually formed and stay in the correct position relative to the classmates in front of and behind them. Similarly, locations such as the library, the hallway, the cafeteria, or the playground set parameters for how loud students speak, for how much or how fast they move around, for the kinds of verbal or physical interactions they have with each other, and for many other social behaviors.

People: With Whom Should Performance Take Place?

Students must recognize which people in a setting should be included—or excluded—in different interactions, and they must also tailor their behavior to the people who are near them (Zirpoli & Melloy, 1993). These people, either individually or collectively, set definite limits on the acceptability of social behavior. For example, Mrs. Armstrong's students can ask favors, share secrets, or roughhouse more freely with their close friends than with other classmates. Group size and composition are other factors that define patterns of student behavior. In a large group activity or with Mrs. Armstrong watching, the students' behavior would usually be more formal, less personal, or more subdued than in a small group of friends. Thus, the topics and language students use, the games they play, the mannerisms they show, and many of the other things they do are largely dependent on who is in the group or who is nearby.

Amount: How Much Performance Is Necessary?

Students must also gauge the amount of behavior that is acceptable under the circumstances. They need to recognize how long a particular behavior should last, how many times it should be repeated, and how loudly, strongly, and intensely it should be performed. Too much or too little behavior may not meet the expectations that apply. During independent work time, most of Mrs. Armstrong's students stay on task long enough to complete the majority of their homework assignment before class ends. During the rest of this time, they must look busy enough to escape her harsh looks. Similarly, during discussions, the students must speak often enough to be a part of the activity, yet avoid speaking too many times or too long on a particular topic.

Materials: What Resources Should Be Used for Performance?

For many activities, students make use of supplies, tools, toys, equipment, or other objects to carry out an interaction. The performance conditions determine when or how these materials are to be used. During social studies class, Mrs. Armstrong's students must recognize when they are to use an atlas or globe, and then they must share and use the equipment properly. Similarly, during a basketball or football game, students must not only use the ball to play the game but also avoid the temptation of juggling, bouncing, or handling the ball in ways that may disrupt the game or annoy the other players.

In this way, the various elements of performance conditions set important limits or parameters that students must observe to execute their social skills effectively. In the next section we discuss the problems that can arise when students do not understand or do not attend to performance conditions—problems that can be investigated by a performance conditions assessment.

Performance Conditions and Problems in Social Behavior

Students must accurately interpret and react to performance conditions if they are to choose the correct skills for their social interactions and use them properly. If they do not recognize the conditions for using their skills or understand what the conditions mean, they will usually behave incorrectly, even though they may have the skills for competent performance. Problems in negotiating performance conditions can usually take two forms: (a) the students have difficulty integrating or placing their behavior into the flow of the situations around them, or (b) they have difficulty reacting properly to the varying conditions of their environment. The next sections describe both of these types of problems, showing how they can occur in each of the categories discussed earlier.

Problems with Placement and Reaction

Students who have difficulty with the *placement* of their behavior in ongoing activities usually have a particular desire or aim in mind. However, they may not recognize the opportunities for using their skills, or they may misplace their behavior in the flow of interactions. They often use the correct skills to achieve their aim, but they apply them under the wrong circumstances and with undesired results.

Students who have difficulty with *reaction* typically act without considering the prevailing conditions of a situation, or fail to respond quickly enough when conditions change during the course of an interaction. Often, their behavior falls out of alignment with ongoing conditions because they do not have a clear aim in mind and they fail to adjust or adapt their actions properly.

Examples of Problems with Placement and Reaction

To illustrate these two types of problems, consider Granville, who has trouble placing his behavior in ongoing activities, and Alfred, who has difficulty reacting properly to changing conditions. We will show how problems in these students' behavior can arise in the five areas described above. We draw these examples from a variety of situations, rather than just from the target skills for Granville and Alfred, to illustrate that problems in placement and reaction can have widespread effects in all facets of school performance.

Time

Placement: Granville wants to borrow 50 cents from his friend Greg so he can buy a soda. He approaches Greg while Greg is talking to a group of friends, and interrupts the conversation. Annoyed, Greg says he will not lend Granville the money, and an argument ensues. Granville's aim was to borrow money for a soda, but he made the request at the wrong time in the conversation.

Reaction: While they are waiting for a class football game to begin, Alfred and Eric play chase and engage in mock-fighting. After the game starts, Alfred continues sporadically mock-fighting with Eric. This causes Alfred to miss a ball that was kicked to him and his teammates are very annoyed. Alfred did not react properly when the conditions changed from informal play to playing the game.

Location

Placement: During a small group activity, Granville goes back to his desk to cut out pictures for a collage. Meanwhile, the rest of his group is sitting together in another area of the classroom, sharing ideas, and working together on the assigned project. The next time he meets with his group, Granville argues with them because they did not put his name on the project. Granville wanted to receive credit for the group's work, but he did not stay where he could work with them.

Reaction: When he first comes in from the playground, Alfred talks just as loudly and acts just as energetically as he did outside. Many of his classmates, who do not notice or mind his boisterous behavior when outside, think he is obnoxious or immature when inside. Alfred does not react correctly to changing locations from the playground setting to the classroom setting.

People

Placement: Granville is having trouble on his social studies worksheet during independent work time, so he asks Karen, who sits next to him, for help. Karen, who prefers to work alone, ignores him. Instead of asking for help from Mrs. Armstrong or another student, Granville calls Karen "stuck up," and gets in trouble for teasing her during the class period. Even though Granville was right to ask for help on the assignment, he directed his questions to the wrong person.

Reaction: Alfred is clowning around again with Eric before class. Eric thinks Alfred is funny and they have a good time together. When Sally and her friends come in, Alfred tries to clown for her in the same way. But Sally thinks such antics are "childish" and "weird," and she and her friends ignore Alfred or roll their eyes and shake their heads at one another. Alfred did not adapt his behavior to fit the change in the peer group.

Amount

Placement: While working on his collage for a social studies project, Granville becomes interested in the pictures he is cutting out. He spends a long time looking through the magazines, and cuts out the pictures very carefully, several times changing his mind and snipping up pictures he decides he does not really like. By the end of the class period, he has cut out only four or five pictures for his project, while the rest of the students have completed their projects. Granville spent too much time selecting pictures.

Reaction: Mrs. Armstrong holds a follow-up discussion on a small group activity. During the course of the discussion, Alfred tries to describe all the things his small group has done, talking twice as long as anyone else. The other group members become irritated with him and protest whenever he puts his hand up. Alfred did not alter his behavior when the other students showed that he had said enough about their project.

Materials

Placement: During independent work time, Granville is trying to complete a math homework assignment. Instead of finding a pencil, he uses a felt-tip pen. By the time he does three or four problems, his worksheet is a mess, and he crinkles it up in frustration. Granville's aim was to complete the worksheet, but he chose the wrong materials to use.

Reaction: Alfred and Eric are playing with Alfred's electronic game during recess. Later, while Mrs. Armstrong is teaching the day's lesson, she hears a telltale "beep-boop-beep" and sees that Alfred is still playing with the game. She confiscates the game until school is over, and Alfred's classmates tease him about it for the rest of the day. Alfred continued playing with the game when he should have put it away. He did not adjust his behavior to fit the requirements of the setting.

In each of these examples, Granville and Alfred are unable to negotiate the various conditions and demands of their environment. Granville misdirects or misplaces his behavior, failing to choose the right opportunities to achieve his aims, or to meet the expectations of the setting, even though he fully intended to do so. On the other hand, Alfred misreads or ignores what people expect from him and fails to match his actions to the existing performance conditions. He does not alter his behavior to fit a new set of circumstances when the conditions in the environment change.

Performance Conditions and Inconsistent Behavior

As the examples show, the difficulties students have responding to performance conditions can cause them many different types of problems. One fairly typical result is that the students' behavior is inconsistent (Hoy & Gregg, 1994). On some

TABLE 8.1 Steps in planning a performance conditions assessment

Step 1:	List information about the student and the target skill
Step 2:	Check off general performance issues to investigate
Step 3:	Describe specific questions to assess
Step 4:	Plan and schedule assessment procedures

occasions, they respond properly to the performance conditions and act in accordance with the demands of the setting, but on other occasions, their behavior is inappropriate, awkward, or out of alignment with ongoing activities and interactions. Granville sometimes ignores or walks away from a disagreement, or even acknowledges that he made a mistake; but at other times he uses abusive language and starts fighting. This inconsistent performance is a frequent characteristic of students who display incompetent behavior and is often an indication that they are unable to negotiate or react to the conditions of performance. An assessment of the students' response to environmental conditions will help you establish clear objectives or directions for addressing this kind of problem. We explain how to plan the assessment in the next section.

Preparing a Performance Conditions Assessment

When you assessed basic abilities and component steps, you were looking very carefully at the students themselves, mostly focusing on their behavior rather than on the circumstances around them. Now you will make an important shift, looking at the target skill for the first time from the students' own point of view, to understand how they perceive and react to their surroundings and to investigate how well they respond to the guidelines these conditions set. Figure 8.1 is an example of a worksheet you can use to plan and conduct an assessment of performance conditions, and shows the notations Mrs. Armstrong used for Granville's assessment.

This worksheet has a different form from the ones used for the other stages of specific level assessment, because this assessment focuses not on the performance conditions themselves, but on the limits they set for student behavior. In planning, you identify key issues you wish to investigate about the way the students respond to these limits. In the sections that follow, we explain the steps for identifying these issues and for planning an assessment of performance conditions. Table 8.1 gives a summary of these steps.

Step 1: Listing Information about the Student and the Target Skill

As before, begin by listing information pertinent to the assessment, such as your name, the date, the student's name and grade level, the assessment setting and

Figure 8.1 Mrs. Armstrong's performance conditions assessment worksheet for Granville.

Worksheet 8.1: Performance Conditions Assessment — Page 1 of 5

Name: *Mrs. Armstrong* Date: *Nov. 2*

Student: *Granville* Grade: *5*

Target skill: *Cooperates with other students in completing small group activities*

Category #1: **Time**

General issues to assess (Check off those that apply):

x whether the student uses the target skill at the right times

___ whether the student uses the target skill at the wrong times

x whether the student uses the target skill better at some times than others

x whether the student performs some other behavior at the times the target skill should be used

Specific questions to assess:

Does Granville cooperate on at least some types of activities during group time? Does he cooperate more (or less) effectively during hands-on map work than with his own projects? Does he work better with the group in the mornings/afternoons? When Granville is not on task, what does he do instead? Does he talk about outside topics (e.g., other schoolwork, recess activities, TV shows)?

Category #2: **Location**

General issues to assess (Check off those that apply):

___ whether the student uses the target skill in the right places

___ whether the student uses the target skill in the wrong places

x whether the student uses the target skill better in some places than in others

___ whether the student performs some other behavior in the places the target skill should be used

Specific questions to assess:

Does Granville cooperate with classmates more (or less) effectively in other instructional settings (e.g., the library, Mr. Wagner's or Ms. Hernandez's classroom)?

Figure 8.1 *(continued)*

Worksheet 8.1 (continued)	Name: *Mrs. Armstrong*	Page 2 of 5

Category #3: **People**

General issues to assess (Check off those that apply):

x whether the student uses the target skill with the right people

x whether the student uses the target skill with the wrong people

x whether the student uses the target skill better with some people than with others

x whether the student performs some other behavior with or toward the people the target skill should be used with

Specific questions to assess:

Does Granville stay with the students in his own work group? Does he interact with them during group time? Does he try to work with classmates who are not in his assigned group? Does Granville cooperate more (or less) effectively with certain types of classmates, e.g., boys versus girls? Are there specific classmates with whom he works particularly well or poorly? How does he interact with the people in his group when he gets off task?

Category #4: **Amount**

General issues to assess (Check off those that apply):

x whether the student uses the target skill at the right amount (level, frequency,

___ whether the student uses the target skill at the wrong amount (level, frequency,

x whether the student uses the target skill better at some amounts (levels,

Specific questions to assess:

Does Granville interact for the full time demanded by the activity? Does he cooperate with classmates more effectively on shorter, or on longer, activities?

Figure 8.1 *(continued)*

Worksheet 8.1 (continued)	Name: *Mrs. Armstrong*	Page 3 of 5

Category #5: **Materials**

General issues to assess (Check off those that apply)**:**

_x_ whether the student uses the target skill with the right materials

_x_ whether the student uses the target skill with the wrong materials

___ whether the student uses the target skill better with some materials than with others

___ whether the student performs some other behavior with the materials than target skill should be used with

Specific questions to assess:

Does Granville use the worksheets and text materials I give to his group? Does he try to work cooperatively using play objects or school supplies that are not needed for the assignment ?

Procedures for assessing issues and questions:

Time	*Observe and videotape Granville and group during activity. Have small groups three times in the morning, three times in the afternoon. Make note of what Granville does when he's not working with the others or when he gets off task.*
Location	*Go to library for small group on 2 days—see if Granville cooperates differently. Ms. Hernandez and Mr. Wagner will observe Granville for at least 2 days of small group activities in their classes.*
People	*Note how Granville reacts to each group member. After day one, change group makeup each time—move one or another student to other group, move Granville, etc. Make a majority of the group girls on one or two days, instead of the boys he normally works with.*
Amount	*Observe and time Granville's on-task performance, and how long he maintains interactions during the activity. Give some short group tasks, as well as some long ones, to look for differences in his level of cooperation.*
	Structure activities that require various materials (books, worksheets, etc.), and observe Granville's use of them. Observe his use of library materials. Note any play equipment or other outside materials he may use during small group time.

Figure 8.1 *(continued)*

Worksheet 8.1 (continued)	Name: *Mrs. Armstrong*	Page 4 of 5

Assessment schedule:

Day 1	*Assess morning group, use typical conditions.*
Day 2	*Afternoon group, move one or two students, assess in library.*
Day 3	*Morning, switch student(s) in group, give a long task.*
Day 4	*Afternoon, switch Granville to other group—mostly girls.*
Day 5	*Morning, switch student(s), assess in library, assign short tasks.*

Results/comments:

Time	*Granville doesn't seem to time his performance to match his peers at all. Once he begins a subtask he gets engrossed in it (or sometimes bored with it), and then often stays with that one subtask, or sometimes a tangential issue, for the entire period. He was a bit better in the mornings than in the afternoons, but not to any remarkable degree.*
	Granville didn't cooperate in the library significantly more than in the classroom, but he did argue less with group members. Mr. Wagner reported that Granville's behavior was even worse in math class than elsewhere. But Ms. Hernandez said Granville interacted surprisingly well in her class. She noted that Granville seemed to enjoy taking a leadership role with the other students in the special education group.
People	*Granville doesn't get along with David, and he seemed more comfortable when David was not there. He also seems to enjoy working with Brian. Other than that, changing students made little difference. Granville did better in smaller groups—had fewer conflicts, and worked more quietly. Putting him in a new group didn't help much; he didn't argue or fight with the girls, but didn't really work with them either.*

Figure 8.1 *(continued)*

Worksheet 8.1 (continued)	Name: *Mrs. Armstrong*	Page 5 of 5

Results/comments (continued):

Amount	*Granville stays on task, but not always the right task. He spent a lot of time in the library looking at sports books. He tends to spend more time on building/cutting/making activities than on discussing or reading. He works better on one focused task, as long as it's something he likes and can remember.*
	Granville gets distracted by materials, rather than using them to get job done. He'll play with scissors, read the wrong book, etc. He doesn't use the worksheets effectively to guide his work.

Findings—Instructional goals for intervention:

Learn to coordinate actions with work of group (even if work is done separately)

Learn to avoid conflicts with rivals, and seek interactions with friends instead

Learn to use materials more effectively to aid group work

Learn to apply on-task focus to completing task at hand

situation, and the target skill you will be assessing. Figure 8.1 shows this portion of the worksheet completed by Mrs. Armstrong for Granville's assessment.

Step 2: Checking off General Performance Issues to Investigate

To establish the focus for a performance conditions assessment, you need to choose the specific conditions and issues you wish to examine. We have formatted the worksheet in Figure 8.1 so you can check the general issues you wish to investigate in each type of performance condition: time, location, people, amount, and materials. For each of these categories, the checklist addresses four basic areas you may choose to examine.

Whether the Students Use the Target Skill under the Right Conditions

The most basic issue in any of these five categories is whether the students use the target skill in accordance with requirements of the setting. When you do an assessment of performance conditions, you have already investigated how well the students are able to perform the skill and how well they perform the skill's components under typical circumstances. Now you are determining whether they use the skill as it is needed—when, where, with whom, as often or as long as, and with what the conditions demand. In Alfred's assessment, Mrs. Armstrong may wish to know whether he responds when classmates begin recess activities like football or basketball, such as when they begin to choose teams or when the teams line up to start the game. In the Time section of Alfred's assessment worksheet, Mrs. Armstrong would check off the issue to assess "whether the student uses the skill at the right times." Similarly, in Sandy's assessment, Mrs. Armstrong may wish to investigate whether she speaks long enough or loudly enough when she answers a classmate's question. In the Amount section of Sandy's worksheet, she would check the issue "whether the student uses the skill for the right amount (level, frequency, duration, intensity)."

On Granville's worksheet (Figure 8.1) Mrs. Armstrong has checked off this first type of issue in the categories of Time, People, Amount, and Materials. Her checkmarks reflect particular questions Mrs. Armstrong wants to investigate about Granville's use of cooperative skills during small group projects:

- Whether he cooperates on at least some types of assignments during small group discussions (Time)
- Whether he stays with the students in his own work group (People)
- Whether he interacts for the total time she assigns the activity (Amount)
- Whether he uses the worksheets and text materials she has given to his group (Materials)

You can answer some of your most fundamental questions about the students' recognition and response to their environment by looking at the basic issue of whether they actually use the target skill under the various conditions to which it applies.

Whether the Students Use the Target Skill under the Wrong Conditions

Often, students who have difficulty responding to performance conditions will misdirect their behavior or act indiscriminately. They use their skills under inappropriate circumstances, such as at the wrong times, in the wrong places, or with the wrong people, because they disregard important features of the setting or fail to react properly to changes in the activities. Thus, even though students may use the target skill correctly under the right circumstances, they may still have trouble *limiting* their behavior to the times, places, people, amounts, or materials for which it is required.

Mrs. Armstrong may wish to learn whether Alfred limits his playing of outdoor games and his more physical behavior to the playground setting or whether he continues these actions in the cafeteria or school hallways. Under the Location category of his worksheet, she would check off the issue "whether the student uses the skill in the wrong places." In the same way with Sandy, Mrs. Armstrong might assess whether she talks to her teachers during free time instead of talking to her classmates. Mrs. Armstrong would check the issue "whether the student uses the skill with the wrong people" on the People section of Sandy's worksheet.

In Granville's assessment, Mrs. Armstrong plans to investigate this issue in the categories of People and Materials (see Figure 8.1). She will examine these elements:

- Whether he tries to work cooperatively with classmates who are not in his assigned group (People)
- Whether he tries to work cooperatively using play objects or school supplies that are not needed for the assignment (Materials)

By examining issues like these, Mrs. Armstrong can discover whether the students are directing their otherwise correct behavior to the wrong circumstances, or are carrying it over to settings and situations that do not require it.

Whether the Students Use the Target Skill Better under Some Conditions Than Others

As we noted earlier, students who have difficulty responding to performance conditions often display inconsistent behavior. Frequently, these students will perform more effectively under some circumstances than others, indicating that they have particular difficulty negotiating a specific set of conditions. To assess such problems, you can observe how the students perform the target skill under varying conditions. With Sandy, Mrs. Armstrong may wish to investigate whether she participates more actively during short question-answer sessions or during one-on-one activities with another student than she does during longer general conversations. Therefore, she would check off the issue "whether the student uses the skill better at some amounts (levels, frequencies, durations, intensities) than at others" under the Amount section of Sandy's worksheet. With Alfred, she may assess whether his game-playing is more proficient during gym class than during the afternoon recess. To address this question, she would check off this issue under both Time ("whether the student uses the skill better at some times than at others") and Location ("whether the student uses the skill better in some places than in others").

In her assessment of Granville, Mrs. Armstrong checked this issue in the Time, Location, People, and Amount categories because she plans to investigate the following:

- Whether he cooperates with classmates more (or less) effectively during hands-on map work activities, or during projects that he chooses (Time)
- Whether he cooperates with classmates more (or less) effectively in other instructional settings, such as the library, Mr. Wagner's or Ms. Hernandez's classroom (Location)
- Whether he cooperates more (or less) effectively with certain types of classmates, such as boys versus girls (People)
- Whether he cooperates with classmates more (or less) effectively on shorter, or on longer, activities (Amount)

By investigating these types of questions, Mrs. Armstrong can gain information about the students' varying reactions to specific environmental factors that may affect the quality and level of their behavior.

Whether the Students Use the Wrong Behavior to Respond to Conditions

A final reason students may not use their social skills effectively is that they are doing something other than what is expected of them by the demands of the setting or activity. In such cases, they may fail to meet expectations not because they ignore or misread the performance conditions but because they are focused on doing something else instead. Often, they may be trying to respond to the prevailing conditions but may select a response that is inappropriate or misconceived. When students do not respond properly to performance conditions, it is often helpful to observe what they do instead under those conditions, to learn whether competing factors or behaviors are involved. Sometimes, when we look at these other behaviors closely, we will see what students are trying to do, or what they prefer to do, and thereby gain an understanding of what outcomes they are trying to achieve and what types of activities are more interesting or motivating for them.

With Sandy, Mrs. Armstrong may wish to assess how she behaves toward peers when she should be talking with them, to see whether she daydreams, fidgets or acts uncomfortable, or looks away to see what other groups are doing. Thus, in the Time section of Sandy's worksheet, Mrs. Armstrong would check off the issue "whether the student performs some other behavior at the times that the target skill should be used." With Alfred, she may be interested in checking how he behaves toward his playmates when he fails to pay attention to his role in the football games, to see whether he talks with them instead, or tries to impress them with his foolish behavior. In the People section of Alfred's worksheet, she would check off the issue "whether the student performs some other behavior with or toward the people the target skill should be used with."

In Granville's assessment, Mrs. Armstrong marked this area for investigation in the Time and People categories:

- Whether he talks about outside topics during small group discussions, such as other schoolwork, recess activities, TV shows (Time)
- The way he interacts with the people in his group when he gets off task (People)

By examining these issues, Mrs. Armstrong could identify behaviors or environmental factors that are taking the place of the expected skill and keeping students from responding properly to the conditions around them. Notice on the worksheet that this particular question does not apply to the Amount category, since a student performing some other behavior "for that amount" would be covered under the Time category.

Check off the Most Pertinent Items

With a total of 19 possible performance issues to investigate—three or four issues for each of the five performance categories—you must limit your assessment to the items you feel are particularly crucial or interesting, as Mrs. Armstrong did in planning her assessment of Granville. In the Location category, she does not plan to assess whether Granville stays in the small group area, or if not, where he goes, because she already knows that he generally stays with his work group when she tells him to. On the other hand, she checked all four issues in the People category, and three issues each in the Time and Material categories, because she wants to concentrate her assessment on these particular performance variables.

Step 3: Describing Specific Questions to Assess

After checking the general issues for assessment, you should clarify the scope of the assessment by listing the specific questions you wish to investigate in each area. Obviously, a generalized checklist like the one presented in Figure 8.1 can provide only a broad outline of the concerns you have about a student's response to performance conditions. In the case study excerpts above, we indicated that Mrs. Armstrong checked off general issues to assess for Granville, but noted that these issues were really a reflection of certain specific questions about Granville's performance.

For example, in the People section of Granville's worksheet, Mrs. Armstrong checked all four of the general issues to be assessed:

- Whether the student uses the skill with the people he/she is expected to
- Whether the student uses the skill with people he/she is *not* expected to
- Whether the student uses the skill better or differently with some people than with others
- Whether the student performs some other behavior with or toward the people with whom the skill is expected to be used

But each of these general issues reflects one or more specific questions Mrs. Armstrong would like to investigate about Granville's behavior:

- Does Granville stay with the students in his own work group? Does he interact with them during group time?
- Does Granville try to work with classmates who are not in his assigned group?
- Does Granville cooperate more (or less) effectively with certain types of classmates, such as boys versus girls? Are there specific classmates with whom he works particularly well or poorly?
- How does he interact with the people in his group when he gets off task?

To maintain her focus on these questions, Mrs. Armstrong writes them on the worksheet along with the checklist she has made for Granville. Figure 8.1 shows her notation of specific questions on her worksheet beneath the general issues she had checked off for Granville.

By elaborating on the general issues with more specific questions, you can use the worksheet checklist as a brainstorming device to help you sketch out the general dimensions of the assessment and consider a broad variety of factors that may be affecting the students' performance. As you brainstorm, note on the worksheet the specific questions and issues you might investigate for particular students.

Step 4: Planning and Scheduling Assessment Procedures

After you have specified the general performance issues and specific questions you plan to assess, you should decide on procedures to use for the assessment and schedule the activities. Just as the scope of investigation can be quite broad and flexible when you assess performance conditions, the procedures you choose and the schedule for carrying out your investigation may vary considerably. In most cases, you will employ procedures using a combination of natural and atypical conditions in order to answer the full range of questions you have about the students' response to performance conditions. In the following sections, we discuss the advantages and limitations of both approaches.

Assessing under Natural Conditions

You will usually have some questions that can be accurately investigated only by seeing how the students interact under the natural conditions of the setting. You should conduct the assessment in these areas with the same guidelines used for a survey level and component skills assessment, observing in as natural and unobtrusive a manner as possible, to learn how the students respond to typical performance conditions. To learn how Alfred coordinates his playing skills with those of his teammates, Mrs. Armstrong will probably want to observe him during typical games on the playground, keeping as low a profile as possible. These circumstances will allow her to obtain an accurate view of how well he matches his actions to the conditions that usually characterize play activities. Similarly, Mrs. Armstrong may use Sandy's typical interactions with classmates to assess how long she continues with her conversations, and to see what she does when she stops attending to the activities.

Assessing under Atypical Conditions

You will often have other assessment questions that you can answer only by changing certain elements of the natural conditions to learn whether the students' behavior is affected by such differences. With these questions, you will need to manipulate the circumstances, as you did when assessing basic abilities. This will often be the case when you investigate a particular variable in the performance conditions and wish to see what effect changing or removing that factor will have on the students' behavior. For example, Mrs. Armstrong may suspect that Alfred's apparent crush on Sally is one reason he acts up so frequently on the playground, so she may want to examine whether his behavior changes because of Sally's presence. To assess this issue, Mrs. Armstrong could separate Sally from Alfred and the rest of the class during recess by asking her and a few of her friends to play in another area of the playground for a day or two. Then, Mrs. Armstrong would be able to observe whether Alfred's behavior changes when Sally is not close by. Another possibility would be to structure special play activities for Alfred—one day with Sally, and another day without her. By comparing Alfred's typical behavior with his behavior under these relatively controlled circumstances, Mrs. Armstrong could determine whether his performance is adversely affected by Sally's presence. The schedule Mrs. Armstrong develops for her assessment would help her organize and keep track of any changes like these that she plans to make.

As these examples show, the procedures and schedule for assessing performance conditions should be tailored to the issues and questions you wish to investigate. By looking over your checklist and carefully planning procedures to match each point you wish to cover, including both natural and artificial situations, you can conduct an assessment that is very specifically directed to your particular concerns.

Entering Procedures and Schedule on the Assessment Worksheet

Figure 8.1 shows a section of the worksheet for planning procedures. Individual headings are given for each performance category (time, location, etc.) to ensure that your plans address all the areas noted on your checklist. Of course, many of the procedures you choose may cover more than one category at once. Note that the worksheet also includes spaces for drafting an assessment schedule. This will help you coordinate your procedures in a clear time frame.

Figure 8.1 also shows the procedures and schedule Mrs. Armstrong developed for Granville's assessment. She plans to videotape some activities, directly observe others, and use outside observers for the rest. When she carries out the assessment in her classroom, she will change some of the assignments she normally gives to small groups, and she will vary the composition of Granville's group. In the library, she will assess under natural conditions and will ask the school librarian to help make the observations for her. She will also have Mr. Wagner and Ms. Hernandez observe Granville's level of cooperation during similar small group activities in their instructional settings. She plans to carry out the assessment over five days.

The most challenging aspects of assessing performance conditions are defining the areas to investigate and developing a plan to assess them. Once the planning is finished, conducting the actual assessment should be fairly straightforward. We discuss how to conduct assessments in the next section.

Conducting a Performance Conditions Assessment

When you conduct a performance conditions assessment, you observe how the students' behavior is affected by the context in which they interact. You should watch both the students' actions *and* the environmental factors that seem to affect those actions. The assessment will generally adhere to the guidelines for assessing behavior under natural performance conditions, but you may wish to do some exploratory work and hypothesis testing of possible intervention procedures by deliberately altering performance conditions. To ensure an accurate and worthwhile assessment, keep in mind the following considerations.

Watching for Environmental Factors That Affect Performance

The task of watching for important environmental factors for using target skills can be more challenging than it first appears. For the first time in the assessment process, you are observing not only the students' behavior but also the context and circumstances under which the behavior takes place. No matter how well you plan your assessment, you cannot anticipate all the environmental conditions that may influence the students' behavior, or all the different reactions the students may have to these conditions. Be prepared to note any incidents that may be significant, even if you had not planned to observe for them before. Pay especially close attention to two key areas.

Observe environmental conditions or cues that cause, prompt, or set the occasion for the students' behavior. These types of variables signal the students that they should start using the target skills. Watching for these cues will help you identify key conditions in the setting that students may ignore or misinterpret. For instance, Mrs. Armstrong should watch closely for the environmental cues that signal opportunities for Sandy to engage in interactions with classmates, such as when one of them greets her, or when she has a chance to join some friends during transitions between activities. With Alfred, Mrs. Armstrong may want to observe the start of games when students are picking teams, to learn whether he knows what team he is on and whether he is attentive to discussions of the rules and playing conventions. By paying close attention to these factors at the start of interactions, Mrs. Armstrong can determine whether the students are sufficiently prepared to participate when the activities begin and can identify the particular conditions or cues they may overlook or ignore.

Observe points or transitions in the situation at which the students should alter their performance. These types of environmental cues signal students that conditions in the setting have changed, or are about to change, and that they must modify their performance and realign it to fit these altered conditions. Watching

During an assessment you should observe how environmental factors affect the students' behavior.

for these factors allows you to note whether students are able to perceive, and to react properly to, shifts in the activities. During Sandy's conversations with classmates, Mrs. Armstrong would be alert to the moment changes in conversational topics take place, to see whether Sandy is able to follow the conversational cues and adjust her behavior properly to the new conditions of the interaction. When Mrs. Armstrong observes Alfred's performance in game-playing situations, she would look closely for the points at which his actions become misaligned with those of his teammates, as when he forgets to take his turn, or when he starts talking to bystanders instead of following the progress of the game.

By focusing on circumstances in which problems in behavior are most likely to occur, Mrs. Armstrong can determine whether Sandy and Alfred enter the flow of the activity from the start, whether they can adjust to the natural shifts in the activity, and whether extraneous factors are diverting their attention from using their social skills effectively. By noting such problem areas, she will be able to focus intervention plans on overcoming them.

Thinking Ahead to Intervention Procedures

A performance conditions assessment provides an excellent opportunity to form and test preliminary ideas for your intervention plans. In large measure, interventions involve changing performance conditions to improve students' behavior. During the assessment, you will have many opportunities to note environmental factors that have a positive influence on the students' behavior in addition to those that have a negative influence. You can expand these opportunities even further by manipulating some of the performance conditions as part of the assessment process. After you have observed the students under natural circumstances, you may wish to alter the conditions in some strategic ways, to explore the effect of changed performance conditions. Often, the variables that have a major impact on social behavior can provide the cornerstones for effective interventions.

In Alfred's assessment, changing groupings to include and exclude Sally will not only give Mrs. Armstrong information about Alfred's performance but may also provide a framework for an intervention. If Mrs. Armstrong finds that Alfred's behavior improves substantially when Sally is not present, she may want to incorporate procedures in his intervention that teach him how to respond more appropriately and maturely to Sally and the other girls he has crushes on. With Sandy, noting conversational topics she especially enjoys or deliberately avoids may give Mrs. Armstrong information about topics for class discussions and activities that could encourage Sandy to contribute her ideas and opinions more freely. Thus, by thinking ahead to the students' intervention, you can investigate, and possibly try out, some promising intervention procedures.

Summarizing the Results of an Assessment

In this section we explain how to record results and comments, and how to state the findings of the assessment.

Recording Results and Comments on the Worksheet

Like the basic abilities assessment, the performance conditions assessment requires a recording format that is fairly open and flexible. In Figure 8.1, the section of the assessment worksheet for recording results provides separate headings and spaces for each performance category. We used this organization to capture information in the most useful way. Rather than summarizing observations in terms of tallies, we suggest an open-ended format that centers on describing the relationships between the students' behavior and the circumstances under which the target skills apply. The results you enter on the worksheet should pull together and summarize these observations for each performance area.

With Alfred, Mrs. Armstrong would use the results section of the worksheet to indicate how well he recognizes and responds to variables of time, location, people, amount, and materials in the playground setting. Her comments would further note whether conditions at the start of recess affected his decision to join (or not join) sports games with classmates, and how the conditions influenced his attention to and participation in the activities during the games. For instance, she may state in summarizing the Time category that Alfred does not join games unless he is specifically asked to do so by one of his friends; under People, she may note that during the games his attention to activities is severely hampered by his trying to show off for Sally and her friends. With Sandy, Mrs. Armstrong would comment on the effect of each performance condition on her participation in conversational groups with peers. Under Location, Mrs. Armstrong might explain that Sandy speaks more to classmates inside the classroom than out in the hallways, and under People, that her attention to the conversational topic is interrupted when someone new joins the group.

Figure 8.1 shows how Mrs. Armstrong entered results from her assessment of Granville on his worksheet. She used this section to describe the specific problems he displayed in his responses to each performance condition as it pertained to cooperating in small group projects. Under the Time category, for example, she stated that Granville does not coordinate his behavior with the group's activities, and that he becomes engrossed in or distracted by individual subtasks without really understanding how they fit in with the assignment as a whole. Under People, she noted how individual students and grouping arrangements affected his behavior in either a positive or a negative way.

Listing the Findings from the Assessment

You should summarize your findings in terms of the specific performance areas and conditions that should be addressed as instructional goals in an intervention, just as you did for the other stages of specific level assessment. In this space you should state any aspects of the performance conditions that students need to learn about, such as conditions they must respond to or react to more effectively. For example, Mrs. Armstrong might list these goals for Alfred in the Findings section:

- Learn to recognize breaks in the activities when he can talk to and horse around with friends
- Learn better strategies for interacting with Sally and other girls

She might list the following instructional goals in Sandy's findings:

- Learn techniques for joining conversational groups
- Learn to shift conversational topics to those that are more interesting to her

The last page of Figure 8.1 shows the findings Mrs. Armstrong entered on Granville's worksheet.

In summary, performance conditions provide the behavioral context for social interactions and establish the guidelines for acceptability for social behavior. An assessment of these conditions allows you to examine the relationship between students' actions and the various circumstances under which they are expected to use target skills. The performance conditions assessment allows you to determine whether students recognize these conditions and respond to them by using the proper social skills. The results of the assessment will indicate what students must learn in order to use their social skills when environmental conditions call for them.

Summary

Overview of a Performance Conditions Assessment

1. Performance conditions are the environmental factors that provide a context for social interactions.
2. Performance conditions determine what students must do to meet social expectations, and what they can do to pursue their own interests.
3. Attention to performance conditions enables students to tailor their actions to their surroundings and to other people's behavior.
4. An assessment of performance conditions involves examining what students know about using their skills under natural conditions.

Performance Conditions and Achieving Social Competence

1. Performance conditions establish the guidelines of acceptability for student behavior in the following areas:
   a. *time:* when students should use their skills
   b. *location:* where they should use their skills
   c. *people:* with whom they should use their skills
   d. *amount:* how much they should use the skills
   e. *materials:* what objects they should use in conjunction with their skills

Performance Conditions and Problems in Social Behavior

1. Problems in performance conditions can involve either placement of behavior into activities or reaction to changes in the activities.
2. With problems of placement, students have a specific aim in mind, but they misplace their behavior in the activities.
3. With problems of reaction, students fail to respond properly to changing conditions in a situation or activity.
4. Problems either with placement or reaction can result in inconsistent behavior in terms of meeting social expectations.

Preparing a Performance Conditions Assessment

1. Planning an assessment of performance conditions involves the following steps:
   a. listing information about the student and the target skill
   b. checking off performance issues to investigate
   c. planning and scheduling assessment procedures
2. The performance issues to investigate in an assessment are the following:
   a. whether students use the target skills under the right conditions
   b. whether they use the target skills under the wrong conditions

c. whether they use the target skills better under some conditions than others
d. whether they use the wrong behavior to respond to conditions

3. Issues investigated during an assessment should be limited to those of major interest or concern.

4. Specific questions should be formulated to address these general issues.

5. An assessment of performance conditions is usually carried out under a combination of natural and atypical conditions.

Conducting a Performance Conditions Assessment

1. During assessment, attention should be given to environmental factors that affect, or should affect, performance, such as:
   a. variables that should cause, prompt, or set the occasion for behavior
   b. points or transitions in activities where students should alter their behavior

2. Performance conditions can be altered during assessment to test out ideas, strategies, or techniques that could provide the framework for an intervention.

Summarizing the Results of an Assessment

1. The format for recording results should be flexible and open-ended, and should focus on describing conditions that have a major effect on student behavior.

2. The findings of an assessment should state what students must learn about performance conditions to use their skills effectively.

Examples for Chapter Eight

Example 8a

Frank is a student in Mrs. Peters' second grade. He tends to lose his temper and get in arguments during free time, recess, and other unstructured situations. Mrs. Peters has decided to focus on his behavior in the cafeteria, as many of his arguments take place there when he is eating breakfast or lunch with his classmates. The target skill she has selected is "Negotiates disagreements in cafeteria."

This page from Mrs. Peters' worksheet shows the general issues and specific questions she planned to assess in the People and Amount categories.

It is helpful to look for specific conditions under which students use the target skill effectively.

Although questions should be related to the checked general issues, they should also explore other areas of the category.

Performance conditions assessments can investigate the precise circumstances in which problems occur.

Worksheet 8.1 (continued)	Name: *Mrs. Peters*	Page 2 of 6

Category #3: **People**

General issues to assess (Check off those that apply):

- _x_ whether the student uses the target skill with the right people
- ___ whether the student uses the target skill with the wrong people
- _x_ whether the student uses the target skill better with some people than with others
- _x_ whether the student performs some other behavior with or toward the people the

Specific questions to assess:

Are there students with whom Frank frequently disagrees but still negotiates effectively? Whom does he argue with the most? How does he interact with these students when he is not arguing? Does he argue with some students more (or less) than others? Who provokes the arguments? How does he handle disagreements with adults or older students?

Category #4: **Amount**

General issues to assess (Check off those that apply):

- _x_ whether the student uses the target skill at the right amount (level, frequency,
- ___ whether the student uses the target skill at the wrong amount (level, frequency,
- _x_ whether the student uses the target skill better at some amounts (levels,

Specific questions to assess:

How long does it take Frank to lose his temper? Does he try to defuse an argument before resorting to yelling or hitting? Does he get along better with classmates during shorter interactions than longer ones—for example, better during breakfast (15 minutes) than lunch (30 minutes)?

Example 8b

Mr. Zimmerman teaches ninth-grade English. Milton is a student whom school staff suspect may have attention deficit disorder. He fails to stay on task, especially when working in a group, and wanders off topic during class discussions. He doesn't get his work done on time, but manages to earn passing grades. For Milton's assessment, Mr. Zimmerman has identified the target skill "Works with classmates on group assignments."

The performance conditions assessment for Milton focused on how different conditions affect his staying on task and on how he responds to the people and events around him. This page shows the schedule Mr. Zimmerman prepared for the assessment and some of the results he obtained. These results were particularly helpful in preparing effective intervention procedures for Milton.

Performance conditions assessments usually explore a combination of typical and atypical circumstances. (→ Day 2)

Assessments can be scheduled to investigate several performance categories with each observation. (→ Day 3)

Results can be recorded as a wide-ranging summary of how the student responds to specific conditions. (→ Time)

The results of a performance conditions assessment often indicate circumstances or activities that can be used in the intervention to motivate students and help them succeed. (→ Location)

Worksheet 8.1 (continued)	Name: *Mr. Zimmerman* Page 4 of 5
Assessment schedule:	
Day 1	*During the morning, observe Milton across different activities. Talk with Ms. Hammond (art) and Mr. Pope (social studies) teachers about observing him in the afternoon.*
Day 2	*Have groups work in library on projects both in social studies (a.m.) and English (p.m.). Have Ms. Saxton (librarian) observe Milton's work with peers.*
Day 3	*Place Milton in different student groups. Also, observe him in different types of computer activities.*
Day 4	*Continue having Milton work in different groups. Check with the rest of the school staff on Milton's work behavior.*
Day 5	*Plan different types of activities for Milton to work on—short/long, simple/complex. Schedule these during both English and social studies.*
Results/comments:	
Time	*Milton seems to pay more attention and get more work done during the morning than during the afternoon. He usually starts activities listening and following directions, but seems to lose interest halfway through and starts bothering other students or arguing with them. He stays on task more during high-interest activities, but even then does not pace himself well.*
Location	*Milton cooperated pretty well in the library and seemed to get along with his peers. He liked the freedom of looking at the magazines, but did not really stay on task for the group project. Ms. Saxton reported that he helped a number of at-risk students during class with understanding how to add fractions. He liked the responsibility and helped them where the teacher was having trouble. Mr. Pope noted that Milton did an excellent job during social studies class with the hands-on project and wanted to help others in the group.*
People	*Milton seems to get along better with the women teachers than with the men. He enjoys working with students who know less than he does on a subject (at-risk and special education). Milton did not argue with girls when in their group, but did not get a lot accomplished either. He tends to be more interested in what other groups are doing than in working with the students in his own group.*

Mr. Wagner's Case Study

Mr. Wagner's Performance Conditions Assessment

For his performance conditions assessment, Mr. Wagner consulted with Mrs. Armstrong and followed her example when checking off issues to assess. But as the page below indicates, the questions he formulated for the assessment were far less extensive than hers, which made his investigation rather cursory. He conducted the assessment entirely in his own classroom under normal conditions, so he obtained merely another description of Granville's typical behavior. As a result, the findings he derived are too general to give him much direction in planning an intervention:

Learn to use group time more productively.
Learn to get along with Bobby.
Learn to complete projects on time.

Worksheet 8.1 (continued)	Name: *Mr. Wagner*	Page 3 of 5

Category #5: **Materials**

General issues to assess (Check off those that apply):

x whether the student uses the target skill with the right materials

x whether the student uses the target skill with the wrong materials

___ whether the student uses the target skill better with some materials than with others

x whether the student performs some other behavior with the materials the target skill should be used with

Specific questions to assess:

Does Granville use the science supplies properly? Does he use the wrong supplies or equipment? Does he misuse the materials or play with them?

Mr. Wagner's questions are merely a restatement of the issues he checked. His questions should explore this category in more detail.

Procedures for assessing issues and questions:

Time	*Observe Granville when he is working on group project. Watch how he uses the time.*
Location	*Observe where Granville goes when he leaves his assigned group.*
People	*Observe how Granville interacts with the people in his group. Ask him how he feels about his classmates.*
Amount	*Time how long Granville works on projects. Note his time on task and off task.*
	Observe what materials Granville uses in his projects. Note how he uses the materials available to the group.

Mr. Wagner's procedures indicate the limited scope of his assessment. He should expand his investigation to include a variety of conditions and situations. For example, conferring with teachers from Granville's other classes would help to supplement his observations on Time.

Mr. Wagner would learn more about Granville's behavior if he varied the size and composition of Granville's work groups.

Mr. Wagner would learn more about Granville's behavior if he varied the types of projects he assigns.

PART THREE

Planning and Implementing Interventions for Teaching Social Competence

In the beginning of the text, we stressed the importance of directing our attention to the skilled behavior that characterizes social competence rather than to the problem behavior that constitutes social incompetence. Our primary aim, we said, should be to define the skills students must learn in order to improve their social interactions, not to label the problems or deficiencies that students show. The detailed process of analysis and assessment we outlined in the previous chapters has accomplished precisely this aim. Through this process, we have compared the students' behavior to the competent behavior of their peers, identified high-priority expectations for further investigation, and conducted a specific level assessment to discover the skills and abilities students need to learn. We have used the assessment process to shift our attention away from abstract labels and incompetent behavior, and thus transformed the "problem students" into students with specific instructional needs.

Often, when teachers have completed a detailed assessment of student performance, their natural inclination is to devise and implement interventions as quickly as possible. After all, the students need help, and the full extent of their problems and deficits has finally become clear. But it is important to approach interventions as carefully and systematically as assessment itself in order to make the best and most complete use of the information that has been so painstakingly gathered. By planning the intervention carefully, you can be sure that the skills you focus on and the procedures you choose fully reflect the information obtained from assessment. Careful planning will also allow you to implement a more complete, powerful, and far-ranging intervention. Furthermore, this planning will help you organize and coordinate the intervention procedures, and will ensure that they are carried out correctly and consistently.

In Part III, we describe an intervention planning and implementation process that involves five phases:

- Chapter Nine shows how to set clear, precise instructional goals for an intervention based on the findings of a specific level assessment. This chapter also shows how to begin brainstorming the various instructional methods and procedures you will consider for addressing instructional goals.

- Chapter Ten discusses how to choose intervention procedures from the range of possibilities you have considered. It offers ways to enlarge and refine your procedures and to handle special demands, such as addressing complex goals, or dealing with problems of student incentive. Chapter Ten also explains how to coordinate and organize procedures and activities into a single, coherent intervention plan.
- Chapter Eleven describes an approach for monitoring intervention plans that will help you evaluate how the procedures are working in terms of improving students' social behavior.
- Finally, Chapter Twelve discusses how to extend the intervention plan based on the results of the monitoring process and considers several courses of action to take in following up on the intervention.

As this short outline suggests, our approach to devising interventions concentrates much more on developing a well-organized plan than on flashy techniques or tricks. You will note that many of the procedures described in this section involve instructional methods that teachers use every day in normal school situations. We have found that by drawing on their own experience and that of their colleagues, teachers typically find more than enough know-how available to design effective interventions. The primary task is to select procedures that will best address the problems identified during assessment and that will achieve the instructional goals as quickly and efficiently as possible. The key, then, is to approach intervention planning carefully and systematically so as to fully harness your own expertise.

CHAPTER 9

Setting Instructional Goals and Brainstorming Procedures

We began our planning of a specific level assessment by asking the question "*Why* does the student have difficulty performing the target skill?" The results from the assessment have shown us the particular basic abilities, component steps, and/or performance conditions that are at the heart of students' problems. More important, the findings from these assessments have helped to highlight specific instructional goals students will need to learn in order to acquire and use the target skill. In this chapter, we show how to summarize and consolidate the findings from the three stages of the specific level assessment to establish a single set of goals for an intervention. We then discuss some of the basic instructional methods you may use to plan a sound, productive intervention to meet these goals.

Consolidating Instructional Goals from a Specific Level Assessment

The first task in developing an intervention is to formulate concise instructional goals to serve as the focal point for an intervention (Campbell & Siperstein, 1994; Merrell, 1994). In this section, we explain how the findings from the three approaches to a specific level assessment can be combined or consolidated into a few key instructional goals for learning the target skill. We also present some important considerations for using these goals to give a sharp focus to your intervention planning efforts.

Reviewing the Findings

In the chapters on specific level assessment, we discussed the importance of expressing the findings at each stage in terms of specific *instructional goals* that students need to learn in order to acquire and use the target skill. On Mrs. Armstrong's worksheets, she expressed her findings for Alfred, Sandy, and Granville in terms of "learn to" statements, such as "Learn to use greetings effectively" and "Learn to coordinate actions with ongoing group activity." Now, as you review these findings from the different parts of the specific level assessment, you will have available for consideration a variety of tightly defined goals that can be applied directly to your intervention plans.

Notice in this review that each different stage of specific level assessment tends to establish goals with a different focus. For instance, the findings from a basic abilities assessment generally provide the simplest and most elementary instructional goals for an intervention, because they indicate the background knowledge and fundamental behaviors students will need to learn to develop a target skill. The findings from a component steps assessment are particularly helpful for identifying the specific steps or subskills students must learn, as well as any particular linking or sequencing skills the intervention needs to address. Finally, the findings of the performance conditions assessment concentrate on specific ways students must learn to adjust their behavior or adapt their skills to match the existing conditions of time, location, people, amount, and/or materials.

Although the findings will usually show a shift in focus for each of the approaches to specific level assessment, you may notice a certain amount of overlap or repetition among the lists. This is because some of the problems students may have using target skills are likely to span all the assessments you conduct, and this

Setting goals is crucial to the success of any intervention.

will be revealed in the findings. For example, when she looks at the lists of findings she derived from her three stages of assessment for Alfred, Mrs. Armstrong may find that some items are quite similar or repetitive. When she puts all three sets of findings together, her list might look like this:

Findings from Assessment of Basic Abilities

- Learn the rules of games being played
- Learn to coordinate play performance with the actions of peers
- Learn positive, nondisruptive ways to gain the attention of friends (e.g., Sally)

Findings from Assessment of Component Steps

- Learn to follow the proper game sequence
- Learn to comply with the directions of team captains
- Learn to perform the proper actions in the game (wait for turn, etc.)

Findings from Assessment of Performance Conditions

- Learn to look for time cues and to "schedule" behavior
- Learn to direct behavior to appropriate people
- Learn to stay on task in games for longer durations
- Learn better strategies for getting people's attention—particularly for impressing girls

Obviously, many of the items on these lists are closely related to one another or are even identical. If Mrs. Armstrong tries to base an intervention on goals that overlap with one another, her plans could quickly become confused or overly complicated, with separate procedures for areas that are really interrelated. Furthermore, it would be inefficient for her to base intervention plans on a set of instructional goals that is this long and disorganized. If she tries to target too many instructional goals at once, her attention is likely to be divided across too many areas of behavior, and she will have difficulty implementing and coordinating all the intervention procedures.

Therefore, it is important at this point to review the list of findings from the specific level assessment and coordinate, consolidate, and prioritize them into a short list of tight, well-directed instructional goals for the intervention. As a general guideline, findings should be condensed into three to five clearly delineated instructional goals. This smaller number will help you to organize and direct the procedures and activities you develop without dividing your attention or giving the student too many goals to master at once. In the following section, we discuss how to complete this process quickly and effectively.

Consolidating and Selecting Instructional Goals

Consolidating findings is fairly simple. It involves reviewing the list of findings from the three phases of specific level assessment, looking for repetitions, similarities, and differences in priority among the goals listed. To complete this process efficiently, we suggest four basic techniques for revision:

1. Delete items that are repeated or rephrased
2. Combine and summarize related items
3. Look for goals that encompass other goals on the list
4. Deemphasize items that are less important or that can be delayed

In the sections that follow, we describe and illustrate each of these techniques.

Delete Repeated or Rephrased Items

The simplest way to begin is to look for items that repeat the same idea. In such cases, you should select the most clearly worded of the items and eliminate the others. Mrs. Armstrong may notice that the following items represent two different ways of stating the same goal:

- Learn positive, nondisruptive ways to gain the attention of friends (e.g., Sally)
- Learn better strategies for getting people's attention—particularly for impressing girls

Mrs. Armstrong may decide she likes the second phrasing better, as it states more clearly the kind of skill Alfred needs to learn. She would eliminate the first item and keep the second as a goal for Alfred's intervention:

- Learn better strategies for getting people's attention—particularly for impressing girls

Combine Related Items

Even when they are not precisely the same, you can usually find groups of items in the findings list that are logically or behaviorally related in some way, or that address fairly similar concerns. In such cases, you can summarize the group of findings as a single, slightly more comprehensive goal. For example, when Mrs. Armstrong examines the list for Alfred, presented above, she notices several items that relate to learning and following game rules:

- Learn rules of the games being played
- Learn to follow the proper game sequence
- Learn to perform the proper actions in the game (wait for turn, etc.)
- Learn to look for time cues and to "schedule" behavior

Rather than expressing these items as four separate goals and dividing her intervention procedures among them, Mrs. Armstrong could combine them into a more broad-based goal. This will give Alfred a single goal, but one that still addresses the fundamental skills he needs to learn:

- Learn the rules and essential behavior for playing games properly

Look for Encompassing Goals

Frequently when you review your findings, you will see items that include or supersede others on the list. When you look at a group of related goals, for instance, you might notice some that are more broadly worded than others and that really encompass the other items in the group. Such goals can often stand alone as representative of an entire issue or concern, allowing you to eliminate the related but subordinate items from the list. Mrs. Armstrong may notice that the following goals from the findings for Alfred address similar issues of interaction with teammates:

- Learn to coordinate play performance with the actions of peers
- Learn to address behavior to appropriate people
- Learn to comply with the directions of team captains

As she considers these three items, Mrs. Armstrong realizes that the first one is a bit broader than the others and can serve to exemplify the other two goals—because they are essential elements of coordinating play behavior with teammates. Therefore, with only a slight revision in phrasing, she can use the first item to express all three goals in one:

- Learn to coordinate game-playing behavior with the behavior of teammates

Deemphasize Less Important Items

As a final possibility, you may decide that certain findings are not as urgent as the others, and that you do not really wish to direct your efforts to these goals yet. You could have several reasons for such a decision. You may realize the goals are not as important for the students as you previously believed. Or you may suspect that they probably do not require any special attention because the problems are likely to work themselves out as the intervention progresses. Finally, you may decide that these goals, while important, are not as crucial to the students' success as the others you have identified and that you want to give them a lower priority until you have addressed your more pressing concerns. For example, Mrs. Armstrong may postpone working on the following goal from her findings list for Alfred:

- Learn to stay on task in games for longer durations

Mrs. Armstrong may decide that staying on task for longer time periods is not as important a goal as the others. She believes that Alfred's problems with staying on task will diminish on their own when he gains a better understanding of the rules for playing the games and when he learns to cooperate more fully in the play of his teammates. For these reasons, she can eliminate this goal from her intervention plan for now so she can concentrate more fully on the other items on her list. Note, however, that Mrs. Armstrong will keep a record of this goal and will recheck Alfred's on-task performance after the other goals of the intervention have been addressed, in case he might still need follow-up work in this area.

By pulling together and consolidating related items using these four techniques, you can prepare a list of instructional goals that is much shorter and more concise than before, but that still addresses the essential skills students must learn if they are to meet the social expectations you are concerned with.

Finalizing Instructional Goals

In this section we discuss several considerations for setting and finalizing the goals for intervention plans.

Prepare a Worksheet for Instructional Goals

Once you have decided on the final list of instructional goals, you should record the items on a worksheet. Figure 9.1 shows the worksheet Mrs. Armstrong prepared for Granville. Notice that the four goals she listed for him are based on the findings shown in earlier chapters. With this more concise set of goals, Mrs. Armstrong will be better able to concentrate Granville's intervention in the areas he most needs to learn if he is to improve his cooperation during small group activities. This worksheet can serve a double duty: later in the chapter we will show how you can also use it as a brainstorming worksheet, for listing preliminary ideas for intervention procedures and activities.

Consider the Goals' Complexity and Difficulty

When you finalize the instructional goals for an intervention, avoid combining or underemphasizing items that represent a significant challenge for students. Figure 9.1 indicates that Mrs. Armstrong left essentially unchanged the goal "Learn strategies for handling teasing and disagreements with peers," rather than combining or grouping it with other items from the findings list. She feels that handling disagreements and teasing is a complicated area and needs to be treated as its own separate instructional goal—especially since Granville has particular difficulties in this area. As the example illustrates, when items on the original findings list are especially complex or represent significant difficulties for students, you should either leave them as separate goals or group them with much simpler items from the list. This will ensure that your finalized list of instructional goals takes into account the individual needs of students and the complexities of the goal areas themselves.

Focus on the Original Target Skill

As you finish formulating instructional goals and move on to planning intervention procedures, remember that the original target skill should continue to serve as the overall goal of the intervention. The primary purpose of devising an intervention is to help students become more competent in the target skill as originally envisioned (Walker, Colvin, & Ramsey, 1995). Thus, the target skill should establish the overall scope of the intervention but also set the boundaries for the planning activities. The instructional goals you derive from the specific level assessment

Figure 9.1 Mrs. Armstrong's worksheet showing finalized instructional goals for Granville.

Worksheet 9.1: Preparing for Intervention Planning — Page *1* of *5*

Name: *Mrs. Armstrong* — Date: *Nov. 10*

Student: *Granville* — Grade: *5*

Target Skill for Intervention:

Cooperates with other students in completing small group activities

Instructional goals for learning target skill:

Learn to follow written and oral directions for group activities

Learn to organize and plan the assignment before starting work

Learn to coordinate performance with the activities of the group

Learn strategies for handling teasing and disagreements with peers

should serve to clarify and highlight the various subskills that will enable students to meet the broader target skill. In many ways, the goals you set represent intermediate steps toward achieving this broader, more complex goal (Cartledge & Milburn, 1986; Hoy & Gregg, 1994). You will ensure that the intervention plan achieves the purpose you originally desired by keeping the target skill firmly in mind.

Although Mrs. Armstrong will direct her efforts for Granville toward four fairly discrete behavioral areas, she should still focus the overall planning of the intervention on improving his performance in cooperating with peers during small group activities. As Figure 9.1 shows, she has entered the original target skill on the worksheet prominently above her new list of instructional goals for Granville. On the one hand, this reminder helps her keep in mind the ultimate purpose of the instructional goals she has chosen: to help Granville become proficient in working cooperatively with his small group. On the other hand, it also helps her avoid branching out into tangential problem areas that could obscure the focus of the intervention. While defining goals for improving Granville's behavior in the group, Mrs. Armstrong must be careful not to stray into other problem areas, such as his frequent failure to complete related class work or his aggressive behavior during free times. These may be important areas for her to address later, but for now she must hold strictly to the overall skill she has defined as the primary target for Granville if she is to keep her efforts tightly focused and manageable.

Therefore, keep the target skill in mind as you formulate instructional goals to prevent setting goals that are too disconnected or too broad, or that address too many issues at once. Close attention to the target skill will help to ensure that your intervention plans concentrate on the social skills you have identified as a priority, and to prevent you from moving into tangential areas.

In sum, by reviewing and finalizing your findings, you can ensure that the instructional goals you set for students will give you a clear, well-coordinated focus for intervention plans. Once you have set instructional goals, you will be ready to consider the actual methods and activities you might use to address these goal areas.

Procedures for Teaching Social Skills

Completing a list of instructional goals puts the finishing touches on the process of assessment we have outlined in the text. This process began with surveying the students' behavior to catalog expectations that represented problems, continued with selecting a single priority skill area as the target for further work, and then in the specific level assessment looked more closely at the particular reasons the students have difficulty performing this target skill. Now, by setting precise instructional goals, you have expressed the results of this in-depth investigation in a few carefully selected and clearly defined aims that will be useful for students to learn in an intervention.

Finalizing instructional goals also represents the first major step toward launching the intervention planning process, as it sets the particular focus of the intervention activities. Now we are ready to consider the techniques and procedures we might use to achieve these goals. In this section, we outline some basic types of procedures you can use to teach social skills, and we show how to begin brainstorming ways you might adapt and apply these general procedures to address the specific instructional goals you have set for your students.

One of the first things you will notice as you go through the following sections is that the procedures we discuss are similar to the teaching techniques used every day in typical classrooms. One of the keys to designing an effective intervention is recognizing from the start that it is not a magical or mysterious affair. Interventions that work well are much less the result of secret tricks or miraculous techniques than they are of clear, tight, and well-defined goals. Furthermore, ineffective interventions are more often attributable to a lack of focus or to poorly directed goals than they are to a lack of special procedures. Therefore, you should begin by realizing that as long as you have defined solid, well-targeted instructional goals, you can usually address them with fairly straightforward and conventional instructional procedures.

In the sections that follow, we present four broad categories of instructional procedures and give examples of ways you can use them in social skills interventions. Note that at this point we discuss these procedures in fairly general terms rather than give detailed explanations of their use. In this chapter we give an overview of procedures for teaching social skills and present some important guidelines for using them so you can learn about the best circumstances under which to incorporate them in an intervention. Then we describe an approach for brainstorming procedures you might try in your plans. In subsequent chapters, we explain in more detail how to develop these ideas further, and how to expand and refine the procedures you choose to form a comprehensive intervention plan.

Table 9.1 gives a brief description of the procedures we will discuss. We are separating these procedures into four categories for the sake of clarity; in fact, however, most of the procedures we describe can and should be used in combination with one another. Therefore, as you read through the descriptions below, you may wish to think of ways these approaches can be combined into effective and comprehensive interventions for students.

TABLE 9.1 Basic procedures for teaching social skills

Procedure	*Description*
Directions	Telling students how to perform the skills
Rehearsal	Having students practice or plan skills out of context
Modeling	Showing students how skills are performed and having them imitate the skills
Prompting	Giving students reminders of how and when to use skills

Directions

Directions represent the most basic and broadly applicable instructional approach there is for teaching social skills. Directions involve *telling* students how or when to behave, or what results will occur when they do (Cartledge & Milburn, 1986; Spivack & Shure, 1974). You use directions whenever you tell students how to play a new game, give them advice on how to handle disagreements, pass out instructions for an activity, or post a list of rules on the board. In addition to verbal and written instructions, directions can include tape-recorded messages, signs, charts, and many other communication methods. Furthermore, directions need not be strictly authoritarian or teacher-developed; they can be elicited in many cases from students themselves, perhaps by holding a class discussion on how to make friends or how to join a conversation.

Directions are usually the easiest, most straightforward, and most efficient way to provide information about social skills; they should be used whenever possible to address instructional goals (Eisler & Frederiksen, 1980; Knapczyk & Livingston, 1974). The best time to use directions is when you are sure students have the ability to comprehend and to act on information that is presented in an abstract format (Kiselica, 1988). Mrs. Armstrong could teach Granville some alternative ways of handling disagreements during group activities by telling or reading to the fifth-grade class a story that explains how other children have resolved their conflicts with schoolmates. By listening to the story, Granville and his classmates could learn new and more effective strategies for handling teasing and disagreements when working together. But for this approach to be successful, the students would have to understand the purpose and moral of the story and be able to apply the examples to their own social interactions.

Guidelines for Using Directions

The following section gives some important guidelines for using directions to teach social skills.

Limit the amount and type of information provided. Directions should concentrate on supplying information about how to improve social skills at the times students need it or are ready for it and should exclude extraneous information students do not need at the moment. Sometimes, we teachers tend to give students too much information, provide it too quickly, or supply it before they are able to understand it. If Mrs. Armstrong decides to use a role-playing activity to show Sandy how to join conversations, it is important for her to address just one instructional goal at a time. If Mrs. Armstrong tries to include directions not only about using greetings but also about choosing topics for conversation and about recognizing body language, Sandy is likely to be overwhelmed with the amount of information presented. On the other hand, if the focus of the activity is limited to using greetings, Sandy will more easily understand and be able to make use of the directions contained in the role-playing activity.

A similar problem can occur if directions include extra information students do not really need to achieve the instructional goals. For example, when Mrs. Armstrong sets up the role-playing activity for Sandy, she needs to be sure the content of the activity does not stray from its central focus on greetings. If the skits become too long or have too many other elements, the directions may become confused or unclear. Sandy would have difficulty picking out the essential information she needs to reach the instructional goals.

On the other hand, students will quickly understand the directions and be able to apply them to their own social interactions if you supply only the most pertinent information, state it clearly, and limit it to what students are able to comprehend (Eisler & Frederiksen, 1980; Solity & Bull, 1987). In the example presented above for Granville, Mrs. Armstrong should be sure that the story she tells the class describes very specifically several alternative ways of handling teasing and disagreements, rather than covering these topics too generally, because Granville needs specificity if he is to achieve the instructional goal. Mrs. Armstrong could lead a class discussion about the story afterward to be sure that Granville and the other students understand the exact directions she wants to convey.

Use various people and formats to provide the directions. Sometimes other adults or even other students are the best people to give the directions in an intervention, because they may have more credibility or a stronger rapport with students (Lovitt, 1984). Mrs. Armstrong may wish to use directions to help Alfred learn how to gain recognition from his peers. But instead of providing the directions herself, she could have the class, as a group exercise, generate its own suggestions for gaining recognition, or she might invite a sixth grader to the class to give the explanation. These approaches may provide Alfred and other students in the class with a better understanding of positive ways to gain attention because they would present the directions from the students' own perspective.

Similarly, embedding the directions in stories, discussions, or other activities can substantially increase the effectiveness of the procedure if the activities are well-planned. Mrs. Armstrong could have the class write scripts for skits based on their own ideas for gaining recognition. Techniques like these can be very effective in showing students how to use the information they gain from directions in the situations they encounter in their everyday social interactions.

Directions, then, can provide a straightforward and uncomplicated means of teaching social skills. Table 9.2 lists examples of procedures that could be used to teach social skills using directions. Note that these are only preliminary sketches of intervention activities at this point; we will discuss how to develop these kinds of ideas more fully in Chapter Ten.

Rehearsal

A second broad type of instructional procedure you can use is rehearsal. With rehearsal, you arrange opportunities for students to practice their social skills before they use them under natural performance conditions (Oden, 1986). An example of rehearsal is having students practice a speech or class presentation in front of a mirror before they speak in front of the class. These structured practice exercises allow students to refine their skills under circumstances that are more supportive, less distracting, or less threatening than those they will encounter later (Franco, Christoff, Crimmins, & Kelly, 1983; Zirpoli & Melloy, 1993). Sometimes, rehearsal

TABLE 9.2 Some ways to use directions to teach social skills

Post the rules for participating in an activity on a chart in a prominent place in the room.
Give students specific examples of how to give greetings, start conversations, or begin other activities. Have them explain what to do next.
Provide students with a note card or picture book that describes the steps for completing an activity.
Give students a worksheet that explains techniques for engaging in particular types of interactions. Have them discuss how they would put the techniques into practice.
Show students a list of steps for playing a game. Ask them to put the steps in the proper order.
Hold a class discussion about some of the best strategies for working on an activity, such as giving a class presentation or sharing work on a project.
Have two or more students begin a project by alternating in explaining to one another what the next step in the activity should be.
Give students a list of rules or procedures for an activity. Have them read or talk over the rules, and then have them use markers or play figures to show what they would do.
Read or narrate stories of social situations, and have students explain what the likely outcomes will be if the main character acts in various ways.
Have students write descriptions of difficult or troublesome encounters they have with schoolmates or teachers during the day, and ask them to put the descriptions in a "Bad Moments Box." Go over the descriptions with the class and have them talk about strategies for avoiding or handling these encounters.

will help students realize that working on a task or participating in an activity is not as difficult or as scary as they think it is. You would also use rehearsal when it is not feasible to have students practice their skills under natural conditions, such as when they are likely to be very self-conscious about trying out a skill for the first time. Mostly, you use rehearsal to help students become more fluent, precise, and confident in their behavior and build a level of proficiency they could not attain on their own.

Mrs. Armstrong could use rehearsal to help Sandy overcome some of the shyness and apprehension she shows in having conversations with classmates during breaks. Mrs. Armstrong could meet individually with her before these times, go over topics the students are likely to talk about, and have her rehearse some ways of initiating conversations about these topics. With this chance to practice her skills beforehand, Sandy may develop greater proficiency and confidence in her behavior.

Rehearsal can be overt or covert in that students can actually perform the required actions ahead of time, or they can simply plan them out or think them through (Campbell & Siperstein, 1994). In using rehearsal to teach Sandy how to start conversations, Mrs. Armstrong could have her act out, write down, talk about, or mentally rehearse ways to begin conversations before she actually engages in them with classmates. Although rehearsal can take place under closely supervised circumstances, it could also be incorporated into ongoing activities. For example, Mrs. Armstrong could work one-on-one with Sandy, or she could set up a role-playing activity and include other students in the practice sessions.

Guidelines for Using Rehearsal

The following guidelines apply to using rehearsal to teach social skills:

Closely watch over the practice sessions. One advantage of rehearsal is that the arranged practice sessions give you a chance to closely monitor and critique students' first attempts at using a skill, allowing you to indicate what the correct and incorrect behaviors are (Campbell & Siperstein, 1994). You should remedy errors as soon as they occur so students do not practice the behavior incorrectly. This feature of rehearsal can help students learn how to evaluate and fine-tune their own behavior as they engage in social interactions. After students become proficient in their behavior, you should teach them to use their skills independently and under normal conditions so they become self-reliant and assume control over their actions as quickly as possible.

Mrs. Armstrong may feel that Granville could avoid many conflicts if he would apologize when he bumps into other classmates or knocks their papers off their desks. She could structure teaching lessons for the group to highlight the need to apologize and have them rehearse giving apologies to one another in simulated situations. This procedure would allow Mrs. Armstrong and the group to correct and refine individual responses, without having to deal with real-life situations before students understand what the expected behavior is or when to use it. After completing the lessons, Mrs. Armstrong would find it much easier to remind Granville and the other students to use apologies during normal classroom activities, because they would already know exactly what to do and would have practiced it.

Use rehearsal after other procedures. Rehearsal is often most effective when used with directions and other intervention procedures. Rehearsal can serve as an excellent follow-up to videotaped presentations, peer demonstrations, skits, simulations, focused discussion groups, and other activities, because it helps students to try out as well as learn about the new behavior. This combination of procedures can highlight and exemplify the correct responses, and students can practice and compare their behavior to the samples they observe. Rehearsal is also flexible in that students do not have to imitate what they see but can adapt the behavior to fit their own performance style. For example, Mrs. Armstrong might have Alfred watch how other students gain recognition and respect from their peers, and she could help him make a list of guidelines or instructions for gaining positive attention. After he makes these observations, Mrs. Armstrong could have him rehearse the skill by practicing different ways to gain recognition or by talking about how he would approach different situations during game time. His ways of seeking recognition would not have to be exactly the same as those of the other students, as long as they are positive and constructive and satisfy the overall demands of the situation.

Carefully plan the practice opportunities. You should organize the opportunities for rehearsing skills so students start with practice sessions that are very structured and controlled, and progress gradually to sessions that are more like natural circumstances. This approach is especially beneficial when students are learning new behavioral patterns, like a new game or a new way to interact in a situation (Campbell & Siperstein, 1994). You set up the first practice opportunities so students play or interact under conditions that are stable, supportive, and noncompetitive, and progress to more varied, realistic, or challenging situations as the intervention proceeds. At the start of Alfred's intervention, Mrs. Armstrong may have him practice following game rules with her in a one-on-one situation. As his behavior becomes more proficient, she can alter the conditions so they are increasingly pressured or competitive, progressing to the natural performance conditions as the intervention continues. After the one-on-one situation, Mrs. Armstrong could have Alfred practice with one other student, and then with a small group. She could complicate the rehearsal situations even further by involving students with higher ability levels and more competitiveness or by changing the pace of the activities.

Rehearsal, then, is having students practice newly acquired skills before they actually use them under natural performance conditions. With rehearsal, you structure conditions so students give their full attention to developing the skills and to combining them into behavioral patterns. This procedure helps students gain greater proficiency and confidence in their performance and encourages them to carry over their skills to situations in which they should use them. Table 9.3 shows some other examples of how rehearsal can be employed in social skills interventions.

Modeling

Modeling is having students watch someone else perform a behavior so they learn to imitate the actions under similar circumstances (Bandura, 1986; Kerr & Nelson, 1989). A common example of modeling can be seen in instructional videos that use a "first watch me, then you try it" approach to teach everything from cooking and painting to dancing and aerobics. Modeling is an effective procedure for developing social skills because students can actually see someone else performing the behavior that they should use. They can observe how to perform a basic ability, how to link component steps together into a behavioral pattern, and how to coordinate actions in response to performance conditions. Furthermore, they can view the reactions of other people to the skilled behavior and observe the effects and outcomes that result from imitating the same behavior (Cartledge & Milburn, 1986).

Mrs. Armstrong could use modeling to teach Sandy how to initiate conversations by having her watch Mary, another student in class. Sandy can see how Mary gets a group's attention, can hear the greetings she uses, can see how she coordinates her behavior with the group's conversation, and can observe the outcomes of the overall interaction. Based on these observations, Sandy may learn to

TABLE 9.3 Some ways to use rehearsal to teach social skills

Ask students to state or act out what they would do next before proceeding to the next step in an activity.
Rehearse with students ahead of time the types of greetings they could give to classmates or adults, and the various things they could say in a conversation.
Have students act out the responses to a game or activity ahead of time, and then explain what they would do to improve on the actions.
Use a "stop action" approach in which the progress of an interaction stops part-way through, and students rehearse or play act what they should do next and what will likely happen in that case.
Have students think through or recite the steps for resolving a disagreement, sharing work on a task, or asking for help just before such an interaction might take place.
Show a video that illustrates interactions in various social situations. Have students practice alternative ways of responding to the situations.
Have students try out facial expressions, gestures, and other body movements in front of a mirror to practice better animation or coordination in social situations.
Have students rehearse or talk through standard types of statements they could use regularly in conversations about popular topics, e.g., "that's interesting," "that's a good idea," "tell me more."
Read or tell students a story about how other children have handled a difficult social situation. Ask the students to plan or act out how they would adapt the story to their own circumstances.
Have students practice different strategies for asking for help so they can obtain needed assistance from teachers and classmates.

initiate her own conversations by imitating Mary's actions. Similarly, Alfred could learn how to play group games by watching the game playing of other students and imitating their behavior. In this way, Alfred could learn what the rules are and see how they are put into practice in the natural situation, giving him a clear model to imitate in his own behavior.

Guidelines for Using Modeling

Below are some guidelines for using modeling to teach social skills.

Use directions to focus students' attention on the desired behavior. Modeling is a very useful method for teaching most social skills because students can see someone actually performing the expected actions in real situations (Bandura, 1986; McGinnis & Goldstein, 1984; Walker, 1979). But obviously, students must know what to watch for, and they must be able to incorporate what they see into their own behavior. For this reason, modeling is typically more effective when it is combined with directions that help students attend to and interpret the modeled

With modeling, students learn by watching and imitating skilled performance.

behavior (Campbell & Siperstein, 1994). Mrs. Armstrong could discuss with Sandy ahead of time the key points to watch for in Mary's interactions. Similarly, after Alfred watches the other students playing, Mrs. Armstrong could have the class discuss and list the rules for football games in order to help him better organize and interpret his observations. Thus, directions can be used to supplement modeling by highlighting and underscoring the central points of a modeled behavior and by helping students recognize the key elements to attend to in their own actions.

Use modeling with discrete skills and actions. Note that modeling works best when the behavior students are to imitate is discrete and easy to observe (Bull, Young, Blair, & Nelson, 1990). With social skills that have many component steps, modeling is most effective when you can isolate each step and point out how it is performed. With complex skills like making friends, playing recess games, or giving class recitations, students may need to see how each individual step in the sequence is performed if they do not already know how to complete some of the component steps. When the skills are not easy to observe, it becomes more important to add directions or some other procedure to highlight or clarify what the expected behavior is; otherwise, students may not know what to look for (Kazdin, 1989).

Model the skills and actions students will actually use. Whenever possible, the modeled actions should closely correspond to the way students are expected to behave under normal circumstances so they can easily adapt the behavior to their own interactions. Furthermore, the circumstances under which modeling takes place should depict the real-life situations that students usually encounter (Eisler &

Frederiksen, 1980; Goldstein, 1988). By following these considerations, you will help students learn how and when to imitate the required behavior. For example, the games Mrs. Armstrong has Alfred observe should show the format and the rules of the games he usually plays, and should depict the various peer interactions he normally has. Through this approach, Alfred can see a true representation of the behavior he should use and understand how the correct performance is carried out under natural conditions.

Select models carefully. You should use care in selecting models, because students are more likely to imitate people they like and admire than those they dislike or hold in low esteem (Bandura, 1986; Sharan, 1980). Mrs. Armstrong would choose Mary to model conversational skills for Sandy because Sandy seems always to look up to her. And if Mrs. Armstrong expects Granville to observe and imitate the cooperative interactions of other students in work groups, she must be careful to select groups that interact in ways that match how Granville should act, and that include students Granville will emulate. In matching students with models, you may need to consider such factors as the model's skill level, age, gender, ethnicity, background, and status within the group (Cartledge & Milburn, 1986; Goldstein, 1988; Kazdin, 1981). Any one of these factors could influence how well students watch and imitate another person's behavior.

Provide practice opportunities. Another important consideration with modeling is ensuring that students have several opportunities to practice and refine the observed behavior so it can become a part of their repertoire (Knapczyk, 1991; 1992; McGinnis & Goldstein, 1984). If the practice opportunities do not occur naturally in the setting, you may have to structure them for students. These opportunities will help students recognize the most pertinent aspects of the interaction and coordinate their behavior with the ongoing activities. For example, Mrs. Armstrong should structure several practice sessions after Sandy has had a chance to observe how Mary initiates her conversations so Sandy will have a chance to try out the behavior. These sessions will enable Mrs. Armstrong to evaluate whether Sandy is using the correct behavior and is adapting or refining the behavior to fit her interactions. In cases where students are reluctant to try or practice the new behavior, you may have to use encouragement or some other incentive technique to stimulate their interest, attention, and participation in the modeling activities.

Use models that are videotaped. One very effective modeling approach is to have students watch videotapes that show examples of skilled social behavior (Cartledge & Milburn, 1986; Knapczyk, 1992). Mrs. Armstrong could teach Granville and some of his classmates how to respond appropriately to disagreements during group work by having them watch videotapes of various cooperative situations. The segments could show typical episodes of conflict between classmates and depict examples of acceptable responses. After Granville and the other students watch the videotapes, Mrs. Armstrong could have the group describe the events leading up to the disagreements and discuss some alternative ways of resolving them.

Videotapes, audiotapes, and other media have advantages in modeling because they allow you to show behavior and highlight performance conditions that would otherwise be very difficult to point out or reconstruct in the natural setting. The use of media gives you a way to freeze events in time so students can see the acceptable behavior; you can also repeat any segment as often as needed (Dowrick, 1986; Eisler & Frederiksen, 1980; Knapczyk, 1988). Mrs. Armstrong could use videotapes with Granville both to highlight certain skills and techniques at the start of the intervention and to emphasize and reinforce crucial points during later feedback sessions.

Videotapes are also helpful for contrasting skilled behavior with unskilled behavior so students can see when to use the desired behavior. Videotaped examples can pinpoint what they should watch for in a situation and stimulate discussions of the best behavioral strategies to use (Knapczyk, 1988, 1992; McCullough, 1989). In her videotapes, Mrs. Armstrong could include examples of inept or immature ways of handling disagreements to contrast with the more effective strategies. This may give added emphasis to the techniques she is teaching Granville.

If you make your own videotapes, you can usually capture some realistic samples of social interactions during most school activities, but first you will have to allow students to become comfortable with being videotaped. Older students may feel more at ease being taped if they have a few opportunities to plan and rehearse their interactions beforehand. After students become comfortable with being videotaped, they may take an interest in preparing the segments themselves and assume a major responsibility for the instructional activities (Goldstein, 1988). In another approach, you could select students from other classrooms as actors and have them depict situations, interactions, and skills you would like your students to learn (Knapczyk, 1988; 1989; 1992). Mrs. Armstrong could ask several middle school students to help her develop videotapes to use with Granville. She could prepare an outline of the types of interactions she would like the students to portray. Then she could videotape their demonstrations of effective ways to cooperate on class projects or to respond to conflicts and disagreements—ways that would be appropriate for Granville to use in his interactions. Even though it would take extra time and planning to prepare the tapes, Mrs. Armstrong could use them again, after Granville's intervention, with other students or with the class as a whole.

Modeling, then, is an excellent approach for teaching social skills because students can actually see the behavior they are learning. However, the ability of students to imitate or use the behavior after they have observed it will depend on whom they observe, how easily they can pick out and repeat the desired actions, and how well they can apply the behavior to their own circumstances. Table 9.4 gives other examples of how modeling can be used in social skills interventions.

Prompting

Prompting is a simple yet effective intervention procedure for improving social skills. With this approach, you give cues to students just prior to when they should use a skill in an interaction. Prompting typically occurs when students have learned a skill but still need reminders about how or when to use it. Examples of prompting include giving students a nod or a hand gesture to remind them to raise their hands before speaking, or asking "What's the magic word?" when you cue them to

TABLE 9.4 Some ways to use modeling to teach social skills

Have students stand on the sidelines and watch a game or activity. Ask them to imitate the step-by-step process other students go through to participate in the activities or interactions.
Teach certain students ahead of time how to play a new game or activity. Have them explain or demonstrate the new game to the group, and then ask them to oversee the activities.
Have a small group of students prepare a skit for younger students that shows how to interact properly in a particularly difficult or complicated social situation. Ask the younger students to repeat the skit.
Have students role-play a typical problem situation and ask them to demonstrate what will likely happen under various circumstances.
Invite students from a higher grade to supervise recess activities. Their role would be to demonstrate skills for various games and activities and to encourage the younger students to imitate the skills during play activities.
Have students watch a video of an interaction in which the actors display both appropriate and inappropriate behaviors. Ask the students to describe and act out what they did correctly, and explain what they could have done differently to avoid the problems caused by the behavior.
Invite older children or youth to the classroom and ask them to coach students in more appropriate ways of handling difficult social situations.
Ask students to make a video of a social situation. Tell them the purpose of the video is to show examples of how students should act during specific activities. Ask the students to imitate the actions shown on the tape.
Use puppet or cartoon characters to depict social situations, and have students demonstrate with their own actions what the characters did or did not do under these circumstances. Have the characters act out the students' performance to show the outcomes of the suggested behavior.
Show a video of game or sports activities in slow motion or stop action. Have students imitate the actions, and then practice combining the actions into a performance pattern.

say "please." You can provide prompts in verbal, written, or gestural form, or you can even teach students to prompt themselves (Knapczyk & Livingston, 1974).

Mrs. Armstrong could use prompts to help Alfred remember the rules for playing football after he has learned them. She could remind him of the rules before he leaves for recess, tell his play group to review the rules before they start playing a game, or have a teammate signal Alfred about what to do during particular play situations (e.g., how far to stand from the line of scrimmage, which player to guard, or what to do if the ball is thrown to that player). The prompts she or his teammates give should help Alfred keep the expected behavior in mind when he plays the game.

Guidelines for Using Prompting

The following guidelines apply to using prompting to teach social skills.

Make sure the meaning of the prompts is clear. Prompts are usually shortened forms or substitutes for directions, modeling, or other more complicated procedures. The content of the prompts and the types you use must therefore be meaningful to students so they can serve as replacements or reminders for the original procedures (Kerr & Nelson, 1989). Furthermore, the prompts should be as simple and straightforward as possible, and should be limited to communicating the information the students actually need in order to achieve the instructional goals.

Mrs. Armstrong may decide that the simplest way to remind Granville of her directions for acting as a small group leader or for resolving disagreements is to work out a system of hand signals with him. Thus, instead of going over the directions again each time he is in his group, she could give him a subtle "thumbs up" signal when he is following the procedure correctly, and a "thumbs down" signal when he has failed or forgotten to follow the directions. But in order to make this system work properly, she must meet with Granville beforehand to go over the signals and explain how they relate to the directions he learned earlier. She might even practice giving him the signals to make sure he understands what they mean and can apply them directly to his behavior and to the prior instructions.

Use prompts as reminders rather than as a primary teaching device. Prompting is an especially useful procedure for reviewing the sequence and timing of component steps and for highlighting performance conditions. In other words, it is effective when students have the basic abilities to perform the skills they need but cannot coordinate their actions with specific situations or activities (Grubaugh, 1989; Solity & Bull, 1987). However, prompts should not be used to give basic instruction when students do not have the knowledge or ability to perform skills with at least some degree of competence. For example, Mrs. Armstrong may use prompts to remind Sandy what to do to join a conversational group. But she must be sure that Sandy has learned the essential skills beforehand—through directions, rehearsal, or other techniques—so she can carry out the prompted behavior to at least a minimum level of proficiency. In this way, Mrs. Armstrong can ensure that the gestures highlight for Sandy the specific skills she is to use and the performance conditions to which she should attend, and do not simply frustrate and confuse her.

Fade prompts when they are no longer needed. Do not allow prompting to become a permanent crutch for students. You should take steps to remove prompts as quickly as possible, especially when they are not a natural part of the performance conditions (Bos & Vaughn, 1988). If you give prompts to only one student or to a specific group, or if the prompts pertain to skills students should perform on their own without being reminded, withdraw them when they are no longer necessary. In most instances, you can simply stop supplying the prompts when students show they can perform independently. At other times, you will need to fade or remove them gradually. As a rule, you should withdraw or fade prompts immediately after students have learned the skill and understand the relationship between their actions and the performance conditions (Knapczyk & Livingston, 1973).

TABLE 9.5 Some ways to use prompting to teach social skills

Set up a cue or signal system with students to remind them when they are to use a particular skill, e.g., initiate a greeting, take their turn, make a comment.
Ask students' friends to coach or prompt them through a particularly difficult part of an activity or interaction.
Prepare cue cards with pictures or phrases that remind students of the steps they should go through to complete an activity or project.
Use pictures or cartoon characters to remind students of how they should behave toward classmates, or what tasks they should complete, e.g., to share in putting away toys or work materials.
Place sign boards in various locations of the classroom to remind students of the expected behavior for that particular location.
Have students prompt one another on the expected behavior before starting on a new activity, e.g., circle time or reading groups.
Use hand signals or facial expressions to remind students what to do, or not to do, just before they begin an activity or interaction.
Teach students a mnemonic device reminding them of the steps to follow in a situation.
Have students use hand gestures to cue one another about the proper behavior to use in situations, e.g., using good manners, waiting their turn.
Have students recite a song or rhyme that reminds them of the way they should act.

After Granville learns some techniques for resolving differences of opinion during small group activities, Mrs. Armstrong can watch his interactions with classmates and remind him to use one of the strategies whenever he is about to have a disagreement. However, Mrs. Armstrong should stop giving the reminders when Granville is able to perform without them so he learns to use the skill independently.

Prompting, then, is a shortened or substitute form of a more complicated or detailed intervention procedure, and it serves to cue students to use a particular skill. Prompts that are not a normal part of the situation should be withdrawn as the intervention progresses so students do not become overly dependent on them. Table 9.5 gives examples of ways prompting can be used in social skills interventions.

Brainstorming Intervention Procedures

One of the best ways to begin planning an intervention is to brainstorm and jot down potential ideas for methods and activities to use with students. The worksheet we introduced earlier in the chapter for listing instructional goals can be expanded to provide a format for generating preliminary intervention ideas. Figure 9.2 shows

Figure 9.2 Mrs. Armstrong's brainstorming worksheet showing ideas for Granville's intervention.

Worksheet 9.1 (continued)	Name: *Mrs. Armstrong* Student: *Granville*	Page *2* of *5*

Instructional goal:

Learn to follow written and oral directions for group activities

Instructional approaches considered:

X Directions ___ Rehearsal *X* Modeling *X* Prompting

Brainstorming—preliminary ideas for intervention procedures:

Teach Granville a step-by-step procedure for writing down and following directions. Point out the key words or phrases for the steps so Granville can use them as a memory device.

Have Granville repeat directions after they are given. Perhaps vary formats so he goes over directions in one-on-one situations, in small groups, and with the class as a whole using overhead transparencies.

Develop a system of nonverbal prompts with Granville to remind him if he forgets a step in the assignment.

If Granville makes mistakes with directions, ask him what he thought the directions were. If needed, prepare clearer sets of directions for the class.

Before groups start an activity, ask them to go over the directions for the assignment. Maybe Granville could alternate with another group member in explaining the steps for the activity.

Prepare a short video of activities showing how students ask questions about directions on assignments. Use the tape to point out some good questioning techniques for him to use when he has difficulty understanding directions.

Figure 9.2 *(continued)*

Worksheet 9.1 (continued)	Name: *Mrs. Armstrong* Student: *Granville*	Page *3* of *5*

Instructional goal:

Learn to organize and plan the assignment before starting work

Instructional approaches considered:

X Directions *X* Rehearsal *X* Modeling ___ Prompting

Brainstorming—preliminary ideas for intervention procedures:

Prepare a worksheet for Granville that shows the steps for completing an assignment. Have him use the worksheet to develop an outline of the steps he should go through to complete an assignment.

Have Granville review verbally the steps for a project before he starts on an activity.

Give Granville a jumbled list of steps for completing activities and ask him to put them in order.

Have Granville make a video of students working through an assignment and have him analyze the tape for the specific steps they go through.

Have his group go over or review the next step in a task before they start it. Maybe give Granville a list of steps ahead of time so he can see whether the group is correct.

After giving an assignment, hold a class discussion of the steps they should go through. Have Granville write the steps on the board or overhead transparency.

Have Granville observe some of the groups using a checklist of steps to see whether the groups are using the right procedures.

Have Granville observe projects in Mrs. Kelly's fourth-grade classroom and have him develop a planning worksheet of steps for her class. Maybe this would emphasize the importance of planning things ahead of time.

Figure 9.2 *(continued)*

Worksheet 9.1 (continued)	Name: *Mrs. Armstrong* Student: *Granville*	Page *4* of *5*

Instructional goal:

Learn to coordinate performance with the activities of the group

Instructional approaches considered:

X Directions   *X* Rehearsal   *X* Modeling   ___ Prompting

Brainstorming—preliminary ideas for intervention procedures:

Have Granville lead a small group discussion of why it is important to work together with classmates on class projects.

Have Granville watch Marty's group and describe what they do. Have him rehearse or practice the actions on his own, before his group starts their work.

Have the groups, including Granville, prepare role-playing videos showing examples of well-coordinated and badly coordinated work groups.

Teach Granville a step-by-step technique for keeping track of what other group members are doing. Have him explain what he could do to help with the project, or to make the group work more smoothly.

Change the group Granville is in; perhaps Sally's group will ignore the jokes and stories. Maybe he could select his own group members when his behavior improves.

Have Granville be the leader for a while and make him responsible for finding a way to get group members to cooperate. Later, he could work as a co-leader and learn to share responsibilities.

Figure 9.2 *(continued)*

Worksheet 9.1 (continued)	Name: *Mrs. Armstrong* Student: *Granville*	Page *5* of *5*

Instructional goal:

Learn strategies for handling teasing and disagreements with peers

Instructional approaches considered:

X Directions *X* Rehearsal *X* Modeling *X* Prompting

Brainstorming—preliminary ideas for intervention procedures:

Ask Granville to develop some guidelines for handling disagreements and have him present the guidelines to the class or to his group.

Have the class role-play situations involving typical disagreements, and discuss good and bad ways to handle them.

Have Granville practice phrases or techniques for responding to disagreements or teasing that are more diplomatic. Allow him and other classmates to practice these techniques during role-playing activities.

Pick a student Granville likes who also has good conflict resolution skills, and pair them in the group. Have Granville watch and discuss with the student different ways to resolve disagreements.

Make a list of acceptable ways to respond to teasing and other conflicts and post it in the room. Every time Granville or another student responds inappropriately, stop the activity or interaction, and ask the student to pick out an acceptable response to use instead.

how Mrs. Armstrong expanded the worksheet she completed in Figure 9.1 so she could use her instructional goals as a focus for her ideas for Granville.

The figure shows that the worksheet for brainstorming intervention procedures need not be particularly complicated. The format should be flexible and free enough to allow you to explore wide-ranging options and proposals, and to incorporate those that hold the most promise into your intervention plan. At the same time, it is important to stay focused on the instructional goals you have set so the intervention remains firmly centered on the students' needs. Having these goals prominently displayed on the worksheet, as shown in Figure 9.2, will help you keep them in mind while you are thinking of procedures to use with your students. In the following section, we explain the steps for preparing a list of brainstorming ideas for interventions and show how Mrs. Armstrong developed a worksheet of possible procedures to use with Granville.

Step 1: Listing Basic Information and Instructional Goals

Start the worksheet by entering the student's name and grade level, and by listing the final instructional goals you have set for the intervention. For this purpose, you can use the page you developed earlier for listing instructional goals. This form, introduced in Figure 9.1 earlier in the chapter, includes a place for entering Granville's name, grade, and date, and lists the four goals Mrs. Armstrong has established for his intervention. This page can now become the cover page for a brainstorming worksheet on which she will sketch out some preliminary ideas for addressing these four goals in the intervention.

Step 2: Making a Separate Page for Each Goal

Your next step should be to prepare a separate worksheet page for each of the instructional goals you set for an intervention. Keeping the goals separate will allow you to focus clearly on each skill area and to consider and outline potential intervention procedures that specifically address each goal. Figure 9.2 shows that Mrs. Armstrong has continued the worksheet she began in Figure 9.1 by adding four new pages, one for each of the four instructional goals. As the example shows, she has entered each goal in its own place at the top of a page.

Step 3: Checking off Instructional Approaches to Consider

Even when you have focused each page clearly on a specific instructional goal, you can be overwhelmed by the many possible intervention approaches you could consider. Conversely, you may find it hard to get your brainstorming started or to find a direction for your ideas. When Mrs. Armstrong began to develop ideas for Granville's intervention, she had some trouble deciding how to get started. She knew that one goal she should work on is teaching him to handle teasing and disagreements more diplomatically, but she was not sure how to organize her many thoughts and ideas for addressing the goal.

To help you generate ideas and give shape to your brainstorming, you should mark or check off instructional approaches you may wish to consider for each goal. The worksheet format presented in Figure 9.2 shows a checklist on each page listing the four broad categories of procedures discussed in this chapter. Mrs. Armstrong has marked the strategies she felt might be useful for addressing each goal area. By reviewing and checking off instructional approaches for addressing each goal, you will be able to set a general direction for your ideas and establish a solid focus for the rest of your planning.

Step 4: Brainstorming Intervention Ideas for Each Goal

After you have listed each instructional goal and marked some possible intervention strategies, you will have established a strong focus for exploring specific intervention ideas. Now you are ready to formulate a rough sketch of potential methods and activities for addressing each of the goals. This step should be a free-ranging brainstorming activity, incorporating as many different possibilities for addressing the goals as you can think of. Interventions are usually more effective when they involve unusual or inventive approaches—procedures that capture the students' attention, interest, and imagination. Remember, however, to keep your ideas firmly grounded in the goals and directions you have set.

As Figure 9.2 shows, when Mrs. Armstrong considered procedures for teaching Granville to follow directions, she thought of ideas like teaching him a five-step memory system, pairing him with a peer tutor, holding a small group discussion, and using computer exercises to teach some of the direction-following skills Granville lacks. As you can see from Figure 9.2, the result is a worksheet filled with activities that are broad based but still focused on her goals. The ideas Mrs. Armstrong has set down here are preliminary sketches rather than complete intervention plans. She will not do all these things at once, and she will need to develop her ideas further and finalize her plans (Chapters Ten and Eleven will discuss these steps). But to start, her best approach was to generate as many ideas and potential procedures as possible and to write them on her worksheet pages.

In summary, you will find it helpful to begin planning an intervention by setting down preliminary ideas for procedures directed toward meeting your instructional goals. The worksheet described above will allow you to capture your ideas from brainstorming while keeping you focused on the goals you have set.

❍ Summary

Consolidating Instructional Goals from a Specific Level Assessment

1. Reviewing the findings from the specific level assessment will help coordinate and consolidate instructional goals for interventions.

2. The four techniques for consolidating instructional goals are the following:
   a. deleting goals that are repeated
   b. combining goals that are related
   c. looking for goals that supersede or encompass others
   d. deemphasizing goals that are less important or that can be delayed
3. The finalized list of goals can be entered on a worksheet to assist with further instructional planning.
4. The final list of instructional goals should reflect the students' needs, the complexity of the goals, and the original target skill.

An Overview of Procedures for Teaching Social Skills

1. Four broad procedures for teaching social skills are directions, rehearsal, modeling, and prompting.
2. Directions involve telling students how or when to behave in social situations, and what will happen when they do.
3. Guidelines for using directions include
   a. limiting the amount and type of information provided
   b. using various people and formats to provide the information
4. Rehearsal is arranging opportunities for students to practice social skills before they use them under natural performance conditions.
5. Guidelines for using rehearsal include
   a. watching closely over practice sessions
   b. using rehearsal after other procedures
   c. carefully planning practice opportunities
6. Modeling is having students observe someone perform a behavior so they learn to imitate the actions under similar circumstances.
7. Guidelines for using modeling include
   a. focusing students' attention on behavior with directions
   b. using modeling with discrete skills and actions
   c. modeling skills and actions students will actually use
   d. selecting models carefully
   e. providing practice opportunities
   f. using models that are videotaped
8. Prompting is giving cues about performance just prior to students' using the skills.
9. Guidelines for using prompting include
   a. making sure the meaning of prompts is clear
   b. using prompts as reminders rather than as a primary teaching device
   c. fading prompts when they are no longer necessary

Brainstorming Intervention Procedures

1. Brainstorming potential intervention ideas is one of the best ways to begin developing an intervention plan.
2. The steps for brainstorming intervention procedures are the following:
   a. listing basic information about the student and about the instructional goals on a worksheet
   b. developing separate worksheet pages for each instructional goal
   c. checking off instructional approaches to use for each goal
   d. brainstorming specific intervention ideas for each goal

Examples for Chapter 9

Example 9a

Ms. Finley is a kindergarten teacher who is working with Margaret, an overly shy, developmentally delayed student who rarely participates in large group circle activities. Ms. Finley has defined Margaret's target skill as "participates in circle group activities." She has set some fairly basic instructional goals for improving Margaret's participation, including "learn to follow the rules for circle games," "learn to take turns," and "learn to show excitement in playing the games." This page from Ms. Finley's brainstorming worksheet shows some ideas she has for teaching Margaret to show excitement during circle activities.

Worksheet 9.1 (continued)	Name: *Ms. Finley* Student: *Margaret*	Page *3* of *5*

Instructional goal:

Learn to show excitement in playing the activities

> Even very basic goals can be addressed with procedures carried out during regularly scheduled activities.

Instructional approaches considered:

X Directions ___ Rehearsal *X* Modeling *X* Prompting

Brainstorming—preliminary ideas for intervention procedures:

Have the children do a skit involving a children's television character. Pair Margaret with Kelly, who is very animated, and have them take turns showing each other how to act in the skit. Give them suggestions and ideas if needed.

> Different types of models stress the skills students need to learn. Verbal directions add further emphasis to modeling procedures.

Use activities with a lot of animation ("I'm a little teapot," "Itsy bitsy spider") and have Margaret help me lead the group through the activity.

Do the usual circle activities, but modify the activities in funny ways—have the students exaggerate the activities, do them backwards, do them with their fingers on their noses. Have Margaret choose the next way to do the activities.

> Routine activities can be structured to reinforce the skills being taught.

Show the group an exercise videotape. Have Margaret and the group give expressions of how people look when they exercise very hard and are exhausted.

Make silly facial expressions and have Margaret imitate them. Ask her to make silly faces for the group.

During circle time, show pictures of animated facial expressions of young children. Ask Margaret and the group to imitate the expressions.

> Using a variety of procedures and teaching formats helps to reinforce a new skill. Ms. Finley can coordinate several of these approaches.

Prompt Margaret to show animated facial expressions during circle time, and during other activities. Use hand signals or cue cards to show her what expressions to use.

Example 9b

Alan is an eleventh-grade student in Mr. Watson's study hall period. Alan does not use his time in study hall productively, preferring visiting with friends to doing homework. Alan is very brash and annoys the students around him. He takes it for granted that neighbors and Mr. Watson will help him with his work whenever he needs it, but he ignores or refuses other students' requests for his help. He also asks for help simply to get attention or to draw other students off task.

Mr. Watson has chosen "gives help to and accepts help from classmates on assignments" as Alan's target skill. His instructional goals are "learn to recognize when help is needed," "learn to express appreciation to classmates for giving help," and "learn to give help when it is requested." This page shows some of Mr. Watson's ideas for teaching Alan to express appreciation to his classmates.

Worksheet 9.1 (continued)	Name: *Mr. Watson* Student: *Alan*	Page *4* of *5*

Instructional goal:

Learn to express appreciation to classmates for giving help

Instructional approaches considered:

X Directions *X* Rehearsal *X* Modeling *X* Prompting

Brainstorming—preliminary ideas for intervention procedures:

Have Alan observe other students and ask him to report on the different ways in which students show appreciation for helping one another.

Hold a small group discussion and ask students to explain why it is important to show appreciation for another person's help. Have them describe how they feel when someone they help (a) shows appreciation or (b) does not show appreciation.

Use the class discussion to make a list of ways to show appreciation. Go over the list with Alan, and have him practice different phrases and actions for showing appreciation.

Explain to Alan the times at which he should show appreciation, and have him come up with a system of prompts we can use to help him recognize these times.

Make a contract with Alan. He can earn library time for remembering to show appreciation.

Encourage him to prompt himself, and let him keep track of his own progress toward the reward.

Pair Alan with Kevin, with whom he works well, and ask Kevin to prompt Alan to show appreciation for helping him. Use the same prompting system Alan came up with.

Set up a role-playing activity in which students help one another and show gratitude. Have Alan imitate and rehearse different ways to show gratitude.

Have some popular students come to study hall to tutor students, and pair Alan with the most popular boy or girl. Have him use the ways he has rehearsed to show gratitude, and have Kevin prompt him when to use these ways.

Peers are a valuable resource for highlighting competent and incompetent performance.

Involve students as much as possible in their own interventions, and allow them to keep track of their own progress.

The brainstorming worksheet should contain as many ideas as possible. Mr. Watson may later reject this procedure as too juvenile for Alan, but at this point he is withholding such judgments and entering as many suggestions as he can.

Most brainstorming ideas will usually involve a combination of instructional approaches.

Mr. Wagner's Case Study

Mr. Wagner looked over his assessment findings and consolidated them into final instructional goals for the intervention. Note that most of these goals are too broad, too vague, or too concerned with academic skills to help improve Granville's social behavior:

Learn to stop borrowing material.
Learn to read over the assignment and do his own share of the work.
Learn to use group time productively.
Learn to get along with Bobby.
Learn to do projects on time.

On this page from his brainstorming worksheet, Mr. Wagner noted his ideas for teaching Granville to read over his assignment and to do his own work.

Worksheet 9.1 (continued)	Name: *Mr. Wagner* Student: *Granville*	Page *3* of *7*

Instructional goal:

Learn to read over his assignment and do his own share of the work

> This goal combines two distinct skills. It is too broad to address with a single set of procedures.

Instructional approaches considered:

_X_ Directions ___ Rehearsal _X_ Modeling _X_ Prompting

Brainstorming—preliminary ideas for intervention procedures:

Tell Granville to read the assignment after it is given out. Check whether he reads it; if he did not, remind him.

> Mr. Wagner has probably used this procedure many times with Granville. He should try something more innovative.

Have students write a group work statement at the end of each activity, stating who did which part. The students can get points and earn rewards for doing their share.

Tell Granville that he needs to read the assignment before he can begin work. If he has not read the assignment sit him separately and have him read; he can go to the group when he is finished. Otherwise, he is out of luck and will have to do the assignment later.

> Avoid reinforcing failure or negative attitudes. This procedure may simply give Granville an easy way to avoid doing his work.

Show the class a video on "Winning with teamwork." Have a class discussion on why it is important to do your share.

> Procedures should pertain directly to the goals. It is doubtful that Granville will benefit much from this activity.

Give Granville a timer to mark down the amount of time he spends doing his work. Give him a reward if he works more than ten minutes.

Talk with Granville about why it's important to get his work done. Ask him to tell me why he doesn't want to do his assignments, and work with him to reverse his negative image of

> Discussing problems with students is not a substitute for teaching them the specific skills they need to learn.

CHAPTER 10

Developing and Refining Intervention Plans

The brainstorming process we outlined in Chapter Nine is likely to produce more ideas for an intervention than you can implement at one time; therefore, you must refine your plans further by choosing the most promising procedures. At the same time you should make this selection carefully because you might need to use several intervention approaches to respond to the various instructional goals you plan to address. Furthermore, you will have to develop your ideas in much greater detail than the notes you made during the brainstorming activities.

In this chapter, we show how to select the procedures you will use in an intervention, and how to develop and expand them. We also discuss how to address particularly complex instructional goals and how to proceed when students lack incentive to learn target skills. Finally, we explain how to finalize procedures and prepare a coherent and fully organized intervention plan.

Throughout the organizational process, remember the aim of preparing an intervention plan: to design procedures and activities that will help students meet the expectations you have set as priorities. The most challenging task here is to select procedures that will achieve this aim as quickly and efficiently as possible, without significantly disrupting the ongoing routines and schedules of the setting. In this chapter, we present a variety of suggestions for making these selections judiciously so your intervention plans will be as precisely targeted and as broadly effective as possible.

Organizing Intervention Plans

One of the most daunting tasks of preparing intervention plans is deciding where to begin. As Mrs. Armstrong looks over all the procedures she has outlined for Alfred, Sandy, and Granville, she is likely to be overwhelmed by the variety of options she could pursue, and somewhat perplexed over where to start. With so many ideas to consider, she will find it helpful to impose an organizing structure before considering specific ideas. The best way to begin organizing plans is to sequence the instructional goals so you will know what areas of behavior to work on first (Campbell & Siperstein, 1994; Howell, Fox, & Morehead, 1993). In the following section, we suggest some organizing strategies.

Sequencing Instructional Goals

A useful way to begin an intervention plan is to sequence instructional goals in the order you plan to address them. This structure will help you consider the individual skills you need to teach and visualize how the procedures you design will eventually fit together. It is usually best to address the most basic goals and skill areas at the start of the intervention, then to move to more complex areas. Not only are these fundamental skills easier for students to grasp, but they often serve as building blocks for the more complex aspects of the target skill (Kameenui & Simmons, 1990; Zirpoli & Melloy, 1993). Thus, when you have defined instructional goals that involve basic abilities, you will usually address them in the initial part of an intervention, before teaching students to link component steps or attend to performance conditions. Goals that require application of skills to other settings are best left to the end of the intervention after students have learned all or most of the essential skills (Hoy & Gregg, 1994).

Mrs. Armstrong would probably start Alfred's intervention by teaching him to perform according to the game rules, because this area is the most basic of his goals and will most likely contribute to his success in the other skills. Then she could concentrate on the more complex demands of his game-playing interactions, like learning how to coordinate his behavior with his teammates' actions or how to interact with his peers in the context of game activities. Her reason for sequencing the goals this way is that after he learns to play correctly and to follow the rules for a game, he will find it much easier to understand the other aspects of game-playing interactions. Similarly, Mrs. Armstrong would probably teach Granville how to follow directions for small group assignments before she works on more complicated goals like learning how to coordinate his performance with group members and learning to be a group leader. Her instructional goals for Granville could be listed in the following order:

- Learn to follow written and oral directions for group activities
- Learn to organize and plan the assignment before starting work
- Learn to coordinate performance with the activities of the group
- Learn strategies for handling teasing and disagreements with peers

By organizing the goals in a simple-to-complex sequence, you will also be able to spot potential difficulties and problems in behavior that the students' assessments may not have uncovered. As you may have noticed in conducting an assessment, when students have trouble performing the basic elements of the target skill, you may have difficulty identifying their more subtle and complex problems. It is very hard to investigate potential problems with component steps and performance conditions when students lack basic abilities, because completing the steps and responding to conditions often require proficiency in these fundamental skills. Therefore, when you begin an intervention by addressing the basic problem areas, you give students an opportunity to display more clearly their knowledge of the more advanced and complicated skills for meeting expectations. This approach will allow you to uncover problems you may not have seen before.

For example, if Mrs. Armstrong begins Sandy's intervention by teaching her how to give greetings and select topics of conversation, she may obtain new information about Sandy's skill level after she begins to use these basic skills in her interactions with teachers and classmates. After Sandy starts speaking more, Mrs. Armstrong may find that she has difficulty talking about certain topics, or that she is unable to express her opinions and ideas effectively. Mrs. Armstrong may have suspected this from her earlier assessments, but once the intervention begins and Sandy's more basic behavior starts to improve, these problems are likely to become more observable. This information will be very useful to Mrs. Armstrong when she moves to other parts of the intervention and addresses the more complex goals for Sandy, such as teaching her how to change the topic of a conversation to one she wants to talk about. We will discuss ways to address problem areas that are uncovered during an intervention in Chapter Twelve when we explain how to choose a course of action after you have begun an intervention.

Identifying Promising Intervention Procedures

Once you have a sequence for instructional goals, you can more easily look at the procedures you have sketched out and gauge their potential usefulness. You may see that certain ones could fit together and complement one another to address several goals at once. But at this point you should avoid thinking of a final selection of intervention procedures; the best approach is to start with the most promising ideas, the ones that will have the greatest effect on the students' performance of the target skill. Together with the sequence of goals you have set, these procedures will be the starting point for further development of your plans.

Mrs. Armstrong likes many of her ideas for Sandy's intervention, but a few seem more practical and potentially effective than others. One is to set up a conversation group for Sandy with some of the more popular girls in the class, to give her an encouraging environment to learn and practice using greetings and other conversational skills. Mrs. Armstrong will begin her intervention plan by building on this idea. Similarly, with Granville she is most interested in teaching him a step-by-step technique for following directions, as well as having him lead the group activity himself. She does not want to discard her other procedures, but she will start with these two possibilities and consider how to use them to address the goals she has outlined. As she develops these procedures further, she may return to her brainstorming worksheet to see what other methods she could combine with them.

In the next section, we discuss how to proceed once you have sequenced the instructional goals and identified key ideas with which to begin planning interventions. We structure this discussion by giving ten helpful suggestions for expanding, improving, and refining your intervention ideas.

Ten Ways to Develop Intervention Procedures

Transforming preliminary ideas about procedures into fully detailed blueprints for interventions is a task that can take many forms. There is no single developmental process; much will depend on the characteristics of the students, the target skills, the level of program support, scheduling considerations, and other factors peculiar to your circumstances (Cartledge & Milburn, 1986). Rather than describe a definitive step-by-step process, we instead present ten different ways you can develop and improve your intervention ideas. These ten items range from broad approaches to specific reminders of guidelines (see Table 10.1). They are not presented in a strict order because they may be useful in a number of ways. Nor is it necessary to use all of them; you should simply consider these possibilities as you expand and refine your intervention plans.

Elaborate and Expand on Key Ideas

The ideas you outline in a brainstorming session are by necessity incomplete and sketchy. Furthermore, they will tend to be fairly limited in scope. One way to bring more detail and breadth to your procedures is to elaborate on the specific details you will need to consider to implement the ideas. For example, as she thinks more about the idea of setting up a conversation group for Sandy, Mrs. Armstrong realizes that this procedure would involve many details she has not yet considered, including the following:

When and where would these conversations take place?

Which students should be involved?

TABLE 10.1 Ten ways to develop and improve intervention procedures

Elaborate and expand on key ideas.
Combine and coordinate individual procedures.
Involve colleagues in planning.
Be sure intervention plans respond to assessment results.
Build on the students' current strengths and areas of competence.
Promote student involvement and independence.
Integrate procedures into the regular routine of the settings.
Make procedures flexible and easy to remove when behavior improves.
Consult published resources for additional ideas and techniques.
Keep procedures simple and straightforward.

How will the group be structured?

Should she direct the group herself?

What kinds of directions should she give the group?

Will Sandy need to be prepared in advance?

As Mrs. Armstrong begins to address implementation questions like these, her simple idea will begin to take more shape and lead to a more fully planned activity.

This kind of planning can prompt further ideas for expanding the original procedure. As Mrs. Armstrong develops her ideas for Sandy in more detail, she may think of other elements that could be added to the activity. When she considers the structure of the group conversations, she might decide to create a written set of directions to get the group started, or she might decide to have the group play a cooperative conversation game. When she thinks about what the groups will talk about, she might decide to use role playing—having Sandy and the rest of the group hold a conversation acting out the roles of famous people, or having them pretend they are on a talk show. By considering logistical questions like these and elaborating on the details of a particular procedure, you can expand the scope of your ideas and make them more concrete.

Combine and Coordinate Individual Procedures

Another way to expand your brainstorming ideas is to combine procedures with other ideas you have outlined. This could allow you to place greater emphasis on specific areas of behavior, or help you expand the number of areas you are addressing. One idea Mrs. Armstrong likes for Alfred is to pair him with friendly, supportive classmates who could serve as models for how to coordinate his behavior with the actions of teammates. To expand this procedure, she can probably combine it with some of her other ideas. Rather than giving directions herself on what Alfred should watch for during a game, she could have the models give these explanations. She could also have them prompt him to pay attention to what his team and the opposing team are doing with each play.

Mrs. Armstrong could link peer tutoring to other instructional goals for Alfred as well. His teammates could help him not only in coordinating his actions with the team members but also in learning game rules. Alfred's teammates could set up pregame rehearsal sessions to help him practice the rules he needs to follow, and they could prompt him to remember these during the game. These are ways you can coordinate and combine procedures to unify your overall approach to interventions. This technique would help you link individual procedures across several goal areas to form more coherent intervention plans.

Involve Colleagues in Planning

A very powerful resource teachers often overlook when planning interventions is the advice and collaboration of their colleagues and others who are familiar with the students' circumstances. Most school staff members hold a wealth of knowledge,

Consulting with colleagues is one way to expand and improve intervention plans.

experience, and expertise. Consulting with other teachers and school personnel throughout the planning process can help you discover new ideas, gain different perspectives, and find support for your work (Cartledge & Milburn, 1986; Walker, Colvin, & Ramsey, 1995). Other important sources of input in planning interventions are the students' parents or guardians, and people in the community who interact with the students, such as Boy or Girl Scout leaders, religious education instructors, daycare teachers, after-school employers, and many others.

Seeking input from colleagues and other personnel is especially important when you will rely on them later to help implement the intervention plan. By using a cooperative approach from the beginning of the planning process, you will be able to work toward consensus on the primary goals and methods of the intervention and on the general strategies for its implementation (Lehr & Harris, 1988). Preparing plans jointly will also ensure that all the people involved in the intervention concentrate their efforts on the same instructional goals and problem areas, thereby substantially increasing the impact of the procedures.

For example, Mrs. Armstrong asked Ms. Hernandez, the special education teacher, to assist in brainstorming ideas for Granville's intervention. Ms. Hernandez had many useful suggestions, particularly the idea of teaching him a step-by-step technique for following directions. Together, the teachers came up with a five-step procedure for Granville to learn:

1. Read or listen to directions
2. Write down the "doing" statements

3. List tasks to complete and materials needed
4. Review directions and ask questions about tasks not understood
5. Check off tasks as they are completed

Ms. Hernandez also volunteered to work with Granville in her resource room so he can learn the procedure before he has to apply it to the small group assignments in Mrs. Armstrong's class. She thought he should have an opportunity to practice the technique without the distractions and pressures of working with the group. Finally, Mrs. Armstrong and Mrs. Hernandez talked about using a system of hand signals with Granville keyed to the five steps, which could be used in both classrooms. When the two teachers have prepared these plans further, they could meet with Mr. Wagner to learn whether he wishes to use the same procedure in his math and science classes to help Granville use his new skills there. As a group, the teachers could implement the procedures and help one another monitor, evaluate, and fine-tune the activities.

Match Intervention Plans to Assessment Results

As you develop intervention plans, make sure the procedures you choose are consistent with the results you obtained in the assessment (Merrell, 1994). Drawing the instructional goals directly from the assessment findings will ensure a fairly close correspondence, but be sure not to overlook the wealth of other information you have gained from the assessment—the observations, comments, and insights you described about every aspect of the students' performance. This information should suggest techniques students will respond to most favorably.

Even when you begin with clearly defined goals, it is easy to lose sight of the students' real needs when you are in the midst of planning and scheduling intervention procedures. When Mrs. Armstrong plans her intervention for Alfred, she will want to refer to her notes on the assessment worksheets about the problems he has with game rules and motor coordination, and about his responses to teammates during game activities. Without continuing reference to the assessment results to keep her focused, Mrs. Armstrong could get off track and branch out into tangential issues, such as Alfred's annoying and clownish behavior, and thereby reduce the precision and overall effectiveness of the intervention. To keep the intervention closely aligned with the students' needs, you should make frequent references to your earlier results and findings.

Build on Students' Strengths

We have emphasized the importance of focusing interventions on the skill deficits you have discovered from the assessment; at the same time, interventions should build on students' abilities and areas of competence (Ferguson & Jeanchild, 1992; Adelman & Taylor, 1993). In your previous work with the students, or in carrying out their assessment, you may have noticed things about their talents and interests that can serve as a framework for planning interventions. These may be skills the students use particularly well, activities they especially enjoy, or teaching methods they respond to favorably.

Mrs. Armstrong noted from her assessment that Granville seems to take charge of an activity naturally, and she may be able to use this tendency to teach him better leadership skills and encourage him to share his ideas and insights on the small group projects with his classmates. Similarly, Alfred tries very hard to get along with people and has a good sense of humor. Mrs. Armstrong may be able to use this characteristic to teach him specific game-playing skills by having him work closely with students he would like to please. And although Sandy acts very shy and reserved, she seems unusually sensitive and responsive to the feelings and moods of other students. Mrs. Armstrong thinks this quality may be helpful in encouraging Sandy's participation in her conversation group.

When you use students' strengths and talents as the foundation for an intervention, you give them a comfortable starting point from which to learn new behavior, and this can increase their confidence level in developing the target skills (Raffini, 1993). By building on their areas of competence, you can promote better attention to and participation in the intervention activities, and encourage students to take more interest in achieving the instructional goals. You can also help them develop their positive abilities and talents even further by teaching them how to use these skills in a wider array of circumstances and interactions. Finally, by acknowledging their talents and interests, you can strengthen the rapport you have with students and help them realize that teachers do not always concentrate solely on the problems and difficulties students have with their behavior.

Promote Student Involvement and Independence

We typically speak of interventions as something that teachers design and direct, but often the most effective interventions are those the students themselves help plan and implement. Involving students in the planning process will take advantage of their own natural inclination to teach and learn from one another. Whenever it is practical, include students in planning, implementing, and monitoring interventions. This strategy will enhance student interest in and ownership of the procedures, encourage their independence, and promote self-regulation of their behavior (Greenwood & Carta, 1987; Kerr & Nelson, 1989; Wolery, Bailey, & Sugai, 1988). This will also minimize the direct involvement you have in the activities (Burden & Byrd, 1994).

Before designing an intervention to teach Granville to cooperate during small group activities, Mrs. Armstrong could have him and the other students in his group fill out an interest inventory indicating the types of activities and topics they enjoy in social studies class. Their responses could assist Mrs. Armstrong in developing procedures and planning activities that are interesting to all members of the group. Granville and the other group members could also prepare the directions for participating in activities and set some ground rules for organizing and monitoring their behavior. The projects, activities, and directions could help them learn to work cooperatively on their own, and their developing this skill would reduce the need for Mrs. Armstrong to impose her ideas and structure on the group.

Integrate Procedures into the Regular Routine

You should develop interventions that are easy to implement in the natural situations in which the skills are to be used, to ensure that the procedures will be carried out consistently and accurately (Harris & Schutz, 1986). The simplest and most straightforward intervention plans involve procedures that can be integrated into ongoing classroom and school activities (Sugai & Tindal, 1993). For example, when Mrs. Armstrong designs her procedures for teaching Granville to follow directions or to coordinate his work with the group, she needs to make sure the intervention activities will fit in naturally with the typical small group situations in her classroom. Even if some elements of the intervention involve outside work or practice under contrived conditions, these activities must be keyed into the actual setting, with plans for integrating the new skills into the normal classroom environment. This type of planning will allow Granville to improve his behavior in the context of the natural classroom routine. Furthermore, his use of the skills is more likely to be extended and improved as he continues to use them during classroom activities, rather than diminishing after the intervention ends.

Make Procedures Flexible

Although we have stressed the need for careful advanced planning if interventions are to be successful, we must also note that the procedures should be flexible and dynamic so you will be able to alter them over time to suit the changing needs of students (Kerr & Nelson, 1989; Wolery, Bailey, & Sugai, 1988). You should be prepared to modify the procedures as students' competence increases or to alter them to address different aspects of the instructional goals. The degree of control you exert on student behavior and the amount of oversight you give to the procedures should lessen as the new skills become an integral part of the students' performance repertoire (Fox, Shores, Lindeman, & Strain, 1986).

During the initial stages of Sandy's intervention, Mrs. Armstrong may decide to join her conversation group, show how specific skills are used, and have the students rehearse prescribed patterns of behavior. She may even supply the students with cue cards to make the directions very explicit so the interactions follow a strict conversational format. Of course, Mrs. Armstrong wants Sandy eventually to use the correct conversational patterns on her own. Therefore, she should gradually reduce the amount and type of input she gives to the group and change the focus of the procedures as Sandy's skills improve. By incorporating into the intervention plan procedures that are flexible and easy to remove, she can ensure that Sandy will achieve independent use of the skills as quickly as possible.

Consult Published Resources for Additional Ideas

Many books and articles on instructional methods and classroom management have helpful suggestions for teaching specific social and behavioral skills. There are also commercially prepared programs and kits for teaching social skills. We have outlined some of these resources in Appendix B at the end of the text. Such resources can be helpful when you are looking for additional ideas for your interventions. Keep in mind, however, that these materials are typically prepared for a broad, general audience. You will need to adapt them to your specific case, keeping your particular instructional goals and target skills clearly in mind.

Mrs. Armstrong found some very helpful material on conflict resolution in a resource book for elementary school teachers. The book outlined a role-playing activity, including prepared scripts, discussion questions, and alternative suggestions for resolving conflicts. Mrs. Armstrong thinks this activity might work very well for Granville's intervention, but before using the procedures, she will need to adapt them to her own circumstances. She will have to alter the scripts so they closely match the kinds of conflicts that typically occur between Granville and other students. Also, she might want to supplement the activities with a class discussion so students can offer their own suggestions for resolving conflicts, rather than limiting options to the ones in the book. With these adjustments, she will be sure the procedures focus on her goals for Granville, and that they are adapted to the specific circumstances of small group work in her classroom.

Keep Procedures Simple

In this list of suggestions, we have outlined several ways to expand, elaborate, and refine your ideas for intervention procedures. At the same time, you must avoid letting the intervention become too involved or circuitous. Sometimes intervention procedures can become so complicated that students have difficulty grasping the point they are supposed to be learning, or so elaborate that students get caught up in the activities and never apply themselves to learning the instructional goals. Therefore, as you settle on a set of procedures, your aim should be choosing activities that will achieve the goals of the intervention as quickly and efficiently as possible, without also producing negative effects. Some procedures may be very effective in changing behavior, but they may disrupt ongoing classroom routines, not be suitable for certain settings, or make students overly dependent on artificial or unrealistic conditions. If you think any of these effects may occur, you should select an alternative procedure that will be less problematic.

For example, Mrs. Armstrong may have considered starting Alfred's intervention by introducing a new game on the playground. The idea would be to teach Alfred the rules before he plays the game, have him be a team captain, and make him responsible for explaining the rules to other students. Later, she could work with Alfred on transferring his new skills to other games, such as football and basketball. But as she considers the idea more closely, she realizes she is probably making the intervention too complicated. First, teaching a new game during recess would require a fairly significant change in the structure of the playground setting since activities would have to become much more formalized and teacher-directed. Second, Mrs. Armstrong would have to spend considerable time setting up and introducing the new game to a number of students, time she could better spend on improving Alfred's performance. Even though Mrs. Armstrong still thinks the procedure could be very helpful for Alfred, she realizes that another approach would be more realistic and manageable, one that focuses more tightly on Alfred in particular.

These ten guidelines make up a broad-based approach to developing comprehensive and well-directed intervention procedures. Taken as a whole, they provide a process that is applicable to almost any intervention. You should review and consider these guidelines throughout the intervention planning process. By referring to them as you prepare interventions, you can ensure that the procedures and implementation plan will not only be well focused on the target skill but will also have far-reaching benefits for students.

You may find in certain cases that the process we have described for developing your procedures does not fully resolve the difficulties an intervention presents. In the following sections, we discuss two particular cases that require special attention in the organization and preparation of intervention plans. One case involves addressing complex instructional goals; the other involves increasing student incentive in the intervention.

❍ Addressing Complex Goals

Sometimes, you may find it difficult to describe intervention procedures for a particular instructional goal because the skills that must be taught are too broad or complicated to be addressed all at once. One of Mrs. Armstrong's goals for Granville is "Learn to coordinate performance with the activities of the group." As she considers this goal more closely, she realizes that it involves a variety of subskills Granville will need to master, including learning to review directions with the group, learning to compromise with other group members, and learning to keep in step with the group's progress. To address a goal this complex, Mrs. Armstrong will need to do more than define some effective procedures; she will also need to break the goal down so Granville can learn it incrementally. For this kind of complex planning, we discuss two different approaches for coordinating intervention procedures: chaining and shaping.

Chaining

Chaining involves breaking an instructional goal into discrete steps or subgoals, and teaching students to link the individual steps into a complete, more complex pattern of behavior. The process of chaining is rather like building a jigsaw puzzle: you connect the pieces one by one until you have completed the entire picture. With chaining you structure the intervention activities so students learn to perform each successive step of the complicated skill until they can put all the components together into a coherent and complete pattern (Alberto & Troutman, 1990; Campbell & Siperstein, 1994). A simple example of chaining is teaching a song by having students sing each verse separately, then having them put all the verses together to make the whole song. Chaining can be used to structure interventions to teach social skills in the same way.

You will most often use chaining to teach instructional goals that involve linking component steps (Solity & Bull, 1987). Essentially, you organize and sequence the intervention procedures to teach students how to do each step, and then how to connect or join the separate steps so the resulting performance is more complex, better timed, and properly sequenced. Thus, you plan the procedures to help students align their actions with the ongoing activities of a setting and pace and adjust their performance to the demands of the situation. To begin this planning process, you can divide the goal into subgoals or steps, much as you did with the target skill when you prepared a component steps assessment (Chapter Seven). In most instances, you will list the subgoals in sequential order so you can more easily teach students to combine the various skills into a smooth and coherent performance pattern.

When she prepares to teach Granville the instructional goal of coordinating his performance with the activities of the group, Mrs. Armstrong could break this goal into the following subgoals:

- Learn to review the directions for the project with the group
- Learn to help in deciding on the roles of the group members
- Learn to work on and complete own subtasks
- Learn to consult with other group members and ask for help when needed
- Learn to give input on the work of the group members
- Learn to keep track of the group's progress
- Learn to assist in completing the project and turning it in

Mrs. Armstrong now has an organizational plan for addressing an instructional goal that previously was too challenging and difficult for Granville to learn as a single unit. She can teach him how to perform each of these subgoals and how to combine them with the other subgoals and goals he has to learn.

Note that chaining is not an actual procedure but rather a way of linking or organizing instructional procedures. In other words, to address the steps she has outlined for Granville, Mrs. Armstrong will use directions, modeling, and other procedures to teach him the skills he must learn if he is to master each individual subgoal. In addition, she will use these procedures to help Granville connect his new skills to form a complete and well-integrated behavioral pattern (Sulzer-Azaroff & Mayer, 1986).

As another example of chaining, Mrs. Armstrong may feel that Sandy will have considerable difficultly with one of her goals: "Learn to join an ongoing conversation." In planning Sandy's intervention, Mrs. Armstrong might use the following subgoals:

- Learn to identify the topics of conversations
- Learn to choose pertinent comments to add to conversations
- Learn to select the proper language patterns to use to make the comments
- Learn to recognize and wait for pauses in conversations
- Learn to interject comments into the conversations in a timely manner

Mrs. Armstrong can now use this list of subgoals to plan procedures more effectively for her intervention.

Chaining, then, involves structuring intervention goals and procedures in a sequential order to develop a coherent behavioral pattern. Each stage of the chaining process builds on the procedures that came before, so the overall intervention develops a closely linked set of related skills that together will meet the demands of the target skill.

Shaping

Chaining is a particularly useful structuring approach when a complex goal requires a clear sequence of component steps. But other goals may be complicated because they involve a variety of key abilities or subskills that must be developed in more subtle ways. For such goals, you may find it helpful to design an instructional plan based on shaping.

With shaping, you sequence intervention procedures to develop increasingly more precise and refined skills. Each successive opportunity to use a skill leads students closer to learning the overall goal. The approach involves organizing the procedures so that over time the students' behavior becomes more sophisticated, precise, consistent, and reliable (Panyan, 1980; Sulzer-Azaroff & Mayer, 1986).

Shaping is a bit like building a sand castle: you being with a basic, raw form, and smooth it, add to it, and shape it step by step until you arrive at the desired final form. Shaping is the same process you go through to teach academic skills like improving word pronunciation and penmanship. You start with the students' raw reading and writing abilities, and organize lessons that help students become increasingly more accurate and precise in their behavior until eventually they meet your objective. Shaping can be used to organize procedures for teaching social skills in the same way (Middleton, Zollinger, & Keene, 1986).

With shaping, you approach a complex instructional goal by first specifying the successive stages or levels of skill development that students will go through to make their behavior more precise or proficient. Then you structure the intervention activities to advance the students through each of these successive levels. You organize the tasks from easy to difficult, or simple to complex, and teach the students gradually to improve the competence of their behavior. At each stage their performance becomes increasingly more exact, refined, and proficient (Zirpoli & Melloy, 1993).

One goal Mrs. Armstrong has defined for Alfred is "Learn the rules and essential actions for playing games properly." As she considers this goal more closely, she realizes that it involves some subskills Alfred will need to master, including learning more about what the rules are, learning the basic motor skills needed to compete properly, and learning to direct his attention to the proper elements of the game. She recognizes that these subskills are not really sequential but rather involve progressively more refined skills. Therefore, a chaining structure would be less helpful for organizing Alfred's intervention than shaping would be.

With a shaping approach, Mrs. Armstrong could use directions and modeling to teach Alfred a few basic rules and simple strategies for following the action of football games. Some areas he might need to work on are rushing the passer, guarding a receiver, catching a ball while running, and avoiding opponents on kick-off returns. She could begin her initial teaching outside the context of normal game activities to start him on learning the skills. As he begins to use these rough abilities, she could gradually change or add procedures to help him become better coordinated and more accurate in performing the basic elements of the game. Then she could add procedures for teaching him to incorporate these techniques while playing under game-like conditions with teammates. Thus, by organizing intervention procedures to mold and shape his performance, Mrs. Armstrong can help Alfred gradually develop more advanced and sophisticated behavior until he masters the goal of following rules and coordinating actions in real game situations.

When you use shaping, it is crucial to give students clear feedback about their performance. Often you can quickly and efficiently help students perfect their skills by acknowledging and praising their actions as they improve and by pointing out and correcting errors (Panyan, 1980; Wolery, Bailey, & Sugai, 1988). Your feedback should communicate to students which of their actions were more accurate and what they should do to develop their skills further. In this way, you can reinforce your instruction and prepare students for the next successive stages of the intervention. For example, from watching Alfred's first attempts at following football rules, Mrs. Armstrong may see that he needs to learn more about applying the rules for rushing the passer, and to be more aware of the location and movement of the ball. She could have Alfred watch other students demonstrate these elements of the game, and then shape his behavior by putting him in a game situation and giving him specific feedback about ball awareness and about his actions when playing defense. She could also relate this feedback to some of the future goals of the intervention, previewing activities that will teach Alfred to coordinate his running and catching with the actions of his teammates and his opponents.

To sum up, shaping is a way to structure interventions so they begin with students' raw or undeveloped version of the desired performance. Conventional teaching procedures are used to gradually refine, mold, and build on these skills until the students' performance is proficient enough to meet the demands of the target skill. Both shaping and chaining are approaches for coordinating intervention goals and procedures when you need to teach complicated or demanding instructional goals that would be difficult for students to learn all at once. By using shaping and chaining, you can help students develop more precise, more complex, and better integrated behavioral patterns.

Increasing Student Incentive

A second special case you might need to address when preparing intervention plans is students' lack of incentive to perform the target skill or to take part in the intervention itself. In this section we explain how students gain incentive to perform target skills, and we discuss some procedures for increasing their motivation to do so.

We have emphasized many times that to meet social expectations, students must have the required skills. But equally important, students must have the incentive to use their skills to respond to these expectations. Incentive is shown by students' willingness to use their skills to meet the social demands that apply to their behavior (Gagne, 1985; Eby & Kujawa, 1994). In some cases, you may find from assessment that students have the skills and abilities they need to perform target skills, but they lack the incentive to use them. Mrs. Armstrong may have discovered from her assessment that Granville has the ability to work effectively under some circumstances, but instead of applying himself fully to doing assignments, he would rather socialize with his friends or argue about the activity. Similarly, she may have found that while Alfred does need to learn some key game-playing skills, at the same time he is more interested in clowning around than in improving his status through more skilled performance. In cases like these, interventions must focus not only on the actual skills involved in the instructional goals but also on the issue of incentive. The following section discusses incentive and the effects it has on target skills.

Incentive Derives from Students' Understanding of Outcomes

Students derive incentive from the outcomes they expect to produce by their behavior (Raffini, 1993). They say or do things based on the reactions they hope to obtain—or hope to avoid—from the environment. Examples of outcomes include the following:

- Passing, or failing, a test
- Pleasing, or angering, classmates
- Being praised, or being reprimanded, by teachers
- Gaining, or missing, an important piece of information
- Having the correct answer, or having the incorrect answer
- Winning, or losing, a game
- Gaining, or losing, privileges

For example, when Alfred pays attention to Mrs. Armstrong's presentation of the day's lesson and gives a correct answer to a question she asks, several outcomes may follow:

- Mrs. Armstrong may praise him for giving the right answer
- Other students may smile and nod at him
- He may feel relieved that he finally understands the material

In contrast, when Alfred does not pay attention to the lesson and gives an incorrect answer,

- classmates may snicker at his response

- Mrs. Armstrong may tell him to pay closer attention next time
- he may feel embarrassed and discouraged

As these examples show, we can think of outcomes as the reactions of the environment to the students' behavior, or in some cases, to their lack of behavior. Thus, outcomes are the various things that happen because students have acted, or have not acted, in certain ways.

How Outcomes Affect Incentive

Outcomes are very important in determining students' incentive to meet social expectations because they give purpose and direction to their behavior. They provide students with worthwhile reasons for trying (or not trying) to do certain things (Bandura, 1986; Burden & Byrd, 1994). The major reason students do things is to try to produce specific outcomes they have in mind.

Incentive mostly stems from students' past experiences and interactions with the environment, and their knowledge of the present circumstances. Their motivation under a particular set of circumstances usually depends on how they interpret their previous successes and failures with their behavior, and on their understanding of what is likely to happen if they decide to use their skills again. As a general principle, students will try to act in ways that will gain them satisfaction, enjoyment, recognition, good grades, or other favorable outcomes from their behavior. On the other hand, they will usually try to avoid acting in ways that result in dissatisfaction, disapproval, failure, or other unfavorable outcomes (Adelman & Taylor, 1993; Raffini, 1993).

There may be several reasons that students have problems showing incentive to perform social skills. Some possibilities include the following:

- Students do not recognize the positive outcomes of skilled performance
- They do recognize these outcomes, but do not view them as valuable or desirable
- They are intimidated or discouraged by the effort required to produce the outcomes
- They prefer to work toward different, competing outcomes instead

In any of these cases, you are likely to find that you need to enhance the instructional activities you have planned for interventions by adding or emphasizing procedures for increasing the students' incentive to use their skills. In the rest of this section, we describe some procedures for increasing incentive that you can include in intervention plans.

Highlight Natural Outcomes

One of the strongest techniques for increasing students' incentive to achieve instructional goals is to highlight the positive outcomes that result from their competent social behavior (Zirpoli & Melloy, 1993). Often students do not understand

Incentive is derived from student perception of outcomes.

what these benefits are, have had little or no exposure to them, or do not realize they can be satisfying and enjoyable (Adelman & Taylor, 1993). Consequently, they have little or no reason to perform the target skill. Many times you can increase students' incentive to use their skills by pointing out the natural outcomes, accentuating their benefits, and providing more opportunities for students to produce them or experience them firsthand (Polloway, Patton, Payne, & Payne, 1989; Taub & Dollinger, 1975). By using this approach, you may be able to make learning target skills much more meaningful to students.

In thinking back over the school year, Mrs. Armstrong realizes that Sandy has never shown much interest in talking with classmates and making friends, and she thinks that Sandy may never have experienced much success in her interactions with her schoolmates. To counteract this experience, Mrs. Armstrong can make sure the small conversation group she puts together for Sandy's intervention is specifically structured to make Sandy feel welcome and valued. Mrs. Armstrong could supplement this approach by arranging small group lessons, activities in the learning center, and other socially oriented tasks that pair Sandy with supportive group members. In this way, Sandy may become much more aware of the recognition and satisfaction that naturally result from interacting with classmates. This approach may provide the impetus Sandy needs to improve her conversations, because she may start to recognize that talking with classmates is indeed an enjoyable experience.

Guidelines for Highlighting Natural Outcomes

The following are guidelines for highlighting natural outcomes:

Accentuate the benefits derived from natural outcomes. You can highlight natural outcomes by (a) telling students about them, (b) having students watch other classmates produce them, (c) placing students directly and repeatedly in contact with them, and (d) ensuring that students' actions produce them (Bandura, 1986; Kazdin, 1981; Wolery, Bailey, & Sugai, 1988). In some instances, you will need to deliberately plan and structure activities to call attention to these outcomes, or to ensure that students will produce them with their behavior.

Mrs. Armstrong could highlight natural outcomes for Alfred by showing him the enjoyment and mutual respect contestants gain from competing with one another in group games. She could help him see that playing group games is fun even when he is not the center of attention, or point out to him the esteem his peers gain by simply taking part in the games. She could also have the class play a new, unfamiliar game so Alfred would have an equal chance to do well and experience the positive outcomes of playing cooperatively with his peers.

Another way to highlight outcomes is to have students themselves describe what happened when they performed competently. They could explain what events followed their behavior, describe how they felt as a result of it, and indicate what they could do to produce the outcomes again (Adelman & Taylor, 1993). Understanding and experiencing (or reexperiencing) the benefits of skilled behavior is especially important when students are using newly acquired skills.

Have other students demonstrate the benefits from outcomes. Other students are often the best sources for showing and highlighting the outcomes of performance (Wolery, Bailey, & Sugai, 1988). You can take advantage of this by (a) encouraging classmates to acknowledge and celebrate one another's competent performance, (b) fostering pride in students who accomplish difficult tasks, and (c) allowing students who have mastered skills to help others who have not (Edwards, 1993). Peer and cross-age tutoring are very effective methods for highlighting the benefits of skilled social behavior.

Mrs. Armstrong may decide to have Alfred's teammates help teach him the new game skills he is learning. She could have them use the prompts she has prepared and praise him when he executes his new skills correctly. They could also use specific, nonthreatening prompts to remind him when he is getting off task or acting obnoxious and provide him with attention when he performs his proper role in the game. In this way, the reactions of the other students in the setting can be specifically geared to helping Alfred recognize and remember the natural benefits of playing games and interacting in a competent manner.

To use another example, Granville is often sullen, moody, and detached, and he does not seem to realize that showing animation and being pleasant are essential elements of getting along with peers. Mrs. Armstrong could have several of Granville's classmates agree to be especially nice to him in order to coax him out of his sulky moods and encourage him to be more pleasant. Through this approach, perhaps Granville will discover that acting pleasant is worthwhile because it helps him gain greater attention from his teachers and classmates.

Highlighting natural outcomes can help students recognize, experience, and enjoy the outcomes already available to them in the setting. This is an especially good approach to use when students' knowledge of and experience with outcomes is incomplete, when they are acquiring new skills, and when they need to increase the value they place on existing outcomes.

Add Rewards for Performance

If conventional outcomes are not sufficient to provide incentive for students to use their skills, you can give them extra rewards or special privileges for performing target skills (Deci & Ryan, 1985). One advantage of offering rewards is that by making the rewards contingent on the proper use of skills, you can refocus students' attention and interest on meeting social expectations. Adding extra rewards is an especially good approach to use when student misbehavior seems to have greater value than the currently existing outcomes for appropriate behavior. If students believe these extra rewards are worth earning, they will direct their actions toward obtaining them instead of behaving inappropriately (Edwards, 1993).

One of the things Alfred does during game-playing situations is brag about his talents. Mrs. Armstrong could enter into a contract with him stating that if he refrains from bragging during recess, he can take the play equipment back to the gym. If Alfred believes he will really enjoy this experience, he may refrain from bragging and redirect his efforts toward gaining attention through more acceptable means.

We often think of rewards in material terms such as candy or prizes, but they can take many forms. Table 10.2 gives several examples of items and activities that can serve as rewards for competent social performance. As you consider possible rewards to use in interventions, remember that they will improve behavior only when they have a positive value to the students and are worth earning (Walker, Colvin, & Ramsey, 1995; Zirpoli & Melloy, 1993).

Guidelines for Adding Extra Rewards

The following are guidelines for using extra rewards in intervention plans.

Use conventional rewards whenever possible. The rewards you give for skilled performance should be events or activities that are a regular part of the performance environment (Polloway, Patton, Payne, & Payne, 1989). This guideline is important because you want to avoid making students overly dependent on incentives that are not a customary part of the setting (Ryan, 1982). Naturally

TABLE 10.2 Examples of events and activities that can act as rewards

Helping prepare bulletin boards	Having some extra quiet time
Setting up for next activity	Playing instructional games
Being line leader	Working on self-selected activities
Taking notes to the office	Choosing the next class or group story
Receiving extra reading or computer time	Escorting visitors around the school
Having access to a special study carrel or work area	Passing out coats or lunch pails
Correcting assignments	Bringing a special audiotape, book, or play object to school
Tutoring other students	Being the class representative in a school project
Taking class roll	Participating in a schoolwide movie, play, or recreational activity
Operating the overhead or slide projector	Reading a story to a younger group of students
Duplicating materials	Helping the teacher in art, music, or gym class
Updating charts, records, and reports	Assisting the administrative or janitorial staff of the school
Making calendars	
Being group leader	
Supervising or directing activities	
Taking care of recess equipment	

occurring rewards will increase students' experience with conventional school outcomes and possibly enhance the value they place on them (Deci & Ryan, 1985; Malone, 1981). For example, Mrs. Armstrong may be able to improve Granville's behavior in small group activities by giving him and his group extra freedom in choosing topics and activities if they cooperate better and work more as a team. Granville may stop arguing and refocus his attention on the assigned task if the options are exciting and challenging to him. Other rewards Mrs. Armstrong could try are praising Granville when he follows directions, offering him extra computer time when he works cooperatively, or having him collect the projects when he finishes the activity on time. She should use contrived or artificial rewards, like candy or soda pop, only as a last resort.

Use special rewards sparingly. Any extra rewards you give students should be considered temporary measures to move students in the right direction in using their skills. You will need to consider how to get students to continue using their skills after the rewards are no longer available to them (Raffini, 1993; Shrigley, 1985). For example, Alfred enjoys working with the school staff, so Mrs. Armstrong may decide that if he refrains from clowning or acting up during games, he can earn special privileges such as taking lunch tickets in the cafeteria, assisting the janitor in cleaning trash from classroom and playground areas, or delivering messages for the principal. But Mrs. Armstrong does not want to use these added rewards any longer than she has to because they are contrived. The privileges may act as an extra inducement to encourage Alfred to use the proper skills, but he needs to regulate his own behavior without special rewards and to respond to the natural outcomes for interacting acceptably with other students. Therefore, after Alfred has acted more appropriately for a couple of days, Mrs. Armstrong should substitute more conventional rewards for the desired behavior so that he eventually behaves appropriately for the same reasons the other students do.

Link the rewards to the proper skills. For rewards to work effectively, students must make a connection between the rewards that are offered to them and the desired behavior (Kazdin, 1989; Polloway, Patton, Payne, & Payne, 1989). You can establish this link by using the same type of reward each time and by giving the reward immediately after the appropriate behavior. Then, after students make the connection, you can increase the time between the behavior and the reward, and vary the types of reward you use. This approach will allow you to fade the rewards and to add more variety to the intervention.

If Mrs. Armstrong uses a reward system to encourage Sandy to join conversations, she must be sure Sandy clearly understands that she is earning the reward for talking more with classmates. Mrs. Armstrong could give Sandy points when she joins a conversation or adds comments to the discussion, and these points could earn Sandy special privileges, like getting extra time in the computer lab or assisting in the first-grade classroom. Mrs. Armstrong should give the points as soon as possible after the appropriate behavior to establish the connection between the target behavior and the privileges. If Sandy's behavior improves during the first few days, Mrs. Armstrong could remove the point system but continue rewarding her behavior a bit longer. Eventually, Mrs. Armstrong would need to remove all the special rewards and privileges she gives Sandy.

Heighten the value of praise and attention. Potentially the most powerful, effective, and adaptable rewards you can use in an intervention are the attention you and classmates give a student for meeting expectations (Kerr & Nelson, 1989). Praise, recognition, acceptance, applause, and other positive responses to skilled behavior can be extremely potent procedures. But the value of these interpersonal rewards depends on the rapport students have with their teachers and peers (Smith, 1989). Attention is rewarding only if the person giving it is important to students and is held in high regard.

In some cases, you may have to make a concerted effort to build a closer rapport with students to heighten the value of the attention you give them or to establish yourself as a supportive and significant person, and you may have to help other students do likewise (Walker, Colvin, & Ramsey, 1995). These efforts can greatly enhance the effectiveness of the praise, recognition, and other interpersonal outcomes you use in an intervention to encourage students to achieve instructional goals. Some effective strategies for enhancing rapport with students are giving them individualized, personalized attention; honoring their special attributes and accomplishments; sharing in their achievements; and celebrating their successes. You should work to create a positive classroom atmosphere for all your students, especially for those who are usually at the bottom of the class.

Using rewards is a very effective way to increase the students' incentive to learn target skills. You can use rewards to refocus their attention to the activity at hand, to maintain their interest in learning new skills, or to add inducements for working on especially difficult and challenging activities. At the beginning of the intervention, you should supply the rewards frequently to direct their attention to using the proper skills. Then, as the students' behavior improves, you should gradually fade the rewards and give them intermittently, or stop giving them altogether, so students learn to rely on the naturally occurring outcomes.

Coordinating and Scheduling Intervention Procedures

Once you have considered complex goals and students' incentive, and have finished outlining specific procedures for teaching instructional goals, you can begin to integrate the procedures into a single, coherent intervention plan. A carefully organized intervention plan clarifies how the procedures will be directed toward specific abilities and skills, and ensures that the activities will work in combination to help students learn the target skill. In addition, a well-structured plan will help you anticipate the logistical demands of the intervention procedures and determine how best to incorporate the intervention into the routines and activities of the setting. In this section we discuss how to integrate and coordinate intervention procedures and how to prepare a timetable for implementing the intervention plan.

Integrating Intervention Procedures

You should view an intervention as a single coherent process rather than as a collection of separate activities, because a comprehensive scheme for coordinating individual procedures will help students fully learn the target skill. In order for interventions to be successful, students must learn both how to perform the specific skills for meeting the instructional goals, and how to combine and use these skills in complex patterns of performance that match the demands of the setting. A comprehensive plan for how the procedures fit together will help ensure that students develop such patterns.

The instructional goals Mrs. Armstrong set for Sandy include learning to use greetings, learning to select topics of conversation, learning to make comments on other people's opinions, and learning to shift topics of conversations to those in which she is interested and knowledgeable. In addition to developing specific procedures to teach Sandy each of these goals, Mrs. Armstrong must structure the overall intervention to teach her to combine these new skills, to link them with the skills she already has, and to apply them as a unit in the broader context of holding conversations with classmates—the original target skill. To assist with coordinating intervention procedures in this way, we recommend writing out a script that describes both the individual procedures you will use and the overall process of the intervention itself.

Writing an Intervention Script

We began the chapter by showing how to sequence the instructional goals for interventions. Developing a sequential structure for goals will help to direct your thoughts in choosing and organizing the most promising intervention ideas. For the same reason, the best way to consolidate and structure the overall intervention plan is to give a sequential, narrative account of the activities you will conduct. We call this account the *intervention script*. You can think of it as a kind of dress rehearsal for carrying out the intervention procedures.

An intervention script describes the various activities and procedures you will use, in roughly the order in which you will use them. Because it is written as a narrative, it does not need to be as formal or detailed as a day-by-day schedule, but it requires you nonetheless to coordinate your ideas into a single, coherent structure. Once she finished developing her ideas for Granville's intervention, Mrs. Armstrong wrote a script outlining the activities she was planning. The instructional goals she had sequenced earlier provided the basic framework for the intervention. But in writing the script, she found that she also had to decide how to integrate the procedures, how to prepare for the various activities, and how to coordinate other people in her intervention plan.

Figure 10.1 shows the worksheet Mrs. Armstrong prepared for writing Granville's intervention script. As on earlier worksheets, she began by listing key information about Granville, including his name, grade level, and the target skill for the intervention. She also entered her instructional goals for the activities, in the sequence she had established earlier. Finally, she wrote a chronological account of the activities she would use for Granville's intervention.

Notice that this account does not include every detail of Mrs. Armstrong's plans. For example, it does not specify the five-step plan she developed with Ms. Hernandez, nor does it explain fully the procedures she will use for the role-playing activity on conflict resolution. Obviously, she will need to prepare these activities carefully before beginning the intervention; the script she outlines here is intended to be merely an overview of her plans. In addition to describing procedures, you should consider the following issues when writing an intervention script.

Choosing the Conditions for the Intervention

One of your most important decisions when you write the intervention script concerns the situations or conditions in which you will conduct the activities. Often, interventions use a combination of natural and artificial conditions to help students learn the target skill. You should realize that both types of conditions offer advantages and limitations, and should weigh the following considerations in deciding whether to use artificial or natural conditions.

Using artificial conditions In the chapters on assessment, we described artificial conditions as circumstances that differ in some significant way from the typical conditions of the setting. When you create new or contrived situations, you

Figure 10.1 Mrs. Armstrong's worksheet showing finalized instructional goals for Granville.

Worksheet 10.1: Writing an Intervention Script — Page *1* of *2*

Name: *Mrs. Armstrong* — Date: *Nov. 15*

Student: *Granville* — Grade: *5*

Target skill: *Cooperates with other students in completing small group activities*

Sequence for addressing instructional goals:

First: *Learn to follow written and oral directions for group activities*

Second: *Learn to organize and plan the assignment before starting work*

Third: *Learn to coordinate performance with the activities of the group*

Fourth: *Learn strategies for handling teasing and disagreements with peers*

Fifth: ______

Intervention Script:

Granville's intervention will begin with Ms. Hernandez teaching him the five-step technique for listening to and writing down directions. In her resource room, she will conduct several activities that use specific directions, and will teach Granville the prompting system for remembering his new technique. Later I will schedule an activity in social studies that will use the direction-following technique, and will use the prompts that Ms. Hernandez has taught. Mr. Wagner will reinforce our work by using the same kinds of activities in his math class.

Meanwhile, I will pass out a questionnaire for all the students in the class to learn what types of subjects and activities they are interested in. I will ask Granville to use the five-step procedure to plan the activity for his group.

Next, the intervention will focus on teaching Granville to organize his tasks before beginning work. Ms. Hernandez will give Granville an organization worksheet, and she will spend time with him in the resource room to teach him how to use it. Later in the day, Mr. Wagner and I will have Granville use the worksheet for two or three short in-class activities (given to the whole class). I will also work on having Granville link his five-step technique on directions to his new organizing worksheet. Maybe he can use the five-step technique to outline the assignment for the class on the board.

At the same time, I will also teach Granville and the class about coordinating their actions with peers. I will give out role-playing scripts that show both good and bad examples of group cooperation, and I will videotape the skits each group puts on.

(Continued on p. 2)

Figure 10.1 *(continued)*

Worksheet 10.1 (continued)	Name: *Mrs. Armstrong* Student: *Granville*	Page *2* of *2*

Intervention Script (continued):

The next day, I will show the videos to the class. I will ask them to discuss the videos, focusing on ways to cooperate, and the importance of following the group leader. Following this discussion I will talk with Granville to make sure he understood the points that were made. Then I will have the class work on a short small group activity. Granville will serve as a leader for his group. He will use his direction-following technique and his organizing worksheet to help plan and coordinate the group's task. The subject of the assignment will be based on the interest survey taken earlier.

Next, the class will work on the conflict resolution activity based on the one I found in the resource book. They will begin with role playing to show different examples of typical conflicts and teasing situations. Together, the class will discuss the examples, and will come up with positive alternatives for responding to disputes and teasing. Then we can go back to the role-playing activity to practice these new responses. The students will make a list of these "acceptable" responses to conflicts, and I will post it on the board. Later I will discuss the list with Granville, and he will practice some of these responses with Ms. Hernandez.

I will begin to solidify these different procedures by having another group project, with Brian—a student Granville likes—serving as group leader. Granville will use his direction-following technique, his organization worksheet, and the coordinating procedures that he learned on previous days. In addition, if conflicts arise I will prompt him to choose acceptable responses from the new list.

As the intervention winds up, Mr. Wagner and I will both go back to assigning normal groups and activities. As Granville uses his new skills more, we will begin to fade prompts, and I will show Granville how to adapt the organization worksheet to his other classes and to different types of assignments. I will also discuss how he can use his cooperative skills in these other circumstances as well.

should recognize that students can react to their new circumstances in ways you might not anticipate, because the demands of the setting have changed. To account for these changes, or to direct them as you wish, you will need to structure the artificial situation very carefully. You should keep tight control over the activities so students learn the precise skills you want them to develop.

If Mrs. Armstrong uses special practice sessions in the gym to teach Alfred basic game activities such as catching the ball or rushing the passer, she will need to structure these activities and control the circumstances carefully. Otherwise Alfred might see the practice time as an opportunity to get adult attention by clowning or wasting time. Similarly, when she plans the special conversation groups for Sandy's intervention, Mrs. Armstrong will need to start the activities with specific aims and guidelines, such as pre-set discussion topics, time frames for individual participants, and even roles for the students to follow. As Sandy becomes more proficient in using her skills, Mrs. Armstrong should be able to relax her control over the artificial situation, or to redirect her control to allow the conversations to become more free-flowing and natural.

Using natural conditions Unlike artificial situations, natural conditions typically require no unusual degree of control when you use them in an intervention. Because you want the students to learn to apply their skills to the ordinary circumstances of the settings, there is usually no need to structure the situation any differently from the way you normally would. On the other hand, whereas artificial situations are precisely designed to address a single skill area, natural situations present broad and complex performance opportunities that can diffuse the students' attention and interest in learning specific skills. Under normal conditions it can sometimes be difficult to isolate a single instructional goal from all the other performance demands placed on students. Therefore, when you apply intervention activities under natural conditions, you need to stay focused on the specific skills you are teaching, and avoid trying to branch out into other problem areas that might arise in these circumstances. You may also have to make a concerted effort to center students' attention on the particular areas of behavior you want them to work on.

For example, when she works with Alfred in the artificial practice situation, Mrs. Armstrong can structure the activity to focus only on his catching and rushing skills. But once Alfred is in an actual game, Mrs. Armstrong will have to plan very carefully to maintain her focus on these skills, rather than looking at the various other behaviors (and misbehaviors) Alfred is likely to show once he has rejoined his classmates. One way she could do this is to have Alfred keep track of his own performance in rushing and catching and report to her each time the ball changes hands. By focusing Alfred's attention on the skills he is supposed to be learning, Mrs. Armstrong will make it easier for the intervention to stay centered on these areas despite the many distractions and variations the game situation presents.

Adding Other Students

Once you have finalized your intervention script, a good final step before moving on to scheduling is to consider including other students in the setting who could benefit from the intervention. As we have noted throughout the text, it is important to structure assessment activities and interventions with a particular student in mind, to ensure the accuracy of the procedures and effectiveness of the results. However, after you have developed the activities for this particular student, you may think of ways the procedures can benefit other students with similar problems. In such cases, you can expand the intervention to include one or more additional students, or even the entire class.

For example, by designing an intervention to improve Granville's cooperation in small groups, Mrs. Armstrong will be able to give a direct aim to the intervention plans. But she realizes that the procedures she is developing for Granville could also be used to help Luis, another student in her class who has difficulty cooperating with his peers. Although Luis is less aggressive than Granville—he tends to whine and sulk rather than fight when he has a disagreement—Mrs. Armstrong feels that he could probably learn a lot from the activities she has designed for Granville. By including Luis, the intervention plan can have more far-reaching effects without losing its specific focus on improving Granville's social competence.

Scheduling the Intervention

The last step in developing an intervention plan is to prepare a schedule or timeline that gives a time frame for the intervention, including the major steps of the intervention plan for each day. This timeline will help you take stock in advance of the entire schedule of activities for the intervention, so you do not lose sight of its overall aim or overlook any crucial elements of the intervention (Harris & Schutz, 1986). But it is important at the same time to view the timeline as flexible or tentative, and to realize that some later steps or activities in the plan may have to be changed based on the students' progress or their response to the procedures.

To help you coordinate the intervention plan, your schedule should contain the following elements.

Procedures to Be Conducted Each Day

The most important elements of the schedule are the description of the procedures and the major tasks or activities you will carry out each day. Figure 10.2 shows the schedule Mrs. Armstrong developed for Granville and Luis. For each day on the schedule, Mrs. Armstrong has listed the elements of the intervention that will take place as well as any preliminary tasks she will need to complete in anticipation of the next day's procedures, such as planning for a class discussion and writing scripts for role playing.

Personnel to Help with Intervention

Listing the personnel involved in the intervention will remind you to include them in every major decision about the procedure (Harris & Schutz, 1986; Salvia & Hughes, 1990). You should confer with these people to finalize the activities, and later on to help with monitoring the procedures and deciding whether the plan needs modification. If you must obtain approval from the administrative staff to change routines, class assignments, or schedules, you should note this in the plan

Figure 10.2 Mrs. Armstrong's intervention schedule for Granville.

Worksheet 10.2: Intervention Schedule — Page *1* of *2*

Name: *Mrs. Armstrong* — Date: *Nov. 16*

Student: *Granville* — Grade: *5*

DAY	
Monday	Procedures: *Ms. H. to teach Granville & Luis the 5-step technique, and prompting system.* *Plan activity for using 5-step technique in social studies. Use new prompts.* *Give class questionnaire on favorite topics.* *Give out scripts for group cooperation demonstration.*
	Other personnel taking part: *Ms. Hernandez*
	Materials needed: *Questionnaires, scripts*
Tuesday	Procedures: *Ms. H. to give G. and L. the organization worksheet.* *Activities in Mr. W.'s class and my class to use worksheet and directions technique.* *Practice and videotape cooperation skits.*
	Other personnel taking part: *Ms. Hernandez, Mr. Wagner*
	Materials needed: *Worksheets, scripts, video equipment*
Wednesday	Procedures: *Ms. H. & Mr. W. to continue work on organizing and directions with G. and L.* *Show videos to class and discuss cooperation.* *Small group activity with G. and L. leading groups.*
	Other personnel taking part: *Ms. Hernandez, Mr. Wagner*
	Materials needed: *Video equipment, organization worksheets*
Thursday	Procedures: *Ms. H. & Mr. W. to continue work on organizing and directions with G. and L.* *Role-playing activity on conflict resolution. Develop and post list of appropriate responses.* *Small group activity, with Brian and Stephanie as leaders for G.'s and L.'s groups.*
	Other personnel taking part: *Ms. Hernandez, Mr. Wagner*
	Materials needed: *Organizing worksheets, materials for conflict resolution activity*

Figure 10.2 *(continued)*

Worksheet 10.2 (continued)	Name: *Mrs. Armstrong* Student: *Granville*	Page *2* of *2*

DAY:	
Friday	Procedures: *Continue as on Thursday, but expand conflict resolution and group cooperation techniques to Mr. W's class.* *Begin to fade prompts, and let G. and L. begin developing their own versions of the organizing worksheet.*
	Other personnel taking part: *Ms. Hernandez, Mr. Wagner*
	Materials needed: *Blank worksheet forms for G. and L.*

DAY:	
	Procedures:
	Other personnel taking part:
	Materials needed:

DAY:	
	Procedures:
	Other personnel taking part:
	Materials needed:

DAY:	
	Procedures:
	Other personnel taking part:
	Materials needed:

as well. Mrs. Armstrong has listed Ms. Hernandez and Mr. Wagner in her plan for the days they will help her with its implementation. Her notes will remind her to get in touch with them a few days in advance to prepare them for their parts in the intervention.

Resources Needed in Intervention

The intervention procedures may require equipment, supplies, commercial materials, tutors or student helpers, videotapes, and other instructional aids. You should list these items in your plan to ensure that they will be available on the days and at the times they will be needed (Harris & Schutz, 1986). Mrs. Armstrong wants to videotape some skits that show various ways of cooperating and coordinating group work. Listing the video equipment on the worksheet will help Mrs. Armstrong remember to reserve this equipment ahead of time so it is available for her use.

By bringing together these different elements, Mrs. Armstrong can create a schedule for her intervention plan that gives her clear direction for proceeding with the activities. In conjunction with the intervention script she wrote before, this schedule will help her coordinate and carry out her plans for a unified and well-targeted intervention. She can give copies of the script and schedule to Ms. Hernandez and Mr. Wagner to help them understand the procedures and apply them consistently in all their settings.

Note that Mrs. Armstrong's intervention for Granville and Luis takes place over a relatively short period. She can extend the activities if she wishes, but she should start with a plan focused very tightly on a short time frame and a very specific set of skills. By concentrating narrowly on a limited number of skills or instructional goals, Mrs. Armstrong can gear her intervention toward gaining specific, immediate results. She can broaden the scope of the plan or revise activities in subsequent weeks depending on how Granville responds to the procedures.

Writing the intervention script and filling out a schedule completes the basic planning for interventions. At this point you have in hand a complete outline and timeline of activities that will address the instructional goals you have identified and will help teach students to perform the target skills. Now, all that remains before actually starting the interventions is to prepare monitoring procedures so you can make an accurate record of the students' response to the intervention. We will address this task in the next chapter.

❍ Summary

Organizing Intervention Plans

1. Intervention plans can be organized according to the sequence in which the instructional goals will be addressed in the intervention.
2. The sequence of instructional goals should usually be ordered from easy to difficult or from simple to complex.
3. Ideas for intervention procedures should be tied directly to instructional goals and be practical to use with students.

Ten Ways to Develop Intervention Procedures

1. Ideas for interventions can be expanded by considering the details involved in carrying out the procedure.
2. Ideas for interventions can be combined and coordinated to develop a broader intervention approach.
3. Involving colleagues and others in the intervention planning process can help with implementation and coordination of interventions.
4. Intervention plans should take into account the various results obtained during assessment.
5. Intervention procedures should build on and extend the students' strengths and interests.
6. Interventions should encourage student involvement and ownership in activities.
7. Intervention procedures should be integrated with the activities and routines of natural performance settings.
8. Intervention procedures should be flexible and dynamic, and stay aligned with the students' progress.
9. Published materials can be a useful source of intervention ideas, but they may require adaptation.
10. Intervention procedures should be simple and straightforward, and be easy for everyone to implement.

Addressing Complex Goals

1. Special provisions may be necessary when planning interventions involving complex instructional goals.
2. Shaping and chaining are approaches that can assist in addressing complex instructional goals.
3. Chaining is teaching a complex goal as a sequence of subgoals or steps that students learn and link together.
4. Shaping is teaching a complex goal in developmental stages through which students learn to refine their actions.

Increasing Student Incentive

1. Intervention procedures may need to be expanded or adapted to address students' lack of incentive to develop and use target skills.
2. Students derive incentive from the outcomes of their performance.

3. Outcomes give purpose and direction to student behavior.
4. Incentive can be increased by highlighting natural outcomes and adding rewards for performance.
5. Highlighting natural outcomes involves telling students about and giving them experience with the outcomes that naturally follow from competent behavior.
6. Guidelines for highlighting natural outcomes include
   a. accentuating the benefits derived from outcomes
   b. having other students demonstrate the benefits derived from outcomes
7. Adding rewards involves giving students extra attention, privileges, or special outcomes for learning and using target skills.
8. Guidelines for adding rewards include
   a. using conventional rewards whenever possible
   b. using special rewards sparingly
   c. heightening the value of praise and attention

Coordinating and Scheduling Intervention Procedures

1. Intervention procedures should be integrated into a coherent plan.
2. The sequence of instructional goals should serve as the overall framework for preparing an intervention plan.
3. An intervention plan should have a script that gives a narrative account of the way intervention procedures will be carried out.
4. An intervention script should describe intervention procedures and the conditions for the intervention.
5. Other students could be added to an intervention to broaden the impact of the intervention plan.
6. An intervention plan should have a timeline that gives a day-by-day account of activities.
7. The intervention schedule should list the personnel and resources that will be used to carry out activities.

Examples for Chapter Ten

Example 10a

Melanie is a first grader who was referred to speech therapy because she is behind her classmates in verbal skills. She speaks too softly and does not articulate words clearly. She is very reluctant to talk with other students and to share in group discussions, but she does play quietly with friends during free time. Mrs. Duncan has chosen "talks to classmates during group activities" as the target skill.

This page shows Mrs. Duncan's instructional goals and the first half of her intervention script. The final stages of the intervention will focus on teaching Melanie to link the individual skills she learns in these activities and to apply them to other activities and settings.

Worksheet 10.1: Writing an Intervention Script — Page *1* of *2*

Name: *Mrs. Duncan* — Date: *Nov. 17*

Student: *Melanie* — Grade: *1*

Target skill: *Talks to classmates during group activities*

Sequence for addressing instructional goals:

Beginning the intervention with the most fundamental skills allows the goals to build on one another.

- First: *Learn to speak as loud as the other students*
- Second: *Learn to make eye contact while speaking*
- Third: *Learn to greet new participants in an activity*
- Fourth: *Learn to make comments about an activity*
- Fifth: ______

Intervention Script:

Note how colleagues can be involved in interventions in various ways.

These procedures use shaping to teach Melanie to speak loudly enough to be heard by the group.

We will begin the intervention by placing Melanie in a small group with some friends, and showing her the importance of speaking loud enough to be heard by classmates. Mrs. Parsons, Melanie's speech therapist, will help me use puppets to act out two children talking about playing a game. One puppet will speak too softly to be heard, and we will act out some difficulties that can arise in trying to interact but not talking loud enough to be heard. Melanie's group will point out the problems they see. Then the quiet puppet will speak louder and the other puppet will act out some benefits of better communication, and Melanie's group will talk about these benefits. We will then have an audience participation activity with the puppets to give Melanie opportunities to rehearse speaking loudly. Mrs. Parsons will give Melanie feedback on how loudly she speaks and will give her suggestions to improve this skill. Then, when Melanie plays or works on projects, I'll bring a puppet along, giving her prompts with the puppet to encourage her to use her new skill. The other teachers will use the puppets in their settings as well to prompt her.

The puppets make it easy to use the procedures during routine classroom activities and add flexibility to the intervention.

Next, I will use the same type of puppet activity to stress the importance of giving eye contact while speaking to someone. In the audience participation part of the activity, Melanie's group will practice using facial expressions while speaking and using head nods and smiles while listening. Then I will work out some hand and face signals with Melanie to prompt her to look at the people she's talking to in her play and project groups, and will go over the signals with the other teachers.

We will work on greeting new participants in a group starting in music class. Ms. Miller, the music teacher, will teach the class a greeting song to use when someone new joins a play group. They will play a game in which students take turns joining the different groups and the group members use the greeting song to welcome their new friend. In my class, we

(Continued on next page)

Example 10b

In Mr. McKey's industrial arts class, students work in pairs on projects for about half the class period. Bill is a student with learning disabilities who has difficulties reading and following directions, working with a partner, staying in his assigned area, and helping with cleanup. He starts projects before he understands the directions, does not share the work load with his partner, and gets angry when the partner offers suggestions or assistance. The target skill Mr. McKey has established for Bill is to "work with partner on shop activities." This page shows Mr. McKey's instructional goals and the beginning of his intervention script. The rest of the script outlines procedures for teaching Bill to link these individual skills into a complete performance pattern.

Worksheet 10.1: Writing an Intervention Script — Page *1* of *2*

Name: *Mr. McKey* — Date: *Nov. 16*

Student: *Bill* — Grade: *11*

Target skill: *Works with partner on shop activities*

Sequence for addressing instructional goals:

First: *Learn to review and follow directions for projects*

Second: *Learn to exchange ideas and suggestions with partner*

Third: *Learn to respond to partner's comments*

Fourth: *Learn to coordinate actions with partner*

Fifth:

Intervention Script:

Bill's intervention will start with a one-on-one explanation of the target skill and the instructional goals to present a general overview of what we will be working on. Before each period, I will give Bill and Jake (his partner) a copy of the day's assignment, go over the activities, and ask them to preview what they will do in the day's class. They will come up with a statement of what they wish to achieve during the activity. I will review and approve the plan before they begin their work.

Next, the intervention will focus on teaching Bill to exchange ideas with Jake. I will have a class discussion on effective and noneffective ways to exchange ideas and suggestions with fellow workers. I will show a videotape from the library on cooperation in the workplace. I will use a "stop action" approach to highlight problems the video shows arising from poor worker communication, and will have the class brainstorm ideas for effective communication. Then I will have them reenact the situations from the video, using the techniques they came up with to resolve the problems that were shown.

I will follow up on these activities with Bill while he is working on his project by having him point out examples of ways he and Jake are communicating or not communicating effectively.

Next I will work with Bill on giving recognition and feedback to a partner on his suggestions. Students in class will be given another set of job situations to role-play, this time focusing on showing people that you are listening to them (by nodding, smiling, saying "Uh huh"). Afterward, during project time, I will prompt Bill to use these techniques with Jake.

(Continued on next page)

Telling students about the goals and procedures of intervention reduces their confusion and may gain their cooperation and support.

This procedure shows the relation between performance demands and natural outcomes and allows students to select outcomes ahead of time.

Commercial materials should be adapted to fit the demands of the particular intervention.

Students should be given opportunities to practice the skills they learn during the intervention.

Mr. Wagner's Case Study

Mr. Wagner revised his instructional goals and brainstorming ideas for Granville. This page shows his new goals and the intervention script he prepared.

Intervention procedures should help students integrate their new individual skills into a behavioral pattern. Although Mr. Wagner's plan addresses each goal area, it does not show Granville how to link the skills together.

Mr. Wagner's procedures should be restructured to give Granville a more active part in the intervention.

Students should have opportunities to practice and apply the skills they learn. Mr. Wagner should have Granville and the class rehearse asking for help.

Modeling procedures must be structured carefully to ensure that students like the models and know what to look for.

Procedures should promote independent student performance, rather than adult intervention.

Rewards should be attainable within a short time span, such as a class period. Rewards should also relate to natural school outcomes rather than to outside incentives like food or other treats.

Worksheet 10.1: Writing an Intervention Script — Page *1* of *2*

Name: *Mrs. Armstrong* — Date: *Nov. 21*

Student: *Granville* — Grade: *5*

Target skill: *Works on projects with classmates*

Sequence for addressing instructional goals:

First: *Learn to read and follow the assignment sheet*

Second: *Learn to give and ask for help from group members*

Third: *Learn to settle disagreements with other group members*

Fourth: *Learn to complete project on time*

Fifth:

Intervention Script:

I will start the intervention by telling Granville to read the assignment before he gets into his group and begins working on the project. I will check whether he has read it by asking him questions about the assignment, and I will explain any steps he does not understand.

Next, I will have a class discussion on what supplies students should bring to class each day and how to plan ahead for class activities and projects. We will also cover the proper ways and times to borrow supplies. I will post the list of supplies and the borrowing suggestions on the board.

On Day 3 of the intervention, I will cover ways to give and ask for help from other group members. I will set up a role-playing activity in which students encounter problems in their work and need to ask for help. Then I will demonstrate some ways to ask for help, contrasting what students normally do with more diplomatic ways.

During lab work, I will have Granville watch the way other students in the group help one another, and have him imitate their behavior.

Next, I will talk with Granville and Bobby about why it is important to get along during class, and encourage them to stop arguing so much during group work. I will tell them that if they do not agree on something, they should come to me and I will settle the disagreement.

Finally, I will reward Granville when he completes his projects on time. If he finishes all his projects on time for the next two weeks, I will give him a coupon for a free meal at a fast food restaurant.

CHAPTER 11

Monitoring the Intervention

The intervention plan you developed from the activities described in Chapters Nine and Ten will guide your intervention procedures, but you should never consider the plan really finished. Think of interventions less as a one-time quick fix than as part of an ongoing process—a process of teaching students to improve their social competence across a broad array of interactions and circumstances.

As you carry out the intervention plan, you should monitor the activities to ensure that the intervention stays tightly focused on the instructional goals and aligned with the progress the students are making in achieving the goals. Monitoring an intervention will allow you to pay careful attention to what happens, and the results you obtain will direct you in deciding what to do next.

In this chapter, we explain the purposes of monitoring an intervention plan, discuss issues you may want to investigate, and describe monitoring procedures. The approach we present encompasses mostly informal observational methods rather than formal, data-based, research-oriented procedures. We have found that an informal approach can supply teachers with sufficient information to fine-tune procedures and evaluate the effectiveness of the plan while still being practical and reasonable in terms of most classroom routines and teaching responsibilities. Furthermore, this approach gives teachers much more latitude in adapting procedures to stay in line with particular concerns they may have at any point in the intervention.

Benefits of Monitoring Interventions

Monitoring an intervention plan can serve several very useful functions in improving students' social competence. First you can gauge the students' progress to see whether they are actually making gains in learning the skills that are the focus of the intervention (Cullen & Pratt, 1992; Sugai & Tindal, 1993). This check will help you determine whether the intervention is having the effects you desire, and

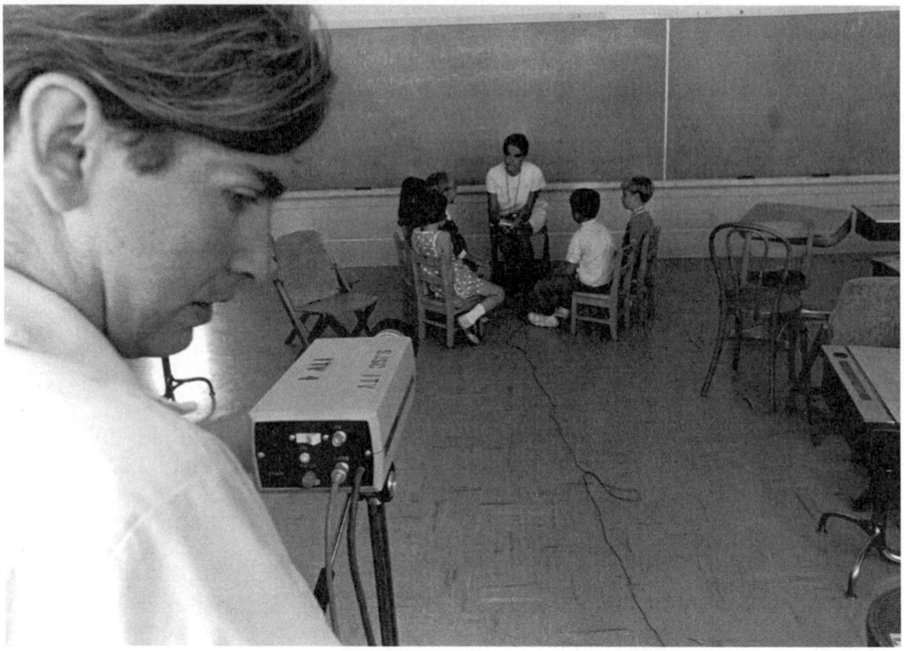

It is important to monitor the progress and the effects of the intervention.

will suggest ways to adjust the procedures as the intervention progresses. Even the best-planned interventions will require adjustments for any number of reasons. Monitoring the students' behavior throughout the intervention will allow you to make these adjustments as soon as they are needed, and will give you a solid basis for planning further action (Kameenui & Simmons, 1990; Walker, Colvin, & Ramsey, 1995). Furthermore, the information you obtain from monitoring will help you decide when students have made sufficient progress in their behavior for you to move on to designing interventions for other high-priority target skills.

Careful monitoring can also serve as a follow-up assessment of the students' behavior, as the intervention results will often provide new insights into their abilities and needs (Kameenui & Simmons, 1990). In undertaking an active intervention program, you can often uncover new information about the students' basic abilities, their proficiency with component steps, and their knowledge of performance conditions; also, you can often answer questions you may have had about the students' incentive. The activities you carry out for the intervention can serve as an active, ongoing assessment at the same time as the procedures help the students develop new skills.

It is important, then, to monitor the intervention as it progresses in order to keep a careful watch over the students' behavior as well as the successes, failures, and unexpected effects of the intervention itself. Monitoring an intervention will allow you to see whether the procedures are adequately addressing the students' immediate problems, and help you tailor the intervention to their needs. It will also provide a wealth of information on what to do next, and serve as a guide for further planning (Cullen & Pratt, 1992).

❍ Preparing to Monitor Interventions

As before, we recommend using a worksheet format to plan and organize the monitoring process for an intervention, for these reasons: (a) interventions usually have many different phases or aspects and can get very complicated before they are finished, and (b) they can produce a variety of effects on student behavior and can reveal surprising things that should be documented. Keeping track of what is happening in an intervention can become quite confusing and difficult if you do not make careful plans ahead of time to consider the issues and concerns on which to focus your attention. In the following sections, we explain the different steps involved in preparing a monitoring worksheet. Table 11.1 lists these steps.

Step 1: Listing Basic Information about the Monitoring Activities

As with all worksheets, it is helpful to begin by entering your name, date, the names of the students participating in the intervention, and any other information you need for documentation purposes. In this case, when planning monitoring activities, you should prepare separate worksheets for each of the students in the intervention. Figure 11.1 shows a format for a monitoring worksheet that Mrs. Armstrong prepared to track Granville's intervention. Note that although Mrs. Armstrong has included Luis in the intervention, she focuses her monitoring worksheet on Granville alone, since the issues she wants to track for him are likely to be different from those she is interested in for Luis.

TABLE 11.1 Steps in preparing a monitoring worksheet

Step 1:	List basic information about the monitoring activities
Step 2:	Enter the target skill
Step 3:	Enter the standard for the original high-priority expectation
Step 4:	Specify a level of confidence for monitoring the standards
Step 5:	Choose other issues for monitoring
Step 6:	List procedures for monitoring
Step 7:	Provide spaces for recording and summarizing results

Figure 11.1 Mrs. Armstrong's monitoring worksheet for Granville's intervention.

Worksheet 11.1: Monitoring the Intervention — Page *1* of *7*

Name: *Mrs. Armstrong* Date: *Nov. 20*

Student: *Granville* Grade: *5*

Target skill: *Cooperates with other students in completing small group activities*

Standard for original priority expectation(s):

Units of Measure	Criterion Level
% of time on task	*85% of group time*
% of work completed	*70% of work completed*

Level of confidence for meeting standard: *At least 5 consecutive days*

Issues or questions to keep track of during intervention:

Does Granville learn to handle disagreements more effectively?

Does Granville learn the 5-step technique for following directions? Does he seem to find it useful?

Does Granville react well to being group leader? Does he approach his position responsibly?

Is Granville able to use the list of alternative ways to handle disagreements? Does he refer to the list when he needs to?

Is Granville ready to be a group leader? When is he ready to follow a different group leader?

Does Granville need more work on following directions? When is he ready to organize tasks on his own?

Does Granville need added incentive? Should he continue being group leader longer than originally planned?

Does Granville use the direction-following technique for other situations besides the group work? Does he use it in other classes?

(Continued on next page)

Figure 11.1 *(continued)*

Worksheet 11.1 (continued)	Name: *Mrs. Armstrong*	Page *2* of *7*
	Student: *Granville*	

Issues or questions to monitor (continued):

Does Granville continue to get in arguments or fights in other situations and settings?

Does Granville form better friendships with group members outside the group work situation? Do his interactions with group members improve in other areas?

Do Granville's academic deficits hold him back in group work, or does he work around them fairly easily once he learns to interact more competently?

What specific areas or circumstances lead to outbursts or problems for Granville?

What outcomes seem to provide incentive for Granville?

Monitoring Procedures

Procedure	Day(s)
Videotape Granville's group	*MTWTF*
Consult with Granville and group	*TWTF*
Logbook—for comments & tallies (check work, behavior, etc.)	*MTWTF*
Consult with Ms. Hernandez and Mr. Wagner	*TWTF*

Step 2: Entering the Target Skill

The most basic reason for monitoring an intervention is to ascertain whether students have acquired the target skill, or are at least making progress in learning it (Walker, Colvin, & Ramsey, 1995). Sometimes, the original purpose of an intervention becomes obscured in planning and working out all the details. Listing information about the target skill on the worksheet will remind you that the real purpose of the intervention is to help the students develop the skills for meeting the expectations you originally identified as priorities.

Mrs. Armstrong should remind herself, when sorting through all the complex ideas and information she has amassed in planning interventions for Sally, Alfred, and Granville, that the primary skills she is addressing are playing in organized games (Alfred), engaging in conversations with peers (Sandy), and cooperating with peers in completing small group activities (Granville). Figure 11.1 shows the target skill she entered on Granville's worksheet.

Step 3: Entering the Standard for the Original Priority Expectation

As you should recall from Chapter Five, the target skill that has been the focus of the intervention plans has its roots in the expectations the students were failing to meet, as revealed during the survey level assessment. In that chapter, we discussed how a key, high-priority item from the "expectations not met" list could be expanded or refined to form the basis for a broader target skill. Now we can return to this original high-priority expectation—and more important, to the standard that describes it—as an efficient and reliable way to gauge students' progress during the intervention. Because it defines a discrete and measurable behavior, the standard for the original priority expectation allows you to judge whether students have actually achieved competence in the central facets of the target skill.

Thus, the standard for the priority expectation will provide the key measure for monitoring your intervention. Although you will ultimately want to record many details about students' performance during the intervention, the standard for the original expectation is the only measure that allows you to judge clearly and objectively whether students are making enough improvement to meet the demands of the situation. Remember that the purpose of the intervention is not simply to improve the students' behavior, but to raise it to meet at least the minimum demands for competence. For this reason, it is extremely important not to lose sight of the original standard, as it represents the most objective basis for judging the effectiveness of the intervention (Howell & Morehead, 1987).

Accordingly, you should enter on the monitoring worksheet information about the standard for the original priority expectation that is the major focus of the target skill. As we discussed in Chapter Three, the standards for expectations can be described in terms of *units of measure* and *criterion levels*. In most cases, you will already have defined these elements when preparing your initial survey level assessment of the students' behavior. For example, the standard Mrs. Armstrong identified for Granville's top priority among the "expectations not met" involved two sets of measurement units and criterion levels:

Expectation	*Units of Measure*	*Criterion Level*
Works cooperatively on assigned activities	% of time discussing topics with classmates	85% on task
	% of work completed	70% of work

Note that even though Mrs. Armstrong rephrased this expectation somewhat when she identified her target skill for Granville, the standard still sets a useful and precise gauge for measuring his progress during the intervention. She listed this information on Granville's monitoring worksheet so that as the intervention procedures take effect she can use the measures to judge whether Granville's performance is beginning to meet the expectation. Figure 11.1 shows how she entered the units of measure and criterion level on Granville's worksheet.

Reviewing Standards

When we first discussed standards in Chapters Three, we stressed that they should be based on as accurate an estimate as you can make of a minimal average performance level for typical students. Now as you review the standards you originally identified for the priority expectation, you might notice that your earlier estimate is less accurate than you might like. The great deal of attention you have paid to the target skill during assessment and intervention planning may have given you new perspectives on the standards that apply, or on the best ways to measure the expectations. Furthermore, the level of typical student performance may have changed somewhat since the first time you estimated it. Therefore, at this point, you should reexamine the units of measure and criteria you originally identified for the expectation rather than copying them directly from the social skills curriculum. The following sections discuss considerations for reviewing and revising standards.

Redefining units of measure The measurement units you use for quantifying student performance should help you judge whether students are meeting the key expectations that make up the target skill for the intervention. For the units to serve this purpose well, you may have to redefine them to bring them more clearly in line with your needs. Remember that when you originally defined the standards for an expectation, each was only one item on a broad list. Now that you are focusing more closely on this single item, you may notice that the units of measure are less useful or accurate than you might like. When Mrs. Armstrong originally defined the standard for Sandy's key expectation "engages in conversations with peers," she used the units of measure "number of conversations per day." Now, as she prepares to monitor Sandy's intervention, she recognizes that this measure does not really capture whether Sandy is actually involved in the conversation, or how long she stays in each conversation. Therefore, Mrs. Armstrong could redefine the measurement units as "amount of time spent conversing." This measure would give her a better picture of how well Sandy is progressing. Of course, Mrs. Armstrong would also have to set a different criterion level to match the new units of measure, but she could quickly do this by estimating the minimum amount of time typical students spend conversing in her setting—for example, "At least 20 minutes per day."

You should use special caution when the original units of measure are expressed in negative terms, such as the number of times students interrupt conversations or the amount of time they are not sitting at their desks. Although these negative units of measure offered a convenient way to assess student problems, they do not always indicate what students should do in the performance of the target skill. For example, the expectation "resolves conflicts without fighting" might originally have been counted with the negative measure "numbers of times fighting." This measure might have been very efficient during the survey level assessment because it gave a natural indication of whether students met the expectation. But for the intervention, we would want to know more than just whether students are still fighting; it would also be important to determine whether they have learned the new replacement behavior of negotiating and resolving conflicts. Therefore, we would want to replace the original negative measure "number of times fighting" with a measure that looks at positive performance, such as "percentage of conflicts resolved through negotiation." In this way, we can ensure that the units of measure we use to monitor the intervention give a clear accounting of the intervention's goal or intent.

Adjusting criterion levels A recheck of standards will also allow you to adjust the criterion levels for the standards if they have changed since you conducted the survey level assessment, or if you feel your original estimate of the standard was not as accurate as you can now make it. It is not unusual for standards to change during the course of a school year as students mature and develop their social skills. Similarly, the large amount of observation and information gathering you have done since you originally defined the expectation may give you a more accurate understanding of the performance level of typical students. In such cases, you should adjust the criterion level before you plan the monitoring procedures. For example, when she reviews the criteria for Granville's priority expectation, Mrs. Armstrong will want to be sure that the levels she identified earlier are still an accurate estimate of typical behavior. If she had found during her assessment of Granville that the other students typically stay on task only about 75 percent of the time, she would need to revise her earlier criterion level of 85 percent. On the other hand, if her observations have confirmed her earlier estimate, she should stay with the 85 percent figure.

Specifying standards for consolidated target skills In some cases, the target skill you originally identified may have been based on a composite of several different items from the original "expectations not met" list. For these, you may be able to identify the one or two high-priority expectations from the list that most closely correspond to the central goals of the intervention, and use these standards on your monitoring worksheet. In other cases, you may find that no one or two items from the list provide an adequate or useful set of standards for monitoring an intervention. When you find that this is the case, you may need to develop a composite standard from among the curriculum items or specify an entirely new standard. As you may recall from the case study in Chapter Five, Mrs. Armstrong defined a fairly broad target skill for Alfred, "plays organized games with peers." She based this skill on several related items from Alfred's "expectations not met" list:

Follows the rules for games

Follows the action of games

Cheers and encourages the performance of teammates

Plays the entire game

Stays in the game-playing area

As she reviews these original expectations and their standards, Mrs. Armstrong realizes that none of the items gives an accurate measure for the overall target skill. Therefore, in preparing her monitoring worksheet for Alfred, she will specify a new standard rather than drawing one directly from her original curriculum. She could define the units of measure as "Amount of game-time spent playing co-operatively," and estimate the criterion level as "At least 75 percent of game time." This standard would give her a more complete measure of the target skill than any of the individual expectations. In most cases, when you need to set a new standard you will be able to estimate an accurate criterion level based on the extensive assessments you have done with your students. In other instances you will have to conduct some quick observations of the students' typical competent behavior in order to estimate the standard level of performance.

Therefore, before entering standards on the monitoring worksheet, you should review them carefully to consider whether the units of measure and criterion levels clearly express the goals you want to achieve with the intervention. When it is necessary to adjust or redefine standards, or set new ones, you will find it helpful to review the process of identifying and describing standards discussed in Chapter Three.

Step 4: Specifying a Level of Confidence for Monitoring the Standards

Comparing student performance with standards will allow you to judge whether an intervention is successful. But when you monitor an intervention, you will obviously not want to end your oversight of the students' behavior the first time they perform at the level of the standards. Even after they have acquired the target skills, it is important to continue monitoring the intervention to be sure the skills have become an established part of their performance routine. In addition, you should often extend monitoring activities even further to evaluate whether students are using their skills in other settings where the skills apply. In this way, the monitoring activities can provide an excellent overall measure of the social validity of the intervention process (Walker, Colvin, & Ramsey, 1995).

For example, Mrs. Armstrong would not stop monitoring Sandy's conversations the first time she engages in conversations for 20 minutes during a day, or stop observing Alfred's play behavior the first time he participates during 75 percent of a recess period. She would continue monitoring the students' behavior to determine whether they consistently meet the expectations or whether they later fall below the criterion level. Only after she sees evidence of sustained competent behavior will she feel confident in ending the monitoring and discontinuing the interventions. Furthermore, with Sandy, Mrs. Armstrong will want to verify that she uses her conversational skills in different school settings and situations and with different students, and not just in social studies with one or two close friends.

The *level of confidence* is a number that describes how long or how consistently the students must continue to meet the standard before we feel assured that they are now meeting the expectation. You could specify, for instance, that students must meet the standard for five days in a row, or for six out of eight consecutive opportunities, for you to be assured of their progress. The level of confidence defines how much competent behavior we must observe before we trust in the intervention's lasting success. By setting a level of confidence and entering it on the monitoring worksheet, you give yourself an overall guide to follow in planning oversight of the students' performance.

A key benefit of establishing a level of confidence is that it provides a flexible gauge for deciding when to continue or fade the intervention plan (Kameenui & Simmons, 1990). It does this by linking the intervention monitoring to the students' actual performance rather than to pre-set time limits. If Mrs. Armstrong sees, for example, that Granville enthusiastically follows the intervention plan and his behavior dramatically exceeds the standard during the entire first week, she will be able to fade the intervention right away based on the level of confidence she has established. On the other hand, she could extend the monitoring beyond the original timeline if her measures indicate that Granville is still struggling with cooperating with his peers, or is generally inconsistent in his behavior either in social studies or in the other settings where he should use this skill.

Another important benefit of establishing a level of confidence is that it will help you avoid making hasty judgments about the students' performance and will ensure that you monitor the intervention long enough to spot any backsliding or regression. Even after an intervention has been successful in teaching students the target skill, their performance may decline after the first few days for any of the following reasons:

- Students forget to attend to some key variables or overlook an important outcome
- They have not had sufficient practice in using their skills
- They have not learned to coordinate their behavior properly with ongoing activities and interactions
- They have difficulty adapting their behavior to changing conditions or to a broad-ranging set of circumstances
- They become complacent or sloppy in their performance

In most instances, you can rectify these problems quickly if you are still overseeing the students' performance, because you can supply additional instruction or incentive to get their behavior back on track. These follow-up procedures could help the students refine their skills further or refocus their attention or interest on performing the required actions before they have made too many errors or bad judgments.

Setting a Level of Confidence

In most instances you should feel confident in ending an intervention if students meet the standard three to five consecutive times in each of the settings or situations you are investigating with the monitoring activities. For example, Mrs. Armstrong should feel secure about Granville's performance if she sees him working with classmates about 85 percent of the time and completing about 70 percent of his work for the project (the standard) over five consecutive days. This level of performance would indicate that Granville can now meet the expectation and can also apply his new skills consistently and repeatedly.

Although the level of confidence should demand a degree of consistency, not every level of confidence need be defined by strictly consecutive performance. For some interventions, particularly those that involve expectations that are less rigid or less consistently applied, you may wish to define the level of confidence as "*x* out of *y* times" rather than as consecutive times. For example, Mrs. Armstrong may decide she will be confident in Sandy's performance if she sees Sandy engaging in conversations for at least 20 minutes (the standard) on three out of five days. This level would allow Mrs. Armstrong to account for normal variations in Sandy's behavior that may arise for any number of reasons, while she still ensures that Sandy is continuing at a generally competent level.

There may be special cases in which you specify levels of confidence that are higher than three to five times. Higher levels of confidence are often indicated with target skills that

- are more complicated and difficult for students to learn
- are not used very frequently in the setting
- are performed with little or no direct supervision
- replace or substitute for extreme or very disruptive behavior
- involve avoiding some danger or risk to the students or peers

You might decide to set the level of confidence for meeting the standard at six to eight times for expectations such as giving a class recitation that students may find complicated or intimidating at first, or playing a drill-and-practice game in math that they may not play very often. You might set the level of confidence at eight to ten times, or even higher, for skills such as running errands for teachers that may require a high degree of independence and initiative, or using self-control strategies for avoiding arguments or fights in school hallways. For Alfred's intervention, Mrs. Armstrong set a confidence level of participating in the game 75 percent of the time (the standard) for ten recess periods in a row. She realizes that Alfred will have to master many adaptations and new skills to coordinate his behavior with that of his teammates and she wants to make sure he continues to use his new skills successfully so they become habits.

Thus, the level of confidence you specify on the worksheet should be linked to the demands of the target skill and the degree of certainty you have in the students' abilities. Figure 11.1 shows the level of confidence Mrs. Armstrong entered on the worksheet for Granville.

Step 5: Choosing Other Issues for Monitoring

Although the standard for the original priority expectation should anchor your monitoring activities to a specific overall goal, it is by no means the only thing you will want to watch for. There are probably as many matters to consider and as many ways to oversee an intervention as there are types of intervention plans. As you prepare to monitor the intervention, think about the other kinds of information that monitoring activities can provide so you can attune yourself to those areas you are genuinely interested in studying (Howell & Morehead, 1987; Kameenui & Simmons, 1990).

Because of the wide variety of issues you could address in monitoring an intervention, you must be selective in the ones to which you pay attention and keep these concerns firmly in mind while carrying out the intervention plan. During Sandy's intervention, in addition to tracking her general progress in engaging in conversations, Mrs. Armstrong could also look for the effects the procedures have on specific aspects of the skill, such as Sandy's choice of conversational topics, her facial expressions and body language, or her articulation of words and speech intonations. Or Mrs. Armstrong could focus on other areas such as Sandy's selection of classmates to talk with during class breaks, her contributions to class discussions, or her reactions to her teacher's suggestions, praise, and feedback.

Like Mrs. Armstrong, you can usually choose from a wide variety of issues to monitor during an intervention—many more, in fact, than you could keep track of or would even be interested in. You should be selective in choosing the most important areas to monitor during the intervention, but you should be aware that your concerns may change during the course of the intervention as the students make progress in their skill development. You will need a broad, dynamic approach, choosing several representative, well-targeted issues rather than limiting your attention to one narrow area of concern or spreading yourself too thin by working from a long list of questions. In the following sections we discuss several types of monitoring issues and explain how keeping track of them can help you make important decisions about continuing or adjusting the intervention plan. These issues are listed in Table 11.2.

Performance of the Target Skill

As we discussed in the chapters on specific level assessment, performing target skills involves a variety of tasks, including mastering basic abilities, linking component steps, and negotiating performance conditions. For this reason, you will probably have several specific questions about the students' performance during the intervention—more than you can answer with a simple tally of the units of measure for the target skill. You may have questions about the students' performance of particular techniques you are trying to teach, or you may want to look

TABLE 11.2 Types of issues to monitor during interventions

Issues relating to the performance of the target skill
Issues relating to the students' reaction to the intervention procedures
Issues relating to coordinating the ongoing intervention with the students' progress and needs
Issues relating to how well the students carry over their new skills to other situations and skill areas
Issues relating to obtaining additional assessment information about the students' performance

for changes in their interactions or improvements in their level of attention. Issues such as these may take on particular importance for those subskills you identified earlier (in Chapter Nine) as instructional goals for the intervention.

Mrs. Armstrong might identify the following issues for her students. Note that many of them are related to the areas she defined as instructional goals:

Sandy

- How well does Sandy learn to give greetings? Does she apply them in conversations?
- Does Sandy pick up on cues and recognize when to speak?
- Does Sandy try to speak more often with friends than she did before?

Alfred

- How well does Alfred follow the rules of the game?
- Does Alfred show any changes or improvements in his game-time interactions?
- Does Alfred pay attention more during the game?

Granville

- How well does Granville understand directions and organize his tasks?
- Does Granville show improvement in his interactions with group members?
- Does Granville handle criticism or suggestions from classmates more effectively now?

Listing concerns or questions like these before the intervention begins will help Mrs. Armstrong look for key elements in the students' progress in acquiring the target skill. It will thus lead to a more detailed and complete understanding of the students' behavior during the intervention, particularly in cases in which their overall performance is mixed, inconsistent, or contradictory.

Students' Reaction to the Intervention Procedures

Students' behavior during the intervention reflects more than their attainment or nonattainment of particular skills. They often react quite strongly to the intervention itself, and their responses may be directed as much to the procedures as to the underlying skills being taught. Student reactions to particular intervention procedures can range from interest, excitement, and enthusiasm to boredom, resistance, and outright resentment. Monitoring these reactions will give you valuable information about the intervention's potential for success and can help you pinpoint the activities that will be most effective in improving the students' skills (Cullen & Pratt, 1992; Howell & Morehead, 1987).

It is particularly important to track the students' reactions to the intervention activities during the first days of the intervention when their overall skill level may remain unchanged or inconclusive. You can easily become discouraged when the students do not immediately alter their behavior after the intervention begins, and you may be tempted to discard what is, in fact, a very effective plan. Often students need a couple of days to adapt and learn from the new procedures and activities you are using. In such cases, there may be no immediate evidence that they are making improvement in their interactions or progress in meeting the expecta-

A key issue to monitor is the way the students react to the intervention procedures.

tion. But you can gain some assurance that the procedures are working by closely watching their reactions to the procedures and noticing subtle changes in their behavior.

With interventions that include incentive-building strategies, it is important to watch for the students' reaction to the outcomes that have now become available to them. You may find that they react strongly to the new outcomes you are using and are very enthusiastic about taking part in the intervention. On the other hand, they may seem unable to understand the outcomes or to realize they are capable of earning these outcomes; and some may not consider them experiences worth working to obtain. Monitoring these issues right from the start can show you whether the students are responding favorably to the incentive procedures or are, at least, interested in and attentive to the activities.

When preparing to monitor her students' reactions to the intervention procedures, Mrs. Armstrong might identify the following concerns:

Sandy

- How does Sandy respond to the role-playing activity? Does she seem to enjoy it?
- What happens when a teacher joins her conversation group?
- How does Sandy seem to feel about the intervention? Is she flattered? Shy? Does the intervention improve or worsen her outlook?

Alfred

- Does Alfred understand the overall purpose and goals of the intervention? Does he seem interested in succeeding?
- How does Alfred react to the peer model or coach? Do they work well together?
- Does Alfred react well to prompting? Does he respond to my prompts?

Granville

- Does Granville learn the technique for following directions? Does he seem to find it useful?
- Does Granville react well to being group leader? Does he approach his position responsibly?
- Is Granville able to use the list of alternative ways to handle disagreements? Does he refer to the list when he needs to?

Coordinating the Ongoing Intervention with Students' Progress

Another area in which monitoring will be important is anticipating and reacting to the students' progress over the course of the intervention. Careful monitoring will allow you to fine-tune the intervention procedures to keep them in line with the gains the students are making at each stage of the intervention plan (Cullen & Pratt, 1992). This function of monitoring is particularly important when your intervention plan involves successive skills that students must master. As you observe the students becoming proficient in one element of the intervention, you can move the intervention along to concentrate on the next procedures or goals. You may find as you monitor the students' progress that you need to speed up or slow down the implementation of the intervention plan, or even shift the emphasis of your procedures, to adapt to the students' needs.

Your observations of the students' progress will also help you decide when to fade certain aspects of the intervention so students are encouraged to assume greater responsibility for their behavior. These observations are especially important when you are using artificial or extra rewards because you will want to remove them as soon as the students begin to recognize and respond to natural outcomes.

Mrs. Armstrong might define the following issues as central considerations in coordinating and timing her interventions for Sandy, Alfred, and Granville. She will pay close attention to these concerns as the intervention progresses:

Sandy

- When is Sandy ready to move from conversing with the teacher to conversing with peers?
- Is Sandy's use of greetings solid enough for informal settings and situations?
- Will Sandy need continued prompting after the first two or three days, or does she learn to pick up on cues naturally?

Alfred

- When is Alfred ready to take responsibility for following game rules on his own? Will the prompting procedure need to be continued beyond the original timeline?
- Does Alfred need more practice on his game-playing skills and strategies, or more work on his interactions with teammates?
- Does Alfred have enough incentive to work on his skills, or should more be added as the intervention progresses?

Granville

- Is Granville ready to be a group leader? Is he ready to follow a different group leader?
- Does Granville need more work on following directions? Is he able to organize tasks on his own?
- Does Granville need added incentive? Should he continue being group leader longer than originally planned?

Students' Ability to Carry Over New Skills to Other Situations

You will probably structure the intervention to develop new skills in one or two clearly defined but limited sets of conditions, but students will have to use the skills eventually in several different circumstances. Sometimes, students will naturally transfer their skills to the different settings where they are needed; other times they will not. One issue you should monitor during the intervention is whether the students are generalizing their new skills properly (Walker, Colvin, & Ramsey, 1995; Zirpoli & Melloy, 1993). If you find they do not make the generalization on their own, you would have to expand the intervention to help them.

A related issue is how well the students transfer their improved behavior to entirely new skill areas. Often, a successful intervention will have effects beyond just the single expectation for which it was designed. Mrs. Armstrong may find, for example, that Sandy's improvement in conversing or Granville's improvement in group work can become a springboard to a broad improvement in social interactions. By watching for this kind of general improvement, Mrs. Armstrong will be able to build on the successes of the intervention by targeting and reinforcing the other skill areas where the students show improvement, or by helping the students make this generalization if they do not do it on their own.

Mrs. Armstrong's list of monitoring issues might include the following concerns relating to carryover:

Sandy

- Does Sandy adapt her greetings to other school personnel (e.g., principal, counselor)?
- Does Sandy apply the skills to informal conversations before class begins, or does she use them only in the intervention situation?
- Does the intervention give Sandy added confidence to participate in class discussions? Does her improvement carry over to other kinds of interactions?

Alfred

- Does Alfred improve in other game-playing activities—for example, in small group games?
- Do Alfred's interactions with teammates improve as his play behavior improves?
- Does Alfred's behavior improve or change in other settings (classroom, cafeteria, etc.), or in other interactions (e.g., class discussions)?

Granville

- Does Granville use the five-step plan for following directions for other assignments besides group work? Does he use it in other classes?

- Does Granville continue to get in arguments or fights in other situations and settings?
- Does Granville form better friendships with group members outside the group work situation? Do his interactions with group members improve in other areas?

Providing Additional Assessment Information

You can use the monitoring of an intervention as an ongoing assessment of performance to obtain a wealth of new or updated information about students' behavior and abilities. Many times you can discover from the intervention much about the students' learning and performance characteristics that you may have missed during the assessment process (Cullen & Pratt, 1992; Kameenui & Simmons, 1990). For example, it is often very difficult to know what incentives will work for students until you actually try them out in the intervention. By carefully observing the students' behavior during the intervention, you can find what will or will not serve as incentives for them to improve their participation in the intervention or increase their interest in using their skills. Monitoring such issues carefully can supplement the assessment results and help you keep the intervention on track.

This source of assessment information is particularly beneficial when the intervention does not appear to be having the desired effect—that is, when the students are not making satisfactory progress in the skills that were the focus of the intervention. In such cases, you will want to modify the intervention procedures to make them more effective, but first, you must determine why the students are not developing the skills properly. Closely watching their performance during the activities can supply useful information about what impediments exist, and can suggest the adjustments you should make in the intervention to advance their skill levels.

Mrs. Armstrong defined the following concerns as important areas to watch during the interventions. By paying careful attention to these issues, she will be able to gather key information about the abilities and needs of Sandy, Alfred, and Granville:

Sandy

- Are there students or groups with whom Sandy finds it particularly easy or difficult to converse?
- Can Sandy adapt her new skills to a number of different school situations?
- How well can Sandy continue with a conversation once she has started or joined it? After she uses her greetings, does she know what to do next?

Alfred

- How does Alfred respond to particular playmates? Is he able to use his new skills when Sally is present, or does he revert to his clowning behavior?
- Will Alfred need additional work on his coordination skills and motor performance?

- Does Alfred interact more competently when he is paying attention to the game, or when he really wants to win?

Granville

- Do Granville's academic deficits hold him back in group work, or does he work around them fairly easily once he learns to interact more competently?
- What specific areas or circumstances lead to outbursts or problems for Granville?
- What outcomes seem to provide incentive for Granville?

Adding the Monitoring Issues to the Worksheet

As the sections above demonstrate, monitoring an intervention can address many important issues, both in verifying the effectiveness of the intervention and in adjusting and modifying procedures. To effectively negotiate these concerns, you should make a list of the issues to monitor as the intervention progresses, and enter the list on the worksheet. Following the examples above, you can express these issues in the form of direct, focused questions, basing them on what you wish to know about the students or what you predict will happen to their behavior. Figure 11.1 shows the issues Mrs. Armstrong plans to monitor during Granville's intervention.

Step 6: Listing Procedures for Monitoring

Choosing the procedures for monitoring an intervention plan is fairly straightforward after you have decided on the issues to investigate. As with the procedures for assessment described in Part II of the text, you should use as many of your normal teaching and supervisory activities as possible both to save extra planning and preparation and to keep the observations unobtrusive and objective. In the next sections, we briefly discuss procedures for monitoring the standards for the original high-priority expectation as well as procedures for keeping track of the other issues you have identified as crucial in the intervention.

Procedures for Monitoring Standards

It is important to make proper provisions for evaluating the students' performance of the original priority expectations because this is the best way to judge the overall success of the intervention. In an earlier step we discussed how to identify the standards for meeting the original expectation. Now, you will need to prepare formalized, data-based procedures to monitor and quantify the students' behavior, so you can compare the behavior against these specific standards (Maag, 1989; Walker, Colvin, & Ramsey, 1995). In most cases, the procedures should be the same as or equivalent to those you used during the survey level assessment. The results you obtain will then give the best indication of whether the students are meeting the original expectation or are at least making substantial progress in their behavior.

In her survey level assessments, Mrs. Armstrong used direct observations and made tallies on a recording form to measure Alfred's play behavior during recess and Sandy's conversations during class breaks. Now, during the intervention, she can use the same techniques to evaluate the students' progress in these areas. While she is carrying out Alfred's intervention, Mrs. Armstrong should count the number of minutes he pays attention to the game and plays along properly to learn whether his performance has improved enough to meet the 75 percent criterion she has identified on her monitoring worksheet; and she should continue to keep a regular tally of his performance as the intervention progresses.

In the same way, you should frequently measure the students' behavior and compare the results against the specified criterion levels for the expectations you are concerned with, and you should continue making these recordings until the students' performance has reached the confidence level you set for the intervention. The level of the students' behavior you observe at each of the measurement intervals will give you a firm basis for deciding what to do next in their intervention plan.

Procedures for Monitoring Other Issues

The procedures you use to answer your other questions about the intervention procedures or about the students' behavior can be as formal as those you use with the target skill, or they can be very informal, depending on the depth and scope of your concerns (Maag, 1989). To investigate whether Sandy carries over her conversational skills to Mr. Wagner's science class, Mrs. Armstrong could do any of the following:

- Ask Sandy how she did in the class.
- Confer informally with Mr. Wagner or some of Sandy's classmates.
- Make videotapes of Sandy's behavior.
- Conduct regularly scheduled formal observations herself or have Mr. Wagner make them.

In most cases, the types of procedures you could use will follow directly from the questions or issues you wish to address, if you have stated and focused them clearly. The background work you did previously in conducting the survey level and specific level assessments will also direct you to the most effective means for keeping track of what happens during the intervention, whether you use video, outside observers, logbooks, or other techniques. With Sandy's intervention, the challenge for Mrs. Armstrong is more in defining the issues she wants to monitor than in devising the methods she will use. After all, she can effectively measure Sandy's performance with the same types of procedures she used in her earlier assessments.

Your main concern will be to describe the procedures on the monitoring worksheet so they match the issues you have outlined. If Mrs. Armstrong is particularly interested in how Sandy reacts to the role-playing games or in whether she carries over greetings to other circumstances, she should probably use direct observation, video, or some other method that will give her a detailed look at these behaviors. However, with an area of less concern to Mrs. Armstrong, like whom Sandy talks with during lunch or recess time, Mrs. Armstrong may simply ask Sandy, because looking at the behavior would not be so crucial.

Thus, the procedures you use to monitor an intervention should correspond directly to the target skill and to issues you have chosen to address. You should use the most formalized and exacting procedures with the concerns and questions that are the most important for you to investigate. Figure 11.1 shows the types of monitoring procedures Mrs. Armstrong plans to use with Granville's intervention.

Step 7: Providing Spaces for Recording Results

The last step in preparing a worksheet is to provide space for entering the monitoring results. The most important consideration is to employ a format that is easy to use, is flexible, and allows plenty of room for making entries. The following sections discuss how to prepare daily records as well as charts and graphs to make a complete document of the students' performance.

Making a Daily Log of the Results

You should use the monitoring worksheet to keep a daily log of the students' behavior (Burden & Byrd, 1994). Your entries could include any of the following:

- a record of grades, test scores, and scores on assignments
- notes from informal observations
- tallies from formal observations and videos
- summaries of comments made by other students
- accounts of interviews with the students themselves
- reports from parents and school personnel
- any other information you feel is important or interesting to document in evaluating the students' progress

At some points in the intervention, you will wish to focus more closely on the target skill and on the other issues you identified beforehand as especially important, but at any time you are likely to find interesting results or insights that you may not have anticipated or that will be helpful in fine-tuning the procedures. You should record these findings carefully, as they can provide a solid basis for your decisions on how to alter the intervention plan. For example, during her initial observations, Mrs. Armstrong may find that Sandy responds particularly well to the role-playing activities. Mrs. Armstrong should record this information on her worksheet so she can remember to use the activity again during the later phases of the intervention. Similarly, other students may tell Mrs. Armstrong that Sandy's behavior improves considerably when a teacher is not a part of the group. Mrs. Armstrong should note this finding as well because she may need to find a way to give input into Sandy's interactions without

Figure 11.2 Pages from Mrs. Armstrong's monitoring worksheet showing her daily log of results.

Worksheet 11.1 (continued)	Name: *Mrs. Armstrong* Student: *Granville*	Page *3* of *7*

Intervention Results for (day) *Monday*

Ms. H. taught G. to use 5-step technique for following directions. She worked on it with G. in resource room. Ms. H. said G. needed prompting, but he did use the technique properly when reminded.

In my class, in group work, G. wrote directions for group, with only one error. G. worked pretty well with group completing questionnaire on social studies topics for discussion. He spent only about 50% of his time on task, but completed 80% of his work, and had no major disagreements.

I told G. he did well, and suggested he use the directions worksheet in Mr. Wagner's class too.

Intervention Results for (day) *Tuesday*

Ms. H. introduced the new worksheet for organizing tasks. G. learned to use the new worksheet fairly quickly, and Ms. H. prompted him to use his direction-following technique at the same time.

We videotaped the skits on group cooperation. G. was to be a lead player, but he seemed uneasy and acted silly, so I had him sit down. But he did seem to enjoy watching the others in the skits.

In follow-up work, G. used his worksheet to follow directions and plan the assignment. Worked well with his group. Time on task: 65%. Work completed: 14 of 20 questions (70%).

Figure 11.2 *(continued)*

Worksheet 11.1 (continued)	Name: *Mrs. Armstrong* Student: *Granville*	Page *4* of *7*

Intervention Results for (day) *Wednesday*

We looked at video of skits, and discussed ways to cooperate in small groups. We made a set of guidelines for group leaders and group members. Asked G. to be a small group leader. He wrote down the directions right away on his worksheet.

G. was good as leader. Followed guidelines carefully, despite some disagreements with others. His group was one of the first to finish. On task: 95%. Work completed: 80%.

Intervention Results for (day) *Thursday*

G. and class worked on conflict-resolving techniques. Used role playing to demonstrate conflicts, and class made a list to post of acceptable responses. I talked with G. afterward and he seemed to understand how to use the list.

During group work, Brian served as leader. G. used his worksheet to write directions. G. seemed grouchy because he didn't get to be leader again. He was distracted a lot, and started to get in an argument, until he was prompted to consult the conflict-resolving list. Time on task: 50%. Work completed: 40%.

Figure 11.2 *(continued)*

Worksheet 11.1 (continued)	Name: *Mrs. Armstrong* Student: *Granville*	Page *5* of *7*
Intervention Results for (day) *Friday*		
Intervention Results for (day) ______		

participating directly in her peer group conversations. Figure 11.2 shows the format Mrs. Armstrong used to record daily results on her worksheet, and includes her entries for the first four days of Granville's intervention.

Graphing and Charting Behavior

In addition to keeping a daily log of the intervention results, you might want to prepare a graph or chart of the students' behavior in order to summarize some of the findings. Charts and graphs are especially useful when you regularly record a specific behavior, as you would with the students' performance of the target skill (Howell & Morehead, 1987; Sugai & Tindal, 1993). With a chart or a graph, you can tell at a glance whether there are any special trends, tendencies, or consistencies in the students' performance. As with any worksheet, you should develop separate graphs or charts for each student you are monitoring, and perhaps for each behavior you are tracking. You should label each chart or graph with the student's name and the specific behavior to be summarized. These initial preparations will be very helpful to you in interpreting the results.

The conventional way of preparing a chart is to draw two or more columns, and to label the top of each column with a heading that explains what the entries will be. The left column usually signifies the day on which the recordings are taken, and the right columns depict the results obtained on those days (Burden & Byrd, 1994; Zirpoli & Melloy, 1993). Mrs. Armstrong plans to monitor Granville's use of his directions and organizing procedures by giving him daily quizzes about the group activities. Figure 11.3 shows a chart she added to her worksheet to record Granville's results on the quizzes, and includes his scores for the first four days of the intervention.

The customary way to label a graph is to specify the days on which you make recordings along the horizontal axis, and to list intervals in the units of measure for the behavior along the vertical axis. Generally, you begin numbering the units of measure with a "0" at the base of the vertical axis, such as "0 times," "0 minutes," or "0 percent." Then, you would number upward in equal increments along the axis (e.g., by 2's, 5's, or 10's) until you have indicated the highest level the behavior will likely reach.

You make your entries on a graph by first writing the date on which the students' behavior is observed on the bottom line. Then you go up the vertical axis and mark the point that represents the level of the students' performance observed on that date. Connecting the points across the successive days on which you measure the behavior will give you a visual report on how the students are progressing. Figure 11.4 shows two graphs Mrs. Armstrong added to her worksheet to summarize the percentage of time Granville was on task and his percentage of work completed. She made a horizontal line across the graphs at the 85 percent and 70 percent levels, respectively, to remind her of the criterion levels for the expectations. These graphs give Mrs. Armstrong an ongoing record of Granville's behavior and help her judge quickly whether his performance is meeting the standard. Again, the figure shows entries for the first four days of Granville's intervention.

The monitoring worksheet you develop should give you an easy, straightforward way to track the students' behavior and the intervention procedures. Once

Figure 11.3 Worksheet page showing chart for recording Granville's quiz scores.

Worksheet 11.1 (continued)	Name: *Mrs. Armstrong*	Page *6* of *7*
	Student: *Granville*	

Charts for recording student performance.

Chart title: *Granville's quiz scores*

Days/times:	Results:
Monday	*13/20*
Tuesday	*17/20*
Wednesday	*16/20*
Thursday	*17/20*
Friday	

Chart title:

Days/times:	Results:

Figure 11.4 Worksheet page showing graphs for Granville's performance of the target skill.

Worksheet 11.1 (continued)	Name: *Mrs. Armstrong* Student: *Granville*	Page *7* of *7*

Graphs for recording student performance.

Graph Title: *Granville's time on task*

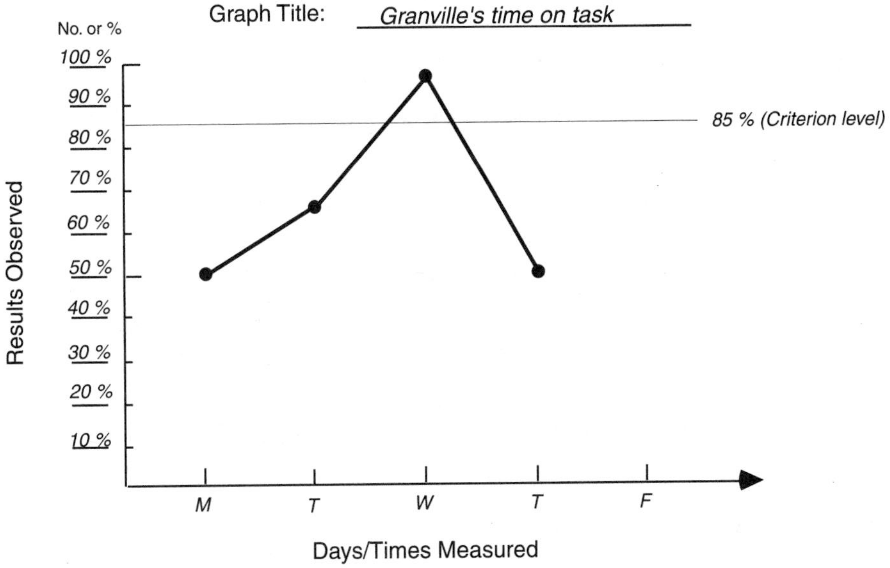

Graph Title: *Granville's work completed*

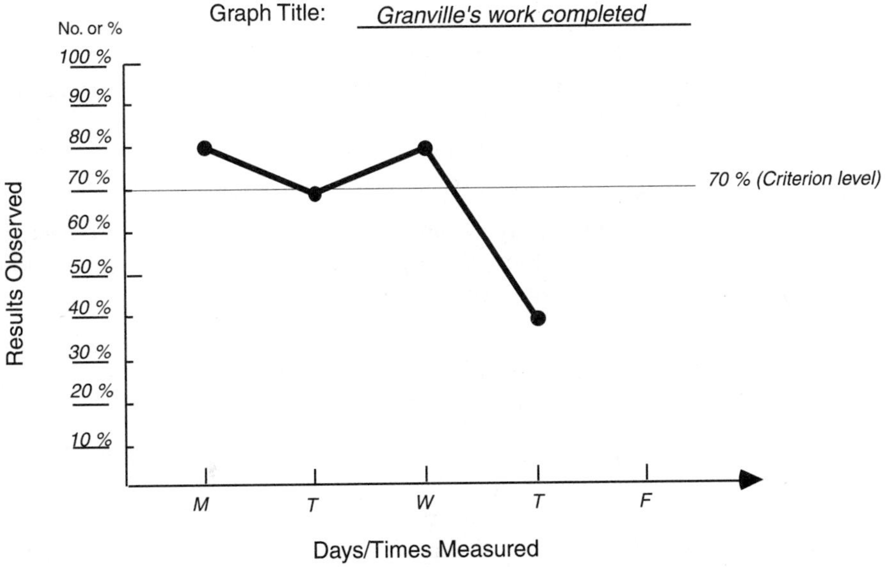

you have prepared the worksheet, you will be ready to begin the intervention right away. The results you enter on the worksheet will help you make adjustments in the intervention plan, determine whether students are acquiring and using the target skills, and answer any other concerns you have about the students' behavior or the intervention procedures. In the next chapter, we discuss how to interpret these results and how to follow up on the achievements and setbacks of the intervention.

Summary

Benefits of Monitoring Intervention Plans

1. Monitoring an intervention plan helps gauge the students' progress in acquiring and using target skills.
2. Monitoring assists in deciding whether the intervention is having positive effects on students' performance.
3. Monitoring aids in fine-tuning intervention procedures to keep them aligned to the students' progress and needs.
4. Monitoring provides additional assessment information about the students' learning and performance characteristics.

Preparing to Monitor Intervention Plans

1. Preparing to monitor an intervention involves the following steps:
   a. listing basic information about monitoring activities
   b. entering the target skill
   c. entering the standard for the target skill
   d. specifying a level of confidence for monitoring the target skill
   e. choosing other issues for monitoring
   f. listing procedures for monitoring
   g. providing spaces for recording and summarizing results
2. Standards for expectations that are the focus of an intervention should be reviewed to ensure that they give the most accurate description of the overall goals of the intervention.
3. Level of confidence is the number that describes how long or how consistently students must continue to meet the standard before monitoring activities can be ended.
4. Issues to address when monitoring an intervention can relate to the following:
   a. performance of the target skills
   b. reaction of students to the intervention procedures
   c. coordination of intervention activities with students' progress and needs

d. carryover and generalization of skills to other situations and skill areas
e. gaining additional assessment information about students' learning and performance characteristics

5. Procedures for monitoring target skills should be formalized and data based, and should generally parallel the methods used in a survey level assessment.

6. Procedures for monitoring other issues can be either formal or informal depending on the depth and scope of concerns.

7. Results from monitoring activities should be entered on a daily log, chart, graph, or other data collection format.

Examples for Chapter 11

Example 11a

Wilfred, a student in Mr. Grady's ninth-grade geography class, speaks out of turn during class discussions and often makes comments that do not pertain to the discussion. Mr. Grady's target skill is "participates in large group class discussions"; he is using peer tutoring and role-playing activities to teach the skill. On this worksheet, Mr. Grady has outlined the standard, the level of confidence, and some of the monitoring issues.

Sometimes the standard will measure both the performance of the target skill and the non-performance of a problem behavior.

Level of confidence should account for normal variations in behavior and opportunities for using skills.

Some teachers find it helpful to label monitoring questions according to the type of issues addressed.

Monitoring issues should anticipate what the intervention might bring to light.

Worksheet 11.1: Monitoring the Intervention — Page *1* of *8*

Name: *Mr. Grady* — Date: *Nov. 23*

Student: *Wilfred* — Grade: *9*

Target skill: *Participates in large group class discussions*

Standard for original priority expectation(s):

Units of Measure	Criterion Level
# of relevant comments added to discussion	*At least 2 per class*
# of times distracting group	*No more than 1 per class*

Level of confidence for meeting standard: *4 out of 5 days per week for three weeks*

Issues or questions to keep track of during intervention:

Performance of the target skill:

Does the intervention increase the number of comments Wilfred makes? Are his comments related to the topic?

Reaction to intervention procedures:

How does Wilfred react to being a part of the role-playing activities in the intervention?

How does he relate to the peer tutors used in the intervention?

What types of prompts work best for Wilfred? How does he react to the prompts?

Obtaining additional assessment information:

Does Wilfred maintain interest in the topic when he has to wait his turn to speak or when he cannot speak so often?

Does Wilfred recognize the cues for when to make comments?

Does he respond to feedback that is directed to the group as a whole?

Carryover and generalization of skills:

Does Wilfred participate better in small group activities? In his other classes?

(continued on next page)

Example 11b

Mrs. Chang is a preschool teacher working with Gloria on choosing a partner during play activities. Gloria is not skilled or coordinated in her play; she mostly wanders from area to area during indoor and outdoor play times. The target skill for Gloria's intervention is "Plays with a playmate during free play activities." Mrs. Chang feels that a partner would help focus Gloria's attention on the activities and would, over time, help her develop better play skills. This page of the monitoring worksheet shows the results of the first two days of the intervention.

Focus comments on how the targeted students perform during the intervention.

Results should indicate whether students meet the standard each day. The standard for Gloria's target skill is "Plays with playmate for 10 minutes out of 20."

Include specific notations of student behavior in the daily log of results.

Results should indicate unanticipated problems and possible solutions.

Worksheet 11.1 (continued)	Name: *Mrs. Chang* Student: *Gloria*	Page *3* of *8*

Intervention Results for (day) *Monday*

During circle time I used the flannel board to teach the children a phrase and a set of gestures they could use when picking playmates. We all said the phrase together ("would you like to play with me?"), and then I had the children practice by asking me to play. Gloria seemed interested in the activity. Afterwards, I heard her saying the phrase to herself.

Mr. Hogan, the aide, worked with Gloria during free play. Together they picked Sam to play with, and Mr. Hogan prompted Gloria to use the phrase and gestures she had learned. Mr. Hogan helped Gloria and Sam get started playing with blocks. He said Gloria stayed at the play area, but needed a lot of prompting and suggestions of things to do with the blocks. She didn't seem very interested in building projects with Sam.

Mr. Hogan said Gloria played with Sam for 12 minutes.

Intervention Results for (day) *Tuesday*

During circle time we practiced the phrase for picking friends. Gloria remembered the phrase, but she wanted to pick Mr. Hogan rather than her neighbor.

During free play, with prompting from Mr. Hogan, Gloria chose a playmate on her own—Kelly. She used the phrase and gestures, and smiled and clapped her hands when she did it right. Kelly and Gloria played dress-up in the housekeeping areas, but Mr. Hogan said Gloria didn't share very well. Whenever Kelly picked out something to wear, Gloria took it away. After a few minutes Kelly walked away. Tomorrow, I will need to work with Gloria on sharing. Maybe I can use the circle time to teach some sharing phrases, and model some techniques for Gloria during free play.

Time playing with Kelly: 5 minutes.

Mr. Wagner's Case Study

Mr. Wagner made a few revisions in his intervention script, and then prepared a monitoring worksheet. As before, his effort included some flaws. The standard he listed on his worksheet, "No more than 1 argument per week," gave little indication of performance on the target skill ("Works on projects with classmates"). Most of his monitoring questions centered on Granville's reactions to the intervention; he didn't include any issues relating to obtaining more assessment information or to generalization and carryover of skills.

Once Mr. Wagner began the intervention, he found that it didn't go as smoothly as he had hoped. This page shows the results he listed on the third and fourth days.

The daily log should focus on Granville's performance, not on Mr. Wagner's activities and judgments.

This activity has become counterproductive. Mr. Wagner should revise his approach rather than force Granville to comply with the procedure.

Mr. Wagner's decision to have individual students account for their share of group assignments has encouraged them to work competitively rather than cooperatively. He should change this procedure.

Mr. Wagner abandons this activity without replacing it with another procedure for teaching Granville to read the directions. This results in another dispute.

Rewards must be perceived by students as valuable and obtainable, or they will not provide incentive.

Mr. Wagner is translating his frustration with the intervention into frustration with Granville. Rather than focus on another student, he should review the intervention goals and procedures and try some new approaches with Granville. We discuss this process in Chapter Twelve.

Worksheet 11.1 (continued)	Name: *Mr. Wagner* Student: *Granville*	Page *4* of *7*

Intervention Results for (day) *Wednesday*

I led a role-playing activity with Granville and the class about different ways to give and ask for help when working on projects. We talked about different types of help students may need. The students seem to have gotten a lot out of this activity. I think it went well.

I continued working with Granville on reading directions. He said he didn't need to go over the instructions with me, because he already knew how to read through them. But he couldn't answer most of my questions about the activity, so I had him read the instructions again. He grumbled a lot and took 25 minutes to finish, but finally he was ready to join the group.

At the end of class Granville got in a fight with the group because they didn't want to let him put his name on the sign-up sheet, since he was still reading the directions while they did most of the work. I had to make him leave the group and finish working on his own.

Number of arguments: 1

Intervention Results for (day) *Thursday*

Today Granville sulked and refused to go over the directions with me. He said he had already read them. I didn't want him to get behind the rest of the group like yesterday, so I let him join the activity.

About halfway through the activity Bobby and Granville got in a fight because Granville had done the steps in the wrong order and he wanted Bobby to help him catch back up. I talked to Granville afterwards and told him this is what happens when you don't read the directions first. I reminded him that he would never get that coupon if he didn't start cooperating and getting his work finished, but he said he didn't care.

I'm beginning to think maybe I picked the wrong student for the intervention, because Granville just doesn't seem to want to cooperate. Maybe next time I should pick Bobby and see if I can get him to stop arguing with Granville, rather than the reverse.

Number of arguments: 1

CHAPTER 12

Analyzing Intervention Results and Determining Next Steps

Typically, most of the thought people put into interventions is focused on planning and preparation; but equally important for long-term success is the way you react to the results you see after the intervention begins. No matter how carefully you have prepared an intervention, you cannot predict how the students will respond to the procedures you have planned. In some cases, their behavior may improve radically in a very short time; in other cases, their actions may not change at all—or may even become more problematic. Throughout the intervention, you may at different times be gratified, discouraged, or just perplexed by the intervention's results.

It is natural to view changes in student behavior as an indication of either the "success" or "failure" of the intervention plan. But careful review of the results provides far more than a source of self-congratulation or condemnation. During the intervention, you will obtain a wealth of new information about the students' abilities and performance characteristics, and about the factors affecting their learning and incentive. No matter how the intervention is progressing, the results and the information you obtain will provide useful, important insights about what to do next.

In this chapter, we explain the courses of action you can take based on the results obtained from the monitoring activities presented in Chapter Eleven. We discuss whether to continue, discontinue, or change the intervention plan, and describe the adjustments you may need to make in the intervention procedures. The chapter presents several scenarios depicting the different types of results you are likely to obtain from an intervention. We separate these into two broad categories: (a) interventions that are working as planned, and (b) interventions that are not working as planned. For each scenario, we give several options for how you should proceed.

When Interventions Are Working As Planned

Few moments in teaching are as rewarding as when you see a student who has had significant difficulties in social interactions begin to make progress and learn new skills during an intervention. All your hard work, attention, and planning seem insignificant balanced by the unprecedented progress of a single student over a few short days. But even the most gratifying intervention results leave you with important decisions to make about how to proceed with your plan. How long should the intervention continue? Should the procedures be refocused on other skills, or do the new skills need further refinement?

The monitoring issues you raised before beginning the intervention (in Chapter Eleven) will help you anticipate many of these questions, but you are still likely to have important concerns to address and decisions to make, even when an intervention has very positive results. In this part of the chapter we look at some of these issues using Sandy's example to show an intervention that goes well, and we discuss the options Mrs. Armstrong would need to consider in deciding how to proceed with Sandy's intervention. Table 12.1 provides an outline of the scenarios and options for an intervention that is working as planned.

Sandy's Intervention: A Progress Report

Day 1: To begin Sandy's intervention on improving her conversations, Mrs. Armstrong decided to work with her in the classroom during recess periods when there would be few distractions. On the first day, Mrs. Armstrong introduced the activities by talking with Sandy casually about conversing with other students. She told Sandy she would like to help her be more comfortable and confident in conversations and help her learn things to say, so she could become better friends with the students she likes. Additionally, Mrs. Armstrong told her that each time she engages in a conversation with classmates, she could earn points toward stickers and computer time. With this explanation, Sandy seemed eager to start.

She and Mrs. Armstrong discussed different types of greetings to use with peers, and Sandy adopted these quickly. Next, Mrs. Armstrong showed Sandy a prompting system of hand gestures she would use to signal Sandy at the time to give greetings. Sandy seemed self-assured with her progress during this first activity; she seemed pleased when Mrs. Armstrong told her she could practice again the next day so she could learn to use the greetings in more realistic situations.

Day 2: On the second day, Mrs. Armstrong again worked with Sandy on greetings, but this time she asked Mary and Karen, two students Sandy likes, to help Sandy practice the greetings. The girls seemed interested in helping Sandy, and Mrs. Armstrong was surprised with how well Sandy responded to their attention. Sandy used the greetings confidently in the practice situations and responded readily to prompts the few times Mrs. Armstrong needed to give them. The three girls and Mrs. Armstrong then discussed different topics that would be age-appropriate to talk about during various school situations. Mrs. Armstrong said they would do some role-playing activities for practice the next day. She also showed

TABLE 12.1 Outline of scenarios and options to consider when interventions are working as planned

Scenario I	The student has acquired the target skill and shows signs of expanding performance to other skill areas and settings.
Options	• Fade the intervention procedures • Select another target skill to work on • Select other students for the intervention
Scenario II	The student is making progress toward acquiring the target skill but has not expanded his or her behavior beyond the intervention situation.
Options	• Continue intervention and add procedures to encourage carryover • Work with other teachers and students in applying expectations across settings consistently • Add incentive procedures to encourage carryover
Scenario III	The student is making progress toward acquiring the target skill but is still working for artificial rewards.
Options	• Adjust procedures to highlight natural outcomes • Fade procedures more gradually and build student's confidence level • Integrate clearer outcomes as a permanent part of the routine of the setting
Scenario IV	The student is making progress toward acquiring the target skill but is still far from reaching criterion level.
Options	• Continue the intervention and recheck progress • Continue the intervention, but shift procedures to stay aligned with student's progress

Sandy how they could adapt the prompting system to indicate appropriate and inappropriate topics.

Day 3: Before recess began the third day, Donna and Beatrice, two other popular girls in the class, asked if they could join Mary and Karen in helping Sandy's conversation and in doing some of the role playing. Mary had told them about the activity, and they thought it would be fun to help Sandy, too. Mrs. Armstong was particularly pleased and surprised at this development, and Sandy seemed flattered by the attention from the other girls. Although Mrs. Armstrong had originally planned to take part in the role-playing conversations, she quickly saw that her own contributions were more distracting than helpful. Instead, she stayed outside the group and prompted Sandy as needed. In the role playing, Sandy responded well and needed little prompting to use her new greetings. She did try to introduce some immature subjects, like dolls and cartoon characters, but did not seem to resent the others' changing the topic. Mrs. Armstrong's prompts on topics were picked up by the whole group, and they began to prompt Sandy themselves when the topic seemed inappropriate.

During the activity, Sandy really came out of her shell; she was as interested and excited about identifying good and bad topics as the other girls were. Mrs. Armstrong was quite surprised to see that Sandy could be pleasant, animated, and even funny when given a chance, and the girls seemed to enjoy interacting with her. By the end of the period, Sandy had earned many more points than she needed to get extra computer time.

Day 4: The plan for the fourth day was to continue with choosing age-appropriate topics and then to move on to learning how to change from topic to topic during a conversation. But Sandy had done so well in her interactions with the other girls the day before that Mrs. Armstrong decided to concentrate entirely on the topic-switching exercises. Sandy did fine at the activity and needed even fewer prompts than the day before. The girls seemed to work best without Mrs. Armstrong's input, largely ignoring her after they got started, and they pushed their free-flowing conversations with Sandy well beyond the limited exercises that Mrs. Armstrong had outlined. By the end of the period, Sandy was so involved in the interactions with the girls that Mrs. Armstrong had difficulty telling her about the points she had earned.

Deciding What to Do Next

After the first four days of the intervention, Mrs. Armstrong finds herself pleased at Sandy's progress but a bit uncertain about what to do next. She does not want Sandy's improvement to stagnate and wants to take advantage of her unexpected progress; but she is worried about ending the intervention too soon and losing the ground she has gained. She realizes that she needs to look closely at Sandy's performance so far and consider the options for how to proceed.

In cases like Sandy's, you should review carefully all the intervention results, in particular the students' performance of the target skill, to determine how far their progress extends. These results will help you identify the goals to set next for the students, and the options you can pursue to achieve these goals. In the sections that follow, we use Sandy's example to show several different scenarios that you might encounter when an intervention goes well, and we show through Mrs. Armstrong the various options that are available to you to address these circumstances.

Scenario I

The student has acquired the target skill and shows signs of expanding performance to other skill areas and settings.

The easiest result to deal with, of course, is the most desirable one: the students not only acquire the target skill and begin using it to meet expectations (or show significant progress toward doing so) but also expand this new competence to other settings or skill areas. Although such an ideal result seems too good to be hoped for, it is in fact not uncommon. In many cases, the attention and focus the intervention gives the students can provide just the nudge they need to make great strides not only in the target skill and the intervention activities, but in other settings and skill areas.

Follow-up planning will ensure an intervention's continuing success.

When she takes a closer look at Sandy's progress, Mrs. Armstrong may find that Sandy not only meets the expectation for holding conversations during unstructured times in social studies class and during recess, but that she has also improved during Mr. Wagner's math and science class periods as well as during art and gym. In addition to conversing more with the students in her intervention group, Sandy may have improved her interactions with many other classmates and with her teachers and other school personnel. Mrs. Armstrong might even find that Sandy's success in the intervention has led to her improvement in other skills, such as taking a more active part in playground activities or volunteering to help classmates with their schoolwork.

When students have acquired the target skill and are carrying over their performance to other settings or skill areas, your main focus should be deciding the best way to move on to new projects while fading out the intervention as smoothly as possible. You have several options for achieving this aim.

Option 1 *Begin to fade the intervention procedures.* One of the best ways to capitalize on a really effective intervention is to fade the procedures you have used, backing away from the intervention and letting the students proceed at their own pace and direction. You should remove any aspects of the intervention that are not a natural part of the performance setting, while you continue to keep a watchful eye on the students for a little longer to ensure that they maintain their performance at or above the level of the standards.

If she finds that Sandy has expanded her skills extensively, Mrs. Armstrong could fade the intervention procedures and let Sandy refine and continue to develop her conversational skills on her own through the normal give-and-take of social interactions. Even so, Mrs. Armstrong should continue to oversee Sandy's performance a little longer to make sure the new skills have become an established part of her performance routine, and to be available to help her make adjustments in her behavior if the need arises.

Option 2 *Select a new priority target skill for the student to work on.* You may also want to consider other areas you could work on with the students and begin planning an intervention to address these problems with another set of procedures. You would review the priorities you set earlier for the students and select another target skill to work on with them. The insights you gained from designing an intervention to address the first skill area should give you many ideas for shortcutting the intervention planning process for the new one.

For example, Mrs. Armstrong may decide that the best way to capitalize on Sandy's success in holding conversations is to move to a related expectation, such as "participates in class discussions." Using the information she has already gathered about Sandy, she could quickly plan a new intervention to address this area, one that builds on Sandy's current success.

Option 3 *Select other students for the intervention.* If you find that the intervention is very successful, another possibility is to use the procedures with other students who show similar problems in their behavior. Sometimes the work you do with an individual student or a small group can serve as a field test or pilot study for trying out new ideas and activities. With some minor modifications in the procedures, you may be able to use the intervention with other students to effect many of the same changes in their behavior. Once Mrs. Armstrong determines that the intervention should be faded for Sandy, she may wish to consider whether other students in her class could learn better conversational skills with the same procedures that worked so well with Sandy.

Scenario II

The student is making progress toward acquiring the skill but has not expanded his or her behavior beyond the intervention situation.

Often, interventions can have positive but more limited effects than those outlined above. An intervention may be successful within its own context or situation, but the students may not transfer their skills to other circumstances in which they should be using them (Berler, Gross, & Drabman, 1982). Mrs. Armstrong might find that Sandy has made great strides in her conversational skills and has begun to meet the expectation for holding conversations during free time in social studies class, especially when interacting with her new friends from the intervention group. But she might also find that Sandy is having trouble applying these skills more broadly. She may discover that Sandy avoids conversing with larger groups or with students she does not know well, or that in other classes and settings she tends to revert to her old habit of silence.

When you find that students learn the requisite skills but do not instinctively carry them over to broader circumstances, you will need to encourage the students to expand their progress to these other situations. Several options to help you with such cases are discussed below.

Option 1 *Continue the intervention and add procedures to encourage carryover of new skills.* To generalize their progress as they move from situation to situation, students must sometimes make significant adaptations in the new skills they have learned. Students like Sandy frequently fail to carry over their new skills because they simply do not know how to make such adjustments. And the controlled or limited conditions under which interventions often take place do little to prepare the students to make these adaptations on their own. In such cases, you may need to add to the intervention other activities or performance opportunities that teach the students how to adjust their behavior. You may have to take the intervention into other natural performance environments so you can deliberately show the students how to adapt their behavior and successfully carry over their skills (Cartledge & Milburn, 1986; Gelfand & Hartman, 1984).

In the role-play group, Mrs. Armstrong could have the other students work with Sandy to model a variety of school situations where different types of conversations take place, including other classroom situations, playground activities, hallway passing time, and other circumstances. In this way, Sandy could learn to adapt the skills she has learned in the intervention to a wider variety of conversational conditions and situations.

Option 2 *Work with other teachers and students to apply social expectations consistently across different settings and activities.* Another factor that can affect carryover of skills is students' failure to recognize all the conditions in which they should use the target skill. In such cases, you would have to broaden the scope of the intervention to include these conditions as well, or enlist the aid of other people who could help the students recognize settings or situations in which they should use the skill (Cartledge & Milburn, 1986).

Mrs. Armstrong could ask Mr. Wagner, Mrs. Kellerman, and other school personnel to use her system of prompts with Sandy to help Sandy recognize the circumstances under which she should greet others and use her conversational skills. Mrs. Armstrong could also arrange to have the intervention group interact with Sandy as much as possible in those settings. These procedures may help Sandy understand how the expectations apply to other settings, and encourage her to use the target skill throughout the school day.

Option 3 *Add incentive procedures to encourage carryover of the new skills.* Sometimes students do not find sufficient incentive to carry over their skills to other circumstances, either because they are content with their current progress or because they do not perceive the benefits of using their skills in the other situations. You may have to adjust the intervention plan by highlighting or enhancing the outcomes available in these situations (Greenwood & Hops, 1981). One possibility is to add procedures that help the students understand or place more value on the natural outcomes available under these circumstances; another possibility is to incorporate some of the incentive procedures you used in the intervention in the activities and practices of the new setting.

For example, Sandy may feel that the success she is having with her new friends is enough, or she may not see the advantages of applying her conversational skills to other settings. Mrs. Armstrong could use the current conversational group to discuss with Sandy the benefits of expanding her skills to other places, perhaps using role playing to show the positive outcomes of having conversations with other groups or in other situations. If she feels that a more concrete incentive is needed for now, Mrs. Armstrong could expand the points-and-stickers system she has used by applying it in new situations. She could enlist the aid of Mr. Wagner, Mrs. Kellerman, or others to help keep track of points that Sandy earns in their classrooms.

Scenario III

The student is making progress toward acquiring the target skill but is still working for artificial rewards.

A third scenario involves students who have learned the target skill, but use it only to gain artificial rewards or outcomes. This situation often arises when interventions rely heavily on incentive-building procedures. In these cases, students may use the intervention activities as a crutch to shore up their progress, or may respond favorably only to the novelty aspects of the intervention. The students may begin to meet the expectation only because they can earn special privileges or points, or because the intervention is new or departs from the normal routine. For example, Mrs. Armstrong may find that Sandy's progress in the intervention activities does not extend much further than the special conversation sessions themselves. Without the extra attention, prompting, and praise Sandy receives from the girls and Mrs. Armstrong, and without the points, stickers, and special computer time, Sandy quickly reverts to her old ways.

In cases like this, it is important to help students learn to use their skills for the intrinsic benefits resulting from the situation rather than for temporary or artificial outcomes (Raffini, 1993; Stokes & Baer, 1977). The focus of the intervention should therefore shift toward teaching the students to recognize and work for the natural, sustaining outcomes of their skilled behavior. We suggest several options for accomplishing this result.

Option 1 *Adjust the intervention procedures to highlight the natural outcomes of behavior.* When students revert to their old problem behavior after the intervention procedures are removed, they usually do not recognize or value the natural benefits arising from the competent behavior. Such regression can be a fairly common problem when interventions use artificial outcomes to increase student incentive. In these cases, you would have to adjust the incentive features of the intervention to highlight the natural outcomes of the students' changed behavior, emphasizing those aspects that are particularly interesting and satisfying to them (Raffini, 1993).

In working with Sandy, Mrs. Armstrong could have the girls in the discussion group talk about the natural benefits of conversing with peers. She could have Sandy and the others make a list of good things that can happen when you talk to classmates, and perhaps a second list of what they think about classmates who are good at conversing. When she recognizes the value that her peers place on conversational skills, Sandy might develop more incentive to use her new skills for their own sake, rather than to earn stickers or extra praise.

Option 2 *Fade the intervention procedures more gradually and build the student's self-confidence.* Sometimes interventions can work very well, yet also create kind of a safety net for students, teaching them to depend too much on the procedures for support and not on their own abilities. This problem often occurs when the intervention takes place outside the natural conditions, such as when teachers work one-on-one with the students on a skill that is typically used in a group situation or with peers. The conditions for the intervention provide such a reassuring and rewarding context that the students are reluctant to break away from these conditions and use the skills on their own.

A way to alleviate this problem is to fade the intervention procedures gradually while also giving the students additional opportunities to practice their skills under more varied circumstances (Kameenui & Simmons, 1990). You would add to the intervention more and more of the features that characterize the natural performance conditions. This technique is especially useful with skills that are difficult for students to learn, as it gives them more time to become proficient in the skills and integrate them into a smooth performance pattern.

Mrs. Armstrong could use the role-playing group during recess to model the natural circumstances of the classroom setting. Sandy and the girls in the group could practice specific conversations that might take place during free time in social studies. When Sandy has had some practice, Mrs. Armstrong could have the group replay the conversations in the actual classroom situation. Gradually, she could encourage the group to move on to more free-form conversations in less-structured situations, and then to expand their conversational group to other classmates. In this manner, Mrs. Armstrong could fade the intervention as she ensures at each step that Sandy has the proficiency and self-confidence to proceed.

Option 3 *Integrate clearer outcomes or extra rewards as a permanent part of the overall routine of the setting.* Some students need more assurance, support, or incentive to use their skills than other students, and you may need to adjust the routines of the natural setting to get these students to maintain their behavioral levels (Edwards, 1993; Raffini, 1993). In some cases, you may be able to incorporate extra praise or special privileges into the students' normal routine, or use the rewards intermittently when the students begin to lose interest in using the target skill. In other instances, you may have to continue the intervention indefinitely by including novel activities regularly in the students' routine or by giving extra privileges, rewards, or points for competent performance.

Mrs. Armstrong may discover that Sandy thrives on special attention and recognition, and that she will remain quiet and not use her conversational skills properly unless she is given extra praise and encouragement for doing so. No matter how hard Mrs. Armstrong has tried to get Sandy to work for natural outcomes, she may still have to give Sandy additional praise for conversing proficiently. She would offer these extra incentives as subtly and as infrequently as possible to avoid increasing Sandy's dependence on them even more, but she may find she has to continue using them indefinitely.

Scenario IV

The student is making progress in acquiring the target skill but is still far from reaching the criterion level.

In the last scenario for successful interventions, the students are showing important progress in meeting the expectation, but they have yet to reach the level of the standards. In some cases they may have developed several of the required skills but need to work on others. Mrs. Armstrong may find that despite Sandy's remarkable progress in the first few days of the intervention, some crucial areas still need work. Sandy might be having trouble with a specific skill area, such as using greetings at appropriate times, expressing her thoughts clearly, or making points without overemphasizing or exaggerating them. Or she could be having trouble applying her progress steadily, as her overall performance is inconsistent.

This example highlights the importance of focusing on the original expectation when you monitor the intervention so you can make accurate judgments on the effectiveness of the procedures. Without referring to the original goal, Mrs. Armstrong could assume that the intervention is a complete success because Sandy is actively participating in the activities—even though she may not have made sufficient progress in her conversations to reach the criteria for natural situations.

When students' progress in acquiring and using the target skill is substantial but not yet complete, it is usually best to leave the intervention in place but to make adjustments in the procedures to continue their progress. The options below can help you decide how to proceed.

Option 1 *Continue the intervention and recheck the student's performance later.* Students frequently need to continue refining their actions on their own for a while to develop a smooth and effective behavioral pattern. They often need time to practice their new skills or to figure out how to assimilate the new behavior with their existing skills (Kameenui & Simmons, 1990). It is not unusual for an intervention to accomplish its basic purpose in teaching students what to do and how and when to do it, yet not get them to the point that they meet the expectation at the standard level indicated. A wise approach in such cases is to leave the intervention in place and continue monitoring the students' behavior. You should watch for any new problems that may arise or for situations the students cannot handle on their own so you can quickly alter the procedures or give the students support to maintain their steady progress. This continued oversight of the intervention will allow you to provide prompts if students need further assistance in refining their actions, and to offer encouragement if their incentive starts to falter.

Mrs. Armstrong might feel that Sandy's failure (despite her progress) to meet the standards for holding conversations simply indicates that she needs more time to practice and refine the skills she has been learning. Mrs. Armstrong could leave the intervention in place, and recheck a few days later to see whether Sandy's progress has continued. At the same time, she may review the intervention procedures to fine-tune the activities and eliminate elements that may not be useful at this particular time. She should also note whether Sandy's incentive to interact with classmates sustains its high level, and should be prepared to shift her procedures if Sandy's progress starts to stagnate.

Option 2 *Continue the intervention, but shift the procedures to align with any new areas of behavior the student needs to develop.* When students are making progress toward meeting a complex or difficult expectation, the intervention needs to remain flexible and to stay current with their abilities and needs (Burden & Byrd, 1994). With interventions that are effective early, you can be caught off guard by the students' success. When students learn skills swiftly, their rapid progress can leave them looking for new challenges—and at the same time, can bring them up against new barriers and deficits.

In cases when students are progressing quickly, they typically need more work practicing and refining their skills, but they may have other requirements or difficulties that must be addressed as well, or they may be eager to advance in new directions. As the intervention proceeds, it must stay aligned with both the barriers they face and the advances they make while it continues to polish their new skills.

Mrs. Armstrong might find that Sandy's rapid progress in using greetings and conversing with the intervention group has left her eager to continue but vulnerable to other skill deficits. Sandy's continued lack of knowledge about topics, for example, might be proving a bigger barrier than Mrs. Armstrong had suspected once Sandy enters normal, nonintervention situations. Mrs. Armstrong may realize that she will have to place more emphasis on this area as the intervention continues. Also, now that Sandy is talking with the group, a new problem might have come to light: she has a tendency to say embarrassing or inappropriate things in conversations—things that could open her up to ridicule in a less-structured situation. Mrs. Armstrong sees that teaching Sandy to avoid inappropriate comments needs to be another new focus of the intervention. Finally, with her increasing self-confidence, Sandy's aspirations for making friends might have grown, and she now really wants to become a true companion of the other girls in the group—but she does not know how to advance from what she has learned so far to making solid friendships. Mrs. Armstrong may find that she will have to bring into the intervention a broader focus on learning to build friendships. Thus, while Mrs. Armstrong will continue the intervention until Sandy meets the standards for holding conversations, she must also shift her focus to include procedures that help Sandy adjust and advance her skills in new areas. Otherwise, the progress Sandy has made could give way to frustration, leaving her in a worse plight than before the intervention started.

In summary, when an intervention is going as you desire, you have many options for how to proceed, depending on how firmly the students have learned their new skills and on what areas might still need improvement. To decide which of the scenarios described above best fits the students' situations, as well as which option or options to pursue, you should review the intervention results carefully. Pay particular attention to the instructional goals and standards for the expectation and to the issues you identified for monitoring on your worksheet. You may have to adjust the plan in any number of ways to ensure that the students' progress is steady and on course, and to promote the level of independence needed to meet the expectation under natural performance conditions. Now let's turn to interventions in which the students do not make the progress you had hoped for, and discuss some options you have in such cases.

When Interventions Are Not Working As Planned

Just as a successful intervention can be one of the most rewarding experiences a teacher can have, an intervention that is not working can be one of the most frustrating. With all the careful thought and meticulous planning you put into preparing interventions, you can become quite discouraged when the procedures fail to make any significant difference in the students' behavior. Often, a teacher's first reaction in such cases is a feeling that the student is unteachable: "I can't get through to her." "He's just impossible!" But blaming the students for interventions that fail to work is not a productive approach; it is more likely to lead you to excuses and inaction than to any coherent plan for how to proceed next.

When an intervention is not working, remember the mind-set with which we started this entire process back in Chapter One: rather than focusing on the students' problems and failures, we need to look at what the students must learn to do to achieve social competence. The failure of the intervention to accomplish its aims does not change this basic approach; rather, it indicates that you need to review the students' deficits and learning characteristics further and to reestablish your aims—perhaps shifting your focus only slightly, perhaps establishing entirely new objectives (Zirpoli & Melloy, 1993).

When an intervention fails to work as planned, you should view the activities as an opportunity to probe and rethink the students' needs rather than a sign that the students are intractable (Sugai & Tindal, 1993). Ideally, of course, you would have spotted these needs earlier, during the assessment process, and accounted for them when you were developing the intervention plan. But in reality, there probably will be times you miss or misinterpret assessment information, or miscalculate the effects of the procedures you plan. Unfortunately, you will not discover such problems until you have begun to carry out the intervention and realize the students are not making satisfactory progress in their behavior. On seeing that the plan has gone awry, you must carefully review your monitoring results to determine what has gone wrong and decide how to redirect the intervention.

Table 12.2 provides an outline of the scenarios and options to consider when interventions are not working as desired. In this part of the chapter we look at these issues in more detail, using Alfred's example to show an intervention that does not go well, and we discuss various scenarios and options that

TABLE 12.2 Outline of scenarios and options to consider when interventions are not working as planned

Scenario I	The student is not making progress because the instructional goals are misdirected.
Options	• Eliminate instructional goals that are not central to acquiring the target skill • Shift emphasis given to instructional goals • Add instructional goals to intervention • Shift focus of intervention to new skill areas • Continue intervention and watch for further effects
Scenario II	The student is not making progress because procedures are ineffective or misdirected.
Options	• Revise or remove procedures that are ineffective • Check procedures to ensure they address instructional goals • Readjust pace of procedures to match student progress • Alter context in which procedures are used • Develop new procedures
Scenario III	The student is not making progress because intervention does not address incentive needs.
Options	• Place more emphasis on natural outcomes or add extra incentives • Change context to help student build confidence in using skills • Reduce competing behaviors

Mrs. Armstrong would need to consider in deciding how to proceed with Alfred's case.

Alfred's Intervention: A Progress Report

Day 1: Mrs. Armstrong had Alfred and Martin, another student she was including in the intervention, do a board activity in the classroom covering the basic rules for playing football. She used counters to represent the positions of the players and had Alfred move the counters to show different game situations. She found that his ability to explain the rules for football generally improved after the activity. To test his knowledge of rules further, she prepared a quiz of 25 different game situations and asked Alfred first to explain the rules and then to move the counters on the board to show how the rules applied. He seemed interested in the activity and enjoyed the challenge of answering the questions and moving the counters to the various positions. She found that Alfred was able to explain the rules correctly on the quiz for 17 of the 25 situations. When he moved the counters to show the actual game situations, however, he was correct on only 8 of 25 situations.

Also on day 1, Mr. Haskell, the gym teacher, worked with Alfred on some playing techniques for football, such as kicking and catching. Mrs. Armstrong checked with Mr. Haskell after the period, and he said that Alfred quickly learned most of the techniques and was able to use them in playing a modified version of football with him and Martin. He added that although Alfred's play skills were not particularly well coordinated, with work he could be as good as the average fifth grader.

Day 2: On the second day of the intervention, Mrs. Armstrong had Alfred review the game situations discussed on the previous day and gave him a revised version of the quiz. The review did not go well, as Alfred responded correctly to only 10 of 25 situations. He and Martin began arguing during the activity so Mrs. Armstrong had to review the rules separately with each student.

She then had the two boys join their classmates on the playground in a regular football game. Her plan was to have them play for only a few minutes so they could get the feel of the game, after which she would try some modeling and rehearsal activities with them on the sidelines. Mrs. Armstrong paired Alfred with Gordon, a teammate, and asked Gordon to explain to Alfred the various actions of the game. Alfred enjoyed playing in the game with his classmates again, and Gordon and Alfred seemed to work well together. Mrs. Armstrong had Ms. Nichols, the playground supervisor, videotape the game. Mrs. Armstrong recorded the amount of time that Alfred participated properly in the game activities and found that it was about 60 percent. He did not want to leave the game when Mrs. Armstrong asked him to and he pouted for a few minutes afterward.

His mood changed considerably, however, when Mrs. Armstrong started to role-play some game situations and techniques on the sidelines, and he and Martin were quite amused by her antics. Some of the other students walked by and asked what was going on, and Alfred and Martin had a good time joking with them about Mrs. Armstrong's role playing. After about ten minutes of this, Mrs. Armstrong started feeling a little foolish and decided to change her tactics. She instead talked Alfred and Martin through some game situations and had them observe their classmates. This seemed to go much better.

Day 3: Mrs. Armstrong reviewed the videotape that Ms. Nichols had made the day before and found that her colleague had done an excellent job of taping the game activities. The class was so interested in the tape that Mrs. Armstrong decided to have the entire class view it before going out to recess. She tried to have Alfred narrate the game activities and explain some of the rules they had worked on, but he mostly made fun of the different things the students were doing in the background. Mrs. Armstrong had also planned to teach Alfred and Martin a memory device for following the directions of group leaders, but she did not have time to carry out the plan before the recess bell rang.

During recess Mrs. Armstrong again paired Alfred with Gordon, and once again had Ms. Nichols videotape. Alfred enjoyed being on Gordon's team and listening to Gordon's directions. When Alfred and Gordon's team was on offense and the two could be close to each other, Alfred followed Gordon's directions very well and there was a notable improvement in his behavior. However, when the boys were on defense and played at different positions on the field, Alfred's attention wandered. On several occasions, he started talking to Sally instead of listening to what Gordon was telling him. Mrs. Armstrong recorded the amount of time that Alfred participated properly in the game activities and found that it was only about 50 percent of the game. After recess, Mrs. Armstrong gave Alfred the quiz of game situations again, and this time he answered 18 of the 25 situations correctly.

Day 4: Mrs. Armstrong used the previous day's tape in a large group discussion and role-playing activity to teach different ways to get attention and seek recognition from peers during recess activities, another goal of the intervention plan. Mrs. Armstrong showed examples of student behavior during the game, including things Alfred had done, and asked the class to indicate which actions would make them respond positively, and which negatively. Alfred seemed interested in the activity, and was particularly struck when Sally and the others said they would react negatively to some of his behavior. Mrs. Armstrong made sure to include examples of good ways to gain recognition as well, including good behavior by Alfred, and had Alfred and the rest of the class role-play some positive ways to gain recognition.

After the classroom activity, Mrs. Armstrong and Alfred discussed what the class had said. Alfred seemed to understand that he needed to find better ways to get recognition, since clowning did not work all the time. Mrs. Armstrong gave Alfred the quiz on game rules again, and he did quite well, scoring 21 out of 25.

On the playground, Mrs. Armstrong decided to fade the use of Gordon, and had Alfred play without a partner. Despite the apparent success of the morning's activities, however, Alfred did not pay much attention during the game, and was soon up to his old tricks, yelling out to Sally and clowning for anyone who would pay attention. Mrs. Armstrong recorded that he participated in only about 35 percent of the game.

Deciding What to Do Next

After the first four days of the intervention, Mrs. Armstrong finds herself frustrated by Alfred's lack of progress, and perplexed about what to do next. The results of the intervention have been uneven at best, and despite his interest in the activities, Alfred's performance of the target skill has actually worsened over the past few days. She realizes that rather than continue with the original plan, she needs to take a closer look at Alfred's performance, reevaluate the intervention, and consider her options for how to proceed.

In cases like Alfred's, it is important for you to look carefully at the intervention results to determine where the plan has gone awry. You might find that the goals of the intervention did not really match the students' needs as well as you thought. Or you might determine that the specific procedures and activities the intervention used were not suited to the students' learning characteristics or to the overall goals of the intervention. You might also decide that the intervention plan did not fully account for the students' need for incentive.

In the sections that follow, we use Alfred's example to illustrate three possible scenarios that you should consider when an intervention does not go well, and we show through Mrs. Armstrong the various options available to you to modify or redirect the intervention plan.

Scenario I

The student is not making progress because the instructional goals are misdirected.

The most fundamental and complicated problems with interventions are usually with their instructional goals. Frequently, an intervention will not work well because its basic aims do not match the students' needs and learning characteristics (Sugai & Tindal, 1993). When you revise an intervention plan, you should ask yourself first: "Is the intervention focused on the right goals for the student?"

To help answer this question, we need to review the idea of an instructional goal. Recall that in Chapter Nine we discussed how the various findings from the specific level assessment should be combined to form the basis for an intervention plan. At that point, you decided which basic abilities, component steps, and performance conditions posed difficulties for the students and established these as the goals of the intervention activities. If you now see that the students are not making satisfactory progress during the intervention, you should reexamine each of these areas in light of any new information you have gained so far from the monitoring process. The results should help you determine whether these aims are still

Instructional goals may need to be revised if the students are not making progress in the intervention.

appropriate. Other instructional goals may need to be added to the intervention's focus, or some goals are not as important to the students' progress as you originally believed.

From her specific level assessment of Alfred, Mrs. Armstrong had established the following instructional goals for his intervention:

- Learn the rules and essential behaviors for playing games
- Learn to coordinate behavior with the play of peers and the directions of group leaders
- Learn to pay attention to game activities for longer durations
- Learn positive ways to gain recognition from peers

Reviewing the results from the past few days, Mrs. Armstrong might realize that these goals probably were not the best choices for Alfred's intervention. For instance, the activities began with a strong emphasis on learning the rules of the game, and this emphasis continued throughout the four days. But now, as Mrs. Armstrong compares the results of Alfred's daily quiz on rules to his performance of the target skill, she notices that his ability to explain the rules had little effect on his playground behavior. In fact, the day he did his best on the rules quiz, he did his worst at participating in the game. She suspects that she might have been mistaken to focus so strongly on the rules. Similarly, Mrs. Armstrong notices that her efforts to have Alfred learn to coordinate his behavior with the play of peers seemed to have little lasting effect. He seemed to enjoy playing with Gordon, but he was easily distracted when Gordon was not nearby.

In cases such as this, when the instructional goals for the intervention seem in retrospect to have been misdirected or misaligned with the students' needs, you should review the goals for ways to modify or shift the emphasis of the intervention. Options for this scenario include the following.

Option 1 *Eliminate instructional goals that are not really central to the student's acquiring the target skill.* In an intervention plan you should concentrate on the aspects of performance that are most directly related to the students' acquiring the target skill. Otherwise, you may get sidetracked by other important skills that the students need to learn but which are not central to the primary aim of the intervention. In the initial planning, it is sometimes difficult to identify these important but nonessential focus areas. But when an intervention stalls or fails to work, you may notice that some of your primary goals may be side issues or distractions to students rather than steps toward learning the target skill. You can usually hasten the students' progress by deleting these areas from the plan or temporarily postponing further attention to them, to give the intervention a tighter and sharper focus. By deemphasizing these areas, you will be able to concentrate on the factors that are the most crucial to the students' acquiring the target skill.

Mrs. Armstrong will probably decide to drop the intervention's emphasis on learning game rules. In retrospect, she realizes that Alfred's interactions have not benefited much from teaching him the rules, and that his behavior during the game does not seem related to how well he knows the rules. Therefore, she will most likely decide to deemphasize the goal involving rules and focus more on the other parts of the intervention.

Option 2 *Shift the emphasis you give to the instructional goals in the intervention plan.* Just as you may find instructional goals that are not as important as you originally thought, you may also notice instructional goals that you placed in a secondary position in your plan but that the intervention results suggest are primary. In such cases, you should consider shifting the emphasis of the intervention to give more attention to these instructional goals. When the students continue to have problems in meeting the expectation and you can address only a limited number of problem areas at one time, it is particularly important to focus on the most significant goals in an intervention. Often, shifting the focus or selecting new procedures for more difficult problem areas can have a very strong effect on the students' behavior.

Now that she has seen Alfred's reaction to her intervention plan, Mrs. Armstrong might decide that the goal "learn positive ways to gain recognition from peers" is really most central to what Alfred needs to learn. She noted that Alfred's reaction to the class discussion and role playing showed that he understood the importance of learning this skill, and she feels that if she shifts the intervention to focus more directly on learning positive ways to gain recognition, Alfred will be more likely to benefit from the activities.

Option 3 *Add other instructional goals to the intervention plan.* When students are not progressing satisfactorily, it is also important to make sure the intervention focus includes all the necessary skills for acquiring and using a target skill. Perhaps you overlooked an area essential to the students' progress that needs to be added to the goals. Sometimes an intervention can uncover problems in basic abilities or component steps you may not have seen earlier. Particularly when interventions focus primarily on incentive issues, problems often surface as students begin making a new effort to perform but still lack the skills to be successful. In such cases, you must react quickly to adjust the intervention so that it teaches the needed skills. Otherwise, continued failure or lack of progress can quickly overwhelm the students' newfound incentive, and they can revert to their earlier behavior.

Mrs. Armstrong might have noticed from the class discussion that Alfred really does want to gain recognition from his peers—especially, she suspects, from Sally—but his behavior during the game shows that he does not have the confidence or the self-discipline to do this through normal game-playing behavior and interactions. Perhaps, Mrs. Armstrong decides, if Alfred were to learn to find a role in the game where he could be a valued part of the team, he would not be as inclined to seek attention through clowning. Therefore, she might decide to add "learns to take a role in the game where he can be valuable to the team" to her list of instructional goals and to make this goal a central focus of her intervention plan.

Option 4 *Shift the focus of the intervention to a new area or target skill.* In some cases, your review of the intervention results may show that the plan's ineffectiveness is due not to misplaced instructional goals but to the target skill itself. The students may have other, more basic deficits that must be addressed before the target skill can be addressed; or the target skill may be too advanced or complicated for the students' current level. In cases like these, it is probably best to shift or redesign the intervention to focus on the more basic or significant skills the students need to learn.

Mrs. Armstrong might decide when she reviews the results for Alfred that she was mistaken to select playing games on the playground as the target skill. Although she still feels that this is important for Alfred, she realizes that the playground setting and the game-playing activity involve a very complicated set of conditions and skills. A large part of Alfred's difficulty during the intervention arose from the complexity of the social demands in the situation and the variety of distractions he had to negotiate to attend to the activities. Mrs. Armstrong might decide to refocus the intervention on a less complicated area, perhaps in a more structured setting such as the social studies class, so the intervention activities would not put as high a demand on Alfred's concentration.

Another occasion to refocus the target skill is when an intervention has successes that were never planned, and the students benefit from the procedures in ways you never envisioned. Sometimes the procedures you use in the intervention may help the students develop skills or overcome problems different from those you had anticipated. In cases like these, you should try to understand the effect of these unintended yet favorable results and adjust the intervention's focus to respond. You may decide that the progress the students have made in this new area points to a more important or more promising target skill than the one you originally selected.

Mrs. Armstrong might notice that Alfred seemed to gain a lot from working with Mr. Haskell in the gym on the first day of the intervention. On further consideration, and discussion with Mr. Haskell, she might realize that this kind of closely directed activity in a small, supervised group kept Alfred on task and led to productive interactions between him and Martin, at least for that day. From this observation, Mrs. Armstrong might decide that learning to work within a small group on supervised tasks could be a good focus for restarting Alfred's intervention. She could implement her plan during gym class, since Alfred seems to benefit from working with Mr. Haskell, and could include Sally in Alfred's group, to give him greater incentive and to allow him to work on gaining her esteem. By using a strategy that she knows will work, Mrs. Armstrong could craft a new intervention plan that is tighter and more controlled than the earlier one, and that is directed toward an area in which she has seen Alfred react positively.

Option 5 *Continue the intervention plan and watch for further effects.* In some cases, it is best to adopt a "wait and see" attitude with an intervention, as students may make important but delayed responses to the procedures. Before making changes in their behavior, they may need time to:

- Adjust to differences in the way people are responding to them
- Sort through what they are learning from the procedures

- Overcome their initial apprehensions about using the new skills
- Judge how worthwhile the incentive components are

During this time, you may be able to observe some subtle changes in the students' behavior that will give you confidence that the plan might work after all. Some indicators are whether they watch closely what is going on with the intervention, or whether they respond more positively to you during nonintervention times. When you see some indirect but positive reactions to the intervention, you should continue with the plan a little longer, perhaps making some minor adjustments in the goals or procedures to strengthen the intervention.

Mrs. Armstrong might feel that although Alfred's play behavior has not changed much, he does seem to like talking about game rules and watching from the sidelines to see how other students play. She might not be sure what other effects the intervention is having on Alfred, but she does note that he shows interest in the procedures, and she is reluctant to discontinue the intervention as long as it is having some kind of positive effect. She could keep the intervention in place for a few more days and watch how Alfred responds next. At the same time, she should review the procedures and the goals to find any modifications she can make to speed things along.

Scenario II

The student is not making progress because the intervention procedures themselves are ineffective or misdirected.

Misdirected goals might be the most common source of trouble for intervention plans, but another problem that often surfaces when interventions are not working is inappropriate procedures. In some cases, the procedures you planned may have been too complicated for the students, leaving them confused or unsure of what to do. On the other hand, the activities might have lacked dynamism, or might have been too similar to normal routines, thus failing to capture the students' interest and attention. Sometimes you might find that a procedure fails to teach the intended instructional goals, or that the context for the intervention activities is distracting or uninteresting to the students.

When Mrs. Armstrong reviews Alfred's intervention results, she might see that many of the procedures she chose were just not appropriate for Alfred. For instance, she realizes that having Alfred narrate the video for the class was a mistake; rather than giving him an experience in a leadership role, it gave him an opportunity to clown in front of the class. Similarly, she can see that modeling the game activities herself was not a good idea, as Alfred found the activity more amusing than enlightening. Mrs. Armstrong notes that even the procedures that did not have negative effects, such as pairing Gordon with Alfred, were often of dubious value. Although Alfred enjoyed playing with Gordon, he did not seem to learn much from the activity.

In a case like Alfred's, it is important to review not only the goals of the intervention but the procedures themselves. You should revise or replace the procedures that are not effective or that fail to directly address the goals of the intervention and the students' learning needs. Your options include those discussed below.

Option 1 *Revise or remove procedures that are ineffective.* The most obvious action you can take when you find that procedures are ineffective or misdirected is to change or remove them. When an intervention is not working well, sometimes the procedures you have been using may simply not be useful for the students or for teaching the target skill. Whether the problem is one of logistics, presentation, complexity, or simple miscalculation, often the best solution is to completely revise the procedure or remove it outright. By jettisoning or reworking procedures that have proven ineffective, you will be able to focus your efforts on the more promising aspects of the intervention, and you will free the students of the distraction or confusion that ineffective procedures can cause.

Mrs. Armstrong decided quickly to abandon the modeling activity she conducted on the second day of the intervention when she discovered that it merely made Alfred laugh. By moving on to something else, Mrs. Armstrong was able to regain Alfred's attention quickly. Similarly, she might decide that the in-class videotape activity needs a lot of rethinking before it can be an effective tool for Alfred. She realizes that having him narrate the video to the class was a mistake, and she decides she will have to change the activity significantly—perhaps making a game out of it, or perhaps including more specific questions or tasks for Alfred to address—before she will try it again.

Option 2 *Check the intervention procedures to make sure they address the instructional goals.* When you review the instructional procedures and activities, another issue is to be sure they are clearly in line with the goal areas. Sometimes procedures are ineffective because they have been chosen more for their interest or novelty than for their instructional value. The format may be too distracting for the students to pay attention to the overall goals involved, or the students may get so caught up in the activity that they are unable to attend to and sort out the information they need to develop their skills properly. In such cases, you may have to streamline or redirect the procedures so they concentrate more directly and deliberately on the skills you are teaching.

Mrs. Armstrong might find that Alfred enjoyed playing with Gordon but that they spent their time together mostly talking about things unrelated to game activities. As a result, Alfred learned little about playing football because Mrs. Armstrong had not linked his pairing with Gordon directly to the goal of teaching Alfred to coordinate his play behavior with his peers. If she decides to use this procedure again, she will have to give Gordon a specific set of guidelines and tasks to carry out so he will be an effective model for Alfred in teaching specific game techniques. This would align the procedure much more clearly with the instructional goal, and it would be less of a distraction and more of an aid to Alfred.

Option 3 *Readjust the pace of the procedures to match the student's progress.* Another impediment to the students' progress may be that the intervention procedures are moving too slowly—or too quickly (Burden & Byrd, 1994; Walker, Colvin, & Ramsey, 1995). On the one hand, you might find that the students are capable of learning more rapidly than you had anticipated, and that they are becoming impatient with the slow pace of the intervention procedures. This is a particular problem when the students' progress is being hampered by activities designed to teach them goals or skills that they already know, or that they learned quickly at the intervention's start. On the other hand, you should also watch for procedures that move too quickly for the students, or that fail to break the skills being taught into manageable units. These problems may require the students to learn and to assimilate the new skills more quickly than they are able, and may thus also cause frustration and discouragement.

Usually, you should suspect these types of difficulties when students show considerable effort and interest in trying to learn from the intervention at first, but then begin to falter as the pace becomes too challenging or too dull and their incentive and attention begin to wane. In such cases, it is important to readjust the pacing of the intervention activities to bring it in line with the students' learning characteristics and level of interest.

Mrs. Armstrong might find that one reason for Alfred's failure to improve is that she is trying too many things at once. As she looks over her summary of results, she can see that working on rules, motor coordination, and seeking recognition all in a few short days is too ambitious a plan for Alfred, and that she needs to slow down the pace of the intervention so the individual procedures stop competing with one another for his all-too-fleeting attention. In the days ahead, she might decide to try the procedures more deliberately, one at a time, and to explain to Alfred the instructions and aims for each one. In this way, she may be able to focus Alfred's efforts more sharply and thereby significantly increase the procedures' effectiveness.

Option 4 *Alter the context in which the procedures are used.* Another factor you should consider when you review the intervention procedures is whether the activities employ the most effective context for developing the students' skills (Walker, Colvin, & Ramsey, 1995). Conditions you might evaluate include the setting and situation for the activities, the materials used in the procedures, and the people helping to implement the plan. In some cases, you might find that these factors present a distraction for students rather than encouraging them to give their full attention to the intervention's goals (Burden & Byrd, 1994). Some indications that the circumstances for an intervention may need to be altered are:

- The students are unable to attend to the procedures and techniques you are using.
- They show discomfort in working in the grouping arrangement (one on one, small group, and so on).
- They become preoccupied with things that are not related to acquiring the target skill.

- They are so concerned with the incentive features of the intervention that they do not concentrate on the instructional activities.

In any of these instances, you should change the context for the intervention and minimize the distracting elements so the students can give their full attention to the intervention procedures (Zirpoli & Melloy, 1993).

Mrs. Armstrong might decide that her modeling activity was not a bad idea but that she was not the best person to demonstrate the game rules and play activities, particularly out on the playground. If she changes the context to have Gordon or some other student model the actions, the procedure may work perfectly well. Similarly, Mrs. Armstrong might conclude that the real problem with using the video was that Alfred was narrating it in front of the entire class, a situation that proved too great a temptation for his clowning. She could decide to change the context to a one-on-one or small group activity to see whether the procedure will be more effective if Alfred has fewer opportunities to be distracted.

Option 5 *Develop new procedures to address the instructional goals.* The last approach to consider when procedures have proven ineffective is to develop new ones. You might find when you review the intervention results that the procedures are simply inadequate for addressing the students' instructional needs, and that the best approach will be to come up with entirely different activities. But do not throw the new plans together in a haphazard fashion; otherwise, they may prove no more effective than the old ones. You should consider the reasons the old procedures failed and be careful not to fall into the same traps a second time.

In such cases you can go back to the original brainstorming worksheets you used when you were first planning the intervention (see Chapters Nine and Ten). You might discover ideas on the worksheets that could be adapted now, or you might be able to devise some new variations on your previous thoughts, considering the wealth of information you have gathered during the intervention. Furthermore, the worksheets will serve as a reminder that it is still important to direct any new procedures toward the instructional goals you established originally for the intervention.

Mrs. Armstrong might decide that Alfred's intervention needs some fresh ideas for procedures. She might consult with Ms. Hernandez and other teachers, and ask their assistance in reworking procedures she discarded earlier in the planning process or in exploring new activities to try with Alfred. They could focus their attention on teaching Alfred more appropriate ways of gaining recognition, and change the context for the intervention to a more structured classroom situation that is easier to control. One possibility might be to put Alfred, Sally, and two or three other students in a small group to play different types of word games. During the game, the students could be limited to a specific list of appropriate phrases and actions; anything they say or do that is not on the list would mean a point against them. By playing the game, Alfred would be able to practice appropriate ways to interact and gain recognition, and Mrs. Armstrong could more easily work with him one on one to teach him the required skills. Later, after he has achieved this instructional goal, she could redirect the intervention toward showing him how to carry over the skills to playground games.

Scenario III

The student is not making progress because the intervention does not adequately address the student's need for incentive.

So far, in our discussion of options for reworking an intervention plan, we have assumed that the students are sufficiently motivated to develop the target skills. But a slow rate of progress in the intervention may also signal a lack of interest or willingness on the students' part to acquire and use the new skills. Therefore, when an intervention is not working as planned, you should also reevaluate the incentive features of the intervention. It is usually best to examine these factors after you have reviewed the instructional goals and the procedures, because you can often overcome problems with an intervention by readjusting or changing these portions of the plan. But there may still be occasions when you need to revise your plans to increase the students' incentive.

Mrs. Armstrong might discover when she considers Alfred's behavior that he does not show much interest in taking part in the intervention activities. Although he is not particularly hostile or resistant to her efforts, he makes little attempt to apply himself to the activities, and he is easily distracted when he does. Mrs. Armstrong realizes she must address Alfred's need for incentive if she expects him to work at improving his behavior. In cases like this, you can choose from several options.

Option 1 *Place more emphasis on the natural outcomes of performance or add extra incentives for the student to learn the new skills.* Sometimes students will not make progress in their behavior because they do not fully understand the importance of learning the skills or do not consider it worthwhile to make the effort involved in changing their behavior. In these cases, you should restructure the intervention in a way that gives the students precise reasons for learning the skills and that emphasizes the benefits they can derive from using them. You may need to highlight natural outcomes more than usual; if this does not work or is not feasible, you may need to add extra rewards or privileges for learning the new skills (Campbell & Siperstein, 1994).

When Mrs. Armstrong reviews her results, she may realize that Alfred is not especially interested in taking part in the intervention or in learning to play more effectively with his peers. Although he wants his classmates to like him, he does not seem to connect the goals of the intervention with the outcomes of gaining greater respect or esteem from his peers. To address this problem, Mrs. Armstrong would need to develop more specific procedures that would highlight for Alfred the natural outcomes of improving his game playing and interactions. She might use the class discussion on gaining recognition to develop a list of outcomes that result from interacting effectively. She could then discuss the outcomes with Alfred and emphasize the importance of cooperating in the intervention so he could learn how to gain this recognition. She might also need to supplement this approach by developing a point system that Alfred can use to monitor and reward his own progress. The points could be exchanged for computer time or other classroom privileges, but would need to be faded when Alfred becomes more attuned to natural outcomes.

Option 2 *Change the context of the intervention to help the student build confidence in using the new skills.* Occasionally, students may seem particularly resistant to an intervention because they lack the self-assurance and confidence to learn the new skills (Campbell & Siperstein, 1994). They may show their resistance by being uncooperative with the activities to save face with their peers, or by putting up a front of disinterest or disregard for the procedures so they do not have to admit to a skill deficit. In these cases the students may want to learn the new skills very much, even though they try hard to hide it by ignoring or openly defying your intervention attempts. Many times, changing the circumstances of the intervention to include more individualized activities or out-of-context situations can overcome this resistance. These circumstances can alleviate the students' concerns about failing in front of their peers or about admitting by their cooperation with the activities that they lack certain skills. It is helpful to build into this new context more opportunities for students to practice their skills so they can gain greater self-assurance and reduce their apprehensions about making mistakes when they interact with others in natural performance conditions.

Mrs. Armstrong might notice that Alfred is more self-conscious than she thought, and that he clowns around during the game-playing activities because he is not confident about his ability to gain recognition through his ordinary play skills. In this case, Mrs. Armstrong might decide to have Alfred work on improving his skills for gaining recognition in the context of one-on-one sessions and small, carefully controlled groups before extending the intervention to the normal playground situation. In this way, Alfred could learn and practice the skills he needs without the added pressure caused by his own desire to stand out from the other students.

Option 3 *Reduce competing behaviors.* As we discussed in Chapter Ten, competing behaviors are the actions students perform instead of those that meet social expectations. Sometimes, an otherwise very good intervention plan is not successful because students are so set on performing competing behaviors that they fail to pay attention to what you are trying to do with the intervention. In these cases, you may have to adjust your plans by starting first with procedures that redirect the students' attention and that improve their concentration on the intervention activities (Walker, Colvin, & Ramsey, 1995; Kameenui & Simmons, 1990).

One approach to reducing competing behaviors is to change the context of the intervention so students do not have the same opportunities to engage in the problem behaviors. Without a chance to perform the competing behaviors in the new context, the students may instead attend to the activities you have planned (Donnellan, LaVigna, Negri-Shoultz, & Fassbender, 1988). Another approach is to punish the problem behaviors and effectively quell the students' desire to engage in them. The students may begin to focus their attention on the intervention once the competing behaviors are not so rewarding as they were before (Wacker, Berg, & Northrup, 1991).

Mrs. Armstrong might find that Alfred is not cooperating with the intervention because he cannot seem to resist the chance to clown around in front of his classmates, particularly Sally. Mrs. Armstrong may decide to alter the context of the intervention to remove this temptation by having Alfred work one on one with her or in a strictly controlled and supervised workgroup. If the problem persists, she could add an unpleasant outcome by isolating Alfred from the others whenever he acts clownish. By enforcing the opposite result (i.e., solitude) from what Alfred's behavior seeks to achieve (i.e., camaraderie), Mrs. Armstrong could eventually eliminate his competing behavior.

A wide variety of very effective techniques for reducing competing behavior are described in the literature on behavior management. We have suggested some of these resources at the end of the chapter.

Your decisions about what to do when students are not making the progress you had hoped for should be based on a careful consideration of the results you obtained while monitoring the intervention. Unsuccessful results usually indicate that the intervention plan is not addressing the source of the students' problems. You should take a close look at the instructional goals of the intervention and reexamine the procedures and activities you are using to determine whether you should make adjustments in the instructional and incentive approaches. Reexamining the students' behavior and the intervention procedures will help you decide how to modify the intervention plan to get it back on the proper course.

Making a Checklist of Scenarios and Options

As you consider how to proceed with an intervention, we suggest that you prepare a checklist of scenarios and options, similar to the ones presented in this chapter, and use it to guide your review of the intervention results. Figure 12.1 shows the checklist Mrs. Armstrong prepared for Granville. It is divided into two separate sections—one to use when interventions are working as planned, and the other for when they are not so successful. Each section outlines scenarios for results that might occur and lists under each scenario the options for further action, along with spaces for check marks. It also includes a page for notes on what actions you should take next.

With such a checklist, you can review the monitoring results obtained during the intervention, including the students' performance of the social expectations you are concerned with. Then you can look for the scenarios that best match what you saw in the intervention, and check off the options that seem most appropriate as general strategies for what to do next. Use the page of notes to outline specific plans for carrying out the options you have marked, such as ideas for revising goals or redirecting procedures.

Following is a progress report of Granville's intervention that explains how Mrs. Armstrong used the checklist shown in Figure 12.1 to plan a further course of action for him. Note that this progress report corresponds with the results she recorded on Granville's monitoring worksheet presented in Chapter Eleven (Figure 11.2).

Figure 12.1 Mrs. Armstrong's checklist for determining how to proceed with Granville's intervention.

Worksheet 12.1: Options for Proceeding with an Intervention Page _1_ of _3_

Name: _Mrs. Armstrong_ Date: _Nov. 27_

Student: _Granville_ Grade: _5_

Section I: When the intervention is generally working as planned.

The following scenarios describe generally positive results from the intervention:

The student has acquired the target skill and shows signs of expanding the new skills to other skill areas and settings.

___ Fade the intervention procedures.
___ Select another target skill for the student to work on.
___ Select other students for the intervention.

The student is making progress toward acquiring the target skill but has not expanded his or her behavior beyond the intervention situation.

_X_ Continue the intervention and add procedures to encourage carryover of new skills.
_X_ Work with other teachers and students to apply expectations consistently across different settings and activities.
___ Add incentive procedures to encourage carryover of the new skills.

The student is making progress toward acquiring the target skill but is still working for artificial outcomes or rewards.

___ Adjust the intervention procedures to highlight the natural outcomes of behavior.
___ Fade the intervention procedures more gradually and build the student's confidence level.
___ Integrate clearer outcomes or extra rewards as a permanent part of the overall routine of the setting.

The student is making progress toward meeting the target skill, but is still far from reaching the criterion level.

_X_ Continue the intervention and recheck the student's progress later.
___ Continue the intervention plan, but shift the procedures to stay aligned with the student's progress and needs.

Figure 12.1 *(continued)*

Worksheet 12.1 (continued)	Name: *Mrs. Armstrong* Page *2* of *3* Student: *Granville*

Section II: When the intervention is generally not working as planned.

The following scenarios describe reasons the student might not be making progress:

The student is not making progress because the instructional goals are misdirected.

___ Eliminate instructional goals that are not central to acquiring the target skill.
___ Shift the emphasis given to the instructional goals in the intervention plan.
___ Add other instructional goals to the intervention plan.
___ Shift the focus of the intervention to new skill areas.
___ Continue the intervention and watch for further effects.

The student is not making progress because the intervention procedures themselves are ineffective or misdirected.

___ Revise or remove procedures that are ineffective.
___ Check the intervention procedures to ensure that they address the intended instructional goals.
___ Readjust the pace of the intervention procedures to match the student's progress.
___ Alter the context in which the procedures are used.
___ Develop new procedures to address the instructional goals.

The student is not making progress because the intervention does not adequately address the student's need for incentive.

___ Place more emphasis on natural outcomes of performance, or add extra incentives for the student to learn the new skills.
___ Change the context of the intervention to help the student build confidence in using the new skills.
___ Reduce competing behaviors.

Figure 12.1 *(continued)*

Worksheet 12.1 (continued)	Name: *Mrs. Armstrong* Student: *Granville*	Page *3* of *3*

Notes on further courses of action:

Ideas for improving Granville's maintenance and carryover of skills for cooperating in small groups:

Work with Mr. Wagner and Ms. Hernandez to develop a more consistent structure and format for small group activities in the various classes Granville attends.

Institute a planning procedure in all fifth-grade classes in which group members start activities by reviewing and writing down the steps they will go through to complete the activity. Have teachers approve each group's plan before students start their work.

Have the groups outline ahead of time what the role of the small group leaders should be, and how other members should respond to the leader.

Ideas for encouraging Granville to extend conflict-resolution strategies to recess and other nonstructured times:

Recommend that play groups review procedures for resolving disagreements as part of their discussion of game rules and playing conventions before the games start.

Have play groups assign a classmate on a daily rotating basis to act as referee for all recess games. Give this student the title "Student Playground Supervisor," and have him or her work closely with the adult supervisors.

Explain to playground supervisors the conflict-resolution strategy Granville should use. Ask supervisors to try to be close by when Granville is likely to have disagreements with teammates, to remind him of the steps he should use before a disagreement begins.

If Granville needs further encouragement and incentive, work out a reward system in which he could supervise younger students, be a weekly referee, or earn other privileges if he plays without any fights or major conflicts for a certain number of days, e.g., Monday through Thursday.

Granville's Intervention: A Progress Report

Day 1: On the first day of the intervention, Ms. Hernandez taught Granville how to use the five-step technique she had developed. The procedure gave him a simple and straightforward way to keep track of the directions teachers write on the board or give orally to the class. Later, Mrs. Armstrong reviewed the new technique with Granville and had him practice using it with the class as she explained the directions for the day's social studies activities. Afterward, she divided the class into small groups, asked the groups to go over a questionnaire on current events they would like to discuss, and gave Granville the task of writing down the directions for his group using the five-step technique. She checked the accuracy of the directions he wrote and found that his work had only one minor error. Then she asked him to go over the directions with his group and to lead the group in filling out the questionnaire.

Granville did fairly well with this activity. Although he spent only about 50 percent of the time discussing topics with the group, he did complete 80 percent of the work assigned and had no major arguments with other students.

After the social studies class, Mrs. Armstrong told Granville that he did a good job with his group, and she suggested that he use the assignment worksheet in Mr. Wagner's classes to help remember directions for Mr. Wagner's assignments. After school, she checked with Mr. Wagner about Granville's performance. She found that Granville did need some prompting to use the worksheet, but his notes were very accurate and his work completion scores were about 75 percent.

Day 2: Ms. Hernandez began the second day of the intervention by giving Granville a worksheet that included sections both for writing down directions and for notes on how to follow them. She went over the worksheet and had him use it with some practice assignments. She told Mrs. Armstrong that Granville was able to use the worksheet fairly easily.

During her social studies class, Mrs. Armstrong set up a role-playing activity using some scripts she developed with Ms. Hernandez. The scripts outlined several examples of good and bad ways to interact with classmates during small group work. She planned to videotape the role-playing skits so she could go over them again with Granville and the class the next day. She asked Granville to be one of the key players in the activity, but after he started acting silly and self-conscious, she had him sit down and watch. He did pay close attention to the activity, and he seemed to enjoy watching his classmates act out various situations. During the small group follow-up activity, he used his worksheet to jot down the directions and to list the steps for the assignment. He worked well with his group in answering questions about ways to interact and work cooperatively with group members. Mrs. Armstrong, in recording his performance, found that he spent 65 percent of the time working on the assignment with classmates, completed 14 of the 20 questions correctly, and again had no arguments. However, later in the day during recess, Granville got into a vehement encounter with some classmates because they teased him about his silly behavior during social studies class. Mrs. Armstrong had to separate the boys for the rest of the recess period.

Day 3: Mrs. Armstrong started the social studies period by showing the class the videotape of the skits they performed the day before, and the class reviewed several ways of working in small group arrangements. In addition, Mrs. Armstrong had the class formulate two sets of guidelines: one for serving as a small group leader, and another for being a group member and following the directions of the leader. Later in the class, she gave a small group assignment and asked Granville to serve as his group's leader. She left the guidelines on the board and asked the leaders to start their work by reviewing the guidelines.

Mrs. Armstrong noticed that after she asked him to be group leader, Granville immediately wrote the directions for the assignment on his worksheet and outlined the steps for completing the activities. He performed the job of group leader very well. Although he had some disagreements with others in the group, he was careful to follow the guidelines closely, and his group was one of the first to complete the assignment. He spent almost 95 percent of the time working with classmates on the activity, and completed 80 percent of the group work.

Day 4: On the fourth day of the intervention, Mrs. Armstrong began by working with Granville and the class on techniques for resolving disagreements. She used a role-playing activity to show different types of conflicts and disagreements, and to act out episodes of teasing that get out of hand. She had the class list acceptable responses for handling conflicts and posted the list on the board. The activity seemed to go well; Mrs. Armstrong talked to Granville about how to use the list of responses outside the classroom, and he seemed to understand.

During the group work, Brian, a student Granville usually gets along with pretty well, served as group leader. Granville filled out his assignment worksheet, but he seemed disappointed at not being group leader again, and he was rather cross and distracted during much of the activity. He was on task for only about 50 percent of the time, and completed only 40 percent of his work. He also got into an argument with Brian and Jermaine about the assignment, but when Mrs. Armstrong prompted him to consult the conflict resolution list the class had just made, he sulkily made up with the students. He did, however, start the argument again in the hallway after class, and he was reprimanded quite severely by Mr. Wagner.

Deciding What to Do Next

After four days, Mrs. Armstrong thinks that Granville's intervention is generally going pretty well, but she feels she should take stock of the results so far and get some direction for what to do in the days ahead. To help her review Granville's results and make decisions on how to proceed, Mrs. Armstrong fills out the checklist of intervention scenarios and options for proceeding presented in Figure 12.1.

Mrs. Armstrong compares the scenarios to Granville's performance, and she sees that the most useful match is clearly "The student is making progress toward acquiring and using the target skill, but still is far from reaching the criterion level." The results indicate that Granville is not yet meeting the expectation "Cooperates with peers on small group projects," as his performance is generally below the 75 percent on-task level and the 70 percent work completion level specified as criteria. But his interest in the intervention and his dramatically improved behavior are signs that the intervention is having a positive effect.

Under this scenario, she checks off "Continue the intervention and recheck the student's progress later." She feels that Granville's positive response to the intervention procedures and his willingness to use the new worksheet for directions and assignments are signs that the intervention plan is having a positive effect on him. She decides to continue for a few more days to see whether Granville will begin to extend and consolidate the gains he has made so far.

At the same time, she also checks off two items from the scenario "The student is making progress toward acquiring the target skill but has not expanded performance beyond the intervention situation." The options she marks are "Continue the intervention and add procedures to encourage carryover of new skills" and "Work with other teachers and students to apply expectations consistently across different settings and activities." Mrs. Armstrong realizes, from talking with Mr. Wagner and Ms. Hernandez, that Granville needs to apply more broadly the techniques he has learned for writing down assignments and for working with classmates on projects. She feels he can solidify his gains if he is encouraged to use the worksheet in other classes. Moreover, she understands that she must work more with Granville on adapting and practicing the conflict resolution strategy she and the class developed so that he uses it throughout the school day. Figure 12.1 shows the check marks Mrs. Armstrong made for Granville and the notes she made for encouraging carryover and generalization of these skills. Note that Mrs. Armstrong has made no check marks on Part II of the worksheet, as these scenarios do no not apply to Granville.

In summary, you can use a checklist to help you decide how the various scenarios and the options discussed in the chapter apply to an intervention. By comparing the monitoring results to the scenarios and checking off options you might wish to pursue, you can create a general course of action for what to do next with your intervention plan.

❍ Summary

When Interventions Are Working As Planned

1. When students have acquired target skills and show signs of expanding their performance, the course of action to take should include one or more of the following:
   a. fading and removing the intervention procedures
   b. selecting new high priorities to work on
   c. selecting other students for the intervention

2. When students are making progress in acquiring target skills, but have not expanded their performance, the course of action to take should include one or more of the following:
   a. adding procedures that encourage carryover of skills
   b. working with others to apply expectations consistently across settings and activities
   c. adding incentive procedures to encourage carryover

3. When students are making progress in acquiring target skills but are still working for artificial outcomes or rewards, the course of action to take should include one or more of the following:
   a. adjusting procedures to highlight natural outcomes
   b. fading procedures more gradually and building students' self-confidence
   c. integrating clearer outcomes or rewards in the routine of the setting
4. When students are making progress in acquiring target skills, but are still far from reaching criterion levels, the course of action to take should include one or more of the following:
   a. continuing with intervention and rechecking progress later
   b. continuing with intervention, but shifting procedures to keep them aligned with students' progress

When Interventions Are Not Working As Planned

1. When students are not making progress because the instructional goals are misdirected, corrective action should include one or more of the following:
   a. eliminating goals that are not central to acquiring the target skills
   b. shifting emphasis given to instructional goals
   c. adding other important instructional goals
   d. shifting to new target skills or performance areas
   e. continuing with intervention and watching for further effects
2. When students are not making progress because the procedures are ineffective, the course of action to take should include one or more of the following:
   a. revising or removing ineffective procedures
   b. checking procedures to ensure they address instructional goals
   c. readjusting pace of procedures to match students' progress
   d. altering context in which procedures are used
   e. developing new procedures to address instructional goals
3. When students are not making progress because the intervention does not address students' incentive needs, the course of action to take should include one or more of the following:
   a. placing more emphasis on natural outcomes or adding extra rewards
   b. changing context to build students' self-confidence
   c. reducing competing behaviors

A checklist of scenarios and options for how to proceed with an intervention will help in revising intervention results.

Suggested Resources for Behavior Management Techniques

Alberto, P. A., & Troutman, A. (1990). *Applied behavior analysis for teachers.* Columbus, OH: Merrill/Macmillan.

Donnellan, A. M., LaVigna, G., Negri-Shoultz, N., & Fassbender, L. (1988). *Progress without punishment: Effective approaches for learners with behavior problems.* New York: Teachers College Press.

Edwards, C. H. (1993). *Classroom discipline and management.* New York: Macmillan.

Kazdin, A. E. (1989). *Behavior modification in applied settings.* Pacific Grove, CA: Brooks/Cole.

Walker, H. M., Colvin, G., & Ramsey, E. (1995). *Antisocial behavior in school: Strategies and best practices.* Pacific Grove, CA: Brooks/Cole.

Wolery, M., Bailey, D., & Sugai, G. (1988). *Effective teaching: Principles and procedures of applied behavior analysis with exceptional students.* Boston: Allyn & Bacon.

Zirpoli, T. J., & Melloy, K. (1993). *Behavior management: Applications for teachers and parents.* New York: Merrill.

Examples for Chapter 12

Example 12a

Ms. Bailey teaches a first-period study skills class to a mixed group of special education and remedial students. She usually has them work in pairs on homework assignments, complete projects, and study for tests. Carolyn is a remedial student who has been reluctant to work with a partner; she has usually strayed from the task, daydreamed, and ignored her classmates. For Carolyn's intervention, Ms. Bailey gave her class written directions for working with partners and agreed with Carolyn on a prompting system for reinforcing the new guidelines. Ms. Bailey also had peer tutors from advanced placement classes come in to work with each pair of students, modeling effective work strategies and encouraging the partners to cooperate. Finally, Ms. Bailey taught her students a self-monitoring procedure for keeping track of their progress.

During the intervention Carolyn has begun to work much more with her partner. She has come to depend too much on her tutor, however, and has not carried over the target skill to her other classes. After reviewing Carolyn's results, Ms. Bailey checked off the following options for next steps in Section I of her worksheet:

Continue the intervention and add procedures to encourage carryover of new skills.

Work with other teachers and students to apply expectations consistently.

Fade the intervention procedures gradually and build the student's confidence.

This page shows the plans she outlined for continuing Carolyn's intervention.

Notes can be organized by the different courses of actions planned.

Fading involves withdrawing elements of the intervention that are not natural features of the situation.

Varying the circumstances for students' performance will solidify their use of target skills.

Continue to monitor the students' behavior throughout the intervention.

Worksheet 12.1 (continued)	Name: *Ms. Bailey* Student: *Carolyn*	Page *3* of *3*

Notes on further courses of action:

Ideas for fading intervention procedures
- *Begin standing farther from Carolyn and let her work with less prompting.*
- *Encourage tutors to let Carolyn work more independently by checking her work less often.*
- *Show tutors how to redirect Carolyn's questions back to her work rather than answering them directly.*

Ideas for continuing intervention to encourage further progress
- *Change Carolyn's partners and have her work on a variety of assignments so she learns to apply her new skills more broadly.*
- *Monitor how Carolyn reacts to different partners and different types of tasks.*

Ideas for improving carryover of skills
- *Work with Carolyn's other teachers to develop a consistent approach for having students work on assignments in class.*
- *Go over self-monitoring procedure with other teachers. Discuss ways it could be implemented in other settings.*
- *Show Carolyn how to adapt the self-monitoring technique.*
- *Show other teachers how to use the prompting procedure to remind Carolyn to work cooperatively.*

Example 12b

Antonio is a student in Mrs. Lamont's first-grade class who does not comply when she gives him directions or corrective feedback. Antonio often talks back, pouts, argues, or in other ways behaves defiantly. Mrs. Lamont based much of her intervention on trying to improve Antonio's motivation to follow directions, but the procedures did not have much effect on his behavior. Although he was at first more attentive to tasks, he had difficulty remembering what to do and needed constant prompts. He seemed to get frustrated with the prompting, and shouted "No!" or "Shut up!" when Mrs. Lamont began reminding him what to do.

For continuing Antonio's intervention, Mrs. Lamont checked off the following items from Section II of her worksheet:

Add other instructional goals to the intervention plan.

Alter the context in which the procedures are used.

Develop new procedures to address the instructional goals.

This page from Mrs. Lamont's worksheet shows the specific ideas she outlined for addressing these options.

Unsuccessful interventions will often reveal other problems students may have in using target skills.

Redirecting instructional goals can involve refocusing on more basic skills.

Outlining specific procedures can give focus to your plans.

Courses of action can include seeking help from school or community resources.

Worksheet 12.1 (continued)	Name: *Mrs. Lamont* Student: *Antonio*	Page *3* of *3*

Notes on further courses of action:

Giving Antonio extra rewards for complying with directions worked only with very simple directions; otherwise he still does not comply. I now see that he is unable to understand and follow directions, especially those involving two or more steps and those involving a delay between steps. I need to refocus the intervention on teaching Antonio a strategy for remembering two- and three-step directions.

Maybe I could work with Antonio individually when I give directions and have him memorize the directions using a song or using stickers or drawings on index cards. I could test out the procedure starting with simple directions and move to more complicated ones, using games or other enjoyable activities to hold Antonio's interest. I can pair Antonio with Larry to model the procedures.

I also noticed in the intervention that Antonio gets frustrated quickly and does not consider what has been said to him before reacting and yelling. If I could teach him to delay his response for a few seconds, this might give him time to consider the prompting or directions that are being given. I could teach him a counting procedure or a short song he can sing to himself when he is corrected or prompted.

I will discuss possible procedures with Ms. Diaz, the language therapist. I should also check with Antonio's parents and his other teachers to see if these are general problems for him.

Mr. Wagner's Case Study

Mr. Wagner has been reviewing the results of his intervention with Granville. He has had some success teaching Granville to borrow supplies before class starts, but in other areas he has been less successful. On Section II of his worksheet, Mr. Wagner checked the following options for continuing:

Add other instructional goals to the intervention plan.

Continue intervention and watch for further results.

Develop new procedures to address the instructional goals.

This page shows Mr. Wagner's notes on what to do next.

Mr. Wagner's revised procedures may get Granville to do his work, but they will not improve his social interactions. Be sure any new procedures address the target skill.

Mr. Wagner outlines a problem here, but gives no indication of what he will do to address it. When stating new goals or skill areas, you should also plan out intervention procedures to use.

Instructional goals should define specific behavioral objectives. Mr. Wagner's notes focus on broad, vague impressions about Granville rather than on particular observations about his behavior and needs.

Worksheet 12.1 (continued)	Name: *Mr. Wagner* Student: *Granville*	Page *3* of *3*

Notes on further courses of action:

Granville still argues and gets in disagreements with his group. Even when he reads his directions, he gets far behind the rest of the group. Maybe it would be easier for Granville to concentrate on the assignment if he could work on his own. I could give him directions one-on-one and then have him work on a portion of the project by himself. That way he could focus on learning the directions without the distraction of arguments and conflicts with group members.

Granville is getting better at asking to borrow materials before class, but I need to teach him how to handle situations when he asks for something but classmates choose not to lend it. This is causing many arguments and conflicts before class.

One reason Granville has so much trouble with the intervention is his poor attitude about his work. He resists learning the directions and talks back when I try to keep him on task. He just doesn't seem interested in learning the material. Maybe if I could help him improve his outlook about the schoolwork he could apply himself more to it. I'll add the instructional goal "learn to take an interest in schoolwork" to the intervention plan.

PART FOUR

Broader Applications in Teaching Social Competence

The major focus of this text has been on designing interventions to improve the social competence of individual students. We have outlined a highly deliberate and systematic process for preparing interventions, involving an extensive series of assessment and planning procedures. Our reason for such a detailed approach is to show you how to design an entirely new strategy for handling the more difficult or complicated problems in social behavior you may encounter with students. By breaking down the process in this thorough fashion, we have been able to illustrate the enormous complexity and variety of factors that influence students' social competence in school settings.

We do not mean to indicate, however, that you must use every one of these procedures or follow the guidelines to the letter each time you design interventions. You will often be able to streamline the process we have outlined, skimming over some of the procedures while concentrating on the most helpful aspects, based on what you already know about the factors that affect the students' social behavior. We also do not suggest that designing interventions for one or two students at a time is the only way—or even the best way—to teach social skills. You may wish to expand on some of the procedures we have described, modifying them for broader applications in the classroom or in the school as a whole.

In this last part of the text, we explore different options for using and adapting the concepts we have presented to address a wider array of circumstances in which to help students improve their social skills. In Chapter Thirteen, we explain how to streamline assessment and intervention planning so you can reduce the time and work involved in designing interventions and thus tailor the planning process to your specific needs. In Chapter Fourteen, we describe ways you can use the concepts as a framework for preparing instructional lessons directed at groups of students rather than individuals. Finally, in Chapter Fifteen, we discuss how to extend your teaching of social competence by collaborating with other teachers and school personnel to plan social skills instructional programs across school settings at a specific grade level, and across grade levels and schools.

CHAPTER 13

Streamlining the Teaching of Social Competence

Throughout the text, we have described the procedures for teaching social competence in a deliberately detailed and systematic manner. For each step in the process, we have discussed a broad range of issues, options, and guidelines. This thorough approach to assessment and intervention is important for two reasons. First, social skills are rarely analyzed with the degree of attention required for teachers to gain an accurate understanding of student deficits and learning outcomes. Second, the effectiveness of interventions is aided more by clear planning and consideration of the target students' needs than by any other factor. Even so, once you have learned the steps we have outlined, each of them can be carried out in a much more informal way than we originally described. In fact, the entire investigation and planning process can often be condensed into a week or two.

You should realize, however, that you cannot choose effective shortcuts in a process of this kind unless you understand thoroughly the principles behind each step. You will not know what activities or procedures you can shorten unless you know what is involved in each step and in the process as a whole. Now that you have this background, you can make informed choices about how best to modify the process to suit your own circumstances. In this chapter, we review the various steps of the intervention planning process, discuss ways to streamline or condense each of the steps, and explain some factors to consider as you decide how detailed your planning should be.

When to Use a Systematic Approach

Streamlining the intervention planning process has several significant advantages. Obviously, it allows you to develop interventions more quickly than a systematic approach would permit. It also allows you to build more efficiently on your prior knowledge of the setting and of the planning procedures, and is particularly useful for implementing short interventions to address more minor problems in social skills. But before we explain how to streamline intervention planning, we should insert a note of caution. Although there are many ways to simplify the activities we have presented, there will still be times when you should be as systematic and deliberate as possible in designing interventions. The next sections describe several circumstances in which a systematic approach has definite advantages in teaching social competence.

Addressing the Most Difficult and Long-Standing Behavior Problems

You should use most of the activities discussed in the text when you are working through the particularly difficult and complicated problems in student behavior. In these instances, taking a systematic approach in addressing these problems will enable you to examine closely the source of the students' difficulties and to generate effective strategies for improving their behavior.

One of the times you will find a detailed breakdown of activities particularly useful is when your natural teaching instincts and your everyday instructional adaptations are not effective in improving the students' behavior—you have tried everything in your instructional bag of tricks, but none of the approaches has satisfactorily addressed the problem situation. Looking at the situation again, this time in a more deliberate fashion, will often give you new insights or suggest possible solutions you have not considered before.

In reflecting on her work with Granville, Mrs. Armstrong sees that it was important for her to go through all the separate steps in designing an intervention because the more informal and intuitive approaches she had been using before had not improved his uncooperative behavior in the classroom. She had made many adjustments in her lessons and disciplinary responses to Granville before but had made no progress because Granville's problems were so broad-based and complex. She realized that she needed to look at the problems in a more objective and methodical manner if she was to find an effective solution. As the case study showed, the steps Mrs. Armstrong followed allowed her to stand back and take an impartial look at Granville's problems, to gather information and ideas from a variety of sources, and to focus her attention on specific, achievable intervention goals. The extra time and care Mrs. Armstrong spent on these activities was worthwhile because she was able to make major adaptations in the way she normally approaches problems in student behavior, and at the same time design an intervention that significantly changed Granville's social behavior.

Working on New Problems

Following a systematic approach is also helpful when you are working in areas of behavior or in circumstances you have not encountered before or have not looked at in great depth. Analyzing the problem area in a deliberate, step-by-step manner will improve your understanding of the factors that contribute to the problem and will often lead you to solutions for overcoming it. As we mentioned before, ideas for possible intervention procedures often follow easily and naturally from a close examination of the social expectations of the setting and an assessment of how students respond and react to these expectations.

For example, before she examined Sandy's behavior carefully, Mrs. Armstrong had thought that having conversations with peers was only a matter of being motivated enough to talk about things that interest you. She had tried to improve Sandy's interactions with procedures like giving her extra attention and reassurance, and encouraging other students to be more friendly toward her. Mrs. Armstrong decided to adopt a more deliberate approach after these methods did not substantially improve Sandy's behavior. By being more systematic, Mrs. Armstrong was able to gain a much better understanding of the complex demands for peer interaction that exist among fifth graders, and to determine exactly where Sandy was having difficulty meeting these demands. As a result, Mrs. Armstrong developed an intervention that was better organized and that focused precisely on Sandy's skill deficits.

Working with Students Having Severe Learning and Behavior Problems

A systematic approach can also help you improve the social competence of students who have special needs, such as students with learning disabilities, diminished self-concepts, attention deficit disorders, behavioral disorders, mental retardation, or other types of disabilities. Often, these students' learning styles and performance characteristics require a detailed analysis of their problems in achieving social competence as well as a broad exploration of procedures and techniques for improving their interactions (Polloway, Patton, Payne, & Payne, 1989; Merrell, 1994; Walker, Colvin, & Ramsey, 1995). In their social interactions, students with disabilities may have to use skills and behaviors that differ significantly from those of most other students. Students usually learn to initiate and sustain conversations through the normal give and take of discourse, but we may have to teach students with disabilities different strategies for performing these behaviors. They may have to choose comments and topics in a far more deliberate and selective manner than other students do, or they may have to rehearse conversational patterns before initiating the interactions. The work on strategy training by Alley and Deshler (1979), Archer (1989), and others highlights the need of some students to learn more systematized patterns of social performance. The detailed process we have outlined in the text can be used to design and teach new patterns of behavior that will enable these students to interact more effectively in school activities.

The chronic nature of problems in social behavior may also be a reason to use formal assessment and intervention procedures such as those we have described. Some students have severe skill deficits that are manifested in defiant, quarrelsome, or self-contemptuous demeanors, or that cause the students to act in ways that directly impede their development of social skills (Koslin, Haarlow, & Karlins, 1986). For example, the frequency or intensity of aggressive actions some students display can contribute to their social isolation and rejection by peers, can encourage classmates to provoke them to even greater levels of aggressive behaviors, or can cause school personnel to remove them from regular classrooms, separating them physically from the influence of positive peer role models (Knapczyk,

Addressing long-standing or severe problems requires a systematic approach.

1989; 1992). Students whose social skills deficits are long-standing and severe often need formalized approaches to social skills instruction, coupled with behavior management techniques (Rutherford, Nelson, & Forness, 1988; Walker, Colvin, & Ramsey, 1995).

Under challenging circumstances like these, you must have a detailed process to use when your initial, more informal and conventional attempts to improve social skills are not successful. If you need a framework for solving particularly difficult or unique problems in social behavior, you should carefully apply the steps in the planning process and work through the problems until you find an effective solution.

With most students, however, you will not need to go through each one of the individual activities discussed in the text every time you design an intervention; there are many ways to shortcut the process. In the rest of the chapter, we describe ways to streamline the intervention planning process; but first, we provide an update on Mrs. Armstrong, so we can use her circumstances to discuss some streamlining options.

Streamlining the Assessment and Intervention Process

The key to successful streamlining is understanding each step in the assessment and intervention process so you can consider how much investigation and planning you will need to complete each activity. Now that Mrs. Armstrong has completed interventions for Granville, Sandy, and Alfred, she recognizes many ways she can simplify her activities in the future. To illustrate how she can use this knowledge the next time she prepares interventions, let us return to the case study.

Mrs. Armstrong's New Interventions

As Mrs. Armstrong is finishing her original interventions, she begins to think of starting the process again, this time targeting Marcia and Monte, two other fifth graders who show problems in their social interactions. She is also thinking of trying another intervention with Alfred. *Marcia* is a quiet student who, like Sandy, does not talk much in class. Her problems are less severe than Sandy's in that her grades are satisfactory and she does have some friends she talks to and plays with outside class. But Mrs. Armstrong believes that Marcia would be more interested in the class and would probably improve her grades if she would take more initiative during group activities, ask more questions in class, and participate more frequently in class discussions.

Meanwhile, *Alfred's* intervention went so poorly that Mrs. Armstrong believes she should refocus her efforts with him. She is thinking of working on Alfred's behavior in the classroom setting, where the circumstances are more controlled and less complicated than on the playground.

Monte is a student who has a significant range of problems in social behavior. He acts immature in his interactions, participates poorly in classroom activities, does not seem to have any close friends, and often gets in trouble with teachers and school personnel, especially in the cafeteria. Mrs. Armstrong would like to investigate Monte's behavior more closely so she can improve his interactions with teachers and students.

With what she has learned in her previous activities about conducting assessments and implementing interventions, Mrs. Armstrong believes she can plan interventions much more quickly this time—in part because of the information she has already gathered about the demands for achieving social competence in school, and in part because she now has a clearer understanding of the steps involved in assessing student needs and developing effective interventions. In the next section, we explain some ways to streamline the intervention planning process and to use a worksheet to guide the activities.

Reviewing the Steps in the Intervention Planning Process

Before shortcutting any stage of the assessment and intervention process, you need a clear understanding of what that stage is designed to do. For this reason, we focus much of this chapter on a review of the various steps outlined in the text. In the next sections, we reexamine every step and for each one present the following:

- *A short review* of the procedures and the questions you should answer before moving to the next step.
- *Three options for streamlining* showing how the step can be carried out with varying levels of detail and complexity.

TABLE 13.1 Steps in streamlining the social skills instructional process

***Part I.* The social skills curriculum and survey level assessment**	
Step 1:	Identify the social skills curriculum
Step 2:	Conduct the survey level assessment
Step 3:	Set priorities and choose target skill
***Part II.* Specific level assessment**	
Step 4:	Assess basic abilities
Step 5:	Assess component steps
Step 6:	Assess performance conditions
***Part III.* Developing and conducting interventions**	
Step 7:	Set instructional goals
Step 8:	Brainstorm and develop procedures
Step 9:	Coordinate and schedule activities
Step 10:	Monitor the intervention

- *Reminders* giving a few key guidelines to remember when you are considering the step.

For illustration purposes, we use Marcia's case to demonstrate the most streamlined approaches, Alfred's case to demonstrate the intermediate level of streamlining, and Monte's case to show the most thorough, step-by-step procedures. With real students, you will use a combination of these options, focusing a good deal of time and attention on certain steps and completing other steps more quickly. Table 13.1 outlines the steps we will discuss in this section.

Part I: The Social Skills Curriculum and the Survey Level Assessment

The opening chapters of the text focused on the need to define the social demands—or the social skills curriculum—that apply to the settings you are addressing. These demands form the basis of the survey level assessment, in which you measure the students' performance against the standards for the peer group and determine what social expectations the students fail to meet. From the results of this assessment, you can assign priorities and pick target skills. Here we review this initial stage of planning and discuss options for streamlining the activities.

Step 1: Identifying the Social Skills Curriculum

Review: The basic purpose for listing the social skills curriculum is to obtain a broad overview of the social demands met by typical students in a setting. This overview helps you understand the social environment and demands of school settings (Weinstein, 1991). As you recall from Chapters Two and Three, the social skills curriculum you develop is a list of the expectations students meet to demonstrate their social competence in each situation, along with standards indicating the level of performance that constitutes minimum competence. When you streamline this step, you should consider how much new information you will need to gather to answer the following questions:

- What are the situations in the setting?
- What social expectations do average students meet in each situation?
- What standards define the minimum level of typical performance for meeting expectations?

We can suggest three streamlining options for defining the social skills curriculum.

Option I: Most streamlined approach The easiest way to streamline this step is to use the list you completed earlier. Once you have developed a social skills curriculum for a particular setting, it will remain accurate and valid as long as people in the setting continue to behave in essentially the same ways. For this reason, you can re-use a social skills curriculum to carry out survey level assessments as long as the setting and its routines have not changed substantially.

Mrs. Armstrong will not need to spend much time preparing a social skills curriculum before she begins assessing Marcia's skills in classroom settings, because of her previous work in the setting. She may fill in some gaps in her original analysis, recheck some of the standards, or update the information if some changes in demands have occurred since her last analysis, but for the most part she will be able to use her list as it stands. Because of the general consistency of the setting, Mrs. Armstrong's curriculum list represents an ongoing resource that she can use to prepare assessments for any number of students in her class.

Option II: Moderate streamlined approach In other cases, you might not have developed a social skills curriculum for the setting, or you might be expanding your previous curriculum to include new situations. But even when you have to prepare a new listing of expectations and standards, you may find this task fairly easy. If the setting is one you normally supervise or oversee, such as your own classroom, the playground, or the locker area, you may be familiar enough with the social expectations to list them quickly after just one or two short observations to take notes and to verify your perceptions. Your experience and knowledge of the circumstances could make the typical demands for social behavior easy to define and the standards for meeting them clear.

When Mrs. Armstrong looks at Alfred's behavior, she might decide to focus on how he passes time in the hallways, since much of his clowning seems to carry over from there. Although she has not previously developed a list of typical student behavior in the hallway setting, she realizes that she can do this quickly. She can easily describe the expectations by listing the routines and conducting one or two quick observations in the situation to note how typical students behave there between classes. When she converts her notes to a list of expectations for the situation, many of the items on her new list will probably be quite similar to those she has already listed for other loosely structured situations, such as free time in class and on the playground. Once Mrs. Armstrong has made a list of the hallway expectations, she can verify and refine her work with one or two follow-up observations, or by conferring with other instructors who monitor the activities.

Option III: Least streamlined approach Although you can often find shortcuts for defining the social skills curriculum, in some cases you must approach this step more systematically and precisely. You might, for instance, want to conduct as broad a survey of skills as possible, or you might not know much about the social demands of the setting. In such cases you should review the information contained in Chapters Two and Three, and take the time to prepare a complete and detailed social skills curriculum for the setting.

Mrs. Armstrong has generally been able to make progress with Monte in her classroom, but because his behavior in the cafeteria is still a problem, she thinks the lunchroom might be the best setting in which to concentrate her work. She knows Monte has problems with adults and students during lunchtime because teachers and cafeteria workers often complain about his behavior. But she does not really know much about the setting because she does not normally supervise in the cafeteria. She suspects that some of Monte's problems may involve the way he treats younger students, and she realizes that in her previous work she has not explored her students' typical interactions with children from other grades. For these reasons, to gain a full understanding of the social demands her fifth graders meet during lunchtime, Mrs. Armstrong will need to make a systematic study of the social expectations that apply there. Chapters Two and Three discuss a number of procedures, guidelines, and cautions that will help her gather and list the information she needs.

Reminders for listing the social skills curriculum No matter how quickly or slowly you prepare the social skills curriculum, you should always include these considerations:

- *Take into account the array of social expectations* in the setting that are critical for students' social competence.
- *Base your listing on what typical students actually do* in the setting rather than what you hope or wish they would do.
- *Remember to consider student-set and self-set expectations* in addition to teacher-set expectations and rules.

Step 2: Conducting the Survey Level Assessment

Review: The social skills curriculum provides the basis for assessing how well individual students respond to the demands met by typical classmates. This process, called the survey level assessment, allows you to inventory the students' abilities and problem behavior, and to prepare a comprehensive listing of expectations they fail to meet in the setting. The list of expectations not met will indicate the students' deficits and instructional needs, and will enable you to set clear priorities for interventions. A survey level assessment is designed to address this basic question:

- Which expectations from the social skills curriculum does the particular student fail to meet?

The following are options for streamlining this step.

Option I: Most streamlined approach You can usually shortcut a survey level assessment if you have had sufficient experience with the students to know their deficits without conducting lengthy observations. In such cases, you can use the list of social expectations as a skills checklist, considering what you already know about the students' behavior and abilities for each expectation. In this way you can identify the major sources of the students' difficulties and specify the key expectations they fail to meet. You should also personalize the assessment by adding to the list any expectations that you know the students do not meet but that are not included in the original curriculum.

Mrs. Armstrong is fairly confident that she has a good understanding of the expectations Marcia does and does not meet as she has worked fairly closely with Marcia during the school year. Marcia's social problems do not seem complex or extensive; instead of conducting a lengthy assessment at this point, Mrs. Armstrong could look over the expectations on the survey level assessment and check off the particular items she knows Marcia has trouble meeting. She will also add a few items that are not on her curriculum worksheet but that present difficulties for Marcia, such as following along with the flow of a discussion.

Option II: Intermediate streamlined approach In other cases, you might still have a few specific questions despite your generally solid knowledge of the students' social behavior. In these cases, you can expand on the approach outlined above by conducting an abridged version of a survey level assessment to fill in gaps in your knowledge of the students' performance and to give you a more objective basis of observation. You could concentrate some short observations on one or two particular areas of behavior, such as conversational skills or resolving disagreements, if you have not examined these aspects of performance before. Or you could focus the assessment on a single situation, like class start-up time, if you would like to look more closely at the students' behavior under these circumstances.

Mrs. Armstrong already knows a good deal about Alfred's behavior and has already begun to make a list of the expectations he fails to meet, but she would like to investigate a couple points more closely. She might decide to observe his conversations during class start-up time, for example, since her knowledge of his conversational skills with peers is limited. And she might want to take a closer look at his behavior in the hallway, since she has not really observed him in that setting before. Coupled with her prior knowledge of Alfred's behavior, these quick observations would give Mrs. Armstrong an accurate listing of the expectations that present problems for him.

Option III: Most streamlined approach You may need to conduct a full-scale survey level assessment of students' social performance when they display a wide array of problem behavior, when you have not worked extensively with them in the past, or when their difficulties are particularly puzzling, complicated, or resistant to informal intervention. In these instances, a fairly formal assessment will help you gain a broad and objective view of the students' behavior.

Mrs. Armstrong has identified several extensive areas she should investigate with Monte, based on the reports she has received. She would like to assess how well he obeys the rules of the cafeteria, interacts with adults and responds to their directions, uses table manners, and gets along with peers and younger children. The procedures and guidelines in Chapters Four and Five can help her develop a survey level assessment for Monte that will be comprehensive, detailed, and accurate. In addition, Mrs. Armstrong will need the assistance of the cafeteria supervisors to get a complete account of Monte's behavior in that setting. The suggestions included in the text will help her make effective use of other personnel in conducting the assessment.

Reminders for completing survey level assessments When you are shortcutting survey level assessments, it is important to remember these points:

- *Consider the entire range of problems* students may have with their behavior, not just the things that are annoying or obtrusive.
- *List your observations in terms of expectations students do not meet,* not in terms of the problems they display.
- *Focus your attention on social behavior,* not just on violations of classroom rules and routines.

Step 3: Setting Priorities and Choosing a Target Skill

Review: The main reason for setting priorities is to specify the most important expectations from among the students' deficits, and thus to narrow the focus of an intervention to a single target skill. Setting priorities is one of the most important steps in preparing for an intervention because it allows you to concentrate your efforts on the single area of behavior that will have the greatest impact on improving students' social competence, rather than dissipating your energies across a variety of different problems.

Despite its importance, however, setting priorities and defining the target skills is fairly simple. The basic questions you should answer with this step are very straightforward:

- What priority level should you assign to each expectation the student does not meet?
- Which priority area should be the target skill for the intervention?

The following are options for streamlining.

Option I: Most streamlined approach Sometimes you can easily see which expectations not met should be designated top priorities, either because they stand out as major issues for the students, or because they are likely to have much more impact than the other items. In cases like these, you can quickly select the items that are most significant. You can then choose the single most important item to serve as the target skill, or alternatively, expand or consolidate the priority items to form a more broad-based target skill.

When Mrs. Armstrong looks over the list of expectations Marcia does not meet, she might notice that several items relating to class participation seem to stand out as more important than the others, especially since Marcia is fairly proficient in other social areas. She may decide that rather than choosing any single item like "raises hand before speaking," "adds comments to discussion," or "answers teacher questions," she will combine these into the broader target skill "participates actively during class discussions."

Option II: Intermediate streamlined approach In other cases, your choices for setting priorities will not be so clear. You might find several important items on the list of expectations not met, or you might have to decide between very different possibilities when choosing a target skill. In such cases, it is helpful to review the guidelines for establishing priorities that are outlined in Chapter Five. This review will help you weigh competing considerations and will assure that the items you choose as target skills are the most central and crucial to improving the students' social competence.

When she looks over the expectations Alfred fails to meet in the hallway and classroom, Mrs. Armstrong may have a hard time choosing a target skill. On the one hand, she has found that while the other students are joking with one another, Alfred tends to clown and engage in horseplay. Since this behavior is what stands out most during this time, she is thinking of making "engages in playful teasing and joking with peers" the target skill. On the other hand, she realizes that Alfred's clowning represents his inept attempt to stay in the flow of peer interactions, and she thinks that "initiates and sustains conversations" might be a better choice. To help her decide, Mrs. Armstrong could look over the list of guidelines. She might decide to focus on holding conversations because it is more broadly functional, will likely carry over to a wide range of situations, will improve his relationships with a larger number of peers, and is a prerequisite for many more advanced social skills.

Option III: Least streamlined approach At times you are likely to find that the list of expectations not met is so long or so complicated that you need to give careful consideration to each item before selecting a target skill. This more deliberate approach will be particularly important when you have not worked extensively with the students before, or when the range of problems is unusually complicated. In these cases, you should go back to the information in Chapter Five and conduct a careful selection of priorities.

Mrs. Armstrong has found from her assessment activities that Monte fails to meet a fairly large number of expectations, including "follows through on the directions of adults," "chooses compatible playmates," "shows good table manners," "keeps hands to self," "talks with neighbors about school events and class work," and "avoids or settles arguments." By choosing priorities in the systematic fashion described in Chapter Five—considering several guidelines, assigning a priority level of 1, 2, or 3 to each expectation, and finally deciding on a target skill for the intervention—Mrs. Armstrong can be sure she is considering the full range of Monte's problems and needs.

In Monte's case, she might conclude that his teasing and joking cause the broadest and most severe problems for him. On the one hand, he teases younger students until they cry or complain to adults. On the other hand, when he is teased, he becomes angry and flustered, swears, or displays some other inappropriate behavior. His behavior also creates problems for him with adults because he argues with them or defies their attempts to intervene. Mrs. Armstrong would thus choose "engages in playful teasing with classmates" as the target skill for Monte's intervention.

Reminders for setting priorities and picking a target skill No matter what approach you take for this step, you should follow these general guidelines:

- *Review the guidelines for choosing priorities* listed in Chapter Five if you have to choose between more than one potential target skill.
- *Choose a target skill that will have the greatest effect* on students' overall performance.
- *If appropriate, expand or consolidate high-priority items* to form a more broad-based target skill.
- *Avoid the natural impulse to choose problems that are most visible or annoying;* if you use shortcuts merely to encourage this haphazard approach, the intervention will be misdirected from the start.

Part II: Specific Level Assessment

Part I of the assessment process allows you to survey student deficits and choose a specific skill area to address with the interventions. The next stage is to conduct a specific level assessment to investigate *why* the students are not using the target skill. This assessment gives you a detailed and precise look at the students' performance by focusing on the basic abilities, component steps, and performance conditions the skill involves. These procedures offer an opportunity to examine the students' behavior from several different perspectives and vantage points so you can identify the particular areas of behavior that will be the primary goals for the intervention. The following sections outline the individual steps in the specific level assessment and discuss options for streamlining.

Step 4: Assessing Basic Abilities

Review: The basic abilities assessment looks at how students' raw abilities affect their performance of the target skill. The purpose of this stage of the specific level assessment is to determine whether students have the background knowledge and key enabling skills they need to make the judgments, perform the tasks, and display the other fundamental skills necessary for showing proficiency in the more advanced target skill. Conducting a basic abilities assessment requires you to address the following questions:

- What basic abilities does the target skill involve?
- How well does the student perform these abilities?
- What abilities might the student need to learn in the intervention (i.e., instructional goals)?

The following options are available for streamlining this step.

Option I: Most streamlined approach When you have worked quite closely with students in the past, you may be able to conduct much of the basic abilities assessment mentally, drawing on your prior knowledge. This process can go fairly quickly in cases where you already know the students have the necessary abilities (for instance, if they can use the target skill when they try their best), or when you already know that they lack important abilities (for instance, if they have a readily apparent learning or skill deficit). In such cases, you could make a quick list of key abilities needed to use the target skill, and mark down the ones (if any) you know students are lacking.

Mrs. Armstrong realizes she is already familiar enough with Marcia's abilities to conduct the basic abilities assessment quite quickly. She could make a short list of key abilities Marcia needs to participate in class:

- Is able to follow a class discussion.
- Is able to recognize when to speak.
- Is able to formulate a pertinent comment.
- Is able to speak at appropriate volume.

From her one-on-one work with the student, Mrs. Armstrong knows Marcia has all these abilities except the third one; she gets flustered easily and has difficulty expressing herself orally. Therefore, Mrs. Armstrong would list "Learn to formulate pertinent comments" as an instructional goal, to serve as a focus for Marcia's intervention.

Option II: Intermediate streamlined approach Even when you are quite familiar with the students you are assessing, you may still have questions about their ability level. In such cases, once you have outlined the fundamental abilities students must display and considered your prior knowledge about their ability level, you might need to structure one or two pointed assessment activities to fill in gaps in your knowledge.

Mrs. Armstrong might identify the following basic abilities Alfred must have to engage in conversations with his peers:

- Is able to follow course of conversation.
- Is able to speak on age-appropriate subjects.
- Is able to identify shifts in conversational topics.
- Is able to wait turn to speak.

Mrs. Armstrong realizes that Alfred's problems in this area are quite different from those Sandy had earlier. She knows, for example, that he can understand age-appropriate topics and can wait his turn to speak. But she will want to double-check some abilities. Using a simple check mark system and a reward to provide incentive, Mrs. Armstrong could quickly assess whether Alfred is able to follow the course of a conversation if he puts his mind to it, or whether he can identify shifts in topics if he pays close attention.

Option III: Least streamlined approach Although shortcuts are possible, a basic abilities assessment can become fairly complicated, especially when you lack crucial information about the students' abilities or have difficulty defining the pertinent abilities to investigate. You might decide that the issue of basic abilities seems central to your concerns for the students and that you want to investigate this area in depth. In such cases, it is helpful to prepare a detailed worksheet and conduct a formalized assessment as outlined in Chapter Six. In this way, you can be sure you will be gathering accurate, detailed information, and you will be able to focus on the question of abilities with a significant degree of attention and thoroughness.

As Mrs. Armstrong tries to identify the basic abilities for "engages in playful teasing with classmates," she realizes she has more questions than answers about Monte's ability level. As a result, she has difficulty picking out the central abilities she should investigate, and even more trouble deciding whether Monte has the abilities. She concludes that she will need to use a complete worksheet and conduct a full-scale assessment of Monte's basic abilities so her findings will be valid and clearly directed.

Reminders for basic abilities assessments Whether you go through this step mentally or conduct formal observations, keep these guidelines in mind when assessing basic abilities:

- *Phrase basic abilities in terms of what students are able to do,* as in "Is able to identify the topics of conversations."
- *Investigate students' abilities,* not their inclinations (what they *are able to* do, not what they *do*).

- *Begin each of your instructional goals with the phrase "learn to . . ."*—for example, "learn to identify topics in conversations."

These suggestions will help you formulate the findings as potential goals for the intervention.

Step 5: Assessing Component Steps

Review: The component steps assessment is designed to let you see how well students link together the discrete steps that make up the target skill. In a component steps assessment, you begin by breaking the target skill into a series of steps, then looking at how the students perform each step and how well they link the steps together into a coherent pattern of performance. This assessment addresses the following questions:

- What sequence of component steps does the target skill involve?
- Which of the steps represent difficulties for the student?
- Which steps might the student need to learn in the intervention (i.e., instructional goals)?

Below are some streamlining options.

Option I: Most streamlined approach If you have a solid knowledge of students' performance and difficulties, you may be able to go through the component steps assessment quite quickly and informally. To begin, you could review the sequence of steps that students must follow to meet the expectation, and then identify the steps where the performance pattern breaks down or becomes confused.

Mrs. Armstrong believes she is pretty familiar with Marcia's performance and her problems with class participation. Instead of conducting a lengthy, formal assessment, Mrs. Armstrong could sketch a list of the steps students follow when participating, and mark the steps (such as "pays attention to the discussion" and "raises hand to answer questions") that she knows Marcia has trouble completing. These steps will form the basis for her assessment findings, such as "learn to pay attention to the discussion," and "learn to raise hand and answer questions."

Option II: Intermediate streamlined approach At times you might have a fairly clear idea of which component steps students do not complete, but you may think some more investigation is in order. You might know the students do not complete the early steps in the sequence, but you might not know whether they have problems with some of the later steps because they may never get that far. In cases like these, you can simply mark down the steps you already know present problems and then conduct some quick assessment activities to investigate the remaining steps.

Mrs. Armstrong may know that Alfred does not choose appropriate peers for conversations and does not greet people appropriately, clowning or joking with them instead. As a result, he is out of most conversations before they begin, and Mrs. Armstrong does not really know how he would perform at later steps, such as limiting his comments to appropriate lengths, or responding to someone who joins the group later on. To fill in these gaps, she could assist Alfred in starting conversations with a group of peers, and draw back as the discussions progress to observe how well he completes the later component steps.

Option III: Least streamlined approach As with basic abilities, there will probably be times when you are not familiar enough with the students' performance to make judgments about which component steps they complete, or when you want to look more carefully at their performance of component steps because you feel this issue is central to the students' problems. In such cases, you probably should prepare a worksheet and conduct a full assessment as outlined in Chapter Seven. After assessing Monte's basic abilities, Mrs. Armstrong knows a lot more about his performance, but she does not feel confident enough to specify the component steps he has difficulty completing. Therefore, she will plan to conduct a full-scale assessment of him over the next few days.

Reminders for component steps assessments When you investigate the issue of component steps, here are some things to keep in mind:

- *Consider what students do under natural circumstances* (as opposed to basic abilities, which involve what they are able to do).
- *Identify clearly the starting and ending points* in the component steps sequence.
- *Begin each of your instructional goals with the phrase "learn to . . ."*— just as you did in the basic abilities step.

Step 6: Assessing Performance Conditions

Review: The performance conditions assessment is the most complex and subtle step of the specific level assessment process because you are investigating the circumstances in which students use the target skill. Completing a performance conditions assessment involves addressing more complicated issues, like these:

- What particular elements of timing, location, people, amount, or materials present difficulties or barriers to the student's performance of the target skill?
- Does the student respond appropriately to the cues these conditions provide?
- Does the student perform better under some conditions than others?
- What aspects of performance conditions might the student need to learn about (i.e., instructional goals)?

The following are options for streamlining.

Option I: Most streamlined approach Through working with students, you might already have some very clear ideas about their response to performance conditions. You may know how their social behavior changes as they move from location to location, which people they interact with best, and how well they recognize timing cues for their performance. In such cases, you need only note these observations and record some findings about the particular conditions students might work on in the intervention.

Mrs. Armstrong has already observed enough to know that when Marcia is in the back of the room, she is quieter than when she is in the front, that her comments in class are too short in duration, that she is more nervous in large groups and around boys than in small groups or with girls. Instead of conducting a detailed assessment, Mrs. Armstrong could simply note these items and formulate two or three goals ("Learn to make longer comments," "Learn to speak in larger groups," and so on) for possible work in the intervention. She would also want to note the conditions that Marcia responds to well so she can make use of this information when she plans the intervention.

Option II: Intermediate streamlined approach Despite your knowledge of the students' responses to performance conditions, you may still have areas you want to investigate a bit more. Perhaps you want to check how students perform the target skill with different groups of people, or take a closer look at how they time their performance. In such cases, you can supplement your notes with some observation procedures that concentrate on the areas where you have questions.

Although Mrs. Armstrong knows about Alfred's performance of conversational skills under some circumstances, she would like to investigate how his performance might vary between the hallway and the classroom, and which students he converses with most effectively. She could make some observations of his conversations in the hallway, and structure a few conversation groups in the classroom to check his performance with different types of students.

Option III: Least streamlined approach As the examples above show, streamlining a performance conditions assessment usually requires you to have particular familiarity with the students being assessed. In cases where you have not been able to observe them carefully, you will probably need to conduct a more detailed assessment of their response to performance conditions, as outlined in Chapter Eight. You should also consider a more complete assessment when you suspect that the students' behavior is strongly affected by their surroundings, or that teaching them to recognize and negotiate social conditions will probably be a central focus of the intervention.

The more Mrs. Armstrong learns about Monte's performance, the more she suspects that his greatest difficulties involve responding to the conditions for social interaction in the cafeteria. Mrs. Armstrong is not sure, however, to what degree Monte's problems relate to the other people in the cafeteria, to the location, or to other aspects of the lunch routine. To investigate these areas more thoroughly, Mrs. Armstrong will need to conduct a fairly systematic performance conditions assessment to obtain as complete a picture as she can of Monte's needs.

Reminders for performance conditions assessments In whatever streamlining approach you take, keep in mind the following points about the performance conditions assessment:

- *Consider all the different aspects of performance conditions,* even if you do not actually assess them all.
- *Note the conditions for which or under which students perform well* in addition to conditions that represent difficulties for them.
- *Once more, use the "learn to . . ." format* for your list of instructional goals.

Part III: Developing and Conducting Interventions

As we have stressed throughout the text, successful interventions depend less on how fancy or elaborate your procedures are than on how closely you match procedures to students' instructional needs. Even when you streamline the process of setting instructional goals and preparing the intervention plans, be sure that your goals are firmly in line with the information you have gathered, and that your procedures and activities are tightly focused, concise, and manageable even if you do not use extensive preplanning. Otherwise, you will find yourself involved in activities that stray from addressing the students' real needs, or that become too extensive or complicated for you to keep under close control. In the following sections, we discuss ways you can streamline the process of setting instructional goals and planning interventions.

Step 7: Setting Instructional Goals for Interventions

Review: If you have given careful attention to the steps of the specific level assessment, setting instructional goals for interventions should be a fairly straightforward task. This normally involves reviewing the findings or goals you set in the specific level assessment (steps 4, 5, and 6) and consolidating them into a few specific goals for the intervention. The instructional goals represent the skills or behavior students need to learn to make progress toward acquiring the target skill. The step of selecting these goals can be summed up in the following question:

- Based on the findings from the specific level assessment, what do the students need to learn to master the target skill?

The following are options for streamlining this step.

Option I. Most streamlined approach Often, you will be able to condense or consolidate the findings from your specific level assessment into a few clear instructional goals. Frequently the findings fall into simple groupings or tend to have repeated elements. In such cases, it is usually a simple task to pick out three to five solid goals on which to focus interventions. For example, when she looks over her findings for Marcia, Mrs. Armstrong might be able to narrow her list to the following instructional goals:

- Learn to attend to the topics of discussions.
- Learn to add pertinent comments of satisfactory length.
- Learn to speak in larger groups.

With these goals in mind, Mrs. Armstrong would be confident she can quickly develop an effective intervention for Marcia.

Option II. Intermediate streamlined approach In some cases, especially when you have made shortcuts in the survey level and specific level assessments, you might not be as certain of the strength and accuracy of your results. In these instances, you should double-check your conclusions with some quick follow-up observations. You can also discuss the validity and desirability of your goals with other personnel or even with students. In this way, you can make sure that the measures you used earlier, even though they were shortcuts, will give you a set of clearly directed goals for your intervention plans.

After Mrs. Armstrong reviews the assessment results from earlier steps, she might list the following preliminary goals for Alfred:

- Learn to select appropriate groups for conversing.
- Learn to greet peers appropriately.
- Learn to wait turn and listen to others.
- Learn to speak appropriately to girls.

As she thinks about these areas more carefully, she might feel she should double-check her conclusions, especially considering how badly misdirected her previous intervention with Alfred was and how many corners she has already cut in preparing this one. To recheck her goals, Mrs. Armstrong could conduct several short observations of Alfred's conversations and could discuss the goals with Mr. Wagner and Ms. Hernandez. Finally, she could show the goals to Alfred himself, both to prepare him for the upcoming intervention and to make sure he considers the goals worth attaining.

Option III. Most streamlined approach You should go through the process presented in Chapter Nine when you are trying to consolidate a complicated mix of findings, or when you are not sure how to organize and structure them for intervention plans. Mrs. Armstrong might observe that her findings for Monte are fairly extensive, and she now has many items to consider as she consolidates her list. Among her preliminary list of goals are the following:

- Learn to identify peers who might be potential friends.
- Learn to choose topics of conversation that are mutually interesting to peers.
- Learn to sustain conversations for longer durations without teasing.
- Learn to decide when and when not to tease.
- Learn to react to teasing by smiling, walking away, or otherwise not overreacting to the situation.

The process outlined in Chapter Nine will help her decide which items to combine as well as which to postpone for later work or to jettison completely.

Reminders for setting instructional goals The following are some guidelines to remember when you are setting instructional goals:

- *Continue to use the "learn to . . ." format.* This will help ensure that your goals represent legitimate aims for students.
- *Make sure the goals will help students meet the target skill.* It is important to remember the overall purpose of the intervention.
- *Avoid setting goals that are unrealistic or overly ambitious.* If students have serious deficits, it is better to set intermediate, achievable aims initially.

Step 8: Brainstorming and Developing Intervention Procedures

Review: The actual procedures and activities you develop for interventions need not be complicated or far reaching, but there should be enough contrast between them and the normal routine for the activities to be effective in eliciting changes in students' behavior. In addition, the procedures should be in line with the instructional goals established for the interventions. This step for devising intervention procedures includes both the free-ranging kind of brainstorming we described in Chapter Nine and the suggestions for further development and improvement we discussed in Chapter Ten. Often when you are streamlining the planning process, you will find that you can address these aspects of formulating procedures in combination and quickly devise a solid intervention plan.

Questions you will need to address when devising intervention procedures include these:

- In what order should the instructional goals be addressed?
- What procedures might be effective in addressing the instructional goals?
- How can your ideas for procedures be developed or improved?
- How will you address complex goals or the need for incentive?

To answer these questions, you will have to weigh carefully the resources available and the needs of the students. Below are some options for streamlining this step.

Option I: Most streamlined approach Many times, you will be able to make significant changes in students' social behavior, and do so very quickly, without planning complicated intervention procedures. In some cases, you may already have developed some promising ideas for intervention approaches while you were assessing the students' performance or planning instructional goals. In other cases, your more conventional teaching practices may work well to overcome the students' problems if you become more precise and consistent in using them, or if you focus them specifically on the instructional goals for the intervention. Usually you can overcome all but the most difficult problems in social behavior by helping students in the following ways:

- Making minor adjustments in normal activities and routines.
- Giving more explicit directions.

- Explaining expectations better.
- Making subtle changes in teaching lessons, formats, and instructional materials.
- Giving students more personalized attention and support.

All these fairly simple and straightforward changes from existing conditions can highlight or clarify what students must do to improve their social skills and emphasize the benefits they can derive from using these skills. Directed specifically at teaching the instructional goals, the changes can form the backbone of a quick but effective intervention plan.

As she reflects on Marcia's problems during the assessment, Mrs. Armstrong might be able to think of many good ideas for helping her develop the skills she needs. Mrs. Armstrong knows that Marcia responds very well to peer modeling and prompts, and that her incentive level for continuing to improve her status among her peers is already very high. Mrs. Armstrong feels that if she can build Marcia's confidence by starting with smaller groups and single-sex groups, and can improve Marcia's discussion skills by having her practice formulating responses and paying attention within her peer group, a very effective intervention could be put in place right away with only minimal planning.

Option II: Intermediate streamlined approach Sometimes, of course, planning intervention procedures takes more time, particularly when students' problems are difficult, or when students have been resistant to intervention efforts in the past. At these times, it is helpful to include in your brainstorming session colleagues, parents, or anyone else who might offer useful suggestions for improving the effectiveness of the intervention procedures.

Mrs. Armstrong will use this strategy in planning Alfred's intervention to help ensure that she is on the right track. She would like to structure the intervention around very specific role-playing activities that concentrate on conversational skills, and she will have Alfred work in the same group with Sally and other girls to provide context and incentive for him to improve his interactions. But remembering the failure of her previous intervention plans for Alfred, Mrs. Armstrong does not want to take any chances. She will write out her intervention ideas and will discuss them with Mr. Wagner and Ms. Hernandez. She also discusses her plans with Alfred's parents to get their views on how he is likely to respond to the procedures. Last, she will go over the plans with Alfred to gauge his likely reactions.

Option III: Least streamlined approach When you must consider a broader or more extensive range of procedures than you can address at one time, you should review Chapters Nine and Ten. The suggestions for intervention strategies in these chapters, as well as the suggestions for further development—such as working with colleagues and consulting other texts and instructional guides—can help you design creative, nonconventional approaches to improving social skills when the more common methods of providing instruction have not worked in the past. These resources will provide you with a wide array of instructional and incentive procedures for developing social skills in students, and you can combine and modify these procedures in many different ways to achieve a variety of instructional goals.

For example, Mrs. Armstrong can see that Monte's intervention procedures may need to be fairly extensive because his problems are complicated, and he has already shown himself to be fairly resistant to conventional forms of intervention. By going through the goals one by one and brainstorming a variety of possible procedures, as the text suggests, Mrs. Armstrong will be able to prepare a more comprehensive and more dynamic intervention. She also will benefit from the ten suggestions for improving interventions outlined in Chapter Ten, such as including in her planning the input and advice of the people who supervise cafeteria activities. Furthermore, she understands that she will need to make a particular effort in the intervention to address Monte's need for incentive. Following the full procedures outlined in the text will help her complete this complex process and devise the most effective intervention for Monte.

Reminders for developing intervention procedures Below are some guidelines for selecting intervention procedures:

- *Keep the procedures consistent* with the instructional goals of the intervention.
- *Select procedures that are realistic* in the context of existing lessons and classroom routines.
- *Make the procedures dynamic* enough to represent an interesting change for students.

Step 9: Coordinating and Scheduling the Intervention Activities

Review: All interventions for improving social skills involve some change or adjustment in the approach you use with students. The purpose of coordinating the intervention plan is to ensure that these changes coincide with the instructional goals of the intervention and that they are applied in a coherent, consistent, and timely manner. Clear intervention plans will help you coordinate and integrate the changes with ongoing activities, schedules, and routines, and use your resources efficiently. Chapter Ten discusses how to prepare an intervention script to coordinate the overall intervention plan as well as how to prepare a schedule to list the procedures, materials, and personnel you will employ each day. To complete this planning process you will need to address the following issues:

- How will the various intervention activities fit together?
- How will you schedule and coordinate the intervention procedures with ongoing routines and activities?
- What materials, personnel, and activities do you need to consider?

Option I: Most streamlined approach In some instances, the most effective and straightforward way to plan interventions is simply to put the new procedures in place and carry through with the intervention quickly, without making detailed plans or worksheets for implementing it. This approach is most applicable when the procedures are simple and straightforward, or when they involve making fairly minor adjustments in your teaching lessons or classroom routines.

Mrs. Armstrong might decide to implement her intervention plans for Marcia right away, without drawing up a formal script or schedule. The procedures she will carry out with Marcia require only minor changes in the existing routines of the classroom, and she can use the same format for Marcia's small group that she used in Sandy's intervention. Furthermore, Mrs. Armstrong wants to capitalize on Marcia's current readiness to learn; she realizes that the student's enthusiasm will be a real asset if she can start the intervention without delay.

Option II: Intermediate streamlined approach Of course, it is not always a good idea to begin an intervention without a written plan of some kind. When interventions involve more complicated or varied procedures, when the plans must be carefully coordinated over several days or with other settings and personnel, or when the problems being addressed are particularly difficult, it is usually advisable to write out at least a short sketch of the procedures and a schedule for implementing the activities.

Unlike Marcia's case, Alfred's intervention will require Mrs. Armstrong to do a little more planning because it will involve more complicated role-playing activities and will need to ensure that Alfred stays interested and on task. Mrs. Armstrong knows that if she implements the activities in an offhanded or haphazard fashion, Alfred will likely take this as an opportunity to return to his silly or clownish behavior. At the same time, her ideas are simple enough that she can probably outline them quickly without an extensive worksheet. Because the activities will be implemented in her own setting, she is confident that she can quickly incorporate them into her normal classroom planning. After she has prepared the materials for the role playing, she can draw up a simple description and timeline for the activities and make a quick list of the students who will be grouped together. Then she will be ready to begin the intervention.

Option III: Least streamlined approach The key factor that allows for streamlining intervention plans in the examples above is the relative simplicity of the intervention procedures. On the other hand, when your intervention requires a significant change in the normal routines, you will need a detailed and comprehensive plan to help keep activities in line with the instructional goals. Developing such a plan might require preparing timelines, scheduling equipment, designing new materials and lessons, coordinating personnel, and completing other related tasks. As Chapter Ten indicates, many of these details can be coordinated in an intervention script and schedule. All these aspects of a plan are particularly important when you use an instructional or incentive approach for the first time or in a new way, when you incorporate the procedures in new types of lessons and activities, when you focus on several students at once, or when you involve other people in helping with the intervention.

Mrs. Armstrong plans to carry out much of Monte's intervention in the cafeteria because this is where he is having the most difficulty. But using this setting will require the cooperation of other students and personnel, and a careful coordination with normal lunchtime routines and interactions. In addition, the procedures she has planned to improve Monte's incentive are fairly untested, in that she will be highlighting the natural outcomes of making friends and talking about conventional topics to replace his customary use of teasing as a way to gain attention. With all these considerations, Mrs. Armstrong realizes the intervention could quickly become unwieldy and disorganized without a clear script and schedule. By carefully preparing a detailed blueprint for the intervention, she will be sure she is considering the factors that are most important in influencing the intervention's effectiveness.

Reminders for preparing intervention plans Whether you draft intervention plans mentally or write them out on a detailed worksheet, you should consider the following points:

- *Apply the procedures in a deliberate and well-organized manner,* even if they are fairly informal.
- *Keep the activities manageable* and avoid implementing too many new procedures at once.
- *Include other students* in the plans (as Mrs. Armstrong did earlier with Luis) if you feel they might also benefit from the procedures.

Step 10: Monitoring the Intervention

Review: Monitoring the progress of interventions serves three important purposes: (a) it allows you to oversee and track the intervention activities, (b) it lets you evaluate the progress students are making in their behavior, and (c) it provides a basis for adjusting the procedures and deciding what needs to be done next. The results you obtain from observing the students' performance will help you decide whether to continue the intervention as planned, change the procedures in some deliberate way, or fade or discontinue the interventions altogether. When you plan your monitoring activities, you will need to answer the following questions:

- How will you keep track of the students' performance of the target skill?
- How will you know when the students are using the target skill effectively in all the settings that apply?
- What other questions or issues will you wish to monitor during the intervention?

Option I: Most streamlined approach The monitoring you do in interventions can vary greatly depending on the amount of progress students are making in acquiring target skills and on the complexity of the intervention procedures. In some cases, only one or two quick spot checks comparing the students' behavior to the standards will allow you to verify their achievement of the instructional goals.

Similarly, you may be able to keep track of most of the key issues you want to watch just by supervising the setting in your normal fashion.

Mrs. Armstrong might decide that she does not need an extensive monitoring procedure for Marcia, especially because of Marcia's relative competence in other social areas. Mrs. Armstrong could watch unobtrusively to learn whether Marcia enjoys practicing her participation in the small group, and whether she carries over this practice into real discussion situations. Mrs. Armstrong is confident that by observing Marcia's participation informally she will be able to tell fairly easily how the intervention is going and when it is time to start fading or discontinuing the procedures.

Option II: Intermediate streamlined approach Not every intervention can be effectively monitored with casual observation. In some cases, the procedures may be addressing several issues at once, or the nature of the activities may make it difficult for you to attend closely to the students' performance. Even with these cases, however, you may still be able to shortcut the monitoring process by noting the key issues to watch for (in addition to tracking the target skill) and making some elementary plans for evaluating these areas.

Mrs. Armstrong knows she will have to take more care with monitoring Alfred's intervention than with Marcia's because the procedures for Alfred are more complicated and difficult to supervise, and because Alfred's performance is likely to prove more problematic than Marcia's. At the same time, she is confident that she can devise her monitoring plan fairly quickly. She might begin by listing a few key issues, such as whether Alfred is beginning to enter conversations more effectively or whether he is learning better ways to address Sally and the other girls in his group. She then could make some plans for keeping track of these issues. She might decide, for example, to videotape the setting, because she will not be able to watch Alfred for much of the time. She also could plan to ask a few unobtrusive questions of the other students in Alfred's conversation groups, as they are likely to observe his behavior more closely than she can. By developing a few simple procedures like these, Mrs. Armstrong will be certain she can get a clear idea of how well Alfred is adapting to the intervention procedures and whether he is making progress toward learning the target skill.

Option III: Least streamlined approach You should use more formal, detailed methods of monitoring when the intervention results are likely to be complex or difficult to track, or when the issues you need to monitor are varied or involved. Detailed monitoring is especially important when you are working on very complicated problems, as these can cause you difficulty in determining the skills students need to learn at each successive step of the intervention, or in predicting with accuracy the types of instructional methods or incentive techniques that will work best with them. When students show many behavior problems, you can lose sight of the instructional goals and your attention can stray from the tight focus of the intervention, even when you have selected very useful and effective procedures. In these cases, it is important to prepare a monitoring worksheet, as described in Chapter Eleven, so you can keep track of exactly what is happening in the intervention.

Mrs. Armstrong realizes that her intervention for Monte will require very close monitoring. In part, this is because she is using untried procedures, is implementing them in a new setting, and is having other people assist with the activities. But it is also because the problems Monte displays are fairly complicated, and Mrs. Armstrong is unsure of how he will react to the activities. By planning out a careful, detailed monitoring worksheet, Mrs. Armstrong will be prepared to watch for any subtle effects the intervention might have as she evaluates the effectiveness of the procedures and makes adjustments if necessary.

Reminders for monitoring interventions You should remember these basic principles when taking shortcuts in monitoring an intervention:

- *Be sure you can obtain a detailed and complete overview* of how the intervention plans are proceeding.
- *Be prepared to spot subtle changes* in the students' behavior.
- *Keep an eye on the target skill and the top priority expectations;* remember that these are the main focuses of the intervention activities.

❍ Using a Worksheet to Guide Streamlining

In the examples above, we used Marcia's case to illustrate the most streamlined approaches, Alfred's for the intermediate streamlining, and Monte's for the intervention with the fewest shortcuts. The real advantage of streamlining, however, is that it allows you to tailor your investigation and planning to individual students by focusing more carefully on certain steps and quickly moving through others. This flexibility allows you to concentrate on the issues you find most important or have questions about, and to deal swiftly with the issues that are more straightforward.

In a more realistic version of the specific level assessment for Alfred, Mrs. Armstrong might focus most of her attention on his responses to performance conditions, and she could prepare a detailed worksheet and assessment plan for that step. At the same time, she might use a quick run-through approach to examine his basic abilities and component steps, as she is less concerned with his performance in these areas. Similarly, with Monte's intervention, Mrs. Armstrong might spend only a little time developing procedures and activities, but she might devote considerable time to preparing her script and monitoring the intervention, because other school staff and students will be involved and she must ensure that the activities of all these participants are coordinated.

As you review and select the key areas of assessment and intervention on which you will concentrate, a worksheet can help guide your decisions. Figure 13.1 shows a worksheet that Mrs. Armstrong used to help her decide how to streamline her intervention planning; it includes the entries she made for Monte. Her worksheet outlines the steps in the overall process, helping her select the activities on which to focus her attention in gathering information and planning interventions. The elements in her worksheet are discussed below.

Figure 13.1 Mrs. Armstrong's streamlining worksheet, showing planning for Monte's intervention.

Worksheet 13.1. Streamlining the Intervention Planning Process. Page *1* of *5*

Name: *Mrs. Armstrong* Date: *Dec. 4*

Student: *Monte* Grade: *5*

Setting(s): *Cafeteria, perhaps other unstructured settings*

Description of student behavior:

Monte is an average student academically, but he just barely gets by with his schoolwork. He does not participate well in most assignments unless he is paired with students who are willing to lead him through activities. Under these circumstances he cooperates very well and responds willingly to suggestions and feedback.

The problems Monte has in school are most apparent in unstructured settings like the cafeteria, playground, and rest rooms. At first glance, Monte gives the impression of being socially adept, but on closer examination his interactions appear to be superficial. He likes to join peer groups and be included in their activities, but he is merely tolerated by the groups because he lacks the experience and sophistication to contribute meaningfully to their interactions. Monte is somewhat naive, immature, and clumsy, and he uses these qualities to try to improve his status with peers; however, his awkwardness results in his being teased by peers. He usually goes along with and even joins in on the teasing, but only to a point. Then he gets upset and flustered, or starts swearing and name calling. This behavior makes him appear even more awkward and students usually tease him some more.

Monte also picks on younger students, and this behavior causes him a lot of trouble with adults, especially during lunchtime. When teachers try to intervene in his teasing, he often talks back to them, ignores their warnings, and disobeys their directions.

Areas or concerns to investigate:

Peer interactions during unstructured times

Approaches to making friends and seeking attention from peers

Interactions with younger students

Cooperating with adults and following their directions

Figure 13.1 *(continued)*

Worksheet 13.1 (continued)	Name: *Mrs. Armstrong* Student: *Monte*	Page *2* of *5*

Part I: Social Skills Curriculum and Survey Level Assessment

Step 1: Identifying the social skills curriculum

* What are the situations in the setting?
* What social expectations do average students meet in each situation?
* What standards define the minimum level of typical performance for meeting expectations?

Notes—how you plan to investigate these issues:

I will observe two or three days in the cafeteria next week. First, I need to list the activities in the routine starting when students enter the lunch line. Then I will describe the expectations and standards. This will involve doing observations, talking with lunch supervisors, and perhaps talking with some fifth graders.

Step 2: Conducting the survey level assessment

* Which expectations from the social skills curriculum does the student fail to meet?

Notes—how you plan to investigate this issue:

I will need to conduct a full assessment of Monte, particularly focusing on expectations that pertain to seeking attention from peers, interacting with younger children, and talking with adults and following their directions.

Step 3: Setting priorities and choosing a target skill

* Which expectations not met by the student should stand as priorities for intervention?
* Which priority area should serve as the target skill for the intervention?

Notes—how you plan to investigate these issues:

I'll need to look closely again at the guidelines for setting priorities, because there are a lot of expectations Monte doesn't meet. Choosing skills that are functional, that improve his status in the group and that are valued by peers and adults will be important considerations in selecting priority 1 expectations.

Figure 13.1 *(continued)*

Worksheet 13.1 (continued)	Name: *Mrs. Armstrong* Student: *Monte*	Page *3* of *5*

Part II: Specific Level Assessment

Step 4: Assessing Basic Abilities

* What basic abilities does the target skill involve?
* How well does the student perform these abilities?
* What abilities might the student need to learn in the intervention ("Findings")?

Notes—how you plan to investigate these issues:

I must look closely at Monte's basic abilities for engaging in playful teasing. Sometimes it looks like he doesn't know what to do besides being angry, or even why students tease him so much. I'll have to prepare a worksheet for the assessment. One area I know I should look at is whether Monte is able to recognize and interpret people's reactions to his behavior.

Step 5: Assessing component steps

* What sequence of component steps does the target skill involve?
* Which of the steps represent difficulties for the student?
* Which steps might the student need to learn in the intervention ("Findings")?

Notes—how you plan to investigate these issues:

I should do a comprehensive assessment with Monte. I'll need to watch closely for when teasing among peers begins, when it ends, and when Monte's behavior starts to cause problems for him—when the teasing goes beyond being playful.

Step 6: Assessing performance conditions

* What elements of performance conditions present difficulties for the student?
* Does the student respond appropriately to the cues these conditions provide?
* Does the student perform better under some conditions than others?
* What aspects of performance conditions might the student need to learn ("Findings")?

Notes—how you plan to investigate these issues:

With this assessment I need to look at the areas of Time, People, and Amount. I wonder how well he keeps up with the progression of the group's interaction, whether certain people or the group size cause him problems, and whether he recognizes his limits and the group's limits for teasing. There will probably be a number of other areas I should look at as well. This assessment needs to be fairly detailed.

Figure 13.1 *(continued)*

Worksheet 13.1 (continued)	Name: *Mrs. Armstrong*	Page *4* of *5*
	Student: *Monte*	

Part III. Developing and conducting interventions

Step 7: Setting instructional goals for interventions

* Based on the findings from the specific level assessment, what does the student need to learn to master the target skill?

Notes—how you plan to address this issue:

I have nine different findings from my specific level assessment, so I will have to consolidate and combine some areas. I need to check back on how to do this so my goals are tightly focused. Maybe I can hold off working on some of these areas for now.

Step 8: Brainstorming and developing intervention procedures

* What procedures might be effective in addressing the instructional goals?
* In what order should the instructional goals be addressed?
* How can your ideas for procedures be developed or improved?
* How will you address complex goals or the need for incentive?

Notes—how you plan to address these issues:

I should meet with all the teachers who supervise the fifth-grade lunch period and share my results. Then we can brainstorm some intervention procedures. Maybe Mr. Wagner and Ms. Hernandez have some ideas too. We should address each instructional goal separately and decide the order in which we'll work on them.

Step 9: Coordinating and scheduling intervention activities

* How will the various intervention activities fit together?
* How will you coordinate the intervention procedures with ongoing routines?
* What materials, personnel, and activities do you need to consider?

Notes—how you plan to address these issues:

We need to be well organized because there will be four of us working with Monte. We will prepare a script to help us coordinate the procedures. I can start in the classroom with some videotape modeling and rehearsal activities, and maybe Mr. Wagner can give directions and rehearsal before Monte goes to lunch. But most of the intervention should take place in the cafeteria. We all need to make sure Monte practices his skills as he learns them, so we should plan for this too. Our plan should also involve some of the students who tease him a lot. I need to review how to prepare a comprehensive plan.

Figure 13.1 *(continued)*

Worksheet 13.1 (continued)	Name: *Mrs. Armstrong* Student: *Monte*	Page *5* of *5*

Part III (continued).

Step 10: Monitoring the intervention

* How will you keep track of the student's performance of the target skill?
* How will you know when the student has learned the target skill sufficiently?
* What other questions or issues will you wish to monitor during the intervention?

Notes—how you plan to address these issues:

Some key areas we should look at include these:

Is Monte still being teased as much as before?
Does he react to the teasing any better in peer groups?
Does he interact or fit in better?
Does he still pick on younger children?
How is he reacting to the procedures we are using?
Are teachers still reporting that he talks back or ignores them?

We will need to prepare a monitoring form to help us all keep close tabs on these areas. I will need to review this section of the text again.

Description of Student Behavior and Circumstances

The worksheet begins with a place for describing the students and/or situation you will be working with. In this space, Mrs. Armstrong has made some notes on what she knows about each student's behavior and circumstances. When she is working with new students like Monte, she provides basic information about the problems they are having in their interactions as well as their strengths or talents on which she can build an intervention. For students like Alfred with whom she has already worked, she would center her notes on what she hopes to achieve next and the specific behavioral areas she wishes to address. The description also includes a brief note on the situations Mrs. Armstrong will be investigating, especially important in this case as she has not looked at these settings before.

Outline of Steps in the Assessment and Intervention Process

The body of the streamlining worksheet lays out the steps of the assessment and intervention process, and lists questions for the information you need to obtain. Depending on what you already know about the students and their circumstances, you may be able to answer the questions easily with a little reflection, or you may need to do some in-depth observation or investigation. Remember, although you will stress some steps more than others, *none of them should be ignored.* You should review the questions each step presents and consider carefully how you will answer them for the students and situations you are investigating.

Notes on How to Complete Each Step

On the worksheet under each step there is a section for you to make notes about how you will proceed. After reviewing the questions listed for a step, you can describe in your notes the approach you will use to address these issues for the selected students. Figure 13.1 shows Mrs. Armstrong's notes on how she will answer the questions listed for each step, including an indication of the information she already has and a description of the approach she will use to obtain any additional information she needs. Notice that Mrs. Armstrong does not use this note-taking section to list expectations, assessment results, goals, or intervention plans; if she needs to write out these elements of her plan, she can use the worksheets presented in the earlier chapters. The notes she takes on this worksheet help her review each step and make plans for completing the intervention planning process.

As Mrs. Armstrong's entries indicate, she is careful to carry out her plans for completing each step before she proceeds to the next step. This approach allows her to account at each stage of her planning for the information she has gained from the previous steps. For example, her notes for assessing Monte's basic abilities in Step 4 are centered on the target skill "Engages in playful teasing with classmates." Without first completing the process she outlined in Step 3 for selecting a target skill, she could not make these plans for further assessment. Similarly, the notes she makes in Step 9 for coordinating the intervention will not be helpful unless they are based on work she has already completed.

Streamlining can thus be a very important tool for adapting the procedures and principles outlined in the text to the needs and characteristics of individual students. No matter what approach you take to streamlining, however, do not ignore completely any of the steps in the assessment and intervention process. When you decide to shortcut a particular step, you should consider the questions and issues the step involves and be sure to achieve the basic aims of the step even if you do not go through it in detail. In this way your assessments and interventions will remain clearly focused and aligned with the students' needs, and you will avoid the pitfall of using streamlining merely to develop haphazard and slipshod interventions.

❍ Summary

When to Use a Systematic Approach

1. Streamlining the intervention planning process will help to improve the student's social skills as rapidly as possible.
2. The amount of shortcutting will depend on an understanding of social expectations and the students' abilities and circumstances.
3. A systematic and deliberate approach should be used in the following circumstances:
   a. when addressing difficult and long-standing problems in behavior
   b. when working on problems not encountered before
   c. when working with students who have severe learning and behavior problems
4. Streamlining activities should be tailored to the individual students for whom interventions are planned.
5. When streamlining a plan, all the steps in the assessment and intervention planning process should be considered.

Streamlining the Assessment and Intervention Process

1. The key to successful streamlining is understanding each step in the assessment and intervention planning process.
2. The steps pertaining to the social skills curriculum and survey level assessment are the following:
   a. identify the social skills curriculum
   b. conduct the survey level assessment
   c. set priorities and choose a target skill
3. The steps in specific level assessment are the following:
   a. assess basic abilities
   b. assess component steps
   c. assess performance conditions

4. The steps for developing and conducting interventions are the following:
   a. set instructional goals
   b. brainstorm and develop intervention procedures
   c. coordinate and schedule intervention activities
   d. monitor interventions

Using a Worksheet to Guide Streamlining

1. The worksheet to guide streamlining activities includes the following parts:
   a. a description of student behavior and circumstances
   b. an outline of the steps in the assessment and intervention process
   c. notes on how to complete each step

Examples for Chapter 13

Example 13a

Paulie is an above-average first grader. Ms. Quincy is concerned about Paulie's interactions with peers, his participation in classroom discussions, and his following teacher directions. She is also concerned about his physical and emotional behavior, because he has been diagnosed as having childhood depression. At times he becomes so entranced that he does not react when called upon or when other students talk to him. Ms. Quincy has noticed that he sometimes seems tired, slurs his speech, and walks with a halting, unsteady gait.

On this page of the streamlining worksheet, Ms. Quincy planned the first steps for assessing Paulie's difficulties with social behavior and his suspected health problems.

Worksheet 13.1 (continued)	Name: *Ms. Quincy* Student: *Paulie*	Page *2* of *5*

Part I: Social Skills Curriculum and Survey Level Assessment

Step 1: Identifying the social skills curriculum

* What are the situations in the setting?
* What social expectations do average students meet in each situation?
* What standards define the minimum level of typical performance for meeting expectations?

Notes—how you plan to investigate these issues:

It is usually possible to revise or expand an existing social skills curriculum to include new situations or skill areas. ➤ *Expand social skills curriculum for the class to include small group activities. Add expectations for volunteering and following directions.*

Step 2: Conducting the survey level assessment

* Which expectations from the social skills curriculum does the student fail to meet?

Notes—how you plan to investigate this issue:

Information from a survey level assessment can provide crucial information in diagnosing physical and psychological problems. ➤ *Conduct a thorough assessment of Paulie focusing on interactions with classmates and teacher and on participation in group activities. Check with foster parents and other teachers to see how he interacts in other settings. Talk with Ms. Thurman, the nurse, Ms. Gomez, the school psychologist, and Mrs. Winston, the physical therapist, about his physical behavior.*

To follow up on suspected medical or psychological problems, seek assistance from other school and community resources. ➤ *Other areas to check:*

- *Is he under a doctor's care? Has he had a recent physical exam?*
- *Does he take medication? If so, check with nurse on dosage level and possible side effects of the medication.*
- *Ask nurse to check on seizures, allergies, other medical problems.*

Step 3: Setting priorities and choosing a target skill

* Which expectations not met by the student should stand as priorities for intervention?
* Which priority area should serve as the target skill for the intervention?

Notes—how you plan to investigate these issues:

Even when health care professionals have been consulted, it is important to carry through with assessment and intervention planning rather than wait for a diagnosis. ➤ *My assessment of Paulie showed a wide variety of expectations Paulie does not meet. I need to review the guidelines for setting priorities in Chapter Five.*

Example 13b

Roland, a tenth grader, is below average academically and receives at-risk services. He responds well in class to teacher directions and feedback, but he annoys people by volunteering for almost every question regardless of whether or not he knows the answer. During unstructured times, Roland usually watches peer activities from the sidelines because he has difficulty joining groups and sustaining interactions. To compound these difficulties, many students complain about or make fun of his body odor.

Mr. Hudson, the at-risk coordinator and school counselor, decided to work with Roland to improve his social interactions. After completing Steps 1 to 6, Mr. Hudson selected "Joining peer groups and holding conversations" as the target skill, and has conducted an informal specific level assessment of Paulie's behavior during group conversations. This page shows the notes Mr. Hudson made for setting instructional goals and developing intervention plans.

Worksheet 13.1 (continued)	Name: *Mr. Hudson* Student: *Roland*	Page *4* of *5*

Part III. Developing and conducting interventions

Step 7: Setting instructional goals for interventions

- Based on the findings from the specific level assessment, what does the student need to learn to master the target skill?

Notes—how you plan to address this issue:

I have ten different findings. I will need to consolidate them into about three or four instructional goals. I will check Chapter Nine and review the guidelines again. Keep "learn to improve personal hygiene" as separate area.

A review of the text can help recall key concepts and guidelines for planning interventions.

Step 8: Brainstorming and developing intervention procedures

- What procedures might be effective in addressing the instructional goals?
- In what order should the instructional goals be addressed?
- How can your ideas for procedures be developed or improved?
- How will you address complex goals or the need for incentive?

Notes—how you plan to address these issues:

Roland should respond well to modeling, role playing, prompts, and discussion groups. It should be fairly easy to come up with some procedures now that the goals are set. I will go over the goals with Roland to see what ideas he has for procedures. Also, I should check with his teachers to see which classmates I can involve in activities.

I'll work with Mr. Hadley in gym on a way to improve Roland's hygiene. I should also call his foster parents to see if I can get their help.

Some steps in the planning process can usually be completed without detailed worksheets or extensive effort.

Note that Mr. Hudson completes each step before making plans for addressing the next step.

Step 9: Coordinating and scheduling intervention activities

- How will the various intervention activities fit together?
- How will you coordinate the intervention procedures with ongoing routines?
- What materials, personnel, and activities do you need to consider?

Notes—how you plan to address these issues:

I can schedule about 15–20 minutes before school to carry out the intervention and can meet with Roland after school to review activities. Before and after his classes, I can have Roland's teachers oversee his interactions and prompt or coach him. We will use Worksheet 10.1 to organize our plan with a script.

Chapter worksheets are helpful for steps that require detailed planning or complicated procedures.

Mr. Wagner's Case Study

Mr. Wagner has decided to develop an intervention plan for Milly, whose performance in his class is below average. Milly is hesitant about participating in class activities unless Mr. Wagner calls on her or works with her individually. When he goes over an activity with her she usually starts the assignment but quickly loses interest. If classmates try to help her, she acts as though she doesn't want the help. She also does not participate well in study or project groups. This page shows the first three steps of Mr. Wagner's streamlining worksheet.

Worksheet 13.1 (continued)	Name: *Mr. Wagner* Student: *Milly*	Page *2* of *5*

Part I: Social Skills Curriculum and Survey Level Assessment

Step 1: Identifying the social skills curriculum

* What are the situations in the setting?
* What social expectations do average students meet in each situation?
* What standards define the minimum level of typical performance for meeting expectations?

Notes—how you plan to investigate these issues:

I will use the "small group activity" situation from my social skills curriculum. This seems to have been a good area for working with Granville.

> The planning process must be personalized to match the characteristics of individual students. Mr. Wagner should review the social skills curriculum and consider adjustments or additions that will ensure the best context for assessing Milly's behavior.

Step 2: Conducting the survey level assessment

* Which expectations from the social skills curriculum does the student fail to meet?

Notes—how you plan to investigate this issue:

I know Milly has difficulty giving and accepting help, staying on task, and asking questions of the teacher. However, I think her basic problem is with motivation and low self-esteem.

> Streamlining should be used to guide thoughtful and deliberate planning, not to state preconceived notions about the student's behavior. This step should note ways of investigating Milly's deficits.

Step 3: Setting priorities and choosing a target skill

* Which expectations not met by the student should stand as priorities for intervention?
* Which priority area should serve as the target skill for the intervention?

Notes—how you plan to investigate these issues:

A priority area for Milly is "cooperates with partners in doing group project." I will use this as my target skill.

> Entries on the worksheet should describe plans for completing each step, rather than answer the questions.

CHAPTER 14

Teaching Social Competence to Groups of Students

When discussing social skills, most teachers express their primary concerns as the problem behavior of a few particular students in their classrooms or schools. For this reason we have focused our discussion on designing and implementing interventions for individual students. But while the methods we have presented can be very effective in examining student deficits and generating practical solutions, this approach is essentially reactive—like looking for fires and putting them out. A broader and more beneficial approach to improving social skills is one that is proactive. With a proactive approach, the procedures are implemented not as individual interventions but as instructional lessons that are carried out as an integral part of classroom and school programs.

By broadening social skills instruction to groups of students, you can help them advance to even higher levels of social maturity and competence in their interactions—essentially preventing the fires before they start. In this chapter, we show how to apply the concepts we have presented in the text in more far-reaching and effective ways, by integrating social skills instruction into your ongoing educational program. We also explore ways to help students improve their social skills above and beyond minimum levels of competence.

❍ Adapting the Intervention Approach to Groups of Students

The principles of teaching social skills to groups of students are essentially the same as those you have learned in working with individual students. The basic foundation for this approach is the social skills curriculum we discussed in Chapters Two and Three. As we mentioned in those chapters, you can use the process of developing a social skills curriculum to analyze the expectations of any setting you wish to examine, and to prepare lessons and interventions to bring students' behavior up to the average standards of performance. Now our focus shifts

Techniques for planning interventions can also be applied to group instruction.

to developing programs of instruction for the group as a whole, to help students go beyond this minimum level of competence.

A well-defined social skills curriculum is central to this effort. As the term *curriculum* suggests, the list of social expectations we described in Chapters Two and Three can be far more than just a tool for assessing individual student problems. It can be used in much the same ways as you would use a math or social studies curriculum, to plan and implement social skills instruction for all your students. In the following sections, we offer suggestions for using the social skills curriculum to design instructional lessons for your whole class. Table 14.1 lists the steps we will discuss.

Most of the steps for planning group lessons are comparable to the ones you would follow in developing an individual intervention. Therefore, we will direct our discussion toward the activities that are unique to working with larger groups, or that require major adaptations in the procedures we have described before, and move quickly over information we have already covered in previous chapters. Our presentation will, by necessity, describe a formalized and systematic approach to preparing lessons, but after considering what is involved in completing the steps, you should be able to shortcut the process, as discussed in Chapter Thirteen.

Step 1: Choosing the Settings, Situations, and Groups You Will Address

You should begin planning group instruction by identifying the subject matter area or the setting in which the lessons will be carried out, and the group that will par-

TABLE 14.1 Steps in developing group instruction for teaching social skills

Step 1:	Choose the settings, situations, and groups you will address.
Step 2:	Identify expectations you will consider addressing.
Step 3:	Assign priorities and choose target skill(s) for the lessons.
Step 4:	List key abilities, steps, and conditions for the target skills.
Step 5:	Conduct informal assessment and list instructional goals.
Step 6:	Brainstorm prospective procedures for addressing instructional goals.
Step 7:	Develop and improve lesson plans.
Step 8:	Coordinate and schedule lesson plans.
Step 9:	Prepare monitoring procedures for overseeing the lessons.

ticipate in the lessons. This information will set the context for the specific skill areas and procedures you will teach. As always, it is a good idea to use a worksheet to help guide your planning. Figure 14.1 shows the worksheet Mrs. Armstrong filled out for her class. The worksheet shows that she is planning her lessons for her morning fifth-grade social studies class.

Step 2: Identifying Expectations to Consider Addressing

As in designing effective interventions, the most crucial step in planning social skills instruction for the class is deciding what to teach. Many teachers' first impulse when approaching social skills instruction is to look for new techniques or commercial programs that seem promising or flashy. Although many of these can be helpful for teaching certain types of social skills, they cannot substitute for first constructing a well-targeted instructional plan. For this reason, you should first concentrate your planning on setting the *goals* rather than the *methods* of instruction. Such a plan is based on a careful consideration of the full range of social expectations students must master.

The social skills curriculum can be used as a starting point for identifying the particular expectations or skill areas that will provide the foundation for a well-designed program of instruction. You can begin deciding what to teach by looking over the social expectations for each situation you are concerned with and listing those you might focus on. If you have not previously prepared a social skills curriculum for this particular setting, you should be able to adapt or expand on the information you have obtained about other settings, following the process outlined in Chapter Thirteen for shortcutting curriculum description.

This step corresponds roughly with the survey level assessment we described in Chapter Four. Your objective is to select from the list of expectations several

Figure 14.1 Mrs. Armstrong's worksheet for planning group instruction.

Worksheet 14.1. Planning Social Skills Instruction for Groups of Students. Page *1* of *3*

Name: *Mrs. Armstrong* Date: *Dec. 11*

Step 1. Groups/Settings to be included in instruction

5th-grade morning social studies class—class discussions and breaks between classes.

Step 2. Social expectations to consider addressing in instruction

A. List expectations in the setting that pose problems for many students:

Criticizes other students' work in a diplomatic manner
Recognizes and responds to nonverbal cues
Accepts criticism and feedback from peers

B. List expectations that are unclear, implicit, or applied inconsistently:

Expresses personal opinions within context of class activity
Shows tolerance for other students' feelings and moods
Responds appropriately to teacher and peer feedback

C. List expectations you want to modify, emphasize, or add to the curriculum:

Stays on topic in class discussions
Talks on age-appropriate subjects
Uses "cool" language
Defers to judgments of popular students

D. List groups of expectations that can be taught together as a unit:

Chooses conversational topics that match interests of the group
Uses greetings effectively
Takes turn to speak
Accepts other students' opinions

Figure 14.1 *(continued)*

Worksheet 14.1 (continued)	Name: *Mrs. Armstrong*	Page *2* of *3*

E. List expectations that students have difficulty applying or carrying over to other settings:

Handles disagreements and teasing in a diplomatic manner (negotiates without

Step 3. Priority expectations/target skill(s) for instruction

Participates appropriately in whole class discussions

Also: Responds appropriately to criticism

Expresses opinions in nonthreatening manner

Step 4. Key abilities, steps, and conditions to consider for teaching target skill

Is able to remember background information on discussion subject

Is able to recognize verbal and nonverbal cues

Listens to the teacher's directions and guidelines for discussing the topics

Reviews materials or visuals pertaining to the topic

Recalls what has already been said about the topic

Considers ideas and opinions about the topic and weighs what others have said

Formulates comments or questions about the topic

Waits turn or watches for an opening in the discussion before speaking

Makes statements or expresses opinions in a diplomatic manner

Times comments and reactions to ongoing conditions

Recognizes how long and how often to speak

Reacts appropriately to neighbors and other classmates

Figure 14.1 *(continued)*

Worksheet 14.1 (continued)	Name: *Mrs. Armstrong*	Page *3* of *3*

Step 5. Instructional goals for group instruction

Learn to *listen to teacher directions and prepare for discussion*

Learn to *consider ideas and opinions of others in discussion*

Learn to *wait turn or watch for openings before speaking (some students)*

Learn to *formulate diplomatic, nonjudgmental comments and questions (some students)*

Learn to ______________________

Step 6. Brainstorming ideas for addressing goals

You may use Worksheet 9.1 to complete this step.

Step 7. Developing and improving lesson plans

You may use Worksheet 9.1 and the suggestions in Chapter Ten to complete this step.

Step 8. Coordinating and scheduling lesson plans

You may use Worksheets 10.1 and 10.2 to complete this step.

Step 9. Preparing monitoring procedures to oversee the instruction

You may use Worksheet 11.1 to complete this step.

TABLE 14.2 Guidelines for choosing expectations to consider for group instruction

- Look for expectations that pose problems for many students.
- Look for expectations that are unclear, implicit, or applied inconsistently.
- Look for expectations you want to modify, emphasize, or add.
- Look for expectations that can be taught together.
- Look for expectations that students have difficulty carrying over.

items or skill areas for which you think students can benefit from deliberate, focused attention. The following guidelines, summarized in Table 14.2, will help you make this selection.

Look for Expectations That Pose Problems for Many Students

One reason social skills are often overlooked when teachers plan instruction is that most students learn these skills naturally or incidentally as part of other ongoing activities. But as you look through the social skills curriculum, you are likely to notice some expectations that pose difficulties for a significant number of students. As Mrs. Armstrong reviews her social skills curriculum, she can probably pick out certain items that pose problems not only for individual students like Sandy, Alfred, or Granville, but for a substantial minority of the class. She may note that many of her students have problems giving or accepting criticism, or that several have difficulty picking up on nonverbal cues in conversations and class discussions. Even for the majority who do meet these expectations, Mrs. Armstrong may find that they could benefit from practice to refine their behavior and develop more consistent and stronger performance patterns. The worksheet in Figure 14.1 shows these particularly challenging expectations as Mrs. Armstrong listed them.

Look for Expectations That Are Unclear, Implicit, or Applied Inconsistently

Social expectations are often much less clear-cut than subject matter demands, because they are not tied to concrete instructional materials and lessons, or outlined in published curriculum guides. They can change dramatically, depending on circumstances; they may involve unstated or peer-set demands; or they may be inconsistent with other expectations in the situation. For instance, in a given situation, it is not unusual for teachers to have one set of demands and for classmates to have another set. Most students learn to recognize and negotiate these complexities with a reasonable degree of success. But for some students, the subtle and hidden expectations and the discrepancies that may occur among them can represent a confusing and frustrating maze of demands. Other students may not even recognize these types of complexities. As you look over your list of social expectations, watch for items that from the students' point of view may seem particularly unclear or inconsistent. By choosing these items for instruction, you can not only help students develop the skills they need to meet the expectations, but you can also clarify for the students what the expectations actually are and how to interpret them (Bauer & Sapona, 1991; Campbell & Siperstein, 1994).

When Mrs. Armstrong considers the difficulties Granville and some of his classmates have working in small groups, she may see that the expectations for this situation are actually quite complex. Students must not only follow her instructions in completing the assignments, but they must also negotiate and coordinate their behavior with their classmates' demands, which sometimes seem to conflict with what Mrs. Armstrong expects. She may continue to tell students to keep their discussion on the topics she assigns, whereas individuals within the group may try to direct the discussion to their more immediate interests and concerns. Mrs. Armstrong may wish to teach the whole class how to reconcile differences in social demands like these, or show them how these differences can sometimes complement one another or be used to their advantage in doing the assigned work. She might wish to teach them how to express their personal opinions or pursue their interests in the projects she assigns on current events. She may also note a few other related expectations that seem unclear or implicit, such as responding to teacher and peer feedback or being more responsive to other students' feelings or moods. Figure 14.1 shows that she added these expectations to her worksheet.

Look for Expectations You Want to Modify, Emphasize, or Add

In Chapter Three we stressed the importance of defining expectations by what students actually do, not by what we want them to do. We indicated that with this approach, the social skills curriculum would accurately portray the demands of the setting, and would assist you in comparing an individual student's behavior to that of the peer group. In teaching social skills with a group focus, however, you have an opportunity to influence these expectations in a carefully planned fashion (Ford, Davern, & Schnorr, 1992; Campbell & Siperstein, 1994). As you look over the curriculum, you may spot expectations that you wish to modify to raise the students' minimum or average levels of behavior. You could exert more control over expectations that apply too haphazardly or that should be integrated more closely with ongoing classroom routines. You could modify standards that are too lax—or too demanding—and help students perform to the level of the new standards. You may wish to add new expectations to improve the students' overall level of competence. Finally, you could change or try to deemphasize peer-set demands that work in opposition to students' achieving academic goals or that encourage childish, petty, or immature behavior. You should make note of expectations like these that you wish to alter or add to the curriculum so you can include them as possible areas to address in your classroom program.

Mrs. Armstrong may feel that the standard for the expectation "stays on topic in class discussions" is more relaxed than she wants it to be, because many of the students get off track, start bickering, and lose sight of the original objectives for the activities. She thinks she should make this expectation more demanding so it will give students a clearer purpose for their interactions. She may also conclude that she needs to exert more influence over the expectations for peer interactions during independent work times and transitions between activities because the expectations in these situations—mostly set by students—can be arbitrary and petty at times. She feels that if she were to encourage the class to set clearer guidelines for these informal interactions, the less socially competent students could more easily identify and meet the expectations. Thus, you can list any new or more advanced expectations you would like your class to meet, or include areas in which the stronger application of existing expectations would be beneficial to the group. Figure 14.1 shows the expectations Mrs. Armstrong may address in her instructional plans for the group.

Look for Expectations That Can Be Taught Together

For purposes of clarity, we have treated expectations as distinct demands in each situation and have tried to address them individually for conducting assessments and designing interventions. In reality, of course, many expectations are closely linked to one another when they are put into practice in school settings. Students often must respond to several expectations simultaneously or shift their behavior quickly to meet different types of expectations as conditions in the setting change. When you design social skills instruction for the class as a whole, you may want to teach students about the relationships among expectations, or teach the expectations in related groupings to help students develop more effective and dynamic behavioral patterns. Mrs. Armstrong may note that choosing conversational topics that match the interests of the group is closely tied to other conversational skills the students have difficulty with, such as using greetings effectively, taking turns in speaking, and showing sensitivity to other students' moods and feelings. She may wish to develop instructional lessons that highlight these and other related expectations so she can teach them as a coherent unit on improving conversations. Figure 14.1 shows examples of items Mrs. Armstrong might decide to work on.

Look for Expectations That Students Have Difficulty Carrying Over

Even when they have the skills for competent social performance, students often have difficulty applying these skills to the various circumstances where they should be used. It is not unusual for students to display proficient social behavior in structured classroom settings but fail to demonstrate the same behavior in less formal situations. When you see that students in your class have problems carrying certain skills over to other settings and situations, you can direct your group lessons toward improving these areas of performance.

Mrs. Armstrong has often noticed that students handle their disagreements and teasing in a fairly friendly, straightforward, and diplomatic manner when she or one of the other teachers is close by or when the students are working on assigned tasks that include clear guidelines for their behavior. Under less supervised or more informal circumstances, however, the students often revert to petty bickering, arguing, and making threats. Mrs. Armstrong believes that the students have the necessary skills but that she needs to help them learn to apply the skills to a wider variety of situations, particularly those in which teachers are not close by.

She could consider areas like these in the instructional lesson she plans for the class and has added them to her planning worksheet as shown in Figure 14.1.

Listing Expectations on the Planning Worksheet

As you choose expectations and skill areas you might want to address in your lesson plans, you can write them on the planning worksheet. Note that Mrs. Armstrong will not address all the items she listed on the worksheet; like the "Expectations Not Met" list that resulted from the survey level assessment, this list summarizes the range of social skills that she will consider for instruction. Remember that with this step you should consider the full range of expectations that present difficulties for students and list any items that could substantially improve their maturity and social development.

Step 3: Assigning Priorities and Choosing Target Skill(s)

The next step in planning lessons is to look over your new list of expectations and decide which you will focus on first in your lessons. In setting priorities, consider the instructional needs of the entire group, and choose areas that will have the greatest long-term impact on increasing the students' social competence. This analysis should result in a list of the expectations that will produce the broadest and most significant benefits to students when you teach the skills to the class.

When you design an intervention for an individual student, you limit it to a single target skill to keep your plans direct and manageable; but with group lessons you have more latitude in deciding the depth and scope of the instruction. You may wish to prepare lessons for just one or two key expectations and save others for later, or you may wish to address a range of interrelated or complex skills in a more comprehensive program. Similarly, you may wish to work with one group of students on one skill area and another group on another skill area.

The basic point is to set instructional priorities that are manageable and that can be coordinated within your teaching routine and schedule (Zirpoli & Melloy, 1993). Just as you would not teach the math curriculum by covering set theory and long division at the same time, or by introducing radicals and quadratic equations in a single week, you should be careful not to overload your teaching of social skills. As with an academic curriculum, you should aim to cover enough material to advance the students' learning but not so much at one time that they lose their focus or are unable to apply what they learn.

Mrs. Armstrong might decide to postpone working on her less pressing priorities to focus on expectations for holding large group class discussions; she believes that enhancing this skill area will immediately improve the students' academic achievement as well as lay the foundation for better peer relationships. Later in the semester, she can develop a follow-up unit on improving conversational skills, which can build on the skills students learn from the first lessons. She could extend the lessons to include short activities on one or two individual expectations, such as responding to criticism or giving opinions in a nonthreatening manner, but for the most part she will limit her focus to keep it manageable. Figure 14.1 shows the priority items and target skill Mrs. Armstrong listed on her worksheet.

Step 4: Listing Key Abilities, Steps, and Conditions for Target Skills

Before carrying out your ideas for teaching specific target skills, consider carefully what the skills involve and what students must know and do to master them. Analyzing this information is similar to breaking target skills into basic abilities, component steps, and performance conditions, which you did in preparation for the specific level assessment. Although you need not be so detailed and formal here, the effects should be the same:

1. To gain a clear understanding of the skills and conditions involved in performing the target skill
2. To determine which aspects of the target skill students need to learn

Thus, you should consider the various elements of the target skill that can pose difficulties for students and list them as potential areas for instruction.

Mrs. Armstrong could review the basic requirements for participating in large group discussions in class and make a list of elements students need to master to increase their competence. Her notes might include the following items:

- Is able to remember background information on the discussion topic
- Is able to recognize verbal and nonverbal cues
- Listens to the teacher's directions and guidelines for discussing the topic
- Reviews materials or visuals pertaining to the topic
- Recalls what has already been said about the topic
- Considers ideas and opinions about the topic and weighs what others have said
- Formulates comments or questions about the topic
- Waits turn or watches for an opening in the discussion before speaking
- Makes statements or expresses opinions in a diplomatic manner
- Times comments and reactions to ongoing conditions
- Recognizes how long and how often to speak
- Reacts appropriately to neighbors and other classmates

Note that the first two items on this list are basic abilities for participating in large group discussions, the next seven items are component steps, and the last three are performance conditions. Figure 14.1 shows that Mrs. Armstrong added these items to her worksheet, and she will consider them as potential goals for her instruction.

Step 5: Conducting Informal Assessment and Listing Instructional Goals for Lessons

Once you have listed the abilities, steps, and conditions, you should consider which of them pose the most problems for the group. Although you will not need to make a detailed assessment of each student's behavior as you did in specific level assessment, you should conduct an informal investigation to determine the most significant problems students have with the target skill and to establish a clear focus for the instructional lessons. For example, you might plan one or two special activities that isolate basic abilities in order to see whether students' difficulties are their background knowledge or fundamental behavior. You could also observe closely to discover whether students have problems with particular component steps of an activity. And you could watch their reactions to specific performance conditions to determine whether they need instruction in this area. In each instance, your aim is to investigate the elements of the target skill you listed above in Step 4 and identify problems that are characteristic of the group's performance.

Mrs. Armstrong might schedule a special question-answer activity to assess how well her class is able to remember background information on topics they usually discuss in social studies. She could also watch closely during large group discussions, determining how well the students listen to her directions, review the materials and visuals, and recall what has been said about a topic. Using simple assessment activities like these, Mrs. Armstrong could achieve a thorough understanding of the difficulties her students have performing the target skill.

After you have assessed the range of abilities, steps, and conditions students must master to learn the target skill, you should select three to five key items as instructional goals for your lessons. As we illustrated in Chapter Nine when discussing goals for interventions, you may wish to consolidate or link some elements to form more broad-based goals; but be sure your goals are not too wide ranging. The main consideration is to select items that will have the greatest effect in helping students improve their overall performance of the target skill. After Mrs. Armstrong completes her informal assessment of key abilities, steps, and conditions, she can set her goals by identifying the specific skills her students most need to learn, just as she did when she set individual instructional goals for Granville, Sandy, and Alfred. As before, she will probably want to consolidate or group items that might be related or redundant.

One new variable to consider when you select goals for group instruction is whether you need to set different goals for particular subgroups of students. Usually you will formulate a single set of instructional goals for the whole class, especially when you are working on a new area of behavior in which all the students need to develop the required skills. But in some cases you may wish to establish separate goals that differentiate among the skills needed by individuals or groups of students. This approach will allow you to emphasize particular skill areas in the lessons based on the distinct needs of the students. For example, Mrs. Armstrong might wish to establish some areas as goals for the entire class, and set others for individual students or subgroups. Figure 14.1 shows that she consolidated her list of skills into two goals for the entire class. She has also decided to stress "learn to wait turn or watch for openings in the discussion before speaking" with certain of her students and "learn to formulate diplomatic, nonjudgmental comments" with some others.

Step 6: Brainstorming Procedures for Addressing Instructional Goals

The next step in planning group-oriented instruction is to devise procedures and activities you might use to teach the social skills. The brainstorming you do here is similar to the process you used earlier to generate methods for interventions. For each of the instructional goals you have identified for the group, you should develop as many ideas as possible for instructional procedures. You can adapt most of the approaches outlined for individual interventions in Chapters Nine and Ten to lessons for larger groups of students. You will find that directions, modeling, prompting, and rehearsal, when applied broadly or used in combination, can serve as an excellent basis for group lesson plans. This step will take a good deal of thought, but you can keep your ideas organized by using a planning worksheet similar to the one we described in Chapter Nine. Mrs. Armstrong decided to adapt the worksheet she used earlier for Granville, Sandy, and Alfred's interventions to help her identify possible activities for her group lessons. As before, she would use a separate page for each instructional goal and would make a list on each page of possible procedures for teaching the goal. You can easily adapt the worksheet presented in Figure 9.1 to brainstorm group instructional procedures.

Step 7: Developing and Improving Lesson Plans

After you have generated a variety of prospective procedures for teaching the instructional goals to the group, you should begin to select your most promising ideas and look for ways to expand and improve your plans. For this step, you can review the section titled "Ten Ways to Develop and Improve Intervention Procedures" presented in Chapter Ten. Most of the principles and suggestions in that section can be used to strengthen your group instruction plans. One of Mrs. Armstrong's ideas is to use a role-playing activity to let students practice better participation in class discussions. She could improve this procedure by involving the students themselves in planning the focus and the format of the activity, as Chapter 10 suggests. She could develop this idea further by combining the role playing with other ideas, such as teaching the students a list of polite phrases for introducing new or contradictory ideas to the discussion, or ringing a bell to prompt them when they make comments that are rude or confrontational.

One suggestion from the list in Chapter Ten bears special mention here: consulting published resources. Much of the commercial material available for social skills instruction is specifically designed to give you ideas and activities for preparing group lessons. You can draw from a wide variety of training programs, curriculum guides, instructional models, activity guides, and other commercial materials to help you develop instructional plans. Appendix B lists some of these materials.

Be prepared, however, to make adjustments to any commercial materials you select so that they will squarely address the goals you have set for your students. Commercial materials are usually quite broad-based, presenting methods and techniques for a wide array of skill areas. They tend to focus more on generalized problems in behavior than on discrete skills and the use of these skills under a particular set of circumstances (Giangreco, 1992; Zirpoli & Melloy, 1993). For instance, the materials may lay out some general steps for holding conversations with classmates and adults, but they would not indicate when or where students should use these steps or what topics would or would not be acceptable under a particular set of conditions. Therefore, you will usually need to adapt the materials you use or expand on the activities they suggest.

Mrs. Armstrong visited the school district's instructional materials center and checked out some commercial materials to use with her class during the times she has set aside for social skills instruction. Some of the materials were highly recommended by the center's coordinator, but just by paging through them, Mrs. Armstrong sees that she will have to choose carefully and expand on the lessons she selects. She does find several helpful activities for improving large group discussions, including techniques for sharing information and building consensus, and she discovers ideas for teaching students to be more diplomatic in their criticism and feedback. But she will need to adapt the activities, monitor the students' progress in learning the skills, and develop some additional lessons to ensure that students learn to apply the skills to their actual discussions in class.

Coordinating Lessons with the Classroom Program

In Chapter Ten we discussed two particular issues that may need attention when you develop interventions: addressing complex goals and increasing student incentive. The principles and methods we discussed in those sections can apply equally well to plans for group instruction. You may find that shaping or chaining is a good way to approach a particularly complex goal, or that highlighting natural outcomes or adding extra rewards helps your students derive the incentive they need to learn the target skill.

But group instruction also gives rise to a new issue that you will need to consider: how the procedures will be integrated with the ongoing routine of the setting. With individual interventions, this was not a major concern; if you wished, you could remove from the classroom the single student with whom you were working. With a larger group, you do not have this flexibility, and you will need to consider more carefully how the lessons you prepare will fit into the overall context of the class. In general, you will follow one of the following approaches in creating your plan:

1. Develop special lessons and activities specifically designed for social skills instruction, and set aside times for these lessons in the students' daily or weekly class schedule.
2. Incorporate particular methods or activities that advance the development of social skills within ongoing subject matter lessons.

We discuss each of these in more detail in the next sections.

Planning special lessons and activities to teach social skills One way to organize social skills instruction with groups of students is to plan special lessons and activities, and set aside separate times in the instructional schedule to work on these skills (Campbell & Siperstein, 1994; Zirpoli & Melloy, 1993). This approach is particularly effective at the preschool and elementary school levels where it may be possible to devote a separate time each day—perhaps 15 to 20 minutes—to social skills instruction. During this time you could carry out instructional activities and practice exercises that focus on particular key areas of social behavior for the entire class. Many researchers, such as Bos and Vaughn (1988), Cartledge and Milburn (1986), Goldstein (1988), and Smith (1989), suggest this method. Recognizing the level of problems shown by many at-risk students, the researchers advocate including specially designed social skills lessons in the instructional routine in addition to the regular subject matter content lessons.

Mrs. Armstrong has decided to schedule about 30 minutes on two or three days a week to address the expectations for holding large group discussions. She plans to use directions, modeling, and rehearsal, with videotaped examples of the skills she wants students to learn. She plans to expand these activities to highlight specific natural outcomes, thus building incentive and self-confidence levels for the few students who need these supplemental procedures.

Incorporating social skills instruction in subject matter lessons Another approach for teaching social skills to groups of students is to incorporate the teaching within the existing curriculum and instructional activities of the classroom. Although this approach will work at all levels of schooling, it is particularly helpful at the middle and high school level, where teachers are typically more constrained by content considerations in their departmentalized programs. The basic idea is to combine social skills instruction with subject matter instruction when you plan lessons and activities. You select the subject matter content of the lessons as you normally would, by reviewing the instructional objectives for the week or the teaching unit. Then you structure the teaching presentations and class activities to address specific areas of social behavior (Oden, 1982; 1986; Johnson, 1981). For example, in a general science unit on weather, you could plan lessons on topics such as climate or wind currents. The students could work on these units with small group assignments that enable you to address or reinforce specific areas of social behavior as well as cover the scientific concepts covered in the lessons.

Two techniques you can use to incorporate social skills instruction with subject matter content instruction are *peer tutoring* and *cooperative learning*. We briefly explain these procedures in the sections that follow and provide a list of suggested resources at the end of the chapter.

Peer tutoring is an effective teaching technique for combining subject matter instruction with social skills instruction because of the variety of opportunities you can create for the students to learn from one another's behavior. Peer tutoring is closely related to modeling, but is less structured and less formal. You arrange students in pairs or small groups so one student who has learned a task assists another student who needs to learn the task. The teaching-learning interactions between students can help them develop both subject matter content skills and the various

Social skills can be taught within the context of subject matter instruction.

social skills you wish to address, depending on how you structure the activities (Goodman, Powell, & Burke, 1989; Lazerson, Foster, Brown, & Hummel, 1988).

For peer tutoring to be effective, you should plan the lessons so students develop the target social skills and reach the subject matter objectives as well (Bell, Young, Blair, & Nelson, 1990). You must plan the grouping arrangements so that students who are compatible will be working together. With compatibility determined, you could pair a student who needs to learn the academic lesson with one who needs to refine some social skills so the tutoring situation is beneficial to both of them.

The tasks students work on should be easily taught by one student and easily learned by the other. Such tasks will provide a firm and consistent basis for improving social skills while avoiding the conflicts or frustrations that could arise from assignments that are beyond the students' capabilities (Gerber & Kaufman, 1981; Scruggs & Richter, 1985). Examples of activities that are good to use in a peer tutoring arrangement include these:

- Drilling on math concepts
- Practicing oral reading and vocabulary
- Studying for tests
- Evaluating homework assignments
- Reviewing outlines for projects

- Working on science laboratory experiments
- Reviewing game rules and practicing sports activities

You would need to set the ground rules for the instructional interaction so the tutor does not do the work for the other student, but models appropriate work habits (Fowler, 1986). Depending on the age levels and maturity of the students involved, the tutors may have to learn some basic presentation techniques ahead of time, such as how to give directions and prompts or how to provide feedback and encouragement (Knapczyk, 1989; Lazerson, Foster, Brown, & Hummel, 1988). This preparation will reduce the possibility that students will become overly dependent on their tutors for doing the assigned work.

Mrs. Armstrong is so pleased with the way Sandy responded to working with her more skilled classmates during the intervention that she has decided to apply a similar approach during some subject matter lessons, such as homework review exercises. After completing a concise, informal assessment of the students, she will pair them, taking into account their academic ability and social competence. In this way, while one student is learning subject matter material, the other student will be developing interpersonal skills. She plans to use her listing of priority social expectations as well as her subject matter curricula to help her concentrate on the skills that will be most helpful to the students in improving their academic achievement and social competence.

Cooperative learning is a teaching approach in which students work in pairs or small groups on assigned content material, such as the day's math lesson or an ongoing language arts project (Eby & Kujawa, 1994; Johnson & Johnson, 1986; Sapon-Shevin, 1986). Unlike peer tutoring, the students in this case are learning together and working on cooperative projects. The structure of the lessons and the process the students follow to complete assigned tasks help them develop a variety of social skills, including these:

- Choosing ideas and topics for the assignment
- Sharing ideas
- Asking for assistance from classmates
- Negotiating differences of opinion
- Assuming different roles and responsibilities
- Being diplomatic and sensitive to other people's opinions

In cooperative learning, the activities are specifically designed so completion of an activity depends on the input and performance of all the group's members, and each student has a major stake in the final product or grade. The group itself does the following:

- Establishes the goals of the task
- Decides what contributions each member will make to the group's performance

- Creates a division of labor so each member has a specific role
- Monitors completion of each task component (Salend & Sonnenschein, 1989)

As students advance in their cooperative skills, you can tie the structure and outcomes of the activity to a system of group accountability. Grades or outcomes for the final project can be given equally to all the members, because each student is responsible for making a major contribution to the project, even though each of the contributions may be substantially different from the others (Mesch, Lew, Johnson, & Johnson, 1986).

For cooperative learning activities to work well, you need to plan the groups' structure and operation carefully. The lessons and grouping arrangements should allow students to develop social skills over time, building on the more basic skills they have developed from their past experiences or from previous activities (Eby & Kujawa, 1994). During the initial stages of the learning process, you may also have to use a more teacher-directed approach, such as giving students a written outline for completing the assignment or for participating in group interactions. The subsequent lessons may then focus on different, more advanced social skills that enable the students to integrate what they have learned with a new set of skills and activities, and also to assume more responsibility for structuring and running the cooperative groups (Johnson & Johnson, 1986; Linney & Seidman, 1989).

You should choose activities that are fairly open-ended, to encourage a high level of cooperation and participation from all members of the groups. In planning these activities, take into account the varied talents and ability levels of the members in both subject matter skills and social skills. Projects that work particularly well in a cooperative learning framework include problem-solving or product-oriented activities, such as the following:

- Planning a debate
- Preparing a science fair display
- Planning rules for a new instructional game
- Making a class presentation
- Preparing visuals for a learning center

Although the task or assignment itself should be fairly straightforward, you may need to give students directions on how to accomplish their individual and group tasks, to help them develop and practice key interpersonal skills. The responsibilities for the overall management and operation of the group should eventually be turned over to the group members so they will learn the target social skills. Again, the keys to the success of cooperative learning are knowing ahead of time what skills you wish students to learn from the lessons, and planning activities that will help them develop these interpersonal skills (Eby & Kujawa, 1994).

After using role playing and practice exercises to teach some basic cooperative skills, Mrs. Armstrong plans to structure small group cooperative learning activities to help her students practice and apply these skills. She will have them work in groups to prepare class recitations using visual aids, focusing on the relationship between a historical event and their daily living experiences. She will design the activities to emphasize such skills as expressing ideas and opinions in a group, critiquing different points of view, and building group consensus.

Peer tutoring and cooperative learning are just two of the many approaches you can use to create opportunities for students to improve their social competence in the context of subject matter lessons. These opportunities allow you to oversee, direct, and encourage the types of social interactions that address target skills under fairly controlled but natural circumstances (Friedman, Cancelli, & Yoshida, 1988). By incorporating such techniques into a well-planned program of social skills instruction, you can give the social skills curriculum a prominent place in your instructional program.

Step 8: Coordinating and Scheduling Lesson Plans

Once you have developed the procedures you will use to teach the target skill, you should coordinate your plans so the lessons address your instructional goals precisely and deliberately. Careful planning will allow you to integrate the activities smoothly into ongoing lessons and routines, and to make sure your procedures complement the other academic and instructional goals you have for students. As with an intervention, a helpful technique for completing your plan is to write a script narrating the procedures and activities you will use. You should also schedule your activities carefully, taking into account any personnel, materials, or equipment you will need. Mrs. Armstrong adapted the planning worksheets shown in Chapter Ten to sketch out a script of the procedures she plans to use. In addition, she prepared a timeline for implementing the activities, and listed the materials or equipment she will use, along with other personnel who will help with the lessons. Like Mrs. Armstrong, you can easily adapt the worksheets presented in Figures 10.1 and 10.2 to develop your group lesson plans.

One important difference between individual interventions and group instruction in social skills is the flexibility of the time frame for carrying out your plan (Cartledge & Milburn, 1986). Whereas an intervention for an individual student should ideally be carried out over just a few days, group lessons give you much more leeway. The scheduling of your lessons will depend on the complexity and detail of the expectations you have chosen to address. Mrs. Armstrong's lessons for improving her students' performance in large group discussions will naturally take longer than working on their hand-raising. At the same time, the reverse of this principle is also true: the time frame you choose will determine the depth and breadth of what you teach. You could prepare a few individual one-time activities to spotlight particular skills or problem areas you want the students to work on; or you may teach a series of ongoing units to concentrate on a particularly complicated skill area over several weeks. The shorter format can prove useful for teaching or reinforcing very specific social behaviors, such as using proper greetings or following a certain classroom rule, or it can lay the foundation for more comprehensive lessons or skill practice exercises later on. The longer-term format is most helpful for teaching related clusters of expectations, such as participating effectively in group discussions or learning new playground games, and for overseeing the application and carryover of expectations across a variety of classroom or school situations. In either case, you should plan ahead for the lessons and integrate them as much as possible with ongoing activities and routines.

Step 9: Preparing Monitoring Procedures

The last step in developing an instructional lesson plan is preparing to monitor the activities. As with individual interventions, the monitoring you do for group lessons should help you decide whether to change or fine-tune the activities, and when to move on to other areas. The issues you monitor should center on the target skills that are the focus of the lessons, on the instructional goals for the expectations, and on any other questions you would like to examine. Mrs. Armstrong will use a worksheet similar to the one shown in Chapter Eleven to monitor the progress of the class during her lessons. You can use the worksheet presented in Figure 11.1 to help with your monitoring activities.

One challenge you will encounter in monitoring group lessons is evaluating the performance of several students at once. Two possible approaches you could take to monitor your lessons are (a) collecting information on the entire group, and (b) collecting information on a subgroup. In large measure, the method you choose will depend on the amount of time you have for monitoring and the questions and issues you would like to investigate.

Collecting Information on the Entire Group

One monitoring approach is to collect information on the performance of each individual student in the class—by observing each of them directly or through video, or by keeping individual logs, charts, or records of their behavior. Individual observation would give you the most detailed and precise information about the students and the effectiveness of the lessons, but it would also be the most complicated and time-consuming to carry out. Sometimes the records you already keep in your normal teaching routine can help you monitor the behavior of the entire class, by measuring such issues as how many assignments students turn in on time or how accurate their work is. Record books, graphs, and wall charts are good ways to organize and summarize the information you collect. When you are using observational procedures, you might be able to monitor each student's performance by rotating your monitoring activities across the class, observing some students one day, other students the next day, and so on. You would continue this process until you have checked each student's performance as many times as you need to answer your questions about their behavior.

Mrs. Armstrong could use the grades she gives on quizzes following group discussions to evaluate whether her lessons on holding discussions are improving the students' understanding of the material they are assigned. She could summarize her monitoring results in terms of how many students in class have made better grades in their work or whether the average scores for the class are higher now than they were before the lessons. Additionally, she could monitor the specific skills for holding discussions by observing a different group of students each day, taking notes on the students in row 1 on Monday, the students in row 2 on Tuesday, and so on.

Collecting Information on a Subgroup

Another option for monitoring is to keep a regular accounting of the performance of only part of the class. You may, for example, decide to keep detailed records on a representative sample of students from the class, and base your judgment of the lesson's effectiveness on their performance. If the sample of students makes the progress you had hoped for, you would conclude that the class as a whole is making the same type of progress. Another approach is to select a small group of students who need to make the greatest progress in the skills you are teaching, and gauge the effect of the lessons on their performance. The results you would obtain from monitoring these particular students' behavior could give you the best indication of whether you are accomplishing the aims you set out for all students in class, as they would focus your evaluation on the most challenging members of the group.

In Mrs. Armstrong's case, rather than trying to observe all her fifth graders, she could pick three or four of her average students and use their performance as a basis for judging the effectiveness of the lessons. On the other hand, she could select the three or four students she thinks have the most to learn about holding discussions, closely monitor their performance, and fine-tune the lesson based on their progress. Mrs. Armstrong could enter the students' names on a worksheet similar to the one she used to monitor interventions for Granville, Alfred, and Sandy. On the worksheet she would list the target skill and questions she plans to answer and the procedures she will use. She could also summarize her observations on a graph or a chart as she did with her individual interventions.

In summary, you can use the process we described in the text to teach social skills as part of the overall classroom instructional program. You should start with the social skills curriculum and establish instructional goals as you would in teaching subject matter skills. You can carry out the instruction by setting aside special times in the classroom schedule or school day, or by incorporating social skills instruction into established routines and lessons. In this way, you advance the social skills of your students beyond the minimum levels of competence.

❍ Summary

Adapting the Intervention Approach to Groups of Students

1. The approach presented in the text for planning interventions can be applied to the instruction of groups of students.
2. The steps for planning group instruction of social skills are the following:
   a. choosing the setting, situation, and groups for the instruction
   b. identifying expectations that could be addressed by the instruction
   c. assigning priorities and choosing target skills
   d. listing key abilities, steps, and conditions for the target skills

   e. listing instructional goals for the lessons
   f. brainstorming possible procedures for achieving the instructional goals
   g. developing and improving instructional plans
   h. coordinating and scheduling the lesson plans
   i. preparing monitoring procedures

3. Group lessons should address the following:
   a. expectations that pose the greatest problems for students
   b. expectations for which the demands are unclear
   c. expectations you wish to modify, emphasize, or add to the curriculum
   d. expectations that can be taught in combination
   e. expectations students have difficulty applying and carrying over to other settings

4. Target skills should be limited in scope to skills that will have the greatest long-term impact on the students' competence.

5. Group instructional lessons should be coordinated with the current instructional program and routine.

6. Separate time periods within the students' instructional day can be set aside for social skills instruction.

7. Social skills instruction can be incorporated into already planned subject matter lessons.

8. Peer tutoring and cooperative learning are effective techniques for teaching social skills in the context of subject matter lessons.

9. Peer tutoring involves arranging students into teaching/learning pairs based on their individual academic and social skills.

10. Peer tutoring may require special training of tutors in teaching techniques.

11. Cooperative learning involves designing lessons and activities to promote sharing, teamwork, and mutual learning of academic and social skills among groups of students.

12. Cooperative learning should be built around well-planned activities and group accountability.

13. Monitoring group instruction can involve collecting information on all students in the group or on a selected subgroup of students.

❍ Suggested Resources for Cooperative Learning and Peer Tutoring

Campbell, P., & Siperstein, G. (1994). *Improving social competence. A resource for elementary school teachers.* Boston: Allyn & Bacon.

Good, T., & Brophy, J. (1987). *Looking into classrooms* (4th ed.). New York: Harper & Row.

Graves, N., & Graves, T. (1985). Creating a cooperative learning environment: An ecological approach. In R. Slavin, S. Sharan, S. Kagan, R. Hertz-Lazarowitz, C. Webb, & R. Schmuck (Eds.), *Learning to cooperate, cooperating to learn*. New York: Plenum.

Jenkins, J., & Jenkins, L. (1989). *Cross-age and peer tutoring: Help for children with learning problems*. Reston, VA: The Council for Exceptional Children.

Pierce, M., Stahlbrand, K., & Armstrong, S. (1989). *Increasing student productivity through peer tutoring programs* (Monograph 9-1). Burlington: University of Vermont, Center for Developmental Disabilities.

Slavin, R. (1990). *Cooperative learning: Theory, research, and practice.* Englewood Cliffs, NJ: Prentice-Hall.

Slavin, R., Karweit, N., & Madden, N. (1989). *Effective programs for students at risk*. Boston: Allyn & Bacon.

Walker, H., Colvin, G., & Ramsey, E. (1995). *Antisocial behavior in school: Strategies and best practices*. Pacific Grove, CA: Brooks/Cole.

Warger, C. (1992). *Peer tutoring: When working together is better than working alone*. Reston, VA: The Council for Exceptional Children.

Examples for Chapter 14

Example 14a

Mr. Nordstrom, a kindergarten teacher, is planning group instructional lessons for five students who have difficulty playing games with classmates. Billy and Sam tend to bully other students, dominate activities, and not share toys and equipment. Tonya and Carl dominate activities too, but with gentle coercion and their sweet personalities. Martha plays in pairs with other children, but shows little tolerance for the other four students' behavior, yelling and screaming whenever they get close to her play area.

The first page of Mr. Nordstrom's planning worksheet shows the expectations he considered addressing in group instruction. After completing this list he combined several priority items into the target skill "Plays cooperatively with other children," with further emphasis on "Makes compromises and shows tolerance for playmates."

Worksheet 14.1. Planning Social Skills Instruction for Groups of Students. Page _1_ of _3_

Name: *Mr. Nordstrom* Date: *Dec. 13*

Step 1. Groups/Settings to be included in instruction

Planning for group instruction can be directed toward a subgroup in the class. → *Billy, Martha, Carl, Tonya, Sam*

Group games—both inside and outside

Step 2. Social expectations to consider addressing in instruction

A. List expectations in the setting that pose problems for many students:

Allows others to participate

Do not be overly concerned with categorizing expectations. Particular items may fall into more than one area. → *Plays games by the rules*

Encourages and claps for playmates

B. List expectations that are unclear, implicit, or applied inconsistently:

Follows conventional rules for playing

Goes over rules before playing games

Some expectations may be considered because of the problems individual students have meeting them; for instance, Martha and Sam have particular difficulty with this demand. Nonetheless, Mr. Nordstrom will be careful to maintain his group focus as he plans instruction. → *Smiles and laughs with other children*

Talks with playmates about activity

C. List expectations you want to modify, emphasize, or add to the curriculum:

Participates in at least one group game per day

Plays competitive games and cooperative games

D. List groups of expectations that can be taught together as a unit:

Accepts outcomes of game

Makes compromises and shows tolerance for playmates

Joins an ongoing activity

Lets others join an activity

Example 14b

Ms. Kingsley teaches allied health and sex education to a mixed group of tenth and eleventh graders. She divides the class period between large group discussion and individual or small group work on assignments and projects. The students are lively participants and enjoy the discussions, but they have difficulty applying the same focus to the group work. Rather than staying on task, they discuss personal matters, criticize each others' work, tease and joke too loudly, and are generally so noisy no one can do the assigned work.

The following page of Ms. Kingsley's worksheet shows some of the expectations she considered addressing; the target skill she selected for her lessons; and the abilities, steps, and conditions she would investigate before setting instructional goals. Ms. Kingsley felt that if the students could direct their enthusiasm toward working cooperatively on group tasks, their more productive and supportive interactions could help them develop more satisfying friendships outside of class as well.

Worksheet 14.1 (continued)	Name: *Ms. Kingsley*	Page *2* of *3*

E. List expectations that students have difficulty applying or carrying over to other settings:

Negotiates disagreements and makes compromises
Teases and jokes with teachers
Offers positive feedback and supportive suggestions to peers

Be sure to include student-set expectations and nonacademic demands when you consider expectations to address in group instruction.

Step 3. Priority expectations/target skill(s) for instruction

Uses lively interaction to complete group activities

Ms. Kingsley consolidated several expectations into a broader target skill in order to expand the focus of the instructional lessons.

Step 4. Key abilities, steps, and conditions to consider for teaching target skill

Is able to understand directions for assignments
Is able to divide and share roles in completing tasks
Is able to formulate positive feedback and suggestions
Listens to teacher's directions
Selects group leader and divides roles
Reviews the directions for assignments
Plans the steps together for completing the task
Encourages group members to share in the activity
Takes turns sharing opinions
Offers encouragement and positive feedback to group members
Reminds group members to stay on task
Smiles and laughs with others in group
Accepts different students in group
Recognizes and responds to nonverbal cues from group members

Consider all three areas from the specific level assessment when listing the possible focus of group lessons. Follow-up observations will help set the instructional goals.

Mr. Wagner's Case Study

Mr. Wagner is planning a group instructional lesson to help teach his students how to behave better. He considered several expectations for instruction, including "Waits turn before speaking," "Stays on task during independent work," and "Respects the opinions of classmates." Other expectations he considered are shown in Section E of his worksheet.

As he states in Step 3, Mr. Wagner decided to focus on the students' behavior during teacher presentation, when they tend to talk out loud, tease one another, and fail to pay attention. Mr. Wagner's entry in Step 4 shows the abilities, steps, and conditions he will consider addressing.

Worksheet 14.1 (continued)	Name: *Mr. Wagner*	Page *2* of *3*

E. List expectations that students have difficulty applying or carrying over to other settings:

- *Respects space of others*
- *Keeps voice level down*

> Expectations for group instruction should be described in behavioral terms. Mr. Wagner should redefine these items or give examples of what he means.

Step 3. Priority expectations/target skill(s) for instruction

- *Listens and follows along with teacher presentation*

> Mr. Wagner is focusing once more on his own rules and wishes for classroom management. Remember to consider expectations from the students' point of view, and choose a target skill that will help them become more happy, confident, and controlled in their social interactions.

Step 4. Key abilities, steps, and conditions to consider for teaching target skill

- *Is able to understand classroom rules*
- *Is able to hear teacher's voice*
- *Is able to listen to instructions*
- *Sits in seat when bell rings*
- *Keeps eyes on teacher*
- *Listens to directions for activity*
- *Writes notes on key directions*
- *Raises hand before speaking*
- *Goes to group to begin work*
- *Recognizes when it's time to be quiet*
- *Avoids teasing other people*
- *Shows respect for teacher and others*

> Some of these items are not likely to be problem areas for the group as a whole.

> Mr. Wagner's list does not include many of the social aspects of the activity. Be sure to consider the range of social interactions the target skill requires.

CHAPTER 15

Collaboration in Teaching Social Competence

We stated at the beginning of this text that achieving social competence requires more of students than mastering individual skills and behaviors; it involves recognizing and reacting to a complicated curriculum of social demands and requirements. By using the methods discussed in the preceding chapters, you can make this curriculum a much more prominent part of your instructional program, and use it to help students acquire and employ the network of social skills they need for meeting the expectations of your classroom.

Students do not learn most social skills in a single term or a single setting, however; they develop them incrementally from year to year and grade to grade. Although a single teacher can often make a profound impact on student behavior, student deficits have usually been built over time in a number of settings. Accordingly, once you have integrated social skills instruction into your own classroom, you can broaden and intensify the effect of your work by extending your focus to include other school settings. In this chapter, we explain how you can collaborate with other teachers and school personnel to extend the concepts of social skills instruction from your classroom to other settings within your grade-level program, and even to other grade levels and schools.

Coordinating Social Skills Instruction with Other Settings

Unlike earlier chapters, which suggested specific procedures or approaches for teaching social competence, this chapter does not propose any particular process for extending your efforts to other settings. Instead, we discuss the benefits and goals of working with other teachers to coordinate the teaching of social competence, and give guidelines and suggestions for sharing the procedures and concepts with other school personnel. Throughout the chapter, we present two different approaches to extending social skills instruction to other settings. One is working within your own grade-level program with other people who share responsibility for the same students you teach. The other is working with teachers from grade levels—or even school units—that precede and follow your own, to coordinate the social expectations and instruction of students as they move from one grade to the next. Although the methods and manner of working with other teachers will be the same in either case, the nature of your work and the goals you address are likely to be quite different. In the sections that follow, we introduce each of these two approaches and outline the benefits of coordinating social skills instruction both within and across grade levels.

Working with Personnel within the Same Grade Level

You should realize that your classroom setting is not isolated from the rest of the school environment—at least not from your students' point of view. The demands students must meet in your classroom are only one part of a much larger collection of social expectations they must negotiate from the moment they arrive at school in the morning to the moment they leave school in the afternoon. To achieve social competence in school, students must be able to respond effectively to the total array of social expectations across all the settings in which they interact (Cartledge & Milburn, 1986).

For example, the difficulties students have in responding to social demands in Mrs. Armstrong's social studies class are likely to be intensified and compounded by inconsistencies and shifts in expectations as the students move to other settings such as Mr. Wagner's math and science classes. Mr. Wagner typically uses a large group lecture-discussion format in his teaching, and he keeps students arranged in their assigned seats. Mrs. Armstrong, on the other hand, schedules small group activities for much of her class period and allows freer movement of students during her lessons. Mr. Wagner tends to have a more explicit and formalized set of classroom rules than Mrs. Armstrong, but he is also more relaxed about their enforcement. He is inclined to joke with the class more than Mrs. Armstrong does, and he gives the students more latitude in handling their petty disagreements during class time. While students are more careful to raise their hands and to line up for recess in Mr. Wagner's class, they also tend to whisper and argue more and to clown around occasionally.

Most fifth graders can instinctively recognize the differences between Mrs. Armstrong's and Mr. Wagner's classes, and they respond appropriately to the social expectations that apply. But for a student like Granville, who has difficulty recognizing and responding to social expectations even within a single setting, the differences in demands across settings can be quite baffling. If he moves around the room in Mr. Wagner's class as he is allowed to in Mrs. Armstrong's class, he will get into trouble. On the other hand, while Mr. Wagner tolerates Granville's complaints and threats, Mrs. Armstrong is quick to admonish him. Alfred may have similar problems; the clowning that Mrs. Armstrong finds tiresome and disrespectful is regarded as harmless or even funny by Mr. Wagner. And these are only two of the settings in which the fifth graders participate. Mrs. Kellerman's art class, Mr. Haskell's gym class, and the playground and cafeteria settings may have shifts in routines and demands for behavior that are equally diverse and conflicting.

Social skills instruction can be enhanced by collaborating with other school personnel

Given the fluctuations and variations in school settings, it would not be surprising if there were several fifth graders, in addition to Granville and Alfred, who have at least some difficulty handling the changes they encounter across settings during the school day. Although Mrs. Armstrong has worked hard to clarify and teach social skills in her settings, her students are likely to have continued difficulty achieving social competence unless she can extend and coordinate her efforts with these other settings.

In this chapter, we explain how you can work with other personnel at your grade level to review the social demands for the various settings in which students interact during the school day, and to plan a more comprehensive approach to social skills instruction. Coordinating instruction within a particular grade level can lay the foundation for a generally stronger and broader educational program for your students. It can improve communication and cooperation among school personnel, expand the scope of instructional activities, and give a focus to lessons, routines, and interventions that pertain to students' social behavior (Sheridan, Kratochwill, & Elliott, 1990; Sugai & Tindal, 1993). A coordinated program of social skills instruction can help all the teachers concentrate their instructional energies more efficiently and effectively by clarifying the key areas of behavior to emphasize and teach in their settings (Cohen & Fish, 1993). Moreover, these benefits need not be limited to a single grade-level program. In the next section, we explain how changes occur in expectations for social behavior as students progress through their schooling, and show how coordinating social skills instruction across grade levels and administrative units can help respond to these changes.

Working with Personnel across Grade Levels and Schools

Throughout the text, we have spoken of social expectations as if they were fixed or frozen in time—a fairly concrete and static set of demands and standards for behavior. But in fact, they are dynamic and progressive in that we expect students to mature and develop socially as they grow older and advance in grade level. The required behaviors for meeting social expectations become more demanding, and the standards that apply to them become more stringent with each new grade level the students enter. Even in a single classroom or school setting, the demands for social behavior become more complex and more exacting by the end of the year than they were at the beginning (Kameenui & Simmons, 1990).

Learning to respond to progressively more advanced social expectations is thus a natural part of the students' growth and development. Teaching students about social expectations serves not only to improve their behavior in their current circumstances but also gives them a foundation on which to build other areas of social competence, areas that change and advance as do the goals in any other curriculum area. Social skills curriculum items such as "works with other students on assignments" or "shows consideration for other students' opinions" are not isolated goals; they build on a framework of skills from previous learning experiences, and they prepare students for the more complex and sophisticated expectations of their future placements (Dissent, 1987).

The idea that the social skills curriculum progresses over time is in keeping with the basic longitudinal nature of our entire educational system. At each grade level, students pick up where they left off the year before, and advance enough to be ready for the next year's demands. An illustration of this process is the cumulative nature of subject matter curricula and instructional programs, which progress with each year's schooling, building on what the students have learned in previous years. Instruction in reading, math, and other subjects proceeds in an orderly manner through the school years, enabling students to make continuous progress in their academic achievement. The students' ability to understand concepts, complete assignments, and grow academically is based on the skills they have learned in the prior grades. This same type of progression is in effect with social demands; students' ability to interact with teachers and classmates, participate in instructional activities, and engage in other types of social behavior is dependent on what they have learned before at each level in their schooling. Thus, each successive year of schooling requires students to develop an even more advanced and complex array of social skills.

In Chapter One we stated that a major portion of the social skills curriculum is usually implicit or hidden. Many of these implied expectations are linked to the students' previous grade-level experiences. This connection explains why, when Mrs. Armstrong's students behave in a particularly childish or rowdy manner, she admonishes them to "act like fifth-grade students." What she means, of course, is that the expectations for social behavior at the fifth-grade level are more advanced than those at previous grade levels, and students need to respond appropriately to these demands. Furthermore, they will need to develop additional skills as the year progresses so they will be ready the following year to "act like sixth-grade students." The games students play during recess, the topics they discuss during free times, and most other aspects of their social behavior differ markedly with each passing year. Thus, the expectations in formal classroom settings, as well as in informal play or recreational settings, will become more advanced as students proceed from one grade level to the next. Students must be adequately prepared to respond to these differences; otherwise, they will most likely show problems in their social behavior.

For at-risk students like Granville, Sandy, and Alfred, the implications of this process are profound. Because public education is carried out over several years, the problems such students have meeting social demands are not fixed, but assume a longitudinal nature of their own. Often, these students do not acquire the skills they need to adjust to changes in expectations across grade levels. They are often unable to develop the needed skills on their own, or to learn the skills incidentally through interactions with classmates and teachers (Cohen & Fish, 1993). As a result, in addition to causing problems in students' current interactions, social skills deficits can develop into long-standing, deeply ingrained patterns of academic and social failure. For example, fifth grade is not the first year that Granville has had difficulty cooperating with classmates, that Alfred has had problems playing during recess, or that Sandy has been reluctant to join conversations. These problems have grown over several years, but they are now causing behavior that seems more disruptive, immature, or obnoxious to teachers and classmates than before, because the discrepancy between these students' behavior and that of their peers has become greater.

To address behavior problems effectively, social skills instruction should be coordinated not only within grade-level settings but across grade levels as well. In academic areas, this kind of coordination is naturally set in place by the curriculum materials teachers use and the textbook adoption policies of their school districts. Publishers of instructional curricula and textbooks devote much time and research to ensuring that texts, supplemental materials, exercises, and workbooks provide continuity in students' academic development. We take this coordination for granted, and we assume that if we use the materials deigned for our particular grade level, our teaching will fit properly into the orderly progression of instruction. Unfortunately, you cannot rely on commercial materials to create this continuity for you in social skills instruction. As a consequence, you must consider how you can build this continuity by collaborating with teachers at other grade levels.

For example, Mrs. Armstrong may wish to collaborate with Ms. Warren, Mrs. Devetski, and Mr. Henson, the fourth-grade teachers at Madison Elementary, on improving the transition of students across the fourth- and fifth-grade levels. Alternately (or additionally), she might work with Mr. Taggert and Ms. Harrison, the sixth-grade social studies teachers at Jefferson Middle School where her students will go next year, and coordinate expectations across the fifth- and sixth-grade levels. In the sections that follow, we discuss some techniques and guidelines for comparing and coordinating expectations, instructional approaches, and teaching routines both within grade-level settings and across grade levels. We begin by explaining how to set the objectives for collaborating with other teachers.

Deciding What to Accomplish by Coordinating Social Skills Instruction

When you develop a coordinated program of instruction, you must first specify what you hope to accomplish and what outcomes you will try to produce so you will have a clear objective in view. Although the approach you will use for working with other teachers is essentially the same whether they work at the same or other grade levels, your objectives are likely to be quite different in each case. In the following sections, we first discuss some of the aims you could set for working with teachers in your own grade level, and then some of the outcomes you could look for in working with teachers from other grade levels or schools.

Collaborating with Personnel within a Single Grade Level

The following are some objectives you could work toward within grade-level settings to coordinate social skills instruction.

Extending Instructional Lessons to Other Settings

One aim of grade-level coordination can be to work with other personnel on extending and adapting to their settings the lessons and activities you have already developed for your students (Campbell & Siperstein, 1994). Many of the activities you design for social skills instruction in your classroom will be equally applicable and important for your students when they are in other settings (Sugai & Tindal, 1993). When you share your goals and priorities with other staff members, you may find they have many of the same interests and aims, and you may be able to gain their assistance in coordinating your efforts throughout the entire grade level.

We described in the last chapter how Mrs. Armstrong planned lessons to teach her class to participate more effectively in large group discussions. At the same time, she may have noted, or heard from other teachers, that the fifth-grade class as a whole is somewhat limited in their ability to hold discussions, and that they show these difficulties in most subject areas. She might decide to share her ideas for lessons and activities with the other fifth-grade teachers, and ask them whether they too would like to concentrate some of their teaching efforts on improving students' discussion skills. She could show the teachers how she uses the teaching techniques in her classroom and discuss how they can adapt and extend her activities in their own subject matter areas, or she might develop exercises and practice lessons they could use to reinforce and strengthen the new skills. In these ways, Mrs. Armstrong may be able to significantly increase the effectiveness and the impact of the instructional lessons she is using in her own classroom.

Teaching Students to Respond to Inconsistencies in Demands among School Settings

A second important area you could address in improving program coordination is alleviating the problems students may have adjusting their behavior to shifting demands throughout the school day (Campbell & Siperstein, 1994). As we noted, changes in the rules, demands, activities, and instructional approaches among settings can be very confusing to students, particularly when they have difficulty recognizing and reacting to social expectations in the first place.

One approach for helping students negotiate differences among settings is to teach them about the expectations that apply to each of the settings and about the shifts in behavior they need to make. This approach will work best when the other teachers and school personnel overseeing the students' interactions collaborate with you in clarifying and highlighting changes among settings. Mrs. Armstrong and Mr. Wagner might talk with their respective classes about the variations in expectations that arise from their classroom rules, teaching styles, student response preferences, and other features of their instructional programs. They could encourage Mrs. Kellerman, Mr. Haskell, and the other school staff who work with the fifth graders to do the same. In this way, the students would learn about the differences in expectations that occur from setting to setting without having to guess about these demands or try to sort them out by themselves.

Reducing the Inconsistencies in Expectations among Settings

Another way to minimize students' difficulties in responding to shifting demands is to reduce the changes in expectations that occur among the grade-level settings. To accomplish this, you would work with other staff members to establish a more uniform set of expectations for social behavior so as to increase the consistency of what students are expected to do. If in some classrooms, Mrs. Armstrong's students are expected to raise their hands before speaking, to talk quietly while lining up for recess, or to go to the teacher's desk when they have questions, the fifth-grade teachers could work together to make sure these demands are applied in the same ways throughout all their settings.

Teachers can improve students' social behavior significantly by coordinating social expectations, because the students will no longer have to make so many difficult and subtle adjustments in their behavior to be successful in their interactions. Obviously, some differences in expectations will remain: individual factors such as classroom routines, teaching styles, and subject matter content will continue to require some shifts that students must learn to negotiate. But many variations among settings are fairly arbitrary and unrelated to reaching subject matter objectives. By reducing these subjective differences, teachers may find it easier to emphasize the most important aspects of their programs, the ones for which differences in expectations are truly essential for students to attain social competence and improve academic achievement.

Working toward greater consistency in social demands is particularly important for teachers in departmentalized middle school and high school programs in which students move from setting to setting on a daily basis. The strategy can also be crucial to the effectiveness of special education and remedial programs; support programs like art, gym, and music; and noninstructional activities like recess or passing time in the school hallways. In all these circumstances, a more uniform and predictable set of social expectations can reduce or eliminate some of the problems students have in their interactions, especially those difficulties that arise when students must adapt their behavior from one set of expectations to another.

Collaborating with Personnel across Grade Levels or Schools

Unlike the work you do with teachers from your own grade, your collaboration with teachers from other grade levels seeks not to match or unify social demands and instructional lessons, but rather to develop continuity between the expectations and activities of two successive programs. This continuity could require linking social expectations across kindergarten and first-grade programs, across eighth-grade junior high and ninth-grade high school programs, or across any other two successive programs. Working across grade levels in this way can provide profound benefits for your students and your instructional program. The next sections suggest some specific objectives you could work toward in coordinating activities with teachers at other grade levels.

Gaining a Better Understanding of New Students' Skills

When you work with teachers in the grades your students complete the year before coming to your class, you can gain a much better understanding of the types of skills and level of skill development students will have when they enter your program at the beginning of the year. By comparing your own social skills curriculum with the activities and demands of the previous grade, you can learn much about how the students behave and where their social development and instruction leaves off at the end of the previous year. This knowledge will help you determine which social skills you can immediately integrate into your instructional activities, which skills will need further refinement and practice, and which skills you cannot assume the students have. For example, when she meets with Mrs. Devetski, Mrs. Armstrong might learn that the fourth-grade students do a lot of teamwork on assignments, but usually in pairs or in threes rather than in the larger groups she uses in her own social studies class. Similarly, she might discover that the fourth graders have little experience in the kinds of class presentations that are a common part of her fifth-grade setting. With this information, Mrs. Armstrong can plan to build on these new skill areas more slowly at the start of the school year, to ease the students' transition to her setting.

Setting the Focus for Social Instruction in Your Setting

When you work with teachers in the grade-level programs following your own, you can get a much clearer idea of the types of social skills you should teach or emphasize during the current school year. By comparing your own expectations to those of the next grade level, you can identify the major changes or developments your students must make in their behavior during the current year. These expectations can then serve as the focus of your social skills instruction because they will enable students to be adequately prepared for the next level of their schooling. The expectations provide a framework as you plan instructional lessons, just as the grade-level curriculum objectives guide your teaching in reading or math. You could emphasize in your program the specific skills that students will need to use in the next setting, or that the next teachers view as especially important. At the same time, you could deemphasize skill areas that will not play an important role in future settings.

When she meets with Mr. Taggert and Ms. Harrison from Jefferson Middle School, Mrs. Armstrong might find that her activities for increasing proficiency in large group discussions will indeed be useful for her students, since most of the middle school classes use this format. She could also prepare new lessons for the class on working more effectively in groups, since the social studies teachers at Jefferson have just adopted a new curriculum that places a heavy emphasis on teamwork and cooperative learning projects. By coordinating her social skills instruction with the conditions in effect at Jefferson, Mrs. Armstrong could ensure that her efforts focus on the skill areas and the expectations that will be most important for her students to learn.

Providing a Framework for Coordinating Interventions

When you build continuity into instructional programs across grade levels, you also improve your ability to plan interventions for individual students, as you can make provisions for teaching social skills from the very start of the year. This benefit is especially important for students who enter your setting without having mastered all the expectations for the previous level—your entry level. These students' prior teachers would be able to tell you specifically which expectations the students have not met, and you could establish priorities for their interventions right from the beginning of the year. You may even be able to do some preliminary planning of procedures based on this information, in much the same way you make provisions in the academic areas for students who may be a little behind their grade-level classmates.

Mrs. Armstrong may be able to obtain useful information from Ms. Warren, Mrs. Devetski, and Mr. Henson about individual students who will be in her fifth-grade program next year. By focusing her inquiry on specific expectations from her social skills curriculum, Mrs. Armstrong can go beyond the usual warnings and gripe sessions teachers often engage in and learn valuable information from her colleagues about students who could benefit from rapid assessment and intervention when they enter her program in the fall. Of course, she would want to make sure that the information the other teachers give her is not outdated, biased, or prejudicial in any way. She will plan a preliminary assessment of the students' behavior when they enter her class to verify the recommendations the teachers have given her and to learn whether the students have improved their social skills during the summer break.

In a similar way, your work with teachers at the next grade level could focus on discussing how they could continue the interventions you started with your students, or how they could expand or follow up on the instructional lessons you have given your class. Not only would the teachers learn about the skills your students have been working on, but they would also obtain suggestions for effective teaching methods to use with the students to start the next year. For example, when she meets with the teachers from Jefferson Middle School, Mrs. Armstrong could discuss the interventions she developed for Granville, Alfred, and Sandy, and she could share the expectations and skill areas she thinks will still present difficulties for the three students in the following year.

Using a Worksheet to List Objectives

Once you have considered the various possibilities for working with teachers within or across grade levels, a short worksheet can help you clarify the specific aims you wish to accomplish before you actually approach these colleagues. You should include a listing of the personnel you plan to work with, and the settings that will be the focus of the coordinating activities. Figure 15.1 shows the worksheet Mrs. Armstrong filled out for working with Mr. Wagner and the other fifth-grade teachers at Madison Elementary School. She could use the same format to list her objectives in working with the fourth-grade teachers or the middle school teachers.

Using a worksheet at this point will help you limit the scope of your plans to objectives that are clearly manageable. Furthermore, it will help you avoid involving too many people at once in these efforts, a move that could hamper your pursuit of the objectives. Although it is important to keep grade-level staff apprised of what you are doing with the coordinating activities, an effective alternative to including everyone in the activities is to involve people at varying levels of participation. You could, for example, have some staff members collaborate at a very active level, especially those with whom you work well or those who will make a major contribution to your efforts. You could keep other members informed of the activities, and perhaps involve them more directly later, after the initial planning and field testing are completed.

In thinking about how to extend her social skills instructional activities, Mrs. Armstrong realizes from the start that she will have to be very limited and focused in what she hopes to accomplish. The fifth-grade staff at Madison Elementary School includes four general education fifth-grade teachers, three special education/remedial education teachers, three support personnel, and two other staff members who assist with supervision of the playground and cafeteria areas. She will have to limit both the number of people and the settings she will work with, and to define fairly narrowly the skill areas or problem behaviors she will address. After considering these issues, she could decide to expand her work with Mr. Wagner, because she already has a solid working relationship with him and because the differences in expectations across their programs seem to pose more problems for students than do most of the other settings in which the fifth graders participate. She could decide to work on a more limited basis with Mrs. Kellerman and Mr. Haskell because she is interested in the way her students respond to the social expectations of the less rigidly structured art and gym classes.

Mrs. Armstrong would also want to limit the scope of her work with the fourth- and sixth-grade teachers. She could decide to work primarily with Mrs. Devetski, who shares a planning period with her, and Mr. Taggert, who will probably have Granville, Sandy, and Alfred in his social studies classes at Jefferson

Figure 15.1 Mrs. Armstrong's planning worksheet for working with other teachers.

Worksheet 15.1. Setting Objectives for Working with Other Personnel within and across Grade Levels

Name: *Mrs. Armstrong* Date: *Dec.18*

Other personnel to work with:

Mr. Wagner

Ms. Hernandez

Mrs. Kellerman

Mr. Haskell

Objectives for collaborative work:

Some areas to work on:

- *Build more consistency in social expectations across 5th-grade classrooms, including art and gym*
- *Share social skills curriculum with teachers*
- *Help other teachers describe expectations for their classrooms*
- *Look for similarities in expectations across classrooms*
- *Compare standards for similar expectations*
- *Clarify differences in expectations—look for expectations we might want to change*
- *Develop a plan to teach students about the expectations across 5th-grade settings to help us start the school year*

Middle School next year. By limiting her initial efforts to working with these two teachers, Mrs. Armstrong can build a solid contact with the other grade levels before making more ambitious plans. She could also decide to limit her focus to building some general continuity across the grade levels, rather than starting out immediately with instructional programs or activities. In this way, she can wait until she gains more familiarity with the other teachers and their settings before suggesting particular social skill areas to work on.

Suggestions for Approaching Other Personnel

For many teachers, the most daunting aspect of coordinating social skills instruction both within and across grade levels is the prospect of burdening other school personnel with additional tasks. Many teachers feel uncomfortable making demands of their already overworked colleagues. Also, there is often a vague taboo against prying into what other teachers do in their settings—a fear of seeming nosy or judgmental (Deal & Peterson, 1990; Villa & Thousand, 1992). This fear of prying is particularly strong in schools where the faculty and other personnel do not regularly work together on planning lessons, interventions, and other instructional tasks. But even in schools like these that have a strong "hands off" tradition, the work you have done on your social skills curriculum, interventions, and instructional lessons will assist you in approaching colleagues in a nonthreatening, nonintrusive manner. In this section we give some suggestions for collaborating with school personnel in ways that lead to a productive and cooperative working relationship.

Using the Direct Approach

Often you can request teachers' cooperation directly, explaining what you hope to accomplish and asking for their assistance. From working together on other projects and activities, you may have built a solid collegial relationship that can serve as the springboard for coordinating social skills instruction. Or you may have involved the teachers in interventions for individual students in the past, or sought their ideas in planning instructional lessons for your class. In such cases, they may already be interested in learning about the approaches you are using to teach social skills and may want to learn how to adapt them to their own circumstances. Mrs. Armstrong knows that Mr. Wagner is familiar with what she has done with Granville, Alfred, and Sandy because he assisted her in some of the planning, assessment, and intervention activities. At this point she would find it very easy to approach Mr. Wagner about coordinating expectations across their settings; he already recognizes the importance of improving students' social behavior and has expressed an interest in working with her further on expanding and broadening her teaching efforts.

Using the Indirect Approach

In other cases, you may have to obtain the cooperation of other teachers or staff members in a more roundabout way. With some staff members, you may have to

Administrators can assist with collaboration among teachers from different schools.

open lines of communication for the very first time and gradually build a rapport with them before even discussing the issue of coordinating social skills instruction (Villa & Thousand, 1992). The indirect route may be the best choice when you approach teachers from other schools with whom you have never worked before. In such cases it is usually helpful to start by talking about your own setting rather than theirs; you can share your list of expectations, explain the priorities you have defined for your setting, and describe the work you have done in teaching social skills to your students. Then, as a firmer foundation for working together is established, you can discuss the need for and the benefits of a better coordinated program.

When your working relationship with staff is somewhat tentative, it is usually best to approach them initially by seeking their assistance in improving your own instructional program. For teachers within your own grade level, you could ask for advice about addressing certain skill areas, or seek their aid in working with a particular student about whom you both have concerns. For teachers in other grade levels, you can ask their help in smoothing your students' transitions between your two settings. Mrs. Armstrong has never worked closely with Mrs. Devetski and is unsure how she will react to the idea of coordinating instruction across fourth- and fifth-grade settings. But on occasion, the two teachers have discussed some of the problems their students have in adjusting socially from the self-contained fourth-grade classrooms to the departmentalized structure of the fifth-grade program. In approaching Mrs. Devetski, Mrs. Armstrong will first ask for suggestions on ways to help students make the transition between grades, specifically focusing on the social aspects of performance, such as improving peer relationships or increasing participation in classroom activities. Their conversation could eventually lead to a discussion of how to coordinate their programs to prepare students better for adapting to the social demands of the fifth grade.

When you contact teachers from other schools, you will probably need to be quite deliberate in planning what you hope to accomplish, and you should be ready to provide the teachers with basic information about the social demands you are addressing in your settings. You should also obtain administrative approval and support for the activities. Before Mrs. Armstrong meets with Mr. Taggert, she should inform the principals at both Madison Elementary and Jefferson Middle School about her objectives for coordinating social skills instruction between the school programs. She could begin her conversation with Mr. Taggert by showing him her social skills curriculum and asking for suggestions for expanding or clarifying it to better anticipate the demands of the middle school settings. She could follow this by discussing common concerns or problems they have both observed, asking for his ideas for possible procedures or activities for improving students' behavior, and working together to develop solutions. With this kind of introduction to break the ice, it is usually very easy to interest your colleagues in at least a basic coordination of social skills instruction (Sheridan, Kratochwill, & Elliott, 1990).

When you engage other teachers in this sort of dialogue, the increased communication and the benefits to students usually make up quickly for any initial uneasiness or inconvenience you may experience. If you feel you are demanding too much from other teachers, remind yourself that having students who are more socially competent and better prepared for the demands of their classes will compensate these teachers for the time and effort they may spend in developing a coordinated program (Stainback, Stainback, & Moravec, 1992).

❍ Coordinating Social Expectations among Settings

Once you have gained the interest and commitment of the other personnel, you can begin discussing ways to coordinate and teach social skills in your settings. You can begin this process by looking at ways to link the social expectations among the settings, as doing so involves only comparing the different settings; the actual program changes would come later. In this section, we discuss some strategies for comparing and reconciling differences in social expectations among settings. This can be a fairly open-ended process, so we will not present a specific worksheet for planning your strategy beyond the one we showed earlier for outlining basic objectives. The social skills curriculum you prepared earlier for your own setting is usually an effective starting point for promoting better coordination of social expectations.

The key to the comparison process is to use the social skills curriculum as a common neutral ground that you all can work from together. In sharing your curriculum, you should avoid appearing judgmental and take care not to put other personnel on the defensive for things they do differently. In addition, you should structure the discussions to refrain from focusing on the students' characteristics, backgrounds, and labels; focus instead on their problem behaviors and the difficulties the students have meeting expectations, or on areas of behavior that can be improved to increase the students' social competence. You can start the process of comparing and coordinating instructional programs by talking to other teachers and personnel about your classroom routine and the teaching activities you use, showing them your list of expectations, and bringing them up to date on your overall program planning. Mrs. Armstrong could give a copy of her social skills curriculum to Mr. Wagner, Mrs. Kellerman, and Mr. Haskell, and discuss how the expectations for her classroom compare to the demands in theirs. Together, they can talk about key areas of agreement in expectations, routines, and activities; identify and negotiate differences in social demands; set common instructional priorities; and use the list of expectations as a framework for considering possible areas to work on together.

Working from the Similarities in Social Expectations

At the start of your coordinating activities, you should concentrate on the similarities between the expectations across settings rather than on the differences. A focus on similarities will allow you to compare social expectations, build greater consistency in their application, and develop an organized approach for carrying out social skills instruction and interventions. The curriculum items you share with other teachers offer a concrete means for describing and highlighting commonalities across settings.

One way to use the expectations that are similar across settings is to help the other teachers and staff formulate their own social skills curriculum. They can copy, restate, or broaden the common expectations from your already documented curriculum, and thus gain a head start in developing social skills curricula for their own settings. The similar expectations you find can also assist you and the other teachers in setting priorities for instruction across settings, sharing teaching methods and activities, planning new instructional approaches and lessons, and creating additional opportunities for students to practice and carry over their skills (Villa & Thousand, 1992).

Working from the Differences in Social Expectations

When you coordinate social skills instruction with other teachers, you need not be limited to the similarities you discover in your programs. The curriculum list can also provide an excellent framework for investigating and negotiating differences between expectations so students can learn to make smoother transitions across settings. Mrs. Armstrong and Mr. Wagner may find that they both have expectations for the amount of student participation in class discussions. However, the criterion level in Mrs. Armstrong's class may be that students contribute between three and five times to a discussion, whereas the level in Mr. Wagner's class is that students contribute about one time. This difference in criterion levels could pose a problem for some students: trying to meet the higher standard they have learned in Mrs. Armstrong's class, they may be perceived as talking too much in Mr. Wagner's classes and be admonished by him for trying to dominate the activity. After discussing this problem, the teachers may be able to work out a solution for applying the expectation more consistently across the settings. As this example suggests, many differences among settings can be eliminated by simple efforts to coordinate social expectations and conditions.

Of course, there may be substantial differences among settings that you will need to consider more carefully. Mrs. Armstrong may find that the sixth-grade teachers at Jefferson Middle School use very different situations and activities in their instructional routines, that they place a different emphasis on certain behaviors, or that they have completely different expectations and standards for what they consider acceptable or satisfactory. To keep track of differences like these, you might suggest that each teacher formulate a separate list of social expectations—an individual social skills curriculum. After the curricula for the settings are sketched out, you may find that you can negotiate several of the differences in social expectations by making minor shifts in the format or emphasis of classroom activities.

Other differences may not need to be changed at all because they are fairly subtle or because they occur in areas where students have few problems. You will undoubtedly elect to keep some differences in the expectations as natural variances between settings because of the instructional styles you use or the subject areas you teach. For example, Mrs. Armstrong generally encourages students to engage in an open sharing of ideas and answers when they work on homework in class, whereas Mr. Taggert expects his sixth-grade students to do their own work. The teachers might decide that this difference in expectations is central to the way they teach social studies; the increased personal responsibility placed on students reflects the progressive demands of the middle school curriculum. They could continue with these separate expectations but prepare their students to adjust to the more advanced requirements when they move to middle school. Thus, even when expectations vary across settings, the transition for students can be eased by the teachers' recognition of different demands and their commitment to communicating these differences to their students, while at the same time showing a unified emphasis on key social skills.

A special consideration in comparing expectations across grade levels is accounting for changes during the school year. Remember that the behavior expected of students at the beginning of the year may differ markedly from the behavior expected of them toward the end of the year. When you compare expectations with another teacher, make sure that you specify the points in the school year that serve as your primary referents. You will usually compare the social expectations at the end of the one year with those that apply at the beginning of the following year. Comparing social skills curricula at these points will give an accurate representation of the progress students must make in their behavior as they move between grades and will help you establish precise guidelines for smoothing their transitions.

Coordinating Instructional Activities among Settings

As you compare social expectations among settings, you may also want to design procedures and activities to promote better social skills and interactions among the students. In this section we offer suggestions for planning instructional activities across settings. You can use the procedures and worksheets presented in earlier chapters to organize your planning.

As in preparing intervention plans and instructional lessons, the first task in designing activities for use in multiple settings is to establish clear, reasonable, and manageable instructional goals for students (Graden & Bauer, 1992). To guide your planning, you may wish to review the procedures listed in Chapter Fourteen for selecting expectations to address in group instruction and for choosing priorities and target skills. After showing the other fifth-grade teachers her list of expectations for social studies class, Mrs. Armstrong could use the worksheet from Chapter Fourteen to help select expectations that her colleagues might want to address in their instruction. Using the worksheet, the teachers could discuss their priorities for the fifth-grade class, either for individual students or for the group as a whole. Together, they could establish target skills and explore ways to address them with a coordinated plan.

When you work with other teachers, remember that there is no single correct way to prepare instructional activities. The plan you devise could be as simple as a fundamental agreement to emphasize particular social expectations and skills during school activities. Mrs. Armstrong and Mr. Wagner could agree to work on improving the dynamics of large group lessons in their classrooms. They could work with the other fifth-grade teachers to establish a common structure for the groups or to enact a collective set of interaction ground rules so the work Mrs. Armstrong does with her specially planned activities would be reinforced in the other teachers' settings. If they wish to extend this approach, the teachers could brainstorm instructional procedures they could use to address this priority area. For instance, they could all place the students in the same types of seating arrangements, assign similar tasks and projects, and use the same types of directions and prompting procedures to develop and reinforce the target skills. In this way, all the teachers' instructional lessons could be carefully coordinated to encompass similar social demands, ground rules, and skill development activities.

Coordinating instructional procedures can be just as effective when working across grade levels as it is within grade-level programs. After Mrs. Armstrong and Mrs. Devetski have taken some steps to clarify and coordinate the social skills curricula across their fourth- and fifth-grade settings, they could discuss ways to collaborate on planning instructional procedures and activities as well. Focusing on the target skill of cooperating on group projects, the teachers could begin their lesson plans in Mrs. Devetski's class toward the end of the fourth-grade year and continue the procedures in Mrs. Armstrong's class the following year. In this way, the students would be much more likely to make a smooth transition to the more demanding group work characteristic of the fifth-grade setting.

Coordinating instructional programs across grade levels in this way can be particularly helpful when students must change from one school to another.

Consider, for instance, the wide-ranging changes in social expectations that occur when students move from a preschool program to an elementary school classroom, or from a junior high or middle school to a high school. These transitions could be greatly smoothed by a well-coordinated program of social skills instruction in both settings. Of course, such an approach poses special challenges: when we imagine program links between different schools or academic units, we tend to think right away of the difficulties of working with other principals, program coordinators, and department heads. But in fact, instructional plans can usually be coordinated much more effectively and informally through the most simple and direct channels of communication: teacher-to-teacher contact.

At mid-year, Mrs. Armstrong could meet with Mr. Taggert and Ms. Harrison at Jefferson Middle School to discuss the transition of her students to their classes next year. She would go through essentially the same process that she did with the fourth-grade teachers: select priority expectations and goals for instruction and plan lessons and activities to help smooth the students' transition to middle school. A key to this process is finding willing teachers in your local school district and making inroads with them in coordinating social skills instructional programs. The social skills curriculum for your setting is an important tool in this process because it provides a framework for communicating the demands for social competence to the other teachers.

In summary, you can coordinate your teaching of social skills with other school personnel to improve educational programs for students. One possibility is to develop a more consistent social skills program across settings at your grade level; another possibility is to develop a more continuous social skills program across grade levels and administrative units. The key step in this process is to establish clear and manageable aims for what you hope to accomplish in coordinating social skills instruction.

❍ Summary

Coordinating Social Skills Instruction with Other Settings

1. Two approaches to extending social skills instruction are the following:
   a. collaborating with school personnel at your grade level
   b. collaborating with school personnel at grade levels immediately preceding and following your level
2. Social demands in a single setting are only one part of the array of expectations students must meet to achieve social competence.
3. Differences in social expectations among grade-level settings can create problems in students' social behavior; collaborating with school staff can alleviate these problems.
4. Social demands change over time and become more advanced and challenging for students.
5. The progression of social demands across grade levels can create problems for students; collaborating with school staff can help address these problems.

Deciding What to Accomplish by Coordinating Social Skills Instruction

1. The first step in coordinating social skills instruction is deciding what objectives to accomplish.
2. Possible objectives for collaborating with personnel within a single grade level are the following:
   a. extending instructional lessons to other settings
   b. teaching students to respond to changes and inconsistencies in expectations
   c. reducing the number of shifts and inconsistencies in expectations
3. Possible objectives for collaborating with personnel across grade levels or schools are the following:
   a. gaining a better understanding of the skills new students have
   b. setting the focus for social instruction
   c. providing a framework for coordinating interventions
4. The objectives for collaborating with school personnel should be entered on a worksheet as an aid to planning activities.

Suggestions for Approaching Other Personnel

1. School personnel can be approached directly—by describing objectives and asking for the teachers' assistance—or indirectly—by first building rapport with the teachers and then giving them a rationale and explanation for activities.
2. The effort teachers make when coordinating instructional programs is compensated by the improvement in their students' social competence.

Coordinating Social Expectations among Settings

1. The social skills curriculum can be used to coordinate expectations across school settings.
2. Discussing similarities in expectations can lay the groundwork for a broader analysis and coordination of expectations.
3. Discussing differences in expectations can help to remove inconsistencies across settings or to prepare students to adjust to them.

Coordinating Instructional Activities among Settings

1. Coordinating instructional activities can reduce problems in students' social behavior and advance their performance beyond minimum levels of competence.
2. Developing instructional activities across successive grade levels can make the transition across settings easier for students.

Examples for Chapter 15

Example 15a

Mrs. Kim teaches preschool at a community agency serving children three to five years old. The children are grouped by age and developmental level; Mrs. Kim teaches the oldest group. She is concerned that many students have problems at the start of the school year because of their low level of social development and maturity. She is also troubled by reports the agency has received from local schools that many of the children have lacked key skills for kindergarten upon leaving the agency program. She feels that a coordinated effort to improve social skills instruction can lay the groundwork for addressing these problems, and she received approval from the agency director and the local school principal to assemble a task force. Mrs. Kim then decided to give structure and direction to the group's discussion by formulating some preliminary objectives. This is the worksheet she prepared.

Worksheet 15.1. Setting Objectives for Working with Other Personnel within and across Grade Levels

Name: *Mrs. Kim* Date: *Dec.15*

Other personnel to work with:

Mrs. Godfrey, volunteer
Ms. Santiago, teacher (3 yr. olds)
Ms. Brown, teacher (4 yr. olds)
Mrs. Franco, Program Coordinator
Ms. Yarborough, Parent Council
Mrs. Carter, teacher (kindergarten)

> Seek the support of those directly and indirectly responsible for instructional programs. Parents and administrators can be key participants in program planning.

Objectives for collaborative work:

At first meeting (December 18), describe deficits children show in my class and discuss problems children have making transitions between levels. Ask group members for their perspectives and discuss what they would like to achieve in the area of social skills.

> It is helpful to include projected dates for holding meetings and completing objectives.

Share social skills curriculum with task force members (by January 5)—seek their cooperation and support for working on social skills instruction between the agency and Kennedy Elementary School.

> In addition to the objectives themselves, the worksheet can be used to outline major steps toward achieving your aims.

Discuss similarities in expectations across program levels (by January 31). Choose one or two key settings to concentrate on and help other staff describe their social expectations. Compile expectations into a working school/agency cooperative curriculum.

Discuss dissimilarities in expectations across settings (by March 31). Consider options for developing greater continuity in expectations across program levels.

Develop a plan for improving the transition of children from one program level to the next (by April 30).

> Linking objectives to specific results keeps them from becoming vague or impractical.

Example 15b

Mrs. Ruiz is the special education resource room teacher at a large high school. Students come in throughout the day for tutoring on homework assignments, projects, and tests. She also teaches a study hall class, working with students on social skills and study habits.

Although her work addresses most subject areas, Mrs. Ruiz is concerned about the number of students who ask for help on industrial arts assignments. From talking with students and teachers in industrial arts, Mrs. Ruiz has learned that many of her students find it difficult to ask for assistance on assignments, to cooperate with partners on small group activities, and to participate in study and work groups. Although she has been working on these areas with students individually and in small groups, they still seem unable to apply the skills to the industrial arts settings.

Mrs. Ruiz has conducted several observations in the industrial arts classroom and has asked to attend the next department meeting. She would like to share some of her work in teaching social skills and explore areas for collaboration so her students can participate more effectively in classroom activities. This worksheet shows the objectives she has set for the meeting.

Worksheet 15.1. Setting Objectives for Working with Other Personnel within and across Grade Levels

Name: *Mrs. Ruiz* Date: *Dec.17*

Other personnel to work with:

Mr. Carlson, industrial arts teacher
Mr. Garrison, industrial arts teacher
Ms. Foster, industrial arts teacher

Objectives for collaborative work:

Give a general overview of how social skills can affect academic achievement, learning activities, peer interactions, and classroom disciplinary practices.

Describe some of my projects in teaching social skills. Focus on specific examples—teaching David to ask questions, having Harold work with peer tutors.

Share the results of my projects. Highlight the ways more competent social skills affected the students' grades, their interest in activities, and their interpersonal relationships.

Discuss how techniques for improving social skills can be adapted to industrial arts settings. Have teachers present options.

Propose follow-up discussion of social skills teaching techniques at February's meeting to explore other options for improving social competence. Set up times for follow-up observations.

Starting a dialogue about social skills with school staff can lead to a coordinated effort to develop instructional approaches.

Talking about particular students can help capture the interest of other teachers and lower any initial resistance.

One of the best ways to encourage collaborative work is by observing in the settings where other teachers work.

Mr. Wagner's Case Study

After talking to Mrs. Armstrong about her work, Mr. Wagner decided he would also like to try working with personnel in other settings. He brainstormed some plans for extending social skills instruction, and made a short list of his ideas on his worksheet.

It is important to specify whom you will meet with. Mr. Wagner should list the individual teachers he plans to contact.

Although working with community agencies can be very effective, Mr. Wagner's plans are both premature and overly ambitious. He should outline the topics he wants to discuss with Mr. Lomax and Mr. Scully instead of focusing on long-term plans.

Mr. Wagner's objectives are too vague and wide-ranging to be practical. He should narrow his focus to one of these projects and more thoroughly develop his plans for making contacts.

It is usually best to begin discussions with other teachers by talking about your own settings, rather than theirs. Mr. Wagner should talk about what students need to learn in his classroom to be ready for the sixth grade.

Worksheet 15.1. Setting Objectives for Working with Other Personnel within and across Grade Levels

Name: *Mr. Wagner* Date: *Dec. 24*

Other personnel to work with:

Mrs. Goldstein, school counselor

Ms. Lomax, coordinator of Extended Day Program

Mr. Scully, director of Boys and Girls Club

Sixth-grade teachers at Jefferson Middle School

Objectives for collaborative work:

Ask Mrs. Goldstein if the school can support an after-school tutoring group for children through the extended day program.

Ask Mr. Lomax and Mr. Scully to start an after-school sports program on school grounds to improve students' athletic and social skills. The program could include the middle school as well, with the older children acting as models for the younger ones.

Start after-school clubs for students (Literature Club, Photography Club) to work on self-esteem.

Get together with sixth-grade teachers from Jefferson Middle School. Talk with them about the social behavior of their students, and ask what kinds of activities they use in their settings.

APPENDIX A

Expectations for Social Behavior

The following real-life examples were taken from the worksheets of teachers who completed course projects with us; they will be useful in several types of school settings and situations at five program levels:

1. Preschool to kindergarten
2. Primary (grades 1–3)
3. Intermediate (grades 4–6)
4. Middle school/junior high school (grades 7–8)
5. High school (grades 9–12)

The lists clarify the concepts in the first chapters of the book by providing concrete examples of social expectations met by typical students.

You can use this appendix as a guide when you prepare your own social skills curriculum. The expectations presented here will give you a clearer picture of the social behavior of your own students and of how to describe this behavior in terms of expectations for social competence. Although we have listed fairly common school situations and behaviors, they are not likely to match your own settings precisely; the lists do not replace direct observation of your students. You should use this catalog as a model, adapting the expectations to the behavior and demands you observe in your own students.

Guidelines and Reminders

- We have tried to avoid excessive repetition of expectations and situations. When preparing your own social skills curriculum, however, remember that many expectations will apply in several situations.
- We have categorized our lists by grade level, but many of the situations and expectations can be adapted to younger or older students. For example, the lunchtime behavior of junior high school students may well be similar to that described in the upper elementary or high school lists.

- The expectations we have listed represent typical student behavior, not necessarily the behavior their teachers prefer.
- These expectations do not represent behaviors that every student performs every day. To make them functional in a social skills curriculum, we would need to define standards for each of them, describing their extent and frequency. This process is discussed in Chapter Three.
- Make sure that the standards you define in your social skills curriculum are based on the actual performance levels of your students. We do not provide samples of standards because units of measure and criterion levels must be linked to the real-life situations where performance will be assessed.
- No catalog of social expectations can be absolutely comprehensive. What makes these lists valuable is the range of social behavior they describe. They give a broad and vivid picture of the way typical students interact. This is what you should strive to achieve in your own social skills curriculum.

Preschool to Kindergarten Level

Setting: Outside School
Situation: Morning Arrival

Shows anticipation when arriving in car or bus (moving forward, stretching to look out windows).

Waves to greet teacher.

Seeks teacher's attention.

Waits in assigned area.

Calls to friends to come join group.

Sits by friends.

Talks about belongings, popular characters, and so on.

Shows affection by hugging teacher.

Gestures good-bye to caregiver or parent.

Walks with other children.

Puts away belongings (coat, backpack).

Moves to play areas.

Setting: Large Group Instruction Area
Situation: Language Lessons with Stimulus Cards

Talks excitedly about activity ("What are we going to do?").

Quiets down when teacher enters area.

Responds to teacher's greeting by word or action.

Listens to directions.

Answers teacher's questions in unison with group.

Waits until teacher finishes directions before taking up language cards.

Shows interest in game by holding cards in hands, showing cards to neighbors, or talking about cards.

Waits turn to speak about cards.

Contributes ideas or thoughts to the discussion.

Participates in games and activities along with the group.

Follows leadership of other students in activities (imitates actions or follows directions).

Smiles and whispers to friends.

Shows excitement with group.

Setting: Reading Area
Situation: Story Time

Responds to new environment with curiosity.

Sits in circle with classmates.

Negotiates to sit near friends.

Speaks with peers about seating ("Sit here," "Scoot over.").

Responds to closeness of other children in positive manner (touching, patting, or giggling).

Keeps eyes on teacher.

Becomes calmer as story time begins.

Participates in activity through facial expressions, clapping, or laughing.

Sings with group as teacher leads.

Attempts to learn words and motions.

Listens as teacher reads.

Looks at pictures in book.

Moves to convey interest (inches forward or stretches to see).

Responds to story situations with appropriate emotions (humor, fear, or sadness).

Asks questions about story.

Joins in discussion of characters (may or may not stay on topic).

Answers questions and makes predictions about the characters.

Catches self when interrupting (hand over mouth, "Oops!").

Giggles and smiles at peers during story.

Talks with classmates after story ("Did it scare you?").

Anticipates next activity ("Can we see Barney today?").

Setting: Classroom Play Area
Situation: Free Play Time

Selects partner to play with.

Chooses place or activity to play.

Uses words and gestures to express ownership (rather than hitting).

Shows interest and excitement.

Asks adult or other children to join them in play.

Shares activities and play objects with playmates.

Talks while playing ("Look at this!" "You take the truck.").

Works toward a common goal with a playmate.

Moves between several play centers or play groups.

Watches and comments on other children's play.

Asks to join group or activity.

Waits turn to play with toys or games.

Chooses another toy or activity when preferred one is chosen by someone else.

Uses toys and play objects for their intended purpose.

Stops playing when directed by teacher.

Setting: Classroom Play Area
Situation: Cleanup Time

Begins picking up when directed by teacher.

Cooperates with teachers and other children in putting away toys.

Asks questions when uncertain what to do.

Responds to reminders to stop playing and get back to cleaning up.

Talks with other children while cleaning area.

Responds to directions and suggestions of other children.

Races other children to finish first.

Reminds others to help with cleanup.

Helps others when finished picking up own area.

Goes to instruction area when pickup is complete.

Talks with neighbors while waiting for teacher to begin next activity.

Setting: Classroom
Situation: Transition to Playground

Displays eagerness and excitement for outdoor activities.

Listens to and follows teacher's directions.

Scurries to door with group.

Asks for assistance when needed ("Help me zip this.").

Seeks a partner ("Hold my hand," "Walk with me.").

Defends position ("I was here first.").

Laughs, chats, and touches in the hall ("What do you want to play?" "That witch is spooky.").

Walks, hops, or jumps along the way.

Responds to teacher corrections.

Walks hurriedly, bunching up into a group.

Squeals, shouts, and runs to the playground.

Setting: Playground
Situation: Free Play during Recess

Rushes to play areas.

Joins friends and classmates.

Talks with friends about toys, cartoons, and games.

Takes turn talking and choosing topics.

Gives nonverbal encouragement to friends by patting, laughing, or smiling.

Participates in tag or running games.

Shouts and teases others during games ("I'll catch you!" "I'm faster than you!").

Shares humor with peers ("Let's scare the teacher.").

Seeks teacher recognition ("Watch me!" "He caught me!").

Squeals, laughs, and runs randomly.

Follows teacher's suggestions for choosing play activities.

Mixes and mingles with several different children.

Asks teacher for help when needed (falling down, losing ball, shoes untied, or settling disputes).

Runs to line-up at teacher direction.

❍ Primary Level: Grades 1 to 3

Setting: Classroom
Situation: Presentation of Day's Lesson

Listens to teacher's directions and instructions.

Volunteers for class jobs (passing out papers or reading directions).

Gets out required materials.

Helps classmates find materials, shares pencils and other supplies.

Pays attention to teacher.

Raises hand and volunteers to answer teacher's questions.

Whispers or motions to neighbors.

Responds to correction by paying better attention.

Talks quietly with others while teacher checks homework sheets.

Comments to teacher when homework sheet is presented.

Compares results with neighbor.

Setting: Classroom
Situation: Transition to Reading Groups

Gets out materials for reading.

Goes to reading tables (may rush or may lag behind a little).

Helps others get chairs down from table.

Sits with students of same gender.

Encourages friends to join group.

Negotiates disputes over seating.

Accepts teacher direction on grouping (boys and girls sitting together or friends splitting up).

Talks quietly with neighbors until activity starts.

Setting: Classroom (Group Tables)
Situation: Reading Out Loud

Sits close and touches.

Leaves space between seats.

Suggests activities (favorite way to read aloud or games).

Finds story in book.

Pays attention to teacher (eye contact and listening).

Volunteers enthusiastically for teacher questions (waving hand, "Me! I know!").

Shows excitement about wanting to read next (makes noise, sits up, or waves arm in the air).

Looks for approval from teacher when finished reading.

Looks at student reading several times during passage.

Follows along (or pretends to) when others are reading.

Nods quietly while other person reads.

Offers help and encouragement to peers (pointing out place or whispering word).

Checks to see if teacher is watching.

Gives an excuse, jokes, or looks guilty when caught not having place.

Offers guesses and shows curiosity about story.

Relates story to personal experiences.

Helps put chairs back before returning to desks.

Setting: Classroom
Situation: Vocabulary Game (Two Teams)

Talks excitedly with teammates about upcoming game.

Watches teacher as vocabulary words are held up on cards.

Offers guesses and shows curiosity about the new words.

Raises hands or looks attentive to get teacher's attention.

Volunteers eagerly to say new vocabulary word ("Choose me!").

Encourages teammates.

Helps team members with hard words (whispers answers).

Responds to other students' slow responses by looking at neighbors (may make faces or roll eyes).

Shows excitement or frustration with team's performance.

Smiles when praised by teacher or peers.

Discusses new vocabulary with neighbors.

Obtains neighbors' attention with gestures or light touching.

Tells teacher when other team's answer is wrong.

Follows the lead of dominant students in group in judging answers or correcting errors.

Reminds others of game rules.

Cheers and claps when team wins.

Expresses disappointment (but not anger) when team loses.

Setting: Cafeteria
Situation: Lining up to Go Outside

Finishes eating quickly and cleans up when table is called.

Encourages others at table to hurry.

Lines up with table group.

Reminds peers of rules when violated.

Talks with others while waiting.

Touches and jostles in line.

Plays with friend's hair (girls).

Takes turns lifting one another (boys).

Plans recess activities.

Helps form teams for recess.

Asks friends to join teams.

Jokes with teacher (begging for early dismissal, complaining about rules).

Follows teacher out of building.

Setting: Playground
Situation: Nonorganized Activities

Chooses playmates.

Discusses rules or guidelines for playing.

Plays by rules of activity.

Shares toys or takes turns playing.

Uses toys for their intended purpose.

Defers to the owner of toys by allowing owner to have first choice or have more say in the activities.

Reports to teacher signs of potential trouble.

Cooperates in picking up toys when activity is finished.

Asks to join play groups.

Accepts other playmates into group.

Talks about activity while playing.

Stops playing when whistle blows.

Discusses activity with playmate as they walk to line.

Lines up in a timely manner (may lag a little behind the group).

Stays with line while walking through the hall.

Talks quietly.

Places toys in designated place on entering classroom.

Setting: Playground
Situation: Playing on Playground Equipment

Races to equipment.

Plays in groups of same age and gender.

Laughs and jokes while playing.

Uses equipment as gathering place for friends.

Teases classmates of opposite gender.

Teases classmates by taking something (shoe, hat, or ribbon).

Responds to teasing by laughing, chasing, or teasing back.

Resolves conflicts within group (without teacher).

Sits and talks on equipment (girls).

Pushes rules for equipment: running up slide or swinging sideways (boys).

Follows playground rules when teacher is watching.

Moves freely between activities and equipment.

Slide Area

Decides which slides to use for different types of play.

Stands in line to wait turn.

Talks with others while in line.

Encourages others to slide ("Hurry up!").

Shows excitement with sliding by sharing and comparing experience with friends ("Did you see me?").

Cooperates with friends to form trains to slide down together (when teacher is not looking).

Takes turns being first in train.

Swings

Shares swing within a group.

Pushes friends' swings.

Asks to take turn.

Smiles or claps while watching others swing.

Asks friends to push.

Competes with friends to swing highest.

Jumps out while swinging.

Talks about activity with friends.

Takes turn without hogging swing.

Saves swing for friend.

Other Equipment

Does flips on monkey bars.

Sits on bars and talks.

Congratulates peers on challenging feats.

Copies new tricks ("Now let me try.").

Seeks attention from friends ("Look at this one!").

Laughs about mistakes.

Uses Timberform as an imaginary place (fort, ship).

Negotiates play situation before beginning ("You be the pirates.").

Develops a plan of attack for chasing others.

Accepts and follows leader's plan .

Setting: Playground
Situation: Talking in Small Groups

Chooses group based on age, friendship, or gender.

Plays while talking (boys).

Stands (not playing) while talking (girls).

Moves quickly between topics.

Follows topics set by group leaders (popular students).

Suggests new topics.

Talks about family, toys, or pets (girls).

Talks about self, other boys, or bikes (boys).

Listens to other group members.

Interrupts occasionally to show interest when others are talking ("Yeah, that happened to me too.").

Uses casual tone with friends.

Speaks more formally when teacher or nongroup member approaches.

Talks at appropriate volume (so group members can hear, but others are not disturbed).

Walks around in small group.

Interacts with other groups.

Visits with teacher, talks about shared interests.

Setting: Classroom
Situation: Lining up to Leave School for the Day

Talks with classmates while getting ready to go home.

Takes time getting things together.

Encourages others to be quiet or sit up straight.

Looks at teacher expectantly while waiting to line up.

Lines up quickly when name is called.

Seeks out friends in line by turning around or changing places.

Laughs, teases, and jokes with others.

Shows off cool backpack or toys to other students.

Listens to other students' exaggerated stories.

Joins in and elaborates on story.

Shares last-minute comments with teacher and says "good-bye."

Leaves class with the group.

❍ Intermediate Level: Grades 4 to 6

Setting: Social Studies Classroom
Situation: Presentation of Lesson

Listens, pays attention to teacher.

Looks for recognition from teacher by whispering, smiling, or holding up hand.

Raises hand before speaking.

Responds to questions asked by teacher.

Volunteers to help teacher pass out materials.

Takes notes on presentation or copies assignment from board.

Gains attention of peers by glancing at them, smiling.

Gives feedback on others' answers.

Offers suggestions to neighbors in answering questions.

Checks progress against neighbor's notes.

Helps others who are called on by whispering answers or making gestures.

Asks questions when help is needed.

Talks quietly with classmates at the end of presentation.

Setting: Math Classroom
Situation: Homework Review and Boardwork Activity

Takes out book and homework at teacher's request.

Shares materials or supplies when asked.

Pays attention to teacher with frequent eye contact.

Volunteers to work problems on board.

Goes to board when called on.

Asks questions for clarification.

Asks neighbors to repeat what teacher says.

Talks quietly with neighbor about problems being worked ("What did you get for number five?").

Encourages and supports classmate's answer when agreeing with it.

Offers alternative answer when disagreeing.

Communicates nonverbally with friends across the room (gesturing, mouthing words).

Makes certain teacher is not looking before teasing or clowning.

Responds to teacher's eye contact by getting back on task.

Talks with neighbor about assignment or next activity when boardwork is finished.

Setting: Science Classroom
Situation: Worksheet Activity

Listens, watches, pays attention when teacher holds up worksheet.

Asks questions about assignment.

Shares supplies with neighbors as needed.

Works quietly at desk.

Raises hand for assistance.

Seeks approval of teacher ("Is this right?").

Checks progress with neighbors.

Helps other students when asked.

Follows feedback and directions of neighbors.

Exchanges smiles or gestures with neighbors, friends.

Greets other teachers who enter room.

Listens to teacher talking with other students, tries to answer questions or join in the discussion.

Responds to teacher's eye contact or other prompts by getting back to work.

Checks to see who else is done after finishing.

Draws or reads while waiting for others to finish.

Talks quietly with others who have finished.

Encourages others to finish up work.

Gives praise to friends who finish, invites them to join conversation.

Helps pass up papers when activity ends.

Setting: Science Classroom
Situation: Grading Worksheets

Talks and whispers about assignment when trading papers.

Raises hand and volunteers proudly to share answers.

Trades glances, rolls eyes, and whispers answers to others.

Reacts to right and wrong answers ("Yess!" "Awww.").

Marks answers on neighbor's worksheet.

Checks neighbor to make sure own worksheet is graded correctly.

Smiles, laughs, or makes funny faces while returning worksheets.

Compares grades with neighbors.

Gets out materials for next activity.

Setting: Language Arts Classroom
Situation: Small Group Activity

Listens to teacher's directions and group assignment.

Visits with friends while going to group.

Talks with group members until teacher repeats assignment.

Whispers with neighbor during teacher's directions (but listens to directions).

Talks over assignment with group.

Offers suggestions and ideas for carrying out assignment, makes compromises.

Laughs or smiles at funny remarks.

Shares in doing work on the assignment.

Follows suggestions of group leader.

Shows tolerance for other's ideas, suggestions, and comments.

Raises hand or volunteers to get help from teacher, when needed.

Works out disagreements within the group.

Accepts suggestions or criticism from group members.

Stays on task long enough to get assignment completed on time.

Continues talking with group members about the assignment or other topics when teacher ends the activity.

Setting: Cafeteria
Situation: Entering Cafeteria, Getting into Line

Enters cafeteria quickly (running or walking fast).

Pushes and shoves playfully (boys).

Talks and acts mature (girls).

Lingers at door and waits for friends.

Cuts in line to join friends.

Talks in loud happy tones.

Laughs and smiles upon joining friends.

Gossips with friends.

Flirts with others by "accidental" hitting or teasing.

Talks and visits with teachers on duty.

Talks and laughs in food line.

Pushes, shoves, or teases others.

Keeps moving with line.

Setting: Cafeteria
Situation: Eating with Friends

Greets friends at table.

Saves places for those still getting food.

Jokes and shares personal stories (about teachers, classmates, and assignments).

Makes plans for recess activities by choosing teams and discussing game rules.

Steals food from friends' trays.

Laughs about cafeteria food.

Shares food with friends.

Cleans up language and changes subject when teacher approaches.

Quiets down when teacher raises hand or asks for attention.

Encourages others to quiet down so table can be dismissed.

Pushes in chair, disposes of trash, and returns trays and dishes.

Joins friends before leaving room.

Teases or pushes playfully while leaving.

Setting: Playground
Situation: Playing Organized Games

Participates in choosing teams and team leaders (popular students act as leaders).

Approaches group leaders to ask to join game ("Can I play?").

Accepts and includes new players ("Sure! Stand over here.").

Decides and agrees on rules, teams, and boundaries.

Follows directions and suggestions of team leader.

Plays by rules of game (may try to bend rules).

Encourages teammates ("Good play!" "Come on, Brian!").

Joins in on competitive interplay with opponents ("My grandma throws better than that!").

Teases other players.

Plays physically and tries hard.

Plays with girls and boys equally.

Shows disapproval through gestures and expression.

Supports teammates in disagreements about plays and rules.

Resolves disagreements without teacher's intervention.

Continues playing until whistle signals end of recess.

Tries for one or two last plays after whistle blows.

Discusses outcome of game with teammates while lining up (may dispute specific plays or the final score but not vehemently).

Supports teammates in discussion of game's outcome.

Quiets down (but continues whispering) upon entering building.

❍ Middle School/Junior High School Level: Grades 7 and 8

Setting: General Science Classroom
Situation: Class Start-up and Preview

Whispers, smiles, and giggles at friends while sitting down.

Talks with friends and neighbors until bell rings.

Engages in playful teasing, jokes, and harmless pranks with friends.

Borrows or lends school supplies and lunch money.

Quiets down when teacher enters room.

Exchanges greetings with teacher.

Listens to announcements (may look at books or whisper to friends).

Responds to announcements by smiling and motioning to neighbors or exchanging knowing glances with friends.

Supplies additional information to class about particular announcements.

Asks questions of teacher for clarification.

Talks in lively tones after announcements end.

Quiets down when teacher begins talking.

Listens to teacher's opening comments and remarks.

Nods and smiles to show agreement and understanding.

Responds to nonverbal correction from teacher (sharp glance or pause in presentation).

Gets out materials at teacher's direction.

Starts next activity with the group.

Setting: Social Studies Classroom
Situation: Small Group Discussion

Talks and jokes while rearranging chairs.

Negotiates to join group with friends.

Complies with teacher's grouping.

Gets quiet as teacher introduces activity.

Asks for clarifications about activity.

Begins group activity.

Cooperates in working on the assignment (contributes ideas and suggestions).

Argues with group members in good-natured way and resolves disagreements without teacher intervention.

Talks, laughs, and shares personal examples with the group.

Returns to topic when directed by teacher or group leader.

Checks group progress with teacher.

Listens as teacher talks to other groups nearby.

Compares ideas with other groups.

Talks and visits with friends when task is complete (while waiting for other groups to finish).

Listens to presentation by group leaders.

Shares in discussion of group's work with the teacher and class.

Claps for each group after presentation is complete.

Listens and smiles as teacher praises group.

Talks with animation while returning seats to normal place.

Setting: Social Studies Classroom
Situation: Review of Homework Assignments

Talks quietly with neighbor about work done (or not done).

Checks with neighbor on last-minute questions or answers about assignment.

Quiets down and waits for instructions.

Listens to teacher presentation.

Raises hand to volunteer answers.

Asks questions when help or clarification is needed.

Gives excuses when not having an answer or knowing that answer is wrong.

Looks to neighbor for help when called on (may give a helpless or imploring look if help is not immediately forthcoming).

Keeps questions and comments on topic of discussion.

Helps collect work when review is completed.

Shares expected grade with neighbor, gives excuses for getting some answers wrong.

Listens and takes notes during presentation of next assignment.

Joins group in complaining and groaning about the difficulty or length of the assignment.

Negotiates good-naturedly for more time to complete homework ("How about giving us the weekend?").

Comments to neighbors about next assignment.

Setting: Math Classroom
Situation: Class Dismissal

Talks with neighbors about class activities, assignments, and personal experiences.

Asks teacher for clarification of assignment.

Gathers personal items (books, purse, or backpack).

Stays in seat until bell rings.

Moves desk back to proper position.

Seeks out friends when leaving the room and talks, jokes, or playfully teases them.

Goes over plans to meet with friends later in the day.

Exchanges good-byes with teacher.

Pushes and shoves when leaving the room (boys).

Talks and visits with teacher after class.

Teases and acts silly when arriving in the hallway.

Setting: School Entrance Area
Situation: Entering Building at Start of the Day

Looks for friends and exchanges greetings.

Talks with friends and classmates while walking into building.

Holds door for next person.

Goes quickly to locker area.

Deposits books and gets materials for first class.

Joins peer groups (same age and gender).

Talks about common interests or timely topics.

Shows interest in what others are saying (nodding head, "Uh huh.").

Bunches with group and watches other students in area.

Gossips and comments with group on nearby students.

Delivers notes from friends to boys or girls in other groups.

Greets and talks with teachers and other passing adults.

Goes to office to handle personal concerns.

Takes care of bathroom and grooming needs, checks appearance.

Arrives at classroom on time.

Setting: Commons Area
Situation: After-Lunch Conversation Groups

Joins in without disrupting group interaction.

Interacts with peers rather than teacher.

Chooses a group with a mutual interest.

Talks in huddle with group.

Talks about appearances and compares self to others (girls).

Complains about school rules.

Relates other students' problems to own life.

Expresses admiration or envy for other students' situations.

Discusses future changes (high school or dating).

Discusses current school or town events.

Shifts to a new topic when group has lost interest in current topic.

Uses physical contact with friends (playing with hair or light shoving).

Moves freely between groups.

Flirts with boys or girls.

Engages in playful teasing.

Responds to teasing, jokes, or pranks by smiling or teasing back.

Moves to locker area as lunch period ends.

❍ High School Level: Grades 9 to 12

Setting: Band Room
Situation: Getting Ready for Class

Enters room talking with friends and greeting classmates.

Exchanges greetings with teacher.

Talks with teacher about assignments, practice lessons, upcoming activities, and other school-related topics.

Waits turn while getting instrument from storage, apologizes for bumping into people.

Shares in playful pranks with classmates.

Responds to pranks by laughing, pretending to be angry, or telling them to "Just wait until next time!"

Sets up music stand and assembles and tunes instrument, coordinates activities with those close by.

Greets and talks with neighbors, laughs and jokes about awkward behaviors in setting up for class.

Helps others complete their setup.

Gets music ready for class by asking neighbors about class activities, helping others find correct place, exchanging comments about music selections.

Tunes instrument and laughs and jokes about sour notes, shares humorous events with neighbors.

Offers and accepts constructive feedback on tuning activities.

Talks, jokes, and engages in playful teasing with neighbors.

Finishes tuning instrument and waits for teacher to begin class.

Comes to attention when teacher starts class (may continue whispering, smiling, or exchanging glances with neighbors).

Setting: Literature Classroom
Situation: Large Group Discussion

Talks loudly while waiting for discussion to start.

Listens to teacher's introduction.

Hesitates before beginning discussion (reticent about going first).

Offers short answer to direct query from teacher.

Clarifies or elaborates on statements when asked.

Backs up comments and opinions by citing examples from the textbook or personal experiences.

Defends position or acknowledges errors when someone disagrees with statement.

Adds comments more freely as discussion progresses.

Adds new observations on subject (rather than going on tangents or repeating what has already been covered).

Looks at teacher when teacher speaks.

Listens to classmates' comments.

Exchanges glances to show disagreement.

Nods and whispers "yes" when agreeing.

Follows up on other students' comments with own ideas, suggestions, opinions.

Gives feedback and criticism in a diplomatic, noncombative manner.

Shares ideas with neighbor quietly before making comments to the whole class.

Writes short notes to neighbors (when teacher isn't looking).

Exchanges smiles and whispers with friends.

Joins with group in smiling or laughing at funny comments or stories.

Gathers books and gets ready to leave when bell rings.

Setting: Health Occupations Classroom and Laboratory
Situation: Working on Projects with Partners

Reviews project guidelines with partner.

Discusses steps for working on project, agrees on a strategy for completing activities.

Helps get out supplies and equipment.

Cooperates in completing activities (does a fair share of the work).

Offers suggestions and gives feedback to partner.

Compares work with other groups.

Works out problems and difficult parts of project with neighboring groups.

Talks with teacher about the assignment (describes work done, seeks additional ideas and suggestions).

Shares humorous incidents or comments with partner, teacher, or nearby students.

Talks quietly with students nearby when finished.

Setting: Health Occupations Classroom and Laboratory
Situation: End of Lab Activities and Cleanup

Quickly finishes last steps of project when teacher says to clean up.

Shares final comments about project with partner or neighbors.

Hands in notes or worksheets.

Discusses results with other groups.

Asks teacher about difficult steps or problems ("What were we supposed to get for Part Three?").

Shares in putting away equipment and supplies.

Helps partner finish cleanup activities.

Returns to seat when finished.

Copies assignment from board.

Discusses assignment with neighbors.

Talks with neighbors until bell rings (jokes, talks about next class, or discusses upcoming test).

Waits for dismissal before leaving area.

Setting: Business Education Computer Lab
Situation: Independent Work Activity

Listens to directions for assignment.

Smiles or laughs at classmates' humorous questions or remarks about activities.

Discusses directions for assignment with neighbor (clarifies details and asks about directions).

Asks teacher for assistance if still unclear about directions before beginning work.

Begins work quickly.

Works quietly on assignment.

Looks around occasionally, glances and smiles at friends.

Responds to teacher's look by getting back on task.

Quietly compares progress with neighbor.

Shows work to teacher when she is nearby.

Ask questions for clarification.

Flirts and teases with boys or girls (glances and whispers).

Laughs lightly at teacher's joking responses or remarks.

Negotiates for more time when teacher announces time is almost up.

Hurries to finish.

Talks about activity after turning work in.

Checks appearance.

Talks quietly while getting out books for class.

Setting: Library Media Center
Situation: History Video (Combined Classes)

Looks around room for a good seat.

Greets friends from other class.

Sits with friends.

Talks in lively tones.

Quiets when teacher calls for attention.

Listens to teacher's introduction.

Talks with neighbors about video as teacher sets up equipment.

Offers assistance to teacher.

Responds to video with facial expressions (rolls eyes, smiles, or nods).

Comments on action of video (laughter, "No way!").

Talks quietly with neighbor during video.

Plays with gum, hair, or pencil.

Calls out responses to questions posed by video.

Claps when video ends.

Talks (usually on nonschool subjects) while waiting for bell.

Setting: Hallway Locker Area
Situation: Passing Time before Lunch

Pairs up or joins group while walking to locker area.

Discusses age-appropriate topics (girls, boys, cars, latest videos, or rock stars).

Waits turn to open locker.

Waits for friends.

Varies greetings and mannerisms with different people (close friends, acquaintances, or boyfriend or girlfriend).

Makes after-school plans with friends.

Chooses topics of conversation to match interests of group.

Jokes, teases, or carries out harmless pranks with friends.

Borrows money from friends.

Discusses lunch menu.

Exchanges greetings with teachers along the way.

Moves quickly from locker area to cafeteria (gets to cafeteria on time).

Setting: Cafeteria
Situation: Going through Food Line

Talks about food choices ("What looks good?" "How many grams of fat does that have?").

Jostles and pushes (boys).

Allows friends to cut in line.

Selects food by appearance and size.

Talks with cafeteria workers ("What's good?" "How much does this cost?" "Can I substitute?").

Compares food choices while waiting to pay ("Where did you get that?").

Talks and jokes with cashiers while paying.

Setting: Cafeteria
Situation: Eating Lunch at Tables

Scans cafeteria for friends or empty tables.

Waits for friends before selecting a place to eat.

Negotiates with friends where to sit.

Sits with appropriate group (seniors, football players, or band members).

Exchanges greetings with students at table.

Compares food choices ("This is good," "That's gross.").

Shares food with friends.

Trades food items (bag of potato chips for homemade brownie).

Sneaks food from neighbor's tray.

Displays age-appropriate conventional manners and posture while eating.

Eats appropriate amount (boys: everything; girls: a few select items).

Asks friends if they need anything (napkins, straws, or ketchup) before going back for items.

Jokes, laughs, teases playfully, and participates in harmless pranks with the group.

Changes language and tone of voice when teacher approaches.

Disposes of trash and trays when finished.

Setting: Cafeteria
Situation: Socializing after Lunch

Discusses events and activities (football game, work schedules, dates, or tests).

Talks about boyfriends or girlfriends.

Laughs with others.

Takes turns in conversation.

Discusses feelings.

Supports friends who have problems or worries.

Shares successes with group.

Responds to group's verbal and nonverbal cues regarding type of comments made, topics selected, and language used.

Watches girls or boys.

Moves around cafeteria to talk to other friends.

Asks permission to go to lockers, restroom, or office.

Greets teacher on duty.

Talks to teacher on school subjects.

Shoves and hits friends playfully (boys).

Checks makeup and clothes (girls).

Exchanges good-byes with friends before leaving for next class.

APPENDIX B

Resources and Teaching Materials for Social Skills Instruction

Achenbach, T. M., & Edelback, C. (1986). *The child behavior checklist: Manual for the teacher's report form.* Burlington, VT: University of Vermont.

Alberg, J., Petry, C., & Eller, A. (1994). *A resource guide for social skills instruction.* Longmont, CO: Sopris West.

Archer, A., & Gleason, M. (1989). *Skills for school success.* North Billerica, MA: Curriculum Associates.

Brigham, T. A. (1989). *Self-management for adolescents: A skills training program.* New York, NY: Guilford Press.

Drew, N. (1987). *Learning the skills of peacemaking: An activity guide for elementary-age children on communicating/cooperating/resolving conflict.* Rolling Hills Estates, CA, Jalmar Press.

Elliott, S., & Gresham, F. (1991). *Social skills intervention guide.* Circle Pines, MN: American Guidance.

Goldstein, A. (1988). *The prepare curriculum: Teaching prosocial competencies.* Champaign, IL: Research Press.

Goldstein, A. P., Sprafkin, R. P., Gershaw, M. J., & Klein, P. (1980). *Skillstreaming the adolescent: A structured leaning approach to teaching prosocial skills.* Champaign, IL: Research Press.

Gresham, F., & Elliott, S. (1990). *The social skills rating scale.* Circle Pines, MN: American Guidance.

Hazel, J., Schumaker, J., Sherman, J., & Sheldon-Wildgen, J. (1981). *ASSET: A social skills program for adolescents.* Champaign, IL: Research Press.

Houchens, C. J. (1982). *Houchen's daily personal growth.* Johnsontown, PA: Mafax.

Jackson, J., Jackson, D. A., & Monroe, C. (1983). *Getting along with others: Teaching social effectiveness to children.* Champaign, IL: Research Press.

Kelly, J. A. (1982). *Social skills training. A practical guide for interventions.* New York, NY: Springer.

Mannix, D. *Social skills activities for special children.* West Nyack, NY: Center for Applied Research in Education.

McGinnis, E., and Goldstein, A. P. (1984). *Skillstreaming the elementary child: A guide for teaching prosocial skills.* Champaign, IL: Research Press.

Nowicki, S., & Duke, M. (1994). *Helping the child who doesn't fit in.* Novato, CA: Academic Therapy Publications.

Project Me. (1973). Glendale, CA: Bowmar.

Rinn, R. C., and Markle, A. (1979). Modification of social skills deficits in children. In A. S. Bellack and M. Hersen (Eds.), *Research and practice in social skills training.* New York: Plenum.

Schmitz, C., & Hipp, E. (1987). *Fighting invisible tigers: A stress management guide for teens.* Minneapolis, MN: Free Spirit Publishing.

Sargent, L. R. (1988). *Systematic instruction of social skills.* Des Moines, IA: Iowa Department of Education.

Skills for adolescents: Middle and junior high schools. Granville, OH: Quest International.

Spence, S. (1981). *Social skills training with child and adolescents: A counselor's manual.* London: NFER–Nelson.

Stephens, T. (1992). *Social skills in the classroom.* Odessa, FL: Psychological Associates Resources.

Thinking, feeling, behaving: An emotional education curriculum for adolescents, grades 7–12. Champaign, IL: Research Press.

Vaughn, S. R. (1987). TLC—Teaching, learning, and caring: Teaching interpersonal problem solving skills to emotionally disturbed adolescents. *Pointer. 31,* 25–30.

Waksman, S. A., and Messmer, C. L. (1985). *Assertive behavior: A program for teaching social skills to children and adolescents.* Portland: Enrichment Press.

Walker, H. M., & McConnell, S. R. (1993). *The Walker–McConnell scale of social competence and school adjustment.* Eugene, OR: University of Oregon, Center on Human Development.

Walker, H. M., McConnell, S., Holmes, D., Todis, B., Walker, J., and Golden, N. (1983). *The Walker social skills curriculum: The ACCEPTS program.* Austin: PRO–ED.

Wilkinson, J., and Canter, S. (1982). *Social skills training manual: Assessment, program design, and management of training.* New York: Wiley.

Wise, K., Bundy, K., Bundy, E., & Wise, L. (1991). *Social skills training for young adolescents.* San Diego, CA: Libra Publishers.

American Guidance Services, Publisher's Building, Circle Pines, Minnesota 55014, publishes a variety of programs and kits such as:
My friends and Me
DUSO kits
Toward affective development

Educational Productions, 7412 SW Beaverton Hillsdale Highway, Suite 210, Portland, Oregon 97225, publishes video training programs such as:
Come join in!
Let's talk
Child's play

James Stanfield Company, P.O. Box 41058, Santa Barbara, California 93140, publishes video series and kits such as:
Being with people
Be cool (coping with teasing, anger, bullying, and so on)
Making it!

Research Press, Box 31773, Champaign, Illinois 61821, publishes a variety of programs and kits such as:
Getting along with others: Teaching social effectiveness to children
Think aloud: Increasing social and cognitive skills—A problem-solving program for children

References

Adelman, H. S., & Taylor, L. (1993). *Learning problems & learning disabilities: Moving forward.* Pacific Grove, CA: Brooks/Cole.

Alberto, P. A., & Troutman, A. (1990). *Applied behavior analysis for teachers.* Columbus, OH: Merrill/Macmillan.

Alley, G., & Deshler, D. (1979). *Teaching the learning disabled adolescent: Strategies and methods.* Denver: Love.

Archer, A. (1989). *Participant's manual: Academy for effective instruction.* Reston, VA: Council for Exceptional Children.

Asher, S., Oden, S., & Gottman, J. (1977). Children's friendships in school settings. In L. Katz, M. Glockner, S. Goodman, and M. Spencer (Eds.), *Current Topics in Early Childhood Education.* Norwood, NJ: Ablex.

Bandura, A. (1986). *Social foundations of thought and action: A social cognitive theory.* Englewood Cliffs, NJ: Prentice-Hall.

Bauer, A. M., & Sapona, R. (1991). *Managing classrooms to facilitate learning.* Boston: Allyn & Bacon.

Bell, K., Young, K., Blair, M., & Nelson, R. (1990). Facilitating mainstreaming of students with behavioral disorders using classwide peer tutoring. *School Psychology Review, 19,* 564–573.

Bellack, A. S. (1979). Behavioral assessment of social skills. In A. S. Bellack & M. Hersen (Eds.), *Research and practice in social skills training.* New York: Plenum.

Berler, E. S., Gross, A., & Drabman, R. (1982). Social skill training with children: Proceed with caution. *Journal of Applied Behavior Analysis, 15,* 41–53.

Borich, G. D. (1988). *Active teaching methods.* Columbus, OH: Merrill.

Bos, C. S., & Vaughn, S. (1988). *Strategies for teaching students with learning and behavior problems.* Needham Heights, MA: Allyn & Bacon.

Brendtro, L. K., Brokenleg, M., & Van Brockern, S. (1990). *Reclaiming youth at risk: Our hope for the future.* Bloomington, IN: National Education Service.

Brophy, J., & Good, T. L. (1986). Teacher behavior and student achievement. In M. C. Wittrock (Ed.), *Handbook on teaching* (3rd ed.). New York: Macmillan.

Burden, P. R., & Byrd, D. (1994). *Methods for effective teaching.* Boston: Allyn & Bacon.

Cairns, R. B. (1986). A contemporary perspective on social development. In P. Strain, M. Guralnick, & H. Walker (Eds.), *Children's social behavior: Development, assessment and modification.* Orlando, FL: Academic Press.

Campbell, P., & Siperstein, G. (1994). *Improving social competence.* Boston: Allyn & Bacon.

Campbell, S. B. & Claus, P. (1982). Peer relationships of young children with behavior problems. In K. H. Rubin and H. S. Ross (Eds.), *Peer relationships and social skills in childhood.* New York: Springer-Verlag.

Cartledge, G., & Milburn, J. F. (1978). The case for teaching social skills in the classroom: A review. *Review of Educational Research, 1,* 133–156.

Cartledge, G., & Milburn, J. F. (1986). *Teaching social skills to children: Innovative approaches.* Elmsford, NY: Pergamon Press.

Cartwright, C. A., and Cartwright, G. P. (1984). *Developing observation skills.* New York: McGraw-Hill.

Choate, J. S., Enright, B. E., Miller, L., Poteet, J., & Rakes, T. (1995). *Curriculum-based assessment and programming* (3rd ed.). Boston: Allyn & Bacon.

Cohen, J. L., & Fish, M. (1993). *Handbook of school-based interventions: Resolving student problems and promoting healthy educational environments.* San Francisco: Jossey-Bass.

Combs, M., & Slaby, D. (1977). Social-skills training with children. In B. Lahey & A. Kazdin (Eds.), *Advances in clinical child psychology.* New York: Plenum.

Cone, J. D., & Hawkins, R. P. (1977). *Behavioral assessment: New directions in clinical psychology.* New York: Brunner/Mazel.

Cooper, J. O., Heron, T., & Heward, W. (1987). *Allied behavior analysis.* Columbus, OH: Merrill.

Cullen, B., & Pratt, T. (1992). Measuring and reporting student progress. In S. Stainback & W. Stainback (Eds.), *Curriculum considerations in inclusive classrooms: Facilitating learning for all students.* Baltimore: Brookes.

Deal, T., & Peterson, K. (1990). *The principal's role in shaping school culture.* Washington, DC: U.S. Government Printing Office.

Deci, E. L., & Ryan, R. M. (1985). *Intrinsic motivation and self-determination in human behavior.* New York: Plenum.

Dissent, T. (1987). *Making the ordinary school special.* London: Falmer.

Donnellan, A. M., LaVigna, G., Negri-Shoultz, N., & Fassbender, L. (1988). *Progress without punishment: Effective approaches for learners with behavior problems.* New York: Teachers College Press.

Downs, W. R., & Rose, S. (1991). The relationship of adolescent peer groups to the incidence of psychosocial problems. *Adolescence, 26,* 473–492.

Dowrick, P. W. (1986). *Social survival for children.* New York: Brunner/Mazel.

Eby, J. W., & Kujawa, E. (1994). *Reflective planning, teaching, and evaluation.* New York: Merrill.

Edwards, C. H. (1993). *Classroom discipline and management.* New York: Macmillan.

Edwards, L. L., & O'Toole, B. (1985). Application of the self-control curriculum with behavior disordered students. *Focus on Exceptional Children, 17,* 1–8.

Eisler, R. M., & Frederiksen, L. W. (1980). *Perfecting social skills.* New York: Plenum.

Fagan, S. A., Long, N. J., & Stevens, D. (1975). *Teaching children self-control.* Columbus, OH: Merrill.

Ferguson, D. L., & Jeanchild, L. (1992). It's not a matter of method: Thinking about how to implement curricular decisions. In S. Stainback & W. Stainback (Eds.), *Curriculum considerations in inclusive classrooms: Facilitating learning for all students.* Baltimore: Brookes.

Fish, M. C., & Massey, R. (1991). Systems in school psychology practice: A preliminary investigation. *School Psychology Review, 29,* 361–366.

Ford, A., Davern, L., & Schnorr, R. (1992). "Making sense" of the curriculum. In S. Stainback & W. Stainback (Eds.), *Curriculum considerations in inclusive classrooms: Facilitating learning for all students.* Baltimore: Brookes.

Foster, S. L., Bell-Dolan, D., & Burge, D. (1988). Behavioral observation. In A. S. Bellack & M. Hersen (Eds.), *Behavioral assessment: A practical handbook.* Elmsford, NY: Pergamon Press.

Fowler, S. A. (1986). Peer tutoring and self-monitoring: Alternatives to traditional teacher management. *Exceptional Children, 52(6),* 573–582.

Fox, J., Shores, R., Lindeman, D., & Strain, P. (1986). Maintaining social initiations of withdrawn handicapped and non-handicapped preschoolers through a response-dependent fading tactic. *Journal of Abnormal Child Psychology, 14,* 387–396.

Fox, R., & McNeil, D. (1987). Development of social skills. In A. Rotatori, M. W. Banbury, & R. A. Fox (Eds.), *Issues in special education.* Mountain View, CA: Mayfield.

Franco, D. P., Christoff, K., Crimmins, D., & Kelly, J. (1983). Social skills training for an extremely shy young adolescent. *Behavior Therapy, 14,* 568–575.

Friedman, D. L., Cancelli, A., & Yoshida, R. (1986). Academic engagement of elementary school children with learning disabilities. *Journal of School Psychology, 26,* 327–340.

Gagne, E. (1985). *The cognitive psychology of student learning.* Boston: Little, Brown.

Gelfand, D. M., & Hartmann, D. (1984). *Child behavior analysis and therapy.* Elmsford, NY: Pergamon Press.

Gerber, M., & Kaufman, J. (1981). Peer tutoring in academic settings. In P. Strain (Ed.), *Utilization of peer tutoring as behavior change agents.* New York: Plenum.

Giangreco, M. (1992). Curriculum in inclusion-oriented schools: Trends, issues, challenges, and potential solutions. In S. Stainback & W. Stainback (Eds.), *Curriculum considerations in inclusive classrooms: Facilitating learning for all students.* Baltimore: Brookes.

Goldstein, A. (1988). Prepare: A prosocial curriculum for aggressive youth. In R. Rutherford, C. Nelson, & S. Forness (Eds.), *Bases of severe behavior disorders in children and youth.* Boston: College-Hill.

Good, T., & Brophy, J. (1991). *Looking into classrooms.* New York: Harper & Row.

Good, T., & Weinstein, R. (1986). Teacher expectations: A framework for exploring classrooms. In K. K. Zumwalt (Ed.), *Improving teaching.* Alexandria, VA: Association for Supervision & Curriculum Development.

Goodman, G., Powell, E., & Burke, J. (1989). The buddy system: A reintegration technique. *Academic Therapy, 25,* 195–199.

Graden, J. L., & Bauer, A. (1992). Using a collaborative approach to support students and teachers in inclusive classrooms. In S. Stainback & W. Stainback (Eds.), *Curriculum considerations in inclusive classrooms: Facilitating learning for all students.* Baltimore: Brookes.

Greenwood, C. R., & Carta, J. J. (1987). An ecobehavioral interaction analysis within special education. *Focus on Exceptional Children, 19,* 1–11.

Greenwood, C. R., & Hops, H. (1981). Group-oriented contingencies and peer behavior. In P. S. Strain (Ed.), *The utilization of classroom peers as behavior change agents.* New York: Plenum.

Gresham, F. M. (1986). Conceptual issues in the assessment of social competence. In P. Strain, M. Guralnick, & H. Walker (Eds.), *Children's social behavior: Development, assessment, and modification.* New York: Academic Press.

Gresham, F. M., and Elliot, S. N. (1984). Assessment and classification of children's social skills: A review of methods and issues. *School Psychology Review, 13,* 292–301.

Grubaugh, S. (1989). Non-verbal language techniques for better classroom management and discipline. *The High School Journal, 73,* 34–40.

Hamilton, S. F. (1983). The social side of schooling: Ecological studies of classrooms and schools. *The Elementary School Journal, 83,* 313–334.

Harris, W. J., & Schutz, P. (1986). *The special education resource program. Rationale and implementation.* Prospect Heights, IL: Waveland.

Herbert, M. (1986). Social skills training with children. In C. Hollin & P. Trower (Eds.), *Handbook of social skills training.* Elmsford, NY: Pergamon Press.

Howell, K. W., Fox, S., & Morehead, M. K. (1993). *Curriculum-based evaluation: Teaching and decision making.* Pacific Grove, CA: Brooks/Cole.

Howell, K. W., & Morehead, M. K. (1987). *Curriculum-based evaluation for special and remedial education.* Columbus, OH: Merrill.

Hoy, C., & Gregg, N. (1994). *Assessment: The special educator's role.* Pacific Grove, CA: Brooks/Cole.

Johnson, D. W. (1981). Student-student interaction: The neglected variable in education. *Educational Researcher, 10,* 5–10.

Johnson, D. W., & Johnson, R. T. (1986). Mainstreaming and cooperative learning activities. *Exceptional Children, 52,* 553–561.

Kameenui, E. J., & Simmons, D. (1990). *Designing instructional strategies: The prevention of academic learning problems.* Columbus, OH: Merrill.

Kasen, S., Johnson, J., & Cohen, P. (1990). The impact of school emotional climate on student psychopathology. *Journal of Abnormal Child Psychology, 18,* 165–177.

Kazdin, A. E. (1989). *Behavior modification in applied settings.* Pacific Grove, CA: Brooks/Cole.

Kerr, M. M., & Nelson, C. M. (1989). *Strategies for managing behavior problems in the classroom.* (2nd ed.). Columbus, OH: Merrill.

Kiselica, M. S. (1988). Helping an aggressive adolescent through the "before, during, and after program." *The School Counselor, 35,* 299–306.

Knapczyk, D. R. (1992). Effects of developing alternative responses on the aggressive behavior of adolescents. *Behavioral Disorders, 17,* 247–263.

Knapczyk, D. R. (1989). Reducing aggressive behaviors in special and regular class settings by training alternative social responses. *Behavioral Disorders, 14,* 27–39.

Knapczyk, D. R., & Livingston, G. (1974). The effects of prompting question asking upon on-task behavior and reading comprehension. *Journal of Applied Behavior Analysis, 7,* 171–177.

Knapczyk, D. R., & Livingston, G. (1973). Self-recording and student teacher supervision: Variables within a token reinforcement structure. *Journal of Applied Behavior Analysis, 6,* 481–486.

Knoff, H. (1990). Preventing classroom discipline problems: Promoting student success through effective schools and schooling. In L. J. Kruger (Ed.), *Promoting success with at-risk students: Emerging perspectives and practical approaches.* New York: Haworth.

Koslin, B. L., Haarlow, R. N., & Karlins, M. (1986). Predicting group status from member's cognitions. *Sociometry, 31,* 64–75.

Kounin, J. S. (1983). Classrooms: Individuals or behavior settings. *Monograph in teaching and learning.* Bloomington, IN: School of Education.

Kronick, D. (1981). *Social development of learning disabled persons.* San Francisco: Jossey-Bass.

Kruger, L. J. (1990). Classroom-based approaches to promoting student success. In L. J. Kruger (Ed.), *Promoting success with at-risk students: Emerging perspectives and practical approaches.* New York: Haworth.

LaVigna, G. W., & Donnellan, A. (1986). *Alternatives to punishment.* New York: Irvington.

Lazerson, D. B., Foster, H., Brown, S., & Hummel, J. (1988). The effectiveness of cross-age tutoring with truant junior high school students with learning disabilities. *Journal of Learning Disabilities, 21,* 253–255.

Lehr, J. B., & Harris, H. W. (1988). *At-risk, low-achieving students in the classroom.* Washington: National Education Association.

Linney, J. A., & Seidman, E. (1989). The future of schooling. *American Psychologist, 44,* 336–340.

Lovitt, T. C. (1984). *Tactics for teaching.* Columbus, OH: Merrill.

Maag, J. W. (1989). Assessment in social skills training: Methodological and conceptual issues for research and practice. *Remedial and Special Education, 10* (4), 6–17.

Malone, T. (1981). Toward a theory of intrinsically motivating instruction. *Cognitive Science, 5,* 333–370.

McFall, R. M. (1982). A review and reformation of the concept of social skills. *Behavioral Assessment, 4,* 1–33.

McLoughlin, J. A., & Lewis, R. (1990). *Assessing special students.* Columbus, OH: Merrill.

Merrell, K. W. (1994). *Assessment of behavioral, social, and emotional problems: Direct and objective methods for use with children and adolescents.* New York: Longman.

Mesch, D., Lew, M., Johnson, D., & Johnson, R. (1986). Isolated teenagers, cooperative learning, and the training of social skills. *Journal of Psychology, 120*(4), 323–334.

Middleton, H., Zollinger, J., & Keene, R. (1986). Popular peers as change agents for the socially neglected child in the classroom. *Journal of School Psychology, 24,* 343–350.

Miller, N., & Harrington, H. J. (1990). A situational identity perspective on cultural diversity and teamwork in the classroom. In S. Sharan (Ed.), *Cooperative learning: Theory and practice.* New York: Praeger.

Nelson, C. M. (1977). Alternative education for the mildly and moderately handicapped. In R. D. Kneedler & S. G. Tarver (Eds.), *Changing perspectives in special education.* Columbus, OH: Merrill.

Nichols, P. (1992). The curriculum of control: Twelve reasons for it: Some arguments against it. *Beyond Behavior, 3*(2), 5–11.

Oden, S. (1986). Developing social skills instruction for peer interaction and relationships. In G. Cartledge & J. Milburn (Eds.), *Teaching social skills to children: Innovative approaches.* Elmsford, NY: Pergamon Press.

Oden, S. (1982). The applicability of social skills training research. *Child and Youth Services, 5,* 75–89.

Panyan, M. P. (1980). *How to use shaping.* Lawrence, KS: H & H Enterprises.

Peterson, D. W., & Miller, J. A. (1990). Providing opportunities for student success through cooperative training and peer tutoring. In L. J. Kruger (Ed.), *Promoting success with at-risk students.* New York: Haworth.

Polloway, E. A., Patton, J. R., Payne, J. S., & Payne, R. A. (1989). *Strategies for teaching learners with special needs.* Columbus, OH: Merrill.

Raffini, J. P. (1993). *Winners without losers: Structures and strategies for increasing student motivation to learn.* Boston: Allyn & Bacon.

Renshaw, P. D., & Asher, S. R. (1982). Social competence and peer status. In K. H. Rubin & H. S. Ross (Eds.) *Peer relationships and social skills in childhood.* New York: Springer-Verlag.

Rose, S. D. (1972). *Teaching children in groups.* San Francisco: Jossey-Bass.

Rutherford, R. B., Nelson, C. M., & Forness, S. (1988). *Bases of severe behavior disorders in children and youth.* Boston: College-Hill Press.

Salend, S. J., & Sonnenschein, P. (1989). Validating the effectiveness of a cooperative learning strategy through direct observation. *Journal of School Psychology, 27,* 47–58.

Salvia, J., & Hughes, C. (1990). *Curriculum-based assessment.* New York: Macmillan.

Salvia, J., & Ysseldyke, J. (1995). *Assessment.* (6th ed.). Boston: Houghton Mifflin.

Sapon-Shevin, M. (1986). Teaching cooperation. In G. Cartledge & J. Milburn (Eds.), *Teaching social skills to children: Innovative approaches.* Elmsford, NY: Pergamon Press.

Scales, P. (1990). Developing capable young children: An alternative strategy for prevention programs. *Journal of Early Adolescence, 10,* 420–438.

Scruggs, T. E., & Richter, L. (1985). Tutoring language disabled students: A critical review. *Learning Disabilities Quarterly, 8* (4), 286–298.

Sharan, S. (1980). Cooperative learning in small groups: Recent methods and effects on achievement, attitudes and ethnic relations. *Review of Educational Research, 50(*2), 241–271.

Sheridan, S. M., Kratochwill, T., & Elliott, S. (1990). Behavioral consultation with parents and teachers: Delivering treatment for socially withdrawn children at home and school. *School Psychology Review, 19,* 33–52.

Shrigley, R. L. (1985). Curbing student disruption in the classroom—teachers need intervention skills. *NASSP Bulletin, 69,* 26–32.

Slavin, R. E., Karweit, N. L., & Madden, N. A. (1989). *Effective programs for students at-risk.* Boston: Allyn & Bacon.

Smith, D. D. (1989). *Teaching students with learning and behavior problems* (2nd ed.). Needham Heights, MA: Allyn & Bacon.

Solity, J., & Bull, S. (1987). *Special needs: Bridging the curriculum gap.* Philadelphia: Open University Press.

Spivack, G., & Shure, M. (1974). *Social adjustment of young children: A cognitive approach to solving real-life problems.* San Francisco: Jossey-Bass.

Stainback, W., Stainback, S., & Moravec, J. (1992). Using curriculum to build inclusive classrooms. In S. Stainback & W. Stainback (Eds.), *Curriculum considerations in inclusive classrooms: Facilitating learning for all students.* Baltimore: Brookes.

Stephens, T. M., Blackhurst, A. E., & Magliocca, L. A. (1988). *Teaching mainstreamed students.* Elmsford, NY: Pergamon Press.

Stokes, T. F., & Baer, D. (1977). An implicit technology of generalization. *Journal of Applied Behavior Analysis, 10,* 349–367.

Sugai, G. M., & Tindal, G. A. (1993). *Effective school consultation: An interactive approach.* Pacific Grove, CA: Brooks/Cole.

Sulzer-Azaroff, B., & Mayer, G. (1986). *Achieving educational excellence.* New York: Holt, Rinehart, &Winston.

Tanner, D., & Tanner, L. (1990). *History of the School Curriculum.* New York: Macmillan.

Taub, S. I., & Dollinger, S. J. (1975). Reward and purpose as incentives for children differing in locus of control expectancies. *Journal of Personality, 43,* 179–195.

Thousand, J. S., & Villa, R. (1992). Collaborative teams: A powerful tool in school restructuring. In R. A. Villa, J. Thousand, W. Stainback, & S. Stainback (Eds.), *Restructuring for caring and effective education.* Baltimore: Brookes.

Villa, R. A., & Thousand, J. (1992). Restructuring public school systems: Strategies for organizational change and progress. In R. A. Villa, J. Thousand, W. Stainback, & S. Stainback (Eds.), *Restructuring for caring and effective education.* Baltimore: Brookes.

Wacker, D., Berg, W., & Northrup, J. (1991). Breaking the cycle of challenging behaviors: Early treatment key to success. *Impact, 4,* 10–11.

Wahler, R., & Fox, J. (1981). Setting events in applied behavior analysis: Toward a conceptual and

methodological expansion. *Journal of Applied Behavior Analysis, 10,* 349–367.
Walker, H. M. (1979). *The acting-out child: Coping with classroom disruption.* Boston: Allyn & Bacon.
Walker, H. M., Colvin, G., & Ramsey, E. (1995). *Antisocial behavior in school: Strategies and best practices.* Pacific Grove, CA: Brooks/Cole.
Wasik, B. H. (1990). Issues in identification and assessment. In L. J. Kruger (Ed.), *Promoting success with at-risk students: Emerging perspectives and practical approaches.* New York: Haworth.
Weinstein, C. S. (1991). The classroom as a social context for learning. *Annual Review of Psychology, 42,* 493–535.
Wolery, M., Bailey, D., & Sugai, G. (1988). *Effective teaching: Principles and procedures of applied behavior analysis with expectional students.* Needham Heights, MA: Allyn & Bacon.
Wolf, M. M. (1978). Social validity: The case for subjective measurement or how applied behavior analysis is finding a heart. *Journal of Applied Behavior Analysis, 11,* 204–214.
Zirpoli, T. J., & Melloy, K. (1993). *Behavior management: Applications for teachers and parents.* New York: Merrill.

Subject Index

Activities and worksheets
  assessing basic abilities, 148–167
  assessing component steps, 178–189
  assessing performance conditions, 203–218
  brainstorming intervention procedures, 247–253
  coordinating and scheduling interventions, 280–288
  defining social skills curriculum, 30, 33–48
  defining target skills, 129–132
  finalizing instructional goals, 232–233
  following up interventions, 352–358
  identifying standards, 67–72
  listing social behaviors, 14–16
  monitoring interventions, 297–322
  observing social behavior, 37–43
  planning collaboration across settings, 440–442
  planning group instruction, 406–425
  recording survey level assessment results, 115–119
  streamlining assessment and instruction, 392–399
  survey level assessment, 86–106
Administration, approval of, 285–286, 444
Assessment, 79–82
  conditions for, 88–91, 97–98, 163–164, 185, 213–214
  during intervention, 312–313
  for group instruction, 416
  importance of, 49, 81–82, 133–137,143–144, 196–198
  need for, 132–137
  and planning interventions procedures, 97–102, 160–163, 184–185, 213–215
  specific level, 79, 143–144, 227–232
  and the social skills curriculum, 49
  and standards, 58–59
  survey level, 82–86, 115–119
  see also Basic abilities assessment; Component steps assessment; Performance conditions assessment; Survey level assessment
Assessment findings
  see Instructional goals for interventions

Basic abilities, 144–148
  defined, 144
  listing for group instruction, 415
  and problems in social behavior, 146–148
  see also Basic abilities assessment
Basic abilities assessment
  conditions for, 160–161, 163–164
  conducting, 163–164
  findings from, 166
  for group instruction, 416
  listing abilities, 149–158
  procedures and scheduling for, 160–163
  questions for, 158–160
  steps in planning, 148–162
  streamlining, 379–381
  summarizing results, 164–167
  worksheet for, 148–155, 157–160, 165–167
  see also Basic abilities
Behavioral patterns
  defined, 173
  developed in interventions, 336
  importance of, 175–177
  and problems in social behavior, 178
  see also Component steps

Carryover of social skills, 124–126, 311–312
  as focus of group instruction, 413–414
  in intervention results, 330–331, 332–334

Chaining, 269–271, 418
Collaboration, 431–448
  across grade levels and schools, 434–436
  in assessment, 98–99, 108–109
  in coordinating expectations, 333, 444–446
  in coordinating group instruction, 436–437, 447–448
  in coordinating interventions, 439–440
  in intervention, 263–265, 285–286
  objectives of, 436–440
  securing administrative approval for, 444
  using social skills curriculum for, 444–446
  within grade level programs, 432–434
  see also Teachers and school personnel
Competing behaviors, 351–352
Component steps, 173–178
  and behavioral patterns, 173–174, 175–176, 178
  defined, 173
  importance of, 175–177
  listing for assessment, 179–184
  listing for group instruction, 415
  and problems in social behavior, 177–178
  see also Component steps assessment
Component steps assessment
  conditions for, 185
  findings from, 188–189
  for group instruction, 416
  guidelines for conducting, 185–187
  guidelines for listing steps, 179–184
  overview, 173–175
  procedures and scheduling, 184–185
  steps in planning, 178–185
  streamlining, 381–382
  summarizing results of, 187–189
  worksheet for, 178–182, 185, 187–189
Cooperative learning, 421–423
Criterion levels
  defined, 66–67
  identifying, 71
  in interventions results, 336
  use in monitoring interventions, 300–303
  use in survey level assessment, 96–97
  see also Standards

Directions, 236–237

Expectations, 17–22, 43–48
  academic and nonacademic, 18–19
  changeable over time, 434–435
  coordinating across settings, 333, 432, 437, 444–446
  defined, 17–18
  features of, 18–22
  for group instruction, 407–414
  guidelines for listing, 44–48
  modifying or generating, 412–413
  monitored during interventions, 300–301, 302–303, 313–314
  as observable behavior, 20, 44–47
  and performance conditions, 195–196
  as positive skills, 21–22, 44
  as prerequisites, 128
  priorities for groups, 414
  and problems in social behavior, 133–136
  in the social skills curriculum, 43–48
  setting priorities among, 120–129
  taught as a unit, 413
  verifying, 48
  see also Priorities; Social demands; Standards; Target skills

Following up interventions, 327–358
  aligning with student progress, 337–338, 347
  changing intervention context, 348, 351
  collaboration during, 333
  fading procedures, 331–332, 335
  highlighting outcomes, 334–336, 350–351
  promoting carryover of skills, 333–334
  reducing competing behaviors, 351–352
  revising instructional goals, 342–345
  revising procedures, 346–350
  selecting new students, 332
  selecting new target skills, 332, 344–345
  when interventions are not working, 341–352
  when interventions are working, 330–338
  worksheet for, 352, 357–358

Graphing and charting, 319
Group instruction, 405–425
  abilities, steps, and conditions for, 415
  assessing for, 416
  coordinated across settings, 436–437, 438–439, 447–448
  expectations for, 407–414
  instructional goals for, 416–417
  monitoring, 424–425
  planning and scheduling for, 423–424
  procedures for, 417–423
  steps in planning, 406–429

in subject matter lessons, 419–423
target skills for, 414–415
using cooperative learning, 421–423
using peer tutoring, 419–421
using special activities, 419
worksheet for planning, 414–417

Incentive, 272–280
and carryover, 333
and competing behaviors, 351–352
defined, 273
and outcomes, 273–274
revising interventions to increase, 350–352
see also Outcomes
Instructional goals for interventions, 49–50, 227–234
from basic abilities assessment, 166
and chaining, 269–271
complex, 269–272
from component steps assessment, 188–189
consolidating, 227–232
finalizing, 232–234
from performance conditions assessment, 218
revising, 342–345
sequencing, 260–261
and shaping, 271–272
and the social skills curriculum, 49–50
and standards, 60–61
streamlining development of, 384–386
Instructional programs, expanding, 50, 405, 431–432, 447–448
Interaction *see* Social skills
Intervention planning
and chaining, 269–271
choosing conditions, 281–284
collaboration during, 263–265
developing procedures, 262–269
organization of, 259–261
scheduling, 285–288
and shaping, 271–272
writing a script, 281
see also Intervention procedures; Interventions
Intervention procedures, 234–247
applied to group instruction, 417
choosing, 261
and complex goals, 269–272
conditions for, 281–282, 348, 351
directions, 236–237
fading, 246–247, 331–332, 335
highlighting natural outcomes, 274–277
integrating, 280–281
linked to instructional goals, 234–235, 252–253, 347
modeling, 240–244
prompting, 244–247
rehearsal, 237–240
revising, 337, 346–350
rewards, 277–280, 334, 335–336, 350–351
steps for brainstorming, 247–253
streamlining development of, 386–390
ways to develop, 262–269
Intervention results, 327–358
successful, 328–330
unsuccessful, 338–341
see also Following up interventions
Intervention script, 281
Interventions, 225–226, 234–319
administrative approval for, 285–286
assessment during, 312–313
and assessment results, 265
coordinated across settings, 439–440
coordinating with student progress, 309–310
following up, 327–358
instructional goals for, 49–50, 227–234
need for a systematic approach, 14–17
planning, 247–253, 259–288
procedures, 234–247
results of, 327–358
revising, 334–335, 337–338, 342–352
student reaction to, 308–309
target skills for, 129–132
see also Following up interventions; Instructional goals for interventions; Intervention planning; Intervention procedures; Monitoring interventions
Level of confidence, 303–306

Modeling, 240–244
Monitoring interventions, 295–322
applied to group instruction, 424–425
benefits of, 295–297
issues for, 306–313
procedures for, 313–315
recording results, 315–322
setting level of confidence, 303–306
steps in planning, 297–322
streamlining, 390–392
use of graphs and charts for, 319
see also Following up interventions

Observations, 37–43
conditions for, 42–43
guidelines for conducting, 42–43
remaining unobtrusive during, 97–98, 108–109
use of video for, 43
using other observers for, 89–99, 108–109
what to look for during, 38–42
see also Assessment
Outcomes
highlighting in group instruction, 418
highlighting in interventions, 274–277, 334–336, 350–351
and incentive, 273–280
integrating into setting, 335–336
and problems in social behavior, 135, 136

Peers
considered in setting priorities, 126–127
demands set by, 11, 13
involved in intervention, 236–237, 240, 243, 276–277
and performance conditions, 199–201
and problems in social behavior
Peer tutoring, 419–423
Performance conditions, 195–203
categories of, 198–200, 201–202, 209, 217
defined, 195
guidelines set by, 198–200
and inconsistent behavior, 202–203
listing for group instruction, 415
and problems in social behavior, 200–203
see also Performance conditions assessment
Performance conditions assessment, 195–196, 203–218
conditions for, 213–214
describing questions to assess, 212–213
findings from, 218
focus of, 198
for group instruction, 416
guidelines for conducting, 215–217
issues to investigate for, 209–212
need for, 196–198
overview, 195–196
procedures and scheduling, 213–215
steps in planning, 203–215
streamlining, 382–384
summarizing results of, 217–218
worksheet for, 203–204, 212–213, 214, 217–218
Priority expectations, 120–129, 332
among expectations not met, 120–129
for group instruction, 414–415
guidelines for setting, 121–129
monitoring, 300
streamlining, 376–378
and target skills, 129–131
see also Target skills
Problems in social behavior, 3, 5–8, 133–136
among groups of students, 411
causes of, 133–136
danger of labeling, 5
inconsistent behavior, 202–203
and need for systematic instruction, 367–370
related to basic abilities, 146–148
related to component steps, 177–178
related to performance conditions, 196
and the social skills curriculum, 49
and standards, 73
Prompting, 244–247

Rehearsal, 237–240
Rewards, in group instruction, 418
use in interventions, 277–280, 334, 335–336, 350–351

Self–esteem, 126–127
Settings, 30–33
coordinating instruction among, 431–448
defined, 31
describing, 33
features of, 31–33
and the social skills curriculum, 30–37
special education and mainstream, 35–37
worksheets for listing, 35–37
see also Situations
Shaping, 271–272, 418
Situations, 30–37
carryover of skills among, 311–312
changes in standards among, 71–72
defined, 31
describing, 33–37
features of, 31–33
and performance conditions, 195–196
and problems in social behavior, 134
and social demands, 9–10
and the social skills curriculum, 30–37
structured and unstructured, 9–10
worksheets for, 35–37
Social competence, 3–6, 7–8
defined, 3–4
importance of positive focus, 7–8

and social demands, 4, 8–9
and the social skills curriculum, 27
standards for achieving, 57–58
see also Expectations; Social demands; Social skills curriculum
Social demands, 8–17, 37–42
complexity of, 8–17
explicit and implicit, 13–14
observing, 37–43
self–set, 11–13
set by peers, 11
set by teachers, 11
and situations, 9–10
see also Expectations; Social competence
Social skills
and basic abilities, 146–148
carryover of, 124–126
and component steps, 175–177
interactions with peers and adults, 41–42
and performance conditions, 200–203
procedures for teaching, 234–247
and social competence, 4
Social skills curriculum, 27–30, 49–50
and assessment, 49
benefits and uses, 49–50
changing over time, 434–435
compared among settings, 438, 444–446
compared to academic curricula, 27–28
defined, 27–28
functions of, 28–30
and instructional programs, 50
and intervention goals, 49–50
and standards, 57–58, 68
steps for identifying, 30–48
streamlining, 372–374
use in collaboration, 444–446
use in planning group instruction, 407–414
use in survey level assessment, 86–86
worksheet for identifying, 35–37, 38–42, 44–48
see also Expectations; Social demands; Standards
Special education, 35–37
Specific level assessment, 79, 143–144, 227–232
see also Basic abilities assessment; Component steps assessment; Performance conditions assessment
Standards, 57–67, 73–74
applied collectively, 73–74
defined, 57–58
in different situations, 71–72
elements of, 62–67
functions of, 58–61, 73–74
identifying, 67–73
and instructional goals, 60–61
and level of confidence, 303–306
and problems in social behavior, 73
procedures for monitoring, 313–314
and the social skills curriculum, 57–58, 68
use in assessment, 58–59, 73, 95–97
use in monitoring interventions, 300–303
worksheet for identifying, 68–72
see also Criterion levels; Units of measure
Streamlining social skills instruction, 367, 370–399
basic abilities assessment, 379–381
component steps assessment, 381–382
development of intervention procedures, 386–388
performance conditions assessment, 382–384
selection of target skills, 376–378
setting instructional goals, 384–386
social skills curriculum, 372–374
worksheet for planning, 392–399
Students
assessment personalized for, 84, 107
involving in interactions, 265–266
matching progress of, 347–348
reaction to intervention procedures, 308–309
Survey level assessment, 82–86, 115–119
choosing students for, 87–88
conditions for, 88–91, 97–98
expectations for, 91–95
guidelines for conducting, 107–109
principles of, 83–86
procedures for, 97–102
recording results of, 102–103, 115–119
scheduling, 103–106
situations for, 88–91
standards for, 95–97
steps in planning, 86–106
streamlining, 374–376
worksheet for, 87–88, 91, 94–96, 102–103, 105, 115–119, 120
Systematic approach to instruction, 14–17, 132–137, 367–370

Target skills, 129–132
and basic abilities, 149
and component steps, 173, 179–184
defined, 129
for group instruction, 414–415
and instructional goals, 232–234
in intervention results, 330–332, 334, 336–337

Target skills (*continued*)
in monitoring interventions, 300–303, 306–308, 313–314
level of confidence for, 303–306
need for assessment of, 132–136
and performance conditions, 209–212
and priority expectations, 129–131
and standards, 302–303
streamlining, 376–378
see also Priority expectations
Teachers and school personnel
collaboration with, 431–448
considered in setting priorities, 126–127
demands set by, 10–11
from other grade levels and schools, 434–436
from same grade level program, 432–434
and performance conditions, 199, 201
role in assessment, 85, 98–99, 108–109
role in intervention, 263–265, 237, 285–286, 333
student interaction with, 41, 126
suggestions for approaching, 442–444
view of problems in social behavior
see also Collaboration

Units of measure
in assessment results, 115–116
basis for selecting, 65–66
defined, 62–63
for different expectations, 63–65
identifying, 68–71
use in monitoring interventions, 301–302
use in survey level assessment, 96–97
see also Standards

Video
use in interventions, 243–244
use in observations, 43, 99–101

Worksheets *see* Activities and worksheets

Name Index

Adelman, H. S., 265, 274, 275, 276
Alberto, P. A., 269
Alley, G., 369
Archer, A., 369
Asher, S. R., 9, 33, 126, 133, 134, 135, 196

Baer, D., 334
Bailey, D., 66, 86, 98, 123, 124, 127, 266, 267, 272, 276
Bandura, A., 240, 241, 243, 274, 276
Bauer, A. M., 11, 31, 412, 447
Bell, K., 242, 420
Bell–Dolan, D., 63
Bellack, A. S., 82, 97
Berg, W., 351
Berler, E. S., 332
Blair, M., 242, 420
Borich, G. D., 95, 103, 144
Bos, C. S., 246, 419
Brendtro, L. K., 11
Brokenleg, M., 11
Brophy, J., 17, 27
Brown, S., 420, 421
Bull, S., 44, 123, 237, 246, 269
Burden, P. R., 57, 60, 135, 266, 274, 315, 319, 337, 348
Burge, D., 63
Burke, J., 420
Byrd, D., 57, 60, 135, 266, 274, 315, 319, 337, 348

Cairns, R. B., 31, 175
Campbell, P., 3, 9, 10, 13, 21, 31, 144, 146, 173, 196, 227, 239, 240, 242, 260, 269, 350, 351, 412, 419, 436, 437
Campbell, S. B., 5
Cancelli, A., 423
Carta, J. J., 31, 33, 90, 266
Cartledge, G., 27, 84, 123, 129, 146, 173, 176, 177, 234, 236, 240, 243, 262, 264, 333, 419, 423, 432
Cartwright, C. A., 42, 63, 65, 85, 87, 97, 103, 133, 195
Cartwright, G. P., 42, 63, 65, 85, 87, 97, 103, 133, 195
Choate, J. S., 84, 85, 79
Christoff, K., 237
Claus, P., 5
Cohen, J. L., 8, 22, 29, 132, 433
Colvin, G., 29, 232, 264, 277, 279, 296, 300, 303, 311, 313, 348, 351, 369, 370
Combs, M., 5
Cone, J. D., 79
Cooper, J. O., 126, 127
Crimmins, D., 237
Cullen, B., 84, 295, 297, 308, 310, 312

Davern, L., 412
Deal, T., 442
Deci, E. L., 277, 278
Deshler, D., 369
Dissent, T., 434
Dollinger, S. J., 275
Donnellan, A. M., 251
Downs, W. R., 11
Dowrick, P. W., 5, 99, 244
Drabman, R., 332

Eby, J. W., 99, 101, 136, 273, 421, 422

Edwards, C. H., 276, 277, 335
Edwards, L. L., 132
Eisler, R. M., 90, 236, 237, 243, 244
Elliot, S. N., 79, 123
Elliott, S., 433, 444
Enright, B. E., 79, 81, 83

Fagan, S. A., 9, 135
Fassbender, L., 351
Ferguson, D. L., 265
Fish, M. C., 22, 29, 84, 132, 433
Ford, A., 412
Forness, S., 370
Foster, H., 420, 421
Foster, S. L., 63
Fowler, S. A., 421
Fox, J., 195
Fox, R., 267
Fox, S., 5, 29, 33, 37, 57, 59, 83, 85, 103, 129, 146, 161, 196, 260
Franco, D. P., 237
Frederiksen, L. W., 90, 236, 237, 242, 244
Friedman, D. L., 423

Gagne, E., 273
Gelfand, D. M., 333
Gerber, M., 420
Giangreco, M., 418
Goldstein, A. P., 30, 241, 243, 244, 419
Good, T. L., 17, 23, 31, 44
Goodman, G., 420
Gottman, J., 33, 133, 135, 196
Graden, J. L., 447
Greenwood, C. R., 31, 33, 90, 266
Gregg, N., 81, 85, 87, 97, 98, 146, 148, 149, 196, 202, 234, 260
Gresham, F. M., 79, 123, 127
Gross, A., 332
Grubaugh, S., 246

Haarlow, R. N., 369
Hamilton, S. F., 27
Harrington, H. J., 127
Harris, H. W., 37, 127, 264
Harris, W. J., 135, 267, 285, 288
Hartmann, D., 333
Hawkins, R. P., 79
Heron, T., 126, 127
Heward, W., 126, 127
Hops, H., 334
Howell, K. W., 5, 29, 33, 37, 50, 57, 59, 79, 83, 85, 103, 129, 134, 144, 146, 161, 173, 196, 260, 300, 306, 308, 319
Hoy, C., 81, 85, 87, 97, 98, 146, 148, 149, 196, 202, 234, 260
Hughes, C., 9, 50, 81, 85, 90, 97, 179
Hummel, J., 420, 421

Jeanchild, L., 265
Johnson, D. W., 126, 419, 421, 422
Johnson, J., 8
Johnson, R. T., 126, 421, 422

Kameenui, E. J., 37, 260, 296, 304, 306, 312, 335, 336, 351, 434
Karlins, M., 369
Kasen, S., 8
Kaufman, J., 420
Kazdin, A. E., 63, 242, 243, 276, 279
Keene, R., 271
Kelly, J. A., 237
Kerr, M. M., 63, 95, 124, 173, 240, 246, 266, 267, 279
Kiselica, M. S., 236
Knapczyk, D. R., 99, 101, 134, 236, 243, 244, 245, 246, 369, 421
Knoff, H., 31, 73, 133
Koslin, B. L., 369
Kounin, J. S., 33
Kratochwill, T., 433, 444
Kronick, D., 9, 134
Kruger, L. J., 20, 63
Kujawa, E., 99, 101, 136, 273, 421, 422

LaVigna, G. W., 351
Lazerson, D. B., 420, 421
Lehr, J. B., 37, 127, 264
Lew, M., 422
Lewis, R., 149
Lindeman, D., 267
Linney, J. A., 422
Livingston, G., 236, 245, 246
Long, N. J., 9, 135
Lovitt, T. C., 237

Maag, J. W., 313, 314
Malone, T., 278
Massey, R., 84

Mayer, G., 270, 271
McFall, R. M., 4, 29, 44, 57, 85
McGinnis, E., 241, 243
McLoughlin, J. A., 149
Melloy, K., 62, 65, 84, 91, 137, 196, 198, 199, 237, 260, 271, 274, 277, 311, 319, 338, 349, 414, 418, 419
Merrell, K. W., 5, 103, 227, 265, 369
Mesch, D., 423
Middleton, H., 271
Milburn, J. F., 27, 84, 123, 129, 146, 173, 176, 177, 234, 236, 240, 243, 262, 264, 333, 419, 423, 432
Miller, J. A., 127
Miller, L., 79, 84, 85
Miller, N., 127
Moravec, J., 123, 444
Morehead, M. K., 5, 29, 33, 37, 50, 57, 59, 79, 83, 85, 103, 129, 134, 144, 146, 161, 173, 196, 260, 300, 306, 308, 319

Negri–Shoultz, N., 351
Nelson, C. M., 63, 95, 98, 124, 173, 240, 246, 266, 267, 279, 370
Nelson, R., 242, 420
Nichols, P., 5
Northrup, J., 351

O'Toole, B., 132
Oden, S., 33, 133, 135, 196, 237, 419

Panyan, M. P., 271, 272
Patton, J. R., 275, 277, 279, 369
Payne, J. S., 275, 277, 279, 369
Payne, R. A., 275, 277, 279, 369
Peterson, D. W., 127
Peterson, K., 442
Polloway, E. A., 275, 277, 279, 369
Poteet, J., 79, 84, 85
Powell, E., 420
Pratt, T., 84, 295, 297, 308, 310, 312

Raffini, J. P., 136, 266, 273, 274, 278; 334, 335
Rakes, T., 79, 84, 85
Ramsey, E., 29, 232, 264, 277, 279, 296, 300, 303, 311, 313, 348, 351, 369, 370
Renshaw, P. D., 9, 126, 134, 135
Richter, L., 420
Rose, S. D., 11, 73
Rutherford, R., 370
Ryan, R. M., 277, 278

Salend, S. J., 422
Salvia, J., 9, 50, 81, 84, 85, 90, 97, 103, 104, 179, 285
Sapon–Shevin, M., 421
Sapona, R., 11, 31, 412
Scales, P., 5, 8
Schnorr, R., 412
Schutz, P., 135, 267, 285, 288
Scruggs, T. E., 420
Seidman, E., 422
Sharan, S., 243
Sheridan, S. M., 433, 444
Shores, R., 267
Shrigley, R. L., 278
Shure, M., 236
Simmons, D., 37, 260, 296, 304, 306, 312, 335, 336, 351, 434
Siperstein, G., 3, 9, 10, 13, 21, 31, 144, 146, 173, 196, 227, 239, 240, 242, 260, 269, 350, 351, 412, 419, 436, 437
Slaby, D., 5
Slavin, R. E., 126
Smith, D. D., 279, 419
Solity, J., 44, 123, 237, 246, 269
Sonnenschein, P., 422
Spivack, G., 236
Stainback, S., 123, 444
Stainback, W., 123, 444
Stevens, D., 9, 135
Stokes, T. F., 334
Strain, P., 267
Sugai, G. M., 66, 47, 86, 98, 104, 123, 124, 127, 266, 267, 272, 276, 295, 313, 338, 342, 433, 436
Sulzer–Azaroff, B., 270, 271

Tanner, D., 50
Tanner, L., 50
Taub, S. I., 275
Taylor, L., 265, 274, 275, 276
Thousand, J. S., 442, 443, 445
Tindal, G. A., 47, 104, 267, 295, 319, 338, 342, 433, 436
Troutman, A., 269

Van Brockern, S., 11

Vaughn, S., 246, 419
Villa, R. A., 442, 443, 445

Wacker, D., 351
Wahler, R., 195
Walker, H. M., 29, 232, 241, 264, 277, 279, 296, 300, 303, 311, 313, 348, 351, 369, 370
Wasik, B. H., 8, 123
Weinstein, C. S., 373
Weinstein, R., 17, 27, 31, 44
Wolery, M., 66, 86, 98, 123, 124, 127, 266, 267, 272, 276
Wolf, M. M., 123

Yoshida, R., 423
Young, K., 242, 420
Ysseldyke, J., 84, 103, 104

Zirpoli, T. J., 62, 65, 84, 91, 137, 196, 198, 199, 237, 260, 271, 274, 277, 311, 319, 338, 349, 414, 418, 419
Zollinger, J., 271

Photo Credits

4, Polly Brown/Actuality Inc.; **12,** Gale Zucker; **20,** Robert Finken; **32,** Michael Siluk; **32,** Elizabeth Crews; **41,** Elizabeth Crews; **59,** Elizabeth Crews; **67,** Elizabeth Hamlin/Stock, Boston; **82,** David Grossman; **101,** Mary Kate Denny/PhotoEdit; **124,** Elizabeth Crews; **125,** Elizabeth Crews; **131,** Gale Zucker; **147,** Robert Finken; **161,** Laima Druskis/Stock, Boston; **174,** Mary Kate Denny/PhotoEdit; **186,** Martha Tabor/Working Images Photographs; **197,** Gale Zucker; **216,** Michael Siluk; **228,** Michael Dwyer/Stock, Boston; **242,** Elizabeth Crews/Stock, Boston; **264,** Gale Zucker; **275,** Elizabeth Crews; **296,** David Bellak/Jeroboam Inc.; **308,** Elizabeth Crews; **331,** David Grossman; **342,** Elizabeth Crews; **370,** Elizabeth Crews; **406,** Elizabeth Crews; **420,** David Grossman; **433,** Gale Zucker; **443,** Ellis Herwig/Stock, Boston.

Worksheet 1.1: Observing Social Behavior

Name: ______________________________ Date: ____________

Structured situation: ______________________________

Behaviors observed:

1.

2.

3.

4.

5.

6.

7.

8.

9.

10.

Worksheet 1.1: Observing Social Behavior

Name: ______________________ Date: __________

Unstructured situation: ______________________

Behaviors observed:

1.

2.

3.

4.

5.

6.

7.

8.

9.

10.

Worksheet 2.1, Part 1: The Social Skills Curriculum—SITUATIONS

Name: ______________________________ Date: __________

Setting #1 (structured): ______________________________

Situations/Activities:

____
____
____
____
____
____
____
____
____

Setting #2 (unstructured): ______________________________

Situations/Activities:

____
____
____
____
____
____
____
____
____

Worksheet 2.1, Part 2: The Social Skills Curriculum—NOTES Page ____ of ____

Name: ______________________________ Date: ____________

Setting: ______________________________

Situation: ______________________________

Notes on social requirements:

Worksheet 2.1, Part 3: The Social Skills Curriculum—EXPECTATIONS Page ____ of ____

Name: ______________________________ Date: ____________

Setting: ______________________________

SITUATION: ______________________________

EXPECTATIONS	STANDARDS *(Covered in Chapter Three)*	
	Units of Measure	Criterion Level

Worksheet 4.1, Part 1: Description of Student Behavior

Name: ______________________________ Date: __________

Student to be assessed: ______________________ Grade: __________

Assessment setting(s): ______________________________________

Description of student behavior (focus on social skills):

Areas or concerns to investigate:

____

____

____

____

____

Worksheet 4.1, Part 2:
Assessment Worksheet

Name: ______________________ Student : ______________________

Assessment Situation: ______________________ Page ____ of ____

Expectation	**Units of Measure**	**Criterion Level**	**Procedure**	**Assessment Results**					
				Observations					Total
				1st	2nd	3rd	4th	5th	

Comments/Notes:

Worksheet 4.1, Part 3: Assessment Schedule Name:______________________

Student: ______________________ Grade: ______ Date: ____________

Days/Times	**Situations/Procedures**	**Personnel/Materials**

Notes:

Worksheet 4.1 Supplement: OBSERVATION FORM

Observer: ______________________ Date: __________

Student: ______________________ Grade: __________

Assessment Situation: ______________________

Instructions to observer:

Expectations	**Method of Measurement**	**Results**					
		Observations 1st	2nd	3rd	4th	5th	Total

Comments/ Observations:

Worksheet 5.1: Setting Priorities from Assessment Results

Name: ____________________ Date: __________

Student: ____________________ Grade: __________

Expectations Not Met	Priority Level

Worksheet 6.1: Basic Abilities Assessment Page 1 of ______

Name: ______________________________ Date: __________

Student: ______________________________ Grade: __________

Target skill: ______________________________

____

Basic abilities to assess:

1. ______________________________
2. ______________________________
3. ______________________________
4. ______________________________
5. ______________________________

Worksheet 6.1 (continued)	Name: ______________________ Page ___ of ___

Basic ability: ______________________________

Questions to answer about basic ability:

Procedures for answering questions:

Personnel/equipment needed:

Day	Results
1	
2	
3	
4	
5	

Conclusions/comments:

Worksheet 6.1 (continued)	Name: ______________________ Page ____ of ____

Findings—instructional goals for intervention:

____

____

____

____

____

Worksheet 7.1: Component Steps Assessment

Name: ______________________________ Date: __________

Student: ______________________________ Grade: __________

Target skill: ______________________________

Procedures for assessing component steps:

Component Steps	**Assessment Results** (enter "+" for successful performance, "o" for unsuccessful performance)				
	1st	2nd	3rd	4th	5th
______	___	___	___	___	___
______	___	___	___	___	___
______	___	___	___	___	___
______	___	___	___	___	___
______	___	___	___	___	___
______	___	___	___	___	___
______	___	___	___	___	___
______	___	___	___	___	___
______	___	___	___	___	___
______	___	___	___	___	___
______	___	___	___	___	___
______	___	___	___	___	___
______	___	___	___	___	___
______	___	___	___	___	___
______	___	___	___	___	___
______	___	___	___	___	___

Worksheet 7.1 (continued)	Name: ______________________________	Page 2 of 2

Comments:

Findings—instructional goals for intervention:

____

____

____

____

____

Name: ______________________ Date: __________

Student: ______________________ Grade: __________

Target skill: ______________________

Category #1: **Time**

General issues to assess (Check off those that apply)**:**

_____ whether the student uses the target skill at the right times

_____ whether the student uses the target skill at the wrong times

_____ whether the student uses the target skill better at some times than in others

_____ whether the student performs some other behavior at the times the target skill

Specific issues or questions to assess:

Category #2: **Location**

General issues to assess (Check off those that apply)**:**

_____ whether the student uses the target skill in the right places

_____ whether the student uses the target skill in the wrong places

_____ whether the student uses the target skill better in some places than in others

_____ whether the student performs some other behavior in the places the target skill

Specific issues or questions to assess:

Name: ______________________________

Category #3: **People**

General issues to assess (Check off those that apply)**:**

_____ whether the student uses the target skill with the right people

_____ whether the student uses the target skill with the wrong people

_____ whether the student uses the target skill better with some people than with others

_____ whether the student performs some other behavior with or toward the people the

Specific issues or questions to assess:

Category #4: **Amount**

General issues to assess (Check off those that apply)**:**

_____ whether the student uses the target skill at the right amount (level, frequency,

_____ whether the student uses the target skill at the wrong amount (level, frequency,

_____ whether the student uses the target skill better at some amounts (levels,

Specific issues or questions to assess:

Category #5: **Materials**

General issues to assess (Check off those that apply)**:**

- _____ whether the student uses the target skill with the right materials
- _____ whether the student uses the target skill with the wrong materials
- _____ whether the student uses the target skill better with some materials than with others
- _____ whether the student performs some other behavior with the materials the target

Specific issues or questions to assess:

Procedures for assessing issues and questions:

Time	
Location	
People	
Amount	

Name: ______________________________

Assessment schedule:

Day 1	
Day 2	
Day 3	
Day 4	
Day 5	

Results/comments:

Time	
Location	
People	

Worksheet 8.1 (continued)	Name: ______________________________	

Results/comments (continued):

Amount	

Findings—Instructional goals for intervention:

____

____

____

____

____

Worksheet 9.1: Preparing for Intervention Planning

Name: ______________________ Date: __________

Student: ______________________ Grade: __________

Target skill for intervention:

____

____

Instructional goals for learning target skill:

____

____

____

____

____

Worksheet 9.1 (continued)	Name: ______________________ Student: ______________________	Page ____ of ____

Instructional goal:

____

Instructional approaches considered:

____ Directions ____ Rehearsal ____ Modeling ____ Prompting

Brainstorming—preliminary ideas for intervention procedures:

Worksheet 10.1: Writing an Intervention Script

Name: ______________________ Date: __________

Student: ______________________ Grade: __________

Target Skill: ______________________

Sequence for addressing instructional goals:

First: ______________________

Second: ______________________

Third: ______________________

Fourth: ______________________

Fifth: ______________________

Intervention Script:

Worksheet 10.1 (continued)	Name: ______________________ Page ____ of ____ Student: ______________________

Intervention Script (continued):

Worksheet 10.2: Intervention Schedule

Name: ______________________ Date: __________

Student: ______________________ Grade: __________

DAY:	
	Procedures:
	Other personnel taking part:
	Materials needed:

DAY:	
	Procedures:
	Other personnel taking part:
	Materials needed:

DAY:	
	Procedures:
	Other personnel taking part:
	Materials needed:

DAY:	
	Procedures:
	Other personnel taking part:
	Materials needed:

Worksheet 10.2 (continued)	Name: ______________________ Student: ______________________	Page ____ of ____

DAY:	Procedures:
	Other personnel taking part:
	Materials needed:
DAY:	Procedures:
	Other personnel taking part:
	Materials needed:
DAY:	Procedures:
	Other personnel taking part:
	Materials needed:
DAY:	Procedures:
	Other personnel taking part:
	Materials needed:

Worksheet 11.1: Monitoring the Intervention

Page 1 of _____

Name: ______________________________ Date: __________

Student: ______________________________ Grade: __________

Target skill: ______________________________

Standard for original priority expectation(s)	
Units of Measure	**Criterion Level**

Level of confidence
for meeting standard: ______________________________

Issues or questions to keep track of during intervention:

____
____
____
____
____
____
____
____
____
____
____
____
____
____
____
____

Worksheet 11.1 (continued)	Name: ____________________ Student: ____________________	Page 2 of ____

Issues or questions to monitor (continued):

Monitoring Procedures

Procedure	**Day(s)**

Worksheet 11.1 (continued)	Name: ______________________________ Student: ______________________________	Page ____ of ____

Intervention Results for (day) ______________________________

Intervention Results for (day) ______________________________

Worksheet 11.1 (continued)	Name: ______________________ Page ____ of ____ Student: ______________________

Charts for Recording Student Performance

Chart title: ______________________

Days/times	Results

Chart title: ______________________

Days/times	Results

Worksheet 11.1 (continued)	Name: ______________________ Student: ______________________	Page ____ of ____

Graphs for recording student performance.

Graph Title: ______________________

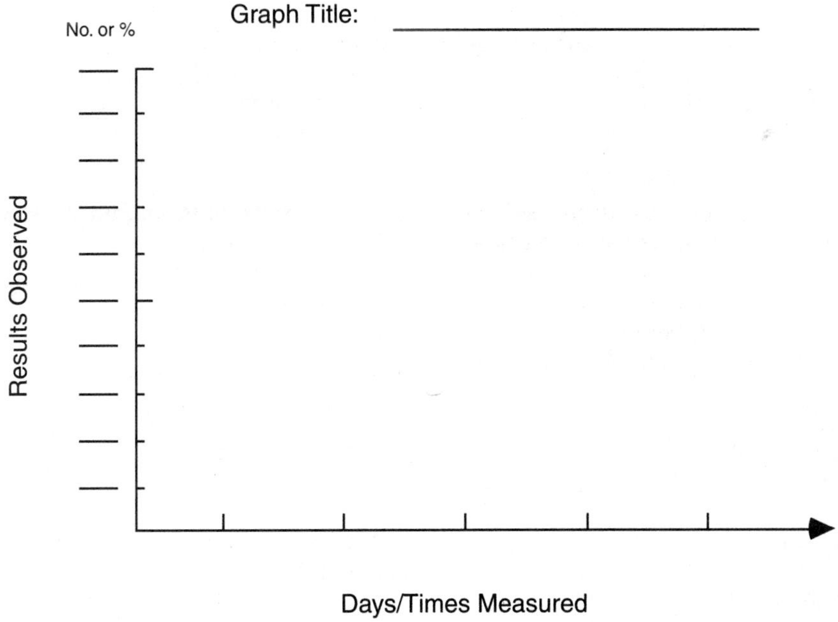

Graph Title: ______________________

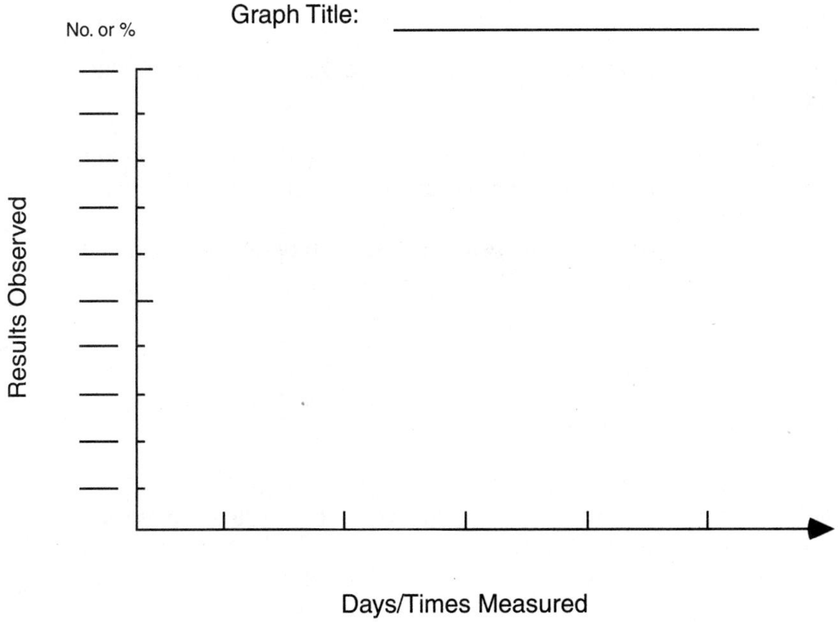

Worksheet 12.1: Writing an Intervention Script

Name: ______________________________ Date: __________

Student: ______________________________ Grade: __________

Section I: When the intervention is generally working as planned.

The following scenarios describe generally positive results from the intervention:

The student has acquired the target skill and shows signs of expanding the new skills to other skill areas and settings.

___ Fade the intervention procedures.
___ Select another target skill for the student to work on.
___ Select other students for the intervention.

The student is making progress toward acquiring the target skill but has not expanded his or her behavior beyond the intervention situation.

___ Continue the intervention and add procedures to encourage carryover of new skills.
___ Work with other teachers and students to apply expectations consistently across different settings and activities.
___ Add incentive procedures to encourage carryover of the new skills.

The student is making progress toward acquiring the target skill but is still working for artificial outcomes or rewards.

___ Adjust the intervention procedures to highlight the natural outcomes of behavior.
___ Fade the intervention procedures more gradually and build the student's confidence level.
___ Integrate clearer outcomes or extra rewards as a permanent part of the overall routine of the setting.

The student is making progress toward meeting the target skill, but is still far from reaching the criterion level.

___ Continue the intervention and recheck the student's progress later.
___ Continue the intervention plan, but shift the procedures to stay aligned with the student's progress and needs.

Worksheet 12.1 (continued)	Name: ____________ Page 2 of ____ Student: ____________

Section II: When the intervention is generally not working as planned.

The following scenarios describe reasons the student might not be making progress:

The student is not making progress because the instructional goals are misdirected.

___ Eliminate instructional goals that are not central to acquiring the target skill.
___ Shift the emphasis given to the instructional goals in the intervention plan.
___ Add other instructional goals to the intervention plan.
___ Shift the focus of the intervention to new skill areas.
___ Continue the intervention and watch for further effects.

The student is not making progress because the intervention procedures themselves are ineffective or misdirected.

___ Revise or remove procedures that are ineffective.
___ Check the intervention procedures to ensure that they address the intended instructional goals.
___ Readjust the pace of the intervention procedures to match the student's progress.
___ Alter the context in which the procedures are used.
___ Develop new procedures to address the instructional goals.

The student is not making progress because the intervention does not adequately address the student's need for incentive.

___ Place more emphasis on natural outcomes of performance, or add extra incentives for the student to learn the new skills.
___ Change the context of the intervention to help the student build confidence in using the new skills.
___ Reduce competing behaviors.

Worksheet 12.1 (continued)	Name: ______________________ Student: ______________________	Page ____ of ____

Notes on further courses of action:

Name: ______________________________ Date: ____________

Student: ______________________________ Grade: ____________

Setting(s): ____

Description of student behavior:

Areas or concerns to investigate:

____

____

____

____

____

Worksheet 13.1 (continued)	Name: ______________________________ Student: ______________________________	

Part 1: Social Skills Curriculum and Survey Level Assessment

Step 1: Identifying the social skills curriculum

*What are the situations in the setting?
*What social expectations do average students meet in each situation?
* What standards define the minimum level of typical performance for meeting expectations?

Notes—how you plan to investigate these issues:

Step 2: Conducting the survey level assessment

*Which expectations from the social skills curriculum does the student fail to meet?

Notes—how you plan to investigate this issue:

Step 3: Setting priorities and choosing a target skill

*Which expectations not met by the student should stand as priorities for intervention?
*Which priority area should serve as the target skill for the intervention?

Notes—how you plan to investigate these issues:

Worksheet 13.1 (continued)	Name: ______________________ Student: ______________________	

Part II: Specific Level Assessment

Step 4: Assessing basic abilities

*What basic abilities does the target skill involve?
*How well does the student perform these abilities?
*What abilities might the student need to learn in the intervention ("Findings")?

Notes—how you plan to investigate these issues:

Step 5: Assessing component steps

*What sequence of component steps does the target skill involve?
*Which of the steps represent difficulties for the student?
*Which steps might the student need to learn in the intervention ("Findings")?

Notes—how you plan to investigate these issues:

Step 6: Assessing performance conditions

*What elements of performance conditions present difficulties for the student?
*Does the student respond appropriately to the cues these conditions provide?
*Does the student perform better under some conditions than others?
*What aspects of performance conditions might the student need to learn ("Findings")?

Notes—how you plan to investigate these issues:

Worksheet 13.1 (continued)	Name: ____________________ Student: ____________________	Page 4 of 5

Part III. Developing and conducting interventions

Step 7: Setting instructional goals for interventions

*Based on the findings from the specific level assessment, what does the student need to learn to master the target skill?

Notes—how you plan to address this issue:

Step 8: Brainstorming and developing intervention procedures

*What procedures might be effective in addressing the instructional goals?
*In what order should the instructional goals be addressed?
*How can your ideas for procedures be developed or improved?
*How will you address complex goals or the need for incentive?

Notes—how you plan to address these issues:

Step 9: Coordinating and scheduling intervention activities

*How will the various intervention activities fit together?
*How will you coordinate the intervention procedures with ongoing routines?
*What materials, personnel, and activities do you need to consider?

Notes—how you plan to address these issues:

Worksheet 13.1 (continued)	Name: ______________________ Student: ______________________	

Part III (continued)

Step 10: Monitoring the intervention

*How will you keep track of the student's performance of the target skill?
*How will you know when the student has learned the target skill sufficiently?
*What other questions or issues will you wish to monitor during the intervention?

Notes—how you plan to address these issues:

Worksheet 14.1. Planning Social Skills Instruction for Groups of Students

Name: ______________________________ Date: ____________

Step 1. Groups/Settings to be included in instruction

____

____

Step 2. Social expectations to consider addressing in instruction

A. List expectations in the setting that pose problems for many students:

B. List expectations that are unclear, implicit, or applied inconsistently:

C. List expectations you want to modify, emphasize, or add to the curriculum:

D. List groups of expectations that can be taught together as a unit:

Worksheet 14.1 (continued)	Name: ______________________________ Page 2 of 3

E. List expectations that students have difficulty applying or carrying over to other settings:

Step 3. Priority expectations/target skill(s) for instruction:

Step 4. Key abilities, steps, and conditions to consider for teaching target skill:

Worksheet 14.1 (continued)	Name: ________________________	Page 3 of 3

Step 5. Instructional goals for group instruction:

Learn to ________________________

Learn to ________________________

Learn to ________________________

Learn to ________________________

Learn to ________________________

Step 6. Brainstorming ideas for addressing goals

You may use Worksheet 9.1 to complete this step.

Step 7. Developing and improving lesson plans

You may use Worksheet 9.1 and the suggestions in Chapter Ten to complete this step.

Step 8. Coordinating and scheduling lesson plans

You may use Worksheets 10.1 and 10.2 to complete this step.

Step 9. Preparing monitoring procedures to oversee the instruction

You may use Worksheet 11.1 to complete this step.

Worksheet 15.1. Setting Objectives for Working with Other Personnel within and across Grade Levels

Name: ______________________ Date: __________

Other personnel to work with:

Objectives for collaborative work:

TO THE OWNER OF THIS BOOK:

We hope that you have found *Teaching Social Competence: A Practical Approach for Improving Social Skills in Students At-Risk* useful. So that this book can be improved in a future edition, would you take the time to complete this sheet and return it? Thank you.

School and address: ______________________________

Department: ______________________________

Instructor's name: ______________________________

1. What I like most about this book is: ______________________________

____

____

2. What I like least about this book is: ______________________________

____

____

3. My general reaction to this book is: ______________________________

____

4. The name of the course in which I used this book is: ______________________________

____

5. Were all of the chapters of the book assigned for you to read? ______________________________

   If not, which ones weren't? ______________________________

6. In the space below, or on a separate sheet of paper, please write specific suggestions for improving this book and anything else you'd care to share about your experience in using the book.

____

____

____

____

____

Optional:

Your name: ______________________ Date: ______________________

May Brooks/Cole quote you, either in promotion for *Teaching Social Competence: A Practical Approach for Improving Social Skills in Students At-Risk* or in future publishing ventures?

Yes: __________ No: __________

Sincerely,

Dennis R. Knapczyk
Paul Rodes

FOLD HERE

NO POSTAGE NECESSARY IF MAILED IN THE UNITED STATES

BUSINESS REPLY MAIL
FIRST CLASS PERMIT NO. 358 PACIFIC GROVE, CA

POSTAGE WILL BE PAID BY ADDRESSEE

ATT: *Dennis R. Knapczyk & Paul Rodes*

Brooks/Cole Publishing Company
511 Forest Lodge Road
Pacific Grove, California 93950-9968

FOLD HERE

Brooks/Cole is dedicated to publishing quality books for the helping professions. If you would like to learn more about our publications, please use this mailer to request our catalogue.

Name: ______________________________

Street Address: ______________________________

City, State, and Zip: ______________________________

FOLD HERE

NO POSTAGE NECESSARY IF MAILED IN THE UNITED STATES

BUSINESS REPLY MAIL

FIRST CLASS PERMIT NO. 358 PACIFIC GROVE, CA

POSTAGE WILL BE PAID BY ADDRESSEE

ATT: *Human Services Catalogue*

Brooks/Cole Publishing Company
511 Forest Lodge Road
Pacific Grove, California 93950-9968

FOLD HERE